ISBN
1859839762

BLACKPOOL

A COMPLETE RECORD
1887-1992

BLACKPOOL

A COMPLETE RECORD 1887-1992

Roy Calley

BREEDON
BOOKS
SPORT

First published in Great Britain by
The Breedon Books Publishing Company Limited
44 Friar Gate, Derby, DE1 1DA.
1992

ISBN 1 873626 07 X

Printed and bound in Great Britain by The Bath Press Limited, Bath.
Jacket printed by BDC Printing Services Limited of Derby.

Contents

Introduction

I WAS delighted to be given the opportunity to write the story and compile the complete statistical record of Blackpool Football Club. As a passionate supporter of the Seasiders for over 25 years, I've looked upon the work as a labour of love and a fascinating insight into what has made our beloved football club tick all these years.

I believe I am right in saying that this is the first statistical history of Blackpool FC, although there have been three previous books written on the club, in 1932, 1972 and more recently in 1987. This book endeavours to bring every possible statistic related to the club to the reader, and hopefully more besides.

As with any statistical work, though, it cannot claim to be 100 per cent accurate as errors are bound to occur. However, the author believes it come as close as possible, given the sources that were available.

The main problem seemed to occur whilst researching World War Two games, where inadequate newspaper coverage hampered the work, a difficulty which was compounded by the peculiar nature of wartime football when one game often counted for two and even three different competitions.

Also, attendances caused a problem in the early years. The Football League did not begin to keep records until the 1925-6 season, so anything before then was usually worked out by the gate receipts, or the local news reporter casting his eye around the ground to decide that 'x' number of thousand were present. This, of course, could be way off the mark, and to make matters worse, the figure did not always stay constant during the 90 minutes.

Watching football in the early part of the century was rather different to today, as often spectators would join or leave a game halfway through, so making accurate figures almost impossible to establish.

With regard to the sources used in research, the majority has come from the pages of the local newspapers. Three are worth mentioning, the *Blackpool Times*, the *Blackpool Herald* and, of course, the *Blackpool Evening Gazette*. Also many other local sources have been used to cross-check when necessary.

Finally, my choices for the games to remember and, more particularly, the player biographies, are quite simply my personal choice. They were selected because I believed they were significant for their respective eras. The players were not all stars and it is quite possible that your favourite has been left out. For that I apologise and hope to do a lot better next time. Thank you for buying the book and I hope you enjoy reading it.

Roy Calley
July 1992

Acknowledgements

In the course of writing this book, I have had help from many people who I would now like to thank: Roger Harrison for supplying all the statistics from 1958 onwards, and the scores for all the seasons before. The Football League for making their records available to me, the staff at the Reference Library in Blackpool for their patience. Also to all the reporters who have followed Blackpool FC for their respective newspapers over the years, the *Blackpool Evening Gazette*, the *Blackpool Times* and the *Blackpool Herald*. At the club, my thanks to Geoff Warburton, who alone was a voice of encouragement.

For all the excellent photographs I must thank the *Blackpool Evening Gazette*, Cliff Muspratt, Mr Beveridge and, above all, John Cross, who came to my rescue at the last moment with a wealth of archive material which he kindly leant to me.

Finally, thank you to Anton Rippon at Breedon Books for giving me the opportunity to write the book, and, of course, to all the players who have worn the tangerine shirt, or otherwise, over the years and helped Blackpool Football Club to become one of the country's most loved and respected.

Foreword

I was brought up within a stone's throw of Bloomfield Road. One of the young boys I played football with in the back street was Jimmy Armfield, who went on to captain Blackpool and his country, and my first estate agency office in Birley Street was opened by Stanley Mortensen, who scored such brilliant goals for Blackpool and England.

There was no greater thrill in life than to stand on the Kop at Bloomfield Road and watch Blackpool surge to three FA Cup finals in six years or to the top of Division One. I believe those days can come back to Bloomfield Road.

The story of any football club, however, is not just written on the field of play. Clubs cannot survive without finance and administration. The men and women whose hard work keeps Blackpool FC going, including my fellow directors, are all part of the Seasiders' story.

But, for me, the real heroes are the fans. Our fine home record during the last two seasons is a fine achievement for the manager and players but they could not do it without our committed, passionate fans. Without them, we would not have won promotion from Division Four. It is for them and to support the wider community in Blackpool, that my family is prepared to sink resources and energy into the Club's revival.

Among the most passionate of those fans is Roy Calley. He has produced a fine book, which covers in every detail the fortunes of Blackpool FC from its foundation. It will form an important part of the history of this Club and the town of Blackpool.

OWEN OYSTON
Chairman, Blackpool FC.

The Blackpool Story

BLACKPOOL, both as a town and a seaside resort, has always had a reputation for being entertaining, brash and breezy, and so it is hardly surprising to find that during most of its history, the local football club has also boasted those attributes. Players of such note and talent as Stan Matthews, Stan Mortensen, Jimmy Hampson and Alan Ball have, over the years left, their indelible mark, not only on Blackpool FC, but on the footballing world in general, and so in turn ensuring that the club from Bloomfield Road remains one of the most famous and well-loved in the country.

Blackpool Football Club is still best remembered for its great team of the 1950s, and especially for the famous 'Matthews Cup Final' of 1953, when they came back from a 3-1 deficit with 20 minutes remaining, to snatch a 4-3 victory over Bolton Wanderers in the dying seconds and so win the FA Cup for the first and so far only time.

During that post-war period the Seasiders made three Wembley appearances in six years and flirted with the League Championship on more than one occasion. They also supplied the national teams with many international players, notably for England in 1953 when four Blackpool men lined up at Wembley, causing the *Daily Mirror* to announce that 'Blackpool FC are playing Hungary today', albeit a day that English football would later want to forget.

Yet the story of Blackpool Football Club is not just about the great team of that era. For instance, two decades earlier the town had a team of which it could also be proud, with players such as Jimmy Hampson and Peter Doherty delighting both home and opposing supporters alike; and later, much later, there were the famous triumphs in Italy in the early part of the 1970s.

There have, of course, also been many frustrations and failures over the years, typified by the fact that today, the Tangerines are residing in the bottom half of the Football League, although publication of this book coincides with a return to the Third Division — from 1992-3 of course, the Second Division — an event which every Blackpool supporter hopes is the herald to greater days once more.

It is generally believed that Blackpool Football Club was formed on 26 July 1887 and came about through a breakaway group from the existing St John's FC. Mr Ken Parr of Blackpool claims to have documentary proof that the Blackpool club was formed ten years earlier. Certainly, in a recently published history of Blackburn Rovers there is reference to a game against 'Blackpool' in December 1880, but whether this is the same club as ours is not clear. Without further details we must go with the generally accepted version of how the club was formed.

The St John's club had been in existence for around ten years and had risen from the ashes of the disbanded Victoria Club. Five members of the St John's club — Revd N.S.Jeffrey, Sam Bancroft, Dick Swanbrick, Dick Worthington and W.J.Brown — felt it necessary for the town of Blackpool to have a football club bearing that name, and after a disagreement with the other members of St John's they left the meeting, went next door to the Stanley Arms Hotel and immediately founded Blackpool Football Club.

Gradually the St John's players changed sides and joined the new club, so making the former defunct, and it was with these players that the Blackpool club staged its first competitive game, at Chorley where they recorded a 2-1 victory. In fact that first season was quite a successful one for the fledgling club as they went on to win the Fylde Cup and the Lancashire Junior Cup, and even managed to announce a profit at the end of the campaign of some £20, with £66 being contributed in membership and subscription fees.

That profit was almost trebled by the end of the following season, when Blackpool became one of the founder members of the Lancashire League. Their home, Raikes Hall Gardens (or the Royal Palace Gardens), was part of a vast entertainment complex that included a theatre and boating lake, and as attendances averaged around the 2,000 mark, these early years were quite a financial success.

The fact that the club existed at all was due, in no small part, to the vision of the men that night in the Stanley Arms Hotel, and also to the intense rivalry that quickly built up between Blackpool and their neighbours, South Shore FC. Games between these two were fiercely contested and when the rivals amalgamated some years later, it caused an outcry in the town. Incidentally, the last game between the two ended in a 1-0 victory for South Shore.

It was Blackpool, though, who made headway in the Lancashire League and at the end of the first season they had won more games than they had lost and finished fifth out of 13 clubs. The following three seasons saw them finish runners-up, to Bury in 1890-91 and 1891-2, and on goal-average to Liverpool in 1892-3. A year later, at the end of the 1893-4 season, Blackpool made it their own, winning 15 games out of 22 to finish three points clear of their nearest rivals.

After another runners-up position in 1894-5, they then struggled near the foot of the table and the board wisely decided that they could make no further progress in local football, so on 13 May 1896, Blackpool Football Club became a limited company and were subsequently elected to the Football League. They joined the Second Division along with Gainsborough Trinity and Walsall, the newcomers replacing Crewe Alexandra, Burslem Port Vale and Rotherham County.

It was an ambition realised for one member in particular, Mr Leonard Seed, who was one of the first to be elected to the board of directors. It was his vision and belief that kept the club moving forward in those early years and it is worth mentioning that the Seed family and the Parkinson family have, over the years, been instrumental in preserving Blackpool FC's existence and ensuring the club's future. The supporters of the Seasiders owe them a great debt of gratitude.

It is also interesting to note that Blackpool won their first-ever 'proper' FA Cup game in 1896, when they defeated Burton Swifts in the first round, only to go out, three weeks later, at the hands of Bolton Wanderers. It was reported that the players were on a win bonus of some 10 shillings (50p), whereas their opponents were due to be paid an extra 45 shillings (£2.25) if they were successful!

So what of the players who lined up on that historic day in September 1896, for the first-ever League match involving the Seasiders? Amongst them was Jack Parkinson, a tall, strong forward who was to give sterling service to his club for many years to come, and was one of the few professional players that Blackpool had on the books. In that first season he was the top scorer and proceeded to score goals regularly until he moved to centre-half.

Then there was Charlie Mount, a fast outside-left who had the honour of scoring Blackpool's first League goal, against Lincoln City. Despite his success, however, he was sold during the summer of 1897, a move which caused an outcry amongst local fans.

Blackpool's first taste of League football was quite successful as they finished in a mid-table position and managed to attract reasonable attendances to their Raikes Hall ground. But one year later, all that changed as Blackpool announced a loss of £1,183. The club had started with capital of around £2,000 but the players' wages had amounted to £1,470, and with attendances plummeting to an average of 2,000, the financial position was not healthy.

On the pitch, too, Blackpool had struggled, managing to finish only in 11th position and also failing to make the first round proper of the FA Cup. There were calls from members for the directors to take the club out of the Football League, with all its expense, and consolidate for a few seasons in local football. Thankfully, this was not taken up, and Blackpool struggled on.

The following season saw the club having to move to a new home, the Athletic Grounds in Stanley Park, due to Raikes Hall being earmarked for housing development, and this seems to have been a financial success at least. Blackpool were able to announce a loss of only £441 2s 5½d, despite a severe reduction in admission prices.

Unfortunately, on the field things became decidedly worse as the team could only finish in 16th position, two points ahead of Loughborough Town, and failed to gain re-election, despite the goalscoring talents of Birkett and Parkinson. The Seasiders dropped out with another Lancashire club, Darwen, who had finished bottom. Their places were taken by Chesterfield and Middlesbrough, whilst Loughborough survived for one more season. The Seasiders' FA Cup exploits were not much better and once again they failed to reach the first round proper.

It is interesting to note that despite Blackpool having spent three years in League football, it was their neighbours from South Shore who enjoyed the better support. When the two decided to amalgamate in 1899, it was believed, quite rightly, that one club would be more successful than two.

The amalgamation had been discussed three years previously but had been voted down by the South Shore committee, despite a vote of approval from their president, Thomas Carter. South Shore had enjoyed limited success in the Lancashire League but had made their name in the football world many years previously when, on 14 January 1885, they had defeated mighty Notts County in the FA Cup at Waterloo Road. It was a sensational giantkilling act and spread the club's name far and wide.

After the amalgamation, which was formalised on 12 December 1899, most of South Shore's players joined Blackpool and the club, after a brief return to Raikes Hall, found itself at Bloomfield Road. This had been the new home of South Shore after they had played for many years at Waterloo Road.

The one season out of the Football League was a success for Blackpool, who won the Combination and were duly re-elected at the League's annual meeting on 25 May 1900, Stockport County joining them back in the Second Division at the expense of Loughborough and Luton Town.

For the new campaign they set about rebuilding the team to cope with League football again. Notable signings came in the form of Joe Dorrington, a goalkeeper from Blackburn Rovers, Harold Hardman, a local schoolboy who played at outside-left but went on to bigger things at Everton and later as director of Manchester United, and the return of the great Jack Parkinson, who had enjoyed a brief taste of First Division football with Liverpool. Moving in the opposite direction, though, was Jack Cox, who was sold to Liverpool for the big sum of £150.

Blackpool's first season back saw respectability with a mid-table 12th position but, alas, again no joy in the FA Cup. The 1901-02 season was one of little progress, with another final place of 12th and little in the way of new players. The club was surviving on the meagre income from the gate receipts and the increasing generosity of the subscribers and the men who made up the committee.

In 1903, Mr R.B.Middleton moved to Blackburn Rovers to become their secretary and Tom Barcroft took over his duties at Bloomfield Road. It was, at first, a temporary appointment, yet Barcroft stayed in that position for well over 30 years and stabilised the club as it steered its way through the rough waters of those early years.

Blackpool's 1904-05 players and officials. Back row (left ro right): Hull, Scott. Middle: Rothwell (trainer), H.E.Leivers (assistant secretary), Threlfall, Birkett, Parkinson, Wolstenholme, A.Bond (director), W.Atherton (director), T.H.Barcroft (secretary). Front: Morgan, Kearns, Hogg, Chadwick, McEwan.

Between 1901-02 and 1904-05, Blackpool enjoyed little success with only 14th and 15th positions attained in the League, although there were one or two good signings. The eccentric goalkeeper 'Tishy' Hull was one of the best, a 'keeper who always played wearing a flat cap and alternated between the brilliant and the bizarre.

There was also a significant improvement in attendances with as many as 7,000 turning up for a game against Bolton Wanderers, although it was reported this was boosted by at least 3,000 travelling supporters. However, finances were still in a serious position and for the start of 1905-06, a new board of directors was installed with Charles Ramsden as chairman and Tom Barcroft remaining as secretary, despite a move to vote him off the board.

On the field, a slight improvement came when the team reached the first round of the FA Cup for the first time in nine years. A defeat at Bristol City followed, yet one year later Blackpool enjoyed their finest moment to date. After beating Crystal Palace over three games they were drawn at home to powerful Sheffield United. The board, always mindful of financial restrictions, 'sold' the ground rights and agreed to play at Bramall Lane. Despite the protestations of the supporters, the move was agreed and on 2 February 1906, Blackpool travelled to Sheffield and won a remarkable game 2-1.

It was an outstanding result and earned the Blackpool players nationwide recognition. What made the victory all the more sweet was that the club had still made around £300 from the game. They netted £650 from the next tie at Newcastle United, although unfortunately the side could not match their previous achievement and were soundly beaten 5-0 in front of 35,000 fans.

New faces at Bloomfield Road in the early years of this century. Charles Ramsden (left) became chairman of a new board of directors at the start of the 1905-06 season. Jimmy Connor (right) was one of a number of new players to join the Seasiders.

During this time many players had come to the club and an equal amount had left. Arrivals included Duckworth, Jimmy Connor and a talented Liverpool junior called Gow. In the meantime, out went the tricky outside-left Marshall McEwan (to Bolton Wanderers), inside-forward Harry Hancock (who joined Oldham Athletic) plus regulars Morgan, Kearns, Hogg and Chadwick.

It was also during the 1905-06 season that the club had their first serious brush with the football authorities over crowd behaviour. It came after the 3-0 home defeat by West Bromwich Albion, when referee W.Gilgryst was escorted from the field, protected from furious spectators who were angry at some rather controversial decisions. One of these had included the 'sending-off' of a supporter for abusive language. He was forced to leave the ground with the help of two burly police officers, and at the final whistle nearly 200 fans invaded the pitch. The club was severely censured by the Football League and told to ensure that such scenes would never happen again.

During the same season, the local newspaper reporter, 'The Scribe', requested that Blackpool invest a 'five-pound note' to build a Press box, as he spent the whole of a game against championship challengers Manchester United outside the gates trying in vain to gain admittance, the 7,500 crowd being the capacity at the time.

One year on from the Sheffield United game, the directors were again forced to sell ground rights of an FA Cup tie. This time it was the first-round game against West Ham United, and as recently-opened Upton Park attracted 13,000 on that January afternoon, the club's coffers were boosted to the tune of £300. It had been announced that Blackpool were losing in the region of £50 per week, with expenditure of £80 per week far outweighing any monies coming through the turnstiles. Unfortunately, the FA Cup was not to provide any further financial interest as the Hammers won 2-1. Blackpool then ended the season in 13th position in Division Two.

For the start of the 1907-08 season, a new board had been introduced with the promise of more money being made available. Fred Seed succeeded Charles Ramsden as chairman and the club went about buying new players. Birch was signed from Atherton, with the effective Owers going to West Brom for a large fee, although he made only four appearances for the Throstles before moving to Chesterfield two years later.

Unfortunately, some serious injuries at the start of the season, including a broken leg suffered by inside-forward King, left Blackpool struggling and once again they could only manage a lowly final position, with another disappointing early exit at Manchester United in the FA Cup. That last match, by the way, saw over 3,000 Blackpool supporters travel to watch their team, making most of the noise in the 12,000 crowd at Bank Street, Clayton.

The summer of 1908 saw the arrival of 22-year-old centre-forward George Beare,

Fred Seed (left) had succeeded Charles Ramsden as chairman for 1907-08 and set about buying new players. But three years later, star forward Joe Clennell (far left) moved to Blackburn as the Blackpool club still struggled to survive financially.

Blackpool's staff for the start of the 1908-09 season. Back row (left to right): Trainer, Threlfall, Fisk, Tillotson, Western, S.Whittingham, Sterling, Parkinson, Miller. Second row: Leach, Whalley, Crewdson, Reid, R.Whittingham, unknown, Scott, Connor. Seated: Fish, Biers, Stephenson, T.Barcroft (secretary), Walker, Clark, Latheron. On ground: Lyons, Baddeley.

who had been scoring regularly for Southampton Reserves. Beare had a reasonable amount of success with Blackpool before going on to better things with Everton, and a journalist later wrote of him: 'If he did not enjoy playing football, he would probably have been one of our leading music-hall comedians, as he is an expert card manipulator, a trick cyclist of no little repute and an excellent billiards player.'

Of more mundane talents was a young miner called Whalley, who joined Blackpool from Dinnington Colliery in Sheffield, whilst leaving the team was the hugely popular and talented Bob Whittingham, who signed for Bradford City in January 1909 and a few months later moved to Chelsea for £1,300. Whittingham had a powerful shot and one goalkeeper commented: "I'd rather face his Satanic Majesty than Whittingham."

Although he left Bloomfield Road midway through the season, Whittingham still finished it as the Seasiders' leading scorer and his departure left a huge gap in the forward line. Once again the team struggled badly, finishing in 20th place and having to apply for re-election once more. Thankfully, another trip to Newcastle in the FA Cup provided much-needed financial revenue, where another 30,000-plus crowd saw the Seasiders lose 2-1.

Jack Cox returned to Blackpool at the start of the 1909-10 season, this time as an unofficial player-manager, and it was his guidance and experience which saw the team's fortunes improve considerably as they climbed to a respectable mid-table position. There had, of course, been one or two changes in playing personnel with the amateur centre-forward W.L.Grundy turning his hand to hockey after not being invited back at the end of the previous season.

Also, the veteran Jack Parkinson moved to Barrow on a free transfer after giving the club many years of devoted service. A year or so later, he would be killed in a tragic accident at a local swimming baths.

As the club's finances continued to give cause for concern, they were once again obliged to sell ground rights of another FA Cup game. This time the match against

Manchester United realised takings of £680, with 20,000 spectators seeing the home team win 2-1 at Old Trafford.

In the Second Division, there had been a vast improvement in Blackpool's fortunes with seventh place being reached for their most successful season to date, and with nearly 15,000 turning up for the penultimate home match against Burnley, there was a feeling that maybe the club would not have to sell its best players to survive. As it was, Joe Clennell, Blackpool's star inside-forward, went to Blackburn Rovers and was later sold to Everton for £1,500. He had contributed 18 goals that season, with only centre-forward Morley also reaching double-figures.

The next two seasons of 1911-12 and 1912-13 were disappointing to say the least, with 14th place being followed by a potentially disastrous 20th position as the Seasiders finished rock-bottom. Happily, they survived having to apply for re-election once more and it is interesting to note that not one player was able to score more than 10 goals in either campaign.

The FA Cup had provided little cheer. A marathon tie against Crewe Alexandra in 1912 was followed by yet another decision to sell ground rights in 1913. This time the opponents were Tottenham Hotspur, who showed scant regard for Blackpool's previous giantkilling reputation by putting six past them in the replay at White Hart Lane. Unfortunately there was no financial bonanza this time as an aggregate of only 35,000 fans watched the two games, realising around £750 in gate receipts.

The 1913-14 season saw a slight improvement in the Seasiders' League position as they finished 16th, but an early exit in the FA Cup at Southern League Gillingham was hugely disappointing.

One of the notable signings of that season, though, was Joe Lane from Sunderland. Lane, who had been playing in Hungarian football before joining the Roker club, cost Blackpool £400 and proceeded to repay that immediately, scoring 11 goals in his first season and continuing to find the net regularly for the rest of his time at Bloomfield Road.

Another strong forward, Charlton was seriously injured during the home game against Leicester Fosse in April, suffering a fractured skull after a collision with a defender. For quite some time his life was in danger, but happily he made a full recovery. At the next home match, a collection was made amongst the fans and £211 was raised for Charlton and his family.

At the start of the 1914-15 campaign, Albert Hargreaves, a director and a former referee, suggested to the Football League that they should consider extending the season for financial reasons, but the suggestion was voted down. It proved rather unfortunate for Blackpool as they enjoyed their best form towards the end of the season and a late surge, when they won eight of their last ten games, saw them finish in a respectable tenth position. Once again Joe Lane's goals kept him at the top of the scoring charts with 28, no other player breaking into double figures.

Interest in the FA Cup ended predictably in the first round at home to Sheffield United, but some talented players joined Blackpool's ranks in this last season of League football before the war, which had been declared in August 1914, saw the suspension of the competition.

Billy Rooks and Len Appleton were new signings but, like everyone else, their careers were about to be savagely interrupted, for overshadowing everything was the conflict in Europe. Inevitably, like other professional sports, football was abandoned until hostilities ceased.

The game eventually restarted with unfamilar regional leagues and Blackpool fielded a side during the remaining war years. In the first season they were quite successful, finishing third in the Lancashire Section's principal competition, followed by second in the subsidiary competition, although none of this really meant a great deal.

They were not as successful again until the end of the 1918-19, when they won the subsidiary competition's Section 'A', which comprised only the Seasiders, Burnley, Preston and Blackburn. The leaders of the four sections qualified for the semi-finals of the Lancashire Senior Cup, in which Blackpool lost 1-0 to Liverpool at Bloomfield Road.

They were helped, especially in that first wartime season, by many 'guest' players who found themselves stationed in the town. Amongst them were four famous players from Blackburn Rovers — the great Bob Crompton, Eddie Latheron, George Chapman and Joe Hodkinson. These played regularly for the Seasiders and so earned the club the new nickname of 'Blackpool Rovers'.

Worth mentioning are a 9-0 home victory over Oldham Athletic, when England player Harry Hampton scored four goals, and the Lancashire Cup semi-final against Liverpool in 1919, when Blackpool attacked constantly, only to lose to a last-minute goal.

When full-time football was resumed for 1919-20, Blackpool had by now joined the growing band of clubs who employed a full-time manager. Bill Norman had taken over the position 12 months previously, leaving Huddersfield, the club he had joined after training Barnsley's 1912 FA Cup-winning side.

Norman was a fitness fanatic and organised strict training routines in a bid to make his players the fittest in the land. It worked superbly as Blackpool enjoyed their best season by finishing fourth in Division Two and winning the Central League championship, although interest in the FA Cup was once again ended in an early round.

After four wartime seasons there were, of course, many changes in the playing staff with regulars George Wilson moving to Sheffield Wednesday, Peter Quinn to Preston, Jimmy Jones to Bolton Wanderers and Bobby Booth to Birmingham.

The biggest shock, though, came in March 1920 with the transfer of Joe Lane, also to Birmingham, for a record fee of £3,600. This caused uproar in the town and many fans questioned the ambition of the board, with the team seemingly in its strongest-ever position.

They could not, however, question the financial position which the club now found itself in, as incoming transfer fees plus record gate receipts had realised a profit of £2,383 as opposed to the loss of £1,337 the previous year. It was not all good news, though, as a fire in one of the stands had all but destroyed it and a large bill was paid for the rebuilding.

The 1920-21 continued the improvement with another push for promotion, but unfortunately a poor run-in at the end of the season saw the team again finish in fourth position. This was viewed by the fans as a huge disappointment, particularly as for most of the campaign the team had been at the top of the table.

The FA Cup provided little cheer as Blackpool found themselves embarrassed by non-League Southend United in the second round. And on the goalscoring front, only Heathcote could break into double figures, scoring 18 times.

One of the most significant appearances, though, was that of Georgie Mee, who from December 1920 proceeded to play in every one of Blackpool's League matches until September 1925, well over 190 consecutive games. It was a marvellous achievement which still stands as a record.

On a sad note, the dependable full-back Horace Fairhurst died after receiving a knock on the head during a game at Barnsley. He was a young player who looked to have a tremendous future ahead of him.

The next season was disastrous for Blackpool as the team struggled against relegation to the new Third Division North. They approached the final two games, both against West Ham United, knowing that they had to win both to stay in

Blackpool, 1920-21. Back row (left to right): Campey, McGuinn, Popplewell, Mr Hargreaves (director), Keenan, Mr Stead (director), Smith, Mingay, Garrison, J.Waterson (trainer), Benton, G.Taylor (assistant). Front: Bullock, Charles, Barrass, Bedford, Heathcote, Mee.

Division Two. And with the Londoners striving for promotion, it seemed an impossible task.

Incredibly, Blackpool won 2-0 at Upton Park and scored another victory seven days later, by 3-1 at Bloomfield Road to escape relegation by a single point, with Bristol City and Bradford going down. How the team could have struggled so badly after such an improvement in recent years was hard to explain, especially with the acquisition of another goalscoring machine, Harry Bedford from Nottingham Forest. Bedford was to emulate Joe Lane by scoring the majority of the team's goals in the following seasons.

Also joining the club was Bert Baverstock from Bolton Wanderers, who was made captain. Baverstock was a fine player but a bad injury early on reduced his appearances.

Again without a Cup run to boost the finances, the club announced another loss, this time of £2,994, for the season. The Bloomfield Road ground continued to see improvements, however, as extra capacity on the Spion Kop — now the South Stand — increased the overall capacity to 18,000.

At the end of 1922-3, which had seen the team running for promotion throughout the campaign only to finish fifth, manager Bill Norman and his assistant Allan Ure, who was also Norman's son-in-law, both moved to Leeds United, although Ure was to return to Bloomfield Road many years later.

It was another disappointing outcome to what had seemed at first to be a successful campaign and, with Bedford scoring 32 goals, expectations had been high. Unfortunately, Blackpool could win only three of their last ten games and so slipped out of contention. With criticism from the supporters intense, Norman felt it best to leave.

Yet once again he had been hampered by lack of funds to buy new players, the only real exception being inside-forward Harry White from Arsenal, for £1,125. White, who was also a Warwickshire county cricketer, had played in an England soccer trial in 1919 and had scored 40 goals in 101 League games for the Gunners.

That Norman could sign even one expensive player was a surprise, for Blackpool's overall loss at the end of the season had increased to nearly £4,000 and desperate measures were now required to rectify it.

One pleasing aspect, though, was the increase in attendances at Bloomfield Road, with some 20,000 reported at the game against Barnsley, although how this was possible with a capacity still officially set at 18,000 is open to question.

For the new season there was a new manager when Major Frank Buckley joined Blackpool. He had previously managed Norwich City, although he had been out of the game and was working as a commercial traveller when the Seasiders signed him up. A tactical visionary, Buckley revolutionised the way the team played. He was a controversial figure and also one of the highest-paid managers in the Football League.

The campaign started badly as Blackpool failed to win any of their first seven games, but eventually they started to play as a unit and with the help of another 32 goals from Bedford, they attained fourth place by the end of the season, although they were never really in touch with the promotion race.

It was also at this time that the club adopted the famous tangerine shirts that are now so much part of Blackpool FC. Albert Hargreaves, after officiating in a Holland-Belgium international game, was so impressed by the Dutchmen's colours that he suggested that Blackpool start the season wearing them.

The colours were adopted and received with universal praise from the fans, although the black collars, cuffs and shorts made the kit seem 'uneven'. Eventually, black was dropped after an FA Cup game at Blackburn in 1925, when it was suggested that Blackpool had lost because the players could not see each other in the murky atmosphere!

Before changing to tangerine, the team had appeared in a whole host of different kits. Blue-and-white striped shirts in the 1890s, a mixture of red or white shirts at the turn of the century, and even red, yellow and black during World War One.

After the war they had worn all white, but the introduction of tangerine seemed to be the most popular colour. That did not stop the board introducing another change in 1934, when the team appeared in alternating dark and light blue stripes, but thankfully in 1939 they bowed to public pressure and reintroduced the famous tangerine. It is now inconceivable that Blackpool Football Club should be identified with any other colour.

For 1924-5 there were more off-the-field problems, nearly all financial. A writ had been presented to the club for £3,618 from the builders of the rebuilt stand, the total cost being £4,618 of which only £1,000 had been paid. After a lengthy meeting it was decided to double the share capial, bringing it up to £10,000 so as to pay off the outstanding debt. Also, the board underwent quite a few changes with new members being added in the hope of providing much-needed cash to alleviate a desperate situation.

Sir Lindsay Parkinson resigned as president, to be replaced by Alderman John Bickerstaffe. Also, the new Blackpool Supporters' Club was formed and in its infancy boasted over 300 members.

On the field, the team, without new blood, struggled badly and spent most of the season fighting relegation, although once again Harry Bedford managed 24 League goals with only the consistent Malcolm Barrass also reaching double figures. There was, for once, more than a passing interest in the FA Cup as Blackpool reached the fourth round before losing to Blackburn Rovers by a single goal in front of 60,000 fans.

Two of the club's top players left Blackpool during the next season, both for large fees. Herbert Jones went to Blackburn for £3,850 — one of the largest fees paid for a full-back up to that time — and goalscoring machine Harry Bedford was sold to Derby County for £3,500.

This was a huge loss to the team, yet an enormous financial gain and, surprisingly, Blackpool managed to finish in sixth position. The board spent a large part of the money on the new South Stand, although the final cost of £13,146 was slightly more than they had bargained for. Nevertheless, it had increased the capacity of Bloomfield Road to well over 20,000.

The 1926-7 season saw Rosebroom and Streets move to Chesterfield and Clapton Orient respectively, whilst in came forward Tom Browell from Manchester City for £1,100. Browell, by now well into the veteran stage, had played in the previous season's FA Cup Final and he expected to add experience to the team.

Unfortunately, Blackpool made little progress and could finish in only ninth position, with only a passing interest in the FA Cup. One big success, though, was the form of centre-forward Billy Tremelling, who scored 31 League and Cup goals. Later, he moved to centre-half to accommodate an even richer goalscoring talent in the shape of the great Jimmy Hampson.

Hampson was signed from Nelson for £1,000 in October 1927 and proved to be one of the club's greatest buys. In his first season, he scored 31 goals in 32 League appearances, including four in a home win over Nottingham Forest. His contribution to the team over the next ten years was beyond equal and he could rightly stake his claim to be one of the greatest of all Blackpool players.

There were many other new faces for the 1927-8 season: McIntyre came from Bristol Rovers, Horace Williams from New Brighton, William Grant from East Stirling, Brookes from Scunthorpe and a twin signing for £4,500 of Oxberry and Ramsay from the North-East.

There was also a new manager in the shape of Sydney Beaumont, a former Preston player who replaced Major Buckley, off to take up a new challenge with Wolves. Beaumont was to last only a year, however, and after one unsuccessful campaign in which the Seasiders finished 19th, avoiding relegation by a single point, he departed.

In a bid to cut costs, Blackpool then decided not to appoint another full-time manager, instead giving the title of honorary manager to director Harry Evans, who held this difficult job for the next five years.

Despite another 40 goals from Hampson in 1928-9, Blackpool could finish no higher than ninth and were severely embarrassed at Plymouth in the Cup. The side's inconsistency was starkly exposed in October and November when they recorded successive League results of 1-4, 4-0, 2-8 and 7-0! The last game, against Reading, saw Hampson score five times.

There were a few additions to the squad, with the tough-tackling Jimmy Hamilton joining the Seasiders from St Mirren, and goalkeeper Bill Mercer coming from Huddersfield Town. All in all, though, it had been another disappointing campaign

and the pressure on the team to bring success to the town was now becoming intense.

It was said that the 1929-30 season would be a make-or-break campaign.

And in that season, success was finally achieved as Blackpool challenged for promotion throughout the campaign and kept their nerve in the important run-in. With the help of a victory at fellow challengers Oldham Athletic, in front of more than 45,000 fans, Blackpool not only achieved promotion to Division One, but secured the Second Division title, too, still the only one the club has won in its long history.

Jimmy Hampson's 45 League goals was a Blackpool record for a single season and still stands as such; and the final points total of 58 was equalled only once more before three-for-a-win was introduced.

During the season, Hampson had scored his 100th goal in only his 97th game for Blackpool, and he was also the country's top scorer. The team had played in front of much larger crowds than before, including over 24,000 for the visit of Oldham, and it was believed the same number welcomed the players at the Town Hall after promotion had been gained.

The feat was even more remarkable for the fact that very few additions had been made to the squad, with only Broadhurst and Percy Downes joining the Bloomfield Road staff. It had been a truly memorable season and the players spent the summer months enjoying civic receptions and dinners held in their honour.

Stockport County goalkeeper Crowther grabs the ball during a first-round FA Cup game at Bloomfield Road in January 1930. The Seasiders won 2-1 but were knocked out in the next round. There was ample consolation, though, with promotion to Division One at the end of the season.

There were many changes made for the start of the club's first season of First Division football, not least at the ground itself. During the close season, a vast new terrace was erected on the north side of Bloomfield Road, the Spion Kop, which at its peak could hold 12,000 people. It was not concreted for quite some time, but it did increase the capacity to around 30,000.

The playing staff was strengthened by the arrival of McLelland, Longden, Jack O'Donnell and Jackie Carr from Middlesbrough, yet the 1930-31 season must go down as one of the most disastrous in the Blackpool club's history. The players who had performed so well the previous campaign found themselves out of their depth in the higher division and proceeded to capitulate to virtually all opposition.

The writing was on the wall after the first game, when Arsenal had won, almost contemptuously, 4-1 at Bloomfield Road in front of nearly 29,000 fans. True, the players had pulled themselves together to record a fine win at Manchester City four days later, but the remainder of the season became a nightmare.

Four goals were conceded on five separate occasions, five goals four times, six goals twice, seven goals on three occasions, and finally ten goals on one humiliating

Former England forward Jackie Carr was a veteran when he joined Blackpool in May 1930, having made 421 League appearances for Middlesbrough, with whom he won two Second Division championship medals. Carr stayed with the Seasiders for only a short period, moving to become player-coach at Hartlepool a year later, after Blackpool's disastrous season in Division One.

afternoon at Huddersfield. All told, the defence leaked a First Division record of 125 goals during that sorry season as the Seasiders lost 21 games.

Amazingly, they escaped relegation, with 32 goals from Jimmy Hampson enough to secure First Division football for at least one more year. Also, a '£10,000 goal' from Albert Watson in the final match, at home to Manchester City, became legendary. The equalizer by the half-back was said to be worth at least that amount as it secured the club's immediate financial future with the promise of big attendances for the next year. Finances were still causing concern, as the club now had a bank overdraft of over £17,000.

The 1931-2 season saw an improvement in that 'only' 102 goals were conceded, including another seven at Manchester City plus five separate occasions where five goals went in. Blackpool had bought heavily in the close season, with the top signing being that of Phil Watson from Hamilton Academical for £3,000. Watson took the place of the departed Billy Tremelling, who had moved to Preston.

Walter Lax had been lured from Lincoln City, for whom he had scored 26 goals the previous season, plus Jack Everest from Rochdale and a new goalkeeper, Alec Roxburgh. Attendances were significantly down, which was hardly surprising as the team spent most of the campaign battling against relegation.

They avoided the drop by yet again winning the final two games of the season, against Huddersfield and Sheffield United. Again Hampson was the top scorer, with 23 goals, and once again any interest in the FA Cup ended in the third round.

The next season, however, saw the trap door finally open and Blackpool dropped back to Division Two after only three years in the top flight. Hampson, for so long the great hero who could do no wrong, had scored only 18 goals and now came under criticism from the fans and local newspapers, and there were reports of discontent within the club.

Eric Longden returned to Hull City for a 'nominal' fee, but the tricky outside-right Alec Reid agreed to come to Bloomfield Road from neighbours Preston North End. With the Seasiders finishing at the bottom of the table, there were calls for a full-time manager to be appointed once more. During the summer months that followed, there was also a major boardroom reshuffle with no less than six long-standing directors resigning. It had been an unhappy end to a brief flirtation with the top division.

Eventually a new manager was appointed and Alex McFarlane, a former Scottish international player with 13 years of management experience, took over. McFarlane was a strict disciplinarian, a perfectionist who showed his ruthlessness at the end of his first season by having a mass clear-out of players. Out went McDonough, Crawford, Thomson, Rattray, Bussey, Butterworth, Armes, Tufnell and Williams, all regulars who had contributed greatly to the team over the years.

The exodus was probably prompted by the side's inability to readjust to Second Division football, as they could finish only in a mid-table position, plus the usual brief interest in the FA Cup. Matters were not helped by a series of injuries to Hampson, who managed only 13 goals and was at his least effective since he joined Blackpool.

The following season, with the signing of Richard Watmough for £3,000 from Bradford City, and the acquisition of Middleton from Darlington, a concerted push for promotion was made. The Seasiders missed going up by only three points, finishing in fourth position, a tremendous improvement on the previous season.

Only their failure to win any of the last three games denied them, and it seemed that the team were in a stronger position than for many years. Hampson was back to something like his old self and once again topped the scoring charts with 20 goals. He was joined by a newcomer who had signed for Blackpool from Glentoran a year previously for £1,000. His name was Peter Doherty, a player who went on to become one of his country's greatest ever footballers. The regular partnership of Hampson, Doherty and Bobby Finan, who had joined the club from non-League football, in the forward-line would have been a great spectacle, yet injuries to one or the other meant that the dream was never realised.

For the beginning of 1935-6, Blackpool made one of their best-ever signings. That August, Joe Smith joined the Seasiders from Reading as manager, remained at Bloomfield Road for 23 years and transformed Blackpool into one of the most powerful football teams in the country.

Smith was a relaxed man who thoroughly enjoyed his football, and this showed through in the teams that he produced at Bloomfield Road over the years. One of his first signings was Fred Chandler, from his old club, but essentially he kept together the team from the previous season. Although only tenth place was attained,

Blackpool, 1936-7. Back row (left to right): Hill, Jones, Farrow, Wallace, Witham, Hampson, Cook. Middle: Cardwell, Shipman, Finan, Joe Smith (manager), Dougall, Jones, McIntosh. Front: Middleton, Blair, Watmough.

the huge success of Bobby Finan at centre-forward, where he scored 34 goals, gave an optimistic indicator to the future.

One year on and Blackpool were promoted once more, this time by finishing second to Leicester City. First Division was achieved with minimal outlay on new players, with only Alec Munro costing a substantial fee. He came from Scottish club Hearts for £3,500. Other signings included Danny Blair from Aston Villa, Frank Hill from Arsenal and Willie Cook from Bolton Wanderers.

The twin strike-force of Hampson and Finan had scored 44 goals between them, and with two other forwards, Watmough and Jones, also hitting double-figures, Blackpool seemed a safe bet in Division One. Unfortunately, finances were once again causing problems and the Irish star Peter Doherty had to be sold. He went to Manchester City for the enormous fee of £10,000.

In Blackpool's history, the 1937-8 season will forever be overshadowed for the tragic death of the great goalscorer Jimmy Hampson. He was on a fishing expedition off the Fleetwood coast on 10 January when disaster struck and his body was never recovered.

Although his scoring prowess was not as effective as previous years, Hampson was still adored by the fans and his death came as a sad blow to the club and football in general.

On the field, the team settled themselves well to the First Division and finished in a respectable 12th place, although a heavy Cup defeat at Villa Park in front of 70,000 fans was a disappointment.

Former Blackpool star Peter Doherty (left), now skipper of Manchester City, greets former teammate Jimmy Hampson before a League match.

Amongst the players who were emerging in the team were George Farrow, a right-back from Bournemouth, and Jock Wallace, who was challenging hard for the goalkeeping position in place of Roxburgh. New signings Frank O'Donnell and Willie Buchan, both from Celtic, each cost £10,000, whereas cheaper imports were Eric Sibley and Malcolm Butler.

For 1938-9, Blackpool spent over £60,000 on new players, a huge amount for the day. In came George Eastham from Bolton for £5,000, Tom Lewis from Bradford, the mighty 'Jock' Dodds from Sheffield United for £10,500, and Frank O'Donnell's brother, Hugh, for a further £2,500, plus many others such as Dai Astley, McLaren, Burke and Park.

In the meantime, out went Frank O'Donnell to Aston Villa for £10,500, and the influential Richard Watmough to Preston North End.

Blackpool's team which met Sheffield Wednesday in a wartime Cup Final in 1942. Back row (left to right): Farrow, Hayward, Pope, Savage, Hubbick, Johnston. Front: Gardner, Dix, Dodds, Finan, Burbanks.

It was a huge gamble but one which was to secure success at the club for many years to come. Fifteenth place was achieved with another early exit in the Cup, but the signs were already there. The fans turned out in larger numbers than before and the team seemed as if it was on the verge of greatness. They had even returned to their popular tangerine colours. The omens looked good.

At the outbreak of war in September 1939, Blackpool stood proudly at the top of the First Division after winning their opening three games. Although it was far too early to predict the outcome, many observers felt that the team was the best they had seen and were capable of lifting the Championship.

As things turned out, Blackpool instead had to be content with becoming, with the help of many guest players, one of the country's top teams throughout wartime football.

In that first wartime season's regional league, the Seasiders finished third and reached the quarter-finals of the War Cup, helped by the remarkable scoring feats of Jock Dodds. Not since Jimmy Hampson had Blackpool possessed a player with such an incredible knack for scoring goals. He netted 30 in 18 appearances, including seven in an 11-2 destruction of Oldham Athletic. Over the next few seasons, Dodds scored seemingly at will — eight times in one game against Stockport County, seven against Tranmere and, altogether, a total of over 200 goals during the war years. In 1941-2 alone he scored 66 times.

The team, meanwhile, were sweeping all before them, winning the Northern Section's first competition on three occasions, lifting the Lancashire Cup once plus reaching the War Cup Final on two occasions, winning it in 1943.

They also played in a famous challenge match at Stamford Bridge against the mighty Arsenal, winners of the Southern War Cup, and trounced them 4-2 in what has been described as the best performances ever by a Blackpool side.

All this was achieved with the help of many guest players, who, like in World War One, found themselves stationed in the town. Worthy of mention are Dix (Tottenham), Stevenson (Everton), Paterson (Celtic), Pope (Hearts and Leeds), Savage (Leeds), Hubbick (Bolton) and Gardner of Aston Villa.

There was also an outside-right who was a regular international and played for Stoke City. Stanley Matthews made regular appearances in Blackpool's tangerine shirt during the war years, teaming up with a promising youngster called Stan Mortensen. Had they only known it, this was a tantalising glimpse into the future for Blackpool supporters.

For the Blackpool club, one positive aspect of the war was the wiping out of their bank overdraft, which stood at £33,704. With the Armed Forces requiring Bloomfield Road for various reasons, the rent paid by the War Office helped the club to become solvent once more.

When peace returned to Europe, Blackpool found themselves in an ever stronger position. Despite the sale of Jock Dodds to Irish club Shamrock Rovers, and the departure of Hugh O'Donnell, manager Joe Smith started to gather around him some of the most talented footballers in the country and with the help of Stan Mortensen's 28 goals, the team finished in fifth position, by far the highest final position that Blackpool had achieved to date.

Attendances everywhere were booming and Blackpool's attractive football certainly appealed to the fans as they flocked to Bloomfield Road in their thousands, the game against Blackburn Rovers on Boxing Day 1946 being the ground's very first all-ticket affair. The FA Cup continued to be of little interest, although over the next few seasons all that was to change.

During the summer of 1947, Blackpool made probably their greatest signing when Joe Smith persuaded Stoke City to release Stanley Matthews for £11,500. Matthews had fallen in love with the town and the club after his stay during the war and was eager to don the tangerine shirt once more.

It was to prove a remarkable partnership for the club and man, as Blackpool FC entered the most successful era in its long history, and indeed the famous 'M' plan was to become legendary. Matthews, Mortensen, Munro, McIntosh, McCall and Mudie were names who appeared in the forward line and struck fear into opposing defences.

This was truly a golden era, and with the help of such players like Farrow, Johnston and Shimwell at the back, the team were at times invincible.

Other new names for 1947-8 included Joe Robinson, Albert Hobson and Walter Rickett, but the club released Jimmy Blair to Bournemouth and, sadly, one of

Action around the Blackpool goal during the classic 1948 FA Cup Final between the Seasiders and Manchester United.

Blackpool's best goalkeepers of recent years, Jock Wallace, to Derby County for just £500.

In the League they finished a disappointing ninth, but 1948 saw Blackpool's first ever trip to Wembley for an FA Cup Final. Their route to the semi-finals was, admittedly, rather easy, but the 3-1 victory over Tottenham Hotspur at Villa Park was an absolute classic with the 'Pool 1-0 down with only four minutes to go. Stan Mortensen's equalizer and two further goals in extra-time ensured a trip to the Empire Stadium where they met Manchester United, who had endured a much harder route to the Final as they had to play every one of their ties away from home, Old Trafford still being rebuilt after serious bomb damage during the war.

The 1948 Cup Final was probably one of the best games of football ever seen at Wembley, but it ended with a 4-2 defeat for Blackpool. That seemed a harsh score-line as the Seasiders had been right in it throughout the 90 minutes, but finally United's determination and slightly superior class won the day.

Stan Mortensen's goal meant that he had scored in every round, a feat rarely achieved. Amazingly, four days later the teams met again in a League game at Bloomfield Road, with Blackpool winning 1-0, although the score-line comes nowhere near in reflecting the dominance of the home team that day. At the end of the season, Blackpool bowed out with a 7-0 thrashing of neighbours Preston North End at Deepdale, with Jim McIntosh scoring five. He had been dropped seven days before for the Cup Final.

The 1948-9 season was a huge let-down with only a mid-table position attained in the League, although injuries to both Mortensen and Matthews contributed a great deal to the lack of fire-power up front. Many players left, such as Jim McIntosh who joined Everton, George Dick who went to West Ham United. Other departures were Buchan, McCormack, Farrow and Lewis. Joining were Rex Adams from amateurs Oxford City, Willie Wardle, a former Manchester City player who signed from Grimsby Town, Ewan Fenton, Jackie Wright and a giant of a goalkeeper from Hibernian, George Farm.

Stan Mortensen is thwarted by Spurs goalkeeper Ted Ditchburn on the opening day of the 1950-51 season at White Hart Lane. Blackpool won 4-1 but newly-promoted Tottenham went on to win the First Division title.

Farm was only playing in third-team football for the Scottish Club when Blackpool signed him, yet he went on to become one of the club's greatest 'keepers.

Unfortunately there was no repeat performance in the Cup as Blackpool were knocked out in a fourth-round replay at Stoke.

The following season saw an improvement with a final position of seventh in the League, Mortensen once again scoring 22 goals. A quarter-final defeat at Liverpool ended any further FA Cup involvement, but the Reserves won the Central League championship, scoring 82 goals in the process. They were helped significantly by one Jackie Mudie, who was just beginning to break into the first team.

Other new members included the amateur W.J.Slater and the talented Bill Perry. Out went Joe Robinson, the goalkeeper, unable to challenge George Farm in the first team, Alec Munro and Ron Suart, who joined Blackburn Rovers.

Blackpool's success was reflected by the crowds they were attracting all over the country, over 70,000 turning up at Goodison Park, although ultimately disappointed to find that the great 'maestro', Stan Matthews, was injured and could not play.

At home, too, attendances had improved significantly, with over 12,000 turning up to watch the Reserves beat Burnley. Financially, Blackpool Football Club had never been in a better position.

Another Cup Final appearance in 1951 seemed to overshadow the fact that the team had enjoyed their most successful season in the League by finishing in third place. There had been few additions to the squad with the exception of Allan Brown. He was signed from East Fife for £26,500 a record paid to a Scottish club, and proved over the years to be worth every penny.

McCall was sold to West Brom for £10,500, but essentially the team remained the same as the previous season. The League position was helped by 47 goals from Mortensen and Mudie, with the genius of Matthews on the wing. They were at times almost irresistible and it has never failed to amaze fans why such a talented team never lifted the greatest honour, the League Championship.

Jackie Mudie heads Blackpool's first goal against Mansfield Town in the fifth round of the FA Cup at Bloomfield Road in February 1953.

The Cup run was a far more difficult proposition than in 1948, none more so than the semi-final against Birmingham City which was eventually decided after a replay. For the Final against Newcastle United, the Seasiders were missing the influential Allan Brown, who had sustained a serious injury at Huddersfield some weeks previously.

His absence really showed as Blackpool tried an unfamiliar offside game and they paid the price by losing 2-0, although it could have been worse had Jackie Milburn been a little more ruthless in front of goal. It was probably one of the few tactical mistakes made by manager Joe Smith and left fans feeling that the veteran Matthews would never win an FA Cup medal.

Predictably, the 1951-2 season was something of an anticlimax with the team failing to challenge for honours. Ninth place in the First Division was seen as a disappointment, with an embarrassing early exit from the FA Cup at Upton Park. Ernie Taylor, who had so impressed in the Cup Final, was signed from Newcastle

for £25,000, but Willie McIntosh and Bill Slater both left, to Stoke and Brentford respectively.

Twenty-six League goals were scored by Mortensen, although Matthews could manage only 19 appearances due to injury, and that went a long way to explaining the team's lack of success. The crowds still flocked to Bloomfield Road, though, with over 32,000 watching a goalless draw with Arsenal during the Easter holiday.

The 1952-3 season will always be remembered for the FA Cup Final, yet that season Blackpool did well in the League once more, finishing seventh with over 36,000 watching the opening home game against Preston. New names emerging were Dave Durie, David Frith and the giant Ray Gratrix, but leaving the club were Len Stephenson and Jackie Wright. The forward line of Taylor, Mortensen, Brown and Perry provided most of the goals, but Matthews was still suffering from niggling injuries which meant he could play in only half the first-team matches that season.

The FA Cup Final against Bolton Wanderers will, of course, always be remembered as the greatest of them all. The day Stanley Matthews finally achieved his winners'

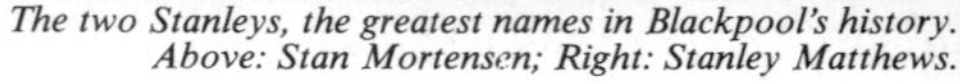

The two Stanleys, the greatest names in Blackpool's history. Above: Stan Mortensen; Right: Stanley Matthews.

medal, the day the team came back from the dead. The Seasiders were 3-1 down with 20 minutes to go, 3-2 down in the final minute, yet still triumphed 4-3.

Mortensen's hat-trick was the first ever scored in an FA Cup Final at Wembley and that glorious May afternoon will ensure Blackpool's fame for evermore. It was the highest point in their 105-year history and one which has little chance of being repeated in the near future.

Their route to Wembley was difficult enough, having to overcome Sheffield Wednesday, Arsenal and Tottenham on the way, and, indeed, only a last-minute error by England full-back Alf Ramsay gave Blackpool their semi-final victory.

The Final, though, was in a different class and everyone who was there, either playing or watching, will remember it vividly for the rest of their days. Spare a thought for Allan Brown, though, for after missing the 1951 Final, he was forced out of the team against Bolton after breaking a leg in scoring the winner in Blackpool's sixth-round victory against Arsenal.

The following season saw another concerted push for the elusive League Championship, but an unhappy Christmas period, when only five points were gained

Allan Brown has just scored the winning goal in the Seasiders' sixth-round FA Cup win over Arsenal. Now he lies in agony with a broken leg and will miss the Final once more.

Blackpool and Bolton Wanderers march out at Wembley for the 1953 Cup Final.

Proud Blackpool with the FA Cup, pictured before the start of the following season.

from ten matches, contributed to a final position of sixth. New players had been added with Jim Kelly being signed from Watford for around £15,000 and Johnny McKenna, an Irish international, from Huddersfield Town.

Leaving were Johnny Crosland, who went to Bournemouth, George McKnight, who went to Chesterfield, and John Ainscough, who went into non-League football. Also, Brown was still recovering from his broken leg and also a cartilage injury, but Mortensen continued to score goals.

The most amazing result of the whole season came, however in, the FA Cup. After a mammoth four-match tie with Luton Town, then two games with West Ham United, the Cup holders went to Third Division Port Vale and were beaten 2-0. It was one of the biggest Cup shocks in history, but paled into insignificance when compared to what was to happen one year later.

In January 1955, Blackpool went down by the same scoreline to Third Division York City at Bloomfield Road in the third round. It was an absolute disaster, and without the goalkeeping of Farm could have been far more humiliating. The 26,000 fans could only watch in despair as their heroes blustered and blundered their way through the 90 minutes as little York cut through a weak defence.

For Blackpool, the League offered little better with a desperate fight against relegation. After so many seasons of success, this came as a shock to both players and supporters and it was a test of character for the team. In fact, with only three games remaining, Blackpool's fate appeared sealed, but a fine 6-1 victory at Manchester City, with Perry scoring a hat-trick, went a long way to saving them.

Why should the same side that had performed wonders previously now struggle

Bill Perry scores one of his hat-trick goals in the 7-3 win over Sunderland in September 1955.

so badly? It was difficult to say, but thankfully First Division football had been ensured for another campaign.

The 1955-6 season was significant for many reasons. First, two of the club's greatest servants, Harry Johnston and Stan Mortensen, both departed to face new challenges. Johnston became manager of Reading, and 'Morty' went to Hull City. Their places were filled by Roy Gratrix and Jackie Mudie, who switched to centre-forward, allowing Dave Durie to take over the inside-left position.

The highest-ever attendance was recorded at Bloomfield Road when over 38,000 crammed into the ground to see Blackpool beat Wolverhampton Wanderers 2-1, but above all the season was significant because of the team's final position in the First Division. Their runners-up spot was the closest they had ever come to lifting the Championship. The fact that it was achieved with a team that was gradually changing, with a lot of new blood breaking through, speaks volumes for the wealth of talent that could be found wearing the tangerine shirts during those golden years.

Two other interesting facts from that season were the quickest goal ever scored by a Blackpool player, when Ernie Taylor netted after only 13 seconds in the FA Cup at Manchester City. Unfortunately the game was later abandoned due to fog and Blackpool predictably lost the replay. And goalkeeper George Farm got his name on the score-sheet, when he took over the centre-forward position after an injury during the home game with Preston. Alas, the rest of the team didn't play half as well and were beaten 6-2.

Gradually the Cup-winning squad of 1953 was beginning to break up, but it

Stanley Matthews scores as Blackpool go nap once more, this time beating West Brom 5-1 in March 1956.

was encouraging to see them being replaced by exciting new players. A young defender, Jimmy Armfield, was showing his talent, with Jim and Hugh Kelly in the half-back line. Up front, Jackie Mudie had quickly taken over the scoring responsibilities from Mortensen, and during the 1956-7 season scored 32 goals, aided by his partner Dave Durie, who scored 20.

That season saw Blackpool slip to fourth place, despite scoring 93 goals. Their interest in the FA Cup ended at the fifth-round stage, but only after a 6-2 drubbing of Fulham in an earlier round when Mudie scored four.

Attendances were down significantly, with only four games at Bloomfield Road attracting over 30,000 fans. This prompted the local newspaper to declare that the Blackpool public did not deserve First Division football, and unless a new comfortable stadium was built it could not see football being played in the town for much longer. Fans are still waiting for the stadium, although in June 1992 it seems that things are at last moving in that direction.

In 1956-7 there were two important departures from Bloomfield Road: Allan Brown joined Luton Town for £10,000, and Jim Kelly quit League football at the end of the season.

Seventh place in 1957-8 was seen as another piece of evidence that the team's best days were behind them, and with no player able to achieve the 20-goal mark, Blackpool's challenge was fast fading. The FA Cup was now no more than at temporary diversion and a heavy defeat at West Ham ended the Seasiders' interest for another season.

The future was not too bleak, though, with the emergence of a new scorer in Ray Charnley at centre-forward, but there were signs that the maestro himself, Stan Matthews, was inevitably bowing to the passing years. There were rumours that

Dave Durie cannot reach this cross, which is punched away by Tottenham's Ted Ditchburn in December 1957. Spurs won 2-0 at Bloomfield Road.

he was on his way back to Stoke City, but by the end of the season he was still a Blackpool player.

Sadly, though, 1958 saw the retirement of the great Joe Smith after 23 years as Blackpool's manager. He had transformed the Seasiders into one of the great sides of the post-war era and only ill-health prevented him continuing. No club has had a better manager.

One of the club's 'old boys', Ron Suart, took over the reigns at the start of 1958-9 and had the thankless task of continuing the great man's work. A quietly spoken, deep-thinking man, Suart did not do badly in his first year in charge, guiding the team to eighth place. Charnley scored 20 goals with Mudie and Perry also breaking double-figures.

The FA Cup saw a run to the sixth round but a single-goal defeat in a replay at Luton was disappointing, especially as the goal came from former Blackpool man Allan Brown. Also, the great Ernie Taylor said goodbye to Bloomfield Road by joining Manchester United in the wake of the Munich disaster.

The following season saw many changes in team personnel, with Ewan Fenton, Jackie Wright and George Farm all departing Bloomfield Road. Joining, however, were Bruce Crawford, a junior; Arthur Kaye from Barnsley; 'Mandy' Hill, a local schoolboy; and goalkeeper Tony Waiters from Macclesfield, who later played for England.

Charnley kept on scoring, 18 in this season, and Stan Matthews kept on defying all the odds by turning out regularly, indeed, now enjoying a new partnership with Charnley. The team, however, failed to make any impact on the Championship, and their 11th place was to be the last time that Blackpool finished in the top half of the First Division.

The most depressing game at Bloomfield Road came in February, when a rampant Manchester United destroyed Blackpool by six clear goals, a score-line more flattering to the Seasiders than their visitors. The FA Cup ended in a fourth-round replay defeat at home to the eventual Finalists, Blackburn Rovers.

The 1960-61 season was a near-disaster with only one win in the first 13 League games. Relegation looked a certainty until six points from the last four matches lifted the club to 20th place and eventual safety, with Preston and Newcastle going down.

There had been many changes, with Hugh Kelly, Brian Snowdon and Peter Smethurst, a South African import who did not make the grade, all leaving, and no less than eight players making their debuts for the club that season. Amongst them was Glyn James, a future Welsh international who was to play many seasons for Blackpool, Gordon West, who shared the goalkeeping duties with Waiters, Ray Parry and Leslie Lea. The latter was to become tremendously popular with the home fans.

Ron Suart's tenure as manager looked in some danger as the fans had now turned on him, especially after a humiliating 6-2 thrashing at Second Division Scunthorpe United in the FA Cup, yet he rode the storm and continued to rebuild the side to his liking.

The new League Cup provided little interest as Blackpool lost a replay to Leeds at Bloomfield Road, where Don Revie scored for the visitors. Finally, it is interesting to note that the first home attendance under 10,000 for over 15 years was recorded when only 9,947 turned up to see West Ham defeated 3-0. It was a glimpse of things to come.

The final proof that the golden days had ended for Blackpool Football Club came during 1961-2, when the great Stanley Matthews returned to Stoke. All the stars, with the exception of Bill Perry, had now gone and Matthews' departure effectively brought down the curtain on a great era for the club. Most observers believed it was the beginning of the end for the team, and indeed it seemed only a matter of time before the trap door would open once more and send the club spiralling downwards.

Thankfully, there was an improvement with 13th place in the First Division, and an excellent run in the League Cup right through to the semi-finals where Blackpool were beaten by Norwich City over two legs, but it had to be said that the competition was still in its infancy and did not compare to today's tournament. There was, for instance, no Wembley Final to look forward to.

Ray Charnley scored 30 goals and Graham Oates made his debut, but overall it was a quite undramatic campaign.

With the maximum wage now abolished, Blackpool, like many other clubs, would now find it difficult to attract the top players to their club, and, indeed, to keep their stars. With limited resources it was a small triumph to see the team finish mid-table once more in 1962-3, but early exits in both cup competitions was a disappointment, especially financially where the club was now relying more and more on extra gate revenue.

Charnley scored 22 goals and a hard-tackling defender, John McPhee, made his debut. Overshadowing that, though, was the first showing of the brilliant Alan Ball, who was to play such a large part in Blackpool's future over the years. Sadly, the final chapter of the 1950s ended when Bill Perry departed.

Another flirtation with relegation in 1963-4 fuelled the critics as they set upon manager Suart, but with the team in a time of transition it was hardly surprising Blackpool could no longer challenge for the top honours. Ball was the top scorer with only 13 goals, although Charnley did score four in a 7-1 League Cup thrashing of Charlton Athletic.

Newcomers included Graham Rowe and attendances were down once more, now averaging around the 16,000 mark — the lowest in Division One.

There was little improvement in 1964-5 with an eventual 17th position, not helped by a mid-season period where the team went 14 games without victory, including nine defeats and seven in a row. Charnley returned to the top of the goalscoring charts with 21, but already the bigger clubs were gathering around the exciting Ball, and it seemed only a matter of time before he was on his way. Newcomers included Ian Moir and Jimmy Robson, but the highly dependable Roy Gratrix had left after 12 years, and the excellent goalkeeper Gordon West had moved to Everton.

At the end of the following season Ball was sold to Everton for a British record fee of £112,000, and so started a trend that was to become depressingly familiar over the years. It was difficult to retain such a talent, especially as Ball had publicly declared his craving for footballing success, although Blackpool did at least keep his name on their books until after the 1966 World Cup Final.

New names Hugh Fisher, Ronnie Brown, goalkeeper Alan Taylor and, for the last game of the season, Emlyn Hughes all made their debuts, although the latter was to make a total of only 33 appearances for the club before Bill Shankly paid £65,000 for his services. Charnley and Ball shared the goalscoring duties, and the team finished a creditable 13th in the table. Once again, though, early exits in the cup competitions became the rule as opposed to the exception.

After so many near escapes over the years, Blackpool were finally relegated to Division Two at the end of 1966-7 after gaining only seven points at Bloomfield Road and winning only one game. That still stands today as the worst home record in the history of the higher division, yet incredibly that solitary home win, over Newcastle, was by six goals.

Away from Bloomfield Road the Seasiders managed to beat both Everton and Liverpool, and so hold the curious record of winning more games in Merseyside

John Johnston follows up his penalty in Blackpool's 2-1 win a Selhurst Park in January 1969.

than in Blackpool, and to make the story even more bizarre, another of their away victories was at Southampton by 5-1.

This was all done with the help of two new exciting forwards, Alan Skirton, from Arsenal, and Alan Suddick, a tremendously talented player from Newcastle United, who came to Blackpool for a club record fee of £60,000.

Predictably, Ron Suart could not hope to survive such a dreadful season and at the turn of the year he was forced to resign after nine years in charge. He was replaced by one of the club's most popular figures, Stan Mortensen, and surely the most popular appointment ever made by the board of directors.

'Morty' immediately began to dismantle the old side. He was not afraid to make unpopular decisions, notably selling Ray Charnley to Preston after a particularly heavy defeat at home to Millwall, yet he brought to the club some quite excellent players. Gerry Ingram came from his old club, Hull City; a big centre-forward Tom White from Crystal Palace; the tricky Tommy Hutchison from Alloa; and the discovery of them all — Tony Green from Albion Rovers. He was one of the most exciting players ever to be seen at Bloomfield Road, and more than adequately filled the gap left by the departure of Ball, one year previously.

Blackpool spent the season challenging hard for promotion, and after six consecutive victories they went into the final game at Huddersfield, knowing that a win would probably secure First Division football. They won 3-1, but after the premature celebrations had died down there was absolute despair in the knowledge

Blackpool, 1968-9. Back row (left to right): Oates, Alcock, Rowe, Ingram, Thompson. Middle: Craven, White, Jones, Taylor, Hutchison, McPhee, Mowbray. Front: Milne, Green, Armfield, Suddick, Skirton.

that their nearest rivals, Queen's Park Rangers, had won at Villa Park by virtue of a last-minute own-goal.

This meant that QPR had deprived Blackpool of a return to the top flight by virtue of a better goal-average — 0.86 to Pool's 0.65. It did not matter that the Seasiders had gained 58 points, the number they had won in the 1929-30 season, when they first gained Division One football. Blackpool were consigned to another season of Second Division football.

For the new campaign Mortensen continued his rebuilding programme ready for another push at promotion. Leslie Lea was transferred to Cardiff City, Ian Moir to Chester City, Gerry Ingram to Preston, Graham Oates to Grimsby and Alan Skirton to Bristol City. As well as leaving room for 'new blood', it helped the rather shaky financial situation at the club, something which had now become a permanent problem.

Bill Bentley was signed from Stoke and took over at left-back, whilst Terry Alcock, signed one year previously from Port Vale, now broke through into the first team. Unfortunately, the season was one of disappointment with the Seasiders ending it in eighth place. Despite a good run in the League Cup, in which they reached the fifth round, the campaign was a let-down.

The board, perhaps panicked into action by a lack of immediate success and disturbed by rumours of player indiscipline, made a most regrettable decision — they sacked Stan Mortensen. Their decision was greeted by the fans with a mixture of shock and anger, as 'Morty' was as popular a manager as he was a player.

Blackpool, 1969-70. Back row (left to right): Pickering, Armfield, Thomson, James, Bentley. Front: Hatton, Burns, Mowbray, Craven, Hutchison, McPhee.

More worrying, his departure began the merry-go-round of managers for which the Blackpool club became so well known in later years.

Yet there could be no complaints about the Seasiders' new manager, Les Shannon, a quiet man who succeeded in bringing promotion to the club in his first season in charge. Shannon added players such as Mickey Burns, who had cost nothing from Skelmersdale, David Hatton and the veteran Fred Pickering, with Harry Thompson now in goal.

The successful campaign saw promotion gained on an emotional night at Deepdale, when a Pickering hat-trick gave the Seasiders a 3-0 victory. The capacity 34,000 attendance included some 20,000 Blackpool fans. It was made all the more sweeter for Pool supporters, as Preston were consigned to the Third Division soon after. The Seasiders, meanwhile, had returned to the First Division, scene of so many past triumphs.

The 1970-71 season, alas, was quite simply disastrous for the Blackpool club. The same team that had done so well the previous season found life in Division One remarkably difficult and failed miserably. Each week saw new levels of mediocrity achieved by the players, as they proceeded to lose to just about everyone. Only four wins were gained and, predictably, Blackpool were relegated at the end of the season, along with neighbours Burnley.

Even the return of Tony Green, after a long lay-off through injury, failed to lift them as the team capitulated to all kinds of opposition. The fact that 28 players were used that season must surely go a long way to explaining the failure, but also manager Les Shannon seemed to have lost the confidence of the players, the fans and the board. After a 4-3 home defeat by Chelsea — when Blackpool had led 3-0 at half-time and Shannon then made an inexplicable decision to substitute the most effective man on the pitch, Fred Pickering — the manager had little option but to go.

It was a sorry end to a brief career at Bloomfield Road. Shannon was quickly replaced by Bob Stokoe, a man who the club had tried to lure away from Carlisle a year or so previously. Unfortunately, it was too late to stop the rot and at the

Alan Suddick scores Blackpool's second goal in the 3-3 draw with Verona, 26 May 1971.

end of the season the town of Blackpool would play host to Second Division football once more.

During the summer of 1971, Blackpool had a chance to regain some pride when they entered the Anglo-Italian Trophy. The competition involved 12 teams, six from each country, with the winners from each group meeting in the Final. Blackpool finished top of the English group by winning two, drawing one and losing one, and scoring far more goals than any other team in their four qualifying matches.

The Final, against Bologna, was played in front of 40,000 fans and saw Blackpool win 2-1 after extra-time. It was a superb victory over a talented side and gave the club a tremendous morale-boost for the coming League season. The next day, thousands of ecstatic Blackpool fans lined the promenade and packed outside the Town Hall to cheer their returning heroes.

For the 1971-2 season, Stokoe began a massive clear-out of players in an attempt to trim a big playing staff. Amongst those leaving were Pickering, Kemp, Taylor, Rowe and Armfield. The latter had retired from playing after the final game of the previous season, after giving 17 seasons of very loyal service to the club.

New faces included goalkeepers Burridge and Wood, Chris Simpkin and Dave Lennard, and finally Keith Dyson. He came in an exchange deal that took Tony Green to Newcastle and also boosted the finances to the tune of £150,000. On the field a creditable sixth place was achieved and there was a good run to the quarter-finals of the League Cup, where Blackpool were beaten by the eventual winners Tottenham Hotspur. All in all, it had been an encouraging debut for Stokoe.

In the summer of 1972, Blackpool attempted to defend their Anglo-Italian Trophy, and once again they made it to the Final. On the way they had won all their group matches, including a remarkable 10-0 home victory over Lanerossi. In the Final they met far stiffer opposition in AS Roma and were soundly beaten 3-1 in front of 70,000 fans.

As for the following season, seventh place was a disappointment, although there was yet another good run to the quarter-final stages of the League Cup, where it took a late goal in the replay to give Wolves victory.

Jimmy Armfield's last appearance for Blackpool came against Manchester United in May 1971.

The main transfer deal involved Tommy Hutchison, who went to Coventry, with Billy Rafferty coming the other way. The biggest change, however, was in the manager's position, with Stokoe leaving Bloomfield Road rather prematurely to join Sunderland. At Roker Park, he enjoyed success by taking Second Division Sunderland to a Wembley FA Cup Final, where they beat First Division Leeds United.

Another Italian interlude during the summer of 1973 — although this time Blackpool were unable to make the Final — was followed by the appointment of new manager Harry Potts. He had been chased by the club in the 1950s, as a player, so he came with high hopes.

Unfortunately the Seasiders' promotion push could not be sustained and they finished fifth, with little interest in the cup competitions. The squad had been strengthened with the additions of veteran Wyn Davies and a future prolific scorer in Mickey Walsh, plus a promising defender in Paul Hart.

For the next two seasons, though goals were scarce and Blackpool scored only 38 and 40 respectively. Final positions of seventh and tenth were also disappointing and in May 1976, Potts left Bloomfield Road.

Although there had been little success on the field, Potts had succeeded in the transfer market, buying sparingly but effectively and selling star players for large profits. Mickey Burns had gone to Newcastle for £175,000 and goalkeeper John Burridge also moved for a large fee.

Another 'old boy', Allan Brown, took over the hot seat for the start of 1976-7

George Best fires in a free-kick against the Blackpool 'wall' at Craven Cottage in 1977.

and he immediately made some shrewd signings, notably that of Bob Hatton who teamed up with Walsh and formed one of the most effective striking partnerships the club had seen for many years. Also joing the Seasiders was Iain Hesford, another fine goalkeeper who was to make his name at Bloomfield Road. The team finished fifth, which was encouraging, and thankfully they had rediscovered their scoring touch. The future looked promising.

The 1977-8 season, however, will always be remembered as arguably the most disastrous in the club's history. From a seemingly safe mid-table position in March, Blackpool won only one of their last 16 games and were relegated to the Third Division for the first time in the club's history.

One felt that this had all come about because the board had made another one of their incomprehensible decisions in sacking Allan Brown, when the Seasiders were in ninth position in the table and had scored ten goals in the previous two home games.

The reasons were never explained fully, but it started the downward spiral that was to continue for many years. Predictably, players left the club in their droves, including Wood, Walsh and Hatton, the latter two after scoring 36 goals between them in the previous campaign.

Wayne Entwistle heads the first goal in Blackpool's 4-0 FA Cup victory of non-League neighbours Fleetwood in 1980.

Jimmy Meadows, who had been given the temporary manager's job, was replaced by the returning Bob Stokoe as the club faced up to life in the Third Division. Despite Derek Spence's goals, the team found it difficult to adjust and could finish only 12th, with attendances lower than ever. At the end of the season Stokoe walked out for the second time, never to return.

Stan Ternent was then thrown into the chair, and, indeed, he did quite a good job in keeping the team around the middle of the table, with the Tony Kellow-Derek Spence partnership looking quite promising. Ternent, though, never had the chance to improve on an encouraging start. The Blackpool board persuaded old favourite Alan Ball to become manager and so in February 1980, Ternent was dismissed.

Ball returned to Bloomfield Road on a tide of enthusiasm from the Blackpool public, and he was treated like a returning 'messiah'. Unfortunately, his time there turned into a nightmare. Blackpool finished 18th, avoiding relegation only in the last match.

The signs were not good. Ball spent a lot of money on new players, who did not subsequently live up to the reputations they had earned in the past. He also introduced a whole bunch of youngsters, who were unable to cope with League football. At the end of the 1980-81 season, Blackpool were in the Fourth Division and Alan Ball had departed.

The Blackpool club was now in serious financial difficulty. They had paid a club record £116,000 for Jack Ashurst two years previously and not recouped any of that sum; and attendances were at an all-time low. There was talk of the local council stepping in to help and, indeed, of a supermarket chain willing to buy the Bloomfield Road ground, but it was all rather worrying for the club's loyal supporters.

On the field, though, Blackpool adjusted quite well to Fourth Division football, finishing 12th after leading the table for some time. This was all under the managership of Allan Brown once more.

A striker by the name of Dave Bamber was making a big name for himself, although by now both Kellow and Spence had moved on. There was an excellent FA Cup run which eventually saw a heavy defeat at Queen's Park Rangers, but at least it helped financially. In April, though, Brown's second stint as manager came to another premature end as pressures from above forced him to resign.

During the summer months there was something of a 'coup' in the boardroom, with the new set of directors promising greater stability and a more positive outlook. They searched for an ambitious young manager and found him in Sam Ellis.

Ellis was a Lancastrian who had been a successful player and was now learning the management ropes under Graham Taylor at Watford. It was probably the best appointment made for many years. Ellis brought a new pride to the club, with a willingness to win instilled into the players.

His first season was, admittedly, a bad one as the team finished 21st and had to seek re-election, but it was all part of a rebuilding process implemented by the manager.

Of course, there was never any money to spend, so Ellis scoured the youth teams and free-transfer market for his buys. He also made some money by selling Dave Bamber and Colin Morris for large fees, and Bamber's replacement, Paul Stewart, began to emerge as a goalscorer. At the end of 1983-4 season, Blackpool had just missed out on promotion, finishing in sixth place. There had also been a successful FA Cup run which saw the Seasiders beat Manchester City in front of 15,000.

The following season, with the help of new signings Ian Britton, Eamon O'Keefe and Mike Walsh, the team finished in second position and gained promotion to the Third Division. It was a great achievement and one which was celebrated by the whole town.

The club which had forever seemed to be going downwards had not only stopped the trend, but reversed it. Sam Ellis was a folk-hero at Bloomfield Road and it was hardly surprising that many top clubs were now watching him closely. One of the most embarrassing moments, however, came in the first round of the FA Cup at Bloomfield Road, where Blackpool were humiliated by non-League Altrincham. Incredibly, one year later the scene was re-enacted, this time in the second round, and again Altrincham won.

Back in the Third Division, Blackpool did very well, staying in the top four right through to Christmas, but then a serious injury to O'Keefe kept him out of the first team and took away much of the Seasiders' fire-power. For O'Keefe it was a disaster as the injury all but ended his career.

Eventually, 12th place was attained but there were more worrying signs off the field. The club were facing hefty bills for the upkeep of the now delapidated Bloomfield Road ground, with a Manchester supermarket chain looming threateningly. It seemed at one stage that the final home game of the season, against Bournemouth, would be the last time the team would be seen in the town, with the talk of a move to Preston. Thankfully, after yet another power struggle in the boardroom, the club survived.

In 1986-7, there were many player changes. Paul Stewart was sold the following March for a huge fee to Manchester City, but before that Conroy and Britton had departed. Alex Dyer went to Hull City, but a new defender, Steve Morgan, was emerging. Also, the once-prolific scorer Craig Madden came to Blackpool.

The season started well enough and, indeed, by February the Seasiders were still handily placed for promotion, but after the sale of Stewart they faded away to finish ninth. Even more worrying, though, were the poor attendances, only 1,900

Ian Britton celebrates after scoring Blackpool's second goal in their 2-0 home win over Hereford United in April 1985. It drove the Seasiders nearer to promotion.

turning up for the game against Fulham and so creating a new and unwanted record for the club. The style of play used by Ellis' men was now under some criticism and the pressure to bring more success was now intense.

The 1987-8 season saw tenth position attained with Blackpool having an outside chance of the new play-offs, but a poor run-in at the end of the season deprived them. The 'discovery' of the season was that of Mark Taylor, who scored a remarkable 21 goals and became an immediate favourite with the fans. Unfortunately, he was to suffer a serious injury soon after which kept him out of the game for some considerable time.

There was success in the cup competitions, with a good run in the FA Cup which saw Blackpool dreadfully unlucky not to beat their familiar cup rivals, Manchester City, at home, plus a fine home victory over Newcastle United in the League Cup. Alas, there was no hiding the fact that Ellis' love affair with the fans had ended and success was now demanded for the following season.

Despite the arrival of many new players such as Andy Garner from Derby County and the added fire power of Tony Cunningham, in April 1989, Ellis paid for failure with his job. The team were struggling near the foot of the table and after a 4-2 home defeat by Reading, the manager's contract was terminated by 'mutual consent'. It was a sad ending to the third-longest-serving manager in Blackpool's history.

By winning four of the last five games, the Seasiders stayed up, but it had been

Blackpool, 1986-7. Back row (left to right): A.Dyer, K.Stonehouse, N.Law, C.Methven, C.Greenall, B.Thomson, S.Morgan. Middle: P.Stewart, D.Moore, B.Siddall, P.Harrington, W.O'Rourke, R.Sendall, P.McGinley. Front: K.Taylor, M.Davies, E.O'Keefe, M.Walsh, J.Deary, B.Butler, N.Matthews.

a close call. Again, there was little interest in the cups, apart from a fine two-legged victory over First Division Sheffield Wednesday in the League Cup.

Many new players were brought into the club for the start of the 1989-90 campaign, including Carl Richards, Steve McIlhargey in goal, Gordon Owen and Gary Brook. These had all been bought by a new manager, Jimmy Mullen, who had been given the job on a wave of public acclaim after he had helped the team to survival the previous season.

Even more interesting was the power struggle in the boardroom, with local entrepreneur Owen Oyston having an increasingly bigger financial stake. He was to be made chairman soon afterwards, and it is fair to say that without the constant input of cash from the Oyston family, the club would have died some time ago.

Mullen's tenure as manager was brief. After spending thousands of pounds on players who subsequently disappointed, and with the team heading for relegation to Division Four once more, his contract was ended less than 11 months after his appointment. The only bright spot in a depressing season was an amazing FA Cup run which lasted until the second replay of the fifth round game at Queen's Park Rangers.

Unfortunately, that could not compensate for the fact that Blackpool Football Club started a new decade in the Fourth Division.

The story of that first season back in the basement is quite incredible. Graham Carr, who had been so successful at Northampton, was appointed as manager, yet after only four months and with the team down in 18th position, he was sacked. His assistant, the largely unknown Billy Ayre, was put in charge and proceeded to transform the team.

With only one signing — the return of the great favourite Dave Bamber — the Seasiders simply tore up the table, losing only three games out of their first 28. Ayre had instilled new confidence in the players, a belief that had been sadly lacking for the previous few years, and as the season drew to a close, Blackpool were in the heart of the promotion battle.

They went into the final game of the season at Walsall in second place, with only one point required for promotion. But in front of a massive following, the players 'froze' and were beaten 2-0. The play-offs beckoned and after disposing of Scunthorpe United in the semi-finals, Blackpool could look forward to their first Wembley appearance for 38 years. Sadly, on the day that the club made it there, one of their most famous players, Stan Mortensen died. A great day tinged with sadness.

Some 15,000 fans witnessed a night of high emotion at Wembley for the Play-off Final. The game went from end to end before finishing 2-2 after extra-time, and for the first time, penalties would decide promotion in the Football League.

In the sudden death Dave Bamber, who after a wonderful season was enduring a personal nightmare, missed his spot-kick and Torquay United were promoted, whilst Blackpool, who had finished seven points ahead of them in the final table, were consigned to another season of Fourth Division football.

It was a cruel blow, yet Ayre had put pride back into the club and was rewarded soon afterwards with a new contract and a directorship.

For 1991-2, Blackpool were firmly the favourites for not only promotion but for the championship, too. Little money was spent on new players, yet nearly half-a-million pounds was realised with the sale of the immensely talented Alan Wright to big-spending Blackburn Rovers.

The Seasiders began the campaign in the manner they meant to go on, and were in the top four throughout the season. Along the way they broke all kinds of home

Trevor Sinclair battles with Scunthorpe's Graham Alexander at Wembley.

records, and by the end of the season the team had managed a run of 31 wins in 35 League games stretching back to the previous season — a remarkable record.

Unfortunately, on their travels they were not as confident and could win only five times. Also, a behind-the-scenes argument amongst the board, involving the chairman Oyston and the local media proved a distraction. However, it was a case of *déjà vu* when Blackpool approached the last game of the season, at Lincoln, needing one point to go up.

With the help of Dave Bamber's 28 League goals, the push had been more than sustained throughout the season and promotion seemed a certainty. Yet again, in front of a huge following, the team failed to perform and were beaten 2-0. Once again the play-offs beckoned.

Two games against Barnet saw a 2-1 aggregate win and for the second successive season, Blackpool would be at Wembley. Their opponents, Scunthorpe United, had finished five points behind them, so the feeling of history repeating itself was even stronger.

On a red-hot May day, some 13,000 tangerine-clad fans witnessed another dour struggle with the final score being 1-1 after extra-time. Yet again penalties were needed and if nerves were on edge before the game, they would be shattered by the end of it.

Thankfully, Blackpool won the day, as the inexperienced Scunthorpe players failed miserably in front of goal. The Seasiders were at long last promoted and, no matter how close it had been again, they could now look forward to life in the new Second Division, following the formation of the Premier League.

It had been said that if the team had failed, then it was almost certainly going to be broken up. As it is, many of the same players should be appearing in the tangerine shirt for the start of the 1992-3 season, as Blackpool Football Club look to the future with a new sense of optimism, to the start of a new era.

Blackpool celebrate after their Wembley Play-off triumph in 1992.

The 1980s – A Time of Trauma

LIKE so many football clubs in the lower leagues, Blackpool have suffered traumatic times, both on the field and off it. Their lowest point came during the mid-1980s when, on more than one occasion, it seemed as if the town would be saying goodbye to the club for evermore. Only last-minute deals and, eventually, a financial benefactor have kept Blackpool FC's head above water, and even now with the team recently promoted to the new Second Division, the future is far from certain.

The decline can be traced back to the 1970s, after the team were relegated to the Third Division for the first time in its history. Attendances were predictably low, so very little revenue was being realised through the turnstiles, and the players who remained were still being paid Second or even First Division wages, whilst playing in the Third.

It was a continuing spiral which wasn't helped by the board's poor judgement when choosing new managers, especially those who cost a 'king's ransom' when joining the club. The 'Tangerine-Club', which had been erected opposite the ground in the early part of the 1970s, had for many years brought in valuable revenue, but even that came under threat a decade later. By the middle of the 1980s the club was in serious financial straits.

After the Bradford fire disaster, stringent safety measures were introduced at all grounds, and Blackpool were one of the many who found the financial burden almost crippling. The ground was in a state of almost total disrepair, and with the recent ruling that all match receipts should go to the home club, revenue was even scarcer.

It was with all of this in mind, that in 1985 steps were taken to try to ensure the future of the club, whether in the town or not. The club's assets were converted into a property company with its shareholding transferred, whilst the board began negotiations with a Manchester group of developers. They wanted to buy Bloomfield Road for a future supermarket development and relocate both the football club and nearby Rugby League club to a position a few hundred yards away. The clubs would share an all-seater stadium which would form a vast entertainment complex.

Unfortunately, the plans were frustrated by the council who refused to give planning permission to the idea, and so towards the end of the 1986-7, the rugby team had to play its fixtures at Bloomfield Road as they couldn't afford the safety measures imposed on their ground. They eventually moved to Wigan, then split into two teams representing Chorley and Trafford, and only now feel able to return to the town.

The football club, meanwhile, had arranged a loan of £150,000 in stages to guarantee its immediate future, following many appeals and a supporters' march through the town. In fact, the fans had shown their immense loyalty by organising many fund-raising schemes, including a promenade 'fun run' which went a long way to paying for Colin Methven from Wigan Athletic. There were regular rumours of the club leaving the town to share grounds with various neighbours, notably Preston North End, although this was, of course, vehemently opposed by the fans.

Towards the end of the 1980s, local entrepreneur Owen Oyston moved in and secured the club's future by paying off many debts. In fact, the club and its fans

Owen Oysten (right), the millionaire businessman who has come to Blackpool's rescue, with Mr Melling who was forced off the board shortly after this photograph was taken.

owe the Oyston family a great debt of gratitude as they have so far injected over £2 million of their own money to keep Blackpool FC afloat.

The future, though, is still not secure. Ambitious plans for a new 'super stadium' have been thwarted regularly by the council and with Bloomfield Road in a decrepit state, patience is wearing thin. The club has been living from hand to mouth for many years now, and with the team playing its best football for many seasons, the future should be promising.

Promotion in May 1992 was still overshadowed by the uncertainty over the new stadium, but the following month progress at last appeared possible as the council approved the scheme.

The Bloomfield Road Story

BLOOMFIELD Road today stands as a testament to many years of neglect, a ground that has been allowed to fall into disrepair by successive boards, and one which has remained essentially untouched for over 60 years. It is hard to believe now that, at one time, the ground was regarded as one of the most modern in the country, and in fact in 1932 played host to a full international fixture.

The story of Blackpool FC's grounds goes well back beyond the existence of Bloomfield Road, as the club had two homes before settling on their current one. Their first, at the time of the club's formation, was in the Royal Palace Gardens or Raikes Hall as it was more commonly known.

The gardens were part of a vast entertainment complex which included such attractions as a theatre, a skating-rink, a boating-lake and facilities for all kinds of sports such as tennis, cricket and bowling. It was the cricket field that was made available to the club during the winter months, although this was met with some predictably strong opposition from the all-white fraternity.

The shape of the field was, for obvious reasons, unusual for football, but at least it offered covered accommodation for the spectators. On the northern side of the ground, and immediately adjacent to the popular boating-lake, there ran a large all-seater stand that could comfortably accommodate around 1,000 people, although the remainder of the ground was cordoned off by little more than a single rope.

The entrance fee was fixed at 3s 6d and Blackpool's first-ever home match was against Leek, which they won quite comfortably by 4-1.

Raikes Hall remained the club's home until August 1897, when they were forced to move out after it had been decided to earmark the whole complex for future housing development.

They immediately moved to the Athletic Grounds in Stanley Park, situated near to where the cricket ground is today, although not on the site of the current atheltic track deep in the park complex.

At first it seemed a popular move as the first home match, against Burnley in the League, attracted a crowd of 4,000, the mayor 'ceremoniously' kicking-off the game. It seemed a fine alternative and was quite comfortable by the standards of

Bloomfield Road pictured in 1905. The small stand on the west side of the ground seated 300 people.

the day. On the west side there ran a covered stand, with a short length of uncovered seating opposite, and a full racecourse ran around the 24-acre perimeter.

Unfortunately, its remoteness from the town meant that soon attendances started to suffer, the game against Small Heath in 1899 realising only £27 in gate receipts. Also, there had been many complaints from local residents who were unhappy with the unruly elements that were attracted to the club, bad language apparently being a serious problem, so the club were under pressure to move again.

The final game played there, against local rivals South Shore, attracted only 300 people, so it was decided to leave the ground after only two years, despite signing a five-year lease with the landlords.

Blackpool moved back to Raikes Hall for a very short time, as up until then only 71 housing plots had been sold, but in December 1899, the club finally arrived at its resting place, Bloomfield Road.

It was the new home of South Shore FC, who had recently moved from their old ground in Waterloo Road, and at the time was rather quaintly called 'Gamble's Field' after the local farmer who owned the land. It offered little in the way of accommodation with only a small stand on the west side seating around 300, the rest being completely open. After the amalgamation of the clubs it was renamed Bloomfield Road, and Blackpool played their first match against Horwich in a friendly, winning easily 3-0.

It was many years before the ground saw any significant improvement. By 1906 the local Press were pleading with the club to provide a decent Press box as they found it difficult to watch a game from the touch-lines. In 1907, a paddock was built in front of the stand to increase the capacity, but ten years later a serious fire all but destroyed it and necessitated a complete rebuild.

Two years later, the Spion Kop, now the South Stand, was erected and could hold 1,000 standing spectators. With the building of the concrete East Paddock, the capacity had now been raised to a respectable 18,000. That last venture very nearly broke the club as a writ was issued against the directors for non-payment of £3,618 with only £1,000 of the total bill settled to that point. It needed a hastily convened meeting and a decision to double the share capital to £10,000 before the club's accountant could relax once more.

On the north side of the ground a curious little oddity had sprung up, nicknamed the Motor Stand, and so Blackpool were one of the few clubs in the country to have stands on all four sides by the 1920s. In 1925 a new construction was erected on the south side of the ground, costing around £13,000 and eventually holding over 4,000 people. It also housed a new boardroom, offices, dressing-rooms, baths and refreshment bars and was looked on as the most modern in the Football League.

In the summer of 1930, after promotion to the First Division, a massive new terrace was built at the north end of the ground which, after being concreted, could hold 12,000 spectators and so increased the capacity to 30,000. The Motor Stand, which had been standing on the same spot, was then moved to a position between the new structure and the West Stand, and so Bloomfield Road was complete and essentially the ground of today.

From that moment to the present day, the only changes have been cosmetic. After World War Two massive repairs were needed, not because of bomb damage, but due to the fact that the Armed Forces had used it extensively. The club could not complain, however, as the rent they had received had more than paid off the current bank overdraft.

Also a roof was added to the Kop and with the extension of the East Paddock, the capacity was raised to 38,000 in 1954. Floodlights were erected in the summer of 1957, and with extra seats in the West Stand the club had a ground of which they could be proud.

Snow-bound Bloomfield Road pictured in the mid-1960s.

Representative games had become commonplace at Bloomfield Road, with the first being a women's international game in 1920 involving England and Ireland, but the only time a full international game was played was on 17 October 1932, when England met Ireland. The Football League played five games there, the first being in 1931 and the last as late as 1960, and there were two Amateur internationals involving England in 1927 and 1936.

Attendances had gradually risen as the team progressed, peaking on 17 September 1955, when 38,098 turned up to see a victory over Wolves in Division One, but gradually the decline set in and it is unlikely that the team will ever again play in front of a home gate that large.

Indeed, the capacity was reduced to 30,000 in the late-1960s, with the addition of new seats, although that figure looked rather optimistic when Everton were the visitors in 1970. With spectators sitting on the touch-lines and climbing the floodlight pylons, the official attendance was 30,705, but the actual figure must have been different.

During the early 1970s, the board introduced a radical measure of putting seats in the East Paddock, but this proved so unpopular that it was scrapped within 12 months.

One of the most unfortunate incidents took place at the start of the 1980s, when it was decided to take the roof off the Kop, safety reasons being cited as the reason. It cost nearly as much to dismantle the roof as it would have to repair it.

That sort of thinking set the trend and over recent years, Bloomfield Road has become a pitiable venue at which to stage League football. New safety measures have seen the capacity reduced from 18,000 to 12,000, and now down to the current 9,600. And with half the Kop closed, the other half open only to away supporters and the East Paddock segregated, the ground now has a strange feel about it. The atmosphere comes almost exclusively from the southern end, unless, of course, there is a large away contingent present.

The familiar exterior of Blackpool FC's home.

Recently, the old North-West Stand was pulled down because of safety measures, and with the West Paddock recently being voted as the 'most uncomfortable in England' there surely looks to be no future for the Bloomfield Road ground as we know it.

Chairman Owen Oyston has, on many occasions, submitted plans for a new 25,000 all-seater stadium adjoining a vast entertainment complex, a venture which is surely essential if the future of the football club is to be secured. Critics can point out that these schemes have been mentioned before. Indeed, as long ago as 1935 the club were looking towards a new stadium and in 1971 the 'Wembley of The North' was to be built on Stanley Park. Eventually a zoo took over the land earmarked for the stadium.

But with the new Premier League demanding all-seater stadiums, and with clubs in an even more precarious financial situation, it is essential that this complex is realised. The future of Blackpool Football Club depends on it. There was good news in June 1992, when it appeared that planning permission had, at last, been granted.

An aerial view of Bloomfield Road taken after the Kop roof was pulled down in 1981.

The shape of things to come? Where Blackpool Football Club may herald in a new millenium.

Blackpool Managers

Bill Norman
1919-1923

AT the beginning of the 1919-20 season, Blackpool joined the growing number of football clubs to appoint a full-time manager, whereas before, team selection had been the responsibility of a committee comprising directors, captain and vice-captain.

Blackpool's first full-time team boss was Bill Norman and in his four seasons in charge he would help Blackpool to challenge seriously for promotion on three occasions.

Norman had been trainer of the Barnsley side which won the FA Cup in 1912 and he held a similar post at Huddersfield Town before joining Blackpool in the close season of 1919. He struck an imposing figure with his waxed moustache, and he always dressed impeccably, expecting his players to do the same.

He immediately organized spartan training routines, helped by his son-in-law, Allan Ure, who was also the club's trainer, and this disciplined approach soon earned him the nickname of 'Sergeant-major'.

Rebuilding the team after World War One was always going to be a difficult job and although Norman could rely on a number of established players, he was also prepared to delve into the transfer market, which he did on frequent occasions, his greatest signing being that of Harry Bedford.

In his first season, Blackpool missed out on promotion by a whisker after making the running for the majority of the campaign, although the sale of top marksman Joe Lane had hardly endeared him to the supporters. In that 1919-20 season, Blackpool Reserves also won the Central League title for the first time.

The following year saw a similar charge for the higher division until a poor run-in once again denied the Seasiders promotion. After spending heavily before the 1921-2 campaign, it must have come as something of a shock to see Blackpool struggling against relegation with only a double victory over West Ham at the end of the season saving Blackpool from dropping into the Third Division North.

This had given Norman's critics — and there were many — all the ammunition they needed, but he stuck to his task and took Blackpool to the top of the table for the majority of the 1922-3 season.

Once again, though, the team collapsed towards the end of the campaign and promotion was missed once more. Whether it was this, or the criticism he was receiving, it is hard to tell, but during the following summer he and Ure left Blackpool and headed for Leeds United, Norman as assistant manager to Arthur Fairclough, with whom he had worked at Barnsley.

Norman helped take Leeds into Division One but when they were relegated in 1927, both he and Fairclough resigned. Norman joined Hartlepools United as manager and although his years at the Victoria Ground were ones of struggle, he did discover the great W.G.Richardson, who later starred for West Brom. He left Hartlepools in April 1932. Ure, incidentally returned to Blackpool as trainer in 1928.

One story perhaps sums up Bill Norman's approach. One day at Hartlepools, the players complained that it was too cold to train. To prove them wrong, Norman stripped naked and rolled in the snow!

Major Frank Buckley
1923-1927

AFTER Bill Norman's departure, the Blackpool board successfully lured Major Frank Buckley to Bloomfield Road with the promise of an extremely high salary and enough money available to strengthen the squad. In the event — and despite a total change of tactics — Buckley did not really have much more success than his predecessor.

Buckley's previous managerial experience had been limited to a spell with Norwich City, but after leaving them in July 1920, he was out of football and working as a commercial traveller when Blackpool took him on.

As a centre-half he had achieved England honours in a career which encompassed Aston Villa, Brighton, Manchester United, Manchester City, Birmingham, Derby County and Bradford City. He retired during World War One but played one game for Norwich in September 1919, when he was the Canaries' secretary-manager. His one international cap came in 1914, when England suffered a shock 3-0 defeat by Ireland at Ayresome Park.

During the war, Buckley had risen to the rank of major in the 17th Middlesex Regiment — the famous Footballers' Battalion — and he used the rank for the remainder of his life. One of his five brothers, Chris, played for Aston Villa and was later chairman of that club.

Major Buckley's managerial style was controversial and, some say, years ahead of its time. Indeed, on more than one occasion he found himself in trouble with the footballing authorities for his methods. He was an imposing figure, nearly 6ft tall, and was always well dressed, his favourite fashion being plus-fours.

Despite this, though, he was a 'tracksuit' manager and had a special talent for developing young players and his youth policy was the first of its kind at Bloomfield Road.

In his first season in charge, he improved on the previous year by taking Blackpool to fourth place in Division Two, but once again this was something of a disappointment, particularly as the Seasiders had headed the table for most of the campaign.

The following year, as Blackpool struggled to avoid relegation, there was dissent amongst the fans and a group of them formed the club's first supporters' club. One of their main complaints concerned the style of management introduced by Major Buckley. The fans suggested that the players had lost their enjoyment of the game and that this was the reason for the team's lack of success. Buckley ignored them and went about rebuilding the side, which included selling established players such as Herbert Jones and top scorer Harry Bedford.

In the following season of 1925-6, the team played quite well but could only finish sixth, this time being hampered by a very poor start to the campaign. They did not fare much better the next year either, when after paying out a lot of money on new players, Blackpool could only finish just above halfway. It was a huge disappointment for Buckley and when Wolverhampton Wanderers courted him, he did not think twice.

He had made a major contribution to Blackpool, however, and even though he had not brought First Division football to the Bloomfield Road club, Buckley had brought about a new professional approach and, most important of all, a successful youth policy.

At Molineux he guided Wolves from the lower reaches of Division Two into runners-up spot in Division One and to an FA Cup Final. In 1944 he became manager of Notts County — at the staggering wage of £4,000 a year — and later managed Hull City, Leeds United and Walsall. Born at Urmston in November 1882, he died in Walsall in December 1964.

Sydney Beaumont
1927-1928

SYDNEY Beaumont's reign as Blackpool manager was as short as it was unsuccessful. He took over from Frank Buckley in the summer of 1927 and immediately began to dismantle the side and bring in big-money signings. His ideas were completely different from those of his predecessor and his radical change of tactics caused problems as the team immediately struggled, losing five of their first six League games under his charge.

At times his team selection bordered on the bizarre and his tactics were even more bewildering. One change that did work very effectively, however, was that of moving Billy Tremelling from centre-forward to the half-back line and so striking up a rich partnership with Jimmy Hampson. Indeed, Sydney Beaumont could also claim responsibility for bringing the great Hampson to Blackpool in the first place.

Beaumont was a former Preston North End player and this hardly endeared him to the Blackpool supporters. A native of Biggleswade, he had an unremarkable playing career, making 25 League appearances for Watford, one for Preston and 15 for Merthyr Town before drifting into non-League football in Wales.

He joined Blackpool after a spell managing Third Division South club Aberdare Athletic, where he had seen unemployment in the town, a miners' strike and the club's wooden grandstand burn down before they were voted out of the Football League.

As Blackpool struggled even more in the depths of Division One, criticism of the manager intensified. Eventually, in the spring of 1928, with the team in the bottom three, he resigned.

The directors, mindful of financial pressures, decided against replacing him with a full-time manager and instead appointed Harry Evans to carry the title of honorary manager for the next five seasons, aided by the club's trainers.

Alex 'Sandy' McFarlane
1933-1935

AFTER Blackpool had been relegated to the Second Division at the end of 1932-3, there were strong calls from the supporters for the reintroduction of a full-time manager.

Since the departure of Sydney Beaumont in 1928, the club had relied on the services of one of the directors, Harry Evans, who had acted as 'honorary manager'. Although this had been a success — particularly as in 1930 Blackpool had gained promotion to Division One for the first time — it had been felt by the fans and club alike that a full-time team boss was needed to give the side a sense of direction they had been missing in the previous couple of seasons.

The directors looked around and finally settled on Alex McFarlane, a former Scottish international inside-forward who had played for Airdrie, Newcastle United, Dundee (with whom he had won a Scottish Cup winners' medal in 1910) and Chelsea.

A tactician extraordinaire, McFarlane had plenty of managerial experience, with two spells each in charge of Dundee and Charlton Athletic. He first joined Dundee as manager in March 1919 and guided them to the Scottish Cup Final in 1925 before taking over as secretary-manager of Charlton in May that year.

He saw Charlton relegated in his first season but after rejoining the club after another spell with Dundee, he steered Charlton to the Third Division South championship in 1929.

With little money to spend, his feat at The Valley had been remarkable but he resigned midway through a disastrous 1932-3 season.

McFarlane arrived at Blackpool with a reputation for sternness, a strong sense of discipline and also for the ability to spot up-and-coming youngsters. He was a fine judge of a player and when he signed a two-year contract in the summer of 1933, the Blackpool club had every reason to be optimistic.

McFarlane was never a popular manager with the players and, indeed, local newspapers were full of stories of dressing-room discontent. But he did bring a period of stability to the club.

In his first season in charge — and Blackpool's first back in Division Two — he guided them to a mid-table position, quite respectable perhaps but certainly not good enough for the new manager. That summer he completely dismantled the side, allowing no less than nine players to leave Bloomfield Road as he brought in fresh faces. One of his best signings was that of Peter Doherty for £1,000, a player later to be sold for ten times that amount.

The following season was a success with the club just missing out on promotion, finishing in fourth place. The seeds had been sown for the future and McFarlane could look back on a job well done. He had put new pride in the club and had given the fans a lot to look forward to. He was a perfectionist in everything he did and some may say that it was this relentless quest which not only made him unpopular with the players but which also led the board to decide not to renew his contract.

Whatever, his time at Bloomfield Road could be regarded as a success and when he left in 1935, the club were on the verge of greatness. Blackpool was his last appointment and he apparently drifted out of football at the age of 57.

Joe Smith
1935-1958

JOE Smith was arguably Blackpool's greatest-ever manager, his 23-year reign being not only the longest but also the most successful in the club's history.

Smith was born in 1890 and spent nearly all of his playing days with Bolton Wanderers, either as an inside or centre-forward. He helped them to reach two FA Cup Finals, in 1923 and 1926, and also played for England before and after World War One.

Smith was acknowledged as one of the best players ever to play for the Trotters and with the help of teammate Ted Vizard, he scored a then club record 38 goals in one season for them. When he retired from playing, he became manager of Third Division South Reading and in four years at Elm Park, he proved that he could make the transition with ease. He led Reading to runners-up spot twice and to third and fourth in the other two seasons.

In August 1935, Smith was invited to take over as manager at Bloomfield Road, an offer which he accepted immediately, a love of the seaside apparently being one of the main deciding factors.

The transformation he brought to the club was nothing short of remarkable as the sternness and harshness associated with his predecessor were replaced by smiles and informality. Smith was never a 'tracksuit' manager and it has to be said that tactics were not his strongest point, but he did have an incredible ability to motivate players and nearly everyone who played for him had the utmost respect for Joe Smith.

His record speaks for itself: in his second season in charge he engineered a promotion-winning side and then with shrewd purchases and the moulding of existing players, he created one of the greatest sides in the country. The famous 'M' forward line of the early 1950s was responsible for three FA Cup Final appearances and regular challenges for the League Championship.

In fact, well before that in the late 1930s, Smith built a side that was so superior that many people believe that if it had not been for the intervention of the war, Blackpool would have swept all before them.

He was responsible for bringing many of the country's top stars to play for Blackpool, notably Stanley Matthews, who many believed at the age of 31 was past his best. That, of course, was proved totally wrong.

As a manager, Smith never bullied his men, preferring to motivate or maybe even massage their egos. He was a good loser and even in defeat he was ready with a joke and a 'never mind we'll win the next one' attitude. His informality set a precedent at the club and many managers who followed tried to emulate him, but with nowhere near the same success.

His greatest achievement was, of course, guiding Blackpool to their dramatic FA Cup victory over Bolton Wanderers at Wembley in 1953, but in many ways a greater achievement was the transformation of a struggling Second Division club into one of the most powerful and attractive teams in the country.

Remember that 21 of the 23 seasons he was in charge were spent in the First Division and it is fair to say that the club's gradual decline started after his retirement, which came about in 1958 because of ill-health and old age.

The Blackpool club never forgot him, awarding him a hefty 'golden handshake' and also buying him a house in the town. It was the least they could have done for him, as he truly was — and still is — the greatest manager of Blackpool Football Club during its long history.

Joe Smith died on 11 August 1971 and it is said that grown men wept at his funeral. His like will probably never be seen again, more's the pity.

Ron Suart
1958-1967

RON Suart was the first player to return to Bloomfield Road as a manager and for nine seasons he sat in the hot seat during what could only be described as a turbulent time.

When Joe Smith announced his retirement due to his ill-health, the club looked around for a suitable successor, a man who would be capable of continuing the work that Smith had done over the previous 23 years. A daunting task for anyone, especially as at this stage the maximum wage had been abolished and Blackpool, like other clubs, were to suffer at the hands of their larger, wealthier neighbours.

Ron Suart came with an impeccable pedigree. As well as being an excellent player whilst at Bloomfield Road, he had successfully made the transition to football management. After his playing days ended at Blackburn Rovers, he travelled a few miles down the road to become player-manager of non-League Wigan Athletic, before taking over at Scunthorpe United.

A mild-mannered quietly-spoken man, his appointment was well received by the fans and Press alike. He had a keen eye for young talent and during his spell he brought such players

as Alan Ball, Ray Charnley and Graham Rowe to the club. Unfortunately, though, with the abolition of the maximum wage and the new freedom which players now had, he was unable to prevent many of his stars moving on. Also, the club could never hope to match the success of the previous decade and, indeed, after Suart's first season in charge, the team never again finished in the top half of Division One.

Attendances started to drop and Blackpool were soon to be known as a spent force in English football. The critics rounded on Suart and after a 6-2 humiliation at Second Division Scunthorpe in the FA Cup, he was asked to resign. He refused and tried desperately to restore pride to the club, but as each season passed it became increasingly obvious that relegation was on the cards.

The fact that it did not happen until the end of the 1965-6 campaign was a testament to Suart's ability to motivate his players and the mix of youth and experience he had created.

With apparently a great deal of interference from the board over team selections and transfers, Suart found the job almost impossible. In 1966-7, Blackpool won only six League games — and only one of those at Bloomfield Road — and were relegated to Division Two. In January 1967, Suart offered his resignation which was accepted.

He joined Chelsea and spent seven years there as assistant manager, first to Tommy Docherty then Dave Sexton, before becoming manager at Stamford Bridge in October 1974. It was never intended to be a long-term appointment and in April 1975, as Chelsea struggled at the foot of Division One, Suart was replaced by Eddie McCreadie. As at Bloomfield Road, he had never panicked as crises arose and he retained everyone's respect.

Stan Mortensen 1967-1969

STAN Mortensen's appointment as manager of Blackpool in February 1967 was universally popular with the fans. Always a favourite during his playing days, he had remained a Blackpool man, even during his time at Hull City, Bath City and Southport. He was still a local businessman and town councillor, so when he was asked to save the sinking ship that was Blackpool Football Club in 1967, he took to the task with relish.

Unfortunately, Mortensen's appointment came too late for him to preserve First Division status, yet within 12 months he had transformed the same side into match-winners and was denied promotion only on the final day of the season. He quickly proved that he had a keen eye for young talent, for whilst buying Henry Mowbray from Albion Rovers, he noticed a young lad named Tony Green.

Within a week Green was at Bloomfield Road for a fee of just over £15,000 and he went on to play a central part in Blackpool's revival the following year. Four years later, the same player was transferred to Newcastle United for a fee ten times the amount Blackpool had paid.

Mortensen blended youth and experience in his team. He gave them confidence to believe in themselves and, more than anything, he told his players to enjoy their game. He was also not afraid to make unpopular decisions, one of the most unpopular being the dropping and eventual sale of Ray Charnley.

Charnley had played over 200 times for Blackpool and was a kind of folk-hero with the fans, but after a 4-1 home defeat by Millwall,

Mortensen could see that something was wrong. He dropped Charnley and replaced him with new signing Gerry Ingram. It worked perfectly as Blackpool became a force in the Second Division.

However, that first season ended in despair for 'Morty' and his players. Despite seven consecutive victories and a points total of 58, the team were pipped to promotion by Queen's Park Rangers by just 0.21 of a goal. It was a bitter blow to the club and the man, but to Mortensen's credit he never complained but just congratulated his players and promised the fans that they would make sure next season.

For the 1968-9 campaign, there were comings and goings at the club with one of Mortensen's shrewdest signings being that of Tommy Hutchison from Alloa Athletic. The team was shaping up nicely and they should have been promotion favourites, yet strangely they never really 'gelled' and their final League position of eighth was a huge disappointment.

Mortensen was still hugely popular with the fans and most of them believed that success was just around the corner. Bearing this in mind, the decision by the board to terminate his contract in April 1969 seems inexplicable.

There had been rumours of discontent amongst the players, and talk of a lack of discipline, yet not one of them seemed to have a bad word for the manager. It was probably one of the worst and most inexcusable decisions taken by a board in the long history of the club. The reasons have to this day still not been disclosed, but 'Morty', being the gentleman that he was, never showed any bitterness. In fact he stayed close to the club for the rest of his life, often sitting in the stand to cheer on the team.

Many people believe that his dismissal was the start of the downward spiral of the club's fortunes. One thing is certain — it was a long time before Blackpool found another manager of Stan Mortensen's calibre.

Les Shannon
1969-1970

AFTER Stan Mortensen's departure, the Blackpool board searched long and hard for a suitable replacement. They eventually settled on the former Burnley and England 'B' inside-forward and wing-half Les Shannon, who had managed Bury to Division Two in 1968.

Shannon was a man light years away from his predecessor at Blackpool. He was quiet and seemingly distant from his players, yet he quickly commanded their respect.

Shannon did little to change the team at first, except for adding to the squad some very experienced players, notably Fred Pickering and Dave Hatton. He also managed to pick up from Skelmersdale, for no fee, Mickey Burns, a player who was to blossom whilst at Bloomfield Road.

The expectations of the manager were high, as only promotion back to the First Division would be enough to satisfy a now highly critical set of supporters, yet by October things did not look too promising. Only three wins in their first ten games saw Blackpool near the bottom of the table. Yet gradually they began to play together and make a concerted push for the top.

Eventually promotion was gained in the penultimate game of the season — Deepdale of all places — and Shannon was a hero with the fans. He had given Blackpool First Division football in his first season in charge and his team had done it without the help of their star player Tony Green, who had been injured.

Why it all went wrong during the next campaign is a mystery. The team which had played so much like a unit one year previously were now hopelessly out of their depth in the higher division. Shannon, in a desperate effort to stop the rot, constantly changed the team

and used no less than 22 players in the first 14 matches.

The critics were out gunning for him and the supporters, who had been behind him not long before, were now calling for his dismissal. Eventually, after a 4-3 home defeat by Chelsea, he resigned. The board had refused to give him a vote of confidence and the fans, furious at his decision to substitute Fred Pickering in the aforementioned game, demanded his head. Shannon had been in charge for 17 months and now became another managerial casualty in the Bloomfield Road merry-go-round.

After some years coaching in the Middle East, Shannon returned to live on his native Merseyside and recently he was an advisor to the Channel Four TV series, *The Manageress*.

Bob Stokoe
1970-1973 and 1978-1979

BOB Stokoe was first approached by Blackpool in the summer of 1969, after the departure of Stan Mortensen. At the time he declined, preferring to remain at Carlisle United, but just over 18 months later he became the ninth official manager in Blackpool's history.

Stokoe, who appeared in Newcastle United's 1955 FA Cup winning side, was almost a one-club man as a player, making nearly 300 League and Cup appearances for the Magpies as a versatile half-back before being transferred to Bury in 1961.

He eventually became manager at Gigg Lane and was also boss at Charlton, Rochdale (twice), Carlisle (three times) and Sunderland, as well as his two stints as Blackpool's manager.

Stokoe was a strict disciplinarian and one of his first jobs on arriving at Blackpool was to clear out the 'dead-wood' as he called it. Too late to save First Division status, he began to systematically rebuild the side to his liking.

Out went goalkeepers Taylor, Blacklaw and Thompson, plus Graham Rowe and the ever-popular Fred Pickering, and in their place came Dave Lennard, Chris Simpkin and big George Wood in goal. Stokoe also agreed to the sale of Tony Green to his old club, Newcastle, bringing striker Keith Dyson in the opposite direction.

In the meantime, he took Blackpool on a successful European jaunt, namely the Anglo-Italian Tournament, in which they beat Bologna in the Final and made many friends on the way. Stokoe, it seemed, was the answer to Blackpool's prayers.

His first season in charge saw a respectable sixth place, but this was still not quite what the fans expected and they quickly became disenchanted. The style of football employed was not to their liking and, indeed, stories on the back pages of the national Press were harming the club.

Another successful Anglo-Italian venture in the summer of 1972 kept the critics at bay, even though the team were beaten in the Final by AS Roma, but the feeling around Bloomfield Road was that the 1972-3 campaign would be critical.

Once again, there were changes in playing personnel before the season began, with Frank Barton and Billy Rafferty coming in and Tommy Hutchison being sold to Coventry City.

The team started reasonably well and were handily placed for a promotion push when Stokoe left Bloomfield Road. He had been lured back to his native North-East by a club he felt had more potential than Blackpool. It annoyed the fans as he had stated that he intended to remain at Bloomfield Road for at least five years. Blackpool's team faded and Stokoe took Second Division Sunderland to a famous FA Cup Final victory over First Division Leeds United.

Five years later, he returned to Bloomfield

Road with the Blackpool club in dire straits. They had just been relegated to the Third Division for the first time in their history and were looking for a man to rebuild the shattered remains of a once-proud playing tradition.

It proved an almost impossible task as Stokoe was forced to sell his best players just to pay off the outstanding loans and bank overdraft. Out went men like Wood, Hart, Hatton and Walsh, for very nearly a million pounds, to be replaced by youngsters still learning their trade.

That first season in Division Three was a difficult one and the transition was not easy, Blackpool eventually finishing in mid-table. Before the start of the 1979-80 season, Stokoe resigned again.

Harry Potts
1973-1976

BLACKPOOL quickly appointed Harry Potts as manager after Bob Stokoe's untimely departure in 1973 and so established a link which had first been talked about in the 1950s.

Then Potts was an effective inside-forward for Burnley, with whom he had gained an FA Cup winners' medal in 1947. Blackpool, constantly looking to strengthen their team, made a record £25,000 bid for him, only to be turned down by the Burnley board.

Potts eventually went to Everton before being appointed chief coach at Wolves. He managed Shrewsbury Town before becoming manager of Burnley in January 1958 and spent 12 years in charge at Turf Moor, guiding one of Burnley's greatest sides into Europe as League Champions and to an FA Cup Final during some heady days for the Clarets. But he was eventually 'kicked upstairs' to become general manager before joining Blackpool after Stokoe's departure, becoming the Seasiders' sixth post-war manager.

Potts was a genial man, even-tempered and certainly a football thinker. Yet after a particularly good start he allowed the team to deploy negative tactics which eventually proved his undoing. His first season in charge nearly saw him emulate Les Shannon by taking Blackpool to promotion, but after leading 1-0 at Sunderland with only seven minutes to go in their final match, the team lost 2-1 and so missed out to Carlisle United.

Potts bought wisely but expensively, most notably on players such as John Evanson, Paul Hart and the old campaigner Wyn Davies. Although these players were worth the money, the club demanded an instant return of good results and so Potts was constantly walking a tightrope.

After this good start it was disturbing to see the team deteriorate into a negative unit, unable to sustain any real kind of promotion challenge. In the next two seasons they could manage only 38 and 40 League goals respectively, despite the obvious scoring talents of Mickey Walsh.

Also, the selling of Mickey Burns to Newcastle for £175,000 hardly endeared Potts to supporters, even though the sale was forced upon him by severe financial pressures.

At the end of the 1975-6 campaign a strong 'Potts out' faction made themselves heard and with the team managing to finish only tenth, the board sacked him in May that season.

It was difficult to understand how a successful team could have become so insular and lacking in ambition. If Potts had continued the good work he had started in his first season, then he would surely have lasted longer.

One of the highlights of his time at Bloomfield Road was a notable FA Cup win over Burnley

in January 1976, a result which hastened the departure of Jimmy Adamson as the Clarets' manager. Potts returned for a second spell in charge at Turf Moor, from June 1977 to October 1979, and was later a scout for the now-defunct non-League high-flyers, Colne Dynamos.

Allan Brown
1976-1978 and 1981-1982

AFTER Harry Potts' dismissal, the Blackpool club returned to one of its most popular players to manage the team. Allan Brown had already proved himself in football management at non-League Wigan Athletic, Luton Town, Torquay United, Bury and Nottingham Forest, and older supporters, remembering his exploits on the field for Blackpool in the 1950s, looked to the future with optimism.

Brown strengthened the attack. In came Derek Spence and the old campaigner Bob Hatton, who teamed up superbly with Mickey Walsh, and once again the club found themselves in the heart of the promotion race.

Brown's style was relaxed, helped by the knowledge that he was popular with the fans, and this came through in the team's play. In his first season, Blackpool finished in fifth position, just one point short of promotion. In those first 12 months he sold Terry Alcock, Dave Hatton and the hugely-popular goalkeeper John Burridge, but replaced them with youngsters and it was obvious that he had in mind a complete rebuilding of the squad.

The start of the 1977-8 campaign saw Blackpool installed as favourites for promotion, with Brown making encouraging statements about the future. Blackpool's play was open and enjoyable and although they conceded many goals, they could also score them.

This was all part of Brown's philosophy of enjoying the game and it obviously translated to the fans, who were turning up in increasingly large numbers. He sold George Wood to Everton for a large fee, but quickly replaced him with Iain Hesford, a goalkeeper with tremendous potential. Also joining the Bloomfield Road set-up as an apprentice was Londoner Jeff Chandler, who later went to Leeds United for £100,000.

The team were shaping up nicely and were occupying a position just on the verge of the promotion race when the unthinkable happened. After an acrimonious meeting with the board, Allan Brown left Bloomfield Road. The reason remains obscure even today, but it seems that Brown could no longer tolerate the alleged interference the board were making in team selection.

His departure came two days after Blackpool had scored five goals at home for the second match running. Supporters were shocked and wasted no time in making their feelings known. Meanwhile, the team fell away, winning only one more game and eventually suffering relegation to the Third Division for the first time in the club's history.

In early 1981, Brown returned to Bloomfield Road with the job of picking up the pieces after Alan Ball had left. The team were sliding into Division Four and Brown was called upon to perform a rescue act.

It was an impossible task, especially as the club were in even worse financial difficulties than ever before, and Blackpool faced the Fourth Division for the first time. By April 1982, Brown was on his way again. The team had failed to adjust to the lower league and could finish only midway up the table.

Stan Ternent
1979-1980

LIKE Jimmy Meadows before him, Stan Ternent was asked to step into the managerial job at short notice after the untimely departure of the previous occupant. Unlike Meadows, though, Ternent was given the job on a permanent basis.

Ternent, a former Burnley and Carlisle wing-half, had worked well with Bob Stokoe as coach at Blackpool, so his familiarity with the players was an asset as far as the board were concerned and his appointment was seen by the fans as an attempt to bring some stability to the rather shaky vessel that was Blackpool Football Club in August 1979.

Ternant immediately started to reshape the side, spending large sums on new players. Jack Ashurst was secured from Sunderland for a club record fee of £116,000 and also coming in were Dave Bamber, Colin Morris, Peter Noble and Tom McAllister.

Yet despite all these new signings, the team's fortunes did not improve and by early 1980, Blackpool were in the bottom half of the Third Division.

For some time, the board had been pursuing former Blackpool favourite Alan Ball and in February, Stan Ternent's brief reign as the Seasiders' manager came to an end. His had been the sixth different name on the manager's door in ten years.

Ternent, a native of Gateshead, was later assistant manager at both Bradford City and Crystal Palace and manager of Hull City from November 1989 to January 1990.

Alan Ball
1980-1981

ALAN Ball was one of Blackpool's greatest players, yet his 12-month managerial reign must go down as the most traumatic and disappointing in the club's history.

Ball's appointment was well received by the Blackpool supporters. Here was a man who had started his football career at Bloomfield Road and had gone on to great things in the game, yet had always publicly expressed a wish to end his football days at Blackpool.

He returned with enthusiasm, a desire to bring back the good times to the club, and still had enough energy to take the field from time to time.

The year that followed saw Blackpool's fortunes slump even further. Large sums were spent but the quality of the buys did not seem to justify the big fees and a style of play that was completely foreign to the fans and players alike.

Joining a club towards the end of a season is always difficult and it proved no less so for Ball. The club was sliding towards relegation and only some determined performances in the last few games ensured survival. The fans showed no dissent, though, as he was still a universally popular figure.

They were prepared to give him time and when he publicly proclaimed that the team would be promoted at the end of the next season, everyone looked to the future with optimism.

Ball brought along several new faces, although the signings of veterans Ted Macdougall and Willie Morgan did not seem to make much sense, but he was prepared to gamble on

youngsters. John Deary was one of the better signings, but too many of the new faces were heralded as stars of the future, only to have their dreams shattered in the rough and tumble of lower league football.

One of the most unpopular moves made by Ball, and one which prompted criticism from the fans, was the sale of Tony Kellow, a huge favourite at the club.

The 1980-81 season began in familiar fashion with Blackpool struggling near the foot of the table. The early optimism had been quickly replaced by anger as the team's performances failed to match up to Ball's promises. The media started to get on his back and, despite requests for him to change the style of play before it was too late, he persisted.

There were also rumours of player dissent and a lack of communication. None of this helped the position and after the FA Cup victory over neighbours Fleetwood Town, Ball publicly criticised the fans for allegedly not wanting the team to win as much as he did.

This was guaranteed to turn the popular support against him. Eventually it all became too much for both the club and the manager. After defeat at Brentford, Alan Ball's contract was terminated with immediate effect. The dream had ended in ruins.

Sam Ellis
1982-1989

SAM Ellis arrived at Bloomfield Road in the summer of 1982 with no management experience, but a keenness to learn. Within three years he had done what no manager had done at Blackpool for 15 seasons, gained promotion.

Ellis was a fine player for Sheffield Wednesday in the 1960s, starring at centre-half. As a teenager he made his FA Cup debut in the 1966 Final against Everton, when his team lost 3-2, and then moved to Mansfield Town, Lincoln City and eventually Watford.

At Vicarage Road, he became coach and assistant manager to the present England boss, Graham Taylor, and played a great part in Watford's meteoric rise through the divisions. Then Ellis turned down a new contract with the club, preferring to cut his teeth with a club in a lower division. When the Blackpool job was advertised he applied and was accepted.

By this time Blackpool were trying desperately to throw away the shackles that had held them down for the previous ten years or so. A new board had promised stability and were now looking to the future, as opposed to the in-house bickerings of recent times.

Ellis was given hardly any money to spend and so was forced to scour the free-transfer market, as well as bringing along the younger players already at the club. At the same time he was forced to sell one of the stars, Colin Greenall, to Sheffield United just to pay the tax man. It was certainly a baptism of fire for the new manager.

His first season was a learning experience. The team finished in the bottom four of the Fourth Division and were forced to apply for re-election, but Sam Ellis had a belief in the future. The fans, too, had taken to him, especially as the team seemed more committed now than at any time in the previous 12 years.

One year on, Blackpool finished sixth, just out of the promotion places. This had been achieved with the acquisition of yet more free-transfer signings, most notably Mike Walsh from Everton and the excellent Ian Britton.

In fact, in his first two years in charge, Ellis had not spent more than £60,000 on new players, whilst being forced to sell many of his stars just to alleviate the still desperate financial position. One of the notable triumphs of that season was a 2-1 FA Cup victory over Second Division Manchester City at Bloomfield Road.

Promotion was gained in 1984-5 and Ellis'

popularity with the fans at Bloomfield Road was at an all-time high. It had been done, once again, with the minimal amount of financial outlay, new signings Alex Dyer and Eamon O'Keefe being particularly effective.

Ellis also brought on a strong centre-forward by the name of Paul Stewart, who was to be sold two years later to Manchester City for £250,000. His management style was not always appreciated by everyone at the club, though, with tales of dressing-room unrest and trips to the amusement centres instead of training, but it continued to work.

The first season back in the Third began well enough, but soon it became obvious that the long-ball game was not highly tuned enough for success and the manager went into the transfer market in a bid to strengthen the side. Also, there were strong approaches from Manchester City for his services, which he turned down, initially to the fans' delight.

The next few seasons were disappointing, though, as the team promised so much, yet delivered so little. Each time they would start the campaign as promotion challengers, only to fall off midway through.

All of this conspired to end the love affair between the Blackpool faithful and Sam Ellis. Despite some good additions to the squad in Tony Cunningham, Andy Garner and Colin Methven, the team struggled and with relegation a serious prospect once more, Ellis' contract was terminated by mutual consent in April 1989.

He went to Bury, where he had a fair amount of success, before finally joining Manchester City as assistant to Peter Reid, some five years after the Maine Road club had first approached him.

Jimmy Mullen 1989-1990

JIMMY Mullen was appointed manager of Blackpool largely on the strength of the last five games of the 1988-9 season.

After the departure of Sam Ellis, Mullen was asked to take charge of the team until the end of the season with the task of ensuring Third Division survival. With the help of Len Ashurst, he guided Blackpool to four victories in the last five matches and just avoided relegation. Soon afterwards, his appointment was confirmed.

Jarrow-born Mullen, a defender with Sheffield Wednesday, Rotherham United and Cardiff City, was assistant manager at Cardiff and Aberdeen and player-manager of Newport County before joining Blackpool in May 1989 and his appointment was, at first, very popular.

That popularity soon waned, though, as the team lurched from one crisis to another, seemingly fixed to the foot of the table. Money had been spent on new players who, frankly, failed to live up to their billing.

Strikers Gordon Owen and Gary Brook did not fit in, and Carl Richards found Mullen's management style difficult. Blackpool were a team going nowhere and within 11 months Mullen's contract was terminated. The one bright spot was a quite amazing FA Cup run which saw the team in the fifth round for the first time in over 30 years.

Blackpool were eventually relegated back to the Fourth Division and Mullen went on to manage neighbours Burnley. He was successful at Turf Moor, taking the Clarets to the Fourth Division championship in his first season in charge — at the expense of Blackpool.

Graham Carr
1990

GRAHAM Carr's reign as manager at Bloomfield Road was as short as it was unsuccessful. He came in the close season and left at the end of November, just four months later, so becoming Blackpool's shortest-serving manager.

Carr had arrived with an excellent pedigree at management level. He had transformed an unfashionable Northampton Town side some years previously into champions with a record amount of points and goals, and he was regarded as a folk-hero at the County Ground.

The style of play was never pretty but certainly effective, and the question was, could he do it for Blackpool? The answer was a definite no. Carr's attitude was questioned and he upset the fans almost immediately when he allowed the Player of the Year Colin Methven to join Carlisle United, saying that he was neither good enough nor quick enough for Fourth Division football.

As the season progressed and the team made no headway, Carr's position was under pressure, not helped by the fact that he had been slow in agreeing to move to the area. Finally, after a 4-0 defeat at Tranmere Rovers in the Leyland DAF Cup, he was dismissed.

Soon afterwards, Carr joined Maidstone United but that move did not work either and he left within a few months, citing personal reasons for his departure.

Billy Ayre
1990-

AFTER Graham Carr's speedy departure, his assistant, Billy Ayre, was thrown into the hot-seat. Almost unknown outside the lower leagues, his appointment was greeted reservedly by Blackpool supporters, yet in the space of two years Ayres has become the club's most popular and certainly most successful boss since Stan Mortensen.

As a player he had spells with Scarborough, Hartlepool United, Halifax Town and Mansfield Town, and as a manager his only previous experience was at Halifax, where he enjoyed little success.

A North-Easterner by birth, his 'no-nonsense' attitude worked with the players and fans as he proceeded almost immediately to turn around the fortunes of the team. With the permanent signing of Dave Bamber, Blackpool climbed from their lowly position of 18th to second on the last day of the season, losing only three League matches on the way.

The team were playing attractive football and a new feeling of self-belief could be seen amongst the players, something which had been lacking before.

Ayre became a folk-hero with the Bloomfield Road faithful, and his 'showbiz' entrance on to the pitch before each home game was becoming legendary. Unfortunately, the season was to end in disappointment as the last match was lost at Walsall, followed by the Wembley penalty shoot-out disaster, and another season in the Fourth Division beckoned.

Ayre was able to keep the same team together for the following season and under his guidance they continued where they had left off. Throughout the season they remained in the top four, although a lack of funds to strengthen the squad made his job even more difficult.

Once again, after a late-season collapse, Blackpool went into the final game with promotion almost assured if they could gain at least a point. Once again they failed, and for the second year running, Ayre had the monumental task of lifting his players for the play-offs. It is a testament to his motivating powers, and his managerial ability that he was able to do it successfully and guide the team to promotion at Wembley, albeit by penalties once more.

Ayre is incredibly popular with the players and the fans, and there is no doubt that he has a great future as a manager. In a way he reminds supporters of Sam Ellis at his peak, able to build a good, strong side with very little money, although Ellis eventually left the club in unhappy circumstances.

It is hoped that Ayre is given the backing he deserves from the board, so that he can continue to build on what he has already achieved at the club. His future seems assured, it is just hoped by all Blackpool supporters that it is to be at Bloomfield Road.

Blackpool Stars

Alan Ainscow was a promising youngster who rose through Blackpool's ranks to be tipped as 'the next Tony Green'. Ainscow, who was born in Bolton on 15 July 1953, was a midfield terrier of outstanding ability who joined the Seasiders as an apprentice in July 1971. In the Anglo-Italian Final against Bologna in 1971, still without a League appearance, he played the game of his life before being substituted at the end of normal time, due to exhaustion. His League debut came at the start of 1971-2, when he scored in a win over Swindon Town, but it took some time for him to break in regularly. After the departure of Tommy Hutchison, however, he became almost ever-present. He could play on either flank, although later he found himself in a much deeper role and in 1972-3 he was joint top-scorer with Alan Suddick. Ainscow, though, was at his best winning balls from midfield and supplying the front men. In July 1978 he was transferred to Birmingham City, for whom he made 108 League appearances, and later had relatively short spells with Everton, Barnsley (loan), Wolves and Blackburn, as well as playing in Hong Kong. Alas, his early potential was never fully realised and he never equalled the achievements of Tony Green and Alan Ball, two players with whom he was constantly being compared in his early years. He was, though, immensely popular with the Blackpool fans and one of the most exciting young players the club has seen.

	LEAGUE		*FA CUP*		*FL CUP*		*TOTAL*	
	App	*Gls*	*App*	*Gls*	*App*	*Gls*	*App*	*Gls*
1971-72	8/10	3	0/1	0	1	0	9/11	3
1972-73	34/3	10	0/1	0	6	0	40/4	10
1973-74	18/1	3	1	0	0	0	19/1	3
1974-75	31	4	1	0	1	0	33	4
1975-76	35	2	0	0	1	0	36	2
1976-77	17	2	2	0	1	0	20	2
1977-78	35	4	1	0	0	0	36	4
	178/14	28	5/2	0	10	0	193/16	28

ALAN AINSCOW

'GEORDIE' ANDERSON

When 'Geordie' Anderson arrived at Blackpool in 1899, he was, according to the local newspapers, a little 'worse for wear'. This did not refer to his state of mind, but to the fact that he was regarded as a veteran. Anderson had made nearly 200 appearances for his previous club, the mighty Blackburn Rovers, where he had also been captain. He was signed because he had recently moved to the town and had expressed a preference for playing for Blackpool in the clean and bracing fresh-air. Blackpool, of course, were happy to sign a strong, reliable defender. As it turned out, he played most of his games in attack, due to the presence of Harry Stirzaker at centre-half. Anderson revelled in his new role and during 1901-02 he was top scorer with 12 goals, the only man to achieve double figures. He worked with the up and coming youngsters at the club, and after his playing days were over he was given a temporary position as team coach. Anderson played some great games for the club, but none more so than in February 1904, at home to Burton United, when, along with new signing Whittle, he tore the opposing defence apart, scoring a hat-trick in the 4-1 win. The local newspapers heaped lavish praise upon him, suggesting that if the team had consisted of 11 Anderson's, they could win the League, the FA Cup — and the Boat Race, too!

	LEAGUE		*FA CUP*		*TOTAL*	
	App	*Gls*	*App*	*Gls*	*App*	*Gls*
1900-01	7	2	-	-	7	2
1901-02	29	12	-	-	29	12
1902-03	21	8	-	-	21	8
1903-04	21	7	-	-	21	7
	78	29	-	-	78	29

JIMMY ARMFIELD

After the 1962 World Cup in Chile, Jimmy Armfield was voted by the Press corps as 'the best right-back in the world'. It was a supreme honour and one which he thoroughly deserved. Born in Denton, Manchester in September 1935, his family moved to Blackpool where he spent his school years and quickly began to shine at sports, notably Rugby Union and football. It was during a practice match at Bloomfield Road that manager Joe Smith spotted Armfield and offered him a trial. On 27 December 1954 he made his debut at Portsmouth to begin a 17-year association with the club, during which he made a record 569 appearances, which included ten years as captain. If any player could be described as a 'one-club-man' then Jimmy Armfield must be that player. His main attributes were speed, superb distribution, outstanding tackling and an enormous capacity for hard work. Time and time again, especially during the team's difficult days in the 1960s, he would somehow find an extra ounce of energy when all seemed lost, and in turn motivate the men around him. This was one of the many things that made him such a great captain, not only for Blackpool but also England. He developed the overlap, so loved by defenders nowadays, to such an art form, that fans used to flock to the grounds to see him in action. He struck a partnership with Stanley Matthews in the late 1950s which would time and again mesmorise opposing markers. Armfield was voted Young Player of the Year in 1959 and was unlucky not to become Footballer of the Year in 1966, being narrowly beaten by Bobby Charlton. He lifted the Blackpool Player of the Year title instead, a tribute to his marvellous loyalty and leadership. Unfortunately he shared in little success whilst with the club, the exception being promotion in 1969-70. After the game at Preston he was chaired off the field by jubilant supporters, with a smile on his face and pride in his heart. He, more than anyone, had helped Blackpool back to Division One. His international career began in 1956, when appeared for the Under-23 side, and he made his full England debut on 13 May 1959 against Brazil in front of over 120,000 fans. There then followed 43 caps, a record for the club, which included 15 games as captain. As well as the 'best right-back in the world' honour, he was also voted as 'best right-back in Europe' for three successive seasons from 1962 to 1964. He bowed out of international football in 1966 to be replaced by George Cohen of Fulham, and so missed an opportunity to appear in a World Cup Final. He played his last game for Blackpool in May 1971, and was rewarded with a testimonial on his 35th birthday. Thousands turned out to pay tribute to him. He later managed Leeds United with some success and is now a football radio commentator and journalist.

	LEAGUE		*FA CUP*		*FL CUP*		*TOTAL*	
	App	*Gls*	*App*	*Gls*	*App*	*Gls*	*App*	*Gls*
1954-55	2	0	0	0	-	-	2	0
1955-56	32	0	1	0	-	-	33	0
1956-57	38	0	4	0	-	-	42	0
1957-58	27	0	1	0	-	-	28	0
1958-59	32	0	6	0	-	-	38	0
1959-60	41	1	3	0	-	-	44	1
1960-61	40	0	1	0	1	0	42	0
1961-62	37	0	2	0	6	0	45	0
1962-63	39	0	2	0	2	0	43	0
1963-64	35	0	2	0	2	0	39	0
1964-65	40	2	1	0	1	0	42	2
1965-66	35	1	2	0	2	0	39	1
1966-67	29	0	0	0	2	0	31	0
1967-68	41	1	2	0	2	0	45	1
1968-69	34	0	1	0	4	0	39	0
1969-70	40	1	3	0	2	0	45	1
1970-71	27	0	2	0	1	0	30	0
	569	6	33	0	25	0	627	6

JACK ASHURST

Jack Ashurst is Blackpool's most expensive player, costing the Seasiders £116,666 when he joined them from Sunderland in October 1979. Born in Coatbridge on 12 October 1954, Ashurst spent most of his career with the Roker Park club, whom he joined as an apprentice in October 1971. He would have made many more than his 129 full League appearances for the Rokerites, but for the presence of Dave Watson at centre-half. Ashurst was in their squad for the 1973 FA Cup Final, although injury ruled him out of the Wembley game. He made his Blackpool debut under Stan Ternent in November 1979, in a draw at Gillingham, replacing the veteran Peter Suddaby at centre-half. Over the next season or so, he was used as a utility player, but then suffered injuries which curtailed his appearances. There was also the pressure of being the club's most expensive player and it was all a huge disappointment to the fans and the club. When Allan Brown rejoined Blackpool as manager, he let Ashurst go. Ashurst moved to Carlisle for £40,000 in August 1981, then played for Leeds United before returning to Bloomfield Road in 1991-2, at the age of 37, when he was with Doncaster Rovers.

	LEAGUE		*FA CUP*		*FL CUP*		*TOTAL*	
	App	*Gls*	*App*	*Gls*	*App*	*Gls*	*App*	*Gls*
1979-80	25	0	2	0	0	0	27	0
1980-81	28	3	2	0	2	1	32	4
	53	3	4	0	2	1	59	4

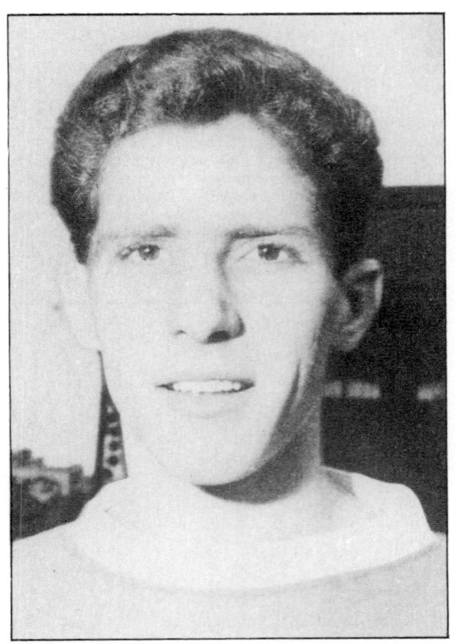

ALAN BALL

Alan Ball was quite simply one of the most exciting players ever seen at Bloomfield Road, a tireless midfielder who became one of the most famous English footballers of the 1960s and '70s. In 1966 he was transferred to Everton for a British record fee of £112,000 and then five years later went to Arsenal for another record fee, this time £220,000. Ball played 76 times for England, including the 1966 World Cup Final when he was only 21 years of age, and continued playing right through to the early 1980s. Born at Farnworth, Lancashire, he had trials with Wolves and Bolton before joining Blackpool in 1962 and Ron Suart gave him his League debut that August, in a win at Liverpool. It took a while for him to break into the team on a permanent basis, but when he did he was tremendously effective, especially when teaming up with Ray Charnley. In 1963-4 and 1965-6 he was the club's top scorer as they fought desperately against relegation. His England debut came in 1965, against Yugoslavia, and following the triumphant World Cup Final campaign, his move to Everton was confirmed. At Goodison he won a Championship medal and an FA Cup runners-up medal, and with Arsenal he gained runners-up medals in the League and the FA Cup again. He later helped Southampton into Division One and then returned to Blackpool (see *Blackpool Managers*) and later managed Bristol Rovers and Portsmouth, whom he also guided to Division One before seeing them relegated 12 months later. Ball also skippered Arsenal and England.

	LEAGUE		*FA CUP*		*FL CUP*		*TOTAL*	
	App	*Gls*	*App*	*Gls*	*App*	*Gls*	*App*	*Gls*
1962-63	5	0	0	0	0	0	5	0
1963-64	31	13	2	0	1	1	34	14
1964-65	39	11	1	1	2	1	42	13
1965-66	41	16	2	0	2	1	45	17
	116	40	5	1	5	3	126	44

Graham Carr's last act as manager was to secure former 'Pool favourite Dave Bamber on a month's loan. Four weeks later, Billy Ayre agreed to pay Hull City £35,000 and complete a full circle in the player's career. Born on 1 February 1959 in St Helens, Bamber joined Blackpool from Manchester University, signing for Stan Ternent. During the next four seasons of struggle he scored 36 goals in 100 games under four different managers. In 1981-2 and 1982-3 he was top scorer before joining Coventry City for £50,000, after the emergence of Paul Stewart at Blackpool. For Coventry he made 19 appearances (three goals) before transfers to Walsall (seven goals in 20 games), Portsmouth (four appearances, scoring once) and Swindon (31 goals in 106 appearances). Then high-flying Watford paid £105,000 for him, but after 18 appearances and three goals he was moved to Stoke City for £190,000. With only eight goals in 43 games for Stoke, Bamber moved to Hull City, where five goals in 28 games was another disappointment. His career was almost at a halt when Blackpool came for him. He scored on his 'debut' at Hereford and ended the season top scorer. An injury towards the end probably cost 'Pool promotion but in 1991-2 he had the best spell of his career to help Blackpool to promotion via the play-offs.

	LEAGUE		*FA CUP*		*FL CUP*		*TOTAL*	
	App	*Gls*	*App*	*Gls*	*App*	*Gls*	*App*	*Gls*
1979-80	6/1	1	0/1	0	0	0	6/2	1
1980-81	12/3	3	0	0	0	0	12/3	3
1981-82	38	15	5	1	2	1	45	17
1982-83	25/1	10	2	1	5	4	32/1	15
1990-91	24	17	1	0	0	0	25	17
1991-92	47	29	2	1	4	6	53	36
	152/5	75	10/1	3	11	11	173/6	89

DAVE BAMBER

When Harry Bedford joined Blackpool he did more than just fill the gap left by Joe Lane's departure — he surpassed Lane's records for the club. Born near Chesterfield in October 1899, Bedford joined Nottingham Forest in 1919 and it was after he had played havoc with Blackpool's defence at the City Ground that the promotion-seeking Seasiders signed him in March 1921. Bedford scored seven goals in his first ten League matches and although it was not enough to bring First Division football — the team faltered badly in the run-in — Bedford was obviously a star of the future. In 1922-3 and 1923-4 he was the country's top scorer, a feat which only Jimmy Hampson equalled with Blackpool. In 1924-5, Bedford's goals helped Blackpool reach the FA Cup fourth round for the first time. He could sniff out a half-chance, had tremendous strength which made up for a comparative lack of speed, and a fierce shot. Surprisingly he gained only two England caps, but once scored four goals for the Football League against the Irish League. In September 1925 he moved to Derby County for a fee of over £3,000, Blackpool again bowing to financial pressure. For five consecutive seasons, Bedford was Derby's top scorer and he later played for Newcastle United, Sunderland, Bradford and Chesterfield. A great player and yet another Blackpool goalscoring machine, Harry Bedford died at Derby in June 1976.

	LEAGUE		*FA CUP*		*TOTAL*	
	App	*Gls*	*App*	*Gls*	*App*	*Gls*
1920-21	10	7	0	0	10	7
1921-22	30	11	1	1	31	12
1922-23	42	32	1	0	43	32
1923-24	40	32	2	1	42	33
1924-25	40	24	7	4	47	28
1925-26	7	6	0	0	7	6
	169	112	11	6	180	118

HARRY BEDFORD

BILL BENTLEY

Bill Bentley was one of football's hard men, at first an aggressive defender who loved the crunching tackle and later developed into an overlapping full-back. He was born at Stoke on 21 October 1947 and began his career with Stoke City, for whom he made 48 League appearances before being transferred to Blackpool in January 1969 for £30,000. He remained at Bloomfield Road for seven seasons, making almost 300 League appearances following his debut in a home defeat by Charlton. Bentley soon established an understanding with Terry Alcock, and later struck up a formidable midfield partnership with him, although at first he worked alongside Jimmy Armfield, perfecting the famous overlap that Armfield had made his trademark. Over the years, Bentley played in a variety of roles — in the heart of defence, in midfield and then in attack, where, although he rarely scored, what goals he did net were usually spectacular: the winner against Burnley in the 1976 FA Cup will live long in the memory. In the 1971 Anglo-Italian Cup Final he stifled the Bologna defence practically single-handed as well as supplying the through-ball for Craven to equalize. Alas, his career was plagued by injury and in July 1977 he was allowed to move to Port Vale, where he ended his League career.

	LEAGUE		*FA CUP*		*FL CUP*		*TOTAL*	
	App	*Gls*	*App*	*Gls*	*App*	*Gls*	*App*	*Gls*
1968-69	17	0	0	0	0	0	17	0
1969-70	28/5	1	2/1	0	2	1	32/6	2
1970-71	32/2	0	0	0	1	1	33/2	1
1971-72	23	1	1	0	1	0	25	1
1972-73	40	1	1	0	7	0	48	1
1973-74	38	2	1	0	2	0	41	2
1974-75	36	3	1	0	1	0	38	3
1975-76	36	0	2	1	1	0	39	1
1976-77	39	3	2	0	4	0	45	3
	289/7	11	10/1	1	19	2	318/8	14

IAN BRITTON

Born in Dundee on 19 May 1954, midfielder Ian Britton began his career at Chelsea, whom he joined in July 1971. After his debut at Blackpool, when he scored the only goal, he made 263 League appearances for Chelsea before transferring to Dundee United in August 1982. With them he enjoyed great success, including European football. In November 1983, Britton moved to Blackpool on a month's loan and impressed Sam Ellis enough for the manager to sign him for a small fee. His debut came as a substitute in a defeat at Doncaster. Small and stocky, he was deceptively quick and loved to go forward. Indeed, in his first season at Bloomfield Road his goals tally was bettered only by Paul Stewart. His best period came when he teamed up with Mike Conroy in midfield. Britton helped the club to promotion in 1985, scoring some important goals, not least in the home win over Hereford when it seemed the team would never breakthrough. He was a favourite with the fans, who were disappointed when he joined struggling Burnley for a nominal fee in August 1986. With Conroy also departed, Blackpool's successful midfield was seriously weakened. Britton continued to make headlines. On the last day of 1986-7 he gave Burnley a 2-0 lead over Orient, when they needed to win to avoid relegation from the Football League. Britton left the Clarets in the summer of 1989 but still lives and works in that area.

	LEAGUE		*FA CUP*		*FL CUP*		*TOTAL*	
	App	*Gls*	*App*	*Gls*	*App*	*Gls*	*App*	*Gls*
1983-84	29/1	9	5	0	0	0	34/1	9
1984-85	46	5	1	0	4	1	51	6
1985-86	25/5	1	1	0	2	0	28/5	1
	100/6	15	7	0	6	1	113/6	16

By the time Tom Browell came to Bloomfield Road in 1926, he was already a veteran, yet he served Blackpool admirably for three seasons. Born in Walbottle, Northumberland, in 1891, he joined his two brothers at Hull City, making his debut for the Anlaby Road club in September 1910. A year later, after scoring 32 goals in 52 games for Hull, he was transferred to Everton for £1,650, a big fee in those days. 'Boy' Browell, as he was known throughout his career, moved to Manchester City for £1,500 in October 1913 and played for them in the 1926 FA Cup Final before Blackpool boss Major Frank Buckley paid £1,100 for him, part of a huge rebuilding process undertaken by the ambitious manager. Browell made his debut in September, in a home draw with Darlington. He teamed up with Downes on the left wing and in his first full season netted 14 goals to become the club's second highest scorer. Those goals included a hat-trick in the final game against Notts County. For 1927-8, he switched to the right side and teamed up with Meredith and the prolific Jimmy Hampson. Eventually, age got the better of him and with the emergence of Jack Oxberry, Browell was released. He stayed in the area, signing as player-coach for Lytham. He later worked as a tram driver and died on 5 October 1955.

	LEAGUE		*FA CUP*		*TOTAL*	
	App	*Gls*	*App*	*Gls*	*App*	*Gls*
1926-27	24	14	1	0	25	14
1927-28	28	9	1	0	29	9
1928-29	14	4	0	0	14	4
1929-30	1	0	2	2	3	2
	67	27	4	2	71	29

TOM BROWELL

During Allan Brown's time at Blackpool the club reached two FA Cup Finals but, despite playing a major part in helping them there, he missed both due to injury. In 1951 he was forced out after suffering a knee injury against Huddersfield; in 1953 he broke his left leg in scoring the 88th-minute winner against Arsenal in the sixth round. Born in Kennoway, Fife, on 12 October 1926, Brown was a Scottish international with East Fife when Blackpool paid £26,500 for him in December 1950. The fee was the largest received by a Scottish club. Brown, a burly inside-forward, could drop the ball exactly on the spot from almost any distance and he also possessed a fierce shot. His debut came in December 1950, in a victory at Charlton, when he replaced Bill Slater, and he made the position his own. When he teamed up with Stan Mortensen they accounted for most of Blackpool's goals. Brown, an almost ever-present, joined a Scottish invasion which included Mudie, Fenton, Kelly and Farm. He played for Scotland in the 1954 World Cup Finals and during his time at Bloomfield Road, Blackpool experienced their most successful years. With Matthews, Mortensen, Perry and Taylor, Brown played in a formidable front line. In December 1957 he was transferred to Luton Town for just under £10,000 and appeared in the 1959 Cup Final against Nottingham Forest, albeit on the losing side. After ending his career with Portsmouth, Brown went into management (see *Blackpool Managers*).

	LEAGUE		*FA CUP*		*TOTAL*	
	App	*Gls*	*App*	*Gls*	*App*	*Gls*
1950-51	16	3	7	2	23	5
1951-52	37	14	1	0	38	14
1952-53	29	15	5	2	34	17
1953-54	27	11	7	2	34	13
1954-55	19	6	0	0	19	6
1955-56	18	6	1	0	19	6
1956-57	17	13	1	0	18	13
	163	68	22	6	185	74

ALLAN BROWN

MICKEY BURNS

This former England amateur international, picked up by Les Shannon from Skelmersdale United, was Blackpool's top scorer in three of his five seasons before being sold to Newcastle for £175,000. Burns, who has a teaching degree, was persuaded to join Second Division Blackpool in 1969. He was a fast winger who could score goals and older fans were soon making comparisons with the great Bill Perry. He scored on his League debut, a win over Portsmouth in August 1969, and helped win promotion back to Division One. He could play on either flank and was top scorer in three of the next four seasons, including the disastrous campaign in the First Division. His best spell was in 1971-2 when he netted 17 League goals. In the Anglo-Italian trophy, he was particularly prolific, notching four in the 10-0 defeat of Lanerossi, and getting the extra-time winner against Bologna in the 1971 Final. Alas, he was unpopular with a section of the home fans, who regarded his style as too individualistic. In the summer of 1974 he asked for a transfer and moved to Newcastle. With the Magpies he played in the 1976 League Cup Final before spells at Cardiff and Middlesbrough, after which he became the PFA's education officer.

	LEAGUE		*FA CUP*		*FL CUP*		*TOTAL*	
	App	*Gls*	*App*	*Gls*	*App*	*Gls*	*App*	*Gls*
1969-70	27/2	6	3	1	2	0	32/2	7
1970-71	26/4	10	1	0	1	0	28/4	10
1971-72	40/1	17	1	0	4	3	45/1	20
1972-73	39	6	1	0	6	2	46	8
1973-74	42	14	1	0	2	3	45	17
	174/7	53	7	1	15	8	196/7	62

JOHN BURRIDGE

At the start of 1971, John Burridge was playing for Workington Reserves in the Northern Alliance. Yet in April that year he made his First Division debut at Goodison Park, playing for Blackpool against Everton after being brought to Bloomfield Road on a month's loan after stand-in goalkeeper Neil Ramsbottom had broken his arm. Blackpool manager Bob Stokoe was already aware of Burridge's potential and had tried to sign him when he was boss at Carlisle United. On his debut Burridge almost single-handedly kept the Everton forwards at bay and one save from Alan Ball was truly world class. His performance that day persuaded the club to sign him permanently for £10,000. A tremendously popular figure, Burridge stayed at the club five years, under constant pressure from George Wood. Rather small for a 'keeper, he spent long hours on the training pitch catching crosses and high balls. Always spectacular, he was the perfect showman and loved to play up to the crowd. One of his finest moments came in the 1971 Anglo-Italian Cup Final in Bologna, when he earned the praise of the normally highly critical Italian fans. His best days probably came after he left Bloomfield Road, when he became something of a journeyman, playing in turn for Aston Villa, Southend United (loan), Crystal Palace, QPR, Wolves, Derby County (loan), Sheffield United, Southampton, Newcastle United and Hibernian.

	LEAGUE		*FA CUP*		*FL CUP*		*TOTAL*	
	App	*Gls*	*App*	*Gls*	*App*	*Gls*	*App*	*Gls*
1970-71	3	0	0	0	0	0	3	0
1971-72	34	0	1	0	3	0	38	0
1972-73	22	0	1	0	5	0	28	0
1973-74	30	0	1	0	0	0	31	0
1974-75	38	0	1	0	1	0	40	0
1975-76	7	0	0	0	1	0	8	0
	134	0	4	0	10	0	148	0

Ray Charnley is Blackpool's most prolific goalscorer behind Jimmy Hampson and Stan Mortensen. Unlike Hampson and Mortensen, though, Charnley's goals came in a struggling team. The tall, stylish centre-forward was born in Lancaster on 29 May 1935 and bought from non-League Morecambe for £1,000 in May 1957. His debut came that September, in a defeat at Luton, and four weeks later he scored twice in Blackpool's biggest-ever home victory, 7-0 against Sunderland, before going off with a serious head injury. Eventually he teamed up with Jackie Mudie, a move inspired by Joe Smith and later used to good effect by Ron Suart. Charnley was Blackpool's top scorer in seven seasons and netted his 100th League goal in his 156th game, a record only marginally bettered by Harry Bedford. Charnley, who narrowly missed the 200 mark, played his best football alongside Alan Ball. In October 1962 he received a belated England call-up against France but it was perhaps too late in the day and he was never picked again. After a bad home defeat by Millwall at the beginning of 1967-8, manager Stan Mortensen made the unpopular decision to drop Charnley and he was soon on his way to rivals Preston, who had rejected him in 1956. He returned to Blackpool nine days later — and scored. Charnley, who ended his career with Wrexham and Bradford, was certainly one of the Seasiders' most exciting players.

	LEAGUE		*FA CUP*		*FL CUP*		*TOTAL*	
	App	*Gls*	*App*	*Gls*	*App*	*Gls*	*App*	*Gls*
1957-58	20	12	1	0	-	-	21	12
1958-59	35	20	6	6	-	-	41	26
1959-60	34	18	3	0	-	-	37	18
1960-61	41	27	1	1	0	0	42	28
1961-62	41	30	2	0	7	6	50	36
1962-63	41	22	2	0	3	0	46	22
1963-64	28	10	2	1	2	4	32	15
1964-65	38	21	1	0	2	1	41	22
1965-66	41	16	2	1	2	2	45	19
1966-67	40	14	1	1	5	6	46	21
1967-68	4	3	0	0	2	0	6	3
	363	193	21	10	23	19	407	222

RAY CHARNLEY

HARRY 'GYP' COOKSON

Born in 1869, Harry 'Gyp' Cookson played in only one full season for Blackpool, but for many years he had been involved with South Shore FC. Cookson was a big, strong forward who liked to score goals. He had been the mainstay of South Shore's forward line for many seasons and helped the club win the Fylde Cup in 1888. When the famous Blackburn Olympic team visited the town, he apparently had the game of his life, scoring a goal in the 1-1 draw which followed a remarkable 3-0 victory over the same side seven days earlier. In 1892-3, Cookson had played for Accrington in the First Division, scoring 15 goals in 30 League and Cup games — including a hat-trick in a 5-2 win at Stoke — before Accrington dropped out of the Football League. At the start of 1902-03, he signed for his home-town club, Blackpool. During that campaign he played alongside Anderson and Jack Parkinson, becoming top scorer with eight goals. It was not a successful season for the club, though, as once again they fought against re-election before finishing 14th. Cookson retired from playing, although he remained at the club to help coach the youngsters. He also kept his connections with the town, living there until he died in 1922, aged just 53. Cookson was one of many players who contributed greatly to the increasing success of the town's two clubs at the turn of the century, although he enjoyed his greatest success at Blackpool's neighbours, South Shore.

	LEAGUE		*FA CUP*		*TOTAL*	
	App	*Gls*	*App*	*Gls*	*App*	*Gls*
1902-03	33	8	-	-	33	8
	33	8	-	-	33	8

JACK COX

Jack Cox's was the first big transfer deal involving a Blackpool player. In February 1898 he was transferred to Liverpool, for the then large sum of £150, so enabling Blackpool to announce a loss of 'only' £441 for the season, as opposed to over £1,000 for the previous campaign. Locally born, Cox went to Blackpool via neighbours South Shore in the close season of 1897. He made his debut in October 1897 against Burton Swifts, scoring both goals in the 2-1 home victory, and went on to score 12 in 17 appearances. He was a fast and tricky outside-left who, coupled together with Jack Parkinson, formed a formidable partnership. Soon far wealthier clubs came after him and Blackpool, mindful of financial restraints, let him go after less than one season in their first team. He helped Liverpool to the League Championship in 1900-01 and 1905-06 and the Second Division title in 1904-05. He also won England honours during the early part of the century, when he was Liverpool's top scorer. In 1909, after scoring 80 goals in 360 League and Cup appearances for Liverpool, he returned to Blackpool on a free transfer, effectively becoming the club's first player-manager. He had lost none of his speed but his goalscoring deserted him and he bowed out in 1911. Despite having his best years with Liverpool, Jack Cox was still one of Blackpool's great early names.

	LEAGUE		*FA CUP*		*TOTAL*	
	App	*Gls*	*App*	*Gls*	*App*	*Gls*
1897-98	17	12	-	-	17	12
1909-10	25	3	0	0	25	3
1910-11	28	3	1	0	29	3
1911-12	15	0	0	0	15	0
	85	18	1	0	86	18

JOHN CRAVEN

When John Craven made his debut for Blackpool in August 1965, in a defeat at Tottenham, he did so at left-back. When he was transferred to Crystal Palace some six years later, it was as a centre-forward and Blackpool's club captain. Craven, who was born at St Annes on 15 May 1947, was a hard-tackling defender when he joined the Seasiders. At first he teamed up with skipper Jimmy Armfield, but after failing to displace Tommy Thompson at left-back, he switched to half-back with some success. Then, after a period in the forward line alongside Gerry Ingram and Alan Skirton, he was put back into the heart of the defence by Ron Suart. It was Les Shannon who converted Craven to the forward line on a permanent basis, and it was his success in teaming up with Fred Pickering and Mickey Burns, that helped Blackpool to promotion. Over the next two years, Craven was one of the club's top scorers and when Bob Stokoe took over, he made Craven skipper to take over from the retired Armfield. Craven led Blackpool to the Anglo-Italian trophy in Bologna, scoring the equalizing goal himself, a personal triumph as he had been praised for the way he had conducted the players through a volatile tournament. In 1971 he was voted Blackpool's Player of the Year, but that September he asked for a transfer and moved to Crystal Palace for £37,000. He later had spells with Coventry, Plymouth, Vancouver Whitecaps and Calgary Boomers.

	LEAGUE		*FA CUP*		*FL CUP*		*TOTAL*	
	App	*Gls*	*App*	*Gls*	*App*	*Gls*	*App*	*Gls*
1965-66	9	0	0	0	2	0	11	0
1966-67	13/1	0	0	0	0	0	13/1	0
1967-68	29/4	2	1/1	0	3	1	33/5	3
1968-69	25/2	4	1	0	3	1	29/2	5
1969-70	39/1	10	3	0	3	0	45/1	10
1970-71	39/1	8	2	1	2	0	43/1	9
1971-72	0/2	0	0	0	0	0	0/2	0
	154/11	24	7/1	1	13	2	174/12	27

Born in Lytham, Johnny Crosland was signed by Joe Smith from Ansdell Rovers during World War Two. A strapping six-footer who could switch from centre-half to full-back, he was unable to break into the first team due to the excellent form of Ron Suart and Harry Johnston. After his debut in September 1946 at Brentford he managed only three more appearances that season. The following season saw him make only a handful of first-team appearances, yet one of them was in the FA Cup Final against Manchester United when Suart was injured. He coped admirably with winger Jimmy Delaney and might have scored himself but, after running nearly the full length of the field, he ballooned his shot wide. Despite these encouraging signs he did not appear in 1948-9. Eventually he competed with Eric Hayward, and with the veteran centre-half succumbing to injuries, Crosland was called on more and more. The England selectors capped him at 'B' level in 1950 before he was given regular first-team football during 1952-3. Alas a series of injuries curtailed his Blackpool career and he was soon sold to Bournemouth for a nominal fee, an unpopular move with the fans. Crosland was never a great player but he was a committed professional who was never given a real chance at Bloomfield Road.

	LEAGUE		*FA CUP*		*TOTAL*	
	App	*Gls*	*App*	*Gls*	*App*	*Gls*
1946-47	4	0	0	0	4	0
1947-48	4	0	1	0	5	0
1948-49	0	0	0	0	0	0
1949-50	16	0	1	0	17	0
1950-51	4	0	3	0	7	0
1951-52	2	0	0	0	2	0
1952-53	25	0	3	0	28	0
1953-54	9	0	2	0	11	0
	64	0	10	0	74	0

JOHN CROSLAND

In his brief stay at Bloomfield Road, Tony Cunningham became something of a hero, for he was a strong, tall, well-built striker who loved to get amongst the goals. Born in Jamaica on 12 November 1959, he was playing for Stourbridge when Lincoln City signed him in May 1979. Cunningham scored 32 goals in 123 League games for the Imps before moving to Barnsley in September 1982. After netting 11 goals in 42 games for the Colliers, his career took him to Sheffield Wednesday (five goals in 27 games), Manchester City (one goal in 18 games) and Newcastle United (four goals in 47 games) before he moved to Blackpool in July 1987, for a fee, fixed by a tribunal, of £25,000. He made his debut on the opening day of 1987-8, in a draw at Gillingham, and it soon looked as if he would become a prolific striker for Blackpool. Maybe too much was expected of him; maybe his temperament let him down, for he was often in trouble with referees. Whatever, as Blackpool struggled, Cunningham was made a scapegoat. At the end of 1988-9, he rejoined Sam Ellis at Bury, where he had considerable success, although in his first game back at Bloomfield Road, he delighted the home fans by getting himself sent off in the first half. After Bury there was a short spell at Bolton followed by a move to Rotherham, where he is at the time of writing.

	LEAGUE		*FA CUP*		*FL CUP*		*TOTAL*	
	App	*Gls*	*App*	*Gls*	*App*	*Gls*	*App*	*Gls*
1987-88	40	10	2	0	3	2	45	12
1988-89	31	8	3	2	5	1	39	11
	71	18	5	2	8	3	84	23

TONY CUNNINGHAM

MIKE DAVIES

Born in Stretford, Manchester, on 19 January 1966, Mike Davies is a successful product of Blackpool's youth system and up to the end of the 1991-2 season he had made over 290 appearances for the Seasiders. Davies made his debut in May 1984, in a home win over Halifax Town. Initially a winger, he won a regular place within a year and ably replaced the experienced Ian Britton, teaming up with John Deary. Davies continued playing wide on the right for the next few seasons under Sam Ellis, scoring important goals in helping the team to promotion. During 1987-8, though, he was at full-back, a move prompted by the arrival of Tony Cunningham. Davies adapted magnificently and despite a brief reversal to his original wide position, he continues to fill the role adequately. A fast, tricky player with tremendous commitment, the flame-haired terrier has often found himself in trouble with over-zealous referees, who have not always appreciated his approach. The supporters, though, have, and in 1987-8 he was voted Blackpool's Player of the Year. One feels that if every man to have worn a Blackpool shirt over the years had showed as much commitment to the cause as Mike Davies, then the Seasiders would never have fallen from grace.

	LEAGUE		*FA CUP*		*FL CUP*		*TOTAL*	
	App	*Gls*	*App*	*Gls*	*App*	*Gls*	*App*	*Gls*
1983-84	3	0	0	0	0	0	3	0
1984-85	15/2	0	1	0	3	0	19/2	0
1985-86	30/6	5	2	0	1	1	33/6	6
1986-87	42	6	1	0	1/1	0	44/1	6
1987-88	36/2	0	6	0	4	0	46/2	0
1988-89	25/5	2	2	0	3	0	30/5	2
1989-90	14/9	0	0/5	0	0	0	14/14	0
1990-91	33/7	1	0/1	0	0	0	33/8	1
1991-92	30/3	1	1	0	4	0	35/3	1
	228/34	15	13/6	0	16/1	1	257/41	16

Born in Ormskirk on 18 October 1967, John Deary was one of Alan Ball's youngsters during Ball's traumatic time as Blackpool's manager. Unlike the rest, though, Deary made the grade and went on to appear in over 300 matches.

JOHN DEARY

He started as an apprentice, signing for the Seasiders in March 1980. He made his debut in September that year, in a win at Fulham, and played in a handful of games that season, mostly in midfield. The management seemed uncertain whether to play him in the heart of defence or deep in midfield. If nothing else it showed his versatility. Eventually he settled into midfield and spent many successful years there. A tough tackler who loved to go forward, in the Fourth Division promotion season of 1984-5 he top-scored. Although Deary was a regular scorer, he was more comfortable in a role supporting such players as Stewart, O'Keefe and, later, Cunningham. His leadership qualities were used to good effect, manager Sam Ellis, whilst not making him captain, often relying on him to provide inspiration when the team were struggling. At the end of 1988-9, after nearly ten years at Blackpool, he decided to move on, his place now coming under increasing pressure. Blackpool's neighbours, Burnley, snapped him up and Deary continued to play superbly at Turf Moor, helping the Clarets back to Division Three in 1991-2.

	LEAGUE		*FA CUP*		*FL CUP*		*TOTAL*	
	App	*Gls*	*App*	*Gls*	*App*	*Gls*	*App*	*Gls*
1980-81	10	0	0	0	0	0	10	0
1981-82	22/5	0	1/1	0	0	0	23/6	0
1982-83	45	6	1	1	4	1	50	8
1983-84	27/4	6	3/1	1	2	0	32/5	7
1984-85	28/3	13	1	0	3	2	32/3	15
1985-86	40	7	1	0	2	0	43	7
1986-87	44	3	1	0	2	1	47	4
1987-88	34/3	3	6	2	2	0	42/3	5
1988-89	35/2	5	3	1	5	1	43/2	7
	285/17	43	17/2	5	20	5	322/19	53

During World War Two, Ephraim 'Jock' Dodds became a legendary figure nationwide because of his phenomenal goalscoring feats. In six years at Bloomfield Road, Dodds scored well over 200 goals, including 66 in 1941-2 alone. He scored eight in a cup game against Stockport in 1941, seven against Oldham the previous season and another seven against Tranmere in their 15-3 thrashing at Bloomfield Road. In that match he scored his first hat-trick in less than three minutes, and a week later scored another almost as quickly. Despite being a massive figure, with huge thighs and a thick neck, he was one of the fastest centre-forwards in the game. Dodds was born at Grangemouth in 1915 but his family moved to Durham when he was 12. In 1932 he signed for Huddersfield Town but two years later joined Sheffield United on a free transfer. At Bramall Lane, however, his career took off; he was the Blades' leading scorer for four seasons and played in the 1936 FA Cup Final against Arsenal, the season he was Division Two's joint top scorer with Blackpool's Bobby Finan. Blackpool signed Dodds in March 1939, for the big fee £10,500, and he made his debut in a defeat at Charlton, where he scored the Seasiders' only goal. He went on to score four in the home victory over Middlesbrough and quickly became a firm favourite. Alas, war intervened and he did most of his scoring for Blackpool in the regional competitions. He also made all his international appearances during the war, once netting a hat-trick to help Scotland to a 5-4 win over England. In November 1946, Everton, now with no Dean or Lawton, signed him and Dodds scored 36 goals in 55 League games for the Toffees before ending his career with Lincoln City, whom he joined October 1948.

JOCK DODDS

	LEAGUE		*FA CUP*		*TOTAL*	
	App	*Gls*	*App*	*Gls*	*App*	*Gls*
1938-39	12	10	0	0	12	10
1939-40	3	3	0	0	3	3
	15	13	0	0	15	13

When Peter Doherty joined Blackpool in November 1933, from Glentoran for £1,500, he already had a reputation as a brave forward and in an age of burly defenders he was never known to shirk a tackle. Doherty was also a master of the long pass and was capable of shooting accurately from just about any position. His partnership with the great Jimmy Hampson is still talked about today by older supporters, although his greatest days came after he left Blackpool. Born in Magherafelt in June 1913, he was turned down by Coleraine before joining Glentoran in June 1930. Blackpool signed him from under the noses of rivals Preston and he soon made his debut, against Bradford. Although Blackpool won 2-1, Doherty failed to impress and it was some time before he gained a regular place. When he did he struck a rich partnership, not only with Hampson but also with Scottish inside-forward Bobby Finan, and their goals in 1934-5 nearly brought promotion. Doherty made his debut for Ireland in 1935, but it is surprising that he made only four appearances for his country whilst with Blackpool. In February 1936 he was transferred to Manchester City for £10,000 and soon repaid that by helping City to the League Championship the following season. During World War Two he guested for Derby before signing for £6,000 and teamed up with Raich Carter to help win the FA Cup in 1946. He joined Huddersfield and later, as player-manager, helped Doncaster win the Third Division North title. He held a number of coaching posts and was Northern Ireland's manager when they reached the 1958 World Cup quarter-finals. He died at Fleetwood in April 1990.

	LEAGUE		*FA CUP*		*TOTAL*	
	App	*Gls*	*App*	*Gls*	*App*	*Gls*
1933-34	19	4	2	1	21	5
1934-35	35	13	1	0	36	13
1935-36	29	11	2	0	31	11
	83	28	5	1	88	29

PETER DOHERTY

Dave Durie came to Bloomfield Road as a deputy to Allan Brown, but eventually succeeded him altogether. Durie, who was born in Blackpool on 13 August 1931, joined the Seasiders in May 1952 and made his League debut in March 1953, in a 3-3 draw at Charlton. He made two more appearances that season, but when Brown struggled with an injury a year later, Durie stepped up at inside-forward. A strong, speedy player, he was probably underrated by supporters, hardly surprising bearing in mind the number of stars in the team at that time. He was a loyal servant and one of the fittest men on the books, despite remaining a part-time professional with outside business interests. With the departure of Brown, Durie became a regular, mostly as a creative inside-forward, and in 1956-7 he and Jackie Mudie scored 52 goals between them, with Durie notching 20. One of his best performances came in the third round of the FA Cup against Mansfield Town in January 1960, when he destroyed the opposing defence almost single-handed to score a hat-trick. That season Ron Suart switched him to left-half and Durie adapted easily. His nickname of 'Legs Divine' came about because he had seemingly 'telescopic' legs that gave his body a strange rocking motion when he ran. Durie was a Methodist Sunday School teacher throughout and beyond his footballing days.

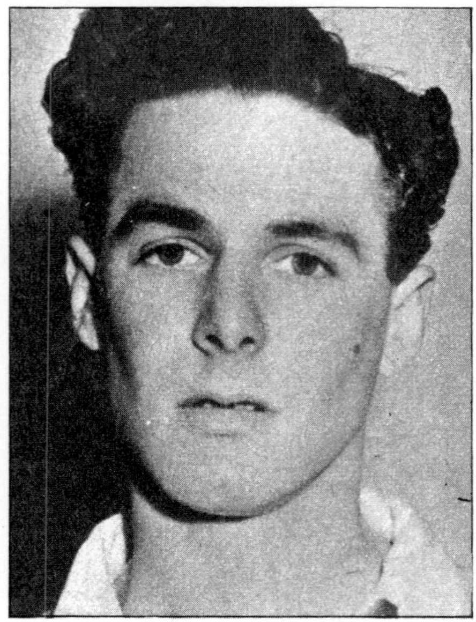

DAVE DURIE

	LEAGUE		*FA CUP*		*FL CUP*		*TOTAL*	
	App	*Gls*	*App*	*Gls*	*App*	*Gls*	*App*	*Gls*
1953-54	7	1	0	0	-	-	7	1
1953-54	3	1	0	0	-	-	3	1
1954-55	3	1	0	0	-	-	3	1
1955-56	15	14	1	0	-	-	16	14
1956-57	37	20	4	2	-	-	41	22
1957-58	33	14	1	0	-	-	34	14
1958-59	38	9	6	2	-	-	44	11
1959-60	32	10	3	3	-	-	35	13
1960-61	36	6	0	0	2	1	38	7
1961-62	40	1	2	0	8	0	50	1
1962-63	40	4	2	0	3	0	45	4
1963-64	12	3	0	0	2	1	14	4
	296	84	19	7	15	2	330	93

Late in 1983, manager Sam Ellis used his Watford connections to sign a few of Graham Taylor's youngsters. One of them was a strong, fast winger by the name of Alex Dyer. Born in West Ham on 14 November 1965, Dyer had been an apprentice at Vicarage Lane but was unable to break into the first team and so in September 1983, Ellis brought him to Bloomfield Road on a free transfer. He made his debut that October, in a home defeat by Rochdale, and immediately became a hit with the fans. Although it took some time to break into the first team regularly, it seemed that he had great potential. He was able to beat his man and had a good attitude. He was full of enthusiasm and energy and with Paul Stewart made a formidable partnership. Dyer was virtually ever-present during the next two seasons, and in one game, a friendly against Manchester City, he tore the opposing defence apart. He seemed a potential star and when Blackpool sold him to Hull City in February 1987, for what appeared to be the ludicrously small amount of £35,000, once again it appeared that the Seasiders had allowed a fine talent to slip through their fingers. In November 1988, Dyer moved to Crystal Palace and two years later was transferred to Charlton for £100,000.

ALEX DYER

	LEAGUE		*FA CUP*		*FL CUP*		*TOTAL*	
	App	*Gls*	*App*	*Gls*	*App*	*Gls*	*App*	*Gls*
1983-84	4/5	0	1/1	0	0/1	0	5/7	0
1984-85	34/2	8	0	0	4	1	38/2	9
1985-86	39	8	2	0	2	0	43	8
1986-87	24	3	0	0	2	0	26	3
	101/7	19	3/1	0	8/1	1	112/9	20

Keith Dyson joined Blackpool in the deal that took Tony Green to Newcastle United for a record fee. A former England Under-23 international, the tall centre-forward, who was born in Consett on 10 February 1950 and who made 76 League appearances for the Magpies, found it difficult to maintain a regular place at St James' Park. He made his debut for Blackpool soon after arriving in October 1971, in a defeat at Fulham, immediately displacing Glyn James from his temporary number-nine shirt. Dyson made a great start to his Blackpool career, scoring 12 goals in his first season, including a hat-trick against Burnley on Easter Saturday, and then teamed up with new signing Billy Rafferty and Alan Suddick. He was a strong player with an excellent temperament, but as time progressed he became unpopular with a section of the highly critical Blackpool fans. The goals dried up and after a while he found himself under pressure from Wyn Davies and, later, Mickey Walsh, and with a series of niggling injuries his appearances became irregular. Dyson never reached his true potential at Bloomfield Road, despite his talent and enthusiasm. After a year spent battling for fitness, he was advised to retire. It was a bitter blow to a man whose career had seemed ready to blossom on his arrival in 1971, but five years later he said goodbye to League football.

	LEAGUE		*FA CUP*		*FL CUP*		*TOTAL*	
	App	*Gls*	*App*	*Gls*	*App*	*Gls*	*App*	*Gls*
1971-72	28	12	1	0	0	0	29	12
1972-73	25/1	9	1	0	5	1	31/1	10
1973-74	26/2	7	1	1	1	0	28/2	8
1974-75	10	2	0	0	0	0	10	2
1975-76	2	0	0	0	1	0	3	0
	91/3	30	3	1	7	1	101/3	32

KEITH DYSON

Horace Fairhurst was born in Bolton in 1895 and played his early football for Darwen. He was a stocky, hard-tackling right-back who struck fear into approaching forwards, and his greatest attribute was his enormous courage. When he joined Blackpool he struck a partnership with Bert Tulloch, and it was their solid defending that helped the team's fortunes to turn around so dramatically. During World War One, he was stationed, like so many other footballers, at Blackpool and appeared in many army games at Bloomfield Road. On his return from Egypt, where he later served, he was signed by Blackpool and made his debut against Oldham Atheltic in the 1917 Principal Tournament. From then on he was almost an ever-present, replacing Jones, who had joined Bolton Wanderers. Blackpool were playing particularly well at this stage, making a strong push for promotion to the First Division with one of the meanest goals-against columns in the League. Fairhurst could dispossess a forward almost by looking at him, for he was such an imposing figure. Yet off the field, he was mild-mannered and even-tempered and very much a family man. His career came to a tragic end on Boxing Day 1920, when he was stretchered off in the game against Barnsley. He had gone into a tackle in typically courageous fashion, but had been left unconscious after a severe bang on the head from an opponent's boot. It was an accident but he never recovered and on 7 January 1921, he died at his home. Fairhurst was only 26 and a promising footballing career had been ended so abruptly.

	LEAGUE		*FA CUP*		*TOTAL*	
	App	*Gls*	*App*	*Gls*	*App*	*Gls*
1919-20	27	0	3	0	30	0
1920-21	20	0	0	0	20	0
	47	0	3	0	50	0

HORACE FAIRHURST

George Farm was probably Blackpool's best-ever goalkeeper. Born in Slateford, Scotland, in July 1924, Farm came to Bloomfield Road in September 1948, from Hibernian for £2,700. He stayed for 12 years, breaking all kinds of appearance records and appearing in two FA Cup Finals — not bad for a player who had been third choice for Hibs. Well-built, he had a distinctive way of holding the ball, preferring to catch it with one hand above and one hand below as opposed to the orthodox style used by most goalkeepers. He was a perfectionist and could often be found on the training ground well after the others had left. He was brave and it didn't matter how he kept the ball out — if that meant heading it, then fine. Farm made his debut in September 1948 at Bolton, replacing out-of-form Joe Robinson. He went on to make more than 500 first-team appearances, including 47 consecutive FA Cup matches. Unfortunately, his performance in the 1953 Cup Final was criticised after he seemingly let in two soft goals, yet Joe Smith kept faith with him. The only time he was replaced — by fellow Scot Bob Wylie — was through an injury. He played for Scotland on ten occasions, including three games in 1959 when he was 35. A year later he was granted a transfer. Manager Ron Suart, who had once been Farm's teammate, was reluctant to let him go, but as soon as Blackpool's indifferent League position improved, Queen of the South took him for £3,000, more than Joe Smith had paid Hibernian 12 years previously. Farm is one of the few 'keepers to have scored a goal. In the 6-2 home defeat by Preston in 1955-6, he injured a shoulder and replaced Jackie Mudie at centre-forward, where he proceeded to open the scoring. From then on the forwards were never to hear the last of it.

GEORGE FARM

	LEAGUE		*FA CUP*		*TOTAL*	
	App	*Gls*	*App*	*Gls*	*App*	*Gls*
1948-49	34	0	3	0	37	0
1949-50	42	0	5	0	47	0
1950-51	42	0	7	0	49	0
1951-52	42	0	1	0	43	0
1952-53	39	0	7	0	46	0
1953-54	34	0	7	0	41	0
1954-55	39	0	1	0	40	0
1955-56	42	1	2	0	44	1
1956-57	42	0	4	0	46	0
1957-58	42	0	1	0	43	0
1958-59	42	0	6	0	48	0
1959-60	25	0	3	0	28	0
	465	1	47	0	512	1

In the years before, during and after World War Two, the half-back line of George Farrow, Eric Hayward and Harry Johnston became legendary. During this time Blackpool became one of the most powerful teams in the country and the famous trio were feared by every team they met. George Farrow joined Blackpool from Bournemouth in 1936 and made his debut in September that year in the home win over West Ham. Initially an inside-left, he soon switched to wing-half where his fierce tackling was far more use. That season he helped the club gain promotion to Division One and for the next 12 seasons contributed to turning the side into one of the best Bloomfield Road has ever seen. His main attributes were strong tackling, accurate long-range passes and a fierce shot. His reputation grew and he was dubbed the 'best uncapped half-back in England'. He was also one of the earliest exponents of the long throw-in. Farrow played for Blackpool for 13 seasons including the war years, but was unfortunate to be transferred to Sheffield United just a few weeks before Blackpool's FA Cup run which led to a Wembley appearance. He probably did not receive better recognition due to the higher profile of skipper Harry Johnston.

GEORGE FARROW

	LEAGUE		*FA CUP*		*TOTAL*	
	App	*Gls*	*App*	*Gls*	*App*	*Gls*
1936-37	33	5	2	0	35	5
1937-38	30	5	2	0	32	5
1938-39	38	1	1	0	39	1
1939-40	3	0	-	-	3	0
1946-47	28	1	1	0	29	1
1947-48	16	3	0	0	16	3
	148	15	6	0	154	15

Ewan Fenton was one of Blackpool's unsung heroes during the successful 1950s and he played for the Seasiders for over 13 seasons. Born in Dundee on 17 November 1929, Fenton played for Jeanfield Swifts before signing professional forms in November 1946 and made his debut in September 1948, in a home draw with Derby County. A cultured right-half, he was brought to understudy Harry Johnston and it was some time before he broke through. In 1952-3, his patience was rewarded and he played through the campaign to finish with an FA Cup winners' medal, his steadiness going a long way to inspiring the famous fight back against Bolton at Wembley. Indeed, calmness was his great strength and in 1956-7 he was appointed captain of the side. Fenton was a shrewd passer of the ball and enjoyed joining the attack, scoring some crucial goals. He was never capped, the nearest he came to representative honours being the powerful British Army XI. After having a transfer request turned down in 1958, he was finally released in May 1959, joining Wrexham for a small fee. He spent just over a year at the Racecourse Ground, although a serious injury threatened to end his career. In 1960-61 he played for Limerick in the European Cup, being then able to boast that he was the only member of Blackpool's great 1953 FA Cup squad who went on to play in Europe.

	LEAGUE		*FA CUP*		*TOTAL*	
	App	*Gls*	*App*	*Gls*	*App*	*Gls*
1948-49	11	1	0	0	11	1
1949-50	0	0	0	0	0	0
1950-51	6	0	1	0	7	0
1951-52	13	0	0	0	13	0
1952-53	23	1	7	0	30	1
1953-54	36	3	6	0	42	3
1954-55	41	6	0	0	41	6
1955-56	25	4	1	0	26	4
1956-57	27	3	4	0	31	3
1957-58	10	0	0	0	10	0
1958-59	3	2	0	0	3	2
	195	20	19	0	214	20

EWAN FENTON

Bobby Finan was another of Blackpool's prolific goalscorers in the years before World War Two, eventually taking over the mantle held by the great Jimmy Hampson. Born in Old Kirkpatrick, Finan began his career as an inside-forward with Yoker Athletic before Alex McFarlane persuaded him to join Blackpool in 1933. His League debut in April 1934 was memorable only for the fact that Blackpool lost 7-0 at Grimsby, but the following season he became a regular. In 1935-6, with Jimmy Hampson injured, Finan deputised at centre-forward and responded to the challenge so well that he ended the season as the Second Division's joint top scorer with 34 goals. When Hampson returned midway through the season he went to inside-right as Finan continued to lead the attack. Finan was fast and strong and not only had a similar style to that of Jimmy Hampson, but also shared a remarkably similar facial appearance to the Englishman. Finan continued scoring freely the next season and once again topped the scoring charts at Bloomfield Road. As he grew older and his speed began to wane, he was moved to outside-left, where he laid on goals for Buchan and later Dodds. During the war Finan's appearances were spasmodic, although he appeared in the famous Cup Final against Arsenal at Stamford Bridge, scoring one of the winning goals. After his playing days ended, he scouted for Blackpool. Bobby Finan was only capped once by Scotland and that during the war, but to Blackpool supporters he was one of the greatest forwards the club has ever seen.

	LEAGUE		*FA CUP*		*TOTAL*	
	App	*Gls*	*App*	*Gls*	*App*	*Gls*
1933-34	2	0	0	0	2	0
1934-35	22	4	0	0	22	4
1935-36	41	34	2	2	43	36
1936-37	41	28	2	2	43	30
1937-38	37	12	2	0	39	12
1938-39	27	5	1	0	28	5
1939-40	3	2	-	-	3	2
	173	85	7	4	180	89

BOBBY FINAN

ANDY GARNER

Andy Garner, who was born at Stonebroom on 8 March 1966, has been a favourite with the fans ever since his move to Blackpool from Derby County in August 1988, for £75,000. Garner made his debut on the opening day, in a 1-1 draw at Chester, and although playing in his first season at centre-forward, he has enjoyed greater success deep in midfield. He has good ball skills and can always score goals, although a lack of pace troubled him when Derby were in the Second Division. But in the lower leagues he has excelled and two of the best goals seen at Bloomfield Road recently came in the 5-2 mauling of Burnley, when Garner twice ran the full length of the pitch with the ball before supplying the crosses for grateful forwards. After the disappointment of the Wembley Play-off Final in 1991, Garner was the subject of intense transfer speculation and it seemed almost certain that he would be leaving Bloomfield Road. Thankfully for Blackpool supporters, though, the proposed move fell through and he remained at the club for another season, although injury then hampered him. Nevertheless, he is still one of the most popular players to play for Blackpool in recent years. Garner, who joined Derby as an apprentice, scored some vital goals in the Rams' Third Division promotion season of 1985-6, including the winner at Blackpool.

	LEAGUE		*FA CUP*		*FL CUP*		*TOTAL*	
	App	*Gls*	*App*	*Gls*	*App*	*Gls*	*App*	*Gls*
1988-89	41/1	11	3	2	5	2	49/1	15
1989-90	45/1	8	7	1	5	1	57/1	10
1990-91	37/2	13	3	1	2	0	42/2	14
1991-92	29/4	5	0/1	0	2/1	0	31/6	5
	152/8	37	13/1	4	14/1	3	179/10	44

Tommy Garrett was a polished, skilful defender who never wilted under pressure. Born in South Shields in February 1926, he was a miner playing for Horden Colliery when Blackpool signed him in 1942, initially as a forward. It was at full-back, though, that he became established — and as a 'footballing' defender at that, always playing his way out of trouble, never slamming the ball aimlessly away. He also spent hours practising heading and was a tower of strength in the air. Garrett made his debut in March 1947-8 but with Ron Suart playing regularly, he had to wait until Suart's departure for Blackburn before making the position his own. He could perform equally well on either flank and played in the 1951 and 1953 Cup Finals, appearing in the latter with a broken nose sustained a week earlier. During this time he made a handful of international appearances, partnering Alf Ramsey in the England defence. In the 1953 FA Cup run, Garrett scored a remarkable goal against Huddersfield, lobbing the ball home from his own half to put Blackpool into the fifth round. After 19 years with the Seasiders he was given a free transfer and signed for Millwall in May 1961, making 12 appearances for the Lions before retiring from League football. Tommy Garrett was certainly one of Blackpool's greatest post-war stars.

TOMMY GARRETT

	LEAGUE		*FA CUP*		*TOTAL*	
	App	*Gls*	*App*	*Gls*	*App*	*Gls*
1947-48	5	0	0	0	5	0
1948-49	4	0	1	0	5	0
1949-50	24	0	2	0	26	0
1950-51	30	0	8	0	38	0
1951-52	36	0	1	0	37	0
1952-53	39	2	7	1	46	3
1953-54	28	0	3	0	31	0
1954-55	37	0	1	0	38	0
1955-56	4	0	1	0	5	0
1956-57	18	0	3	0	21	0
1957-58	23	0	0	0	23	0
1958-59	28	1	0	0	28	1
1959-60	4	0	0	0	4	0
1960-61	26	0	1	0	27	0
	306	3	28	1	334	4

Roy Gratrix was always described as the 'centre-half England never chose', a player who appeared over 400 times for Blackpool yet never fully received the credit he deserved. He was born in Salford in February 1932 and was playing for a local works team, Taylor Bros, when he was signed by Joe Smith. A tall, strong defender, Gratrix succeeded Eddie Shimwell at right-back, making his debut in March 1954, in a goalless draw at home to Middlesbrough, and then played in every match until the end of the season. In 1954-5 he retained his position, teaming up with Tommy Garrett, although occasionally being asked to play at left-back. The following season, with Harry Johnston leaving to manage Reading, Gratrix moved to centre-half and remained in that role for the rest of his playing days. He created a bit of a record at Blackpool, for despite his many appearances he never found himself on the score-sheet, unless one counts an own-goal against Sheffield Wednesday. During the 1950s, the half-back line of Gratrix and the two Kellys was a formidable one. The contrasting styles of Hugh and Jimmy worked perfectly with the rugged but effective style of Gratrix and it is no coincidence that Blackpool had some of their most successful seasons whilst they were together. In September 1964, Gratrix signed for Manchester City, for whom he made 15 League appearances before retiring.

	LEAGUE		*FA CUP*		*FL CUP*		*TOTAL*	
	App	*Gls*	*App*	*Gls*	*App*	*Gls*	*App*	*Gls*
1953-54	9	0	0	0	-	-	9	0
1954-55	33	0	1	0	-	-	34	0
1955-56	40	0	1	0	-	-	41	0
1956-57	42	0	4	0	-	-	46	0
1957-58	42	0	1	0	-	-	43	0
1958-59	40	0	6	0	-	-	46	0
1959-60	40	0	3	0	-	-	43	0
1960-61	39	0	1	0	1	0	41	0
1961-62	42	0	2	0	8	0	52	0
1962-63	35	0	2	0	3	0	40	0
1963-64	34	0	2	0	1	0	37	0
1964-65	4	0	0	0	0	0	4	0
	400	0	23	0	13	0	436	0

ROY GRATRIX

Tony Green was described as the 'new Alan Ball' when he moved to Blackpool but people were soon calling him the 'first Tony Green'. Born in Glasgow, he was still at school when he became a part-timer at Albion Rovers and his speed and goalscoring soon attracted English clubs, notably Fulham and Blackburn. But on Scottish Cup Final day in 1967, it was Blackpool manager Stan Mortensen who signed him for £15,000. It was to be one of the bargain buys of all time. Green made his debut almost immediately and despite Blackpool losing 3-1 at home to West Brom, he was cheered off the field, for it was obvious that he was a star in the making. In 1967-8 his partnership with Suddick helped Blackpool to within a whisker of promotion to Division One and, although he rarely scored himself, he laid on the majority of Ingram's goals. Alas, just when it seemed that he would break into the Scotland squad he suffered a serious ankle injury in training and was out for well over a year, completely missing Blackpool's promotion season of 1969-70. He stayed cheerful and when he reappeared in the home match against the champions Everton, he brought new vitality to the team and hope into the hearts of supporters who had endured a quite miserable season. Green eventually made his international debut in 1971, playing magnificently against England at Wembley. Bids of over £100,000 came in for him but Blackpool resisted until he refused new terms at the beginning of 1971-2. In his last game he helped them to a 4-1 League Cup win over Aston Villa before signing for Newcastle for a club record £150,000, over ten times the amount Blackpool had paid for him. Not long afterwards he suffered another injury which was to force his retirement when he was in his mid-20s. It was one of football's tragedies that he was lost to the game so young and he would surely have won more than six international caps but for that.

	LEAGUE		*FA CUP*		*FL CUP*		*TOTAL*	
	App	*Gls*	*App*	*Gls*	*App*	*Gls*	*App*	*Gls*
1966-67	1	0	0	0	0	0	1	0
1967-68	38	3	2	1	3	0	43	4
1968-69	40	5	1	0	4	1	45	6
1969-70	0	0	0	0	0	0	0	0
1970-71	28/1	3	2	2	0	0	30/1	5
1971-72	14	2	0	0	3	2	17	4
	121/1	13	5	3	10	3	136/1	19

TONY GREEN

COLIN GREENALL

In August 1980, at the age of 16 years 237 days, Colin Greenall made his debut for Blackpool, so becoming the club's youngster-ever League player. Three days later he appeared in a League Cup game at Goodison Park. Born in Billinge, near Wigan, on 30 December 1963, Greenall eventually signed as a full-timer in January 1981, one of a host of young players brought to the club by Alan Ball. Unlike most of the others, though, he stayed the course, developing into a dependable defender. Eventually he took over the central role, combining with skipper Steve Hetzke and Mike Conroy to form a successful defensive partnership. Greenall won England Youth honours and at 20 he was voted the Fourth Division Player of the Year by the PFA. Under Sam Ellis he became a stylish player with just the right amount of aggression. After 183 League appearances in just over five years, Greenall had a contractual dispute with Blackpool and in September 1986 he moved to Third Division Gillingham for £40,000 and Blackpool lost one of their most influential players. Greenall joined Oxford United in February 1988 for £235,000 and they soon made him skipper following the departure of Tommy Caton. In July 1990, he moved to Bury for £100,000 after a loan spell there.

	LEAGUE		*FA CUP*		*FL CUP*		*TOTAL*	
	App	*Gls*	*App*	*Gls*	*App*	*Gls*	*App*	*Gls*
1980-81	11/1	0	1	0	1	0	13/1	0
1981-82	16/2	0	0	0	1	0	17/2	0
1982-83	23/1	1	0	0	1	0	24/1	1
1983-84	39	4	5	0	1	0	45	4
1984-85	44	3	1	0	4	1	49	4
1985-86	43	1	2	0	2	1	47	2
1986-87	3	0	0	0	2	0	5	0
	179/4	9	9	0	12	2	200/4	11

JIMMY HAMPSON

Before the glory days of Matthews and Mortensen, there was one player who Blackpool supporters treated with similar reverence. Jimmy Hampson was an extraordinary goalscorer, feared by defenders, and to this day Blackpool's record goalscorer. Born in Little Hulton in 1906, Hampson started his League career with Nelson, making his debut in 1925. At inside-right he soon became their top scorer and quickly attracted the top clubs. Yet it was Second Division Blackpool who secured his services in October 1927. They agreed a fee of £1,000 and Hampson was tracked down to a local cinema, where he became Blackpool's shrewdest signing. Despite being only 5ft 6in tall, Hampson was converted to centre-forward and proved his worth with 31 goals in the remaining 32 games of the season. Amongst his many attributes were incredible acceleration and a bullet-like shot in either foot. He was often on the receiving end of some rough treatment but accepted it as part of his job. The following season he scored 40 goals to become the Second Division's top scorer and that summer, Arsenal made a near-record bid of £10,000 for him. But Hampson, a quiet man who would perhaps not have been at home amongst the bright lights of London, remained a Blackpool player. In 1929-30, Blackpool won the title and Hampson's goals were the key to the club reaching Division One for the first time. His partnership with centre-half Billy Tremelling, who would often supply the through ball for Hampson, was almost irresistable and he became the League's top scorer that season with 45 goals. Hampson was now a household name and was even honoured by having a model of himself at Louis Tussaud's Waxworks. During three seasons of struggle in Division One, Hampson still managed 72 goals in that time; and after Blackpool were relegated he was their top scorer for the next two seasons, even though he missed quite a few games through injury. Indeed, since his arrival he had scored on average at least 60 per cent of Blackpool's goals each season. He also held the record for the fastest century of goals, netting 101 in 97 games between 1927 and 1930. His international career was brief, due to the presence of 'Dixie' Dean and the fact that Hampson played most of his football in Division Two, but he scored five goals in his three England games, plus nine in four appearances for the Football League. Jimmy Hampson was physically small, but his standing in football in the 1930s could not be overshadowed. He was idolized in Blackpool and when he drowned in a boating accident in January 1938, at the age of 32, the town was stunned. It is said that grown men wept, knowing that the greatest player the club had ever seen had been lost. His body was never recovered, but his legend lives on and his 248 goals in 361 appearances is a club record unlikely to be beaten.

	LEAGUE		*FA CUP*		*TOTAL*	
	App	*Gls*	*App*	*Gls*	*App*	*Gls*
1927-28	32	31	1	0	33	31
1928-29	41	40	1	0	42	40
1929-30	41	45	2	1	43	46
1930-31	41	32	2	1	43	33
1931-32	42	23	2	1	44	24
1932-33	35	18	3	1	38	19
1933-34	23	13	0	0	23	13
1934-35	25	20	0	0	25	20
1935-36	21	6	0	0	21	6
1936-37	42	16	0	0	42	16
1937-38	18	4	1	0	19	4
	361	248	12	4	373	252

HAROLD HARDMAN

Harold Hardman was another of Blackpool's players in the early part of the century who went on to greater success after leaving the club. Born in Kirkmanshulme, Manchester, on 4 April 1882, he was discovered as a schoolboy and thrown into the first team during Blackpool's one-year exile in the Lancashire League in 1899-1900, when he also appeared for Northern Nomads. He made his Football League debut in September 1900 in the home draw with Gainsborough Trinity, and for the next three seasons became an almost ever-present. Essentially an outside-left, he had the ability to switch flanks and sometimes turned out on the right wing. Fast and tricky, although not a great goalscorer himself, he provided the final ball for many of the goals scored by Birkett and Parkinson. Blackpool, though, were a team constantly struggling in the Second Division and Hardman was far too good for the club to retain. In 1903, Everton bought him for just over £100 and he played for them in the 1906 and 1907 FA Cup Finals before joining Manchester United in 1908, the year he won an Olympic soccer gold medal with Great Britain. He later played for Bradford City and Stoke. After his playing days ended he became a well-known administrator and, later, the much-loved chairman of Manchester United. Blackpool never saw the best of Hardman, all his England appearances coming whilst playing for Everton, but he was proof of the new talent policy that the club had introduced during the early 1900s. He was a solictor who practised in Manchester, where he died on 9 June 1965.

	LEAGUE		*FA CUP*		*TOTAL*	
	App	*Gls*	*App*	*Gls*	*App*	*Gls*
1900-01	27	2	0	0	27	2
1901-02	14	2	0	0	14	2
1902-03	30	6	0	0	30	6
	71	10	0	0	71	10

PAUL HART

Son of Johnny Hart, a former Manchester City forward, Paul Hart was an immensely talented defender, skilful enough to play some games in midfield, who joined Blackpool from Stockport County in June 1973, for £25,000, and made his debut in a home win over Fulham four months later. Born in Golborne on 4 April 1953, Hart had made 88 League appearances for Stockport, but played only twice more for Blackpool in his debut season. Eventually, though, he established himself as a regular first-teamer and in 1976-7, when he scored six goals as Blackpool challenged for promotion, he was ever-present. Hart's reputation grew in a struggling side and, with relegation to Division Three virtually assured, he moved to Leeds United for £300,000 in March 1978, as a replacement for Gordon McQueen. After a shaky start, he settled down as a commanding stopper and made over 200 appearances for Leeds before moving to Nottingham Forest in the 1983 close season. There followed spells with Sheffield Wednesday, Birmingham City (he broke his leg in his only game for them) and Notts County (as player-coach) before he managed Chesterfield to a Wembley Play-off Final. Hart was also talked about as a possible successor to Jimmy Mullen at Bloomfield Road.

	LEAGUE		*FA CUP*		*FL CUP*		*TOTAL*	
	App	*Gls*	*App*	*Gls*	*App*	*Gls*	*App*	*Gls*
1973-74	3	0	0	0	0	0	3	0
1974-75	37	4	1	0	1	0	39	4
1975-76	33	2	2	0	0	0	35	2
1976-77	42	6	2	0	4	0	48	6
1977-78	28	3	1	0	2	1	31	4
	143	15	6	0	7	1	156	16

DAVE HATTON

Wing-half Dave Hatton arrived at Bloomfield Road from Bolton Wanderers in September 1969, for £40,000, and by the end of the season the Seasiders were back in Division One. Hatton, who was born in Farnworth on 30 October 1943, made 259 League and Cup appearances for Bolton, captaining the Trotters, before Les Shannon signed him. He made his debut in a home win over Swindon Town and teamed up with Glyn James and John McPhee, adding an extra dimension to the midfield as a skilful ball-winner. Alas, the following year was a disaster with relegation, and Hatton's worst moment came in a 4-3 home defeat by Chelsea, Hatton scoring the winner with a remarkable last-minute own-goal after Blackpool had been 3-0 in front. The next summer, though, he helped the Seasiders win the Anglo-Italian Cup, and the arrival of Peter Suddaby saw him switch to full-back where he played some of his best football, continuing alongside Bill Bentley to the end of his Blackpool days. Allan Brown released him to join Bury in August 1976 and a year later he became player-manager at Gigg Lane, losing the job after the Shakers narrowly avoided relegation to Division Four in 1979.

	LEAGUE		*FA CUP*		*FL CUP*		*TOTAL*	
	App	*Gls*	*App*	*Gls*	*App*	*Gls*	*App*	*Gls*
1969-70	36	0	2	0	0	0	38	0
1970-71	36	0	2	0	2	0	40	0
1971-72	40	4	1	0	4	0	45	4
1972-73	33	1	1	0	5	1	39	2
1973-74	30/1	1	0	0	2	0	32/1	1
1974-75	41	1	1	0	0	0	42	1
1975-76	34	0	2	0	1	0	37	0
	250/1	7	9	0	14	1	273/1	8

Although Bob Hatton played for Blackpool for only two seasons, he will never be forgotten by those who witnessed his goalscoring and his partnership with Mickey Walsh. By the time Hatton, who was born in Hull on 10 April 1947, arrived at Bloomfield Road in July 1976, he had already enjoyed a varied career with Wolves, Bolton Wanderers, Northampton Town, Carlisle United and Birmingham City (for whom he scored 58 goals in 175 League games, helping them into Division One in 1972 and to two FA Cup semi-finals). Allan Brown brought him to Bloomfield Road in an inspired transfer and in his first game he scored twice in a 4-1 win over Bristol Rovers. When the injured Walsh returned, the pair terrorised opposing defences, scoring 36 goals between them with Hatton's share ten. Hatton was the perfect foil for the speedy Walsh, with his excellent control, aerial power and still boundless energy. The following season was a personal triumph for Hatton with 22 goals, including two successive home games when he scored seven. Alas, despite this and 14 goals from Walsh, Blackpool dropped into Division Three for the first time, the team having collapsed after the sudden departure of Allan Brown. Hatton moved to Luton Town that summer and ended his League career with Sheffield United and Cardiff City, totalling 217 goals in 620 League games altogether. He later had a spell in the League of Ireland with Dundalk.

	LEAGUE		*FA CUP*		*FL CUP*		*TOTAL*	
	App	*Gls*	*App*	*Gls*	*App*	*Gls*	*App*	*Gls*
1976-77	39	10	2	0	4	1	45	11
1977-78	36	22	1	1	2	1	39	24
	75	32	3	1	6	2	84	35

BOB HATTON

During World War Two and for a few years beyond, Blackpool had what was widely regarded as the best club half-back line in the country in George Farrow, Eric Hayward and Harry Johnston. Of that trio, Hayward was the one who received the least publicity, yet his contribution to the great Blackpool team of the 1940s and 1950s was as important as anyone's. Born in Newcastle under Lyme on 2 August 1917, he first played for Hanley and Port Vale. A strong, skilful centre-half, he was utterly dependable, always there with a last-ditch tackle or timely clearance. He joined Blackpool in 1937 and during the war played in one of the finest teams in the country, although service in India restricted the number of games he could manage. He played in the 1943 War Cup Final and appeared in the 1948 and 1951 FA Cup Finals. The latter Final saw him marking the legendary Jackie Milburn and Blackpool unsuccessfully tried an offside game to compensate for Hayward's lack of speed against the great man. Two goals and another defeat were testament to a failed experiment. Hugh Kelly had now taken over from Farrow and he and Hayward worked well together, Hayward breaking up attacks and placing the pass for Kelly to start the counter-attack. Hayward remained loyal to Blackpool and after his playing days ended he returned as assistant manager to another old boy, Ron Suart. It was in that capacity that he helped to nurture the talents of Alan Ball, turning a youngster with potential into a player of immense talent. Eric Hayward died in 1976

	LEAGUE		*FA CUP*		*TOTAL*	
	App	*Gls*	*App*	*Gls*	*App*	*Gls*
1937-38	24	0	2	0	26	0
1938-39	41	0	1	0	42	0
1939-40	3	0	-	-	3	0
1946-47	20	0	0	0	20	0
1947-48	41	0	6	0	47	0
1948-49	42	0	3	0	45	0
1949-50	27	0	4	0	31	0
1950-51	37	0	5	0	42	0
1951-52	40	0	1	0	41	0
	275	0	22	0	297	0

ERIC HAYWARD

IAIN HESFORD

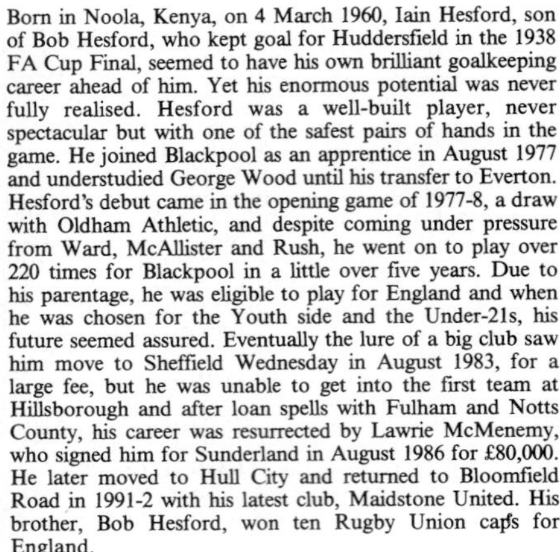

Born in Noola, Kenya, on 4 March 1960, Iain Hesford, son of Bob Hesford, who kept goal for Huddersfield in the 1938 FA Cup Final, seemed to have his own brilliant goalkeeping career ahead of him. Yet his enormous potential was never fully realised. Hesford was a well-built player, never spectacular but with one of the safest pairs of hands in the game. He joined Blackpool as an apprentice in August 1977 and understudied George Wood until his transfer to Everton. Hesford's debut came in the opening game of 1977-8, a draw with Oldham Athletic, and despite coming under pressure from Ward, McAllister and Rush, he went on to play over 220 times for Blackpool in a little over five years. Due to his parentage, he was eligible to play for England and when he was chosen for the Youth side and the Under-21s, his future seemed assured. Eventually the lure of a big club saw him move to Sheffield Wednesday in August 1983, for a large fee, but he was unable to get into the first team at Hillsborough and after loan spells with Fulham and Notts County, his career was resurrected by Lawrie McMenemy, who signed him for Sunderland in August 1986 for £80,000. He later moved to Hull City and returned to Bloomfield Road in 1991-2 with his latest club, Maidstone United. His brother, Bob Hesford, won ten Rugby Union caps for England.

	LEAGUE		*FA CUP*		*FL CUP*		*TOTAL*	
	App	*Gls*	*App*	*Gls*	*App*	*Gls*	*App*	*Gls*
1977-78	14	0	0	0	2	0	16	0
1978-79	33	0	2	0	2	0	37	0
1979-80	30	0	2	0	0	0	32	0
1980-81	42	0	2	0	4	0	48	0
1981-82	39	0	5	0	2	0	46	0
1982-83	44	0	2	0	5	0	51	0
	202	0	13	0	15	0	230	0

STEVE HETZKE

Born in Marlborough on 3 June 1955, Steve Hetzke made over 250 League appearances for Reading, the club he joined as an apprentice in June 1973. A tall, strong central defender, Hetzke was transferred to Blackpool in July 1982, for a modest £12,500 fee settled by a tribunal, and proved a real bargain buy. Hetzke, who in 1976 had a summer in the NASL with Vancouver Whitecaps, made his Blackpool debut on the opening day of 1982-3, in a defeat at Mansfield, taking over from the departed Paul Hart. Hetzke was a tower of strength in a leaky defence as Blackpool finished 21st in his first season. Gradually, the team began to progress and under his captaincy became a force in Division Four. At the end of 1984-5, the Seasiders were promoted, conceding only 39 goals in 46 matches. Hetzke was never a spectacular centre-half, but he always preferred the measured pass as opposed to the hopeful boot out of defence. Midway through 1985-6, his position came under pressure from Nicky Law and in March 1986, Hetzke moved to Sunderland, for whom he made 31 League appearances before ending his career with a handful of games for Chester and Colchester.

	LEAGUE		*FA CUP*		*FL CUP*		*TOTAL*	
	App	*Gls*	*App*	*Gls*	*App*	*Gls*	*App*	*Gls*
1982-83	42	2	2	0	4	1	48	3
1983-84	45	7	5	0	2	0	52	7
1984-85	30	5	1	0	4	0	35	5
1985-86	23	4	2	0	0	0	25	4
	140	18	10	0	10	1	160	19

'Mandy' Hill's was a career that showed great promise when he was young, but eventually a catalogue of injuries deprived him of the success he deserved. Born in Blackpool on 15 February 1940, Hill joined the club in May 1959 as a winger with a reputation as a prolific goalscorer. He was fast and his magical touch on the ball, coupled with a deceptive body-swerve, soon had people talking of a 'new Stanley Matthews'. The management groomed him as a potential successor to the maestro and, indeed, four appearances in England's Under-23 side underlined Hill's potential. He made his first-team debut in October 1959, deputising for the injured Matthews in a home defeat by Manchester City, but then spent the next two years trying to break into the first team as Matthews continued long after most pundits had predicted that he would hang up his boots. Eventually, in 1961-2, with Matthews transferred to Stoke, Hill broke into the side on a regular basis, but then he seemed susceptible to niggling injuries. These injuries became frequent and one particular knock caused him to miss the majority of the next two seasons. By the time it had been cleared up completely, Hill had lost his place to Leslie Lea and was transferred to Tranmere Rovers in September 1964. For Tranmere he made 130 League appearances, but predictably he could never have lived up to his billing as Matthews successor at Bloomfield Road.

	LEAGUE		*FA CUP*		*FL CUP*		*TOTAL*	
	App	*Gls*	*App*	*Gls*	*App*	*Gls*	*App*	*Gls*
1959-60	7	0	0	0	-	-	7	0
1960-61	10	0	0	0	1	0	11	0
1961-62	37	1	2	0	6	0	45	1
1962-63	9	0	0	0	1	0	10	0
1963-64	9	0	2	0	1	0	12	0
	72	1	4	0	9	0	85	1

STEVE 'MANDY' HILL

Born in Barrow-in-Furness on 28 August 1947, Emlyn Hughes made only 28 League appearances for Blackpool before being transferred to Liverpool in February 1967 to begin a remarkable career with England's most successful club. Son of a Rugby League international, Hughes joined the Seasiders from Roose FC of Blackpool in September 1964. His debut came in the final game of 1965-6, a victory over Blackburn, and the following season Ron Suart teamed him up with Jimmy Armfield, a tremendous opportunity for the youngster to learn his trade. Soon, though, Bill Shankly paid £65,000 for the 19-year-old. With Liverpool, Hughes went on to collect the game's greatest honours, captaining the Reds to a host of domestic and European honours as well as being England's skipper for a brief spell — he won 62 caps between 1970 and 1980. He was essentially a full-back, with a strange galloping action which, coupled with his obsessive enthusiasm, earned him the nickname 'Crazy Horse', but he was equally at home in the centre of defence or midfield. After 657 games for Liverpool, Hughes was transferred to Wolves in August 1979, for £90,000, and led them to a League Cup success in 1980 before becoming player-manager of Rotherham United. Hughes had spells with Hull City (he was later a director at Boothferry Park), Mansfield Town (although he did not play a League game for the Stags) and Swansea City. He became a TV celebrity and an outspoken figure in tabloid journalism.

	LEAGUE		*FA CUP*		*FL CUP*		*TOTAL*	
	App	*Gls*	*App*	*Gls*	*App*	*Gls*	*App*	*Gls*
1965-66	1	0	0	0	0	0	1	0
1966-67	26/1	0	1	0	5	0	32/1	0
	27/1	0	1	0	5	0	33/1	0

EMLYN HUGHES

Tommy Hutchison, one of the most gifted players to appear at Bloomfield Road, was bought from Alloa Athletic in February 1968, for just over £10,000 by Stan Mortensen.

TOMMY HUTCHISON

Almost immediately he took the place of Graham Oates at outside-left, making his debut against Plymouth. Hutchison was brought to boost 'Pool's flagging promotion drive, and in the final nine games of the season, with Hutchison playing, they won eight. Promotion was missed on the final day, but 'Hutch' had been impressive throughout. He teamed up with Burns and Suddick in midfield, often winning the ball deep in his own half and taking it forward before supplying the perfect pass. When Bob Stokoe took over, he worked on Hutchison's crossing ability, believing it to be his only weak spot. He did not score many goals, but one of his most spectacular was in a home game against Portsmouth in 1972, crashing the ball home after a brilliant solo run. Later that year First Division Coventry offered cash plus Billy Rafferty and Blackpool let him go. At Coventry and later at Mancheter City he enjoyed most success, winning international honours. His most famous moment came in the 1981 FA Cup Final, for Manchester City against Spurs when he scored for both sides. He later appeared for Burnley, Swansea and had a spell in Hong Kong, returning to Blackpool on loan in 1987. He is still playing non-League soccer.

	LEAGUE		*FA CUP*		*FL CUP*		*TOTAL*	
	App	*Gls*	*App*	*Gls*	*App*	*Gls*	*App*	*Gls*
1967-68	9	0	0	0	0	0	9	0
1968-69	32	2	0	0	5	1	37	3
1969-70	41	2	3	1	3	0	47	3
1970-71	38	1	1	0	2	0	41	1
1971-72	32/2	2	1	0	3	2	36/2	4
1972-73	10	3	1	0	4	0	15	3
1987-88	3/3	0	0	0	0/1	0	3/4	0
	165/5	10	6	1	17/1	3	188/6	14

Born in Llangollen, Glyn James served Blackpool as a centre-half and captain, played for 15 seasons and made over 400 appearances. A strong, tall player, he made his debut at Preston in October 1960, standing in for the injured Roy Gratrix, whose monopoly of the number-five shirt meant that the youngster had to wait nearly four years to succeed him. Once he did, though, he became as effective

GLYN JAMES

him. Once he did, though, he became as effective as his predecessor. James was never spectacular, but his height proved invaluable at the heart of the defence. With the hard John McPhee alongside him, they made a fearsome duo, although James preferred the cultured approach. His leadership qualities earned him Welsh caps, but his greatest moment came in the 1972 Anglo-Italian Final against AS Roma when he held the defence together as the Italians threatened to overwhelm Blackpool. Although they lost, it made up for James' disappointment 12 months previously when he was forced to miss the Bologna Final due to injury. At the start of 1971-2, Bob Stokoe tried him at centre-forward. James replied with six goals in his first five games but after the arrival of Keith Dyson he returned to his familiar role. Towards the end of his career the club arranged a testimonial game, and it was pleasing to see so many appreciative fans turn up to salute one of Blackpool's most loyal players. He remains closely connected with the club and is now a successful local businessman.

	LEAGUE		*FA CUP*		*FL CUP*		*TOTAL*	
	App	*Gls*	*App*	*Gls*	*App*	*Gls*	*App*	*Gls*
1960-61	3	0	0	0	2	0	5	0
1961-62	1	0	0	0	0	0	1	0
1962-63	7	0	0	0	0	0	7	0
1963-64	9	0	0	0	1	0	10	0
1964-65	35	0	1	0	2	0	38	0
1965-66	37	1	2	1	1	0	40	2
1966-67	33/1	0	1	0	3	0	37/1	0
1967-68	32	2	1	0	3	0	36	2
1968-69	42	4	1	0	5	0	48	4
1969-70	38	2	3	0	1	1	42	3
1970-71	35/1	1	2	0	2	0	39/1	1
1971-72	38/1	8	1	0	4	1	43/1	9
1972-73	31/3	1	1	0	4	0	36/3	1
1973-74	42	3	1	0	2	0	45	3
1974-75	12	0	0	0	1	0	13	0
	395/6	22	14	1	31	2	440/6	25

Between 1937 and 1955, Harry Johnston was 'Mr Blackpool', for during this time he made over 400 first-team appearances and captained the club in three FA Cup Finals. Born in Manchester on 26 September 1919, Johnston spent his early years with Droylsden Athletic but, despite living in the shadow of Maine Road, he was a fanatical follower of Manchester United. It was

HARRY JOHNSTON

Blackpool, though, who signed Johnston when he was 15, as a member of the groundstaff, and three years later, in November 1937, he made his League debut at Deepdale. He was one of the youngest players to appear for Blackpool but by the following season he was a regular in the first team. During his career he appeared in all three half-back positions and even moved up to centre-forward when circumstances demanded. After the war, during which he served in the Middle East, he became the rock on which the successful Blackpool team was built and as captain he led them to FA Cup Final appearances in 1948 and 1951, and, of course, to the famous 1953 Final, when he became the first Blackpool skipper to lift the trophy. Although a hard tackler, he was also a perfect gentleman. It was often said that in the 1950s, if Johnston, Matthews and Mortensen were playing, then the away attendance would normally be doubled. In 1950-51 he was voted Footballer of the Year and he was always enormously popular throughout the country. Johnston was the subject of several big bids from other clubs but always remained a one-club player. He played his last game for Blackpool on 25 April 1955, at Newcastle, and later that year became manager of Reading. Harry Johnston had always been a Blackpool man and it was no surprise, some 12 years later, to see him back at Bloomfield Road as chief scout. His international career was all-too brief, at least as far as caps were concerned. He gained only ten in a seven-year period, although had it not been for the consistent Billy Wright he would surely have appeared many more times for his country. Harry Johnston played for Blackpool more times than any other player until Jimmy Armfield broke his record. He was an essential part of the great team of the 1950s and commanding leadership was an inspiration to those around him. When one talks of the great players of the post-war era, the names of Matthews, Mortensen and Johnston are synonymous. When he died, at the age of only 54, the whole town mourned, for Harry Johnston was truly one of the greatest players ever to wear the tangerine shirt.

Harry Johnston's long leg gets the ball away from Roy Swinburne of Wolves.

	LEAGUE		*FA CUP*		*TOTAL*	
	App	*Gls*	*App*	*Gls*	*App*	*Gls*
1937-38	20	1	2	0	22	1
1938-39	35	0	1	0	36	0
1939-40	3	0	-	-	3	0
1946-47	40	0	1	0	41	0
1947-48	36	1	6	1	42	2
1948-49	36	0	3	0	39	0
1949-50	40	2	4	0	44	2
1950-51	38	7	8	0	46	7
1951-52	31	0	1	1	32	1
1952-53	41	0	7	0	48	0
1953-54	37	0	6	1	43	1
1954-55	41	0	1	0	42	0
	398	11	40	3	438	14

HERBERT JONES

Born in Blackpool on 3 September 1896, Herbert 'Taffy' Jones became an integral part of the Seasiders' defence in the early part of the century and later gained full international honours whilst playing for Blackburn Rovers. He started his playing career at South Shore and Fleetwood before joining Blackpool in 1922, making his debut for the club on 16 December against Hull City. A hard full-back, he made a formidable partnership with Leaver and their solidity at the back helped Blackpool's 'goals-against' column to be so impressive. He made only around 100 appearances for the Seasiders before being lured away by the mighty Blackburn Rovers for a then huge fee of £3,850, one of the largest paid for a full-back at that time. Whilst at Ewood Park, Jones made six appearances for England and over 260 for Rovers. Later he was transferred to Brighton before ending his career at Fleetwood, whom he led to the Lancashire Junior Cup Final when he was 40. He continued to follow the fortunes of Blackpool and lived on the Fylde coast until he died in 1973. He was never regarded as a star at Bloomfield Road, more of a 'solid' player, but then all good teams are built on such players.

	LEAGUE		*FA CUP*		*TOTAL*	
	App	*Gls*	*App*	*Gls*	*App*	*Gls*
1922-23	16	0	0	0	16	0
1923-24	28	0	2	0	30	0
1924-25	34	0	7	0	41	0
1925-26	18	0	0	0	18	0
	96	0	9	0	105	0

JIMMY JONES

Born in Newburn-on-Tyne in 1889, Jimmy Jones was a sharp-tackling full-back who joined Blackpool from Gateshead in June 1912. Although relatively small for a defender, he had tremendous pace and a cannon-like shot. He made his debut in September 1912, in a home win over Fulham, and proceeded to take over the left-back position vacated by Charlie Gladwin. From that moment he was almost ever-present in a team that was constantly changing, and kept his place throughout the next few years, including the first two seasons of wartime football. Jones was reliable if unspectacular, and aggressive but fair. He was popular with the Blackpool fans and they were sad to see him leave for Bolton Wanderers in March 1920, for £1,000. His position had come under intense pressure from the talented Horace Fairhurst, and as he was no longer regarded as a definite choice, he decided to move. After 70 League appearances for Bolton, he joined New Brighton of the Lancashire Combination in August 1922 and the following season became their first captain in the Football League. Jones retired in the close season of 1927, after 141 League games for the Rakers, and returned to Blackpool as a publican.

	LEAGUE		*FA CUP*		*TOTAL*	
	App	*Gls*	*App*	*Gls*	*App*	*Gls*
1912-13	32	0	2	0	34	0
1913-14	38	0	1	0	39	0
1914-15	21	0	0	0	21	0
1919-20	22	0	0	0	22	0
	113	0	3	0	116	0

During the early part of the 1933-4 season, manager Alex McFarlane, looking to boost his side's already flagging promotion hopes, began to search further afield for talent. He went to Ireland and found two, Peter Doherty and Sam Jones. Jones was playing for Distillery and needed no persuading to cross the water and play in English League football. A few weeks later, Doherty joined the Seasiders and the two became firm friends, sharing digs near Bloomfield Road. Jones was a stylish but tough-tackling half-back who played over 170 games for Blackpool. He was, like his friend Doherty, an absolute fitness fanatic and would spend hours in extra training. Due to his upbringing he never drank or smoked, believing both to be hazardous to his health at a time when neither activity was particularly frowned upon even by sportsmen. He played alongside a number of centre-halves, but his partnership with Louis Cardwell was especially successful, particularly in 1936-7 when Blackpool regained First Division status. He made his debut in October 1933, in the goalless draw with Oldham, and continued playing right through to the war. He also played in the team that lifted the War Cup in 1943. He could often be seen marshalling his players and urging them to even greater efforts. He played for Ireland on a handful of occasions, yet many people believed he never received the recognition he deserved. A good, solid no frills type of player, for ten years he was one of the mainstays of the Blackpool team.

	LEAGUE		*FA CUP*		*TOTAL*	
	App	*Gls*	*App*	*Gls*	*App*	*Gls*
1933-34	22	1	2	0	24	1
1934-35	41	1	1	0	42	1
1935-36	37	2	2	0	39	2
1936-37	34	0	0	0	34	0
1937-38	24	0	0	0	24	0
1938-39	7	2	0	0	7	2
	165	6	5	0	170	6

SAMMY JONES

Hugh Kelly joined Blackpool for a £10 signing-on fee from Scottish junior club Jeanfield Swifts in 1943 and went on to make over 470 League appearances for the club. Kelly, who was born in Valleyfield in January 1923, was a sturdy wing-half and a superb passer of the ball. He guested for several clubs during the war, notably East Fife, before making his League debut for Blackpool in September 1946, in the home victory over Aston Villa, although he had appeared in the previous season's marathon FA Cup tie with Leeds United. It took some time for him to become established, but by 1948-9 the half-back line of Johnston-Hayward-Kelly was becoming legendary. Kelly played in the 1948 and 1951 Cup Finals, but an ankle injury saw him miss the 1953 Final, although the club asked the FA to produce a special winners' medal for his nomination as '12th man'. In 1955 he took over from Harry Johnston as skipper and helped Blackpool finish in their highest-ever League position, runners-up to Manchester United. Kelly won one Scottish cap, in the 6-0 defeat of the USA in 1952. At the end of 1960-61, unable to command a first-team place, he was given a free-transfer and non-League Ashton United snapped him up as their player-manager. He was later on the backroom staff at Bloomfield Road and was also in business in the town as a grocer and ice-cream manufacturer. He was often called 'Mr Loyal' by supporters and no football team could have wished for a better servant.

	LEAGUE		*FA CUP*		*TOTAL*	
	App	*Gls*	*App*	*Gls*	*App*	*Gls*
1946-47	6	0	0	0	6	0
1947-48	23	0	6	0	29	0
1948-49	38	2	3	0	41	2
1949-50	41	0	5	0	46	0
1950-51	37	1	7	0	44	1
1951-52	32	0	0	0	32	0
1952-53	33	0	2	0	35	0
1953-54	35	0	6	0	41	0
1954-55	35	0	1	0	36	0
1955-56	41	0	1	0	42	0
1956-57	17	0	0	0	17	0
1957-58	36	3	1	1	37	4
1958-59	36	2	6	0	42	2
1959-60	18	0	2	0	20	0
	428	8	40	1	468	9

HUGH KELLY

Joe Lane was Blackpool's first prolific goalscorer and in the season immediately after World War One he helped the Seasiders to their highest-ever finish. Born in Hereford in July 1892, he joined Watford as an amateur in 1906 and then played in Hungarian football before signing for Sunderland in 1912. He joined Blackpool from the Roker club in 1913, for £400, and he went straight into the first team at centre-forward, where he struck a rich partnership with inside-right Charlton. Lane scored on his debut against Leeds City and went on to net a further ten that season, helping Blackpool claw their way back up the table. It soon became obvious that the Seasiders had unearthed a player of some considerable skill, who also had a knack of scoring regularly. The following season his goals helped Blackpool to a respectable mid-table position and the club managed to hold on to him in the face of strong interest from other clubs. During the war, Lane served in Egypt with the Hertfordshire Yeomanry. In the first post-war season his goals helped Blackpool into second place, their best position since joining the League over 20 years earlier. But in March 1920, the board finally bowed to increasing financial pressure and sold him for a club record £3,300 to Birmingham. The move caused an uproar amongst supporters and Blackpool's season collapsed. They finished fourth and missed promotion. The directors, though, had no choice; attendances were poor and the club had always been financially embarrassed. At Birmingham, Lane scored 26 goals in 67 League games to help the Blues regain their First Division status. He later played for Millwall, coached Barcelona and was still scoring goals for Watford Printing FC when he was 43. Joe Lane died at Abbott's Langley in February 1959.

JOE LANE

	LEAGUE		*FA CUP*		*TOTAL*	
	App	*Gls*	*App*	*Gls*	*App*	*Gls*
1913-14	26	11	1	0	27	11
1914-15	38	28	1	0	39	28
1919-20	30	26	3	2	33	28
	94	65	5	2	99	67

Leslie Lea was another player heralded as Stanley Matthews' replacement. Alas, Lea never realised his early potential and had his best days after he left Bloomfield Road. A nippy outside-right, born in Manchester on 5 October 1942, he joined the Seasiders from a Manchester junior club and made his League debut in August 1960, in the opening game of the season against Leicester City. Ron Suart's idea was that Lea would complement Matthews on the right, but he played only a handful of games that season and a combination of niggling injuries and the form of Mandy Hill kept him out for the next season or so. That both Hill and Lea were described by the Press as the natural successors to Matthews is interesting, for neither lived up to their early promise. Lea's breakthrough came in 1962-3 when he teamed up with Pat Quinn, but then the emergence of Alan Ball restricted his appearances. Lea was a talented player with fluent ball control, an accurate cross, and he enjoyed running at an opponent. In November 1967, Stan Mortensen, mindful of his new signing Alan Skirton, transferred Lea to Cardiff City for £20,000. Whilst at Ninian Park he took on the mantle of cult-hero and became one of the Bluebirds' most popular players before ending his career with over 200 League appearances for Barnsley.

LESLIE LEA

	LEAGUE		*FA CUP*		*FL CUP*		*TOTAL*	
	App	*Gls*	*App*	*Gls*	*App*	*Gls*	*App*	*Gls*
1960-61	7	1	0	0	1	0	8	1
1961-62	0	0	0	0	0	0	0	0
1962-63	23	2	2	0	1	0	26	2
1963-64	30	1	0	0	1	0	31	1
1964-65	30	2	1	0	2	1	33	3
1965-66	26	4	2	0	2	1	30	5
1966-67	36	3	1	0	5	1	42	4
1967-68	6/2	0	0	0	1	0	7/2	0
	158/2	13	6	0	13	3	177/2	16

Jimmy McIntosh could be described as one of Blackpool's unluckiest players. During the 1947-8 FA Cup campaign he scored five goals to help the club to Wembley for the first time, and it was a crushing blow when he was told by Joe Smith that, due to injury and a recent loss of form, he would not be playing against Manchester United. Blackpool lost the Cup and a week later McIntosh was recalled for the final League match of the season. In a rearranged game at Preston, he tore the home defence apart, scoring five goals in a remarkable 7-0 victory. The great Jimmy Hampson is the only other player to score five goals for Blackpool in a League game and the victory still stands as the Seasiders' biggest away win. McIntosh was discovered at non-League Droylsden, playing alongside Harry Johnston. A fast, strong, well-built player, he was ideally suited to step into Hampson's shoes, yet his appearances were brief. He made his debut in September 1935, in a defeat at Swansea, and played only three more times that season. Two years and one more appearance later, he was part of the deal that brought Frank O'Donnell from Preston, with Watmough joining McIntosh on his way to Deepdale. Immediately after the war, McIntosh rejoined Blackpool and struck a partnership with Stan Mortensen. In 1947-8 he scored 13 goals in 35 games plus those five FA Cup goals.

	LEAGUE		*FA CUP*		*TOTAL*	
	App	*Gls*	*App*	*Gls*	*App*	*Gls*
1935-36	4	0	0	0	4	0
1936-37	0	0	0	0	0	0
1937-38	1	0	0	0	1	0
1946-47	28	5	1	0	29	5
1947-48	33	13	5	5	38	18
1948-49	13	4	2	0	15	4
	79	22	8	5	87	27

A year after his Wembley disappointment, with the arrival of Willie McIntosh, also from Preston, McIntosh moved to Everton for a 'nominal fee'.

JIMMY McINTOSH

John 'Chopper' McPhee was one of football's hard men. He was born in Motherwell on 21 November 1937 and joined Blackpool from his home-town club — where he was one of Bobby Ancell's 'babes' — in July 1962, for a bargain £10,000. Hard-tackling and fully committed, he was also versatile and during his eight years with Blackpool he played in virtually every position except in goal. He made his League debut in September 1962, at inside-right in a draw at Aston Villa, but soon reverted to half-back, swopping roles with Bobby Crawford. His place came under threat a couple of years later, when Graham Rowe joined the club, but McPhee's all-round ability won the day and in 1965 and 1968 he was the club's Player of the Year. He earned his 'chopper' reputation because of his crunching tackle and there were few forwards who relished going into battle with the Scotsman, yet he rarely found himself in trouble with referees. In July 1969, McPhee was initially blamed for the injury that virtually crippled the brilliant Tony Green, but it was soon established by Green that his tendon had snapped as he ran past McPhee in a pre-season friendly. McPhee's popularity survived and his passion and enthusiasm went a long way to helping gain promotion the next season. In June 1970 he moved to Barnsley and ended his career at Southport. Today he is a Blackpool businessman and still a popular figure in the town.

	LEAGUE		*FA CUP*		*FL CUP*		*TOTAL*	
	App	*Gls*	*App*	*Gls*	*App*	*Gls*	*App*	*Gls*
1962-63	37	6	2	1	3	2	42	9
1963-64	30	5	2	0	0	0	32	5
1964-65	26	1	1	0	0	0	27	1
1965-66	26/4	0	1	0	1	0	28/4	0
1966-67	25/1	0	1	0	4	0	30/1	0
1967-68	42	1	2	0	3	0	47	1
1968-69	38/1	1	1	0	5	0	44/1	1
1969-70	25/4	1	3	0	3	0	31/4	1
	249/10	15	13	1	19	2	281/10	18

JOHN McPHEE

CRAIG MADDEN

Craig Madden was one of the lower divisions' most prolific scorers in the early 1980s. At 5ft 8in, he was small for a striker, but deceptively quick, especially around the penalty area, with marvellous ball control. He was born in Manchester on 25 September 1958 and joined Bury from Northern Nomads in March 1978. For the Gigg Lane club, Madden rewrote the record books, scoring 129 goals in 296 League appearances, including 35 in 1981-2. His prowess was eventually recognised by a bigger club and West Brom signed him March 1986 for £50,000. The move did not work out, however, and after only 12 League appearances, in which he scored three times, Madden moved to Blackpool, again for £50,000, in February 1987. He made his debut in a big defeat at Wigan, scoring the Seasiders' only goal. Thereafter, he was almost ever-present, fitting in well with twin strikers Walwyn and Cunningham. In 1987-8, Madden was Blackpool's third highest scorer but began to fall prey to niggling injuries. Each time he dropped out of the team, it became more difficult to get back in and midway through the disastrous 1989-90 season, Jimmy Mullen allowed him move to non-League Fleetwood Town. He regained his scoring touch and continued to enjoy his football. He also kept his connection with Blackpool, becoming community officer at Bloomfield Road.

	LEAGUE		*FA CUP*		*FL CUP*		*TOTAL*	
	App	*Gls*	*App*	*Gls*	*App*	*Gls*	*App*	*Gls*
1986-87	19	5	0	0	0	0	19	5
1987-88	25/8	11	4/1	3	4	0	33/9	14
1988-89	20/7	4	1	0	0/2	0	21/9	4
1989-90	9/2	4	1	0	2/2	0	12/4	4
	73/17	24	6/1	3	6/4	0	85/22	27

Stanley Matthews must surely be regarded as the greatest player the game has ever seen and for most of his career, Matthews and Blackpool were inextricably linked, the two enjoying more success than at any other time. He was the man who played League football longer than any other, 33 years, and the man who had the longest England career. Born on 1 February 1915 in Hanley, Staffordshire, he was the son of boxer Jack Matthews, the 'Fighting Barber of Hanley' as he was billed. Matthews senior was a fitness fanatic and Matthews junior inherited his father's dedication, although young Stan preferred football and joined Stoke City as an amateur in September 1930. Within two years he signed professional forms and in 1933 helped Stoke to the Second Division title. In September 1934, he marked his England debut with a goal against Wales. Throughout his long career he was famous for his elusiveness and there was no faster player over 20 yards. He had superb balance, his slightly hunched figure over the ball almost inviting opponents to tackle him. They could try, but Matthews would more often than not leave them on their backsides. If he was tackled unfairly he would never retaliate, but just got up and continued to humble opponents in the only way he knew. In 1934, after an England game against Italy, a journalist said that he lacked the 'big-game temperament', but Matthews continued to play for his country well past his 42nd birthday. The first time he played for Blackpool was during World War Two. He was in the RAF and found himself stationed in the town, willingly accepting Colonel William Parkinson's invitation to guest for the Seasiders. His first match was in a defeat at Preston in August 1941, but he went on to star in a Blackpool team that excelled in wartime football. In the 1943 War Cup challenge match against Arsenal at Stamford Bridge, he virtually destroyed the Gunners' defence single-handed. Matthews signed officially for Blackpool on 10 May 1947, for a fee of £11,500, when he was 32. Some suggested that his best years were behind him, but Stoke fans turned up to a public meeting in their thousands in an attempt to get him to stay in the Potteries. The next six years saw Matthews play in three FA Cup Finals and win more international caps. The greatest moment of his career came in May 1953, when he engineered an incredible fightback as Blackpool came from 3-1 behind to beat Bolton 4-3 in the dying seconds of the FA Cup Final. The game will always be remembered as the 'Matthews Final', despite Stan Mortensen's hat-trick and Ernie Taylor's great display. Blackpool were a tremendous draw wherever they went, and if Matthews was playing then one could guarantee the highest attendance of the season at that ground. In the 1957 New Year's honours list he was awarded the CBE and eight years later became football's first knight. He was Footballer of the Year in 1948 and again in 1963, whilst playing for

	LEAGUE		*FA CUP*		*TOTAL*	
	App	*Gls*	*App*	*Gls*	*App*	*Gls*
1947-48	35	1	6	0	41	1
1948-49	26	3	3	0	29	3
1949-50	31	0	3	0	34	0
1950-51	38	0	8	0	46	0
1951-52	19	1	1	0	20	1
1952-53	24	4	7	1	31	5
1953-54	32	2	7	0	39	2
1954-55	33	1	1	0	34	1
1955-56	36	3	1	0	37	3
1956-57	24	2	4	0	28	2
1957-58	30	0	1	0	31	0
1958-59	19	0	6	0	25	0
1959-60	15	0	0	0	15	0
1960-61	27	0	1	0	28	0
1961-62	2	0	0	0	2	0
	391	17	49	1	440	18

SIR STANLEY MATTHEWS

Stoke City at the age of 48. His international career spanned 22 years and whilst playing for Blackpool he made 36 England appearances, the last coming against Denmark in 1957. He returned to Stoke in 1961 and continued playing for another four years, helping them regain First Division status and significantly improving their attendances. He appeared as fit as he had been all those years before. When he retired at the age of 50, all the great stars of the day turned out in his testimonial game at Stoke. He later managed Port Vale and coached around the world, notably in Malta and Canada, before returning to live in his beloved Potteries.

Between December 1920 and September 1925, Georgie Mee created a club record (which still stands) by appearing in 195 consecutive League matches for Blackpool. Mee signed from Notts County in July 1920 and made his debut on 18 September that year, in the 2-0 victory at Coventry when he replaced Donachie at outside-left and made the position his own. Mee was small, well-built and incredibly fast. His bursts down the wing were legendary and his ability to cross the ball accurately helped Harry Bedford to score many of his goals. Mee was not a great scorer himself, preferring to make them, but in March 1922 he netted one of the greatest goals ever seen at Bloomfield Road, hitting the ball home from 40 yards. He was an essential part of the forward line that included Bedford, Barrass, Charles and the man with whom he worked especially well on the left, Heathcote. Despite being Blackpool's top scorer, Bedford was criticised for being 'too lazy off the ball and too slow to react to crosses'. Of course, it was Mee who made up for Bedford's weaknesses with his remarkable speed and accurate centres. In February 1926, Mee joined Derby County for £3,750, along with Jimmy Gill. He helped Derby into Division One that season and to the First Division runners-up spot in 1929-30 before moving to Burnley in September 1932. He later played for Mansfield Town, Accrington Stanley (two spells), Great Harwood and Rochdale before taking a pub in Blackpool. His brother, Bertie, managed Arsenal's double-wining side of 1970-71. Georgie Mee was born in Bulwell in April 1900 and died at Poulton-le-Fylde in July 1978.

GEORGIE MEE

	LEAGUE		*FA CUP*		*TOTAL*	
	App	*Gls*	*App*	*Gls*	*App*	*Gls*
1920-21	29	2	3	0	32	2
1921-22	42	7	1	0	43	7
1922-23	42	1	1	0	43	1
1923-24	42	5	2	0	44	5
1924-25	42	4	7	0	49	4
1925-26	19	2	0	0	19	2
	216	21	14	0	230	21

By the time Colin Methven came to Bloomfield Road in July 1986, he had already made well over 500 League appearances with his two previous clubs, East Fife and Wigan Athletic. Although born in India, on 10 December 1955, Methven is a true Scot with an unrivalled passion for football. He moved to Wigan in October 1979 and was club captain at Springfield Park when Blackpool signed him for £20,000. He made his debut at centre-half, in a home draw with Chesterfield, replacing Nicky Law, and was a virtual ever-present for the next four years. Methven was strong, skilful and had tremendous leadership qualities. His contribution in the heart of the defence was outstanding, his age not slowing his drive and enthusiasm. He was also a 'footballing' centre-half who enjoyed going up for corners. He played right through to the end of 1989-90, being voted Player of the Year for two consecutive seasons by the fans, who were angry when he was sold to Walsall in November 1990, after an earlier loan spell with Carlisle United. Graham Carr, in his early days of management at Bloomfield Road, declared that Methven was 'neither fast enough nor good enough for Fourth Division football'. Methven had the last laugh, though, In the final game of the season, playing for Walsall, he was superb in helping his team to a 2-0 victory, so denying Blackpool automatic promotion to Division Three.

COLIN METHVEN

	LEAGUE		*FA CUP*		*FL CUP*		*TOTAL*	
	App	*Gls*	*App*	*Gls*	*App*	*Gls*	*App*	*Gls*
1986-87	46	5	1	0	1	0	48	5
1987-88	37/5	2	1/1	0	3	1	41/6	3
1988-89	41/1	1	3	0	5	0	49/1	1
1989-90	44/1	3	7	1	5	0	56/1	4
	168/7	11	12/1	1	14	1	194/8	13

Gordon Milne's best playing days were behind him when he came to Bloomfield Road in May 1967, but his strong defensive work proved invaluable in the club's first season back in Division Two. Born in Preston on 29 March 1937, Milne played for Preston Amateurs, Morecambe and Preston North End before joining Liverpool for £16,000 in August 1960. At Anfield he enjoyed his greatest successes. A strong, constructive wing-half, he was capped 14 times by England and was included in the 1966 World Cup squad. And although he missed the 1965 FA Cup Final against Leeds due to injury, he played in two League Championship sides, a Second Division title side and a European Cup-winners' Cup Final before joining Blackpool for £30,000. Milne made his debut in the opening match of 1967-8, on his old hunting ground of Deepdale and he immediately 'gelled' with defenders Glyn James and John McPhee. Blackpool missed promotion back to Division One on the final day of the campaign, although by then John Craven had taken over Milne's role at half-back. The next season saw injury and loss of form severely curtailed his appearances and towards the end of the season Stan Mortensen tried him, unsuccessfully, in the forward line. In January 1970, new manager Les Shannon let Milne go to Wigan Athletic as player-manager and he later held managerial posts with Coventry City, Leicester City, the England Youth team and with Beşkitaş of Turkey.

	LEAGUE		*FA CUP*		*FL CUP*		*TOTAL*	
	App	*Gls*	*App*	*Gls*	*App*	*Gls*	*App*	*Gls*
1967-68	34	2	2	0	3	1	39	3
1968-69	18/3	2	0/1	0	0/1	0	18/5	2
1969-70	8/1	0	0	0	1/1	0	9/2	0
	60/4	4	2/1	0	4/2	1	66/7	5

GORDON MILNE

Joining Blackpool in February 1965 from Manchester United, for whom he made 45 League appearances, Ian Moir was immediately thrown into the first team in a desperate effort to stave off relegation. An exciting winger, Moir made his debut on the left in the drawn game with Leicester City on 13 February and thereafter alternated between right and left flanks. He found himself competing with Leslie Lea, a player who had wrongly been heralded as the replacement for Stanley Matthews, but when he did play, Moir forged a rewarding partnership with Alan Ball. Many of the brilliant midfielder's goals were the result of Moir's work and most supporters were puzzled that he never enjoyed greater success in his career. He had excellent ball skills and could beat his man with ease, although he was sometimes accused of being 'greedy'. At the end of the 1966-7 relegation season, Stanley Mortensen began his rebuilding process and sold Moir to Chester City for just over £10,000. He moved to Wrexham in January 1968, for a similar fee, and helped them to promotion from Division Four in 1970 before being surprisingly released to Shrewsbury in March 1972. Sixteen months later he returned to Wrexham for a short spell and then played in South African football. Moir was born in Aberdeen on 30 June 1943.

	LEAGUE		*FA CUP*		*FL CUP*		*TOTAL*	
	App	*Gls*	*App*	*Gls*	*App*	*Gls*	*App*	*Gls*
1964-65	14	4	0	0	0	0	14	4
1965-66	25	3	0	0	1	0	26	3
1966-67	22	5	0	0	4	2	26	7
	61	12	0	0	5	2	66	14

IAN MOIR

STEVE MORGAN

Born in Oldham on 19 September 1968, Steve Morgan is another excellent product of Blackpool's youth policy and has already been capped by England Under-21s. He made his full first-team debut in April 1986, in an away defeat by Bristol Rovers. A strong, well-built player, he is comfortable in either a defensive or midfield position and spent much of his early career deep in defence alongside Dave Burgess or Mike Davies. Fast and skilful, he possesses an accurate cross, often after an overlapping sprint down the left wing. Morgan was virtually ever-present throughout his first three seasons, although his popularity waned when fans questioned his attitude. Indeed, his style often gave the impression that he was too relaxed, and with Blackpool struggling in the Third Division he was often made a scapegoat by supporters. Towards the end of 1988-9, First Division Wimbledon reportedly offered around £300,000 for him. Cash-starved Blackpool could have used the money but Morgan could not agree personal terms with Wimbledon. A year later, in July 1990, he joined Second Division Plymouth Argyle for less than one-third of that amount.

	LEAGUE		*FA CUP*		*FL CUP*		*TOTAL*	
	App	*Gls*	*App*	*Gls*	*App*	*Gls*	*App*	*Gls*
1985-86	3/2	0	0	0	0	0	3/2	0
1986-87	7/4	0	0	0	0	0	7/4	0
1987-88	46	6	6	0	4	1	56	7
1988-89	43/1	3	3	0	4	1	50/1	4
1989-90	36/2	1	7	0	5	0	48/2	1
	135/7	10	16	0	13	2	164/7	12

COLIN MORRIS

Colin Morris arrived at Bloomfield Road in January 1980, in the £125,000 part-exchange deal that took old favourite Derek Spence to Southend United. Morris made his debut that month, in a home defeat by Oxford United, and immediately proved that he was worth every penny of the fee. Fast and strong, he started in midfield, supplying the front men, Fletcher and Bamber, but soon proved to be better at scoring goals. The following season he was top scorer with 12 League goals in a relegation year and manager Alan Ball praised him as the side spiralled towards Division Four. Certainly his commitment to a lost cause was remarkable and no other player scored more than five goals in that disastrous campaign. With the club in Division Four and Alan Ball departed, it became only a matter of time before Morris was snapped up by a top side. In February 1982, Blackpool accepted a fee of around £100,000 from Sheffield United, a figure that represented the amount the taxman had demanded be paid within seven days but a sum nowhere near representing the worth of the player. He went on to make 240 League appearances for the Blades, scoring 68 goals. Morris, who was born in Blyth on 22 August 1953, began his career with Burnley before moving to Southend in January 1977.

	LEAGUE		*FA CUP*		*FL CUP*		*TOTAL*	
	App	*Gls*	*App*	*Gls*	*App*	*Gls*	*App*	*Gls*
1979-80	21	4	0	0	0	0	21	4
1980-81	44	12	2	1	4	3	50	16
1981-82	22	10	5	2	2	0	29	12
	87	26	7	3	6	3	100	32

Stanley Mortensen is one name which can truly live up to the often over-used term of 'great' footballer. One of the fastest, most powerful forwards in the game, Mortensen scored over 200 goals for Blackpool, including his famous 1953 Cup Final hat-trick, and he managed virtually a goal a game when wearing the England shirt. Born in South Shields in May 1921, he was playing local football when Blackpool signed him in May 1938 to begin an association that was to last for virtually the rest of his life. At first he showed little promise and after 12 months the club were close to terminating his contract. Then, after individual training sessions with Georgie Mee and Bobby Finan, Mortensen speeded up and gradually became a player admired everywhere. Fast, determined and skilful, he worked his way through the reserve teams before war interrupted his progress and he found himself playing in a makeshift Blackpool side and also guesting for other clubs, notably Bath City. Mortensen made his League debut on 31 August 1946, scoring the opening goal in a victory at Huddersfield and going on to net 29 that season to become Blackpool's top scorer. The following season, as Blackpool began to make a serious impact, his 31 League and Cup goals again put him at the top of the list, including a hat-trick in the FA Cup semi-final at Villa Park and a goal at Wembley. By this time he had been joined by Stanley Matthews and it was Matthews for centres and Mortensen for goals as every weekend crowds flocked to see them play. Blackpool were now a powerful force and Morty's goals helped them to maintain their challenge. He was their top scorer right through to 1955 but his greatest moment came in 1953, when he scored the famous hat-trick that helped Blackpool come from behind to beat Bolton Wanderers 4-3 in the Cup Final. His last-minute equalizer is legendary — a 25-yard free-kick straight past the wall and into the net, despite Ernie Taylor's insistence that there was 'no gap'. Somehow Morty found a gap and gave the 'keeper no chance. His international career started in the war when he made a guest appearance for Wales after Ivor Powell went off injured and the Blackpool man generously stepped in. He made his England debut in May 1947, scoring four goals against Portugal, and went on to score 23 times in 25 full internationals. In late 1955 he was transferred to Hull City, yet chose to continue his training at Bloomfield Road. Later he played for Southport, Bath City again and Lancaster City, but he was always lured back to his first love, Blackpool (see *Blackpool Managers*). He became a successful local businessman, a town councillor and, of course, managed the club in the late 1960s. Mortensen was a brilliant player. He had a lethal shot, incredible speed, a remarkable body-swerve and was noted for his torpedo-like headers. He was also truly a great Blackpool man, loved and admired by everyone in the town. It has been said that the month of May was always significant to Stan Mortensen. He was born in May, signed professional terms in May, made his international debut in May, scored his famous hat-trick in May and, finally, in May 1991, he died. The whole town mourned his passing and it was particularly ironic that he passed away on the day that his beloved club had reached Wembley for the first time since 1953. He will never be forgotten.

STAN MORTENSEN

	LEAGUE		*FA CUP*		*TOTAL*	
	App	*Gls*	*App*	*Gls*	*App*	*Gls*
1946-47	40	28	1	1	41	29
1947-48	36	21	6	10	42	31
1948-49	34	18	3	2	37	20
1949-50	38	22	5	3	43	25
1950-51	36	30	8	5	44	35
1951-52	35	26	1	0	36	26
1952-53	35	15	2	3	37	18
1953-54	32	21	2	1	34	22
1954-55	28	11	1	0	29	11
1955-56	11	5	-	-	11	5
	325	197	29	25	354	222

HENRY MOWBRAY

Three weeks before the great Tony Green was signed for Blackpool by Stanley Mortensen, Henry Mowbray was acquired from Scottish club, Cowdenbeath. Mortensen had gone to watch Mowbray, decided to sign him and then noticed Green. The rest is history. Mowbray was a young full-back with tremendous determination and a lot of skill. He could run with the ball and had a perfectly-timed tackle. He was, indeed, the ideal replacement for Tommy Thompson, who had given such sterling service. Mowbray was signed on his birthday, 1 May 1967 — he was born in 1947 at Hamilton — and in August he made his debut in a draw at Ipswich. He fitted in perfectly with Jimmy Armfield for the next couple of years. Then Mowbray was hampered by injury and found himself battling to regain his place from Bill Bentley. It was a difficult decision for Mortensen, then for Shannon: the culture of Mowbray or the aggression of Bentley? More often than not, Bentley won the day and Mowbray played his last match for Blackpool in April 1971. New manager Bob Stokoe had made it clear that he preferred Bentley, so Mowbray moved to Bolton Wanderers, where Armfield was now as manager. He made 31 appearances for the Trotters before leaving League football.

	LEAGUE		*FA CUP*		*FL CUP*		*TOTAL*	
	App	*Gls*	*App*	*Gls*	*App*	*Gls*	*App*	*Gls*
1967-68	27	0	0	0	3	0	30	0
1968-69	12	0	0	0	3	0	15	0
1969-70	24/2	0	2/1	0	1	0	27/3	0
1970-71	25/1	0	2	1	1	0	28/1	1
	88/3	0	4/1	1	8	0	100/4	1

JACKIE MUDIE

Jackie Mudie was born in Dundee in 1931 and signed as an amateur from Lochee Harp before becoming a full-time professional in June 1947. On his League debut, at Liverpool in March 1950, he scored the only goal. A year later, after being second-highest scorer to Mortensen, Mudie played in the FA Cup Final against Newcastle, but after the Final Blackpool signed Ernie Taylor and Mudie lost his place. Eventually he worked his way back and scored the last-minute winner in the 1953 semi-final against Spurs, going on to gain a Cup winners' medal. In 1955, Mudie took over from the departed Mortensen at centre-forward, scoring 22 goals in the first season and 32 the following season, still a First Division record for a Blackpool player. He made 17 appearances for Scotland, scoring nine goals including a hat-trick against Spain that secured Scotland's World Cup Finals place. In March 1961, he was sold to Stoke for £8,500 and scored on his debut after only five minutes. He was small for a centre-forward — 5ft 6in — yet many of his goals were headed, and he played in every forward position except outside-left for Blackpool. In 1992, Jackie Mudie died at home after a serious illness and the club and the town mourned the passing of a fine player.

	LEAGUE		*FA CUP*		*FL CUP*		*TOTAL*	
	App	*Gls*	*App*	*Gls*	*App*	*Gls*	*App*	*Gls*
1949-50	8	1	0	0	-	-	8	1
1950-51	39	17	8	3	-	-	47	21
1951-52	9	4	0	0	-	-	9	4
1952-53	18	5	7	1	-	-	25	6
1953-54	24	11	1	0	-	-	25	11
1954-55	24	7	1	0	-	-	25	7
1955-56	42	22	1	0	-	-	43	22
1956-57	39	32	4	6	-	-	43	38
1957-58	35	18	0	0	-	-	35	18
1958-59	40	14	6	0	-	-	46	14
1959-60	31	9	2	0	-	-	33	9
1960-61	15	4	1	1	1	0	17	4
	324	144	31	11	1	0	356	155

Grahame Oates, who was born in Scunthorpe on 4 December 1943, signed as an apprentice for Blackpool in May 1961. He had been approached by the club earlier, but they were eventually fined for 'poaching' him. Oates, a nippy winger able to dribble, and something of a goalscorer, was seen as 'one for the future' for a team that was changing rapidly in an attempt to halt the slide from the glory days. After making his debut in September 1961, in a home defeat by Nottingham Forest, he played in a handful of games over the next year or so as veterans Bill Perry and Ray Parry continued their good form. Eventually, Oates broke through and for the next four seasons he was a regular on the left wing, scoring eight goals in his first 12 games before playing a supporting role to Charnley's goalscoring talents. Injury then kept Oates' appearances down, however, and with competition from Des Horne, he found it difficult to break back into the side. In 1968-9, Stan Mortensen had begun rebuilding and Oates was one of the players who no longer figured in his plans. In October 1968, Oates joined Grimsby Town for £10,000, ending his League career at Blundell Park.

	LEAGUE		*FA CUP*		*FL CUP*		*TOTAL*	
	App	*Gls*	*App*	*Gls*	*App*	*Gls*	*App*	*Gls*
1961-62	4	0	0	0	1	1	5	1
1962-63	1	0	0	0	0	0	1	0
1963-64	25	8	0	0	1	1	26	9
1964-65	30	12	0	0	0	0	30	12
1965-66	20/1	1	0	0	0	0	20/1	1
1966-67	16	2	0	0	1	0	17	2
1967-68	22/1	3	1	0	3	0	26/1	3
1968-69	1/1	0	0	0	1	0	2/1	0
	119/3	26	1	0	7	2	127/3	28

GRAHAME OATES

Jack O'Donnell joined Blackpool in late 1930 and made his debut on 20 December, in the home game against Grimsby Town. For the next two seasons he became the mainstay of the defence as Blackpool tried desperately to preserve their recently-won First Division status. Born in Gateshead in 1897, he started his career, like so many others from the North-East, by playing for his local colliery team, in his case, Felling. Darlington soon signed him and he earned a reputation as a hard-tackling full-back, the kind who could ruin a top striker's game by close marking and ruthless tackling. Everton paid around £3,000 for his services soon afterwards, showing how highly he was rated, particularly as that kind of fee was rare for a defender. Unfortunately for O'Donnell, the move did not work out and in the autumn of 1930, Blackpool bought him for a similar price. Almost immediately he struck a partnership with the captain, Walter Grant. Unfortunately it was a torrid time for the defenders in those first few years of higher League football; in the first season they conceded 125 goals, followed by 106 in the next. The team as a whole was woefully out of its depth, but the defenders took the majority of the criticism. O'Donnell also had a serious disciplinary problem, and it was reported on three occasions that the club had suspended him for various matters. Eventually it was agreed to end his contract by mutual agreement and O'Donnell played out his career in the lower leagues, notably with Wigan. He was a fine talent and it is fair to say that Blackpool never really saw him at his best.

	LEAGUE		*FA CUP*		*TOTAL*	
	App	*Gls*	*App*	*Gls*	*App*	*Gls*
1930-31	23	0	2	0	25	0
1931-32	32	0	2	0	34	0
	55	0	4	0	59	0

JACK O'DONNELL

EAMON O'KEEFE

Born in Manchester on 13 March 1953, Eamon O'Keefe was a free-scoring centre-forward, who began with Stalybridge Celtic before moving to Plymouth in February 1974. He failed to make the grade at Home Park and returned to non-League football with Hyde United a year later. There followed a spell in Saudi Arabia before his 29 goals helped Mossley win the Northern Premier League. This earned him England semi-professional honours, something which caused trouble a year later when he attempted to make his Republic of Ireland debut against Wales, although he went on to win five caps for Eire. First Division Everton had signed him in July 1979 and he played in 40 League games before joining Wigan Athletic (25 goals in 58 games), then Port Vale (17 goals in 59 games). Blackpool's Sam Ellis paid £17,500 for him in March 1985 and he made a scoring debut in a home win over Peterborough. He helped gain promotion to Division Three and the following season saw him at his best with 17 goals in 22 matches. Alas, injury now bothered him and after making only two appearances in 1986-7 he retired. That summer, 5,000 fans saw Blackpool meet League Champions Everton in his benefit game at Bloomfield Road. O'Keefe scored for Blackpool that night and two years later he made a comeback, returning with his new club Chester City to score a last-minute equalizer to deny Blackpool two points in their battle against relegation.

	LEAGUE		*FA CUP*		*FL CUP*		*TOTAL*	
	App	*Gls*	*App*	*Gls*	*App*	*Gls*	*App*	*Gls*
1984-85	12	6	0	0	0	0	12	6
1985-86	19/3	17	0	0	2	0	21/3	17
1986-87	2	0	0	0	0	0	2	0
	33/3	23	0	0	2	0	35/3	23

Jack Parkinson was top scorer in Blackpool's first-ever League season and went on to make over 360 appearances for them. Born in Blackpool in 1869, he devoted nearly his whole career to his home-town club, playing at centre-forward or inside-right. Later he was the perfect foil for prolific scorers like Jack Cox and Bob Birkett and then moved into midfield, playing at centre-half as the selection committee felt that the modern game was becoming too fast for a veteran forward. He became a celebrity around Blackpool and when the team returned from their victorious Cup tie with Sheffield United, it was Parkinson who was lifted shoulder-high by his adoring fans. In 1899-1900, after Blackpool failed to gain re-election, he played one game for Liverpool, in a Merseyside derby against Everton at Anfield, but returned after a year, when Blackpool were back in the League. From then he was virtually ever-present until his free transfer to Barrow in 1910. In April 1905, after ten years' service, he was given a benefit match against Liverpool. Afterwards he was presented with a gold watch by the directors. He became superintendent of Cocker Street Baths and lost his life there in a tragic accident. He was attempting to rescue a colleague from a tank of boiling sea-water when a plank on which he was standing snapped and Parkinson also fell in. He died shortly afterwards.

JACK PARKINSON

	LEAGUE		*FA CUP*		*TOTAL*	
	App	*Gls*	*App*	*Gls*	*App*	*Gls*
1896-97	27	12	-	-	27	12
1897-98	24	8	-	-	24	8
1898-99	34	9	-	-	34	9
1900-01	31	25	-	-	32	5
1901-02	27	6	-	-	27	6
1902-03	31	6	-	-	31	6
1903-04	29	2	-	-	29	2
1904-05	34	1	1	0	35	1
1905-06	37	1	5	0	42	1
1906-07	31	0	1	1	32	1
1907-08	33	2	1	0	34	2
1908-09	26	0	2	0	28	0
	365	52	10	1	375	53

Bill Perry was the most successful of the South African players who joined Blackpool after the war. Born in Johannesburg in 1931, he was recommended by Billy Butler, manager of Perry's team, Johannesburg Rangers. A year earlier, in 1948, Perry had turned down a move to Charlton, but now lured by a big club he moved to England. He made his League debut in March 1950, in a win at Manchester United, and for the next few years virtually made the outside-left position his own. He was fast, had an accurate centre and after he teamed up with Allan Brown during the team's most successful seasons, those two figured prominently. Perry was never a prolific scorer, but in 1955-6 he netted 20 goals to help Blackpool to their highest-ever League position. And his goal deep into injury time in the 1953 FA Cup Final, when he pounced on a Matthews cross, gave Blackpool their only Wembley success. Due to his father's birthplace he was able to play for England and won three caps, scoring twice in a 4-1 victory over Spain. In 1960 a cartilage operation virtually brought to an end his playing career, and after being in and out of the side he was transfer-listed in the summer of 1962. Southport bought him for around £3,500 and he stayed at Haig Avenue for a while before trying his hand in Australia. Eventually he returned to Blackpool where he went into business.

	LEAGUE		*FA CUP*		*FL CUP*		*TOTAL*	
	App	*Gls*	*App*	*Gls*	*App*	*Gls*	*App*	*Gls*
1949-50	11	0	0	0	-	-	11	0
1950-51	30	4	8	2	-	-	38	6
1951-52	35	4	1	0	-	-	36	4
1952-53	36	12	7	3	-	-	43	15
1953-54	42	15	7	3	-	-	49	18
1954-55	27	10	1	0	-	-	28	10
1955-56	41	20	1	1	-	-	42	21
1956-57	37	7	4	1	-	-	41	8
1957-58	40	18	1	0	-	-	41	18
1958-59	38	12	5	0	-	-	43	12
1959-60	34	9	3	0	-	-	37	9
1960-61	13	6	1	0	0	0	14	6
1961-62	10	2	1	0	2	0	13	2
	394	119	40	10	2	0	436	129

BILL PERRY

Although Fred Pickering was at Blackpool for only two seasons, he played an important role in the club's affairs at the turn of the 1970s. Born in Blackburn in January 1941, he began his career with his home-town club and stayed for five years before joining Everton for £85,000 in March 1964. There he became an England international, scoring a hat-trick on his debut against the USA, yet surprisingly was selected only once more for his country. In 1967, Pickering moved to Birmingham, where he had the happy knack of scoring goals, something which persuaded Les Shannon to pay £45,000 for him. A big, powerful centre-forward, with the decline of Tom White, Pickering was seen as the ideal replacement as Blackpool made a push for promotion. He made his debut with Mickey Burns in August 1969, in a home win over Portsmouth, and went on to become top scorer in his first season. Three of his goals came at Deepdale in the promotion decider, which made him into a folk-hero. Back in Division One, though, he played in only a handful of games and there was controversy. In October, in a home game against Chelsea, Blackpool were leading 3-1 with two goals from Pickering, when with 15 minutes to go, Shannon substituted him. It was a decision greeted by howls of derision from the fans. Blackpool collapsed to lose 4-3 and two days later, the manager resigned. New boss Bob Stokoe sold Pickering back to Blackburn for £10,000 in March 1972. It was an unhappy return to Ewood Park and a bid to revive his career with Brighton also failed.

	LEAGUE		*FA CUP*		*FL CUP*		*TOTAL*	
	App	*Gls*	*App*	*Gls*	*App*	*Gls*	*App*	*Gls*
1969-70	35	17	3	1	2	0	40	18
1970-71	14/1	7	1	0	1	0	16/1	7
	49/1	24	4	1	3	0	56/1	25

FRED PICKERING

GRAHAM ROWE

At 6ft 2in, Graham Rowe was the perfect size for a centre-half and, indeed, at his former club Southport he mostly played in that position. At Blackpool, though, he became a utility player moving from wing-half to centre-half and also on occasions at centre-forward. He was born in Southport on 28 August 1945, and joined Blackpool in the early part of 1961, signing professional forms in July 1963 and making his debut in February 1964 at Wolves, although it took some time to break into the first-team regularly as John McPhee was in such good form. Rowe was heavily built and his weight often contributed to the heavy tackles that he so enjoyed, although like McPhee he was never a dirty player. He came into his own whilst partnering Glyn James and John McPhee in the half-back line, yet on the occasions that he was asked to perform in attack he always coped admirably. In November 1968, whilst playing at centre-forward, he scored a hat-trick in the 6-0 demolition of Bury. A solid and reliable player, he never enjoyed popular status, yet was always appreciated by the fans. In November 1970, he moved to Tranmere on loan and ended his career with Bolton Wanderers, for whom he signed at the end of Blackpool's disastrous 1970-71 season.

	LEAGUE		*FA CUP*		*FL CUP*		*TOTAL*	
	App	*Gls*	*App*	*Gls*	*App*	*Gls*	*App*	*Gls*
1963-64	11	1	0	0	0	0	11	1
1964-65	23	4	1	0	1	0	25	4
1965-66	13	0	0	0	0	0	13	0
1966-67	13	0	0	0	1	0	14	0
1967-68	14/1	1	2	0	0	0	16/1	1
1968-69	17/2	6	1	0	3	0	21/2	6
1969-70	5/1	0	0	0	1	1	6/1	1
1970-71	5	0	0	0	1	1	6	1
	101/4	12	4	0	7	2	112/4	14

When Sheffield United refused Eddie Shimwell permission to run a pub, Blackpool jumped in to sign the unsettled defender for £7,000 in December 1946. It was to be a shrewd purchase as Shimwell went on to play in all three of the Seasiders' FA Cup Finals. Born in Matlock in February 1920, Shimwell, a tough-tackling full-back, good in the air and possessing a powerful clearance, played for Sheffield United throughout the war before Blackpool signed him.

EDDIE SHIMWELL

His debut was delayed when the train from his Chesterfield home was snow-bound and he did not arrive at The Valley until half-time. Instead he opened his Blackpool account four days later, on Christmas Day against Blackburn Rovers, replacing Eric Sibley. From that moment he made the position his own, teaming up in later years with Tommy Garrett, when their contrasting styles were most effective. Garrett was the polished defender, Shimwell preferring the sliding tackle and the shoulder-charge. He scored two important FA Cup goals for Blackpool. The first, against Chester in January 1948, saw him lob the ball home from fully 60 yards, the following wind and a frozen pitch seeing it bounce over the 'keeper's head; later that year, he became the first full-back to score in a Wembley Cup Final when his 14th-minute penalty gave Blackpool the lead. A dislocated shoulder brought about a premature end to his Blackpool days, although for some time he played in the Reserves, still travelling from his Chesterfield home for matches. In May 1957, he was given a free-transfer to Third Division Oldham Athletic. He later played for Burton Albion and became a licensee in Matlock.

	LEAGUE		*FA CUP*		*TOTAL*	
	App	*Gls*	*App*	*Gls*	*App*	*Gls*
1946-47	21	0	1	0	22	0
1947-48	37	0	6	2	43	2
1948-49	37	2	3	0	40	2
1949-50	32	3	3	0	35	3
1950-51	41	0	8	0	49	0
1951-52	33	0	1	0	34	0
1952-53	35	0	7	0	42	0
1953-54	32	0	7	0	39	0
1954-55	11	0	0	0	11	0
1955-56	8	0	0	0	8	0
1956-57	1	0	0	0	1	0
	288	5	36	2	324	7

At nearly 6ft, Alan Skirton did not look like a typical outside-right, yet he had great speed, marvellous ball skills, an accurate cross and a fierce shot. And his size and weight often deterred defenders from tackling him. Skirton, who was born in Bath on 23 January 1939, joined Arsenal from Bath City for £5,000 in January 1959 and scored 53 goals in 145 League games for the Gunners before being transferred to Blackpool in September 1966 for £65,000, although had the club listened to Stan Mortensen, then they could have had him for a lot less, for Mortensen, a former Bath player himself, had earlier recommended Skirton to the Seasiders. Skirton scored on his Blackpool debut — at Highbury of all places — and the next season saw the Seasiders back in Division Two with Skirton their second-highest scorer. That made him popular with the fans and he was also a good influence in the dressing-room. In November 1968, however, Mortensen, seeing the emergence of Ronnie Brown on the right wing, allowed Skirton to return to the West Country and he joined Bristol City for £15,000. It was a shame for the Bloomfield Road faithful, as Skirton had brought enjoyment to their football and become something of a folk-hero. He later played for Torquay United, in South Africa for Durban City, for Weymouth and held commercial posts at Weymouth, Bath and Yeovil Town.

	LEAGUE		*FA CUP*		*FL CUP*		*TOTAL*	
	App	*Gls*	*App*	*Gls*	*App*	*Gls*	*App*	*Gls*
1966-67	25	8	0	0	3	2	28	10
1967-68	37/1	17	2	1	2	0	41/1	18
1968-69	14	0	0	0	3	0	17	0
	76/1	25	2	1	8	2	86/1	28

ALAN SKIRTON

Bill Slater, or W.J.Slater as he was known in his Blackpool days, holds two interesting records: he is the last amateur to have appeared in an FA Cup Final at Wembley, for Blackpool in 1951; and he scored Blackpool's quickest-ever goal, which came after only 11 seconds in December 1949 against Stoke City. Slater, born in Clitheroe in April 1929, joined Blackpool as a schoolboy soon after the war. He made his League debut for the Seasiders in September 1949, in a goalless draw at Aston Villa, but as a nippy inside-forward he found himself competing with Allan Brown for the number-ten position for most of his time at Blackpool. In the Cup Final against Newcastle, he partnered South African Bill Perry, but, unable to guarantee a first-team place, he joined Brentford in December 1951 and moved to Wolves in August 1952, finally becoming a part-time professional. With Wolves he switched to half-back and was capped 12 times at full level by England, being voted Footballer of the Year in 1960, when he led Wolves to victory in the FA Cup Final against Blackburn. He also won three League Championship medals with the Molineux club. In July 1963 he returned to Brentford, after 339 appearances for Wolves, and later played for Northern Nomads. Slater held several posts in physical education and in 1982 was awarded the OBE for his service to sport.

	LEAGUE		*FA CUP*		*TOTAL*	
	App	*Gls*	*App*	*Gls*	*App*	*Gls*
1949-50	9	3	2	3	11	6
1950-51	18	4	1	0	19	4
1951-52	5	2	0	0	5	2
	32	9	3	3	35	12

BILL SLATER

DEREK SPENCE

This tall, lanky striker was most unfortunate in his career at Bloomfield Road. The former Oldham forward was signed by Allan Brown from Bury at the beginning of 1976-7 and made his debut against Brian Clough's Nottingham Forest that October. He complemented the twin striking powers of Mickey Walsh and another new signing, Bob Hatton, although at the end of the season he found his place under pressure from Stan McEwan. A serious injury then kept him out for the whole of the next campaign, significantly being the season that the club were relegated to Division Three for the first time. His international career was also on hold after he had made six appearances for Northern Ireland, all of them as substitute. A year later he teamed up with Tony Kellow, a signing from Exeter City, and they made formidable pair, between them scoring 27 goals, nearly half of the team's total, with Spence top scorer on 16. He returned to the international scene and went on to win 15 caps, scoring three goals. Blackpool, though, were struggling and there were constant team changes, Spence's place coming under pressure from Gary Jones. During 1979-80 he sustained an injury serious enough to force his premature retirement. It was a sad ending to a successful career and he was missed by the Bloomfield Road faithful.

	LEAGUE		*FA CUP*		*FL CUP*		*TOTAL*	
	App	*Gls*	*App*	*Gls*	*App*	*Gls*	*App*	*Gls*
1976-77	24/3	3	2	1	0	0	26/3	4
1977-78	0	0	0	0	0	0	0	0
1978-79	42	16	2	0	5	1	49	17
1979-80	16	2	2	0	2	1	20	3
	82/3	21	6	1	7	2	95/3	24

PAUL STEWART

In 1986-7, Paul Stewart joined the ranks of the prolific centre-forwards that Blackpool have produced, when he notched 21 goals before being sold to Manchester City for £250,000, then a Blackpool record. Born in Manchester, he was brought to Bloomfield Road by Allan Brown and made his debut as substitute for Dave Bamber in a home draw with Rochdale in February 1982. For the rest of the season he alternated between midfield and an out-and-out forward. It was not until the arrival of Sam Ellis that Stewart found his true role, at centre-forward, and Ellis can take credit for making Stewart into the player he is now. It took some time for his scoring promise to be fulfilled, though, Stewart preferring to be a supplier for Deary and O'Keefe, but in his last season he scored 21 goals and helped Mark Taylor net 14. Alas, in March 1987 hard-up Blackpool were forced to sell him. He had always supported City as a boy, but within a couple of years he was the subject of a million-pound move to Spurs. There he found a new role in midfield and confirmed his international future under Bobby Robson and later Graham Taylor. Blackpool had not heard the last of Stewart. They received a cash bonus from his transfer to White Hart Lane and he returned to Bloomfield Road in January 1991 to score the only goal for Spurs in an FA Cup tie. Tottenham went on to win the Cup and Stewart scored in the Final. In June 1992, there was talk of him moving to Liverpool in exchange for Dean Saunders.

	LEAGUE		*FA CUP*		*FL CUP*		*TOTAL*	
	App	*Gls*	*App*	*Gls*	*App*	*Gls*	*App*	*Gls*
1981-82	9/5	3	0	0	0	0	9/5	3
1982-83	34/4	7	0	0	3	1	37/4	8
1983-84	40/4	10	4	1	1	1	45/4	12
1984-85	31	7	0	0	3	1	34	8
1985-86	42	8	2	1	1	0	45	9
1986-87	32	21	1	0	2	0	35	21
	188/13	56	7	2	10	3	205/13	61

HARRY STIRZAKER

Signed from Fleetwood Rangers in 1894, Harry Stirzaker played in Blackpool's first-ever League game, against Lincoln City in September 1896, and became a regular first-teamer for the next five seasons. Stirzaker, a well-built individual, started his career at centre-half but also appeared in the heart of defence and, occasionally, as an attacker. One of those times he scored a remarkable goal against Burslem Port Vale. It came midway through the first half when, after receiving a pass from Bob Birkett, he cannoned the ball towards goal from fully 30 yards. It was hit with such ferocity that it rebounded off one post against the goalkeeper's head, and then against the opposite post before rolling over the line. Whilst Stirzaker and his colleagues were celebrating, the poor 'keeper was being stretchered off unconscious, unaware of what had happened. Stirzaker was rewarded with the captaincy during the 1901-02 season. His commitment was amply displayed in the opening game of that season, when he volunteered to stand in goal, after regular 'keeper, Dorrington, was injured and there was no replacement. Although Blackpool lost that day, Stirzaker performed superbly and conceded only two goals. Along with two other imports from Fleetwood Rangers, Birkett and Jack Scott, he was the mainstay of Blackpool's fledgling Football League team of the early part of the century.

	LEAGUE		*FA CUP*		*TOTAL*	
	App	*Gls*	*App*	*Gls*	*App*	*Gls*
1896-97	27	3	-	-	27	3
1897-98	25	1	-	-	25	1
1898-99	31	1	-	-	31	1
1900-01	33	6	-	-	33	6
1901-02	29	2	-	-	29	2
1902-03	9	0	-	-	9	0
	154	13	-	-	154	13

Ron Suart was the first Blackpool player to return to manage the club. He joined the Seasiders from Netherfield in the summer of 1938 and spent his first season playing in the Reserves. Then, just as it seemed as if he was ready to break into first-team football, war intervened. He was a strong full-back with a reputation as a hard but fair tackler and Blackpool were grooming him for the future. He started his career in junior sides in his home town of Barrow before moving to Netherfield, where he had attracted the attention of many of the top clubs. Suart established himself in Blackpool's first team during the war, first at centre-half where he played alongside George Farrow and Harry Johnston. He made his League debut on 31 August 1946, in the victory at Huddersfield, and eventually moved to full-back. In 1948, Suart suffered the same fate as Jimmy McIntosh when, after playing in all the knockout stages of the FA Cup, he was forced to miss the Final due to a foot injury. Many fans felt that one of the reasons for defeat that day was the defensive frailties that had shown themselves without the sturdy Suart. In 1949 he was granted a transfer. Unable to secure a first-team place, he wanted to try his luck elsewhere and in September, Blackburn Rovers secured his services for just over £12,000. Suart spent six happy seasons at Ewood Park before moving into football management, eventually returning to Bloomfield Road (see *Blackpool Managers*).

RON SUART

	LEAGUE		*FA CUP*		*TOTAL*	
	App	*Gls*	*App*	*Gls*	*App*	*Gls*
1946-47	21	0	1	0	22	0
1947-48	38	0	5	0	43	0
1948-49	39	0	3	0	42	0
1949-50	5	0	0	0	5	0
	103	0	9	0	112	0

Peter Suddaby was a great servant of Blackpool FC during the 1970s. Born in Stockport on 23 December 1947, Suddaby graduated as a teacher and was playing for non-League Skelmersdale United when he was spotted by the Seasiders, whom he joined in May 1970, making his debut under Bob Stokoe in February 1971 in a defeat at Coventry. He played in the back-four, originally on the left before taking over at centre-half to team up superbly with Glyn James. He continued at number-five for the remainder of his career, replacing the experienced Dave Hatton who moved to full-back. Suddaby was strong in the air, possessed a biting tackle and was an excellent leader. He also enjoyed going forward for corners, although goalscoring was not one of his greatest talents. He played for Blackpool right through to the midway point of the 1979-80 season, including, of course, the disastrous campaign that led to Third Division football. To his credit, he did not desert the sinking ship, as others had done during those dark days, but was a true clubman. Eventually, during Alan Ball's managership, he moved on. His place was under increasing pressure and with the arrival of record signing Jack Ashurst from Sunderland, he decided that his future lay elsewhere. In November 1980 he moved to Brighton and ended his League career with a handful of games for Wimbledon.

PETER SUDDABY

	LEAGUE		*FA CUP*		*FL CUP*		*TOTAL*	
	App	*Gls*	*App*	*Gls*	*App*	*Gls*	*App*	*Gls*
1970-71	12	0	1	0	0	0	13	0
1971-72	41	2	1	0	4	0	46	2
1972-73	38	0	1	0	7	0	46	0
1973-74	40	1	1	0	2	0	43	1
1974-75	23/1	0	0	0	1	0	24/1	0
1975-76	38	4	1	0	1	0	40	4
1976-77	42	0	2	0	4	0	48	0
1977-78	39	1	1	0	2	0	42	1
1978-79	42	2	2	0	5	0	49	2
1979-80	15	0	0	0	4	0	19	0
	330/1	10	10	0	30	0	370/1	10

On 22 October 1966, Blackpool beat Newcastle 6-0 at Bloomfield Road. Playing for the Magpies was inside-forward Alan Suddick and so impressed were Blackpool with his commitment that two months later they paid a club record fee of £60,000 for him. Suddick was an outstanding talent. He had a wealth of skills including superb passing ability and a famous 'banana' shot and soon became one of Blackpool's most popular players. He made his debut on Boxing Day, in a home defeat by West Ham, and was virtually ever-present thereafter, teaming up with Tommy Hutchison on the left or deep in midfield. In the 1971 Anglo-Italian Final against Bologna he quite simply took the opposition apart. Three of the best goals ever seen at Bloomfield Road were Suddick's: against Verona in the aforementioned tournament where he kept the ball airborne for an age before crashing it into the net; against Arsenal in an FA Cup replay; and one of his famous 'bender' free-kicks against Oxford United. In 1968-9 he was top scorer with 12 goals, most of them spectacular ones. He missed most of 1970-71 with a leg injury, and then again in 1974-5 with the same problem. For all his talent, his erratic form could infuriate and probably contributed to his lack of international appearances. He played at Under-23 level for England, scoring an own-goal. His talent was never truly realised and, like many stars, his temper sometimes got the better of him. In December 1976 he moved to Stoke City and later had spells with Southport and Bury.

ALAN SUDDICK

	LEAGUE		*FA CUP*		*FL CUP*		*TOTAL*	
	App	*Gls*	*App*	*Gls*	*App*	*Gls*	*App*	*Gls*
1966-67	19	4	1	0	0	0	20	4
1967-68	22/1	9	2	0	0	0	24/1	9
1968-69	41	12	1	0	5	2	47	14
1969-70	42	10	3	1	3	2	48	13
1970-71	16/4	1	0/1	0	2	1	18/5	2
1971-72	41	10	1	0	3	2	45	12
1972-73	42	10	1	1	7	2	50	13
1973-74	39	6	1	0	2	0	42	6
1974-75	5	0	0	0	0	0	5	0
1975-76	27	1	0	0	1	0	28	1
1976-77	11	2	0	0	3/1	0	14/1	2
	305/5	65	10/1	2	26/1	9	341/7	76

Goalkeeper Alan Taylor, who was born at Thornton Cleveleys on 17 May 1943, was unfortunate to be at Bloomfield Road under the shadow of two fine Blackpool 'keepers, Tony Waiters and Harry Thompson. Taylor, an acrobatic goalkeeper with a superb temperament, signed for the Seasiders in October 1963 and spent most of his early days as understudy to Waiters. He made his first-team debut in 1966, when Waiters was injured, but despite keeping a clean sheet in the two games he played, he had to wait nearly a year before being selected again. This time he played three times, but again was denied by the brilliance of Waiters. His breakthrough came after Waiters had retired and his first full season was one of near promotion in which Taylor was outstanding. He continued to be first choice for another 12 months until the arrival of Harry Thompson, then it was back to the Reserves. By 1971, young John Burridge was beginning to make a name for himself and manager Bob Stokoe decided that both Taylor and another reserve 'keeper, Adam Blacklaw, could leave. Taylor, who had been on loan to Oldham and Stockport, signed for Southport in July 1971 and ended his League career with 102 appearances for the Haig Avenue club.

	LEAGUE		*FA CUP*		*FL CUP*		*TOTAL*	
	App	*Gls*	*App*	*Gls*	*App*	*Gls*	*App*	*Gls*
1965-66	2	0	0	0	0	0	2	0
1966-67	3	0	0	0	0	0	3	0
1967-68	39	0	2	0	3	0	44	0
1968-69	38	0	0	0	5	0	43	0
1969-70	3	0	0	0	0	0	3	0
1970-71	9	0	2	0	0	0	11	0
	94	0	4	0	8	0	106	0

ALAN TAYLOR

It is said that after Blackpool's defeat by Newcastle in the 1951 FA Cup Final, Stanley Matthews told Joe Smith that he would like the Magpies' inside-right in the team. Whatever, on 10 October that year, Ernie Taylor signed for Blackpool for £25,000 and went on to become one of the Seasiders' greatest players. Born in Sunderland in 1925, he was a naval submariner when he joined Newcastle in 1942. At only 5ft 4in, Taylor was one of the smallest players in the game, but his defence-splitting passes caused havoc amongst opponents and it was his cheeky back-heel that laid on a goal for Jackie Milburn in the 1951 Final. He made his debut for Blackpool three days after signing and when Matthews recovered from injury, the pair created one of the most respected of right-wing partnerships. In the 1953 Final, Taylor played brilliantly in one of the great comebacks of all time. That year England decided to use the Matthews-Taylor partnership, but it was in the 6-3 defeat by Hungary. Taylor, along with others, was discarded from the international scene but continued to dominate First Division defences. In the FA Cup in January 1956, he scored after only 13 seconds at Maine Road, but the match was abandoned, so Taylor's effort didn't stand. Although not known for his goals, those that he did score were usually spectacular, notably the equalizer against Arsenal in the 1953 Cup sixth round. In 1958 he helped devastated Manchester United to the FA Cup Final soon after the Munich disaster. Soon afterwards he signed for Sunderland, for £6,000, and later played for Altrincham and Derry before emigrating to New Zealand. He returned to England and died at Birkenhead in April 1985.

	LEAGUE		*FA CUP*		*TOTAL*	
	App	*Gls*	*App*	*Gls*	*App*	*Gls*
1951-52	30	5	1	0	31	5
1952-53	39	11	7	2	46	13
1953-54	35	12	7	0	42	12
1954-55	34	6	1	0	35	6
1955-56	37	8	1	0	38	8
1956-57	31	3	3	0	34	3
1957-58	16	8	0	0	16	8
	222	53	20	2	242	55

ERNIE TAYLOR

MARK TAYLOR

Mark Taylor might have come to Blackpool on a free transfer from Hartlepool United, but he soon had fans thinking about the days when Tony Green dazzled them. Born in Hartlepool on 20 November 1964, Taylor joined his home-town club from junior football in January 1984 and stayed for two years before falling out with the management. After a month on loan to Crewe, he arrived at Bloomfield Road in August 1986 and made his debut the following month, in a draw at Doncaster. Taylor was fast and tricky and could score goals. He started on the wing before moving to a central role, backing up Paul Stewart but still managing to score 14 goals in his first season. It was surprising that Hartlepool had allowed him to leave without demanding a fee. In 1987-8, Taylor top-scored with 21 goals and his partnership with the emerging Keith Walwyn proved an effective strike force. Alas, midway through the following season, Taylor suffered an injury which side-lined him for nearly two years. Eventually he fought his way back but the long lay-off had left him short of pace and the familiar light touch on the ball was missing. In March 1992, after a month on loan to Cardiff City, he was transferred to Wrexham for a small fee and it was a disappointing end to what had promised to be a fine Blackpool career.

	LEAGUE		*FA CUP*		*FL CUP*		*TOTAL*	
	App	*Gls*	*App*	*Gls*	*App*	*Gls*	*App*	*Gls*
1986-87	40	14	1	0	0/1	0	41/1	14
1987-88	41	21	5	2	4	0	50	23
1988-89	8/1	3	1	0	2	1	11/1	4
1989-90	0	0	0	0	0	0	0	0
1990-91	16/6	3	0	0	0/1	0	16/7	3
1991-92	2/7	2	1	0	0	0	3/7	2
	107/14	43	8	2	6/2	1	121/16	46

HARRY THOMSON

Between 1968 and 1972, Blackpool had a wealth of goalkeepers. Perhaps the most popular was Harry Thomson, who was bought from Burnley by Les Shannon in July 1969 and made his debut on the opening day of the following season, against Portsmouth, immediately displacing Alan Taylor. At 5ft 9in, Thomson was small for a goalkeeper, yet he was one of the most spectacular that Bloomfield Road has seen. He loved to play to the crowd and on more than one occasion he was censured by the club for his on-field antics. Like most showmen, though, he was erratic and sometimes fell out with referees, too. But once he had overcome his initial nervousness, he could be quite brilliant. During the disastrous 1970-71 campaign, he sometimes kept Blackpool in the game single-handed. When Bob Stokoe took over, Thomson had just been disciplined but the new manager brought him back to the first team. It did not work, though, and after a poor performance against Ipswich, when he let in a bad goal near the end, Stokoe terminated his contract and he ended his career with Barrow. Thomson, who was born in Edinburgh on 25 August 1940, joined Burnley in August 1959 from Bo'ness United and spent almost six years as understudy to Adam Blacklaw at Turf Moor, eventually making around 150 appearances for the Clarets before the arrival of Peter Mellor. His most famous game was against Naples in the 1967 Fairs Cup, after which an Italian newspaper called him 'A god in a green jersey'.

	LEAGUE		*FA CUP*		*FL CUP*		*TOTAL*	
	App	*Gls*	*App*	*Gls*	*App*	*Gls*	*App*	*Gls*
1969-70	39	0	3	0	3	0	45	0
1970-71	21	0	0	0	2	0	23	0
	60	0	3	0	5	0	68	0

Billy Tremelling started as a centre-forward but after an inspired tactical move at the start of 1927-8, he became an attacking centre-half who helped Jimmy Hampson to a record number of goals. Tremelling, who was born at New Hill in 1905, joined Blackpool in the summer of 1924. He made his League debut in March the following year, against Manchester United, but made only one more appearance that season. He needed constant service from midfield men and in the 1920s, Blackpool had nobody to supply it. He continued to score for the Reserves and his chance came again the following season after an injury to Sid Binks. Tremelling managed only three appearances before breaking a leg in the home win over Barnsley. It was not until well into 1927-8 that he regained his place, but he scored 31 goals in 27 League and Cup games, becoming the club's top scorer. He scored a hat-trick in the 6-0 thrashing of Port Vale and it seemed that he was the obvious successor to Harry Bedford. Strangely, the start of the next season saw Tremelling appear at centre-half. This proved to be an inspired move by new manager Sydney Beaumont. He believed that Tremelling could service Hampson and enable the centre-forward to be even more dangerous in front of goal. The change worked and over the next few seasons, Tremelling's passes helped Hampson to be top scorer each time. Tremelling's career at Blackpool came to an end in 1930-31, when he transferred to Preston for a nominal fee. He later captained Preston in an FA Cup Final but in later years he joined the growing number of former players who returned to Bloomfield Road in a coaching role. His brother, Dan, was a Birmingham goalkeeper who played for England.

	LEAGUE		*FA CUP*		*TOTAL*	
	App	*Gls*	*App*	*Gls*	*App*	*Gls*
1924-25	2	0	0	0	2	0
1925-26	3	0	0	0	3	0
1926-27	26	30	1	1	27	31
1927-28	22	4	1	0	23	4
1928-29	12	5	1	0	13	5
1929-30	38	3	2	0	40	3
1930-31	11	1	0	0	11	1
	114	43	5	1	119	44

BILLY TREMELLING

Bert Tulloch was one of Blackpool's finest full-backs and for around ten seasons either side of World War One he was the mainstay of the defence. Strong and committed, his walloping defensive tactics unnerved opponents to such an extent that subsequent raids on the Blackpool goal would invariably come down the opposite flank to where Tulloch was operating. He joined Blackpool in the summer of 1914 and made his debut in a 2-1 home defeat by Leicester Fosse, immediately establishing a regular place. He was two-footed, enabling him to appear on either flank, and quickly struck a partnership with Robson and later Jones. He was skilful and would often dribble the ball out of danger. During his time at the club, Blackpool had some of their most successful seasons with four concerted pushes for promotion and it was no coincidence that the 'goals-against' column showed a marked improvement. With Mingay's erratic goalkeeping, the defenders were probably needed more than at any other time and Tulloch could be seen marshalling his fellow 'stoppers' and making last-ditch goal-line clearances. Some time after his playing days had ended, he returned as trainer and masseur, joining a growing number of former players lured back by the friendly atmosphere.

	LEAGUE		*FA CUP*		*TOTAL*	
	App	*Gls*	*App*	*Gls*	*App*	*Gls*
1914-15	25	0	1	0	26	0
1919-20	35	0	3	0	38	0
1920-21	40	0	2	0	42	0
1921-22	41	0	1	0	42	0
1922-23	29	0	1	0	30	0
1923-24	8	0	0	0	8	0
	178	0	8	0	186	0

BERT TULLOCH

TONY WAITERS

In a long line of splendid Blackpool goalkeepers, Tony Waiters was probably one of the best. Born at Southport on 1 February 1937, he won England Amateur honours with Macclesfield and Bishop Auckland before signing for the Seasiders in 1959, making his debut on Boxing Day that year in a home win over Blackburn. Waiters, who eventually displaced the great George Farm, was a fitness fanatic and was always practising taking high crosses and saving fierce shots. Lean and agile, tall and strong, he soon developed into one of the country's top goalkeepers and in 1964-5 won five England caps, taking the place of the great Gordon Banks. Yet he never achieved the greatness predicted for him and many believed that he gave up the game too early, when he retired in May 1967 to become the FA's North-West Regional coach. Coaching and managerial posts followed with Liverpool, Burnley (for whom he made 38 League appearances), Plymouth, Vancouver Whitecaps, the Canadian Olympic team, Tranmere Rovers and Chelsea. Waiters played for seven seasons at Bloomfield Road and was a firm favourite with the fans, yet he enjoyed none of the top club honours. Maybe it was this that persuaded him to retire so early.

	LEAGUE		*FA CUP*		*FL CUP*		*TOTAL*	
	App	*Gls*	*App*	*Gls*	*App*	*Gls*	*App*	*Gls*
1959-60	17	0	0	0	-	-	17	0
1960-61	24	0	0	0	2	0	26	0
1961-62	20	0	2	0	3	0	25	0
1962-63	42	0	2	0	3	0	47	0
1963-64	39	0	2	0	1	0	42	0
1964-65	42	0	1	0	2	0	45	0
1965-66	40	0	2	0	2	0	44	0
1966-67	34	0	1	0	5	0	40	0
	258	0	10	0	18	0	286	0

Blackpool have had many excellent goalkeepers and one of the best was Jock Wallace. Born in April 1911, at Deantown, Wallace joined Blackpool from Raith Rovers in March 1934 and was on the Seasiders' books for over 14 years. A giant of a man and amazingly agile, he was capable of making quite incredible last-ditch saves. Wallace made his debut at Lincoln in February 1934 and became almost an ever-present, Sandy McFarlane, the man who signed him, describing him as 'a natural talent in goal, a man born to be a goalkeeper'. The following season he played in every game but then a knee injury saw him challenged for his place by Roxburgh, although Wallace was always first choice. During the war he was stationed abroad for a spell and his appearances were brief. Off the field he was a joker and at times a controversial character. More than once he fell out with the board or management and on one notorious occasion he refused to join the team to play Leeds in the FA Cup. His argument was over contractual terms and he eventually joined Derby County for a nominal fee of £500 in February 1948. Derby had a goalkeeping crisis and the veteran Wallace, who was not cup-tied, played for the Rams in the sixth round and semi-final. Ironically, Derby were knocked out and it was Blackpool who went on to Wembley from the other semi-final. Many fans thought that he should have been playing for Blackpool at Wembley. His job done, he left Derby for Leith Athletic in August 1948. He died in 1978. His son managed Rangers, Leicester City, Seville and Scotland.

JOCK WALLACE

	LEAGUE		*FA CUP*		*TOTAL*	
	App	*Gls*	*App*	*Gls*	*App*	*Gls*
1933-34	13	0	0	0	13	0
1934-35	42	0	1	0	43	0
1935-36	34	0	2	0	36	0
1936-37	34	0	2	0	36	0
1937-38	17	0	0	0	17	0
1938-39	33	0	1	0	34	0
1939-40	3	0	-	-	3	0
1946-47	42	0	1	0	43	0
1947-48	25	0	0	0	25	0
	243	0	7	0	250	0

Mickey Walsh scored one of the greatest goals ever seen at Bloomfield Road. It came three minutes from time in a thrilling game with Sunderland in February 1975, a run from the halfway line that ended with a terrific shot that earned him BBC TV's Goal of the Season award. Walsh joined Blackpool in the summer of 1972, from Chorley, and made his League debut in September 1973, in a draw at Fulham. He was meant to complement Wyn Davies up front but circumstances meant that he moved to outside-left, where he was unhappy and struggled to keep his place. During 1974-5, though, he became a virtual ever-present, switching from centre-forward to outside-right, and he was top scorer with 12 League goals in an overall tally of only 38. A strong player with good skill, he netted 17 goals in 1975-6 in an unsuccessful promotion bid, but his best spell came in the next campaign when he teamed up with veteran striker Bob Hatton. They scored 36 goals, 26 going to Walsh for the highest individual tally since Charnley's 30 in 1961-2. Blackpool tried to keep their star forward but after the disastrous 1977-8 season — when they were relegated despite Walsh's 14 goals — the Seasiders sold him to Everton for a six-figure fee. A Republic of Ireland international, he later played for Manchester City and Porto.

	LEAGUE		*FA CUP*		*FL CUP*		*TOTAL*	
	App	*Gls*	*App*	*Gls*	*App*	*Gls*	*App*	*Gls*
1973-74	16/5	3	0	0	0	0	16/5	3
1974-75	35/2	12	1	0	1	1	37/2	13
1975-76	41/1	17	2	0	1	0	44/1	17
1976-77	41	26	2	1	4	1	47	28
1977-78	39	14	1	0	2	1	42	15
	172/8	72	6	1	8	3	186/8	76

MICKEY WALSH

Like his namesake from the 1970s, Mike Walsh contributed much to Blackpool's success. Born in Manchester on 20 June 1956, he started with Bolton in July 1974 and made 177 League appearances for the Trotters, helping them win the Second Division in 1977-8. A strong, skilful defender, he skippered most of his clubs, including Blackpool. In August 1981 he joined Everton in a £90,000 plus player-exchange move and, whilst at Goodison, earned the first of five Republic of Ireland caps. There followed loan spells with Norwich and Burnley and a summer with Fort Lauderdale in the NASL before Walsh signed for Manchester City in October 1983. He joined Blackpool for only £6,000 in January 1984 and his debut the following month was in a 3-0 home win over leaders York City, when he took a deep defensive role alongside David Moore. During five happy years at Blackpool, he led the Seasiders to promotion in 1984-5. Injuries sometimes hindered him but he was influential in a well-organised defence. One of his best games was in a 1988 FA Cup replay at Maine Road, when Blackpool nearly scored a shock win. At the end of 1988-9, with the dismissal of Sam Ellis, Walsh decided to move and it was Ellis, now manager of Bury, who snapped him up. Walsh helped in the Shakers' promotion charge and at the beginning of 1991-2 he was made manager after Ellis' departure. But financial difficulties led him to sell most of his best players and Bury were relegated to Division Four in his first season in charge.

	LEAGUE		*FA CUP*		*FL CUP*		*TOTAL*	
	App	*Gls*	*App*	*Gls*	*App*	*Gls*	*App*	*Gls*
1983-84	20	1	0	0	0	0	20	1
1984-85	35	1	1	0	3	0	39	1
1985-86	25	1	1	0	1	0	27	1
1986-87	34	2	1	0	2	0	37	2
1987-88	25/4	0	5	0	3	0	33/4	0
1988-89	6/4	0	0/1	0	1	0	7/5	0
	145/8	5	8/1	0	10	0	163/9	5

MIKE WALSH

Outside-right Dickie Watmough was signed by Alex McFarlane from Bradford City late in 1934, for a largish fee of £3,300, and immediately struck a partnership with Tommy Jones and Jimmy Hampson. Born in Idle in 1912, Watmough was a fast and tricky winger who as well as being able to score goals, later found a new role by supplying the telling crosses for Hampson's successor, Bobby Finan. His lightning bursts down the right wing became a trademark and after scoring the winner on his debut in October 1934, at home to Norwich, he became almost an ever-present. He scored a further eight goals that season and, more significantly, in the following campaign he helped Finan to become the Second Division's top scorer. Watmough played for the majority of the 1936-7 season, helping Blackpool back to Division One, although after being dropped he was selected for the final game, against Doncaster Rovers, for purely sentimental reasons. He did not adapt to First Division football and a recurring injury also meant that his appearances were limited. When Alec Munro arrived from Hearts, it soon became obvious that he was to be preferred over Watmough. In December 1937, Watmough moved to Preston in an £8,000 exchange deal that brought Frank O'Donnell to Blackpool and also took Jim McIntosh to Deepdale. At Preston, Watmough resurrected his career and won an FA Cup winners' medal. The 1938 Cup Final was his last senior game, for after missing the whole of the following season through injury, he retired. Once 12th man for Yorkshire CCC in a County Championship match, Watmough later became a publican in Eccleshall and scouted for Bradford PA. He died in 1962. A fine footballer, he never quite realised his potential at Bloomfield Road.

DICKIE WATMOUGH

	LEAGUE		*FA CUP*		*TOTAL*	
	App	*Gls*	*App*	*Gls*	*App*	*Gls*
1934-35	32	9	1	0	33	9
1935-36	23	8	2	2	25	10
1936-37	31	12	2	1	33	13
1937-38	14	2	0	0	14	2
	100	31	5	3	105	34

Albert Watson will always be remembered for scoring the '£10,000 goal'. It came seven minutes from the end of Blackpool's crucial home game against fellow relegation candidates Manchester City in May 1931. The score was 2-1 to City and, in an act of almost total desperation, Blackpool's inside-right Jack Oxberry exchanged places with wing-half Watson, who took a square pass from Jimmy Hampson and shot a 20-yarder into the corner of the net to save First Division football for the Seasiders. The goal ensured free meals at local restaurants for Watson for the rest of his life. A strong, heavily-built wing-half who liked to attack, he made well over 360 League appearances for Blackpool, helping them to two promotions. He made his debut in April 1923, in a home win over Rotherham County, and was virtually ever-present from then on. He played alongside the captain, Billy Benton, but never really had the flair or speed of his skipper. Because of this, his contributions were often overlooked by the local Press and supporters. Watson stayed at Bloomfield Road until 1936, when he was granted a free transfer. In later years he scouted for Blackpool and was responsible for discovering many young players who were later to make their mark at the club.

ALBERT WATSON

	LEAGUE		*FA CUP*		*TOTAL*	
	App	*Gls*	*App*	*Gls*	*App*	*Gls*
1922-23	2	0	0	0	2	0
1923-24	15	5	0	0	15	5
1924-25	40	1	7	0	47	1
1925-26	42	2	1	0	43	2
1926-27	38	0	1	0	39	0
1927-28	32	1	0	0	32	1
1928-29	42	3	1	0	43	3
1929-30	37	1	2	0	39	1
1930-31	37	1	0	0	37	1
1931-32	28	7	2	0	30	7
1932-33	35	1	3	0	38	1
1933-34	3	0	0	0	3	0
1934-35	0	0	0	0	0	0
1935-36	22	0	0	0	22	0
	373	22	17	0	390	22

After Billy Tremelling's departure, Blackpool tried Eric Longden at centre-half for a season before settling on Phil Watson, a £3,000 signing from Hamilton Academical. Watson, who was a strong, hard player with lots of skill for a centre-half, joined the Seasiders in February 1932 and made his debut that month, in a home win over Everton, when he had to mark the great Dixie Dean and acquitted himself well. Watson spent most of the remainder of his career at Bloomfield Road, moving to full-back in 1935-6. One of his greatest moments, though, came as a stand-in centre-forward. He played there against Aston Villa in March 1933, when Jimmy Hampson was injured, and responded with a hat-trick in Blackpool's 6-2 victory. A native of Dykehead, where he was born on 23 February 1907, Watson was capped once for Scotland, against Austria in 1934. In December 1937 he moved to Barnsley and ended his career with Queen of the South. Whilst with Hamilton he had played for the Scottish League.

	LEAGUE		*FA CUP*		*TOTAL*	
	App	*Gls*	*App*	*Gls*	*App*	*Gls*
1931-32	15	1	0	0	15	1
1932-33	42	7	3	0	45	7
1933-34	42	1	2	1	44	2
1934-35	34	2	0	0	34	2
1935-36	33	0	2	0	35	0
1936-37	0	0	0	0	0	0
1937-38	5	0	0	0	5	0
	171	11	7	1	178	12

PHIL WATSON

Tom White, brother of the late Spurs and Scotland star John, came to Bloomfield Road in March 1968 from Crystal Palace for £20,000. He made his debut in a home win over Aston Villa, immediately taking over the centre-forward role left vacant by the departure of Gerry Ingram. White was a tall, skilful player whose aerial command led to many of his goals and, although he had lost a lot of his speed by the time he came to Blackpool, he could still play havoc with opposing defences. In his first season he teamed up brilliantly with Tony Green and Alan Suddick, although towards the end of the campaign he found his position under pressure from Graham Rowe and eventually moved to outside-left. Perhaps White did not score as many goals as expected, but he laid on many for Suddick. Injury curtailed his days with the Seasiders and he ended his career with Bury and Crewe. After his playing days were over, he continued his association with Blackpool, becoming a businessman in the town and serving as a director of the club until 1992. In 1990 he was called upon to act as temporary manager after the dismissal of Jimmy Mullen, with the team hurtling towards Division Four. It was a task that he did not relish, but he showed total commitment to what proved to be a lost cause. White, who was born in Musselburgh on 12 August 1939, began his career with Aberdeen before joining Palace in June 1966.

	LEAGUE		*FA CUP*		*FL CUP*		*TOTAL*	
	App	*Gls*	*App*	*Gls*	*App*	*Gls*	*App*	*Gls*
1967-68	11	4	0	0	0	0	11	4
1968-69	22	5	1	0	2	2	25	7
1969-70	1	0	0	0	0	0	1	0
	34	9	1	0	2	2	37	11

TOM WHITE

GEORGE WOOD

A giant of a man at over 6ft tall and weighing 14st, goalkeeper George Wood was bought from East Stirling in January 1972, for £10,000 as cover for the tremendously popular John Burridge. After spending some time in the Reserves, Wood made his debut that April, in a home victory over Oxford United, and then spent the next four years vying for the number-one spot with Burridge before establishing himself in 1975-6. Wood was never a spectacular goalkeeper, but a safer pair of hands you were not likely to see, reminding many older fans of the legendary George Farm. At the end of 1976-7 he was transferred to Everton for a large fee and with the Blues he became a Scottish international. There were then big-money moves to Arsenal and Crystal Palace, where once again he became a big favourite with the fans. He later played with Cardiff (with whom he gained a Welsh Cup winners' medal) and Hereford and returned to Bloomfield Road on loan for three months as the team tried desperately to save Third Division football. It was, he said, like coming home. He can now be found playing in non-League football looking as spritely and agile as ever.

	LEAGUE		*FA CUP*		*FL CUP*		*TOTAL*	
	App	*Gls*	*App*	*Gls*	*App*	*Gls*	*App*	*Gls*
1971-72	4	0	0	0	0	0	4	0
1972-73	20	0	0	0	2	0	22	0
1973-74	12	0	0	0	2	0	14	0
1974-75	4	0	0	0	0	0	4	0
1975-76	35	0	2	0	0	0	37	0
1976-77	42	0	2	0	4	0	48	0
1989-90	15	0	0	0	0	0	15	0
	132	0	4	0	8	0	144	0

ALAN WRIGHT

At 21, defender Alan Wright is one of the game's most exciting prospects, an England international at Schoolboy, Youth and Under-21 levels. Born in Ashton-under-Lyne on 28 September 1971, Wright took over the title of Blackpool's youngest League player when he made his debut as substitute in May 1988, at home to Chesterfield. He had risen from the YTS ranks to the first team in a remarkably short time and was soon challenging Steve Morgan in the heart of defence. Extremely small at 5ft 4in, he has outstanding speed, good ball-control and a maturity beyond his years. Wright signed as a full-timer in 1989, gaining a regular place around the same time. He soon brought stability to a shaky defence and it seemed that nothing could unnerve him, no matter how big the game or stage. At Wembley in the 1991 Play-off Final, he held the defence together under great pressure. Wright has a remarkably cultured left foot, and a favourite move of putting the ball on one side of a player whilst running around the other. After Blackpool's failure to gain promotion in 1991, big clubs, notably Liverpool and Manchester City, were reported to be interested in him. Eventually, the promise of top football became too much and midway through 1991-2, Wright signed for Kenny Dalglish's Blackburn Rovers, the £450,000 fee making him Blackpool's most expensive export.

	LEAGUE		*FA CUP*		*FL CUP*		*TOTAL*	
	App	*Gls*	*App*	*Gls*	*App*	*Gls*	*App*	*Gls*
1987-88	0/1	0	0	0	0	0	0/1	0
1988-89	14/2	0	0	0	1	0	15/2	0
1989-90	20/4	0	5	0	3/2	0	28/6	0
1990-91	48	0	3	0	2	0	53	0
1991-92	12	0	0	0	4	0	16	0
	94/7	0	8	0	10/2	0	112/9	0

Matches to Remember

Match to Remember 1 — 5 September 1896

Lincoln City 3 Blackpool 1

BLACKPOOL'S first-ever Football League game was this Second Division match which ended in defeat at Lincoln. But that the game took place at all is remarkable, with the team taking six hours to travel from the seaside to their destination, where they found the conditions atrocious.

The players, directors and club doctor caught the 7am train from Blackpool North station and then had to endure a journey via Manchester and Birmingham. They had to change trains twice and with their only exercise a quick run up and down the platform, it was hardly surprising that they were not in the best of condition to take on Lincoln.

The game was due to kick-off at 2pm, but due to the fact that it had been raining incessantly and the pitch more resembled a swamp, the referee delayed the start by 15 minutes whilst the players acclimitized themselves.

When the match finally got underway, Blackpool, playing in their blue and white striped shirts, mounted many early attacks, forcing Lincoln's French goalkeeper, Boullemier, into action.

After only five minutes, though, they were caught at the back when Lynes broke away, beat two defenders and shot ferociously. Douglas had no chance and Lincoln were 1-0 ahead.

Undeterred, Blackpool continued to push forward at every opportunity and so it was a devastating blow when they conceded a second goal a minute from half-time.

Lynes once again found the Blackpool defence wanting and broke away. He got the ball to the unmarked Kirton on the right and the Lincoln outside-left made sure with Douglas a helpless spectator.

The players came out reluctantly for the second half as conditions had got progressively worse and most of the 1,500 spectators had decided that a warm fireside was preferable to standing around a muddy field.

Blackpool showed a little more commitment, though, and after ten minutes of the second period they scored their first-ever Football League goal.

It came about after a Lincoln defender had handled the ball on the edge of the penalty area. Mount stepped up and hit a 20-yard free-kick straight past Boullemier.

Much jubilation and hand-shaking followed amongst the 'Pool players, who, fired with new optimism, continued to press forward.

Alas they could not draw level and, indeed, five minutes from time they conceded a third goal when their shaky defence allowed Kirton to once again find room and pop the ball over the head of 'keeper Douglas.

The *Athletic News* reported that Blackpool had a weakness in front of goal, plus a rather poor defence. Surprising, then, that they proceeded to acquit themselves rather well in the League in that first season. In fact, they did not finish as high again until 1911.

Lincoln City: Boullemier; Wilson, Byres, Hannah, Timmis, Smith, Lynes, Fraser, W.Gillespie, M.Gillespie, Kirton.
Blackpool: Douglas; Parr, Bowman, Stuart, Strizaker, Norris, Clarkin, Donnelly, J.Parkinson, R.Parkinson, Mount.

Attendance: 1,500

Match to Remember 2 — 3 February 1906

Sheffield United 1 Blackpool 2

WHEN the draw was made for the second round of the FA Cup, the Blackpool directors must have rubbed their hands with glee. After seeing their team struggle through a three-match marathon first-round tie against non-Leaguers Crystal Palace, the 'Pool had been given a lucrative home draw against the mighty Sheffield United.

The Blackpool club were, as always, in severe financial difficulties with attendances averaging about 3,500, barely enough to pay the club's weekly expenses, so the promise of First Division opposition at Bloomfield Road was very welcome.

Sheffield United were one of the 'giants' of the Football League and could boast players of immense skill and ability, such as Lipsham, Donnelly and Drake. The chances of struggling Blackpool getting the better of them were rather remote, to say the least, particularly as the Seasiders had notched up only five League victories to that point.

About a week or so before the tie, the Sheffield directors, mindful of Blackpool's financial problems, offered to switch the game to Bramall Lane, where a much larger crowd could be expected. At first Blackpool refused, then agreed, only to quote an over-inflated fee for the privilege.

At first it seemed that negotiations had broken down, but eventually a compromise was reached and the game went ahead in Sheffield. Many Blackpool supporters criticized this move, but it was pointed out that if the game was played at Bloomfield Road, the club would make £150. Now they would be guaranteed at least £300, a much-needed windfall for a club in such severe financial straits.

To prove the point, it was also noted that the entire Sheffield team spent the preceding week relaxing in Skegness, a 'luxury' the Blackpool club could only dream about.

Sheffield started the game in confident mood and immediately laid seige to the Blackpool goal. 'Pool's defenders tried valiantly to keep out the marauding masses with some desperate defending, and only the brilliant goalkeeping of 'Tishy' Hull stopped the Yorkshiremen from scoring.

Eventually, though, they succumbed when England's Bert Lipsham scored a fine goal. A corner from the right had not been cleared properly and from the ensuing cross, the former Crewe left-winger smashed the ball past the fully-stretched Hull.

After only 15 minutes, Blackpool were one down and the writing was seemingly on the wall. Their cause was not helped a few minutes later when Scott was carried off with a serious knee injury, leaving Blackpool down to ten men. Thankfully, the defender was made of sturdy stuff and 20 minutes later he rejoined the fray.

Blackpool in 1906. Back row (left to right): Miller (assistant trainer), H.E.Leivers (assistant secretary), Johnson, Hull, Riley, Birkett, Dorrington, Parkinson, Lowe, Threlfall, Rothwell (trainer). Middle: Raisbeck, Reilly, Duckworth, Bate, Jones, T.Barcroft (honorary secretary), Hancock, Bennett, Lavery, Conner, Scott. Front: Anderton, Darlington, Crewsdon, Francis, Gow.

As the game progressed, the Seasiders settled down and started to look dangerous on the breakaway, although it has to be said that Sheffield's 'custodian', Leivesley, was not really troubled and at half-time Sheffield held a slender lead.

It is not known what was said in the Blackpool dressing-room at half-time, but the start of the second half saw the Seasiders moving forward in numbers and pressing the Sheffield goal as if their lives depended on it. And after only two minutes they had equalized through Hancock.

A United attack broke down and Johnson sent a long ball up to the left winger, Bate. He dribbled it up to the corner-flag before being fouled. From the free-kick, taken by Johnson, Blackpool's inside-right headed home. 'Pool were level and the 250 supporters who had made the journey were overjoyed, their team now holding mighty Sheffield United.

A couple of minutes later they were ecstatic as Blackpool took the lead. The Sheffield defender Groves was robbed by Connor on the halfway line and he sent a through-ball to Bate, who in turn found Hancock unmarked on the right.

Hancock hit a stunning 20-yard shot into the corner of the Sheffield net. Within four minutes of the start of the second half, Hancock had put his side in front and they were now poised to pull off an incredible upset.

The Sheffield team were now in a state of near-panic and under severe criticism from their supporters they fell apart. After 55 minutes, Duckworth missed an open goal for Blackpool, and with five minutes left, Hancock nearly completed his hat-trick when he headed the ball against a post with Leivesley standing watching.

As the final whistle was sounded, the Blackpool players embraced each other, some in tears. They had overcome all the odds and deservedly beaten their superiors by two goals to one. The result caused shockwaves throughout the footballing world with newspapers and magazines highlighting the game. Even the local *Gazette* devoted five full-length columns to the team in their match report, the club receiving more publicity than ever before.

Back in the town it was around 10pm when they heard the incredible news, and when the train carrying the team pulled into the station in the early hours of the following morning, there were around 2,000 fans to greet them. Even veteran defender Jack Parkinson was overcome, commenting that he felt as if someone had walked up and given him a ten-pound note!

Unfortunately in the third round Blackpool were drawn away to Newcastle United, where they were soundly thrashed. No matter, the team had had their day and thoroughly enjoyed it.

Sheffield United: Leivesley; Groves, Benton, McCormick, B.Wilkinson, Parker, Donnelly, Bluff, Brown, Drake, Lipsham.
Blackpool: Hull; Crewdson, Scott, Threlfall, Parkinson, Johnson, Duckworth, Hancock, Francis, Connor, Bate.

Attendance: 10,219

Match to Remember 3 — 21 April 1930

Oldham Athletic 1 Blackpool 2

AS the 1929-30 season came to a close, three teams were in with a chance of promotion to Division One. Blackpool were the leaders, and had been for most of the season; Chelsea were in second place with Oldham one point behind in third.

As luck would have it, the fixture list had thrown up a meeting between the two Lancashire sides on the Easter Monday. The brief was simple: the Latics had to win to keep in touch, whilst Blackpool could effectively clinch promotion if they came away from Boundary Park with two points.

Interest in the game was phenomenal, with the ground packed to capacity and the gates closed some 30 minutes before kick-off. Blackpool were the team in form, winning five of their previous six games, and they had brought a large and noisy following with them, although the roar that greated the Oldham players as they took to the pitch could probably be heard for miles around.

It was Blackpool who were the more settled side from kick-off and they came close to scoring in one of the first attacks of the game, when Oxberry finished off a move he had started, only to see his powerful shot crash against the bar.

Gradually, though, the Latics, roared on by their fans, became more and more confident and started to give the 'Pool defence some worrying moments, with former Blackpool man Joe Taylor coming close on more than one occasion.

Moments before half-time, Oldham outside-right Worrall was allowed to run almost the full length of the field before a timely tackle by Tufnell saved the day. It had been a frantic first 45 minutes, yet surprisingly the teams went to the interval goalless.

In the second half, Blackpool stepped up a gear and completely overwhelmed their opponents. Within a minute of the restart, Rattray found Jimmy Hampson free, yet incredibly the great man somehow put his shot well over the bar.

Ten minutes later, Oldham must have felt that it was to be their day. Hampson, after beating two men with consumate ease, was brought down in the penalty area and referee Mr Watson had no hesitation in pointing to the spot. Up stepped Hampson and shot well wide of the post. Blackpool supporters groaned in despair — if Hampson could not score, then who could?

Within ten minutes, however, Hampson had made amends when he took a pass through the middle of the field, shimmied past two defenders and hit a fierce shot into the net, giving Moss no chance whatsoever. It was his 45th League goal of the season, and surely the most important.

Blackpool in 1929-30. Back row (left to right): Wilson, Grant, Pearson, Ramsey, Wait, Watson, Benton. Middle: A. Ure (trainer), Quinn, Lauderdale, Tremelling, Upton, Downes, J. Charles (assistant trainer). Front: Rafferty, Tufnell, Broadhurst, Hampson, Oxbery, Nicol, Ritchie.

Within three minutes the celebrating tangerine-clad fans had even more to cheer as Blackpool went two up. Rattray picked up a loose ball on the right, crossed it to Hampson and watched as he unselfishly drew the defenders towards him before leaving Jack Oxberry in the clear. The pass to the inside-left was perfectly timed and from a very acute angle, Oxberry slammed the ball into the net.

The game was effectively over, although with eight minutes remaining Oldham did pull a goal back. The 'Pool defence was caught unawares, leaving 'keeper Pearson alone to deal with a difficult cross. He misjudged the flight and Worrall beat him to it, putting the ball into the empty goal.

After that, of course, there was frantic play from the Oldham forwards as they looked for the equalizer, but Blackpool's back-row held firm. The final whistle was greeted with an enormous cheer from the travelling faithful, as they knew that promotion had been secured at long last. For Oldham it was a sad end to their season as they allowed Chelsea to pip them the following Saturday.

Later that evening the Blackpool players were met by thousands of fans at the train station, celebrating promotion to the First Division for the first time in the club's history. There was one player above all who they had come to acclaim — Jimmy Hampson. They cheered him as he appeared on the Town Hall steps and would not let him go until he had made a speech. The mild-mannered man was later heard to say that it was more difficult addressing a crowd of 30,000 than scoring a goal in front of them. His goals had earned the team a place in the higher echelons, and they would not let him forget it.

Oldham Athletic: Moss; Ivill, Porter, Adlam, King, Goodier, Worrall, Dyson, Taylor, Hargreaves, Wasson.
Blackpool: Pearson; Grant, Watson, Wilson, Tremelling, Tufnell, Rattray, Broadhurst, Hampson, Oxberry, Neal.

Attendance: 45,304

Blackpool 1 Arsenal 4

THE last Saturday of August 1930 saw the realization of a dream for Blackpool Football Club, as they started their first-ever season in Division One.

After the success of the previous campaign, the whole town had been buzzing and when the fixture list paired the 'Pool with mighty Arsenal on the opening day, the excitement became intense.

In the summer months immediately following promotion, the directors went about bringing Bloomfield Road up to first-class standard and this involved building the massive 'Spion Kop'. This enormous terrace was capable of holding 12,000 people and on this great day it was packed to capacity, helping the club to realize a 'gate' of nearly 29,000, the most that had ever been seen inside the ground.

The game was of such importance to the town that the Mayor and Mayoress, complete with their official regalia, 'opened' the new stand before the game. In his speech, Mayor Gath promised that Blackpool would be a force to be reckoned with in the First Division, and Arsenal were on to a hiding to nothing! The spectators looked forward to a feast of football.

What followed in the next 90 minutes, though, proved a severe and harsh lesson to the players and supporters of Blackpool Football Club. Arsenal proceeded to dismantle the home defence with complete ease and showed that the gap between the division that Blackpool had just left and the one they were in now, was wide.

The first goal came midway through the first half when Lambert converted a penalty after Jack had been brought down. Although that was the extent of the scoring in the first period, it was obvious that there was more to come.

Goal number-two came from a free-kick just outside the area. Jones' powerful shot was saved by Pearson but he could not hold on to it and inside-right Jack snapped up the rebound. There then followed a brilliant individual goal from Bastin to make it 3-0 before Jack added another after some good work by centre-forward Lambert.

Blackpool did manage a solitary goal from Jimmy Hampson — who else? — and they had a seemingly good effort disallowed, but as Arsenal also had one of their efforts turned down by the referee, the Seasiders could hardly complain.

It was fiery baptism for Blackpool and one can imagine the feelings of the players as they left the field on that gloriously hot day. In fact they recovered sufficiently to record a victory at Maine Road four days later, but their defensive frailty had been exposed. During that season, the Blackpool defence conceded 125 goals, something of a record.

Blackpool: Pearson; Grant, Watson, McMahon, Tremelling, Tufnell, Neal, Carr, Hampson, Oxberry, Downes.
Arsenal: Preedy; Parker, Hapgood, Jones, Roberts, John, Hulme, Jack, Lambert, James, Bastin.

Attendance: 28,723

Blackpool 4 Chelsea 0

THIS game between Blackpool and Chelsea promised to be nothing more than an ordinary League clash, yet at the end of the 90 minutes the few hardy souls who braved the elements that October day soon realized that they had witnessed one of the most remarkable football matches in Blackpool's history.

It was not the emphatic scoreline, although that was amazing in itself, but the fact that by the end of the game, Chelsea had only six players left on the field.

For two weeks previously it had rained incessantly on the Fylde coast and most of Blackpool was flooded with the Promenade closed to traffic and pedestrians. Bloomfield Road had not escaped the deluge and, despite excellent drainage, by the morning of the game with Chelsea there were over two inches of water on the playing surface.

Incredibly, the game was given the go ahead, despite fierce protests from the Chelsea management, who quite rightly argued that there should be no way that a game of football could be played on that surface. In fact, when the players stepped out on to the pitch the rain was still coming down and they could be forgiven for thinking that they would be better indulging in water polo than soccer.

Whether it was Blackpool's 'Northern grit' overcoming the 'soft Southerners', we do not know, but it was the Seasiders who adapted to the conditions whilst their opponents had no appetite for the game and proceeded to moan and groan at the referee. This was despite the fact that Blackpool were kicking against the howling wind and driving rain.

By half-time the 'Pool were three goals to the good, coming from Hampson (twice) and Wilkinson. The Pensioners were just not in the mood for the fight and throughout the first half they pleaded with the referee to abandon the game.

Mr Jones ignored their pleas, mindful that the home team had weathered the conditions and scored three times. During the interval, one of the Chelsea officials also approached the referee and appealed again, but once more with no success.

As the teams returned for the second period, the rain was still falling and the pitch was now a sea of water. It was also noticable that only eight Chelsea players had returned, their centre-half retiring with severe cramp and two others refusing point-blank to continue.

Eventually they were persuaded to return and after 60 minutes Chelsea were back to ten men. It did not last long, though, as they very quickly became fed up with the whole situation and walked off again.

Mr Jones, after consulting with his linesman, just shrugged his shoulders and dropped the ball, continuing play. The remaining Chelsea players were throughly disenchanted with the situation and allowed Blackpool to dominate even more.

After 75 minutes, Hampson completed his hat-trick, scoring an absolutely brilliant solo goal, even more remarkable considering the conditions.

Obviously the game was won and so it came as no surprise whatsoever to see another two Chelsea players walk off the field arm in arm, presumably holding on to each other for support. There were now only six blue shirts left on the field of play.

Those remaining players did themselves proud by defending valiantly and so not conceding any more goals. Yet when the final whistle blew, it was the Blackpool players who received the standing ovation. This was not for the victory, although that was most welcome in that desperate season, but because no 'Pool player had needed treatment nor, indeed, even complained about the truly dreadful conditions.

After the game the referee reported the incident to the Football League; in turn, the Chelsea officials reported Mr Jones for his handling of the whole affair. It mattered not as the result was allowed to stand and Blackpool had picked up two points and a certain amount of pride.

It is unlikely that we shall ever see a game like it again, as in today's age there would be no way that any official would ever allow a game of football to be played in conditions like those experienced that October afternoon.

Blackpool: McDonough; Wassell, Everest, A.Watson, P.Watson, Rattray, Wilkinson, Butterworth, Hampson, McLelland, Smalley.
Chelsea: Woodley; Odell, Law, Allum, O'Dowd, Ferguson, Oakton, Rankin, Mills, Miller, Pearson.

Attendance: 7,311

Match to Remember 6 — 15 May 1943

Arsenal 2 Blackpool 4

IT is fair to say that during the years of World War Two, Blackpool had one of the finest teams in the country. With the help of many 'guest' players who found themselves stationed in the town, the Seasiders all but dominated their regional leagues and also found success in the Cup.

During 1942-3 they completed the 'double' of winning the Northern Regional League and the Northern Wartime Cup, the latter by beating Sheffield Wednesday over two legs. They were then invited to compete in a game at Stamford Bridge against the Southern Cup winners, Arsenal, in a game billed as the 'Championship of England'.

The Gunners, who had won their Final by beating Charlton Athletic over two legs, were apparently so confident of success that they had a photograph taken of their team with the trophy *before* the game! It is also interesting to note that after Blackpool had beaten them, the cup was never released and presumably is still somewhere in the vaults of Highbury Stadium.

The game was played in front of a near full house, most of them cheering on the Londoners and creating an intimidating atmosphere for the Seasiders.

Arsenal's pre-match confidence seemed well-placed when, after only seven minutes, they found themselves two goals up. Ray Lewis had given them the lead after four minutes with a shot from the edge of the penalty area; and three minutes later, Dennis Compton made it 2-0.

Many Blackpool players said after the game that at this time they felt as if they were on to a hiding. They were defending desperately as Arsenal pushed forward in numbers to overwhelm their opponents in every department.

Slowly, though, Blackpool began to play as a unit and after 20 minutes Ronnie Dix reduced the arrears with a fine goal. It was just what Blackpool needed and from a position just a few minutes earlier, when they had their backs to the wall, they were now playing the flowing, attractive football that had made them famous throughout the country.

For their part Arsenal kept up their attacking mode and came close to increasing

Jock Dodds receives the League North Cup from Mr A.V.Alexander at Hillsborough in 1943. The Seasiders then met Arsenal and won the wartime 'Championship of England'.

their lead on a number of occasions, but goalkeeper Savage was equal to every effort. It came as no surprise, however, when only 60 seconds from the interval, Blackpool equalized through Burbanks. It made the score 2-2 and set up for an exciting second half.

The game was being broadcast live on radio throughout the country and it was said that the streets of Blackpool were deserted on a traditionally busy May day. With wartime travel severely restricted, the wireless was the only way in which supporters could keep up to date on their team's progress.

The second half was just as frantic with Blackpool gradually beginning to take control. A tactical switch at the interval, involving Dix and Dodds, seemed to confuse the Arsenal defence and after 75 minutes 'Jock' Dodds scored one of his trademark goals from outside the area to make it 3-2.

By now it was the Gunners who were defending desperately and only some superb saves by goalkeeper Marks kept the 'Pool forwards at bay. After 82 minutes, though, Bobby Finan made it 4-2 after a mêlée of players had failed to clear the Arsenal goalmouth.

The victory was complete and Blackpool had confirmed their status as the finest team in the country. The newspapers were full of praise for the victors, with the *Daily Mail* going so far to say that Blackpool's performance was one of the 'greatest by a football team since the game was invented'. High praise indeed, but by all accounts certainly justified.

It was something of a swan-song, though, for within a year, with the war coming to an end, the players who turned out for Blackpool that day began to drift back to their own clubs, although the nucleus of an even greater Blackpool team was now in place.

Arsenal: Marks; Scott, L.Compton, Crayston, Joy, Hale, Kirchen, Drake, Lewis, Bastin, D.Crompton.
Blackpool: Savage; Pope, S.Jones, Farrow, Hayward, Johnston, Matthews, Dix, Dodds, Finan, Burbanks.

Att: 67,000

Match to Remember 7 — 24 April 1948

Blackpool 2 Manchester United 4

FOR many years, the 1948 FA Cup Final has been described as the best Wembley Final ever in terms of skill. The teams had a reputation as fast, skilful and always entertaining, and so when Blackpool and Manchester United made it to Wembley, the whole nation looked forward to the encounter.

Both sides took the pitch wearing unfamiliar colours, Blackpool in white with their opponents in an even stranger blue, and it was Blackpool who seemed to be at a disadvantage. They had come to Wembley seriously understrength with

Eddie Shimwell scores from the penalty-spot against Manchester United at Wembley in the 1948 FA Cup Final.

Suart and McIntosh both missing from the side that had performed so well in the previous rounds.

It was Blackpool, though, who had the first chance of the match and they squandered it badly. Alec Munro, receiving a pass from Matthews, incredibly mis-hit a shot from only a couple of yards out. The game was only two minutes old and Munro then seemed to spend the next 80 regretting that miss.

After 14 minutes, though, the Seasiders took the lead. Mortensen was brought down on the edge of the area by Allenby Chilton and referee Barrick pointed to the spot. There were question marks over the decision, as most people believed the offence took place outside the area, but there were no questions over the way Eddie Shimwell took the penalty. He slammed the ball straight into the net and Blackpool were 1-0 up. Shimwell thus became the first full-back to score in a Wembley Final.

However, the goal seemed to inspire United and frequent forays into the Blackpool goal followed. It came as no surprise when, after 30 minutes, they equalized. A rather harmless cross from Delaney was not cleared by either 'keeper Robinson or Hayward, and in their hesitation they allowed Jack Rowley to nip in. It was a bad mistake and one for which Joe Robinson shouldered most of the blame.

Seven minutes later though, Stan Mortensen, kept up his record of scoring a goal in every round of the Cup when he converted a Matthews free-kick, helped by a touch from Kelly, and so gave Blackpool a 2-1 half-time lead.

The thousands of Blackpool fans in the stadium must have felt that the Cup was destined for the seaside.

The second half saw Blackpool trying desperately to increase their lead with the Manchester defence calmly resisting. Matthews was becoming more and more influential out on the right wing, and Johnston's marshalling of his men in midfield was exemplary.

The football being played that afternoon was possibly the most entertaining that the stadium had ever seen and after the game the Blackpool fans were magnaminous in defeat.

United's equalizer came almost out of the blue and quite controversially. On 70 minutes, Hugh Kelly had been penalized for handball, something which he believed was accidental. Whilst the referee was explaining his decision, Johnny Morris took the free-kick for Rowley to once again take advantage of a mix-up between Robinson and Hayward. It was 2-2 and suddenly the pendulum began to swing towards United.

After 80 minutes, after a fierce Blackpool attack, Anderson made a long, accurate pass to Stan Pearson deep in the Seasiders' half; he in turn fired a 25-yard shot past the helpless Robinson.

Soon afterwards, the fourth goal was scored, another shot by Pearson which was helped on its way by Hugh Kelly. It was 4-2 and the FA Cup went to Manchester. Yet Blackpool had played their part in a superb exhibition of football. Afterwards, David Prole in his report on the game said: 'If United's display was as close to perfection as any team could hope to go, Blackpool's was not far behind.'

Curiously, a few days later the teams met again in a rearranged League match at Bloomfield Road, and Blackpool won 1-0 with a Mortensen goal. It had to be said that the scoreline did not accurately reflect the ease of Blackpool's victory. Three years later they would be back at Wembley in a bid to try again.

Blackpool: Robinson; Shimwell, Crosland, Johnston, Hayward, Kelly, Matthews, Munro, Mortensen, Dick, Rickett.
Manchester United: Crompton; Carey, Aston, Anderson, Chilton, Cockburn, Delaney, Morris, Rowley, Pearson, Mitten.

Att: 100,000

George Farm is beaten by Jackie Milburn's shot in the 1951 FA Cup Final. The Newcastle centre-forward scored both his side's goals.

Match to Remember 8 — 28 April 1951

Blackpool 0 Newcastle United 2

BLACKPOOL'S second appearance in an FA Cup Final was a huge disappointment and certainly an anticlimax for all of their supporters. The team was at the height of its power and had just finished in third place in Division One, the highest the club had ever achieved.

Newcastle were worthy opponents but most observers were of the opinion that a full-strength Blackpool side should be capable of lifting the trophy for the first time in the club's history.

The only casualty was Allan Brown, who had suffered a serious knee injury and was replaced by the amateur Bill Slater. Ironically, Brown also missed the 1953 Cup Final through injury.

It has been said that Blackpool lost this game before the kick-off, due to a tactical error. It had been decided by manager Joe Smith that Newcastle centre-forward Jackie Milburn would be too fast for Hayward, so an unfamiliar offside game was introduced. It was something which the defenders did not feel comfortable with and it ultimately led to the team's downfall on that cold April day.

The early running had been made by Blackpool, with Slater and Mortensen coming close in the first ten minutes, goalkeeper Fairbrother making a superb save to deny 'Morty'. Newcastle were biding their time, though, and as soon as they realized the Blackpool defence's unease with the offside trap. they exploited it as often as possible.

On four occasions Milburn managed to evade the fragile defence and breakthrough, only to be denied by George Farm or the post. Indeed, on one occasion Milburn had the ball in the net but the effort was ruled offside.

Blackpool continued to push forward, but Mortensen was strangely subdued, whilst Matthews was running himself into the ground but had extreme difficulty in shaking off the attentions of Corbett. At half-time there was no score, but the massed ranks of Magpies fans must have felt the more confident for the second period.

Strangely, Blackpool did not abandon the offside trap in the second half — maybe one of the few mistakes manager Joe Smith made in his career — and within five minutes they paid the price.

George Robledo intercepted a pass from Matthews and quickly found Milburn. 'Wor Jackie', taking advantage of the back line's hesitation in waiting for the whistle, raced through and shot hard past the despairing Farm.

After 51 minutes, it was 2-0 with that man Milburn scoring again. With the Seasiders' defence in disarray, Walker took the ball on the right wing and gave a short pass to Ernie Taylor (later to join Blackpool). Taylor, seeing the big centre-forward racing up alongside him, gave a delicate back-pass straight into Milburn's path. Within a split-second the ball was in the corner of the net, shot with deadly accuracy from outside the area.

Effectively, the game was now over, although Blackpool kept pushing forward looking for the elusive goal. As the game progressed, though, it became increasingly obvious that it would never come. Towards the end, Milburn nearly finished it off with a header, but another goal would probably have been an injustice to the hard-working Blackpool team.

As the teams left the pitch, many observers expressed their sadness that Stanley Matthews, who was now ageing, would never win the FA Cup winners' medal that he wanted so badly.

Blackpool: Farm; Shimwell, Garrett, Johnston, Hayward, Kelly, Matthews, Mudie, Mortenson, Slater, Perry.
Newcastle United: Fairbrother; Cowell, Corbett, Harvey, Brennan, Crowe, Walker, Taylor, Milburn, Robledo, Mitchell.

Att: 100,000

Match to Remember 9 — 2 May 1953

Blackpool 4 Bolton Wanderers 3

SO much has been said and written about the 1953 FA Cup Final, that it is almost impossible to do it justice in just a few paragraphs. Although it was not a classic in the footballing sense, the game has come to be regarded as the most famous FA Cup Final of all time.

Dubbed the 'Matthews Final' for obvious reasons, it was a game that included the only ever hat-trick scored in a Wembley FA Cup Final, and a quite remarkable fight-back by Blackpool from 3-1 down to finish winners by scoring two goals in the last minute.

When Blackpool reached Wembley for the third time in six years, the whole nation cheered, for it meant that the world's most famous footballer, Stanley Matthews, had another opportunity to collect that elusive winners' medal.

After the disappointments of 1948 and 1951, no one, except the Bolton fans, wanted to deny him another chance, yet within two minutes of the kick-off it seemed as if the odds were against it happening.

Nat Lofthouse had given Bolton the lead with a goal that had 'Pool 'keeper George Farm squirming with embarrassment. The centre-forward had unleashed a 20-yard shot — the sort which, nine times out of ten, would not have bothered the Scottish international. This time, though, Farm somehow let the ball slip through his arms and could only look back in despair as it rolled into the net.

The goal kept up Lofthouse's record of scoring in every round, but it also served to unnerve not only Farm but the rest of his teammates too. The Bolton forwards went charging upfield, taking advantage of Blackpool's rather shaky defence, and just four minutes later they should have made it 2-0. Lofthouse, again from a pass from Holden, missed a golden opportunity.

These were rather worrying moments for the Blackpool supporters, their team had 'frozen' two years previously against Newcastle and were certainly not looking too confident in the first few minutes of this Cup Final.

There then followed a serious injury to Bolton's Eric Bell, and the Trotters were forced to reorganize. Bell was put out to the left wing, where he spent the rest of the game hobbling in some pain. In those days there were no substitutes, so poor Bell had to endure the remaining 70 minutes.

This, of course, inspired the Seasiders as they calmed themselves and then started pushing forward looking for the equalizer. Taylor and Perry both looked dangerous

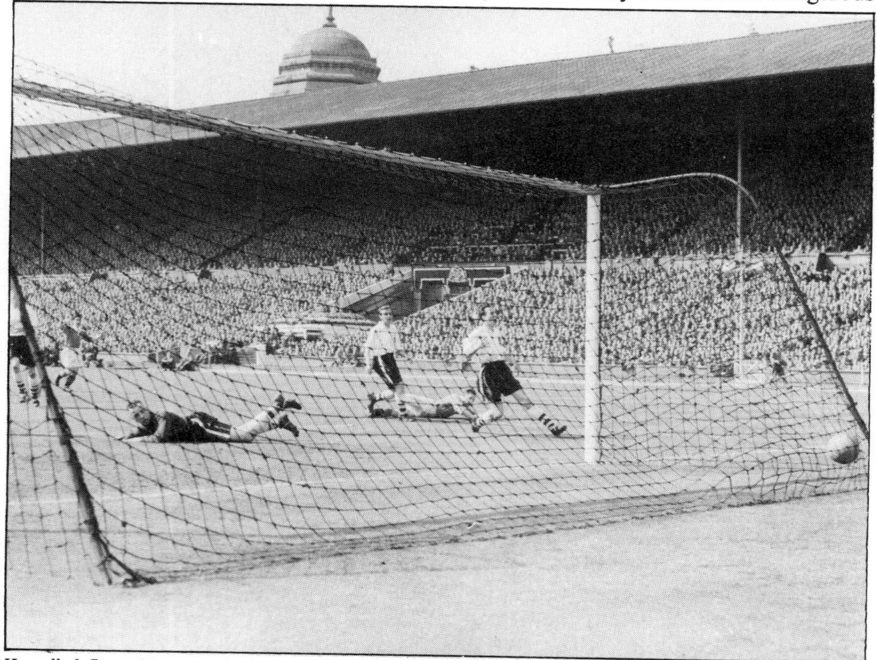

Hassall deflects Mortensen's shot over the line and the Seasiders are level at 1-1 against Bolton in the 1953 FA Cup Final.

and, indeed, both men had opportunities to score, but a combination of poor finishing and rather bad luck kept them at bay.

When Blackpool did equalize, though, it was a classic. Stan Mortensen ran some 20 yards with the ball, shaking off the attentions of two defenders, and hit a terrific shot which left Hanson with no chance. The ball deflected off Hassall, but the goal was Mortensen's all the way and he rightly celebrated.

Blackpool had drawn level and were beginning to play the type of football that had made them so popular throughout the country. Their celebrations were quietened a few minutes later, however, as Lofthouse found himself free from his marker and facing Farm. Fortunately for 'Pool, he blasted well over, another seemingly golden opportunity missed.

Yet after 40 minutes, Bolton were back in the lead, once again with a goal that had to be attributed to George Farm's indecisiveness. Langton floated the ball into the area, and the 'keeper, apparently unnerved by the approaching Muir, hesitated and allowed the inside-right to glance it into goal. It was a terrible disappointment and one that left the half-time score at Blackpool 1 Bolton 2.

During the interval, Joe Smith told his players to carry on with what they were doing, being sufficiently pleased and not prepared to make any tactical changes. It seemed to work. In the first ten minutes of the second half Blackpool piled on the pressure, looking for another equalizer.

Ernie Taylor's snapshot from a cross from Matthews was the best effort, and it certainly looked as if the 'Pool were the more determined side. Yet after 55 minutes, totally against the run of play, Bolton got their third goal.

In a rare Trotters attack, the ball was floated into the area and somehow the crippled Bell had risen above all the defenders and headed past Farm. It was a dreadful shock to Blackpool's supporters, who, up until then, had been convinced that their team could win.

It should also have come as a hammer-blow to the Blackpool players, yet surprisingly it had the opposite effect. It has been said many times by the men who wore tangerine that day, that Bolton's third goal spurred them on. They knew they were the better team, they knew they were the fitter team, especially with so many of Bolton's players suffering from cramp. But most of all they knew they would win.

Whether that was the case or not, the fact is that Blackpool attacked constantly and it was only a matter of time before they scored.

The goal came from another one of those wonderful runs on the right wing from the 'Maestro', Stanley Matthews. Easily outpacing Banks, he crossed the ball deep into the area, Hanson failed to collect it and Mortensen, under extreme pressure, squeezed it into the net. It was 2-3 and the fight-back had begun.

As successive Bolton players went down with injuries and cramp, Lofthouse included, Blackpool grew more and more in confidence. A tactical switch was made between Perry and Mudie and this nearly paid dividends when, after a mix-up in Bolton's defence, 'Morty' saw his powerful shot saved by Hanson and put round for a corner.

Blackpool were now rampant, yet time seemed to be running out. Would Stanley Matthews' dream of a Cup winners' medal remain just that? Most observers must have felt so, but the Blackpool team 'knew' differently.

With only a couple of minutes remaining, Jackie Mudie was 'sandwiched' between two defenders as he made a charge for goal. A free-kick was given just outside the area and up stepped Mortensen. Legend has it that 'Morty' saw a gap appear in the defensive wall and shouted to one of his teammates that he was going to 'have a go'. With that he unleashed a shot so powerful that it flashed past the wall, goalkeeper Hanson and very nearly burst the net.

Stan Mortensen, under extreme pressures, squeezes home Blackpool's second goal to make the score 3-2.

Bill Perry hammers Stan Matthews' cross into the net and Blackpool have scored an epic Cup Final victory.

Skipper Harry Johnston and Stan Matthews are chaired around Wembley with the FA Cup.

The 'Pool were level and Stanley Mortensen had scored the first hat-trick in an FA Cup Final at Wembley, his teammates mobbing him in delight. The Bolton players looked at each other in disbelief; they had the Cup within their grasp, yet now, with barely a minute left, they were level. Extra-time beckoned and one could forgive the Trotters' players for thinking that this was not to be their day.

Straight from the kick-off, Blackpool surged forward again, determined to grab the winner as the Bolton players fell over themselves in a desperate attempt to defend. Matthews, now inspired, yet again beat Banks and crossed for Mudie to shoot just wide.

The seconds ticked away as Blackpool mounted one last attack. Taylor slid another pass to Matthews and, as Banks came out to tackle, the 'Maestro' slid around him, leaving him for dead. Matthews went to the by-line and cut back a hard ground pass behind the retreating defenders, to where Bill Perry was running in to meet it.

In an instant the ball was in the net and Blackpool had won the FA Cup. It was a remarkable end to a remarkable match and many of Blackpool's players were in tears as they mounted the steps to receive their winners' medals from the Queen, none more so than Stanley Matthews, who at the age of 38 had at long last gained a Cup winners' medal. It was probably the most popular victory ever seen at Wembley.

There were many other heroes, of course: Stan Mortensen, who had scored the only ever hat-trick in an FA Cup Final, never complained when the media dubbed it 'the Matthews Final'; and manager Joe Smith had built the side from nothing and had taken his team to their greatest triumph, in the most famous FA Cup Final there has ever been.

Blackpool: Farm; Shimwell, Garrett, Fenton, Johnston, Robinson, Matthews, Taylor, Mortensen, Mudie, Perry.
Bolton Wanderers: Hanson; Ball, Banks, Wheeler, Barrass, Bell, Holden, Moir, Lofthouse, Hassall, Longham.

Att: 100,000

Match to Remember 10 — 5 October 1957

Blackpool 7 Sunderland 0

GAMES between Blackpool and Sunderland in the 1950s were always keenly contested affairs and more often than not would result in an avalanche of goals. This match would be no different.

Before the game most 'Pool supporters were of the opinion that their team had 'nowt to beat', and within only 45 seconds they seemed to be right. Dave Durie rose above the defence to nod in a corner to give Blackpool the lead.

The Sunderland back line were decidedly shaky and within ten minutes had conceeded two more goals, Durie again and Ray Charnley taking advantage of goalkeeping errors to give the Seasiders an already unassailable lead.

A near capacity crowd roared on the home team and with Stanley Matthews

Blackpool's staff at the start of the 1957-8 season. Joe Smith's team scored a big win over the Wearsiders at Bloomfield Road.

in superb form, twisting this way and that, most of Sunderland's players looked as if they preferred to be elsewhere.

At the back, Jimmy Armfield, who had little to do defensively, became more and more ambitious and nearly got on the score-sheet himself.

Just before half-time, though, Charnley got his second and Blackpool's fourth, a superb solo effort. It had been an outstanding 45 minutes for the tall centre-forward as he had almost single-handedly torn the Sunderland defence apart, and as the players left the pitch at the interval he especially was given a hero's ovation.

In the second period the visitors started to play more composed football, desperate to put some respectability into the score-line and they must have been encouraged to see that Bill Perry out on the left wing was carrying an injury and had, by this time, become no more than a spectator.

Also, on 60 minutes Blackpool's forward line was further depleted when Charnley was forced off the field with a serious head injury, not returning until the game was all but over.

In the meantime, though, Blackpool rode a storm of Sunderland pressure and went out to score three quick goals, two by Ernie Taylor and the last by the limping Perry.

The nine and a half fit men had destroyed any resistance their opponents had put up and the 7-0 score-line was far more flattering to Sunderland than it was to Blackpool.

Incredibly, two weeks later in the next home game, virtually the same team, but without the injured Charnley, fell to pieces in front of a powerful Manchester United and lost 5-2. This victory remains Blackpool's biggest ever at home in the Football League. Their biggest away win is also 7-0, against a much-weakened Preston North End at Deepdale in 1948.

Blackpool: Farm; Armfield, Garrett, J.Kelly, Gratrix, H.Kelly, Matthews, Taylor, Charnley, Durie, Perry.
Sunderland: Fraser; Hedley, McDonald, Anderson, Hurley, Elliott, Hannigan, Revie, Spence, O'Neill, Grainger.

Attendance: 33,172

Match to Remember 11 — 22 October 1966

Blackpool 6 Newcastle United 0

DURING the disastrous campaign of 1966-7, Blackpool managed only one home League victory and it came on 22 October, just one week after their first win of the season.

Their opponents, Newcastle United, were expected to provide tough opposition, as indeed most of Bloomfield Road's visitors were that season, yet on that incredible day Blackpool played with a passion and enthusiasm that had rarely been seen previously.

The facts do not really tell the full story. Ian Moir's goals had given Blackpool a 2-0 lead within 16 minutes, Alan Skirton and Ray Charnley had made it four by half-time.

Alan Suddick was on the wrong end of a 6-0 thrashing at Bloomfield Road, but Blackpool were so impressed by his commitment that two months later they paid a club record £60,000 for his services.

In the second half, Jimmy Robson's goal and another by the new signing Skirton brought the score to 6-0, and even Leslie Lea was allowed the luxury of a disallowed goal, yet Blackpool did not have it all their own way.

They were made to fight by a very determined Newcastle side, who, even when 6-0 down in the last ten minutes, exerted such pressure on Blackpool's goal that Tony Waiters was forced to make two world-class saves. It was an end-to-end footballing extravaganza and the difference between the sides was the finishing power of the Blackpool forwards.

Alan Skirton, who had been signed from Arsenal one month previously, played the game of his life and was cheered off the field by the ecstatic fans. He came close to adding to his two goals on many occasions, and only the brilliance of goalkeeper Hollins denied him.

On the opposite side, a young Alan Suddick tried to take on the Blackpool defence almost single-handedly at times, and it needed the combined talents of Fisher, Rowe and McPhee to contain him. In fact, so impressed were the Blackpool board and management that within six weeks Suddick was signed for a record fee.

That day Blackpool gave a brilliant display. They met a very good Newcastle side and against all the odds recorded a victory that was the second largest in the First Division that season.

Incredibly, though, that side, with very few changes, won only two more games all season — both away — and were, of course, relegated.

Those who witnessed such a feast of football that day could be forgiven for thinking that they had seen an illusion, for they were not to see a Blackpool performance like that again all season.

Blackpool: Waiters; Thompson, Hughes, Fisher, McPhee, Rowe, Skirton, Robson, Charnley, Moir, Lea.
Newcastle United: Hollins; Cragg, Clark, Moncur, Thompson, Hey, Robson, Bennett, McGarry, Suddick, Knox.

Attendance: 21,202

Match to Remember 12 — 11 May 1968

Huddersfield Town 1 Blackpool 3

DESPITE winning their previous six games, Blackpool came to this last match of the season knowing that even if they won, they could still be denied promotion to Division One if their nearest rivals, Queen's Park Rangers, won at Aston Villa.

Expectations were high and over 4,000 tangerine-clad fans made their way over the Pennines, their bodies in Huddersfield but their minds at Villa Park.

The game was only given the go-ahead 15 minutes before kick-off after a torrential downpour the previous day and that morning had made the pitch a sea of mud. Yet it would have been difficult not to have allowed it to start, bearing in mind the importance of the occasion.

Blackpool began tentatively, mindful of the pressure bearing down on them, and also in the knowledge that they could not afford to lose. The pitch made any attempts to play serious football laughable and, with the rain still pouring down, it soon became difficult to distinguish one side from the other.

Indeed, it was so bad at one stage that the referee ordered Tony Green to the dressing-room to change his shirt as he could not tell which side he was on!

The first half was a battle, Huddersfield, not under any pressure, making the better chances, whilst Blackpool defended in earnest. On a couple of occasions Worthington came close to breaking the deadlock but last-ditch saves from Taylor denied him.

Unfortunately, though, the goal that Blackpool feared came on 40 minutes from the left-back Legg. All was not lost, though, as the electronic scoreboard showed that QPR were also a goal down at Villa Park at half-time. Even that was fraught with tension, for whoever was manning the scoreboard had a black sense of humour, starting with 'Villa 1, Queen's Park Rangers 1', right through to 'Queen's Park Rangers 10' before settling on nil.

The restart saw a new determination about the Blackpool side and it was not

Tony Green played 'the game of his life' as Blackpool won 3-1 at Leeds Road.

long before they were level with an equalizer from Alan Suddick. Then they went ahead after a comedy of errors and a crazy own-goal by unfortunate full-back McGill.

The Blackpool fans were beside themselves with joy. They had heard that QPR were level but that did not matter if the 'Pool could win.

When the third goal went in after a fierce shot from Alan Skirton, promotion seemed assured and the 'Pool contingent started singing and chanting, making Leeds Road seem like a home venue. Blackpool kept pressing forward but the fourth goal eluded them, Hutchison, on the left, gave McGill the run-around and Tony Green was playing the game of his life.

The final whistle blew and the supporters streamed on to the pitch, chanting manager Stan Mortensen's name. They were promoted and it had taken Morty only one season to achieve it.

After a while, Morty appeared looking shaken, for he knew that they had been denied after all. In the last seconds of the game at Villa Park, a home defender had put through his own goal and so gave QPR a 2-1 victory and promotion.

They had won it by virtue of a better goal average — 1.86 as opposed to Blackpool's 1.65 — and so the 'Pool had to endure another season of Second Division football.

It mattered not that they had scored 58 points, the highest for a team that failed to gain promotion, and at the end of the game fans were seen leaving the ground in tears. It had been one of the most disappointing days in the club's history.

Blackpool: Taylor; Armfield, Mowbray, Craven, James, McPhee, Skirton, Green White, Suddick, Hutchison.
Huddersfield: Oldfield; McGill, Legg, Smith, Nicholson, Cherry, Harper, Worthington, Aimson, Shaw, Dobson.

Attendance: 11,603

Match to Remember 13 — 13 April 1970

Preston North End 0 Blackpool 3

TWO years after the Huddersfield disappointment, Blackpool found themselves in a similar position when they travelled to rivals Preston for the penultimate match of the season.

This time, though, they knew that victory would not only guarantee a return to the First Division, but would almost certainly consign their neighbours to the Third for the first time in their history.

The game was played on a Monday evening in front of a capacity crowd of 34,000, yet it seemed like a home game for Blackpool as the tangerine supporters numbered around 20,000.

Predictably, the atmosphere was tense with so much depending on the outcome for both teams. Yet Blackpool, who had six days earlier managed to gain an excellent draw at fellow promotion candidates Swindon Town, played the better football.

In fact, the away team all but overran a very poor Preston side who were low on confidence and short of ability. It came as no surprise when, on 16 minutes, the 'Pool scored their first goal, a right-wing cross from Mickey Burns being met by Fred Pickering on the far post. A simple nod in gave Blackpool a 1-0 lead.

The away supporters started their celebrations early as Blackpool swept all before them and exerted constant pressure on North End's shakey defence.

It was only the sheer brilliance of goalkeeper Kelly that denied Blackpool a second, and Preston looked dangerous on only two occasions throughout the game, when Archie Gemmill had a couple of long-range efforts saved by Harry Thompson.

On 40 minutes, Blackpool were 2-0 up and once again it was Fred Pickering who scored. Hutchinson put a superb through ball to the overlapping Bentley, who in turn had crossed perfectly for the centre-forward to ram home with his head. The 'Pool fans were ecstatic as the half-time whistle was blown.

The second 45 minutes were very much like the first, with wave after wave of constant Blackpool pressure. After 58 minutes Fred Pickering scored his and Blackpool's third goal. A shot from Tommy Hutchison rebounded off the legs of Kelly and there was Pickering to simply tap into the net.

Until the final whistle the Tangerines just toyed with Preston, with each forward having a pot at goal as and when he pleased. Kelly, who had played a blinder

Fred Pickering leaps into the net after scoring one of his hat-trick goals against Preston at Deepdale.

throughout the game, was forced to make some quite brilliant saves just to keep the score respectable.

There were no more goals, though, and in the final five minutes the home side hardly touched the ball as the 'Pool players passed it around from one to another. Blackpool fans roared their approval and in dying minutes a chant of 'Blackpool, Blackpool' could be heard for miles around.

The scenes at the final whistle were incredible as overjoyed Blackpool supporters poured on to the pitch to cheer their heroes off. The Preston fans, meanwhile, quietly left in total despair as they contemplated Third Division football for the first time. Of all the battles between the 'Old Enemy' this must surely go down as the best, especially if you are a Blackpool supporter.

Preston North End: Kelly; Patrick, McNab, Hawkins, Cranston, Heppolette, Lee(Irvine), Spavin, Lloyd, Gemmill, Temple.
Blackpool: Thompson; Armfield, Bentley, McPhee, James, Hatton, Burns, Craven, Pickering, Suddick, Hutchison.

Attendance: 34,000

Match to Remember 14 — 24 October 1970

Blackpool 3 Chelsea 4

OF all the football matches staged at Bloomfield Road over the years, surely the game played on 24 October 1970 was the most bizarre.

Chelsea's Phillips grabs the ball as Pickering and Suddick wait to pounce.

Blackpool's opponents in the First Division that day were the FA Cup holders 'fashionable' Chelsea, a team full of international players. Chelsea were on the verge of the Championship race, whilst Blackpool were already facing a difficult battle against relegation and were at the foot of the table.

Yet if an outsider had joined the game at half-time he would have thought the roles had been reversed as Blackpool had an incredible 3-0 lead!

The story of that first period was one of complete and total Blackpool domination, of a team playing with confidence and passion that had been so sadly lacking all season.

They had quite simply torn Chelsea apart and should have had more than the three goals, with stand-in 'keeper Phillips looking like a little boy lost as the home forwards bombarded his goal time after time.

The goals had come from Alan Suddick and two from Fred Pickering, his last and Blackpool's third being the pick of the bunch, and as the players left the field they were given a standing ovation. The poor Chelsea players looked completely shell-shocked and at a loss as to what to do. They went into the dressing-room in the unacustomed position of being 3-0 down.

If the first half was incredible, the second was nothing short of unbelievable. Chelsea, obviously with now nothing to lose, came out and played attacking football whereas Blackpool were quite content to sit back on their lead and take maximum points for only the third time that season.

Even when Keith Weller pulled a goal back for the Blues, Blackpool refused to come out of their shell. Their second-half performance was as different to their first as chalk and cheese, and their supporters began to get nervous.

On 60 minutes, Chelsea's manager Dave Sexton made an inspired substitution by replacing Tommy Baldwin with Charlie Cooke. He immediately began to cause Blackpool's defence problems with his long runs down the left wing, yet after 75 minutes the home team still held the upper hand at 3-1.

Then one decision changed the whole complexion of the game. Blackpool manager Les Shannon inexplicably took off centre-forward Fred Pickering, replacing him with John Craven. It was one of the most extraordinary decisions any manager has ever made and the Blackpool fans howled their protests.

After the game, Shannon said that Pickering was carrying an injury, but the player always denied this. Whatever the reason it totally changed the game as Blackpool completely collapsed. Almost immediately Chelsea scored after Osgood had crossed for Dave Webb to beat the lethargic Mowbray and head into the net.

Within a few minutes they were level. Harry Thomson, by now under all sorts of pressure in goal, dropped the ball to allow Weller to score his second. The Chelsea contingent were by this time ecstatic as their team pushed for the winner.

Surely, though, Blackpool could hold out for a point at least? But with less than 90 seconds left, Dave Hatton quite unbelievably sliced a seemingly safe ball into his own net. The players and fans could not believe it.

As the game ended, tangerine shirted players sank to the ground in abject despair, whilst the blue shirted men went off scarely able to believe their luck. Three days later, manager Les Shannon, under a cloud of criticism, did the only thing open to him and resigned. Blackpool went on to relegation.

Blackpool: Thomson; Armfield, Mowbray, Hatton, James, Bentley, Burns, Green, Pickering(Craven), Suddick, Hutchison.
Chelsea: Phillips, Mulligan, Harris, Hollins, Hinton, Webb, Weller, Hudson, Osgood, Baldwin(Cooke), Houseman.

Attendance: 24,940

Match to Remember 15 — 12 June 1971

Bologna 1 Blackpool 2
(after extra-time)

THE Anglo-Italian Tournament of 1971 restored pride in Blackpool Football Club after their disastrous relegation campaign from Division One.

The Seasiders began the competition with morale low, yet after their four qualifying matches they had scored enough goals and points to win themselves a place in the Final at the Stadio Comunale in Bologna. Their opponents were regarded highly in Italy and were, at the time, one of that country's top teams. So, with a home crowd of 40,000 behind them Bologna, were expected to win quite easily.

The game kicked off at 5pm local time and was beamed live on TV back to Britain, although strangely the transmission ended after 90 minutes.

Blackpool line up in the Stadio Comunale before their extra-time victory over Bologna.

The heat was not particularly oppressive but still a mite uncomfortable for players used to an English winter.

It has to be said that the first 45 minutes were hardly exciting, the Italians adopting an all-too familiar cautious approach to their play, whilst Blackpool's players were slightly overawed by the whole occasion.

Bologna relied heavily on the breakaway, the speed of their front two Salvodi and Rizzo giving Blackpool's defenders all kinds of problems. In fact, it was just that sort of surprise attack that gave the Italians the lead on 32 minutes, with the number 11, Pace finishing off a fine move with a fierce shot that left 'keeper Burridge with no chance.

The score remained at 1-0 up until half-time and, really, Blackpool could have no complaints. They'd hardly managed a decent shot on goal all afternoon.

Whatever was said by manager Bob Stokoe during the interval obviously worked, as the players came out in the second half with new enthusiasm and commitment. Tony Green in midfield, who up until then had been largely quiet, now started to run at the Italians, upsetting their rhythm.

Alan Suddick took command of the middle of the field and Bill Bentley, with his constant forays upfield, helped out the attack.

After a period of sustained Blackpool pressure the equalizing goal came on 62 minutes. Bentley put a superb through pass for John Craven in space and the centre-forward crashed it into the net from inside the penalty area.

This upset the home team and as the game progressed it seemed that only Blackpool had the desire and ability to win. Mickey Burns brought out a superb save from veteran goalkeeper Vavassori late in the match and Craven, too, came close to adding to his earlier strike.

Two substitutions were made by Stokoe with Wann and Johnstone replacing Ainscow and Craven. The former was suffering from almost total exhaustion as the heat inside the stadium had risen considerably.

Blackpool celebrate with the Anglo-Italian trophy.

Extra-time came with the home supporters strangely quiet. For most of the game they had been singing and dancing with the stadium bedecked in a sea of blue-and-red, but with another 30 minutes to play they had obviously lost faith in their side. The small band of Blackpool fans, however, were thoroughly enjoying themselves.

After 99 minutes the winner came and a better goal you are not likely to see in any Cup Final. Dennis Wann, inside his own half, hit an inch-perfect 30-yard pass to Mickey Burns who, taking it in his stride, shrugged off the attentions of two defenders and smashed the ball into the net. Blackpool were ahead and Bologna were already a beaten side.

Their heads dropped and from then on they never looked like coming back. Blackpool played the ball around with ease and almost contemptously they dared the Italians to win it back. The final whistle was greeted with a roar from the

Blackpool fans high up in the grandstand, and surprisingly with sporting applause from the home supporters.

The next day the team paraded the cup on the Promenade and at the Town Hall and, to their surprise, a crowd of nearly 50,000 were there to greet them. Not only had they won their first trophy for nearly 20 years, but more importantly they had put pride back in to the name of Blackpool.

Bologna: Vavassori; Roversi, Fedele, Perani, Janich, Gregori, Cresci, Rizzo, Salvodi, Scala, Pace.
Blackpool: Burridge; Bentley, Hatton, Ainscow(Wann), Alcock, Suddaby, Burns, Green, Craven(Johnstone), Suddick, Hutchison.

Attendance: 40,000

Match to Remember 16 — 24 June 1972

AS Roma 3 Blackpool 1

ONE year later, Blackpool returned to Italy to defend their trophy, but this time against a far more able and organized side. Roma, their opponents, were odds-on to win in a game that was played in baking heat where temperatures reached as high as 100 degrees.

The Olympic Stadium was only two-thirds full, yet still had 75,000 spectators present and the noise and spectacle at the start would have been enough to put off even the most experienced of teams.

The first half was evenly matched with both teams coming close to scoring on many occasions. Roma, like their compatriots a year earlier, relied heavily on the breakaway, yet they always looked far more dangerous than Bologna had ever done.

Within ten minutes the Italians should have been ahead when Rigani's header went over the bar from close range. Spadani might have scored but for the good goalkeeping of Burridge.

Blackpool, for their part, were never positive enough, especially in front of goal. Twice in the space of ten minutes they missed seemingly easy chances, the first from Mick Hill and the second from Keith Dyson, who hit the side netting when he should have scored. On both occasions the provider was the ever busy and influential Mickey Burns, who was once again running tirelessly at the opposing defence. At half-time, though the game was still goalless.

The second half started with the temperature even higher and it was obvious that it was not to the Blackpool players liking. After a long, hard season this was not the kind of game that they wanted. The killer blow came on 47 minutes when Capellino took advantage of a loose ball from Dave Hatton and scored to give Roma a 1-0 lead.

The home fans went into ecstacy and Blackpool knew they had a difficult job to keep hold of their title. They did push forward though but always mindful of leaving gaps at the back for the Italian forwards to exploit.

Blackpool had two really good chances to equalize in the second half, first a header from Glyn James that went just wide and later a spectacular scissor-kick from Mickey Burns.

Substitute Terry Alcock scores a consolation goal for Blackpool in Rome's Olympic Stadium.

It was to no avail, though, as the Roma defence held firm and began to take control of the game. By the time Terry Alcock put the ball in the net on 89 minutes, Roma had scored a further two from breakaways.

The Seasiders could have no complaints about the result, as they had not shown enough desire or passion to take on the Italians and their fanatical supporters.

They left the tournament with their heads held high, though, being congratulated as perfect ambassadors for English football. They had gone a long way to restoring dignity to a competition that, over the years, had been stained by violent play from both countries. Unfortunately, though, two years later the tournament was scrapped and Blackpool never got another chance to win back the cup they had won so well in 1971.

AS Roma: Ginvilli; Capelli, Liquori, Salvori, Bet, Santarini, Capellino, Spadani, Rigani, Cordeva, Franzot.
Blackpool: Burridge; Hatton, Bentley, Suddaby, James, Ainscow, Hutchison, Suddick, Dyson, Hill(Alcock), Burns.

Attendance: 75,000

Match to Remember 17 — 1 February 1975

Blackpool 3 Sunderland 2

ONE of the most exciting games seen at Bloomfield Road during the 1970s was this top of the Second Division clash with Sunderland. It had everything that a football fan could want, and those who witnessed it will never forget it.

Sunderland came as the Second Division pacesetters with Blackpool just a few places and points behind them and, with some 5,000 North-Easterners in the crowd, it made for a cracking atmosphere.

Not surprisingly the game started at a furious pace with late tackles and many off-the-ball incidents. Gradually, though, it calmed down and the two sides provided a feast of footballing skills.

It was Blackpool who got the early breakthrough when Terry Alcock opened the scoring on 19 minutes. A corner from Bill Bentley was nodded on by Walsh, for Alcock to power home with his head.

It was just what the home side needed and they then took the game to a clearly rattled Sunderland side. Ainscow came close on a couple of occasions and Bentley was proving a handful for the Sunderland rearguard.

Yet it was not until the 42nd minute that the second goal arrived. A Mickey Walsh cross was not cleared by the defence and there was Wyn Davies to stab the ball home.

It could have been 3-0 a minute later when Bentley made a complete hash of an easy chance. Nonetheless, Blackpool could feel satisfied with their half-time lead.

The second half saw constant and consistent pressure by the visitors, obviously paying heed to a half-time lambasting from their manager Bob Stokoe.

They threw everything at Blackpool's defence and it came as no surprise when, on 51 minutes, they pulled a goal back. Halom's lethal shot was too much for Burridge and it was 2-1.

From then on, Blackpool's defence survived on luck alone, although gradually after a sustained period of pressure they began to relax and started to feed their forwards. Indeed, just when it seemed as if they had weathered the storm Sunderland broke away and got the equalizer with a goal by Kerr on 68 minutes.

It was 2-2 and neither team could complain, as by now mistakes were being made and both sides were coming close to snatching the winner. It was clear that one more goal would be enough.

That goal, when it did come, was probably one of the most spectacular ever seen at Bloomfield Road. With just three minutes left, Mickey Walsh broke free from his markers on the halfway line, shrugged off the attentions of Moncur and Guthrie, and from fully 35 yards unleashed a fierce left-foot shot that flew into the top corner of the net, giving Montgomery no chance.

The home fans went wild and spilled on to the pitch in celebration, Blackpool had snatched a last-gasp 3-2 victory. The goal became famous all over the country as it was voted 'goal of the season' on BBC's *Match of the Day* programme, and has been shown at regular intervals since.

There was one other incident during this remarkable game that has since been forgotten amongst the footballing thrills and spills. Just after Sunderland had equalized they were then given a penalty, taken by Billy Hughes. This was saved rather easily by Burridge, but afterwards on TV it was noted by Jimmy Hill that a groundsman behind the goal was waving his arms and clearly distracted Hughes.

This, thought Mr Hill, was most unfair and was on the brink of ungentlemenly conduct. When the groundsman, Bert Taylor, was asked about the incident he just smiled. "I was just trying to tell the referee that I thought he'd made a poor decision."

Blackpool: Burridge; Curtis, Hatton, Hart, Harrison, Alcock, Ainscow, Davies, Walsh, Bentley, Evanson.
Sunderland: Montgomery; Malone, Bolton, Moncur, Watson, Guthrie, Kerr, Hughes, Halom, Robson, Towers.

Attendance: 16,151

Terry Alcock opens the scoring against Sunderland after catching the Wearsiders' defence napping.

Wyn Davies scores the Seasiders' second after a mistake by Jim Montgomery in the Sunderland goal.

Match to Remember 18 — 1 May 1985

Darlington 0 Blackpool 4

BLACKPOOL approached this top-of-the-table clash knowing that a win would almost certainly secure promotion back to Division Three. Darlington were a place behind the 'Pool and with only three matches remaining after this game, it was essential that Blackpool did not lose.

Over 3,000 fans travelled with the team and they witnessed one of the most positive and certainly most clinical performances of the season from their team. It was a perfect lesson in finishing power as Blackpool all but destroyed their opponents.

Darlington though were the team who appeared the more dangerous in the first half, in fact wasting three glorious chances before allowing Mike Conroy to give Blackpool a 1-0 lead after 25 minutes.

After another home attack had broken down, Ian Britton sent Stewart scampering away on the right. His cross for Conroy was perfect and the number eight smashed the ball home past the despairing Barber.

It was a real blow to the home side, who up until then had made most of the running, and, indeed, their answer was to push even more men forward.

Darlington had been criticised in the past for their negative play, especially by 'Pool manager Sam Ellis, but now they had no option but to play a more open type of game.

Once again they were guilty of missed chances and once again they were punished by Blackpool. On 37 minutes, Eamon O'Keefe receiving a through ball from Windridge, calmly slotted the ball into the net to give Blackpool a 2-0 lead.

Champagne celebrations in the Feethams' dressing-room after the Seasiders' return to the Third Division.

It effectively killed off Darlington's challenge and, indeed, the contest. Just before half-time Windridge was denied a penalty, but even so Blackpool went in at the interval highly satisfied with their contribution.

The second half was one of almost total domination by Blackpool. They managed to score two more goals and throughout the 45 minutes 'keeper O'Rourke had only one real save to make.

The first of those goals came on 60 minutes when a Windridge cross was deflected on to Paul Stewart's head by 'keeper Barber and into the net. Goal number four came on 77 minutes when yet another cross from Windridge — who was playing the game of his life — was met by Deary. His first-time header was brilliantly saved by Barber, but the goalkeeper could not stop the follow-up from the same player.

Blackpool's 4-0 victory had gained three valuable promotion points. Afterwards the 3,000 'Pool fans chanted Sam Ellis's name and would not leave until he acknowledged them, his popularity at an all-time high with the Bloomfield Road faithful.

It had been an important victory, even more so bearing in mind that two weeks later Darlington joined Blackpool in Division Three, finishing with only one point less than the Seasiders.

Darlington: Barber; Aldred, Johnston, Smith, MacDonald, Tupling, McLean, Forster, Haire, Airey, Todd.
Blackpool: O'Rourke; Moore, Price, Deary, Hetzke, Greenall, Britton, Conroy, Stewart, O'Keefe, Windridge.

Attendance: 7,021

Match to Remember 19 — 18 February 1990

Blackpool 2 Queen's Park Rangers 2

THE 1989-90 season had been a disastrous one for Blackpool, with only ten League games won and eventual relegation to the Fourth Division for only the second time in their history.

Yet incredibly they had their best FA Cup run for over 30 years by reaching the fifth round. Admittedly, their four previous opponents, Bolton Wanderers, Chester City, Burnley and Torquay United, were all from the lower divisions. But for a club who had been so starved of success in recent years, this mattered not.

Their opponents in front of a capacity Bloomfield Road crowd were the 'aristocrats' from London, First Division Queen's Park Rangers, and maybe it was the fact that the game had been put back 24 hours to the Sunday, on police advice, or maybe it was the claustrophobic surroundings of a packed Bloomfield Road, but the Londoners left that day mighty relieved that they had escaped with a draw.

Predictably, it was the Seasiders who came out with all guns blazing, attacking right from the start, and after only three minutes they had amazingly taken the lead.

Rangers' international goalkeeper David Seaman misjudged a David Eyres cross and allowed Paul Groves to nod the ball into the open goal. It was the best possible start for the 'Pool and the worst for Rangers.

The crowd were ecstatic and roared their heroes on as the Blackpool players now tore into the Queen's Park Rangers defence. It took the First Division side quite some time to settle down, but eventually they calmed themselves and tried to play the kind of football expected of them.

Blackpool, though, were wound up and just would not allow their opponents to dwell on the ball, and as the game progressed it was they who looked the more likely to score again.

Time and time again they pressed Seaman into action but on each occasion he was equal to the task. Rangers relied on the breakaway as they searched for an equalizer, and with Andy Sinton and Ray Wilkins working well together they began to look dangerous, although it looked as if Blackpool would go into the half-time break still ahead.

Unfortunately Rangers got the goal that came as a real hammer-blow to the Seasiders, arriving just 30 seconds from the whistle. A corner from the left was not cleared properly and that gave Sinton a second opportunity to cross the ball. It was hit low, and all it needed was for Colin Clarke to tap the ball past the stranded 'Pool 'keeper and Rangers were level.

After that devastating end to the first 45 minutes, you would have expected Blackpool to have collapsed under the superior skills of their First Division opponents,

Blackpool applaud their fans after drawing 0-0 at Loftus Road in the first replay against QPR.

but incredibly they came out full of fire and passion, troubling Seaman immediately. He gave the impression that he really would have preferred to have been elsewhere.

Then totally against the run of play, Blackpool went behind to a superb solo goal from Colin Clarke again. He rode the attentions of two defenders before blasting a 20-yard shot into the far corner of the net. The Londoners celebrated, believing that they had now put out the Seasiders, but Blackpool's never-say-die attitude paid off just five minutes later when they equalized.

Andy Garner, who had been superb in midfield, put an inch-perfect pass through for David Eyres to run on to. He controlled it, shimmied to his left, and coolly placed the ball wide of Seaman's outstretched arms.

The goals stopped, but the action continued and as the final whistle sounded, the crowd stood and applauded both teams. It had been a typical cup-tie and Blackpool had been so close to causing an upset. Very rarely during that season had the team played with so much commitment and passion, and very rarely had they played with the type of skill they showed that day.

It took Queen's Park Rangers two further games to dispose of Blackpool, the first being goalless, the second seeing three second-half goals finally ending the marathon. In a season of such misery and despair, this had been a beacon of shining light. What a shame they could not continue it in the League.

Blackpool: McInhargey; Wright, Morgan, Coughlin, Methven, Bradshaw, Gouck, Groves, Brook(Owen), Garner, Eyres.
Queen's Park Rangers: Seaman; Bardsley, Samson, Parker, McDonald, Maddix, Wilkins, Barker, Clarke, Wegerle, Sinton.

Attendance: 9,641

Match to Remember 20 — 31 May 1991

Blackpool 2 Torquay United 2
(Torquay won 5-4 on pens)

SOME 38 years after their last, and indeed most famous, appearance at Wembley Stadium, Blackpool Football Club returned to the venue for a less glamorous but equally important game.

The Fourth Division Play-off Final offered Blackpool a second opportunity to gain promotion back to the Third Division, after they had failed so miserably three weeks previously at Walsall.

Over 15,000 fans made the journey to London on that bitterly cold May evening, and they witnessed a night so full of emotion that it will stay in Blackpool footballing folklore for many years to come.

Both sides were obviously aware of the importance of the game, it effectively deciding the immediate futures of the two clubs. Yet it was not the dull, defensive-minded match that we had all expected. Blackpool attacked from the whistle and came close on a couple of occasions, with Mark Taylor looking especially dangerous.

Indeed, it was the Seasiders who made the 'dream-start' on eight minutes when captain Paul Groves latched on to a through ball from Taylor just inside the box, and coolly slipped it past the outstretched arms of goalkeeper Gareth Howells.

The Blackpool supporters were delirious with joy and now more than ever were convinced that Torquay were there for the taking. From that moment, though,

Blackpool players line-up for a minute's silence in memory of the great Stan Mortensen before their 1991 Wembley game against Torquay United.

things did not really go according to plan. The Devon side, spurred on by their influential midfield rock Wes Saunders, moved forward and gave the Blackpool defence some worrying moments.

Despite exhortations from the bench, the team just could not seem to exercise any dominance over Torquay, and it came as no surprise when, on the half-hour, they levelled the score.

A corner from the right was not cleared by the Blackpool defence, and Loram's high floating cross was met by Saunders, who from five yards out nodded the ball into the net.

Torquay now moved forward in some numbers and, cheered on by their small band of supporters, they laid siege to the Blackpool goal. The tangerine shirts had regrouped, however, and were gradually beginning to take control of the midfield. Indeed, it looked as if the teams would go in at half-time at 1-1.

On 40 minutes, though, disaster struck. Dave Bamber, in a vain attempt to cut out a cross from Holmes, inadvertantly lifted his arm and allowed the ball to cannon off it.

Referee George Courtney had no choice but to point to the spot, and Dean Edwards easily converted. It was the start of what could only be described as nightmare for the lanky striker. Called back into the team after missing the run-in at the end of the season through injury, everything was to go wrong for the club's top scorer.

The second half saw Blackpool come out fighting and completely dominate their opponents, with only the heroics of Howells and some poor finishing by the 'Pool forwards keeping the score at 2-1. As the game wore on, the defending became increasingly more desperate and the attacking play more and more frantic.

When the equalizer did come, however, it was in a bizarre fashion. Mike Davies put a free-kick high into the Torquay area for Dave Bamber to nod down. David Eyres, with his back to the goal, tried a spectacular overhead scissors-kick which crashed off the upright.

It was hit with such force that Torquay defender Chris Curran could only watch in despair as the ball rebounded on to his legs and then into the back of the net. Blackpool had drawn level and the thousands of tangerine-clad fans roared them on as they pushed for the winner.

Incredibly, despite constant attacks on the Torquay goal, it did not come and at 90 minutes the score remained 2-2.

Extra-time was to be played. Thirty more leg-sapping minutes on the Wembley turf, with the knowledge that just one mistake could cost the team a whole season's work. The 'Pool fans got behind their team like never before and on 96 minutes it looked like they had been rewarded when Dave Bamber crashed the ball home, only to see referee George Courtney rule it offside.

Bamber was aghast and the supporters furious, but the decision stood. Blackpool did not come close after that, but they did have to survive a scare in the final minutes, when only the brilliance of 'keeper McIlhargey saved them.

So after 49 matches the League season would be decided by a penalty shoot-out. It seemed totally unfair to ask these players of both sides to determine the next 12 months for their respective clubs by kicking penalties, but those were the rules.

Now whether it was nerves or lack of confidence, or, indeed, the fact that the Devon players were facing their own fans, I really don't know, but the Torquay kicks were far more positive and accurate, whilst most of Blackpool's seem to trickle into the goal.

After the first five kicks each the scores were level at 4-4, Mark Loram and Tony Rodwell the culprits. Sudden death followed and up stepped Torquay's 'keeper, Gareth Howells, to blast the ball firmly past his opposite number. Five-four and the responsibility now lay with Dave Bamber. After an evening of total frustration, his confidence seemed now in tatters. The kick was placed well wide of the goal and Bamber's disastrous night was now complete.

The Torquay players and supporters celebrated whilst at the other end of the stadium the Blackpool team and their followers could only stand and stare in disbelief.

In an instant Blackpool's promotion hopes had been destroyed and they faced another season of Fourth Division football. For Bamber it had been especially cruel, for no player had contributed more to Blackpool's promotion charge than him, yet it had been his unfortunate miss that had finally denied them.

It was left to manager Billy Ayre to sum up all of our feelings when answering a TV commentator after the game he said, "I've never had a worse moment in my life, never mind football"

Blackpool: McIlhargey; Davies, Wright, Groves, Horner, Gore, Rodwell, Taylor, Bamber, Garner, Eyres.
Torquay United: Howells; Curran, P.Holmes, Saunders, Elliot, Joyce, Myers, M.Holmes, Evans, Edwards(Hall), Loram.

Attendance: 21,615

Match to Remember 21 — 23 May 1992

Blackpool 1 Scunthorpe United 1
(Blackpool won 4-3 on penalties)

TWELVE months after their 1991 disappointment, Blackpool returned to Wembley for yet another Fourth Division Play-off Final. Unlike the previous occasion, however, it was not greeted in celebratory fashion. Having to do it all at Wembley after such a promising season, which should have ended in automatic promotion, was viewed as something of an anticlimax by the fans.

The day was a scorcher and around 13,000 fans travelled to London, desperately hoping not to witness a repeat of the previous year. It was obvious that this was the team's last chance, and the players came out with determination etched on their faces.

To show the level of commitment, defender Mike Davies was booked within 80 seconds for an over-zealous tackle on Buckley, and it was clear that Billy Ayre had wound up his men to give their all.

Both teams took their time to settle down as one or two mistakes were made, but it was Blackpool who created the first real scoring chance. Andy Garner, after receiving a pass from Rodwell, hit a 20-yard shot which was saved by Samways. It spurred the Seasiders on and a few minutes later, Dave Bamber's header went just wide after some good early work from Rodwell again.

Scunthorpe came back, cheered on by their small band of supporters, and after 40 minutes they should have taken the lead. A neat one-two between Ian Hamilton and Dave Hill ended with Hamilton blasting over the bar from the edge of the 18-yard box.

It was a poor ending to the best move of the match and within 60 seconds they were punished severely when Blackpool took the lead. Once again superb work from Rodwell, who had won the ball off Longden, ended with a cross for Dave Bamber to head in from the most acute of angles. It was the big striker's 37th goal of the season, and surely the most important.

The second half started with constant pressure from Scunthorpe as the 'Pool defence worked overtime to keep the forwards at bay. McIlhargey was forced to make some desperate saves, but on 52 minutes he was beaten by a 25-yard blast from Tony Daws. It came after some good team work between himself and Ian Helliwell and proceeded to open the game up even more.

Blackpool reacted in the best possible way and all but dominated the game thereafter. David Eyres saw two shots go the wrong side of the post, and Bamber had a penalty claim turned down when it seemed that he was brought down by Longden.

On 75 minutes a free-kick by Eyres was tipped on to the bar by Samways, and with only eight minutes to go, Phil Horner saw his volley go just over the bar.

At the other end, McIlhargey was forced to make a great save from Hill's close-range shot. At full-time, though, the teams were still locked at 1-1 and for the second successive season Blackpool had to face another leg-sapping 30 minutes' extra-time on the Wembley turf.

The best of the chances during the extra period undoubtedly fell to Blackpool, with the clearest going to Bamber, who shot wide from only three yards out.

Then, deep into the second period, Rodwell broke through after a 20-yard run but saw his effort saved by Samways. In truth, it seemed as if only Blackpool were willing to win the game, probably due to the terrible experience of the previous year, but Scunthorpe still looked dangerous on the breakaway.

Eventually, Keith Hackett confirmed all the worst fears of the Blackpool supporters by blowing his whistle and consigning both teams to the penalty competition. For the thousands of tangerine-clad fans, it was now a complete sense of *déjà vu*, as for the second year running, promotion would be decided on the farcical penalty idea. Blackpool fans could be forgiven for believing that history was about to repeat itself.

Ian Hamilton gave Scunthorpe the lead with a perfect penalty that gave McIlhargey no chance, followed by Mitch Cook's left-footed effort to tie the scores at 1-1.

Dave Bamber, minus his shirt, with the Fourth Division Play-off trophy in 1992.

Milhargey makes a brilliant save from Alexander's penalty.

Paul Longden made it 2-1 before captain Groves equalized the scores with a fine shot that just crept under Samways' body.

With the tension almost unbearable and many players and fans refusing to watch, Matthew Elliot gave United the lead. For him it was a repeat of 1991, as he played in the Torquay side that went through the same agony.

Andy Garner stepped up and made it 3-3, to the desperate cheers of the 'Pool contingent.

Then came the moment that will stay with goalkeeper McIlhargey for the rest of his life. Graham Alexander, one of the substitutes, powered his shot towards the corner, only to see McIlhargey dive to his right and save brilliantly.

Suddenly there was hope, and when David Eyres nearly burst the net with his shot to make it 4-3, Division Two was almost a reality.

In an uncanny repeat of 1991, substitute Jason White stepped up, knowing that he had to score to keep alive Scunthorpe's hopes. To the absolute delight of the 13,000 Blackpool fans, poor White blasted the ball high over the bar and the Seasiders were promoted.

The after-match scenes were completely different from the previous year. Blackpool had gained success at last, and this time the fans could drive back up the motorway with their heads held high.

Blackpool: McIlhargey; Burgess, Cook, Groves, Davies(Murphy), Gore, Rodwell, Horner(Sinclair), Bamber, Garner, Eyres.
Scunthorpe United : Samways, Joyce, Longden, Hill, Elliot, Humphries, Martin, Hamilton, Daws(White), Buckley(Alexander), Helliwell.

Attendance: 22,741

Blackpool in the Football League
1896-97 to 1991-92

	P	W	D	L	F	A	Pts	Pos
DIVISION TWO								
1896-97	30	13	5	12	59	56	31	8th
1897-98	30	10	5	15	49	61	25	11th
1898-99	34	8	4	22	49	90	20	16th
1899-1900	Not re-elected							
1900-01	34	12	7	15	33	58	31	12th
1901-02	34	11	7	16	40	56	29	12th
1902-03	34	9	10	15	44	59	28	14th
1903-04	34	11	5	18	40	67	27	15th
1904-05	34	9	10	15	36	48	28	15th
1905-06	38	10	9	19	37	62	29	14th
1906-07	38	11	11	16	33	51	33	13th
1907-08	38	11	9	18	51	58	31	15th
1908-09	38	9	11	18	46	68	29	20th
1909-10	38	14	8	16	50	52	36	12th
1910-11	38	16	10	12	49	38	42	7th
1911-12	38	13	8	17	32	52	34	14th
1912-13	38	9	8	21	39	69	26	20th
1913-14	38	9	14	15	33	44	32	16th
1914-15	38	17	5	16	58	57	39	10th
1919-20	42	21	10	11	65	47	52	4th
1920-21	42	20	10	12	54	42	50	4th
1921-22	42	15	5	22	44	57	35	19th
1922-23	42	18	11	13	50	43	47	5th
1923-24	42	18	13	11	72	47	49	4th
1924-25	42	14	9	19	65	61	37	17th
1925-26	42	17	11	14	76	69	45	6th
1926-27	42	18	8	16	95	80	44	9th
1927-28	42	13	8	21	83	101	34	19th
1928-29	42	19	7	16	82	76	45	8th
1929-30	42	27	4	11	98	67	58	1st
DIVISION ONE								
1930-31	42	11	10	21	71	125	32	20th
1931-32	42	12	9	21	65	102	33	20th
1932-33	42	14	5	23	69	85	33	22nd
DIVISION TWO								
1933-34	42	15	13	14	62	64	43	11th
1934-35	42	21	11	10	79	57	53	4th
1935-36	42	18	7	17	93	82	43	10th
1936-37	42	24	7	11	88	53	55	2nd
DIVISION ONE								
1937-38	42	16	8	18	61	66	40	12th
1938-39	42	12	14	16	56	68	38	15th
1946-47	42	22	6	14	71	70	50	5th
1947-48	42	17	10	15	57	41	44	9th
1948-49	42	11	16	15	54	67	38	16th
1949-50	42	17	15	10	46	35	49	7th
1950-51	42	20	10	12	79	53	50	3rd

	P	W	D	L	F	A	Pts	Pos
1951-52	42	18	9	15	64	64	45	9th
1952-53	42	19	9	14	71	70	47	7th
1953-54	42	19	10	13	80	69	48	6th
1954-55	42	14	10	18	60	64	38	19th
1955-56	42	20	9	13	86	62	49	2nd
1956-57	42	22	9	11	93	65	53	4th
1957-58	42	19	6	17	80	67	44	7th
1958-59	42	18	11	13	66	49	47	8th
1959-60	42	15	10	17	59	71	40	11th
1960-61	42	12	9	21	68	73	33	20th
1961-62	42	15	11	16	70	75	41	13th
1962-63	42	13	14	15	58	64	40	13th
1963-64	42	13	9	20	52	73	35	18th
1964-65	42	12	11	19	67	78	35	17th
1965-66	42	14	9	19	55	65	37	13th
1966-67	42	6	9	27	41	76	21	22nd
DIVISION TWO								
1967-68	42	24	10	8	71	43	58	3rd
1968-69	42	14	15	13	51	41	43	8th
1969-70	42	20	13	9	56	45	53	2nd
DIVISION ONE								
1970-71	42	4	15	23	34	66	23	22nd
DIVISION TWO								
1971-72	42	20	7	15	70	50	47	6th
1972-73	42	18	10	14	56	51	46	7th
1973-74	42	17	13	12	57	40	47	5th
1974-75	42	14	17	11	38	33	45	7th
1975-76	42	14	14	14	40	49	42	10th
1976-77	42	17	17	8	58	42	51	5th
1977-78	42	12	13	17	59	60	37	20th
DIVISION THREE								
1978-79	46	18	9	19	61	59	45	12th
1979-80	46	15	11	20	62	74	41	18th
1980-81	46	9	14	23	45	75	32	23rd
DIVISION FOUR								
1981-82	46	15	13	18	66	60	58	12th
1982-83	46	13	12	21	55	74	*49	21st
1983-84	46	21	9	16	70	52	72	6th
1984-85	46	24	14	8	73	39	86	2nd
DIVISION THREE								
1985-86	46	17	12	17	66	55	63	12th
1986-87	46	16	16	14	74	59	64	9th
1987-88	46	17	14	15	71	63	65	10th
1988-89	46	14	13	19	56	58	55	19th
1989-90	46	10	16	20	49	73	46	23rd
DIVISION FOUR								
1990-91	46	23	10	13	78	47	79	5th
1991-92	42	22	10	10	71	45	76	4th

*2 points deducted

Summary of League Records

DIVISION ONE	1134	405	273	456	1733	1863
DIVISION TWO	1694	650	409	635	2440	2446
DIVISION THREE	368	116	105	147	484	516
DIVISION FOUR	272	118	68	86	413	317
TOTAL	3468	1289	855	1324	5070	5142

1896-97

Manager: None

1	Sep	5	(a)	Lincoln C	L 1-3	Mount	1,500
2		12	(a)	Darwen	W 3-2	Donnelly 2, Mount	
3		19	(h)	Burton W	W 5-0	Connor, Donnelly, Stirzaker, Mount, Clarkin	3,000
4		26	(h)	Manchester C	D 2-2	J.Parkinson, Bowman	4,000
5	Oct	3	(a)	Leicester F	L 1-2	Donnelly	6,000
6		17	(h)	Newton Heath	W 4-2	Mount, J.Parkinson 2, Martin	5,000
7		24	(a)	Burton S	D 2-2	Martin, J.Parkinson	3,000
8	Nov	7	(a)	Manchester C	L 2-4	J.Parkinson, Martin	4,000
9		14	(h)	Lincoln C	W 3-1	Birkett, Mount, Clarkin	1,500
10		28	(h)	Notts C	W 3-2	Stirzaker, Martin 2	2,200
11	Dec	19	(a)	W Arsenal	L 2-4	R.Parkinson, Donnelly	6,000
12		26	(a)	Newton Heath	L 0-2		10,000
13	Jan	1	(h)	Grimsby T	W 1-0	Norris	5,000
14		4	(h)	W Arsenal	D 1-1	Martin	1,000
15		16	(a)	Newcastle U	L 1-4	Bowman	8,000
16		23	(h)	Small Heath	L 1-3	Bradshaw	2,000
17		30	(a)	Loughborough T	L 1-4	Stirzaker	
18	Feb	13	(h)	Walsall	W 3-2	J.Parkinson, Clarke, Parr	1,000
19		20	(a)	Grimsby T	D 2-2	Martin, Clarke	5,000
20		27	(h)	Leicester F	W 3-0	Bradshaw, J.Parkinson, Clarke	
21	Mar	6	(a)	Small Heath	W 3-1	Clarke, J.Parkinson, Martin	5,000
22		13	(h)	Newcastle U	W 4-1	J.Parkinson, Clarkin 2, Bradshaw	3,000
23		20	(a)	Notts C	L 1-3	Bradshaw	7,000
24		27	(h)	Loughborough T	W 4-1	Clarke 2, Bradshaw, Clarkin	2,500
25		29	(a)	Burton W	L 1-3	Martin	
26	Apr	3	(a)	Gainsborough T	L 0-2		
27		10	(a)	Walsall	L 0-2		
28		16	(h)	Darwen	W 1-0	J.Parkinson	5,000
29		19	(h)	Burton S	W 3-0	J.Parkinson 2, Martin	3,000
30		24	(h)	Gainsborough T	D 1-1	Clarkin	3,000

FINAL LEAGUE POSITION: 8th in Division Two

Appearances

Goals

Douglas	Parr	Bowman	Stuart	Stirzaker	Norris	Clarkin	Donnelly	Parkinson J	Parkinson R	Mount	Connor	Thompson	Martin	Birkett	Colville	Gillett	Bradshaw	Winstanley	Clarke	Scarr	
1	2	3	4	5	6	7	8	9	10	11											1
1	2	3	6	5	4	7	8	10		11	9										2
1	2	3	4	5	6	7	8	10		11	9										3
1	2	3	4	5	6	7	8	10		11	9										4
1	2	3	4	5	6	11	10	9		7	8										5
1	2	3	4	5	6	7	8	9		11			10								6
1	2	3	4	5	6	7	8	9		11			10								7
1	2	3	4	5	6	7	8	9		11			10								8
1	2	3	4	5	6	7	8	9		11				10							9
1	2	3	4	5	6	7	8	9	10				11								10
1	2	3	4	5	6		8	9	11				10								11
1	2	3	4	5	6	7	8		9				11				10				12
1	2	3	4	5	6	7	8		9				11				10				13
1	2	3		5	6	7		9	10				11		4	8					14
1	2	3		5	6	7	8	9	10				11		4						15
1		3		5	6	7		9	8			2	11		4		10				16
1	2	3	4	5	6								11		9	7	10	8			17
1	2	3	4	5	6	7		10					8				11		9		18
1	2	3	4	5	6	7		10					8				11		9		19
1	2	3	4	5	6	7		10									11	8	9		20
1	2	3	4	5	6	7		10					8				11		9		21
1	2	3	4	5	6	7		10					8				11		9		22
1	2	3	4	5	6	7		10					8				11		9		23
1	2	3	4	5	6	7		10					8				11		9		24
1	2	3		5	6	7		10					8		4		11		9		25
1	2	3		4	6	7		10				5	8				11		9		26
1	2	3		4	6	7		10				5	8				11		9		27
1	2	3			6	7		10				5	8				11		9	4	28
1	2	3			6	7		10				5	8				11		9	4	29
1	2	3			6	7		10				5	8				11		9	4	30
30	29	30	21	27	30	28	14	27	8	9	4	6	23	1	5	2	17	2	13	3	
	1	2		3	1	6	5	12	1	5	1		10	1			5		6		

1897-98

Manager: None

1	Sep	4	(a)	Burnley	L 1-5	Opp own-goal	2,000
2		11	(h)	Burnley	D 1-1	Martin	4,000
3		18	(h)	Manchester C	L 0-2		3,000
4		25	(a)	Newton Heath	L 0-1		3,000
5	Oct	2	(a)	Gainsborough T	L 1-4	Halsall	
6		9	(h)	Burton S	W 2-1	Cox 2	1,000
7		16	(h)	Small Heath	W 4-1	Clarkin, Cox 2, Birkett	1,500
8		23	(a)	Newcastle U	L 0-2		7,000
9	Nov	6	(a)	Leicester F	L 1-4	Martin	6,000
10		13	(a)	Darwen	L 1-3	Martin	2,000
11		27	(a)	W Arsenal	L 1-2	Martin	6,500
12		29	(a)	Luton T	L 1-3	Clarkin	
13	Dec	18	(h)	Gainsborough T	W 5-0	Cox, Stirzaker, Parkinson, Opp own-goals 2	
14		25	(h)	Newcastle U	L 2-3	Cox 2	3,000
15		27	(a)	Walsall	L 0-6		
16	Jan	1	(h)	W Arsenal	D 3-3	Cox 2, Birkett	1,500
17		8	(h)	Leicester F	W 2-1	Parkinson, Martin	3,000
18		15	(h)	Newton Heath	L 0-4		4,000
19		29	(a)	Small Heath	W 3-2	Parkinson, Martin, Cox	6,000
20	Feb	5	(a)	Lincoln C	L 2-3	Wilson, Birkett	
21		19	(h)	Lincoln C	W 5-0	Birkett 2, Cox 2, Parkinson	1,000
22		26	(a)	Burton S	L 1-2	Birkett	
23	Mar	19	(a)	Grimsby T	L 0-3		4,000
24		26	(a)	Loughborough T	W 2-0	Birkett, Leadbetter	
25		30	(a)	Manchester C	D 3-3	Clarkin, Parkinson 2	1,000
26	Apr	2	(h)	Walsall	D 1-1	Martin	
27		8	(h)	Darwen	W 1-0	Clarkin	4,000
28		16	(h)	Grimsby T	D 1-1	Leadbetter	1,000
29		23	(h)	Loughborough T	W 4-0	Parkinson 2, Birkett, Leadbetter	300
30		30	(h)	Luton T	W 1-0	Clarkin	200

FINAL LEAGUE POSITION: 11th in Division Two

Appearances

Goals

Douglas	Parr	Bowman	McHardie	Stirzaker	Norris	Clarkin	Martin	Wilson	Keach	Halsall	Parkinson	Leadbetter	Stuart	Cox	Birkett	Cardwell	Scarr	Banks	
1	2	3	4	5	6	7	8	9	10	11									1
1	2	3	4	5	6		7	9	10		8	11							2
1	2	3	4	5		7	8	9	4	10		11							3
1	2	3		5	6	7	8		4	10	9	11							4
1	2	3		5		7		8	6	9	10		4	11					5
1	2	3		5	6	7	8		4	9	10			11					6
1	2	3	6	5		7	8		4			10		11	9				7
1	2	3	6	5		7	8		4		9	10		11					8
1	2		6	5		7	8	10	9				4	11		3			9
1	2		6	5		7	8	10	2				4	11	9				10
1	2		5		6	7	10	8	3		9		4	11					11
1	2		5		6	7	10	8	3		9		4	11					12
1	2		5	3	6	7	10	8			9		4	11					13
1			5	3	6	7	2	8	4		9	10		11					14
1			5	3	6	7	2	8	4		9	10		11					15
1	2		5		6	7	4	8				11		9	10	3			16
1	2		5		6	7	8	4	9		10			11		3			17
1	2		5	3	6	7	8	4	9		10			11					18
1	2		5	3	6	7	9	4			10			11	8				19
1	2		5	3	6	7	9	4			10			11	8				20
1	2		5	3	6	7	9	4			10			11	8				21
1	2		5	3	6	7	9	4			10	11			8				22
1	2		5	3	6	7	9	4			10	11			8				23
1	2		5	3	6	7	9	4			10	11			8				24
1	2		5	3	4	7	9	6			10	11	8						25
1	2		5	3	6	7	9	4			10	11			8				26
1	2		5	3	6	7	9	4			10	11			8				27
1	2			5	6		9				10	11	8		7	3	4		28
1	2				5		9				10	11	8		7	4	3		*29
1	2			5			9				10	11	8		7	4	3	6	30
30	28	8	24	25	23	26	29	23	16	5	24	17	10	17	14	6	3	1	
				1		5	7	1		1	8	3		12	8				

3 own-goals. *Match started with only ten players.

1898-99

Manager: None

No	Month	Day	Venue	Opponents	Result	Score	Scorers	Attendance
1	Sep	3	(a)	Glossop	L	1-4	Opp own-goal	
2		10	(h)	Walsall	L	1-2	Leadbetter	1,000
3		17	(a)	Burton S	L	1-3	Parkinson	3,000
4		24	(h)	Burslem P.Vale	L	0-4		1,000
5	Oct	8	(h)	Loughborough T	W	2-1	Birkett 2	500
6		22	(a)	Grimsby T	L	1-2	Birkett	4,000
7	Nov	5	(a)	New Brighton T	L	0-4		500
8		12	(h)	Lincoln C	W	3-0	Stirzaker, Birkett 2	1,000
9		26	(h)	Luton T	L	2-3	Cartmell, Leadbetter	500
10	Dec	3	(a)	Leicester F	L	0-4		4,000
11		10	(a)	Newton Heath	L	1-3	Birkett	4,000
12		17	(a)	Gainsborough T	L	0-7		
13		24	(h)	Manchester C	L	2-4	Hateley, Hoyle	1,000
14		26	(a)	Small Heath	L	0-5		4,000
15		31	(h)	Glossop	L	1-2	Parkinson	
16	Jan	7	(a)	Walsall	L	0-6		
17		14	(h)	Burton S	W	3-0	Parkinson 2, Scott (pen)	2,000
18		21	(a)	Burslem P.Vale	L	1-6	Parkinson	
19	Feb	4	(a)	Loughborough T	W	3-1	Scott, Birkett 2	5,000
20		11	(a)	Barnsley	L	1-2	Stuart	
21		18	(h)	Grimsby T	L	3-6	Birkett 2, Parkinson	4,000
22	Mar	4	(h)	New Brighton T	L	1-2	Parkinson	
23		8	(h)	Small Heath	D	1-1	Scott	1,000
24		11	(a)	Lincoln C	D	0-0		
25		15	(h)	Barnsley	W	3-1	Parkinson, Gamble 2	600
26		18	(a)	W Arsenal	L	0-6		3,000
27		22	(h)	W Arsenal	D	1-1	Gamble	1,000
28		25	(a)	Luton T	L	2-3	Leadbetter, Birkett	
29		31	(h)	Darwen	W	6-0	Parkinson, Parr, Morris 2, Birkett, Williams	
30	Apr	1	(h)	Leicester F	D	2-2	Scott, Morris	
31		3	(a)	Newton Heath	L	0-1		3,000
32		8	(a)	Darwen	W	2-0	Leadbetter, Morris	
33		15	(h)	Gainsborough T	W	4-0	Leadbetter 2, Birkett 2	
34		22	(a)	Manchester C	L	1-4	Birkett	10,000

FINAL LEAGUE POSITION: 16th in Division Two (failed re-election)

Appearances

Goals

Fletcher	Stirzaker	Scott	Scarr	Howson	Mayor	Harrison	Jones	Leadbetter	Birkett	Parkinson	Dickson	Cartmell	Gosling	Banks	Exton	Williams	Harrison F	Harrison W	Parr	Hoyle	Stuart	Nightingale	Hateley	Dewhurst	Elston	Eaves	Atherton	Gamble	Kirkham	Morris	
1	2	3	4	6	5	7	10	11	8	9																					1
1	2	3	4	6	5	7	10	11	8	9																					2
1	2	3	4	5			10	11	7	9	6	8																			3
1	2	3	4	6				11	7	9			5	8	10																4
1	2	3		4				11	9	10		7		8		5	6														5
1	2	3		4				11	9	10				8		5	6	7													6
1	5	3		4				11	7	10				8		9			2	6											7
1	5	3		4				11	9	10		7		8					2	6											8
1	5	3		6				11		10		7		9		8			2	4											9
1	3	9		7				11	8	10						5			2	4	6										10
1	3	9		7				11	8	10						5			2	4	6										11
1	3	9		8				11		10						5			2	4	6	7									12
1	4	3						11	9	8						5			2	7	6		10								13
1	4	3						11	9	8						5			2	7	6		10								14
	4	3						11	9	8						5			2	7	6		10	1							15
	4	3		9				11		8						5			2	7	6		10	1							16
1	3	8						11	9	10				7		5			2		6	4									17
1	3	8						11	9	10				7		5			2			4									*18
1	3	8						11	9	10				7		5			2		6	4									19
1	3	8						11	9	10				7		5			2		6	4									20
1	3	10		6					9	8						5			2	4					11	7					21
1	3	8						11	9	10						5			2	4						7	6				22
1	3	10						11		9						5			2		6					8	4	7			23
1	3	8						11	9	10						5			2	4							6				24
1		3						11		10						5			2		6				7		4	8	9		25
1		3						11		10						5			2		6				7		4	8	9		26
1	5	3						11		10									2	4							6	8	9		27
1	5	3						11	9	10									2	4					7		6	8			28
1		3						11	8	10						5			2	4					7		6			9	29
1	5	3						11		10									2	4					7		6	8		9	30
1	5	3						11		10									2	4					7		6	8		9	31
1	5	3						11		10									2	4					7		6	8		9	32
1	5	3						11	9	10									2	4					7		6	8			33
1	5	3						11	8	10									2	4					7		6			9	34
32	31	34	4	14	2	2	3	33	24	34	1	4	1	10	1	22	2	1	28	21	13	5	4	2	10	3	13	9	3	5	
	1	4						6	15	9		1				1			1	1	1		1					3		4	

1 own-goal

*Played with only ten players

1900-01

Manager: None

1	Sep	1	(a)	New Brighton T	D 0-0		3,000
2		8	(h)	Gainsborough T	D 1-1	Birkett	'Good'
3		15	(a)	Walsall	W 2-1	Birkett, Evans	5,000
4		22	(h)	Burton S	W 2-0	Stirzaker, Birkett	2,000
5		29	(a)	Barnsley	W 1-0	Evans	4,000
6	Oct	6	(h)	W Arsenal	D 1-1	Hardman	4,000
7		13	(h)	Chesterfield	D 1-1	Parkinson	1,000
8		20	(a)	Stockport C	W 1-0	Birkett	4,500
9		27	(h)	Small Heath	D 0-0		'Good'
10	Nov	10	(h)	Lincoln C	W 2-0	Birkett 2	
11		24	(h)	Glossop	D 0-0		1,500
12	Dec	1	(a)	Middlesbrough	L 1-3	Leadbetter	10,000
13		8	(h)	Burnley	L 0-1		3,500
14		15	(a)	Burslem P.Vale	L 0-4		
15		22	(h)	Leicester F	W 1-0	Birkett	2,000
16		26	(a)	Newton Heath	L 0-4		10,000
17		29	(h)	New Brighton T	L 1-2	Evans	2,000
18	Jan	5	(a)	Gainsborough T	W 3-1	Hardman, Birchall, Stirzaker	
19		12	(h)	Walsall	W 1-0	Evans	920
20		19	(a)	Burton S	W 2-1	Birkett, Stirzaker	
21		26	(a)	Grimsby T	L 0-2		
22	Feb	16	(a)	Chesterfield	L 0-2		
23		23	(h)	Stockport C	W 3-0	Parkinson, Stirzaker (pen), Birchall	2,000
24	Mar	2	(a)	Small Heath	L 1-10	Anderson	5,000
25		9	(h)	Grimsby T	L 0-1		2,000
26		16	(a)	Lincoln C	L 0-3		
27		20	(h)	Barnsley	D 1-1	Birkett	500
28		23	(h)	Newton Heath	L 1-2	Birkett	1,000
29		30	(a)	Glossop	L 0-6		
30	Apr	5	(h)	Burslem P.Vale	W 2-1	Stirzaker, Parkinson	800
31		6	(h)	Middlesbrough	W 3-0	Anderson, Parkinson, Opp own-goal	2,000
32		8	(a)	W Arsenal	L 1-3	Stirzaker	6,000
33		9	(a)	Leicester F	L 1-3	Parkinson	3,000
34		13	(a)	Burnley	L 0-4		2,000

FINAL LEAGUE POSITION: 12th in Division Two

Appearances

Goals

Dorrington	Boulton	Burden	Threlfall	Stirzaker	Birchall	Speight	Baxendale	Birkett	Parkinson	Evans	Hardman	Howson	Scott	Leadbetter	Anderson	Taylor	Jones	
1	2	3	4	5	6	7	8	9	10	11								1
1	2	3	4	5	6	7		9	10	8	11							2
1	2	3	4	5	6	7	8	9	10	11								3
1	2	3	4	5	6	7	8	9	10	11								4
1	2	3	4	5	6	7	8		9	10	11							5
1	2	3	4	5	6		8	9	10	11	7							6
1	2	3	4	5	6		7	9	8	10	11							7
1	2	3	4	5	6		8	7	9	10	11							8
1	2	3	4	5	6		8	7	9	10	11							9
1	2	3	4	5	6			9	10	8	11	7						10
1	2	3	4	5	6			8	9	10	11	7						11
1	2	3	4	5	6			9		8		7	10	11				12
1	2	3	4	5	6			9	10	8		7		11				13
1	2	3	4	5	6			9	10	8		7		11				14
1		3	4	5	6			9	8	10	7		2	11				15
1	2	3	4	5			10		8	11			6	7				16
1	6	3	4	5				9	8	11	7		2	10				17
1	6	3	4	5				9	8	11	7		2	10				18
1	4	3		5	6			9	8	11	7		2	10				19
1	2	3		5	6			9	8	11	7		4	10				20
1	2			5	6			9	8	11	7	4	3	10				21
1	2			5	6			9	8	11	7	4	3	10				22
1	2		7	5	6			9	8	10	11	4	3					23
1	2	3	4	5	6			9	10	11	7				8			24
1	2	3	4	5	6			9	10	11	7				8			25
1	2	3	4		6			9	10	11	7		5		8			26
1	2	3	4	5				8	10	11	7		9		6			27
1	2		4	5	6			9	10		7		3	11		8		28
1	7	3	4	5	6		8	9			11		2		10			29
1	7	3	4	5	6		8		9		11		2		10			30
1		3	4	10	6			9	5		7		2		11	8		31
1		3	4	5	6			9	10		7		2	11		8		32
1		3	4	5	6			9	10		7		2	11		8		33
1		3	4	5	6			9	10		7		2	11			8	34
34	29	30	30	33	30	5	11	32	32	27	27	8	19	15	7	4	1	
				6	2			10	5	4	2			1	2			

1 own-goal

1901-02

Manager: None

1	Sep	7	(h)	Bristol C	L 0-2		4,000
2		14	(a)	Burton W	D 1-1	Foster	3,000
3		21	(a)	Stockport C	L 1-3	Birkett	
4		28	(h)	Newton Heath	L 2-4	Anderson 2	3,300
5	Oct	5	(a)	Glossop	L 1-3	Brooks	
6		12	(h)	Doncaster R	W 3-1	Evans, Hardman, Anderson	1,000
7		19	(a)	Lincoln C	D 0-0		4,000
8		26	(h)	West Brom A	D 2-2	Foster, Hardman	5,000
9	Nov	9	(h)	Barnsley	W 2-1	Stirzaker, Birkett	3,000
10		23	(h)	Preston NE	L 1-4	Foster	6,000
11		30	(a)	Burnley	L 0-2		600
12	Dec	21	(h)	Gainsborough T	W 3-0	Foster, Evans, Stirzaker	1,500
13		25	(a)	W Arsenal	D 0-0		5,000
14		28	(a)	Middlesbrough	L 1-2	Parkinson	8,000
15	Jan	1	(h)	Burslem P.Vale	W 1-0	Anderson	4,000
16		4	(a)	Bristol C	L 0-3		2,000
17		11	(h)	Burton W	W 1-0	Parkinson	2,200
18		18	(h)	Stockport C	W 1-0	Parkinson	3,300
19		25	(a)	Newton Heath	W 1-0	Anderson	3,000
20	Feb	1	(h)	Glossop	D 1-1	Threlfall	2,000
21		8	(a)	Doncaster R	L 3-4	Anderson, Parkinson, Anderton	1,500
22		15	(h)	Lincoln C	W 3-0	Anderson 2, Anderton	
23		22	(a)	West Brom A	L 2-7	Anderson 2	7,000
24	Mar	1	(h)	W Arsenal	L 1-3	Parkinson	'Good'
25		8	(a)	Barnsley	L 0-2		
26		15	(a)	Leicester F	L 0-1		
27		22	(a)	Preston NE	D 1-1	Boulton	3,000
28		28	(h)	Leicester F	W 4-0	Anderson, Foster 2, Parkinson	3,000
29		29	(h)	Burnley	W 2-1	Anderton, Anderson	6,000
30		31	(a)	Chesterfield	L 1-3	Anderton	
31	Apr	5	(a)	Burslem P.Vale	W 1-0	Scott	100
32		12	(h)	Chesterfield	D 0-0		
33		19	(a)	Gainsborough T	L 0-3		
34		26	(h)	Middlesbrough	L 0-2		2,000

FINAL LEAGUE POSITION: 12th in Division Two

Appearances

Goals

Match	Stirzaker	Scott	Burden	Brooks	Threlfall	Birchall	Hardman	Anderson	Birkett	Foster	Evans	Higginson	Boulton	Dorrington	Gillett	Parkinson	Anderton	Allen	Barcroft	Billington
1	1	2	3	4	5	6	7	8	9	10	11									
2	5	8	3		4	6	7		9	10	11	1	2							
3	5	3		8	4	6	7		9	10	11	1	2							
4	5	3			4	6	7	8	9	10	11	1	2							
5	5	3		7		6	11	4	9	10			2	1	8					
6	5	3			4	6	7	8		10	11		2	1	9					
7	5	3			4	6	11	8	7	9			2	1		10				
8	5	3			4	6	11	8	7	9			2	1		10				
9	5	3			4	6	11		7	8			2	1	9	10				
10	5	3			4	6	7		9	8	11		2	1		10				
11	5	3			4	6	11	8	7	9	10		2	1						
12	5	3			4	6		8		10	11		2	1		9	7			
13	5	3			4	6		8		10	11		2	1		9	7			
14	5	3			4	6		8	11				2	1		9	7	10		
15	5	3			4	6	11	8	9				2	1		10	7			
16	5	3				6		4	7	11			2	1		9	8	10		
17	5	3			4	6	11	8		7	10		2	1		9				
18	5	3			4	6	7			10	11		2	1		9		8		
19	5	3			4	6		8		10	11		2	1		9	7			
20	5	3			4	6		8	10		11		2	1		9	7			
21	5	3			4	6		8	2	10	11		2	1		9	7			
22	5	3			4	6		8	2	11				1		9	7	10		
23	5	3			4	6		8	2	11				1		9	7	10		
24	5	3			4	6		8	10		11		2	1		9	7			
25	5	3			4	6		8			11		2	1		9	7	10		
26	5	3			4	6		10	2		11					9	8		1	7
27		3			4	6		8	2	10	11		5	1		9	7			
28	5	3			4	6		8	2	11	10			1		9	7			
29	5	3			4	6		8	2	11	10			1		9	7			
30	5	3			4	6		8	2	11	10			1		9	7			
31		5	3		4	6		8		11	10		2	1		9	7			
32		5			4	6		8	3	11	10		2	1		9	7			
*33		5			4	6		8	3	11			2	1		9	7			
34		10	3		4	6		8	5	11			2	1		9	7			
	29	34	4	3	32	34	14	29	26	28	23	3	27	29	3	27	21	6	1	1
	2	1		1	1		2	12	2	6	2		1			6	4			

*Played with only ten players

1902-03

Manager: None

1	Sep	6	(a)	Burslem P.Vale	D 1-1	Heywood	3,500
2		13	(h)	Barnsley	D 3-3	Anderson 3 (1 pen)	2,000
3		20	(a)	Gainsborough T	D 0-0		
4		27	(h)	Burton W	D 3-3	Anderson, Parkinson, Duckworth	2,000
5	Oct	11	(h)	Glossop	D 2-2	Parkinson, Cookson	2,000
6		25	(h)	Stockport C	W 2-0	Birchall, Opp own-goal	1,500
7	Nov	8	(a)	W Arsenal	L 1-2	Threlfall	8,000
8		22	(a)	Lincoln C	W 2-0	Parkinson, Anderson	
9		29	(h)	Small Heath	L 0-1		3,500
10	Dec	6	(a)	Leicester F	L 1-2	Cookson	2,000
11		13	(h)	Manchester C	L 0-3		4,000
12		20	(a)	Burnley	D 1-1	Cookson	600
13		25	(h)	Doncaster R	W 4-0	Hardman 2, Parkinson, Anderton	4,000
14		26	(a)	Manchester U	D 2-2	Heywood 2	
15		27	(h)	Preston NE	D 2-2	Heywood, Cookson	4,000
16	Jan	1	(h)	Bristol C	L 0-1		3,000
17		3	(h)	Burslem P.Vale	L 2-5	Anderson, Cookson	1,000
18		10	(a)	Barnsley	L 0-6		
19		17	(h)	Gainsborough T	W 4-0	Anderson 2, Hardman, Anderton	800
20		24	(a)	Burton W	L 0-2		3,000
21		31	(a)	Bristol C	W 1-0	Cookson	4,600
22	Feb	7	(h)	Burnley	W 2-0	Scott (pen), Hardman	600
23		14	(h)	Manchester U	W 2-0	Cookson, Threlfall	3,000
24		17	(a)	Glossop	L 0-1		2,000
25		21	(a)	Stockport C	L 0-4		
26		28	(a)	Chesterfield	D 1-1	Anderton	
27	Mar	7	(h)	W Arsenal	D 0-0		2,000
28		14	(a)	Doncaster R	L 0-3		2,100
29		21	(h)	Lincoln C	L 2-3	Hardman, Parkinson	1,500
30		28	(a)	Small Heath	L 1-5	Hardman	7,000
31	Apr	4	(h)	Leicester F	W 2-0	Duckworth 2	'Poor'
32		10	(a)	Preston NE	L 1-3	Scott (pen)	
33		11	(a)	Manchester C	L 0-2		4,000
34		13	(h)	Chesterfield	W 2-1	Cookson, Parkinson	3,000

FINAL LEAGUE POSITION: 14th in Division Two

Appearances

Goals

Dorrington	Birkett	Scott	Threlfall	Anderson	Birchall	Duckworth	Cookson	Parkinson	Heywood	Hardman	Stirzaker	Anderton	Wolstenholme	Wright	Parr	Evans	Hull	
1	2	3	4	5	6	7	8	9	10	11								1
1	2	3	4	8	6	7	9		10	11	5							2
1	2	3	4	8	6	7	9		10	11	5							3
1	2	3		5	6	7	8	9	10	11		4						4
1		3	2	5	6		8	9	10	11		7	4					5
1	2	3	4	8	6			9	10	11		7	5					6
1	2	3	4	5	6		8	9	10	11		7						7
	2	3	4	5	6		8	9	10	11		7		1				8
	2			5	6		8	9	10	11		7	4	1	3			9
1	2			5	6		8	9	10	11		7	4		3			10
	2	3		5	6		8	9	10	11		7	4	1				11
	2	6		5			8	9	10	11		7	4	1	3			12
	2	3		5	6		8	9	10	11		7	4	1				13
	3	2		5	6		8	9	10	11		7	4	1				14
	3	2	4	5			8	9	10	11		7	6	1				15
1	2	3	4	5			8	9	10			7	6			11		16
1	2	3	4	5		7	8	9	10				6			11		17
		3	4	2		7	8	9	10		5		6			11	1	18
	2	3	4	8	6		9		10	11		7	5				1	19
	2	3	4		6	7	8	9	10	11			5				1	20
	2	3			6		8	9	10	11	5	7	4				1	21
	2	3	4				8	9	10	11	5	7	6				1	22
	2	3	4		5		8	9	10	11		7	6				1	23
	2	3	4		5		8	9	10	11		7	6				1	24
	2	3	4		5		8	9	10	11		7	6				1	25
1	2	3	4		5		8	9	10	11		7	6					26
		3	4	2			7	9	10	11	5	8	6				1	27
		3	4	2			7	9	10	11	5	8	6				1	28
	2	3	4		9		8	5	10	11		7	6				1	29
1	2	3	4		5		9	10		11		8	6				7	30
	2	3	4			7	9	5	10	11		8	6				1	31
	2	3	4			7	9	5	10	11		8	6				1	32
	2	3	4			7	8	9	10		5	11	6				1	33
	2	3	4				8	9	10	11	5	7	6				1	34
12	30	32	26	21	22	10	33	31	33	30	9	28	28	7	3	3	16	
		2	2	8	1	3	8	6	4	6		3						

1 own-goal

1903-04

Manager: None

1	Sep	5	(a)	W Arsenal	L 0-3		12,000
2		12	(h)	Barnsley	L 0-2		4,000
3		19	(a)	Lincoln C	D 0-0		
4		26	(h)	Stockport C	W 4-1	Pentland, Rooke, Scott (pen), Parkinson	2,500
5	Oct	3	(a)	Chesterfield	L 1-2	Pentland	
6		10	(h)	Bolton W	L 1-4	Pentland	7,000
7		17	(a)	Burnley	W 4-1	Pentland 2, Anderson, Threlfall	3,000
8		24	(h)	Preston NE	L 0-3		6,000
9	Nov	7	(h)	Leicester F	L 1-2	Carthy	2,500
10		21	(a)	Gainsborough T	L 1-3	Anderton	
11	Dec	5	(a)	Bristol C	L 0-5		
12		19	(a)	Glossop	W 1-0	Bennett	
13		25	(h)	Glossop	W 3-2	Anderson 2, Bennett	3,500
14		26	(h)	Bradford C	L 0-1		
15	Jan	1	(a)	Bolton W	L 0-3		11,000
16		2	(h)	W Arsenal	D 2-2	Jackson (og), McEwan	4,000
17		9	(a)	Barnsley	D 2-2	Bennett 2	
18		16	(h)	Lincoln C	W 2-1	Scott, Parkinson	
19		23	(a)	Stockport C	L 1-2	Birkett	
20		30	(h)	Chesterfield	D 0-0		700
21	Feb	13	(h)	Burnley	L 0-5		1,500
22		20	(h)	Burton U	W 4-1	Anderson 3, Bennett	
23		27	(h)	Grimsby T	W 3-0	Birkett (pen), Bennett, Scott (pen)	200
24	Mar	5	(a)	Leicester F	L 1-5	Bennett	
25		9	(h)	Manchester U	W 2-1	Rooke, Bennett	1,000
26		12	(a)	Burslem P.Vale	L 0-5		
27		19	(h)	Gainsborough T	W 2-1	Bennett, Threlfall	500
28		26	(a)	Burton U	D 1-1	Rooke	
29	Apr	1	(h)	Burslem P.Vale	W 1-0	Anderson	1,500
30		2	(h)	Bristol C	L 0-1		1,000
31		4	(a)	Grimsby T	L 0-4		4,500
32		9	(a)	Manchester U	L 1-3	Spencer	10,000
33		23	(a)	Bradford C	W 2-0	Rooke 2	7,000
34		30	(a)	Preston NE	L 0-1		

FINAL LEAGUE POSITION: 15th in Division Two

Appearances
Goals

Hull A	Birkett R	Scott J	Threlfall	Wolstenholme T	Pickford P	Anderton W	Rooke J	Pentland F	Parkinson J	Bennett C	Davies J	Jones J	Anderson G	Carthy J	Hughes D	Miller P	Swarbrick L	McEwan M	Killean E	Whittle H	Hodgson J	Anderson T	Spencer S	
1	2	3	4	5	6	7	8	9	10	11														1
1	2	3	4	6		7	8	9	5	10	11													2
1	2	3	4	5		7	8	9	10	11		6												3
1	2	3	4	5		7	8	9	10	11		6												4
1	2	3	4	5		7	8	9	10	11		6												5
1	2	3	4	5		7	8	9	10	11		6												6
1	2	3	4	5		7	8	9		11		6	10											7
1	2	3	4	5		7	8	9		11		6	10											8
1	2	3	4	5		7	8			11		6	10	9										9
1	2	3				8				10		4	5	9	6	7	11							10
1	2	3	4	6		10	8					5		9		7		11						11
1	2	3		4		7			5	10		6	8	9				11						12
1	2	3		4		7			5	10		6	8	9				11						13
1		2		4		7			5	10		6	8	9				11	3					14
1	2		4			7	6		5			10	8	9				11	3					15
1	2	3	4			7	8		5	10		6		9				11						16
1	2	3	4			7			5	10			8					11	6	9				17
1	2	3	4						5	10			8	9		7		11	6					18
1	2	3	4	6		7			5	10			8	9				11						19
1	2	3	4	6		7			5	9		10	8					11						20
1	2	3	4	6		7			5	9		10	8					11						21
	2	3	4	6		7	8		5	11		1	10							9				22
	2	3	4	6		7	8		5	11			10							9	1			23
	2	3	4	6		7	8		5	11			10							9	1			24
1	2	3	4	6		7	8		5	9				10				11						25
1		3	4	2		7	8		5	9				10				11	6					26
1	2	3	4	6		7			5	9			10	8				11						27
1	2	3	4	6		7	8		5	9			10					11						28
1	2	3	4	6		7	8		5	9			10					11						29
1	2	3	4	6		7	8		5	9								11				10		30
1	2	3	4	6		7	8		5					9				11				10		31
1	2	3	4	6		7			5	10				9				11					8	32
1	2	3	4	6		7	8		5	9			10					11						33
1	2	3	4	6		7	8		5				10	9				11						34
31	32	33	30	29	1	33	23	8	29	30	1	17	21	16	1	3	1	21	5	4	2	2	1	
	2	3	1			1	5	5	2	9			7	1				1					1	

1 own-goal

1904-05

Manager: None

1	Sep	3	(h)	Leicester F	D 0-0		4,300
2		5	(a)	Burslem P.Vale	D 2-2	Hogg, Chadwick	
3		10	(a)	Barnsley	L 1-2	Chadwick	3,000
4		17	(h)	West Brom A	D 0-0		5,000
5		24	(a)	Burnley	W 1-0	Kearns	4,000
6	Oct	1	(h)	Grimsby T	D 1-1	Chadwick	3,500
7		8	(a)	Bolton W	L 0-3		10,000
8		15	(a)	Doncaster R	D 0-0		3,000
9		22	(h)	Gainsborough T	D 2-2	Hogg 2	1,500
10	Nov	5	(h)	Liverpool	L 0-3		5,500
11		7	(a)	West Brom A	L 2-4	Birkett (pen), Waddington	4,951
12		19	(h)	Bristol C	L 2-4	Scott, Hogg	4,000
13	Dec	3	(h)	Glossop	W 4-1	Kearns, Chadwick, Birkett (pen), Waddington	
14		17	(h)	Bradford C	W 2-0	Wilson (og), Waddington	2,000
15		24	(a)	Lincoln C	L 0-1		
16		26	(a)	Burton U	D 0-0		
17		31	(a)	Leicester F	L 1-3	Scott (pen)	
18	Jan	7	(h)	Barnsley	W 6-0	Chadwick 2, Morgan, Kearns, Parkinson, Threlfall	
19		21	(h)	Burnley	W 2-0	Morgan, Waddington	3,000
20		28	(a)	Grimsby T	L 0-2		3,000
21	Feb	11	(h)	Doncaster R	W 1-0	Birkett	2,000
22		18	(a)	Gainsborough T	D 1-1	Chadwick	
23		25	(h)	Burton U	W 1-0	Hogg	2,000
24	Mar	4	(a)	Liverpool	L 0-5		6,000
25		11	(h)	Burslem P.Vale	W 3-0	Waddington 2, Morgan	1,400
26		18	(a)	Bristol C	L 0-2		7,000
27		25	(h)	Manchester U	L 0-1		6,500
28	Apr	1	(a)	Glossop	D 0-0		
29		8	(h)	Chesterfield	D 1-1	Chadwick	
30		15	(a)	Bradford C	L 1-3	Pratt	12,000
31		21	(h)	Bolton W	L 0-2		9,500
32		22	(h)	Lincoln C	W 1-0	Pratt	3,800
33		24	(a)	Manchester U	L 1-3	Morgan	10,000
34		29	(a)	Chesterfield	L 0-2		2,000

FINAL LEAGUE POSITION: 15th in Division Two

Appearances
Goals

FA Cup

1	Jan	14	(a)	Bristol C	L 1-2	Morgan	8,000

Appearances
Goals

Hull	Birkett	Scott	Threlfall	Parkinson	Wolstenholme	Morgan	Kearns	Hogg	Chadwick	McEwan	Lowe	Gettins	Heywood	Waddington	Dorrington	Jolly	Crewdson	Cook	Pratt	Gow	Jones	Reilly	
1	2	3	4	5	6	7	8	9	10	11													1
1	2	3	4	5	6	7	8	9	10	11													2
1		3	4	5	6	7	8	9	10	11	2												3
1	2	3	4	5	6	7	8		10	11		9											4
1	2	3	4	5	6	7	8	9	10	11													5
1	2	3	4	5	6	7	8	9	10	11													6
1	2	3	4	5	6	7	8		10	11			9										7
1	2	3	4	5	6	7	8	9	10	11													8
1	2	3	4	5	6		8	9	10	11				7									9
	2	3	4	5	6	8		9	10	11				7	1								10
	2		4	5	6	8		9	10	11				7	1	3							11
	2	3		5	6	8		9	10	11				7	1		4						12
1	2	3	4	5	6		9		10	11				8				7					13
1		3	4	5	6			9	10	11	2			8				7					14
1	2	3	4	5	6			9	10	11				8				7					15
1	2	3	4	5	6			9	10	11				8				7					16
1	2	3	4	5	6		8		10	11				9				7					17
1	2	3	4	5	6	9	8		10	11								7					18
1	2	3	4	5	6	9			10	11				8				7					19
1	2	3	4	5	6	9	7		10	11				8									20
1	2	3	4	5	6	9		9	10	11				7									21
1	2	3	4	5	6	9		9	10	11						7							22
1	2	3	4	5	6	9		9	10					11		7							23
1	2	3	4	5	6	9		9	10	11						7							24
1	2	3	4	5	6	9		9	10					11		7							25
1	2	3		5	6	9	7	9	10					11			4						26
1	2	3	4	5	6		7	9	10					11					9				27
1	2	3	4	5	6			9	10										9	7	11		28
1	2	3	4	5	6	7		9	10					11					9				29
1	2	3	4	5	6	7		9	10					11					9				30
1	2	3	4	5	6	7		9	10					11					9				31
1	2	3	4	5	6	7		9	10										9			11	32
1	2	3	4	5	6	7		9	10					11					9				33
1	2	3	4	5	6			9	10					11					9	7			34
31	32	33	32	34	34	25	15	27	34	23	2	1	1	21	3	5	2	7	8	2	1	1	
	3	2	1	1		4	3	4	8					6					2				

1 own-goal

Hull	Birkett	Scott	Threlfall	Parkinson	Wolstenholme	Morgan	Kearns	Hogg	Chadwick	McEwan	Lowe	Gettins	Heywood	Waddington	Dorrington	Jolly	Crewdson	Cook	Pratt	Gow	Jones	Reilly	
1	2	3	4	5	6	9			10	11				8				7					1
1	1	1	1	1	1	1			1	1				1				1					
						1																	

1905-06

Manager: None

1	Sep	2	(h)	Burton U	W 2-0	Connor 2	3,000
2		4	(a)	Manchester U	L 1-2	Bennett	9,000
3		9	(h)	Chelsea	L 0-1		3,000
4		11	(a)	Burslem P.Vale	W 2-1	Bennett, Duckworth	
5		16	(h)	Gainsborough T	D 2-2	Bennett, Johnson	
6		23	(a)	Bristol C	L 1-2	Bennett	9,000
7		30	(h)	Manchester U	L 0-1		7,500
8	Oct	7	(a)	Glossop	L 1-4	Birkett	700
9		14	(h)	Stockport C	W 2-0	Hancock, Birkett	1,500
10		21	(a)	Grimsby T	D 1-1	Birkett (pen)	
11		28	(a)	Bradford C	L 1-2	Bate	10,000
12	Nov	4	(h)	West Brom A	L 0-3		2,500
13		11	(a)	Leicester F	L 0-2		
14		25	(a)	Lincoln C	D 1-1	Connor	
15	Dec	2	(h)	Chesterfield T	W 2-1	Duckworth, Gow	2,800
16		16	(h)	Barnsley	D 0-0		3,000
17		23	(a)	Clapton O	D 0-0		
18		25	(a)	Burnley	L 1-4	Lavery	6,000
19		30	(a)	Burton U	D 1-1	Connor	
20	Jan	1	(h)	Leeds C	L 0-3		3,000
21		6	(a)	Chelsea	L 0-6		6,000
22		20	(a)	Gainsborough T	W 1-0	Francis	
23		27	(h)	Bristol C	L 1-3	Gow	5,000
24	Feb	10	(h)	Glossop	W 1-0	Hancock	2,100
25		17	(a)	Stockport C	L 1-2	Francis	
26	Mar	3	(h)	Bradford C	D 2-2	Hancock 2	3,500
27		7	(h)	Grimsby T	W 2-0	Connor, Sanderson	2,000
28		10	(a)	West Brom A	L 0-5		6,500
29		14	(h)	Hull C	L 1-2	Francis	1,500
30		17	(h)	Leicester F	L 0-1		
31		24	(a)	Hull C	D 2-2	Parkinson, Francis	5,000
32		31	(h)	Lincoln C	W 2-0	Scott (pen), Francis	2,000
33	Apr	7	(a)	Chesterfield T	L 0-2		
34		13	(h)	Burnley	L 0-1		4,500
35		14	(h)	Burslem P.Vale	W 2-1	Hancock, Francis	
36		16	(a)	Leeds C	L 0-3		10,000
37		21	(a)	Barnsley	D 1-1	Connor	
38		28	(h)	Clapton O	W 3-0	Hancock, Threlfall, Lavery	

FINAL LEAGUE POSITION: 14th in Division Two

Appearances
Goals

FA Cup

1	Jan	13	(h)	Crystal P	D 1-1	Hancock	2,500
R		17	(a)	Crystal P	D 1-1*	Threlfall	4,000
2R		22	(n†)	Crystal P	W 1-0	Francis	2,500
2	Feb	3	(a‡)	Sheffield U	W 2-1	Hancock 2	10,219
3		24	(a)	Newcastle U	L 0-5		35,000

*After extra-time. †Played at Aston Lower Grounds, Birmingham. ‡Drawn at home, sold ground rights.

Appearances
Goals

Hull	Birkett	Scott	Threlfall	Parkinson	Raisbeck	Duckworth	Connor	Hancock	Bennett	Darlington	Johnson	Gow	Bate	Francis	Reilly	Lowe	Lavery	Crewdson	Jones	Hollingworth	Sanderson	Topping	Brown	Anderton	Musgrove	Copestake	
1	2	3	4	5	6	7	8	9	10	11																	1
1	2	3	4	5	6	7	8	9	10	11																	2
1	2	3	4	5	6	7	8	9	10	11																	3
1	2	3	4	5	6	7	8	9	10	11																	4
1	2	3	4		6		8	9	10		5	7	11														5
1	2	3	4	5	6		8	9	10			7	11														6
1	2	3	4	5	6		8	9	10			7	11														7
1	2	3	4	5	6	7	9		10			8	11														8
1	2	3	4	5	6	7	8	9	10				11														9
1	2	3	4	5	6		8	9	10			7	11														10
1	2	3	4	5	6			8	10			7	11	9													11
1	2	11	4	5	6			8	10			7		9	3												12
1	2	3	4	5	6	7	10	9				8	11														13
1	2	3	4	5		7	10	9			6	8	11														14
1	2	3	4	5		7	10	9			6	8	11														15
1		3	4	5		7	10	9			6	8	11			2											16
1		3	4	5		7	10				6	8	11			2	9										17
1		3	4	5		7	10				6	8	11			2	9										18
1		3	4	5		7	10				6	8	11			2	9										19
1		3	4	5		7	10				6	8	11			2	9										20
1		3	4	5		7	10				6	8	11			2	9										21
1	2			5	4		8					7	11	9			10	3	6								22
1	2	3	4	5			10				6	8	11				9			7							23
1		3	4	5			10	8			6	7		9				2		11							24
1		3	4	5			10	8			6	7		9				2		11							25
1		3	4	5		7	10	8			6			9				2		11							26
1		3	4	5		7	8				6			9				2		11	10						27
1		3	4	5		7	10	8			6			9				2		11							28
1		3	4	5		7	10	8			6			9				2		11							29
1		3	4	5		7		8			6			9			11	2				10					30
1		3	4	5	6		7				8			10				2				11	9				31
1		3	4	5			7				6			10				2			8	11	9				32
1		3	4	5		7	10	8			6			9				2		11							33
1		3	4	5		7	10	8			6							2		11			9				34
1			4	5		7		8			6			10				2		11				3	9		35
1	2		4	5		7	10	8			6						11							3	9		36
1	2	3	4	5			8				6		11				9								10	7	37
1	2	3	4	5				8			6		11				9								10	7	38
38	20	35	37	37	15	24	33	27	12	4	25	20	20	14	1	6	11	13	1	10	2	3	3	2	4	2	
	3	1	1	1		2	6	6	4		1	2	1	6			2				1						

Hull	Birkett	Scott	Threlfall	Parkinson	Raisbeck	Duckworth	Connor	Hancock	Bennett	Darlington	Johnson	Gow	Bate	Francis	Reilly	Lowe	Lavery	Crewdson	Jones	Hollingworth	Sanderson	Topping	Brown	Anderton	Musgrove	Copestake	
1	2	3	4	10		7	5	8			6	11		9													1
1	2	3	4	10		7	5	8			6	11		9													R
1	2	3	4	10		7	5	8			6	11		9													2R
1		3	4	5		7	10	8			6		11	9				2									2
1		3	4	5			10	8			6	7		9				2		11							3
5	3	5	5	5		4	5	5			5	4	1	5				2		1							
			1					3						1													

1906-07

Manager: None

1	Sep	1	(a)	Barnsley	L 2-3	Connor, Francis	
2		8	(h)	Chelsea	D 0-0		5,000
3		15	(a)	Wolves	D 1-1	Francis	6,000
4		22	(h)	Clapton O	L 1-3	Copestake	
5		29	(a)	Gainsborough T	L 0-2		
6	Oct	1	(a)	Burton U	D 0-0		
7		6	(h)	Stockport C	L 0-1		2,500
8		13	(a)	Hull C	L 0-3		8,000
9		20	(h)	Glossop	W 4-1	Connor 2, Threlfall, Dunkley	
10		27	(h)	Chesterfield T	D 0-0		
11	Nov	3	(a)	Bradford C	L 0-3		
12		10	(h)	West Brom A	W 2-1	Grundy, Anderton	5,772
13		17	(a)	Leicester F	L 1-5	Grundy	
14		24	(h)	Nottingham F	L 1-2	Threlfall	6,000
15	Dec	1	(a)	Lincoln C	W 1-0	Francis	2,000
16		5	(h)	Leeds C	W 1-0	Scott	1,000
17		15	(a)	Grimsby T	D 0-0		3,000
18		22	(h)	Burslem P.Vale	L 0-1		2,000
19		25	(a)	Burnley	L 1-2	Dunkley	7,000
20		29	(h)	Barnsley	L 2-3	Anderton, Grundy	2,000
21	Jan	1	(h)	Gainsborough T	W 1-0	Scott (pen)	
22		5	(a)	Chelsea	L 0-3		15,000
23		19	(h)	Wolves	L 1-2	Connor	3,000
24		26	(a)	Clapton O	D 0-0		5,000
25	Feb	2	(a)	Leeds C	D 1-1	Dunkley	5,000
26		9	(a)	Stockport C	D 0-0		
27		16	(h)	Hull C	D 1-1	Francis	1,500
28		23	(a)	Glossop	D 0-0		
29	Mar	2	(a)	Chesterfield T	W 1-0	Maples (og)	
30		9	(h)	Bradford C	W 1-0	Morris	2,000
31		16	(a)	West Brom A	L 0-3		5,500
32		23	(h)	Leicester F	W 1-0	Grundy	
33		29	(h)	Burnley	W 2-0	Grundy, Morris	7,000
34		30	(a)	Nottingham F	L 0-3		
35	Apr	6	(h)	Lincoln C	W 2-0	Grundy, Francis	2,000
36		13	(h)	Burton U	D 1-1	Grundy	2,000
37		20	(h)	Grimsby T	W 4-3	Morris 2, Grundy (pen), Threlfall	700
38		27	(a)	Burslem P.Vale	L 0-3		

FINAL LEAGUE POSITION: 13th in Division Two — Appearances / Goals

FA Cup

1	Jan	12	(a*)	West Ham U	L 1-2	Parkinson	13,000

*Drawn at home, sold ground rights. — Appearances / Goals

Wilcox	Birkett	Scott	Threlfall	Parkinson	Johnson	Copestake	Connor	Francis	Morris	Dunkley	Rimmer	Swan	Wake	Crosswaithe	Lowe	Clarke	Gow	Lavery	Bate	Crewdson	Pearson	Collier	Grundy	Anderton	
1	2	3	4	5	6	7	8	9	10	11															1
1	2	3		5	6	7			10	11	4	8	9												2
1	2	3	4	5	6	7		9	10	11		8													3
1	2	3	4	5	6	7		9	10	11		8													4
		3	4	5				9		11		8		1	2	6	7	10	11						5
1		3	4	5				9		11	2	8				6	7	10							6
1		3	4	5				9		11	2	8				6	7	10							7
1			4	5				9		11	2	8			3	6	7	10							8
1		3	4	5			8		11	10		9				6	7			2					9
1		3	4	5			8		11	10		9				6	7			2					10
1		3	4			7	8					10				6			11	2	5	9			11
1		3	4									10				6			11	2	5		7	8	12
1		3	4						8			10				6				2	5	7	9	11	13
1		3	4			7	8					10				6				2	5		9	11	14
1		3	4	5			8	9				10				6	7			2				11	15
1		3	4	5			8					10				6	7			2			9	11	16
1		3	4	5			8	10								6	7			2			9	11	17
1			4	5			8	10			3					6	7			2			9	11	18
1			4	5			8	9		10	3					6	7			2				11	19
1		3	4		5		8			10						6	7			2			9	11	20
1		3	4	5		7		8		10	2					6							9	11	21
1		3	4		5		8	9								6	7	10		2				11	22
1			4		5		8	11					9			6	7	10		2				3	23
1		3	4	5				8					9			6	7	10	11	2					24
1		3		5	4	7		9		11						6	8	10		2					25
1		3	4	5		7		10		11						6	8	9		2					26
1		3	4	5		7		10								6	8	9		2				11	27
1		3	4	5	11	7		10								6	8	9		2					28
1		3	4	5		7		10	11							6	8	9		2					29
1		3	4	5		7			10							6	8	9		2			11		30
1		3	4	5		7			10							6	8	9		2			11		31
1		3	4	5					10			8				6	7			2			11	9	32
1		3	4	5					10			8				6	7			2			11	9	33
1		3	4	5		7			10			8				6		9		2			11		34
1		3	4	5		7		8	10							6				2			9	11	35
1		3	4	5		7		8	10							6				2			9	11	36
1		3	4	5				8	10							6	7			2			9	11	37
1		3	4	5					10	11		8				6	7	9		2					38
37	4	34	36	31	9	17	13	23	17	15	7	19	3	1	2	34	26	16	4	29	4	2	16	18	
		2	3			1	4	5	4	3													8	2	

1 own-goal

Wilcox	Birkett	Scott	Threlfall	Parkinson	Johnson	Copestake	Connor	Francis	Morris	Dunkley	Rimmer	Swan	Wake	Crosswaithe	Lowe	Clarke	Gow	Lavery	Bate	Crewdson	Pearson	Collier	Grundy	Anderton	
1		3	4	5			8	10		11						6	7			2			9		1
1		1	1	1			1	1		1						1	1			1			1		
				1																					

1907-08

Manager: None

1	Sep	2	(a)	Stockport C	D	1-1	Whittingham	
2		7	(h)	Clapton O	W	5-0	Whittingham 2, Scott, Owers 2	4,500
3		14	(h)	Leeds C	L	2-3	Brindley, Parkinson	5,500
4		21	(h)	Wolves	L	0-2		5,000
5		28	(a)	Gainsborough T	L	1-2	Owers	
6	Oct	5	(h)	Stockport C	L	1-3	King	
7		12	(a)	Glossop	D	2-2	Whittingham, Grundy	
8		19	(h)	Leicester F	D	2-2	Whittingham, Grundy	
9		26	(a)	Grimsby T	D	2-2	Whittingham, Reid	4,500
10	Nov	2	(a)	Stoke	L	1-3	Parkinson	
11		9	(h)	West Brom A	L	0-1		9,145
12		16	(a)	Bradford C	L	0-3		11,000
13		23	(h)	Hull C	D	1-1	Weston	2,000
14		30	(a)	Derby C	L	1-2	Grundy	9,000
15	Dec	7	(h)	Lincoln C	W	4-3	Weston, Grundy 3 (1 pen)	
16		14	(a)	Fulham	L	0-3		10,000
17		21	(h)	Barnsley	D	1-1	Grundy	
18		25	(a)	Burnley	L	1-2	Heywood	12,000
19		26	(a)	Oldham A	L	2-3	Grundy, Gow	4,000
20		28	(a)	Chesterfield	L	2-3	Whittingham, Weston	
21	Jan	1	(h)	Oldham A	W	1-0	Grundy	5,000
22		4	(a)	Clapton O	D	1-1	Brindley	
23		18	(a)	Wolves	L	0-1		7,000
24		25	(h)	Gainsborough T	L	0-1		
25	Feb	8	(h)	Glossop	W	4-0	Whittingham 2, Weston, Grundy	
26		15	(a)	Leicester F	L	1-2	Gow	
27		29	(h)	Stoke	W	1-0	Birch	
28	Mar	7	(a)	West Brom A	L	0-3		7,000
29		14	(h)	Bradford C	W	2-1	Birch, Weston	3,000
30		21	(a)	Hull C	L	2-3	Whittingham 2	7,000
31		28	(h)	Derby C	W	1-0	Grundy	4,000
32	Apr	1	(h)	Grimsby T	W	3-0	Threlfall, Birch, Grundy	
33		4	(a)	Lincoln C	L	0-2		
34		11	(h)	Fulham	W	2-1	Whittingham, Connor	7,000
35		17	(h)	Burnley	W	1-0	Whittingham	9,500
36		18	(a)	Barnsley	D	0-0		
37		20	(a)	Leeds C	D	1-1	Cookson	7,000
38		28	(h)	Chesterfield	W	2-0	Whittingham 2	

FINAL LEAGUE POSITION: 15th in Division Two — Appearances / Goals

FA Cup

1	Jan	11	(a)	Manchester U	L	1-3	Grundy	12,000

Appearances

Goals

Tillotson	Crewdson	Scott	Threlfall	Parkinson	Clarke	Grundy	Whittingham	Owers	King	Brindley	Lowe	Rose	Gow	Cookson	Rimmer	Weston	Reid	Connor	Heywood	Waddington	Fiske	Birch	
1	2	3	4	5	6	7	8	9	10	11													1
1	2	3	4	5	6	7	8	9	10	11													2
1	2	3	4	5	6	7	8	9	10	11													3
1	2	3	4	5	6	7	8	9	10	11													4
1		3		5	6		10	9		11	2	4	7	8									5
1	2	3		5	6	7	8	9	10	11		4											6
1	4	3		5	6	7	8	9	10	11					2								7
1	6	3	4	5		7	8		10	11					2	9							8
1	6	3	4	5		7	8		10	11					2		9						9
1	6	3		5			8		10	11					2	9	7	4					10
1	6	3		5			8	9	10	11					2		7	4					11
1	6			5	3		8	9		11					2	10	7	4					12
1	4	3		5	6	9	8			11					2	10	7						13
1	4	3		5	6	9									2	10	7		8	11			14
1	4	3		5	6	9									2	10	7		8	11			15
1	4	3		5	6	9									2	10	7		8	11			16
1	4	3			6	9							7		2	10		5	8	11			17
	2	3			6		10					5	7			9		4	8	11	1		18
	2	3			6	9	10					5	7					4	8	11	1		19
	2	3			6		10					5	7			9		4	8	11	1		20
	2	3			6	9				11		5	7			10		4	8		1		21
	2			5	6					10			7		3	9		4	8	11	1		22
	2			5	6					10			7		3	9		4	8	11	1		23
	2	3		5	6	9	11						7			10		4	8		1		24
	2	3	4	5	6	9	8						7			10				11	1		25
	2	3	4	5	6		10						7			9			8		1	11	26
	2	3	4	5		9	8			7						10		6			1	11	27
	2	3	4	5		9	8			7						10		6			1	11	28
	2	3	4	5		9	8			7						10		6			1	11	29
	2	3	4	5			8						7			9		6		10	1	11	30
	2	3	4	5		9	8									10	7	6			1	11	31
	2	3	4	5		9	8									10	7	6			1	11	32
	2	3	4	5			8						7				9	6	10		1	11	33
	2	3	4	5	10	9	8										7	6			1	11	34
	2	3	4	5	10	9	8										7	6			1	11	35
	2	3	4	5	10	9	8										7	6			1	11	36
	2	3	4	5	10		8							9			7	6			1	11	37
	2	3	4	5	10	9	8										7	6			1	11	38
17	37	35	20	33	27	26	31	9	10	19	1	6	13	2	13	22	16	23	13	11	21	13	
			1	2		12	15	3	1	2			2	1		5	1	1	1			3	

Tillotson	Crewdson	Scott	Threlfall	Parkinson	Clarke	Grundy	Whittingham	Owers	King	Brindley	Lowe	Rose	Gow	Cookson	Rimmer	Weston	Reid	Connor	Heywood	Waddington	Fiske	Birch	
	2	3	4	5		9				11			7			10		6	8		1		1
	1	1	1	1		1				1			1			1		1	1		1		
						1																	

1908-09

Manager: None

1	Sep	2	(h)	Barnsley	D	1-1	R.Whittingham	4,000
2		5	(a)	Wolves	D	2-2	Reid, R.Whittingham	8,000
3		12	(h)	Oldham A	W	1-0	Weston	10,000
4		19	(a)	Clapton O	D	1-1	Weston	
5		26	(h)	Leeds C	W	1-0	Weston	5,000
6	Oct	3	(a)	Barnsley	L	0-4		
7		10	(h)	Tottenham H	D	1-1	R.Whittingham	6,000
8		17	(a)	Hull C	L	0-2		8,000
9		24	(h)	Derby C	D	2-2	Baddeley, R.Whittingham	6,000
10		31	(h)	Bolton W	L	1-2	Walker	5,500
11	Nov	7	(a)	Chesterfield	L	1-3	Walker	
12		14	(h)	Glossop	W	2-1	R.Whittingham 2	
13		21	(a)	Stockport C	L	0-1		
14		28	(h)	West Brom A	L	0-2		5,500
15	Dec	5	(a)	Birmingham	D	2-2	R.Whittingham 2 (1 pen)	6,000
16		12	(h)	Gainsborough T	W	3-0	Grundy 2, R.Whittingham	2,000
17		19	(a)	Grimsby T	L	1-2	R.Whittingham	
18		25	(a)	Burnley	D	1-1	Whalley	
19		26	(h)	Fulham	W	2-0	R.Whittingham, Beare	5,000
20	Jan	1	(a)	Bradford	L	3-4	R.Whittingham (pen), Baddeley, Lyon	12,000
21		2	(h)	Wolves	W	3-1	Grundy 2, R.Whittingham	3,000
22		9	(a)	Oldham A	L	1-3	Beare	6,000
23		23	(h)	Clapton O	L	1-3	Lyon	
24		30	(a)	Leeds C	L	0-1		8,000
25	Feb	13	(a)	Tottenham H	L	1-4	Walker	15,000
26		20	(h)	Hull C	L	2-3	Reid (pen), Baddeley	5,000
27		27	(a)	Derby C	D	1-1	Swan	3,800
28	Mar	6	(a)	Bolton W	L	1-3	Grundy	4,000
29		13	(h)	Chesterfield	D	2-2	Grundy (pen), Beare	2,000
30		20	(a)	Glossop	L	0-3		
31		27	(h)	Stockport C	W	2-1	Grundy, Beare	
32		31	(h)	Bradford	W	2-1	Beare 2	
33	Apr	3	(a)	West Brom A	L	1-5	Weston	17,426
34		9	(h)	Burnley	D	0-0		6,000
35		10	(h)	Birmingham	W	2-0	Grundy, Beare	5,000
36		12	(a)	Fulham	L	0-3		10,000
37		17	(a)	Gainsborough T	L	0-1		
38		24	(h)	Grimsby T	D	2-2	Whalley, Beare	

FINAL LEAGUE POSITION: 20th in Division Two

Appearances
Goals

FA Cup

1	Jan	16	(h)	Hastings & St Leonards	W	2-0	Whalley, Threlfall	2,000
2	Feb	6	(a)	Newcastle U	L	1-2	Weston	32,137

Appearances
Goals

Fiske	Crewdson	Scott	Threlfall	Whittingham S	Connor	Reid	Beare	Lyon	Whittingham R	Baddeley	Parkinson	Whiteside	Weston	Miller	Latheron	Swan	Stephenson	Walker	Grundy	Gladwin	Whalley	Tongue	Sterling	Clarke	Dawson	Tillotson	Bradshaw	Gillibrand	
1	2	3	4	5	6	7	8	9	10	11																			1
1	2		4	3	6	7	8		10	11	5	9																	2
1	2		4	3	6	7			10	11	5	8	9																3
1	2		4	3	6	7			10	11	5	8	9																4
1	2		4	3	6	7			10	11	5	8	9																5
1	2	3	4		6	7			10	11	5	8	9																6
1	2		4		6		7		8		5	10	9	3	11														7
1	2				6	7	11		9		5			3		4	8	10											8
1	2			9	6		7		8	11	5			3		4		10											9
1	2		4	3	6	8	7		9	11	5							10											10
1	2		4	3	6		7		8	11	5		9					10											11
1	2	3	4		6		7		8	11	5		10						9										12
1	2	3			6	7			8	11	5		10			4			9										13
1	2	3	4		6	7	11		8		5							10	9										14
1	2	3	4		6		7		8	11	5		10						9										15
1		3	4		6		7		8	11	5							10	9	2									16
1	2	3	4		6		7		8	11	5		10						9										17
1	2	3	4		6		7	10	8	11	5										9								18
1	2	3	4		6		7	10	8	11	5								9										19
1	2	3	4		6		7	10	8	11	5								9										20
1	2	3	4		6		7	10	8	11	5								9										21
1	2	3	4	5	6		7	10	8	11									9										22
1	2	3	4		6		7	10		11	5								9			8							23
1	2	3	4		6		10			11	5								9			8	7						24
1	2	3		4	6	7	11			10	5							9				8							25
1	2	3		4	6	7	11	9		10	5					8													26
1	2	3		4	5	7	11			10			9			8								6					27
1	2	3		4		7	11			10	5					8			9					6					28
1	2	3		4	5		11			10						8			9			7		6					29
1	2		4	3	6		7			10	5		8						9						11				30
1	2		4	3	5		8			9			10						7					6	11				31
1	2		4	3	5		8			9			10						7					6	11				32
1			4	3	5	7	8			9			10	2										6	11				33
1	2		4	3	5		8			9			10						7					6	11				34
1	2		4	3	5		8						10						7		9			6	11				35
1	2		4	3		7	8			9			10								5			6	11				36
	2			3	5		8						10						7		9			6	11	1	4		37
1	2			5			8						10						7	3	9			6	11		4		38
37	36	20	28	23	35	16	33	8	22	32	26	6	20	4	1	7	1	7	21	2	5	4	1	11	9	1	2		
						2	8	2	13	3			4			1		2	6		2								

Fiske	Crewdson	Scott	Threlfall	Whittingham S	Connor	Reid	Beare	Lyon	Whittingham R	Baddeley	Parkinson	Whiteside	Weston	Miller	Latheron	Swan	Stephenson	Walker	Grundy	Gladwin	Whalley	Tongue	Sterling	Clarke	Dawson	Tillotson	Bradshaw	Gillibrand	
1	2	3	4		6		7	10		11	5										9							8	1
1	2	3		4	6	7	11			10	5		9			8													2
2	2	2	1	1	2	1	2	1		2	2		1			1					1							1	
			1										1								1								

1909-10

Manager: None

1	Sep	2	(a)	Manchester C	W 2-1	Beare (pen), Dawson	14,000
2		4	(h)	Wolves	W 2-0	Miller, Connor	7,000
3		11	(a)	Gainsborough T	L 1-3	Miller	
4		13	(a)	Fulham	W 1-0	Miller	6,000
5		18	(h)	Grimsby T	W 1-0	Beare (pen)	7,000
6		25	(h)	Manchester C	D 0-0		8,500
7	Oct	2	(h)	Leicester F	L 0-1		
8		4	(h)	Fulham	D 1-1	Beare	4,000
9		9	(a)	Lincoln C	D 2-2	Burt, Dawson	
10		16	(h)	Clapton O	D 2-2	Burt, Cox	
11		23	(a)	Bradford	L 1-2	Morley	
12		30	(a)	Hull C	W 2-1	Morley, Elmore	8,000
13	Nov	6	(h)	Derby C	D 1-1	Morley	5,000
14		13	(a)	Stockport C	L 0-2		
15		20	(h)	Glossop	D 1-1	Cox	
16		27	(a)	Birmingham	W 2-1	Morley, Beare	1,000
17	Dec	4	(h)	West Brom A	W 2-1	Beare, Miller	7,700
18		11	(a)	Oldham A	L 0-2		4,000
19		18	(h)	Barnsley	D 0-0		
20		25	(a)	Burnley	L 1-5	Elmore	12,000
21		27	(a)	Leeds C	L 1-3	Beare	10,000
22	Jan	1	(h)	Leeds C	W 3-1	Miller 3	4,000
23		8	(a)	Wolves	L 1-2	Dawson	8,500
24		22	(h)	Gainsborough T	L 0-2		
25	Feb	12	(a)	Leicester F	L 2-3	Beare 2	
26		15	(a)	Grimsby T	W 1-0	Morley	
27		19	(h)	Lincoln C	W 3-0	Morley, Connor, Elmore	
28		26	(a)	Clapton O	L 1-2	Miller	
29	Mar	5	(h)	Bradford	D 0-0		
30		12	(h)	Hull C	L 1-2	Connor	3,000
31		19	(a)	Derby C	L 1-2	Miller	10,000
32		25	(h)	Burnley	L 2-3	Miller, Morley	10,000
33		26	(h)	Stockport C	W 2-0	Connor, Elmore	9,500
34	Apr	2	(a)	Glossop	W 3-2	Elmore 2, Beare	
35		9	(h)	Birmingham	W 2-0	Cox, Miller	2,000
36		16	(a)	West Brom A	W 3-0	Miller 2, Wolstenholme	6,103
37		23	(h)	Oldham A	L 1-3	Dawson (pen)	5,500
38		30	(a)	Barnsley	L 0-1		

FINAL LEAGUE POSITION: 12th in Division Two

Appearances
Goals

FA Cup

1	Jan	15	(h)	Barnsley	D 1-1	Wolstenholme	5,000
R		20	(a)	Barnsley	L 0-6		10,000

Appearances
Goals

Fiske	Crewdson	Whittingham	Threlfall	Connor	Clarke	Morley	Beare	Miller	Elmore	Dawson	Gladwin	Cox	Drain	Burt	Evans	Goulding	Didymus	Shaw	Bradshaw	Wolstenholme	Dale	Hoade	
1	2	3	4	5	6	7	8	9	10	11													1
1		3	4	5	6	7	8	9	10	11	2												2
1	2	3	4	5	6	7	8	9	10	11													3
1	2	3	4	5	6	7	8	9	10	11													4
1	2	3	4	5	6	7	8	9	10	11													5
1	2	3	4	5	6	7	8	9	10	11													6
1	2	3	4	5	6	7	8		10	11		9											7
1		3	4	5	6	7	8	9	10	11	2												8
1	2	3	4		6	8			10	11		7	5	9									9
1	2	3	4		6	8	7		10			11	5	9									10
1	2	3	4		6	8			10	7		11	5	9									11
1		3		4	6	8	7		10		2	11		9	5								12
1		3		4	6	8	7		10		2	11		9	5								13
1		3		4	6	8	7	9	10		2	11			5								14
1		3		4	6	8	7	9	10		2	11			5								15
1		3	4	5	6	10	7	9	8		2	11											16
1		3	4	5	6	8	7	9	10			11				2							17
1		3	4	5	6	8	11	9	10							2	7						18
1		3	4	5	6	8	11	9	10							2		7					19
1		3	4	5	6	8		9	10			11				2		7					20
1		3	4	5	6	7	9	10				11				2	8						21
1		3	4	5	6	7	9	10				11				2	8						22
1	2			5	6	7		8		11				9		3			4	10			23
1		3		5	6	7	9		8		2	11	4							10			24
1			4	5	6		9	8			3	11								10	2	7	25
1			4	5	6	7	9	8	10		3	11									2		26
1			4	5	6	7	9	8	10		3	11									2		27
1		3	4	5	6	7	9	8	10			11									2		28
1			4	5	6	7	9	8	10	11	3										2		29
1			4	5	6		7	8	9		3	11								10	2		30
1			4	5	6	8	7	9	10		3	11									2		31
1		3	4	5	6	8	7	9	10			11									2		32
1				5	6	8	7	9	10			11				3			4		2		33
1			4	5	6		7	9	8			11				3				10	2		34
1			4	5	6		7	9	8			11				3				10	2		35
1			4	5	6		7	9	8		2	11				3				10			36
1			4	5	6		7	9	8	11	2					3				10			37
1			4	5	6	7	11	9	8							3				10	2		38
38	10	25	31	35	38	32	34	31	34	13	16	25	4	6	4	13	3	2	2	9	12	1	
				4		7	9	13	6	4		3		2						1			

Fiske	Crewdson	Whittingham	Threlfall	Connor	Clarke	Morley	Beare	Miller	Elmore	Dawson	Gladwin	Cox	Drain	Burt	Evans	Goulding	Didymus	Shaw	Bradshaw	Wolstenholme	Dale	Hoade	
1		3	4	5	6		9	8		11						2				10		7	1
1		3	4	5	6		9	8		11	2									10		7	R
2		2	2	2	2		2	2		2	1					1				2		2	
																				1			

1910-11

Manager: None

1	Sep	3	(a)	Leeds C	W	2-1	Connor, Miller	12,000
2		10	(h)	Stockport C	W	2-1	Wolstenholme, Cox	
3		17	(a)	Derby C	D	1-1	Connor	6,000
4		24	(h)	Barnsley	W	1-0	Connor	7,000
5	Oct	1	(a)	Leicester F	L	0-2		
6		8	(h)	Wolves	W	2-0	Clennel, Beare	5,000
7		15	(a)	Chelsea	D	0-0		30,000
8		22	(h)	Clapton O	D	1-1	Clennel	
9		29	(h)	Bolton W	D	1-1	Clennel	6,000
10	Nov	5	(a)	Glossop	L	1-3	Cox	
11		12	(h)	Lincoln C	W	5-1	Cox, Morley 3 (1 pen), Clennel	3,000
12		26	(h)	Birmingham	W	3-1	Morley, Wolstenholme, Clennel	4,500
13	Dec	3	(a)	West Brom A	W	1-0	Hoad	8,840
14		10	(h)	Hull C	W	2-0	Clennel 2	6,000
15		17	(a)	Fulham	L	1-2	Clennel	14,000
16		24	(h)	Bradford	W	4-1	Clennel 2, Morley 2	
17		26	(a)	Burnley	D	1-1	Clennel	15,500
18		27	(a)	Gainsborough T	L	0-2		
19		31	(h)	Leeds C	L	1-2	Connor	4,500
20	Jan	2	(h)	Gainsborough T	D	1-1	Clennel	
21		7	(a)	Stockport C	W	3-1	Bainbridge, Clennel, Connor	
22		21	(h)	Derby C	L	0-1		5,000
23		28	(a)	Barnsley	W	2-1	Wolstenholme, Clennel	
24	Feb	4	(a)	Huddersfield T	D	2-2	Hoad, Clennel	6,000
25		11	(a)	Wolves	W	3-0	Clennel, Morley 2	9,000
26		18	(h)	Chelsea	L	0-2		3,000
27		25	(a)	Clapton O	L	1-2	Wolstenholme	9,000
28	Mar	4	(a)	Bolton W	L	0-1		13,500
29		11	(h)	Glossop	W	1-0	Connor	
30		18	(a)	Lincoln C	W	1-0	Clennel	
31		25	(h)	Huddersfield T	D	1-1	Clennel	4,000
32		29	(h)	Leicester F	W	2-0	Mearns (og), Morley	3,000
33	Apr	1	(a)	Birmingham	L	0-2		13,000
34		8	(h)	West Brom A	D	0-0		6,100
35		14	(h)	Burnley	W	1-0	Morley	14,500
36		15	(a)	Hull C	D	1-1	Morley	3,500
37		22	(h)	Fulham	L	1-2	Hoad	5,000
38		29	(a)	Bradford	L	0-1		2,000

FINAL LEAGUE POSITION: 7th in Division Two — Appearances / Goals

FA Cup

1	Jan	14	(a*)	Manchester U	L	1-2	Clennel	20,000

*Drawn at home, sold ground rights. — Appearances / Goals

Fiske	Gladwin	Goulding	Threlfall	Connor	Clarke	Beare	Wolstenholme	Miller	Clennel	Cox	Dale	Dawson	Crewdson	Morley	Bradshaw	Hoad	Walters	Quinn	Burt	Evans	Bainbridge	Shaw	Thorpe	Kidd	
1	2	3	4	5	6	7	8	9	10	11															1
1	2	3	4	5	6	7	8	9	10	11															2
1	3		4	5	6	7	8	9	10	11	2														3
1	3		4	5	6	7	8	9	10	11	2														4
1	3		4	5	6	7	8	9	10		2	11													5
1	3		4	5	6	7		8	10			11	2	9											6
1	3		4	5	6	7	8		10	11			2	9											7
1	3		4	5	6	7	8		10	11			2	9											8
1	3			5	6	7	8		10	11			2	9	4										9
1			4	5	6		8		10	11	2		3	9		7									10
1	3		4		6		8		10	11			2	9		7	5								11
1	3		4	5	6		8		10	11			2	9		7									12
1	3		4	5	6		8		10	11			2	9		7									13
1	3		4	5	6		8		10				2	9		7		11							14
1	3			5	6		8		10	11			2	9	4	7									15
1	3			5	6		8		10	11			2	9	4	7									16
1	3			5	6		8		10	11			2	9	4	7									17
1	3			5	6		8		10				2		4	7		11	9						18
1	3			5	6		8		10	11			2	9	4	7									19
1	3				6		8		10	11			2			7	5			4	9				20
1				5	6		8		10	11	3		2		4						9	7			21
1	3			5	6		8		10	11			2		4	7					9				22
1	3		4				8		10	11			2				5			6	9	7			23
1	3		4	5			8		10	11			2	9		7				6					24
1	3		4	5			8		10	11			2	9		7				6					25
1	3		4	5			8		10	11			2	9						6		7			26
1	3		4	5			8		10	11			2	7		7				6					27
1	3			5	4		8		10	11			2	9				9		6					28
1	3			5	4		8		10	11			2	11		7				6					29
1	3			5	4		8		10		2			11		7				6	9				30
1	3			5	4				10		2			9		7		8		6	9				31
1	3						8			11	2					7	5	10		6			4		32
1	3				5		8		10	11			2	9		7		9		6			4		33
	3			5			8			11			2	9		7		10		6			4	1	34
	3			5			8					11	2	9		7		10		6			4	1	35
				5			8				3	11	2	9				10		6		7	4	1	36
	3				10		8						2	9		7	5	11		6			4	1	37
	3				10		8						2	9		7	5	11		6			4	1	38
33	35	2	18	31	29	9	36	6	32	28	9	4	30	27	8	24	6	11	1	17	6	4	7	5	
				6		1	4		18	3				11		3					1				

1 own-goal

Fiske	Gladwin	Goulding	Threlfall	Connor	Clarke	Beare	Wolstenholme	Miller	Clennel	Cox	Dale	Dawson	Crewdson	Morley	Bradshaw	Hoad	
1	3			5	6		8		10	11			2	9	4	7	1
1	1			1	1		1		1	1			1	1	1	1	
									1								

1911-12

Manager: None

1	Sep	2	(h)	Hull C	W 3-2	Nesbitt, Milne, Wolstenholme	5,500
2		9	(a)	Barnsley	L 0-1		
3		16	(h)	Bradford	L 0-4		
4		23	(a)	Fulham	L 0-3		10,000
5		30	(h)	Derby C	W 1-0	Wolstenholme	5,000
6	Oct	7	(a)	Stockport C	W 2-1	Nesbitt 2	6,000
7		14	(h)	Leeds C	W 3-0	Quinn, Nesbitt, Wolstenholme	5,000
8		21	(a)	Wolves	L 0-3		10,000
9		28	(h)	Leicester F	D 1-1	Quinn	
10	Nov	4	(a)	Gainsborough T	D 0-0		
11		11	(h)	Grimsby T	L 1-2	Connor (pen)	3,000
12		18	(a)	Nottingham F	L 1-2	Wolstenholme	
13		25	(h)	Chelsea	W 1-0	Wolstenholme	3,000
14	Dec	2	(a)	Clapton O	L 0-2		
15		9	(h)	Bristol C	W 1-0	Wolstenholme	2,400
16		16	(a)	Birmingham	L 1-2	Morley	10,000
17		23	(h)	Huddersfield T	W 3-1	Morley 2, Milne	1,500
18		25	(a)	Burnley	D 1-1	Wolstenholme	22,000
19		26	(a)	Glossop	D 1-1	Milne	
20		30	(a)	Hull C	L 0-3		9,000
21	Jan	1	(h)	Glossop	W 2-0	Milne, Morley	
22		6	(h)	Barnsley	D 0-0		700
23		27	(h)	Fulham	W 3-1	W.Clarke, Connor (pen), Marshall (og)	4,000
24	Feb	6	(a)	Bradford	D 0-0		
25		10	(h)	Stockport C	L 0-1		
26		17	(a)	Leeds C	L 0-1		6,000
27		24	(a)	Derby C	L 1-5	Quinn	5,000
28	Mar	2	(a)	Leicester F	L 0-4		
29		9	(h)	Gainsborough T	D 0-0		
30		16	(a)	Grimsby T	L 0-1		4,000
31		23	(h)	Nottingham F	W 2-0	Thorpe, Wolstenholme	
32	Apr	5	(h)	Burnley	D 0-0		15,000
33		6	(h)	Clapton O	W 1-0	Milne	
34		13	(a)	Bristol C	L 0-2		10,000
35		17	(h)	Wolves	W 1-0	Wolstenholme	6,000
36		20	(h)	Birmingham	W 1-0	Wilson	2,000
37		22	(a)	Chelsea	L 1-4	Milne	27,000
38		27	(a)	Huddersfield T	L 0-4		3,000

FINAL LEAGUE POSITION: 14th in Division Two — Appearances / Goals

FA Cup

1	Jan	14	(a)	Crewe A	D 1-1	Milne	8,000
R		22	(h)	Crewe A*	D 2-2†	Quinn, Wolstenholme	3,500
2R		25	(n)‡	Crewe A	W 2-1	Bainbridge, Cowie	7,500
2	Feb	3	(a)	Bolton W	L 0-1		18,607

*Following an abandoned game (61 mins) on 16 January with Blackpool winning 2-0. — Appearances

†After extra-time. ‡Played at Hyde Road, Manchester. — Goals

Fiske	Crewdson	Gladwin	Thorpe	Connor	Evans	Morley	Wolstenholme	Milne	Metcalfe	Nesbitt	Cahill	Clarke W	Owen	Quinn	Dale	Downhall	Cowie	Dollins	Cox	Bradshaw	Kidd	Bainbridge	Clarke T	Mitchell	Wilson	Spencer	Howard	
1	2	3	4	5	6	7	8	9	10	11																		1
1	2	3	4	5	6	7	8	9	10	11																		2
1	2	3	4	5	6		8	9		11	7	10																3
1	2	3	4	5	6		8	9		11		10	7															4
1	2	3	4	5	6	7	8	9					11	10														5
1	2	3	4	5	6	7	8	9		11				10														6
1	2	3	4	5	6	7	8	9		11				10														7
1	2		4	5	6	7	8	9		11				10	3													8
1	2	3	4	5		7	8				11			10		6	9											9
1	2		4	5	6	8	10			7					3			9	11									10
1	2	3	4	5	6	7	9	9						10					11									11
1	2	3	4	5			9			7				10				9	11	6								12
1	2	3	4	5			9			7				10				9	11	6								13
1	2	3	4	5			9			7				10				9	11	6								14
1	2	3	4	5			9			7				10				9	11	6								15
1	2	3	4	5		10	9	9			7								11	6								16
1		3	4	5		10	9	9			7				2				11	6								17
1		3	4	5		10	9	9			7				2				11	6								18
1	2		4	5		10	9	9			7				3				11	6								19
1	2		4	5		10	9	9			7				3				11	6								20
1	2	3	4	5		10	9	9			7			11						6								21
1	2	3	4	5		10	9	9			7			11						6								22
1	2	3	4	5		10	9				7			11						6					9			23
	2	3	4	5							7	10		11			8				1	9	6					24
	2	3	4	5		8		9				10		11						6	1			7				25
	2	3	4	5								10		11			8			6	1	9		7				26
	2	3	4	5										10					11	6	1	8		7	9			27
	2	3	4	5		8					7			10					11	6	1	9						28
	2	3	4	5		8					7			10					11	6	1	9						29
1	2	3	4	5		10	8	9			7								11				6					30
1	2		4	5	6		8				7	10		11	3							9						31
1	2		4	5	6		10				7			11	3							9			8			32
1	2		4	5	6		10				7			11	3							9			8			33
1	2		4	5	6		10	9			7			11	3										8			34
1	2		4	5	6		10				7			11	3							9			8			35
1	2		4	5	6		10				7			11	3							9			8			36
1	2		4	5	6		10	9			7			11	3										8			37
1			4	5	6			9	8					11	2										10	3	7	38
32	35	26	38	38	18	21	31	21	3	12	21	6	2	27	14	1	3	5	15	17	6	10	2	3	9	1	1	
			1	2		4	9	6		4		1		3											1			

1 own-goal

Fiske	Crewdson	Gladwin	Thorpe	Connor	Evans	Morley	Wolstenholme	Milne	Metcalfe	Nesbitt	Cahill	Clarke W	Owen	Quinn	Dale	Downhall	Cowie	Dollins	Cox	Bradshaw	Kidd	Bainbridge	Clarke T	Mitchell	Wilson	Spencer	Howard	
1	2	3	4	5		10	8	9			7								11	6								1
1	2	3	4	5		9	8				7			10					11	6								R
	2	3	4	5							7			10			8		11	6	1	9						2R
	2	3	4	5							7	10		11			8			6	1	9						2
2	4	4	4	4		2	2	1			4	1		3			2		3	4	2	2						
							1	1						1			1					1						

1912-13

Manager: None

1	Sep	3	(a)	Grimsby T	D 1-1	Heslop	5,000
2		7	(a)	Hull C	L 1-4	Wilson	8,000
3		9	(h)	Grimsby T	W 2-1	Connor (pen), Wilson	6,000
4		14	(h)	Bury	W 2-1	Wilson, Wilkinson	10,000
5		21	(a)	Glossop	L 0-2		3,000
6		28	(h)	Fulham	W 2-0	Heslop, Quinn	5,000
7	Oct	5	(a)	Clapton O	L 0-1		14,000
8		12	(h)	Barnsley	L 0-1		
9		19	(a)	Lincoln C	L 0-1		
10	Nov	2	(a)	Nottingham F	D 1-1	Heslop	12,000
11		9	(h)	Wolves	L 1-2	Wilson	5,000
12		16	(a)	Bristol C	D 0-0		10,000
13		23	(h)	Leicester F	W 2-1	Gillow, Wilson	2,000
14		26	(h)	Bradford	L 0-2		
15		30	(a)	Birmingham	L 2-3	Wilson, Heslop	10,000
16	Dec	7	(h)	Stockport C	D 1-1	Charles	
17		14	(a)	Huddersfield T	L 0-3		3,500
18		21	(h)	Preston NE	L 0-1		6,000
19		25	(a)	Burnley	L 0-4		13,500
20		26	(a)	Leeds C	W 2-0	Quinn, Bainbridge	8,000
21		28	(h)	Hull C	L 1-2	Connor (pen)	3,000
22	Jan	1	(h)	Leeds C	L 0-3		5,000
23		4	(a)	Bury	D 1-1	Gillow	4,000
24		18	(h)	Glossop	D 1-1	Bainbridge	2,800
25		25	(a)	Fulham	L 2-4	Charles, Bainbridge	7,000
26	Feb	8	(h)	Clapton O	W 2-0	Bainbridge, Wilson	
27		15	(a)	Barnsley	L 3-5	Bainbridge, Wilson, Gillow	
28		22	(h)	Lincoln C	D 1-1	Wilson	
29	Mar	1	(a)	Bradford	L 2-4	Bainbridge, Booth	
30		8	(h)	Nottingham F	W 2-1	Connor (pen), Bainbridge	7,000
31		15	(a)	Wolves	L 0-4		2,500
32		21	(h)	Burnley	L 0-2		13,000
33		22	(h)	Bristol C	D 1-1	Quinn	4,000
34		29	(a)	Leicester F	L 1-5	Bainbridge	
35	Apr	5	(h)	Birmingham	W 2-0	Bainbridge, Charles	10,000
36		12	(a)	Stockport C	L 0-2		
37		19	(h)	Huddersfield T	W 2-1	Dollins, Wilson	2,000
38		21	(a)	Preston NE	L 1-2	Charles	

FINAL LEAGUE POSITION: 20th in Division Two — Appearances / Goals

FA Cup

1	Jan	11	(a)	Tottenham H	D 1-1	Charles	18,667
R		14	(a*)	Tottenham H	L 1-6	Charles	16,926

*Sold ground rights — Appearances / Goals

Fiske	Dale	Gladwin	Thorpe	Connor	Booth	Charles	Heslop	Dollins	Wilkinson	Quinn	Wilson	Chapman	Bainbridge	Jones	Kidd	Gillow	Crewdson	Millership	Davies	McCulloch	Keenan	Reeves	Pagnam	
1	2	3	4	5	6	7	8	9	10	11														1
1	2	3	4	5	6	7	8		10	11	9													2
1	2	3	6	5		7	10			11	9	8	4											3
1	2	3	4	5		7	8		10	11	9		6											4
1	2	3	4	5		7	8		10	11	9		6											5
1		2	4	5		7	8		10	11	9		6	3										6
1		2	4	5		7	8		10	11	9		6	3										7
		2	4	5		7			10	11	9		6	3	1	8								8
		2	5		6	7				11	9	8	4	3	1	10								9
		2	5		6	7	8		10	11	9		4	3	1									10
			5		6	7	8		10	11	9		4	3	1		2							11
			5		6	7	8			11	9		4	3	1	10	2							12
			5		6	7	8			11	9		4	3	1	10	2							13
			5		6	7	8			11	9		4	3	1	10	2							14
			4	5	6	7	8			11	9			3	1	10	2							15
1			4	5	6	7	8			11	9			3		10	2							16
1			4	5	6	7	8			11				3		10	2	9						17
1			4	5	6	7		8	10	11				3		9	2							18
1			4	5	6	7		8	10	11				3		9	2							19
1			4	5	6	7		8		11			9	3		10		2						20
1			4	5	6	7		8		11			9	3		10		2						21
			5		6	7	9	8		11			4	3	1	10	2							22
			4		6	7	5	8			9			3	1	10	2		11					23
			4			7	6	8					9	3	1	10	2		11	5				24
			4			7	6		8				9	3	1	10	2		11		5			25
			4	5	6	7				11	8		9	3	1	10	2							26
			4	5		7	6			11	8		9		1	10	2							27
			4	5		7	6			11	8		9	3	1	10	2							28
			4	5	6	7	8			11	10		9	3	1		2							29
1			4	5		7	6			11	10		9	3				2				8		30
1			4	5		7	6			11	10		9	3				2				8		31
1			4	5		7	6		10	11			9	3				2				8		32
1			4	5		7	6		10	11			9	3				2				8		33
1			4	5		7	6	8	10	11			9	3				2						34
1			4	5	6	7		8		11			9	3		10		2						35
1			4	5	6	7		8					9	3		10		2					11	36
1			4	5	6	7		8			9			3		10		2					11	37
1			4	5	6	7		8			9			3		10		2					11	38
22	5	10	38	28	23	38	27	13	15	32	24	2	28	32	16	23	17	12	3	1	1	4	3	
				3	1	4	4	1	1	3	10		9			2								

Fiske	Dale	Gladwin	Thorpe	Connor	Booth	Charles	Heslop	Dollins	Wilkinson	Quinn	Wilson	Chapman	Bainbridge	Jones	Kidd	Gillow	Crewdson	Millership	Davies	McCulloch	Keenan	Reeves	Pagnam	
			4		6	7	5	8			9			3	1	10	2		11					1
			4		6	7	5	8		11	9			3	1	10	2							R
			2		2	2	2	2		1	2			2	2	2	2		1					
						2																		

1913-14

Manager: None

1	Sep	6	(h)	Hull C	D 2-2	Brown, Charles	3,000
2		13	(a)	Barnsley	L 1-2	Brown	
3		20	(h)	Bury	L 0-1		11,000
4		24	(a)	Notts C	L 0-2		
5		27	(a)	Huddersfield T	L 0-1		7,000
6	Oct	4	(h)	Lincoln C	W 2-1	Quinn, Charles	
7		11	(a)	Fulham	D 0-0		6,000
8		18	(a)	Nottingham F	L 0-3		10,000
9		25	(h)	W Arsenal	D 1-1	Quinn	18,000
10	Nov	1	(a)	Grimsby T	L 0-2		8,000
11		8	(h)	Birmingham	D 2-2	Connor (pen), Charles	5,000
12		15	(a)	Bristol C	L 0-1		8,000
13		22	(h)	Leeds C	D 2-2	Lane, Connor (pen)	5,000
14		29	(a)	Clapton O	L 0-2		
15	Dec	6	(a)	Glossop	W 2-1	Charlton, Lane	
16		13	(a)	Stockport C	D 0-0		
17		20	(h)	Bradford	W 2-1	Pagman, Lane	
18		25	(a)	Leicester F	W 1-0	Charlton	10,000
19		26	(a)	Wolves	L 0-1		10,000
20		27	(a)	Hull C	D 0-0		12,000
21	Jan	1	(h)	Wolves	W 2-0	Lane 2	7,500
22		3	(h)	Barnsley	W 3-1	Lane, Charlton, Charles	6,000
23		17	(a)	Bury	L 0-1		10,000
24		24	(h)	Huddersfield T	L 0-1		
25	Feb	7	(a)	Lincoln C	W 2-1	Charles, Lane	
26		14	(h)	Fulham	D 1-1	Connor (pen)	5,000
27		21	(h)	Nottingham F	W 2-1	Buchan 2	
28		28	(a)	W Arsenal	L 1-2	Charles	20,000
29	Mar	7	(h)	Grimsby T	D 1-1	Lane	4,000
30		14	(a)	Birmingham	D 0-0		7,000
31		21	(h)	Bristol C	L 0-1		4,000
32		28	(a)	Leeds C	L 1-2	Lane	12,000
33	Apr	4	(h)	Clapton O	D 0-0		3,500
34		10	(h)	Leicester F	W 1-0	Connor	4,000
35		11	(h)	Glossop	D 1-1	Lane	4,000
36		13	(h)	Notts C	D 0-0		5,000
37		18	(h)	Stockport C	D 2-2	Charles, Turley	4,000
38		25	(a)	Bradford	L 1-4	Lane	25,500

FINAL LEAGUE POSITION: 16th in Division Two

Appearances
Goals

FA Cup

1	Jan	10	(a)	Gillingham	L 0-1		

Appearances
Goals

Fiske	Millership	Jones	Thorpe	Heslop	Booth	Charles	Turley	Brown	Gillow	Quinn	Connor	Buchan	Pagman	Sharp	Robson	Bainbridge	Rushton	Burke	Lane	Charlton	Rookes	Green	Wilson	Kidd	Keenan	
1	2	3	4	5	6	7	8	9	10	11																1
1	2	3	4		6	7	8	9	10	11	5															2
1	2	3	4		6	7	8	9		11	5	10														3
1	2	3	4		6			9		11	5	10	7	8												4
1		3	4	10	6			9		11	5		7	8	2											5
1		3	4		6	8		9		11	5	10	7		2											6
1		3	4		6	8		9		11	5	10	7		2											7
1		3	4		6	8		9		11	5	10	7		2											8
1		3	4		6	8		9		11	5	10	7		2											9
1		3			6	9		9		11	5	10	7		2	4										10
1		3			6	8		9		11	5	10	7		2	4										11
1		3			6	8				11	5	10	7			9	2	4								12
1		3			6	7				11	5	8			2	4			9	10						13
1		3			6	7				11	5	8			2	4			9	10						14
1		3			6			7		11	5	8			2	4			9	10						15
1		3			6					11	5		7	8	2	4			9	10						16
1		3			6						5	10	7		2	4			9	8	11					17
1		3			6						5	10	7		2	4			9	8	11					18
1		3			6						5	10	7		2	4			9	11		8				19
1		3			6	7					5				2	4			9	8		10	11			20
1		3			6	7					5				2	4			9	8	11	10				21
1	2	3			6	7					5					4			9	8	11	10				22
1		3			6	7					5	10			2	4			9	8	11					23
		3			6	7					5				2	4			9	10	11	8		1		24
		3			6	7					5	10			2	4			9	8	11			1		25
		3			6	7				11	5	10			2	4			9	8				1		26
		3			6	7		11			5	10			2	4			9	8				1		27
1	2	3			6	7				11	5	10				4			9	8						28
1	2	3			6	7				11	5	10				4			9	8						29
1	2	3			6	7					5	10	11			4			9	8						30
1	2	3			6	7					5	10	11			4			9	8						31
1	2	3			6	7	8				5		11			4			9	10						32
1	2	3			6	7					5		11			4			9	10		8				33
1	2	3			6	7					5		11			4			9	10		8				34
1	2	3			6	7					5		11			4		10	9			8				35
1	2	3			6	7	8					10	11			4			9						5	36
1	2	3			6	7	8			11	5					4			9			10				37
1	2	3			6	7	8			11	5					4			9			10				38
34	16	38	9	2	38	31	7	13	2	21	36	24	20	3	21	29	1	2	26	22	7	10	1	4	1	
						7	1	2		2	4	2	1						11	3						

Fiske	Millership	Jones	Thorpe	Heslop	Booth	Charles	Turley	Brown	Gillow	Quinn	Connor	Buchan	Pagman	Sharp	Robson	Bainbridge	Rushton	Burke	Lane	Charlton	Rookes	Green	Wilson	Kidd	Keenan	
1		3			6	7					5				2	4			9	8	11	10				1
1		1			1	1					1				1	1			1	1	1	1				

1914-15

Manager: None

1	Sep	2	(a)	Bristol C	L 1-2	Lane	3,000
2		5	(a)	Hull C	W 3-1	Lane 3	6,000
3		12	(h)	Bury	L 3-4	Yarnall, Charles, Green	
4		19	(a)	Leeds C	L 0-2		8,000
5		26	(h)	Preston NE	L 0-2		8,000
6	Oct	3	(a)	Clapton O	L 0-2		
7		10	(h)	Nottingham F	W 3-0	Lane 2, Green	
8		17	(a)	Arsenal	L 0-2		17,000
9		24	(h)	Leicester F	L 1-2	Sibbald	
10		31	(a)	Derby C	L 0-5		4,000
11	Nov	7	(h)	Barnsley	D 1-1	Booth	
12		14	(a)	Lincoln C	W 1-0	Lane	
13		21	(h)	Glossop	W 3-0	Lane 3	7,000
14		28	(a)	Birmingham	L 0-3		5,000
15	Dec	5	(h)	Wolves	W 1-0	Sibbald	4,500
16		12	(a)	Grimsby T	L 0-2		
17		19	(h)	Fulham	D 2-2	Lane, Green	2,000
18		25	(a)	Stockport C	W 2-0	Lane 2	
19		26	(a)	Huddersfield T	L 0-5		9,500
20	Jan	1	(h)	Bristol C	W 2-0	Quinn, Lane	4,000
21		2	(h)	Hull C	L 1-2	Lane (pen)	5,000
22		23	(h)	Leeds C	W 1-0	Lane (pen)	6,000
23		25	(a)	Bury	D 2-2	Quinn, Green	3,000
24		30	(a)	Preston NE	L 0-1		7,000
25	Feb	6	(h)	Clapton O	W 5-1	Lane 2, Booth, Sibbald, Wilson	
26		13	(a)	Nottingham F	L 1-2	Wilson	
27		20	(h)	Arsenal	L 0-2		6,000
28		27	(a)	Leicester F	D 2-2	Lane 2	
29	Mar	6	(h)	Derby C	W 2-1	Quinn, Lane	5,000
30		13	(a)	Barnsley	W 2-1	Lane 2	
31		20	(h)	Lincoln C	D 0-0		
32		27	(a)	Glossop	W 3-1	Appleton, Sibbald, Charles	
33	Apr	2	(h)	Huddersfield T	W 3-2	Charles, Lane, Quinn	4,500
34		5	(h)	Stockport C	W 4-2	Appleton, Sibbald, Charles, Lane	5,000
35		10	(a)	Wolves	L 0-2		7,000
36		14	(h)	Birmingham	W 3-1	Charles, Lane 2	5,000
37		17	(h)	Grimsby T	W 5-0	Charles, Appleton, Lane, Sibbald 2	4,000
38		24	(a)	Fulham	W 1-0	Bainbridge	2,000

FINAL LEAGUE POSITION: 10th in Division Two — Appearances

Goals

FA Cup

1	Jan	9	(h)	Sheffield U	L 1-2	Sibbald	7,500

Appearances

Goals

Kidd	Robson	Jones	Bainbridge	Connor	Rooks	Charles	Turley	Lane	Yarnall	Quinn	Green	Booth	Millership	Tulloch	Sibbald	Wilson	Appleton	Gregson CWS	Mitchell FJ	Thompson	Brooks	
1	2	3	4	5	6	7	8	9	10	11												1
1	2	3	4	5	6	7		9	10	11	8											2
1	2	3	4	5	6	7		9	10	11	8											3
1	2	3	4	5		7	8	9	10	11		6										4
1	2		4	5		7		9	10	11	8	6	3									5
1	3		4	5		7		9	10	11	8	6	2									6
1	2	3	4	5		7		9	10	11	8	6										7
1	2	3	4	5		7		9	10	11	8	6										8
1		3	4	5		7		9	8	11		6		2	10							9
1		3	4			7		9		11	8	6		2	10	5						10
1	2	3	4			7		9		11	8	6			10	5						11
1	3		4			7		9		11	8	6		2	10	5						12
1	2		4			7		9		11	8	6		3	10	5						13
1	3		4					9		11	8	6		2	10	5	7					14
1	3		4					9		11	8	6		2	10	5	7					15
1	3		4					9		11	8	6		2	10	5	7					16
1	3		4			7		9		11	8	6		2	10	5						17
1	3		4			7		9		11	8	6		2	10	5						18
1	3		4			7		9		11	8	6		2	10	5						19
1	3	2	4			7		9		11	8	6			10	5						20
1	3	2	4			7		9		11	8	6			10	5						21
1	3		4			7		9		11	8	6		2	10	5						22
1			2			7	4	9		11	8	6		3	10	5						23
1			2			7	4	9			8	6		3	10	5	11					24
1	2		4			7		9		11		6		3	10	5	8					25
1	2		4			7		9		11		6		3	10	5	8					26
1	2		4			7		9		11		6		3	10	5	8					27
1			4		2	7		9		11		6		3	10	5	8					28
1	2	3	4		6	7		9		11						5	8	10				29
1	2	3	4		6	7		9		11						5	8	10				30
		3	4		6	7		9		11				2		5	8	10	1			31
		3	4			7		9		11		6		2	10		8			1	5	32
		3	4			7		9		11		6		2	10		8			1	5	33
		3	4		6	7		9		11				2	10	5	8			1		34
		3	4		6	7		9		11				2	10	5	8		1			35
		3	4		6	7		9		11				2	10	5	8		1			36
		3	4		6	7		9		11				2	10	5	8		1			37
		3	4		6	7		9		11				2	10	5	8		1			38
30	25	21	38	9	12	35	4	38	9	37	21	27	2	25	27	27	18	3	5	3	2	
			1			6		28	1	4	4	2			7	2	3					

Kidd	Robson	Jones	Bainbridge	Connor	Rooks	Charles	Turley	Lane	Yarnall	Quinn	Green	Booth	Millership	Tulloch	Sibbald	Wilson	Appleton	Gregson CWS	Mitchell FJ	Thompson	Brooks	
1	3		4			7		9		11	8	6		2	10	5						1
1	1		1			1		1		1	1	1		1	1	1						
															1							

1915-16

Manager: None

1	Sep	4	(a)	Southport Cen	L 0-2		1,100
2		11	(h)	Oldham A	W 4-1	Latheron, Chapman 2, Appleton	5,000
3		18	(a)	Everton	L 2-4	Appleton, Latheron	
4		25	(h)	Bolton W	W 2-1	Latheron, Charles	
5	Oct	2	(a)	Manchester C	L 0-3		
6		9	(h)	Stoke	D 1-1	Latheron	
7		16	(a)	Burnley	L 2-5	Latheron, Chapman	6,000
8		23	(h)	Preston NE	W 5-1	Hodgkinson 2, Charles, Latheron 2	
9		30	(a)	Stockport C	L 1-2	Latheron	
10	Nov	6	(h)	Liverpool	W 5-2	Wilson, Latheron 2, Chapman 2	4,000
11		13	(a)	Bury	W 2-1	Charles, Chapman	
12		20	(h)	Manchester U	W 5-1	Chapman, Latheron 2, Appleton, Crompton (pen)	4,000
13		27	(a)	Rochdale	W 3-2	Chapman, Appleton, Crompton	
14	Dec	4	(h)	Southport Cen	D 0-0		
15		11	(a)	Oldham A	L 0-2		500
16		18	(h)	Everton	L 1-4	Chapman	
17		25	(a)	Bolton W	W 2-0	Appleton, Hodgkinson	1,000
18	Jan	1	(h)	Manchester C	W 2-0	Carney, Charles	
19		8	(a)	Stoke	L 1-3	Wilson	
20		15	(h)	Burnley	W 2-1	Hodgkinson, Latheron	4,000
21		22	(a)	Preston NE	W 2-1	Broadhurst (og), Charles	
22		29	(h)	Stockport C	W 4-1	Charles, Green 2, Wilson	
23	Feb	5	(a)	Liverpool	L 0-1		16,000
24		12	(h)	Bury	W 3-1	Charles, Fairclough, Hodgkinson	
25		19	(a)	Manchester U	D 1-1	Fairclough	10,000
26		26	(h)	Rochdale	W 4-0	Quinn 2, Green 2	4,000

FINAL LEAGUE POSITION: 3rd in Principal Competition — Lancashire Section

Northern Group

27	Mar	4	(a)	Bury	W 2-1	Carney, Crompton (pen)	3,000
28		11	(h)	Burnley	L 1-2	Carney	5,000
29		18	(a)	Preston NE	W 3-1	Hodgkinson, Charles, Latheron	4,500
30		25	(h)	Bolton W	W 3-1	Green, Carney, Quinn	3,000
31	Apr	1	(a)	Southport Cen	W 3-2	Booth, Latheron (pen), Quinn	
32		8	(h)	Bury	W 4-2	Latheron (pen), Quinn 3	4,000
33		15	(a)	Burnley	L 1-2	Taylor (og)	4,000
34		21	(h)	Southport Cen	W 3-1	Green 2, Charles	4,000
35		22	(h)	Preston NE	W 2-0	Charles, Quinn	6,000
36		29	(a)	Bolton W	W 2-1	Appleton, Green	

FINAL LEAGUE POSITION: 2nd in Subsidiary Competition — Northern Group

1	2	3	4	5	6	7	8	9	10	11	
F.J.Mitchell	R.Crompton	J.Jones	J.Bainbridge	G.Wilson	R.Booth	J.Charles	R.Green	G.Chapman	E.G.Latheron	L.Appleton	1
..	..	..	..	..	..	..	..	..	..	..	2
..	..	..	..	..	..	..	..	..	..	..	3
..	..	..	..	..	..	..	..	..	..	J.Hodgkinson	4
..	..	..	..	G.Chapman	..	..	..	L.Appleton	..	..	5
..	..	..	..	G.Wilson	..	..	L.Appleton	G.Chapman	..	..	6
..	J.Bainbridge	..	J.Carney	..	..	..	R.Green	..	..	..	7
..	R.Crompton	..	J.Bainbridge	..	..	..	L.Appleton	..	..	..	8
..	..	..	..	..	..	..	..	..	..	..	9
J.Kidd	J.Bainbridge	..	J.Carney	..	..	..	P.Quinn	..	..	..	10
..	R.Crompton	..	J.Bainbridge	..	..	..	J.Carney	..	..	..	11
..	..	..	..	..	..	..	L.Appleton	..	..	..	12
..	..	..	..	..	..	J.Hampson	..	..	..	..	13
..	..	..	..	..	..	J.Charles	..	..	..	..	14
..	J.Bainbridge	..	J.Carney	..	..	..	..	..	L.Lloyd	..	15
..	R.Crompton	..	J.Bainbridge	..	..	..	L.Lloyd	..	E.G.Latheron	..	16
..	G.Wilson	J.Carney	..	R.Crompton	..	R.Green	J.Charles	L.Appleton	..	..	17
..	..	..	..	..	..	P.Quinn	..	..	..	..	18
..	R.Crompton	J.Jones	J.Carney	G.Wilson	..	J.Charles	J.Bainbridge	..	..	..	19
..	..	..	J.Bainbridge	..	..	..	L.Appleton	G.Chaplan	..	..	20
..	..	..	..	..	..	..	R.Green	L.Appleton	..	P.Quinn	21
..	..	..	J.Carney	..	..	..	..	J.Bainbridge	..	Smith	22
..	..	..	J.Bainbridge	..	..	..	..	A.Fairclough	..	J.Hodgkinson	23
..	..	..	J.Carney	..	..	..	..	..	..	..	24
..	..	..	..	..	..	..	..	..	..	..	25
..	..	..	..	..	..	..	..	P.Quinn	..	..	26

J.Kidd	J.Jones	R.Crompton	R.Booth	G.Wilson	J.Bainbridge	J.Hodgkinson	E.G.Latheron	P.Quinn	J.Carney	J.Charles	27
..	R.Crompton	J.Jones	J.Bainbridge	..	R.Booth	J.Charles	J.Carney	..	E.G.Latheron	J.Hodgkinson	28
..	..	..	..	..	J.Carney	..	R.Green	..	..	..	29
..	..	..	..	..	..	..	..	..	..	..	30
..	J.Bainbridge	..	J.Carney	..	R.Booth	..	..	..	..	..	31
..	..	..	..	..	..	..	..	..	..	..	32
..	..	..	..	..	..	..	..	..	..	..	33
..	..	..	..	..	..	..	..	Heywood	Sibbald	Burnham	34
..	..	..	..	..	..	..	..	Sibbald	P.Quinn	..	35
..	..	..	..	..	..	L.Appleton	..	P.Quinn	Sibbald	..	36

Principal Competition – Lancashire Section
Appearances: Booth 26, R.J.Charles 25, E.G.Latheron 25, G.Wilson 25, R.Crompton 24, J.Jones 24, J.Bainbridge 23, J.Hodgkinson 21, G.Chapman 17, J.Kidd 17, R.Green 13, L.Appleton 16, J.Carney 11, F.J.Mitchell 9, P.Quinn 4, A.Fairclough 3, L.Lloyd 2, J.Hampson 1, Smith 1.
Goalscorers: Latheron 13, Chapman 9, Charles 7, Appleton 5, Hodgkinson 5, Green 4, Wilson 3, Crompton 2, Fairclough 2, Quinn 2, Atherton 1, Carney 1, Broadhurst (own-goal) 1.

Subsidiary Competition – Northern Group
Appearances: J.Bainbridge 10, J.Carney 10, J.Jones 10, J.Kidd 10, G.Wilson 10, J.Charles 9, P.Quinn 9, R.Booth 8, R.Green 8, J.Hodgkinson 7, E.G.Latheron 7, R.Crompton 4, Burnham 3, Sibbald 3, L.Appleton 1, Heywood 1.
Goalscorers: Quinn 6, Green 4, Carney 3, Charles 3, Latheron 3, Appleton 1, Booth 1, Crompton 1, Hodgkinson 1, Taylor (own-goal) 1.

1916-17

Manager: None

1	Sep	2	(h)	Preston NE	W	5-1	Bainbridge 2, Carlisle, Croker, Charles	3,000
2		9	(a)	Blackburn R	L	0-4		2,000
3		16	(h)	Burnley	D	1-1	Croker	4,000
4		23	(a)	Manchester C	L	0-4		10,000
5		30	(h)	Manchester U	D	2-2	Appleton 2	4,000
6	Oct	7	(a)	Everton	L	1-3	Croker	15,000
7		14	(h)	Liverpool	L	0-1		1,500
8		21	(a)	Rochdale	L	1-4	Johnstone	
9		28	(h)	Stockport C	L	0-2		2,000
10	Nov	4	(a)	Bolton W	L	1-4	Appleton	
11		11	(h)	Bury	D	1-1	Whiting	4,000
12		18	(a)	Port Vale	L	1-11	Spencer	
13		25	(h)	Stoke	D	1-1	Jones	
14	Dec	2	(a)	Oldham A	D	1-1	Williamson	1,144
15		9	(h)	Southport Cen	L	0-2		
16		16	(a)	Preston NE	L	1-2	Spencer	
17		23	(h)	Blackburn R	W	3-2	Williamson 3	1,000
18		30	(a)	Burnley	L	0-7		2,000
19	Jan	1	(a)	Southport Cen	L	0-1		
20		6	(h)	Manchester C	W	3-1	Bainbridge, Booth, Harland	3,000
21		13	(a)	Manchester U	L	1-6	Unknown	
22		20	(h)	Everton	D	1-1	Clifton	3,000
23		27	(a)	Liverpool	D	2-2	Harland, Smith	12,000
24	Feb	3	(h)	Rochdale	L	0-2		1,000
25		10	(a)	Stockport C	L	0-6		
26		17	(h)	Bolton W	W	5-3	Phillips, Jones, Kelly 2, Williamson	
27		24	(a)	Bury	L	0-2		
28	Mar	3	(h)	Port Vale	W	4-0	Gilham, Williamson, Hampton 2	3,000
29		10	(a)	Stoke	L	0-6		
30		17	(h)	Oldham A	W	9-0	Williamson, Clifton, Hampton 4, Carlisle, Gilham 2	3,000

FINAL LEAGUE POSITION: 16th in Principal Competition — Lancashire Section

Subsidiary Competition

31	Dec	25	(a)	Burnley*	L	0-4		2,000
32	Mar	31	(a)	Preston NE	L	1-2	Williamson	
33	Apr	6	(h)	Burnley	L	2-3	Unknown 2	5,000
34		7	(h)	Blackburn R	W	4-1	Gilham 2, Williamson, Spencer (og)	4,000
35		14	(h)	Preston NE	D	0-0		3,000
36		21	(a)	Blackburn R	W	3-2	Williamson, Davis 2	

FINAL LEAGUE POSITION: 11th in Subsidiary Competition — Lancashire Section

*Counted towards Principal and Subsidiary Competitions

1	2	3	4	5	6	7	8	9	10	11	
J.Kidd	Harker	J.Jones	J.Connor	R.Carlisle	R.Booth	J.Charles	Simmons	J.Bainbridge	L.Appleton	Croker	1
..	J.Collins	..	..	..	..	..	J.Peet	J.Lyner	..	..	2
..	J.Bainbridge	..	..	..	..	..	L.Appleton	L.Chorley	Sibbald	..	3
..	..	..	..	..	..	..	..	..	L.Johnstone	F.A.Mitchell	4
..	..	Croker	..	..	..	..	..	..	..	..	5
..	..	..	..	..	..	..	L.Johnstone	L.Appleton	L.Chorley	..	6
..	..	J.Jones	..	..	..	L.Appleton	..	Kuragh	..	Croker	7
Wilcox	Holmes	..	..	..	Cook	Clifton	..	J.Bainbridge	..	..	8
J.Kidd	..	..	..	..	..	..	..	..	..	..	9
..	J.Bainbridge	..	..	..	R.Booth	..	L.Appleton	Williamson	Spencer	..	10
..	..	..	..	Bull	..	..	Williamson	Whiting	..	..	11
Wilcox	Haydock	..	..	Abbott	..	..	L.Appleton	Williamson	..	..	12
..	Holmes	..	..	..	..	..	Bunn	..	..	..	13
..	..	..	..	..	..	..	..	..	..	..	14
..	..	Dunn	..	..	J.Jones	..	L.Appleton	..	..	..	15
..	..	..	..	..	..	..	..	..	..	..	16
..	..	..	..	..	..	..	..	..	..	..	17
..	..	..	..	..	..	..	..	..	..	..	18
..	..	..	..	..	..	..	..	..	..	..	19
..	J.Bainbridge	..	..	..	R.Booth	..	..	..	..	Harland	20
..	..	..	..	..	..	..	..	..	..	..	21
Stansfield	..	..	..	R.Carlisle	Bold	..	..	..	Smith	..	22
..	Holmes	..	..	..	R.Booth	..	..	..	..	..	23
..	Pickup	Fairhurst	..	..	..	..	..	..	..	..	24
Wilcox	J.Bainbridge	..	..	Phillips	..	..	..	..	..	..	25
Stansfield	..	J.Jones	..	..	..	..	..	..	Kelly	Kellock	26
..	Bold	..	..	R.Carlisle	..	..	..	H.Hampton	..	..	27
..	J.Bainbridge	..	..	..	..	..	Williamson	..	J.Gilham	E.Mosscrop	28
..	J.Gilham	Fazackerley	..	..	..	..	..	..	Smith	..	29
..	..	..	..	..	..	..	..	..	..	..	30

Wilcox	Holmes	J.Jones	J.Connor	Abbott	J.Jones	Clifton	L.Appleton	Williamson	Spencer	Croker	1
Stansfield	Cuffe	..	..	R.Carlisle	R.Booth	..	Williamson	Fazackerley	Smith	G.Mosscrop	2
..	..	..	..	..	..	..	..	..	..	..	3
..	J.Gilham	..	..	..	..	..	..	J.Hampton	..	..	4
Stevenson	Cuffe	..	..	..	Davis	J.Gilham	Fazackerley	Williamson	Roach	..	5
Stansfield	..		..	..	..	..	..	..	..	..	6

Principal Competition – Lancashire Section
Appearances: Connor 30, Clifton 23, Appleton 22, Booth 22, Jones 20, Williamson 20, Croker 18, Carlisle 17, Bainbridge 16, Spencer 12, Wilcox 12, Abbott 10, Holmes 10, Kidd 10, Dunn 9, Stansfield 8, Chorley 7, Charles 6, Harland 6, Johnstone 6, Smith 6, Hampton 4, Gilham 3, Mitchell 3, Mosscrop 3, Bold 2, Bunn 2, Cook 2, Fairhurst 2, Fazackerley 2, Kellock 2, Kelly 2, Philips 2, Bull 1, Collins 1, Harker 1, Haydock 1, Kuragh 1, Lyner 1, Peet 1, Pickup 1, Sibbald 1, Simmons 1, Whiting 1.
Goalscorers: Williamson 7, Hampton 6, Appleton 3, Bainbridge 3, Croker 3, Gilham 3, Carlisle 2, Clifton 2, Harland 2, Jones 2, Kelly 2, Spencer 2, Booth 1, Charles 1, Johnstone 1, Phillips 1, Whiting 1, Unknown 1.

Subsidiary Competition – Lancashire Section
Appearances: Connor 6, Jones 6, Williamson 6, Carlisle 5, Mosscrop 5, Clifton 4, Cuffe 4, Fazackerley 4, Stansfield 4, Booth 3, Gilham 3, Smith 3, Davis 2, Roach 2, Abbott 1, Appleton 1, Croker 1, Dunn 1, Hampton 1, Holmes 1, Spencer 1, Stevenson 1, Wilcox 1.
Goalscorers: Williamson 3, Davis 2, Gilham 2, Unknown 2, Spencer (own-goal) 1.

1917-18

Manager: None

1	Sep	1	(h)	Oldham A	W 3-2	Kirrage 3	2,000
2		8	(a)	Oldham A	D 1-1	Kirrage	2,218
3		15	(h)	Bury	W 1-0	Wilson	
4		22	(a)	Bury	L 1-2	Campey	
5		29	(h)	Stockport C	W 3-1	Thomas 2, Kirrage	
6	Oct	6	(a)	Stockport C	L 1-3	Williamson	
7		13	(h)	Stoke	L 0-5		4,000
8		20	(a)	Stoke	L 1-3	Thomas	
9		27	(a)	Liverpool	L 1-4	Thomas	12,000
10	Nov	3	(h)	Liverpool	L 0-6		3,000
11		10	(a)	Southport Cen	W 2-0	Bold, Williamson	800
12		17	(h)	Southport Cen	D 1-1	Clarke	2,000
13	Dec	1	(a)	Manchester U	L 0-1		
14		15	(h)	Manchester U	L 2-3	Myers, Williamson	3,000
15		22	(h)	Rochdale	L 1-3	Berry	
16		25	(a)	Burnley	D 1-1	Unknown	3,000
17		29	(a)	Rochdale	L 3-6	Beel 2, Moorcroft	
18	Jan	8	(h)	Everton	W 1-0	Moorcroft	
19		15	(a)	Everton	L 2-7	Keenan, Moorcroft	
20		22	(h)	Port Vale	L 0-1		700
21		29	(a)	Port Vale	L 0-4		
22	Feb	2	(h)	Bolton W	L 0-5		3,000
23		9	(a)	Bolton W	D 1-1	Williamson	
24		16	(a)	Preston NE	L 1-2	Moorcroft	
25		23	(h)	Preston NE	W 1-0	Connor (pen)	
26	Mar	2	(a)	Blackburn R	D 2-2	Keenan, Williamson	
27		9	(h)	Blackburn R	W 4-1	Hunter 4	2,000
28		16	(h)	Manchester C	W 1-0	Bold	3,000
29		23	(a)	Manchester C	D 2-2	Booth, Unknown	8,000
30		29	(h	Burnley	W 1-0	Hunter	

FINAL LEAGUE POSITION: 12th in Principal Competition — Lancashire Section

Subsidiary Competition

31	Nov	24	(a)	Burnley	L 1-3	Thomas	500
32	Dec	1	(h)	Burnley	W 5-1	Thomas 2, Keenan, Chadwick 2	1,000
33	Mar	30	(h)	Blackburn R	W 2-0	Hasson, Banks	500
34	Apr	6	(a)	Blackburn R	W 4-1	Bold, McBean 2, Hunter	'Small'
35		13	(h)	Preston NE	L 2-3	Hunter, Berry	3,000
36		20	(a)	Preston NE	W 4-1	McBean 2, Bold, Hunter	

FINAL LEAGUE POSITION: 5th in Subsidiary Competition — Lancashire Section

1	2	3	4	5	6	7	8	9	10	11	
Steventon	Fairhurst	Dunn	McPherson	Connor	Keenan	Robb	Campey	Gilham	Williamson	Kirrage	1
..	..	..	..	..	..	..	..	..	..	..	2
..	..	..	..	Wilson	..	..	..	..	..	..	3
..	..	..	..	Connor	..	Williams	..	..	..	..	4
..	..	..	..	..	..	..	Thomas	..	..	..	5
..	..	..	..	..	..	..	..	..	..	..	6
..	..	..	..	..	..	..	..	..	..	..	7
..	..	..	..	..	..	..	..	..	..	..	8
..	..	..	..	..	..	..	..	..	..	..	9
..	..	..	..	..	..	..	..	..	..	..	10
..	Bates	Bold	..	..	..	..	Campey	..	Thomas	Williamson	11
..	..	..	..	Stirzaker	..	..	Booth	Clarke	..	..	12
..	A.N.Other*	..	Robson	Connor	..	Bell	Myers	Berry	..	Kirrage	13
..	Bates	..	..	..	..	..	..	..	Williamson	Thomas	14
Sperrin	..	..	..	..	..	..	..	..	..	..	15
Steventon	..	..	McPherson	..	..	Williams	Booth	Clarke	Thomas	Chadwick	16
Monaghan	..	..	Robson	Keenan	Connor	Moorcroft	Myers	Ralphs	Williamsom	Beel	17
..	..	..	..	..	..	..	..	..	..	..	18
..	..	..	..	..	..	..	Booth	..	..	..	19
..	Fairhurst	Dunn	Connor	Forest	Keenan	Booth	..	Reed	Ralphs	Moorcroft	20
..	..	..	..	..	..	Moorcroft	Williamson	Ralphs	Williamson	Reed	21
Kidd	..	..	..	..	..	..	Booth	..	..	..	22
Steventon	..	..	..	..	..	..	..	Williamson	Ralphs	Berry	23
..	Quinn	..	..	..	..	..	..	..	..	..	24
..	Fairhurst	Besant	..	..	..	Curtain	..	..	..	..	25
..	..	..	..	..	..	..	..	..	..	..	26
..	..	..	..	..	..	..	Hunter	..	..	..	27
Mitchell	Bates	Bold	Robson	Connor	Forest	Thorpe	..	Keenan	..	..	28
..	..	..	..	Keenan	Connor	..	Booth	Williamson	..	..	29
..	..	Dunn	Connor	..	Booth	Williamson	Hunter	McBean	Berry	Grice	30

*Played with only ten players

Spurren	Bates	Bold	McPherson	Connor	Keenan	Williams	Booth	Clarke	Thomas	Williamson	31
Steventon	..	..	..	..	..	..	..	..	..	Chadwick	32
Mitchell	..	Dunn	Connor	Keenan	Booth	Hasson	Banks	McBean	Berry	Grice	33
..	..	Bold	..	..	..	..	Hunter	..	..	..	34
Monaghan	..	Dunn	..	..	..	Williams	Banks	Hunter	..	McBean	35
..	Bold	Keenan	..	Kinsella	..	..	Hunter	Banks	..	..	36

Principal Competition – Lancashire Section
Appearances: Keenan 30, Connor 28, Williamson 27, Steventon 20, Fairhurst 17, Dunn 16, McPherson 13, Ralphs 13, Booth 12, Thomas 12, Bates 11, Berry 11, Bold 11, Gilham 11, Kirrage 11, Williams 10, Forest 9, Moorcroft 8, Robson 8, Campey 5, Monaghan 5, Myers 5, Beel 3, Bell 3, Besant 3, Curtain 3, Hunter 3, Mitchell 3, Reed 3, Robb 3, Clarke 2, Thorpe 2, Burke 1, Chadwick 1, Grice 1, Kidd 1, McBean 1, Quinn 1, Sperrin 1, Stirzaker 1, Wilson 1.
Goalscorers: Hunter 5, Kirrage 5, Williamson 5, Moorcroft 4, Thomas 4, Keenan 2, Beel 2, Bold 2, Wilson 1, Berry 1, Booth 1, Campey 1, Clarke 1, Connor 1, Myers 1, Unknown 2.

Subsidiary Competition – Lancashire Section
Appearances: Booth 6, Connor 6, Keenan 6, Bates 5, Berry 4, Bold 4, McBean 4, Williams 4, Banks 3, Hunter 3, Clarke 2, Dunn 2, Grice 2, Hasson 2, McPherson 2, Mitchell 2, Monaghan 2, Thomas 2, Chadwick 1, Kinsella 1, Spurren 1, Steventon 1, Williamson 1.
Goalscorers: McBean 4, Hunter 3, Thomas 3, Banks 1, Berry 1, Bold 2, Chadwick 2, Hasson 1, Keenan 1.

1918-19

Manager: Bill Norman

No	Month	Day	Venue	Opponents	Result	Score	Scorers	Attendance
1	Sep	7	(h)	Bolton W	L	1-4	Berry	
2		14	(a)	Bolton W	L	1-2	McBean	
3		21	(h)	Port Vale	D	1-1	McBean	
4		28	(a)	Port Vale	L	0-6		
5	Oct	5	(h)	Preston NE	L	1-2	Hunter	2,000
6		12	(a)	Preston NE	D	2-2	Unknown 2	
7		19	(h)	Manchester C	L	0-3		6,000
8		26	(a)	Manchester C	L	0-4		
9	Nov	2	(a)	Oldham A	D	1-1	O'Doherty	1,517
10		9	(h)	Oldham A	W	2-1	Unknown 2	2,500
11		16	(a)	Blackburn R	W	3-0	McIver, Baker, Jackson	700
12		23	(h)	Blackburn R	W	2-0	O'Doherty 2	5,000
13		30	(a)	Everton	L	0-6		10,000
14	Dec	7	(h)	Everton	L	1-3	Jackson	3,000
15		14	(a)	Rochdale	L	0-1		
16		21	(h)	Rochdale	W	5-1	Quinn 2, Hunter 2, Berry	3,000
17		28	(h)	Manchester U	D	2-2	Hunter 2	
18	Jan	6	(a)	Manchester U	D	1-1	Unknown	
19		11	(h)	Stoke	L	1-6	O'Doherty	
20		18	(a)	Stoke	L	1-2	Lockett	6,000
21		25	(h)	Bury	W	3-2	Connor, O'Doherty, Appleton	2,000
22	Feb	1	(a)	Bury	L	0-1		
23		8	(h)	Burnley	D	1-1	Hunter	
24		15	(a)	Burnley	L	0-3		6,283
25		22	(h)	Stockport C	W	2-0	O'Doherty, Hunter	3,000
26	Mar	1	(a)	Stockport C	W	2-1	Hunter, O'Doherty	
27		8	(h)	Liverpool	W	3-2	Rooke, Hunter, O'Doherty	5,000
28		15	(a)	Liverpool	L	1-3	O'Doherty	24,000
29		22	(h)	Southport Vulcan	W	6-0	O'Doherty, Hunter 4, Unknown	
30		29	(a)	Southport Vulcan	W	2-0	Hunter, O'Doherty	

FINAL LEAGUE POSITION: 11th in Principal Competition — Lancashire Section

Subsidiary Competition

No	Month	Day	Venue	Opponents	Result	Score	Scorers	Attendance
31	Dec	25	(a)	Burnley	L	1-5	Unknown	7,000
32	Apr	5	(a)	Blackburn R	D	1-1	O'Doherty	12,000
33		12	(h)	Blackburn R	W	6-1	Rooke, O'Doherty 2, Hunter 2, Wilson	8,000
34		18	(h)	Burnley	D	0-0		12,000
35		19	(h)	Preston NE	W	3-0	O'Doherty 2, Hunter	10,000
36		26	(a)	Preston NE	W	2-0	Heathcote, Hunter	
SF	May	24	(h)	Liverpool*	L	0-1		10,000

FINAL LEAGUE POSITION: 1st in Subsidiary Competition — Lancashire Section, and qualified for final stages of the Lancashire Senior Cup.*

1	2	3	4	5	6	7	8	9	10	11	
Mahon	Bainbridge	Dunn	Connor	Keenan	Booth	Buckley	Hunter	McBean	Hogan	Berry	1
..	..	..	..	..	..	..	..	..	..	..	2
..	..	Congrove	..	..	..	..	..	..	Bowman	..	3
?	?	?	?	?	?	?	?	?	?	?	4
Mahon	Bainbridge	Congrove	Robinson	Keenan	Booth	Buckley	Hunter	Robson	Bowman	Berry	5
?	?	?	?	?	?	?	?	?	?	?	6
Mahon	Bainbridge	Congrove	Robinson	Keenan	Booth	Buckley	Hunter	Robson	Bowman	Berry	7
..	..	..	..	..	..	..	..	..	..	Orrell	8
..	..	..	..	..	..	..	..	O'Doherty	..	..	9
Steventon	..	Dunn	..	..	..	..	..	..	..	..	10
..	McIver	Baker	Jackson	..	..	..	..	..	..	..	11
..	Bainbridge	Dunn	Robinson	..	..	McIver	Baker	..	Jackson	..	12
..	..	..	..	..	..	..	..	..	..	..	13
..	..	..	..	..	..	Berry	..	..	..	..	14
..	..	..	..	..	..	Quinn	..	..	..	..	15
..	..	..	..	..	..	..	Hunter	..	Appleton	Berry	16
Haslam	Dunn	Bainbridge	..	..	..	..	..	..	Bold	..	17
?	?	?	?	?	?	?	?	?	?	?	18
Steventon	Dunn	Bainbridge	Robinson	Keenan	Booth	Quinn	Hunter	O'Doherty	Bold	Berry	19
..	..	..	Connor	..	..	..	..	Lockett	..	..	20
..	..	..	..	..	..	..	..	O'Doherty	Appleton	..	21
..	..	..	..	..	..	..	..	..	..	..	22
Mitchell	Fairhurst	Jones	..	..	..	..	..	..	..	..	23
Steventon	..	..	Robinson	..	..	..	Connor	..	..	Bold	24
Mingay	..	..	..	..	..	..	Hunter	..	..	..	25
..	..	..	..	..	Berry	..	..	..	..	Watson	26
..	..	..	..	..	Rooke	..	..	..	..	..	27
..	..	..	..	..	..	..	..	..	..	..	28
..	..	..	Keenan	Watson	Booth	Appleton	Heathcote	Hunter	O'Doherty	Rooke	29
..	..	..	..	..	..	..	..	..	..	..	30

Line-ups not available for matches 4, 6 & 18

?	?	?	?	?	?	?	?	?	?	?	31
Mingay	Fairhurst	Jones	Keenan	Watson	Booth	Appleton	Heathcote	Hunter	O'Doherty	Rooke	32
..	..	..	..	..	..	..	Wilson	..	..	..	33
..	..	..	..	..	..	..	..	..	..	..	34
..	Bainbridge	..	..	..	..	..	..	..	..	..	35
..	..	..	..	..	..	Heathcote	..	..	..	..	36
..	..	Rooke	..	..	Quinn	..	..	..	..	Appleton	SF

Line-up not available for match 31

Principal Competition – Lancashire Section
Appearances: Keenan 27, Booth 24, Hunter 22, O'Doherty 20, Bainbridge 18, Robinson 17, Berry 14, Dunn 13, Quinn 13, Steventon 12, Appleton 11, Buckley 9, Connor 8, Fairhurst 8, Jones 8, Orrell 8, Bowman 7, Mahon 7, Mingay 6, Baker 5, Bold 5, Congrove 5, Jackson 5, Watson 5, Rooke 4, McBean 3, Robson 3, Heathcote 2, Hogan 2, Haslam 1, Lockett 1, Mitchell 1, McIver 3.
Goalscorers: Hunter 14, O'Doherty 11, Berry 2, Jackson 2, McBean 2, Quinn 2, Appleton 1, Baker 1, Connor 1, Lockett 1, McIver 1, Rooke 1, Unknown 6.

Subsidiary Competition – Lancashire Section
Appearances: Hunter 6, Keenan 6, Mingay 6, O'Doherty 6, Rooke 6, Watson 6, Appleton 5, Booth 5, Jones 5, Wilson 5, Bainbridge 3, Fairhurst 3, Heathcote 3, Quinn 1.
Goalscorers: O'Doherty 5, Hunter 4, Heathcote 1, Rooke 1, Wilson 1, Unknown 1.

1919-20

Manager: Bill Norman

1	Aug	30	(h)	Leeds C	W	4-2	Wilson, Lane 2 (1 pen), Charles	10,000
2	Sep	1	(a)	Lincoln C	W	3-0	Lane, Heathcote 2	
3		6	(a)	Leeds C	L	0-1		10,000
4		8	(h)	Lincoln C	W	6-0	Lane 3 (1 pen), Sibbald 2, Heathcote	9,000
5		13	(a)	Stoke	L	0-2		
6		20	(h)	Stoke	W	3-1	Heathcote, Lane 2	9,000
7		27	(a)	Grimsby T	D	1-1	Heathcote	4,000
8	Oct	3	(a)	Nottingham F	L	0-2		4,000
9		4	(h)	Grimsby T	W	2-0	Lane 2 (1 pen)	
10		11	(a)	Birmingham	L	2-4	Lane 2	16,000
11		18	(h)	Birmingham	W	3-0	Heathcote, Lane, Rookes	8,000
12		25	(a)	Leicester C	W	3-2	Lane 2, Booth	12,000
13	Nov	1	(h)	Leicester C	W	3-0	Charles, Booth, Lane	
14		8	(a)	Fulham	W	2-1	Sibbald, Lane	12,000
15		15	(h)	Fulham	D	1-1	Rookes	7,000
16		22	(a)	Coventry C	D	0-0		19,000
17		29	(h)	Coventry C	W	2-0	Heathcote, Lane	5,000
18	Dec	6	(a)	Huddersfield T	W	3-1	Quinn, Heathcote, Lane	6,500
19		13	(h)	Huddersfield T	L	0-3		5,000
20		20	(a)	Bristol C	D	0-0		8,000
21		25	(a)	Bury	W	2-1	Lane 2	15,000
22		27	(h)	Bristol C	D	0-0		10,000
23	Jan	1	(h)	Rotherham C	W	5-1	Lane 2, Sibbald, Charles, Quinn	
24		3	(h)	West Ham U	D	0-0		7,000
25		17	(a)	West Ham U	L	0-1		26,000
26		24	(h)	Clapton O	W	3-0	Rookes, Quinn, Lane	8,000
27	Feb	7	(h)	Tottenham H	L	0-1		12,000
28		14	(a)	Tottenham H	D	2-2	Lane 2	38,000
29		21	(h)	South Shields	L	0-3		8,000
30		28	(a)	South Shields	L	0-6		28,000
31	Mar	6	(a)	Wolves	W	3-0	Quinn, Sibbald, McGinn	15,000
32		13	(h)	Wolves	W	1-1	Hunter	7,000
33		18	(a)	Clapton O	L	0-3		
34		20	(a)	Hull C	W	1-0	Berry	10,000
35		27	(h)	Hull C	W	2-1	Sibbald, Hunter	6,000
36	Apr	2	(h)	Bury	W	1-0	Charles	17,000
37		3	(a)	Stockport C	D	0-0		
38		5	(a)	Rotherham C	W	2-1	Heathcote, Hunter	15,000
39		10	(h)	Stockport C	W	1-0	Heathcote	6,000
40		17	(a)	Barnsley	D	1-1	Hunter	
41		24	(h)	Barnsley	L	0-2		8,000
42	May	1	(h)	Nottingham F	W	3-2	Heathcote 3	7,000

FINAL LEAGUE POSITION: 4th in Division Two

Appearances
Goals

FA Cup

1	Jan	10	(h)	Derby C	D	0-0		11,000
R		14	(a)	Derby C	W	4-1	Sibbald, Lane 2, Charles	20,000
2		30	(a)	Preston NE	L	1-2	Quinn	25,000

Appearances
Goals

Mingay	Tulloch	Jones	Keenan	Wilson	Rookes	Charles	Heathcote	Lane	Sibbald	Quinn	Fairhurst	Booth	Appleton	O'Doherty	Tremeling	Jacklin	McGinn	Burke	Hunter	Marsh	Bainbridge	Berry	Baker	Kent	Howard	Dumper	Barrass	
1	2	3	4	5	6	7	8	9	10	11																		1
1	2	3	4	5	6	7	8	9	10	11																		2
1	2	3	4	5	6	7	8	9	10	11																		3
1	2		5		6	11	8	9	10		3	4	7															4
1	2	3	5		6	7	8	9	11			4		10														5
1	2	3	4	5	6	11	8	9	10				7															6
1	2	3	4	5	6	11	8	9	10				7															7
1	2	3	4	5	6	11	8	9	10				7															8
1	2	3	4	5	11		8	9	10		6		7															9
	2	3	4		6		8	9	10	11			7		5	1												10
1	2	3	4		6		8	9	10	11			7		5													11
1	2	3	4		6		8	9	10	11		4	7		5													12
1		3			6	11	8	9	10		2	4	7		5													13
1		3			6		8	9	10	11	2		7		5													14
1		3	4		6		8	9	10	11	2		7		5													15
1		3	4		6		8	9	10	11	2		7		5													16
1		3	4	5	6		8	9	10	11	2		7															17
1	2	3	4	5	6		8	9	10	11			7															18
1	2	3	4	5	6		8	9	10	11			7															19
1	2	3	4	5	6	7	8	9		11							10	4										20
1	2			5	6	7		9	8	11	3						10	4										21
1		3		5	6	7		9	8	11	2						10	4										22
1		3		5	6	7		9	8	11	2						10	4										23
1	2	3		5		7	8	9		11		6					10	4										24
1	2			5	6	7	8	9		11	3						10											25
1	2		4	5	6	7		9	8	11	3						10											26
1	2		4	5	6	7		9		11	3								8	10								27
1	2		4	5			8	9		11	3	6					10		7									28
1	2		4	5			8	9		11	3	6					10		7									29
1	2		4	5	11			9	8	10		6							7		3							30
1	2		4	5	6	7			8	11	3						10			9								31
1	2		4		6				8		3						10	4	7	9		11						32
1	2		5		6	7			8		3						10	4		9		11						33
1	2		5		6	7			8		3						10	4	9			11						34
1	2		5		6	7			8		3						10	4	9			11						35
1	2		5		6	7	8		9		3						10						4	11				36
1	2		5		6	7	8		9		3						10					11	4					37
1	2		5		6	7	8				3						10		9				4	11				38
1	2		5		6	7	8				3						10		9				4	11				39
1	2		5		6	7	8				3						10		9				4	11				40
1	2		5		6	7	8				3						10		9				4	11				41
1	2		5		11		8		9		3												4		6	7	10	42
41	35	22	35	22	39	27	31	30	32	24	27	8	15	1	7	1	20	9	11	4	1	5	7	5	1	1	1	
				1	3	4	13	26	6	4		2					1		4			1						

Mingay	Tulloch	Jones	Keenan	Wilson	Rookes	Charles	Heathcote	Lane	Sibbald	Quinn	Fairhurst	Booth	Appleton	O'Doherty	Tremeling	Jacklin	McGinn	Burke	Hunter	Marsh	Bainbridge	Berry	Baker	Kent	Howard	Dumper	Barrass	
1	2		4	5	6	7	8	9		11	3						10											1
1	2		4	5	6	7		9	8	11	3						10											R
1	2		4	5	6	7		9	8	11	3						10											2
3	3		3	3	3	3	1	3	2	3	3						3											
						1		2	1	1																		

1920-21

Manager: Bill Norman

1	Aug	28	(a)	Bury	D 2-2	Heathcote, Keenan	20,000
2		30	(h)	Bristol C	L 1-2	Heathcote	10,000
3	Sep	4	(h)	Bury	L 0-1		16,000
4		8	(a)	Bristol C	D 1-1	Barrass	20,000
5		11	(h)	Coventry C	W 4-0	Benton 3, Donachie	12,500
6		13	(h)	Clapton O	D 2-2	Barrass, Heathcote	8,000
7		18	(a)	Coventry C	W 2-0	Benton, Heathcote	20,000
8		25	(h)	Leeds U	W 1-0	Heathcote	8,000
9	Oct	2	(a)	Leeds U	L 0-2		9,500
10		9	(h)	Birmingham	W 3-0	Rookes, Heathcote, Benton	9,000
11		16	(a)	Birmingham	L 0-3		30,000
12		23	(h)	West Ham U	W 1-0	Reid	10,000
13		30	(a)	West Ham U	D 1-1	Heathcote	25,000
14	Nov	6	(h)	Fulham	W 1-0	Barrass	8,000
15		13	(a)	Fulham	W 2-1	Benton, Heathcote	12,000
16		20	(h)	Cardiff C	L 2-4	Heathcote 2	12,000
17		27	(a)	Cardiff C	D 0-0		22,000
18	Dec	4	(h)	Leicester C	W 2-0	Reid, Barrass	8,000
19		11	(a)	Leicester C	W 1-0	Barrass	16,500
20		18	(h)	Notts C	L 0-2		7,000
21		25	(h)	Barnsley	W 1-0	Heathcote	12,000
22		27	(a)	Barnsley	W 1-0	Barrass	18,000
23	Jan	1	(a)	Notts C	W 2-1	Heathcote 2	15,000
24		15	(a)	Nottingham F	L 1-3	Ratcliffe	10,000
25		22	(h)	Nottingham F	W 1-0	Mee	9,000
26	Feb	5	(h)	Sheffield W	D 1-1	Heathcote	9,000
27		7	(a)	Sheffield W	W 1-0	Ratcliffe	8,000
28		12	(a)	Rotherham C	W 2-0	Keenan, Heathcote	15,000
29		19	(h)	Rotherham C	L 0-1		
30		26	(a)	Port Vale	W 1-0	Keenan	
31	Mar	5	(h)	Port Vale	W 1-0	Heathcote	
32		12	(a)	South Shields	L 0-1		15,000
33		19	(h)	South Shields	W 3-2	Bedford, Charles 2	8,000
34		25	(h)	Stoke	W 3-1	Heathcote, Barrass, Bedford	15,000
35		26	(h)	Hull C	L 1-2	Bedford	15,000
36		28	(a)	Stoke	D 1-1	Charles	
37	Apr	2	(a)	Hull C	L 1-2	Barrass	9,000
38		9	(h)	Wolves	W 3-0	Bedford 2, Mee	10,300
39		16	(a)	Wolves	L 1-3	Bedford	13,802
40		23	(h)	Stockport C	D 1-1	Bedford	7,000
41		30	(a)	Stockport C	D 2-2	Heathcote, Barrass	
42	May	7	(a)	Clapton O	D 0-0		10,000

FINAL LEAGUE POSITION: 4th in Division Two

Appearances
Goals

FA Cup

1	Jan	8	(a)	Darlington	D 2-2	Ratcliffe, Barrass	16,113
R		12	(h)	Darlington	W 2-1	McGinn, Ratcliffe	8,000
2		29	(a)	Southend U	L 0-1		9,000

Appearances
Goals

Mingay	Fairhurst	Tulloch	Keenan	Halstead	Howard	Charles	Heathcote	Ratcliffe	McGinn	Donachie	Benton	Popplewell	Barrass	Burke	Gavin	Brown	Richardson	Bainbridge	Rookes	Mee	Baker	Hunter	Reid	Lovett	Marsh	Leaver	Bedford	
1	2	3	4	5	6	7	8	9	10	11																		1
1	3	2	5		6	7	8	9	10	11	4																	2
1	3	2	4		6	7	8		9	11		5	10															3
1	3	2	5		6	7	8			11	9		10	4														4
1	3	2	5		6	7	8			11	9		10	4														5
1		2	5			7	8			11	9		10	4	3	6												6
	3		5			7	8				9		10	4			1	2	6	11								7
	3	2	5			7	8			11	9		10	4			1		6									8
	3	2	5			7	8			11	9			4			1		6		10							9
	3	2	5			7	10			11	8			4			1		6			9						10
	3	2	5		4		10	9		11	8						1		6			7						11
		2	5		4		10			7	8				3		1		6	11			9					12
	3	2	5				10			7	8		9				1		6	11	4							13
	3	2	5				10			7	8		9				1		6	11	4							14
	3	2	5				10			7	8		9				1		6	11	4							15
	3	2	5				10			7	8		9				1		6	11	4							16
	3	2	5			7	10				6		9				1				4		11	8				17
	3	2	5			7	8				6		10				1			11	4		9					18
	3	2	5			7	10			11	8		9				1		6		4							19
	3	2	5			7	10			11	8		9				1		6		4							20
	3	2	5				10			7	6		9				1			11	4			8				21
	3	2	5				8	9	4	7	6		10				1			11								22
		2	5			7	8	9	4		6		10		3		1			11								23
			5			7		9	4		6		10		3		1	2		11					8			24
		2	5			7		9	4		8		10		3		1		6	11								25
		2	5			7	8	9	4		10				3		1		6	11								26
		2	5			7	8	9	4		6				3		1			11						10		27
		2	5			7	8	9	4		6				3		1			11						10		28
		2	5			7	8	9	4		6				3		1			11						10		29
		2	5			7	10	9	6		4		8		3		1			11								30
		2	5			7	10	9	6		4		8		3		1			11								31
		2	5			7	10		4		6		8		3		1			11							9	32
		2	5			7	10		4		6		8		3		1			11							9	33
		2	5			7	10		4		6		8		3		1			11							9	34
		2	5			7	10		4				8		3		1		6	11							9	35
1		2	5			7	10		4		6		8		3					11							9	36
1		2	5			7	10		4		6		8							11	3						9	37
1		2	5			7	10		4		6		8		3					11							9	38
1		2	5			7	10		4		6		8		3					11								39
1		2	5			7	10		4		6		8							11	3						9	40
1		2	5			7	10		4		6		8						3	11							9	41
1		2	5		6		10		4		7		8						3	11							9	42
13	20	40	42	1	8	33	40	13	24	19	39	1	32	7	18	1	29	2	17	29	12	2	3	2	1	3	10	
			3			3	18	2		1	6		9						1	2			2				7	

Mingay	Fairhurst	Tulloch	Keenan	Halstead	Howard	Charles	Heathcote	Ratcliffe	McGinn	Donachie	Benton	Popplewell	Barrass	Burke	Gavin	Brown	Richardson	Bainbridge	Rookes	Mee	Baker	Hunter	Reid	Lovett	Marsh	Leaver	Bedford	
		2	5			7	8	9	4		6		10		3		1			11								1
			5			7	8	9	4		6		10		3		1		2	11								R
		2	5			7	10		4		9		8		3		1		6	11								2
		2	3			3	3	2	3		3		3		3		3		2	3								
								2	1				1															

1921-22

Manager: Bill Norman

No	Month	Day	Venue	Opponent	Result	Score	Scorers	Attendance
1	Aug	27	(h)	Derby C	W	4-2	Benton, Mee 2, Heathcote	12,000
2		31	(a)	Bury	L	0-3		12,000
3	Sep	3	(a)	Derby C	L	0-1		10,000
4		5	(h)	Bury	L	0-1		19,000
5		10	(a)	Leeds U	D	0-0		18,000
6		17	(h)	Leeds U	L	1-3	Barrass	13,000
7		24	(a)	Hull C	L	0-2		8,000
8	Oct	1	(h)	Hull C	L	0-1		10,000
9		8	(a)	Notts C	L	1-2	Bedford	
10		15	(h)	Notts C	L	1-2	Benton	
11		22	(a)	Crystal P	L	0-1		15,000
12		29	(h)	Crystal P	L	1-3	Bedford (pen)	
13	Nov	5	(a)	Rotherham C	W	1-0	Charles	
14		12	(h)	Rotherham C	W	3-1	Bedford 2, Sibbald	
15		19	(h)	Sheffield W	L	0-2		
16		26	(a)	Sheffield W	L	1-5	Mee	12,000
17	Dec	3	(h)	Fulham	L	0-2		6,500
18		10	(a)	Fulham	L	0-1		15,000
19		17	(h)	Bradford	D	1-1	Sibbald	7,000
20		24	(a)	Bradford	D	0-0		6,000
21		26	(h)	Leicester C	W	2-0	Bedford 2	
22		27	(a)	Leicester C	L	0-1		
23		31	(a)	Clapton O	L	0-3		20,000
24	Jan	14	(h)	Clapton O	W	2-0	Power, Barrass	6,000
25		21	(h)	Coventry C	W	2-1	Power, Baverstock	5,000
26		28	(a)	Coventry C	W	1-0	Mee	15,000
27	Feb	4	(h)	Barnsley	W	1-0	Power	5,500
28		11	(a)	Barnsley	L	2-3	Power, Barrass	
29		18	(h)	Wolves	L	1-3	Power (pen)	7,000
30		25	(a)	Wolves	L	0-4		11,510
31	Mar	4	(h)	Nottingham F	W	2-1	Mee 2	8,000
32		11	(a)	Nottingham F	D	0-0		12,000
33		18	(a)	Bristol C	W	1-0	Barrass	18,000
34		25	(h)	Bristol C	W	2-0	McGinn, Heathcote	10,000
35	Apr	1	(a)	South Shields	L	1-2	Barrass	8,000
36		8	(h)	South Shields	W	4-0	Charles, Power, Mee (pen), Bedford	5,000
37		14	(h)	Stoke	W	3-2	Barrass, Benton, Bedford	12,000
38		15	(h)	Port Vale	L	0-1		15,000
39		17	(a)	Stoke	D	1-1	Bedford	20,000
40		24	(a)	Port Vale	L	0-1		14,000
41		29	(a)	West Ham U	W	2-0	Bedford, Barrass	18,000
42	May	6	(h)	West Ham U	W	3-1	Bedford, Leaver, Barrass	12,000

FINAL LEAGUE POSITION: 19th in Division Two

Appearances
Goals

FA Cup

No	Month	Day	Venue	Opponent	Result	Score	Scorers	Attendance
1	Jan	7	(h)	Watford	L	1-2	Bedford	10,121

Appearances
Goals

Richardson	Tulloch	Clough	McGinn	Rooks	Benton	Charles	Heathcote	Bedford	Barrass	Mee	Gavin	Keenan	Mingay	Ford	Curran	Sibbald	Hacking	Dyke	Watkinson	Baker	Leaver	Power	Roseboom	Baverstock	Stroud	Lowson	Brown	
1	2	3	4	5	6	7	8	9	10	11																		1
1	2		4		6	7	8	9	10	11	3	5																2
1	2		4	5	6	7	8	9	10	11	3																	3
			4		6	7	8	9	10	11	3		1	2	5													4
	2		4		6	7		9	10	11	3	5	1			8												5
	2		4		6	7		9	8	11	3	5	1			10												6
	2		4		6	7	8	9	10	11	3				5		1											7
	2		4		6	7	8	9	10	11	3				5		1											8
	2		4	6	8			9	10	11	3				5		1	7										9
	2		4	6	8	7		9	10	11	3				5		1											10
	2		4	6	8	7	10	9		11	3				5		1											11
	2		4	6	8	7	10	9		11	3				5		1											12
	2		5	6	4	7	10	9		11	3		1			8												13
	2		5	6	4	7	10	9		11	3		1			8												14
	2		5	6	4		10	9		11	3		1			8			7									15
	2		4	7			10	9		11	3	5	1			8				6								16
	2			7	4		8			11	3	5	1		6	10					9							17
	2			6		7		8	10	11	3	5	1		4	9												18
	2		4	6					9	11	3	5	1			7						8	10					19
	2		4	6	9	7				11	3	5	1									8	10					20
	2		4	6		7		9		11	3	5	1									8	10					21
	2		4	6	9	7				11	3	5	1									8	10					22
	2		4	7	6			9		11	3	5	1									8	10					23
	3		4	6		7			8	11			1		5	10						9		2				24
	3		4	6		7			8	11			1		5	10						9		2				25
	3		4	6		7			8	11			1		5	10						9		2				26
	3			6	4	7			8	11			1		5	10						9		2				27
	3			6	4	7			8	11			1		5	10						9		2				28
	3		6			7			8	11		4	1		5	10						9			2			29
	3		4		6	7		9	10	11			1		5							8			2			30
	2		4		6	7		9	10	11	3		1		5							8						31
	2		4		6	7	8		10	11	3		1		5							9						32
	2		4		6	7	8	9	10	11	3		1		5													33
	2		4		6	7	8	9	10	11	3		1		5													34
	2		4		6	7	8		10	11	3		1		5							9						35
	2		4		6	7		9	10	11	3		1		5							8						36
	2		4		6	7		9	10	11	3		1		5							8						37
	2			4	6	7	8	9	10	11	3		1															38
	3				4			9	10	11		5	1		5						7		8	2		6		39
	3				4			9	8	11			1								7		10	2		6		40
	3				5			9	10	11		6	1									8		2		4	7	41
	3		4		6	7		9	10	11		5	1								8			2				42
3	41	1	34	23	34	33	18	30	31	42	30	15	33	1	25	15	6	1	1	1	4	18	7	9	2	3	1	
			1		3	2	2	11	8	7						2					1	6		1				

Richardson	Tulloch	Clough	McGinn	Rooks	Benton	Charles	Heathcote	Bedford	Barrass	Mee	Gavin	Keenan	Mingay	Ford	Curran	Sibbald	Hacking	Dyke	Watkinson	Baker	Leaver	Power	Roseboom	Baverstock	Stroud	Lowson	Brown	
	2		4	7	6			9		11	3	5	1									8	10					1
	1		1	1	1			1		1	1	1	1									1	1					
								1																				

1922-23

Manager: Bill Norman

1	Aug	26	(a)	Leeds U	D 1-1	Barrass	20,000
2		28	(h)	Clapton O	D 0-0		14,000
3	Sep	2	(h)	Leeds U	W 1-0	Bedford	14,000
4		4	(a)	Clapton O	W 1-0	Bedford	
5		9	(h)	Bradford C	W 3-0	Barrass 3	14,000
6		16	(a)	Bradford C	W 2-0	Bedford 2	12,000
7		23	(h)	Southampton	L 1-2	Bedford	13,500
8		30	(a)	Southampton	D 1-1	Barrass	17,000
9	Oct	7	(h)	Derby C	W 3-2	Roseboom, Bedford 2	12,000
10		14	(a)	Derby C	L 0-1		12,000
11		21	(a)	West Ham U	L 0-2		16,000
12		28	(h)	West Ham U	W 4-1	Bedford 2, Barrass 2	10,000
13	Nov	4	(a)	Notts C	L 0-2		15,000
14		11	(h)	Notts C	D 1-1	Bedford	12,000
15		18	(a)	Fulham	D 1-1	McIvenney	15,000
16		25	(h)	Fulham	W 3-0	Barrass, Bedford, McIvenney	9,500
17	Dec	2	(h)	Crystal P	W 4-0	McIvenney, Barrass, Watkinson, Bedford (pen)	10,000
18		9	(a)	Crysral P	D 1-1	Bedford	5,000
19		16	(h)	Hull C	D 0-0		8,000
20		23	(a)	Hull C	D 0-0		8,000
21		25	(a)	Leicester C	W 2-1	Bedford 2	
22		26	(h)	Leicester C	L 1-2	McIvenney	15,000
23		30	(h)	Sheffield W	W 3-0	Bedford 2, Barrass	10,000
24	Jan	1	(a)	Stockport C	D 2-2	Roseboom, Barrass	18,000
25		6	(a)	Sheffield W	W 3-2	Bedford 3	28,000
26		20	(a)	Barnsley	D 2-2	Barrass, Bedford	7,000
27		27	(h)	Barnsley	L 0-1		20,000
28	Feb	3	(a)	Port Vale	L 0-2		9,000
29		10	(h)	South Shields	W 3-0	Barrass 2, Bedford	9,000
30		17	(a)	Wolves	W 4-3	Bedford 3, Mee	11,793
31		24	(h)	Wolves	W 3-1	Charles, Bedford, Barrass	8,500
32	Mar	3	(a)	Coventry C	W 2-1	Bedford 2	14,000
33		10	(h)	Coventry C	L 0-1		12,000
34		17	(h)	Port Vale	L 0-2		11,000
35		21	(a)	South Shields	L 0-1		
36		30	(h)	Stockport C	D 0-0		15,000
37		31	(h)	Manchester U	W 1-0	Charles	17,500
38	Apr	7	(a)	Manchester U	L 1-2	Leaver	24,500
39		14	(h)	Bury	W 5-1	Charles, Barrass, Bedford 3	12,000
40		21	(a)	Bury	L 0-3		10,000
41		28	(h)	Rotherham C	W 1-0	Bedford	6,000
42	May	5	(a)	Rotherham C	L 0-1		

FINAL LEAGUE POSITION: 5th in Division Two

Appearances
Goals

FA Cup

1	Jan	13	(a)	Derby C	L 0-2		22,745

Appearances
Goals

Mingay	Baverstock	Tulloch	McGinn	Keenan	Benton	Charles	McIlvenney	Bedford	Barrass	Mee	Hird	Watkinson	Roseboom	Edge	Brown	Leaver	Wood	Curran	Baker	Jones	Lowson	White	Martin	O'Doherty	Watson	
1	2	3	4	5	6	7	8	9	10	11																1
1	2	3	4	5	6	7		9	10	11	8															2
1	2	3	4	5	6			9	10	11	8	7														3
1	2	3	4	5	6			9		11	8	7	10													4
1	2	3	4	5	6			9	8	11			10	7												5
1	2	3	4	5	6			9	8	11			10	7												6
1	2	3	4	5	6			9	8	11		7	10													7
1	2	3	5		6	7		9	8	11			10		4											8
1	2	3	4		6	7		9	8	11			10			5										9
1		3	4		6	7		9		11	8		10			5	2									10
1		3			6	7		9	8	11			10		4	5	2									11
1		3			6			9	8	11				7	4	10	2	5								12
1		3			6			9	8	11				7	4	10	2	5								13
1		3			6			9	8	11				7	4	10	2	5								14
1		3	4		6		8	9	10	11		7					2		5							15
1		3	4		6		8	9	10	11		7				5	2									16
1		3	4		6		8	9	10	11		7				5	2									17
1		3	4		6		8	9	10	11		7				5	2									18
1			4		6		8	9	10	11		7				5	2			3						19
1			4		6		8	9	10	11		7				5	2			3						20
1			4		6	7	8	9	10	11							2				5					21
1		3	4		6	7	8	9	10	11							2				5					22
1		3	4		6	7		9	10	11			8				2	5								23
1			4		6	7		9	10	11			8				2	5		3						24
1		2	4		6	7		9	10	11			8					5		3						25
1		3	4		6	7	8	9	10	11						5	2									26
1		3	4		6	7		9	8	11			10			5	2									27
1		3	4		6	7	8	9	10	11						5	2									28
1			4		6	7	8	9	10	11						5	2			3						29
1			4		6	7	8	9	10	11						5	2			3						30
1			4			7	8	9	10	11					6	5	2			3						31
1			4			7		9	10	11					6	5	2			3		8				32
1			4			7		9	10	11					6	5	2			3		8				33
1			4				8	9	10	11						5	2			3		7	6			34
1			4				8	9	10	11						5	2	6		3		7				35
1		2	4		6			9		11			8			5				3		7		10		36
1		2	4		6	7		9	10	11						5				3		8				37
1		2	4		6	7		9	10	11						5				3		8				38
1		2	4		6	7		9	10	11						5	3					8				39
1		3	4		6	7		9	10	11						5	2					8				40
1					6	7		9	4	11						5	2			3		10			8	41
1					6	7		9	4	11						5	2			3		10			8	42
42	9	29	36	7	37	25	16	42	39	42	4	9	13	5	8	28	29	7	1	16	2	11	1	1	2	
						3	4	32	16	1		1	2			1										

Mingay	Baverstock	Tulloch	McGinn	Keenan	Benton	Charles	McIlvenney	Bedford	Barrass	Mee	Hird	Watkinson	Roseboom	Edge	Brown	Leaver	Wood	Curran	Baker	Jones	Lowson	White	Martin	O'Doherty	Watson	
1		3	4		6	7	8	9	10	11							2	5								1
1		1	1		1	1	1	1	1	1							1	1								

1923-24

Manager: Major Frank Buckley

1	Aug	25	(h)	Oldham A	D 2-2	Bedford, Leaver	16,000
2		27	(a)	South Shields	L 0-1		
3	Sep	1	(a)	Oldham A	D 1-1	Bedford (pen)	17,000
4		3	(h)	South Shields	D 1-1	White	15,000
5		8	(a)	Stoke	D 2-2	Mee, Bedford	16,000
6		15	(h)	Stoke	D 1-1	Charles	15,000
7		22	(a)	Crystal P	L 1-3	Bedford	
8		29	(h)	Crystal P	W 2-0	Barrass, Mee	12,000
9	Oct	6	(a)	Sheffield W	D 2-2	Thompson, Bedford	15,000
10		13	(h)	Sheffield W	W 1-0	Barrass	12,000
11		20	(h)	Coventry C	W 5-0	Mee, Watson 2, White 2	10,000
12		27	(a)	Coventry C	L 1-3	Barrass	15,000
13	Nov	3	(h)	Bristol C	W 2-0	Barrass, Bedford	9,500
14		10	(a)	Bristol C	D 1-1	Barrass	10,000
15		17	(a)	Southampton	L 2-3	Bedford 2 (1 pen)	10,000
16		24	(h)	Southampton	W 2-0	Bedford 2	10,000
17	Dec	1	(a)	Fulham	W 3-2	Barrass 2, Meredith	17,000
18		8	(h)	Fulham	W 3-0	Mee, Bedford, Watson	10,000
19		15	(a)	Derby C	L 0-2		18,000
20		22	(h)	Derby C	W 4-0	Bedford 2, Watson, Benton	12,000
21		25	(a)	Stockport C	L 1-2	Bedford	15,000
22		26	(h)	Stockport C	D 0-0		12,000
23		29	(h)	Nelson	D 1-1	Bedford	9,000
24	Jan	5	(a)	Nelson	W 3-2	Bedford 2, Barrass	10,000
25		19	(h)	Bury	W 3-1	Bedford, White, Barrass	10,000
26		26	(a)	Bury	L 0-2		15,000
27	Feb	6	(h)	Manchester U	W 1-0	Bedford	7,000
28		9	(a)	Manchester U	D 0-0		20,000
29		16	(h)	Barnsley	L 0-2		10,000
30		23	(a)	Barnsley	L 1-3	Bedford	10,000
31	Mar	1	(h)	Bradford C	W 2-1	Bedford 2	8,000
32		8	(a)	Bradford C	W 2-0	Bedford, White	13,000
33		15	(a)	Port Vale	W 6-2	Bedford 3 (1 pen), White, Butler, Meredith	
34		22	(h)	Port Vale	W 6-1	Bedford 3, White 2, Meredith	9,500
35		29	(a)	Leeds U	D 0-0		25,000
36	Apr	5	(h)	Leeds U	D 1-1	Bedford	14,000
37		12	(a)	Leicester C	W 2-1	Butler, Bedford	15,000
38		18	(h)	Hull C	D 0-0		16,000
39		19	(h)	Leicester C	W 3-1	White 2, Watson	15,000
40		21	(a)	Hull C	L 1-2	Bedford (pen)	30,000
41		26	(a)	Clapton O	L 0-1		10,000
42	May	3	(h)	Clapton O	W 3-0	Mee, White, Mackenzie	

FINAL LEAGUE POSITION: 4th in Division Two

Appearances
Goals

FA Cup

1	Jan	12	(h)	Sheffield U	W 1-0	White	12,567
2	Feb	2	(a)	Southampton	L 1-3	Bedford	19,519

Appearances
Goals

Mingay	Wood	Tulloch	Martin	Leaver	Benton	White	Mackenzie	Bedford	Barrass	Mee	Jones	Charles	Carruthers	Thompson	Curran	Gadsden	Forbes	Meredith	Watson	Wellock	McGinn	Hacking	Butler	
1	2	3	4	5	6	7	8	9	10	11														1
1	2		4	5	6			9	10	11	3	7	8											2
1	2		4	5	6	8		9	10	11	3	7												3
1	2		4	5	6	8		9	10	11	3	7												4
1	2		4	5	6			9	10	11	3		8	7										5
1	2		4	5	6			9	10	11	3	7		8										6
1	2		4	5	6			9	10	11	3	7		8										7
1	2	3	4		6			9	10	11		7		8	5									8
1	2		4		6			9	10	11				8		3	5	7						9
1	2		4		6			9	10	11	3			8			5	7						10
1	2		4		6	9			10	11	3						5	7	8					11
1			4	2	6	8		9	10	11	3						5	7						12
1				2	6	8		9	10	11	3						5	7		4				13
1				2	6	8		9	10	11	3						5	7		4				14
1			4	2	6			9	10	11	3						5	7	8					15
1		3		2	6			9	10	11					4		5	7	8					16
1		3		2	6			9	10	11					4		5	7	8					17
1				2	6			9	10	11					4	3	5	7	8					18
1				2	6			9	10	11					4	3	5	7	8					19
1			5	2	6		10	9		11					4	3		7	8					20
1		3	5	2	6		10	9	8	11					4			7						21
1		3	5	2	6		10	9	8	11					4			7						22
1		3		2	6			9	10	11					4		5	7	8					23
1				2	6	8		9	10	11	3						5	7			4			24
1		2			6	8		9	10	11	3						5	7			4			25
1				2	6	8		9	10	11	3						5	7			4			26
	2				6	8		9	10	11							5	7		3	4	1		27
					6	8		9	10	11	3						5	7		2	4	1		28
				3	6	8		9	10	11							5	7		2	4	1		29
				5	6	8		9	10	11	3							7		2	4	1		30
				2	6	8		9	5	11	3							7	4			1	10	31
				2	6	8		9	5	11	3							7			4	1	10	32
	2				6	8		9	5	11	3							7			4	1	10	33
	2				6	8		9	5	11	3							7			4	1	10	34
	2				6	8		9	5	11	3							7			4	1	10	35
	2				6	8		9	5	11	3							7			4	1	10	36
	2					8		9	5	11	3							7	6		4	1	10	37
	2					8	10	9	5	11	3							7	6		4	1		38
	2			5		8		9	7	11	3								6		4	1	10	39
				5		8		9		11	3							7	6		4	1	10	40
				2		8		9		11						3	5	7	6		4	1	10	41
					6	9	8		5	11	3					2		7	4			1	10	42
26	20	8	16	28	37	26	6	40	39	42	28	6	2	6	9	6	19	33	15	6	17	16	11	
				1	1	11	1	32	9	5		1		1				3	5				2	

Mingay	Wood	Tulloch	Martin	Leaver	Benton	White	Mackenzie	Bedford	Barrass	Mee	Jones	Charles	Carruthers	Thompson	Curran	Gadsden	Forbes	Meredith	Watson	Wellock	McGinn	Hacking	Butler	
1				2	6	8		9	10	11	3	7			5						4			1
1				2	6	8		9	10	11	3	7			5						4			2
2				2	2	2		2	2	2	2	2			2						2			
						1		1																

1924-25

Manager: Major Frank Buckley

1	Aug	30	(h)	Clapton O	W 1-0	Bedford	15,000
2	Sep	1	(a)	South Shields	W 3-1	Barrass, White, Bedford	
3		6	(a)	Hull C	D 1-1	Bedford (pen)	12,000
4		8	(h)	South Shields	W 5-0	Bedford 4, Meredith	15,000
5		13	(h)	Portsmouth	D 1-1	White	
6		15	(h)	Derby C	W 5-1	Barrass 2, White, Bedford 2	14,000
7		20	(a)	Fulham	L 0-1		22,000
8		27	(h)	Wolves	L 2-4	Barrass, Bedford (pen)	13,000
9	Oct	4	(a)	Barnsley	W 4-2	Butler 3, Meredith	11,000
10		11	(h)	Middlesbrough	D 1-1	Mee	14,000
11		18	(a)	Port Vale	W 2-1	White 2	
12		25	(h)	Crystal P	L 0-1		
13	Nov	1	(a)	Southampton	L 1-2	Meredith	4,000
14		8	(h)	Chelsea	L 1-2	White	12,000
15		15	(a)	Stockport C	L 0-1		
16		22	(h)	Manchester U	D 1-1	Bedford	10,000
17		29	(a)	Leicester C	W 2-0	Bedford, Meredith	20,000
18	Dec	6	(h)	Stoke	L 1-2	Barrass	
19		20	(h)	Oldham A	L 1-2	Bedford (pen)	10,000
20		25	(a)	Sheffield W	W 6-2	Barrass 3, Bedford 2, Meredith	
21		26	(h)	Sheffield W	D 2-2	Curran, Bedford	15,500
22		27	(a)	Clapton O	L 0-1		15,000
23	Jan	3	(h)	Hull C	D 0-0		7,000
24		17	(a)	Portsmouth	D 1-1	Barrass	
25		24	(h)	Fulham	W 4-1	Bedford 2 (1 pen), Streets 2	6,000
26	Feb	7	(h)	Barnsley	L 1-2	White	9,000
27		14	(a)	Middlesbrough	L 1-4	Barrass	12,000
28		28	(a)	Crystal P	W 2-1	Meredith, Bedford	15,000
29	Mar	9	(a)	Coventry C	L 1-2	Barrass	
30		14	(a)	Chelsea	L 0-3		27,000
31		21	(h)	Stockport C	L 0-1		
32		23	(a)	Wolves	L 0-2		7,450
33		28	(a)	Manchester U	D 0-0		30,000
34	Apr	1	(h)	Southampton	W 1-0	Bedford (pen)	8,000
35		4	(h)	Leicester C	W 2-1	Bedford (pen), Meredith	9,000
36		10	(h)	Bradford C	L 1-2	Bedford	17,000
37		11	(a)	Stoke	L 1-3	Butler	
38		14	(a)	Bradford C	L 0-1		15,000
39		18	(h)	Coventry C	W 3-1	Watson, Butler, Curran	9,000
40		22	(h)	Port Vale	W 4-1	Butler, Bedford, Mee 2	8,000
41		25	(a)	Oldham A	L 1-4	Bedford	8,988
42	May	2	(a)	Derby C	D 2-2	Butler, Mee	8,000

FINAL LEAGUE POSITION: 17th in Division Two

Appearances

Goals

FA Cup

1	Jan	10	(h)	Barrow	D 0-0		11,755
R		13	(a)	Barrow	W 2-1	Bedford, Streets	7,154
2		31	(a)	Bradford	D 1-1	Meredith	21,500
R	Feb	4	(h)	Bradford	W 2-1	Streets, Meredith	13,800
3		21	(a)	West Ham U	D 1-1	Bedford	31,000
R		25	(h)	West Ham U	W 3-0	Meredith, Bedford 2	15,190
4	Mar	7	(a)	Blackburn R	L 0-1		60,011

Appearances

Goals

Hacking	Leaver	Jones	Watson	Thorpe	Benton	Meredith	White	Bedford	Butler	Mee	Barrass	Wilkinson	Gadsden	Wood	Curran	Bradshaw	Crompton	Streets	Warren	McGinn	Hamilton	Williams	McIntosh	Tremelling	Wellock	
1	2	3	4	5	6	7	8	9	10	11																1
1	2	3	4	5	6	7	8	9		11	10															2
1	2	3	4	5	6	7	8	9		11	10															3
	2	3	4		6	7	8	9	10	11	5	1														4
	2	3	4		6	7	8	9	10	11	5	1														5
	2	3	4	5	6	7	8	9		11	10	1														6
	2		4	5	6	7	8	9		11	10	1	3													7
	2		4	5	6	7	8	9		11	10	1	3													8
1			4	5	6	7	9		10	11	8			2	3											9
1			4	5	6	7	9		10	11	8			2	3											10
1			4		6	7	8	9	10	11	5			2	3											11
1			4		6	7	8	9	10	11	5			2	3											12
1	5	3	4		6	7	8	9		11	10					2										13
1	5	3	4		6	7	8	9		11	10					2										14
1	5	3	6			7	8	9	10	11	4					2										15
	5	3	6			7	8	9	10	11	4					2	1									16
	5	3	4		6	7	8	9		11	10					2	1									17
	5	3	4		6	7	8	9		11	10					2	1									18
	2	3	4		6	7	8	9		11	10				5		1									19
	2	3	4		6	7	8	9		11	10				5		1									20
	2	3	4		6	7	8	9		11	10				5		1									21
	2	3	6			7	8	9	10	11					5		1	4								22
	2	3	4		6	7	8	9		11	10				5		1									23
	2	3	4		6	7		9		11	10				5		1	8								24
	2	3	4		6	7		9		11	10				5		1	8								25
	2	3	4	10	6	7	8	9		11							1		5							26
	2	3	4		6	7	8	9		11	10				5		1									27
	2		4		6	7	8	9		11					5	3	1	10								28
	2	3		5	6			9		11	10						1	8		4	7					29
	2	3			6	7	8	9		11	10				5		1	4								30
	2	3	4		6	7		9		11					5		1	8				10				31
	2	3	4		6	7		9		11					5		1	8					10			32
	2	3	4		6	7	8	10		11					5		1							9		33
	2	3	4		6	7	8	10		11					5		1							9		34
	2	3	4		6	7	8	9	10	11					5		1									35
	2	3	4		6	7	8	9	10	11					5		1									36
	2	3	4		6	7	8	9	10	11					5		1									37
1		3	4		6	7	8	9	10	11				2	5											38
		3	8		6	7		9	10	11				2	5		1								4	39
		3	8	4	6	7		9	10	11				2	5		1									40
		3	8		6	7		9	10	11					5	2	1	4								41
			8	4	6	7		9	10	11				2	5	3	1									42
11	33	34	40	12	39	41	33	40	18	42	26	5	2	8	26	9	26	9	1	1	1	1	1	2	1	
			1			7	7	24	7	4	11				2			2								

Hacking	Leaver	Jones	Watson	Thorpe	Benton	Meredith	White	Bedford	Butler	Mee	Barrass	Wilkinson	Gadsden	Wood	Curran	Bradshaw	Crompton	Streets	Warren	McGinn	Hamilton	Williams	McIntosh	Tremelling	Wellock	
	2	3	4		6	7	8	9		11	10				5		1									1
	2	3	4		6	7		9		11	10				5		1	8								R
	2	3	4		6	7		9		11	10				5		1	8								2
	2	3	4		6	7		9		11	10				5		1	8								R
	2	3	4		6	7	8	9		11	10				5		1									3
	2	3	4		6	7	8	9		11					5		1	10								R
	2	3	4		6	7	8	9		11	10				5		1									4
	7	7	7		7	7	4	7		7	6				7		7	4								
						3		4										2								

1925-26

Manager: Major Frank Buckley

1	Aug	29	(h)	Southampton	W 2-1	Meredith, Bedford	18,195
2	Sep	2	(a)	Middlesbrough	L 2-3	Bedford (pen), Williams	18,108
3		5	(a)	Nottingham F	D 1-1	Wright	8,685
4		7	(h)	Middlesbrough	L 2-3	Bedford 2 (1 pen)	17,036
5		12	(h)	Derby C	L 1-2	Watson	14,850
6		14	(h)	Darlington	L 0-1		11,791
7		19	(a)	Bradford C	L 0-1		11,006
8		23	(a)	Darlington	W 3-1	Bedford 2, Williams	7,977
9		26	(h)	Port Vale	D 2-2	Leaver, Benton	9,502
10	Oct	3	(a)	Barnsley	L 0-2		7,663
11		10	(h)	Clapton O	W 3-0	Binks, Butler, Meredith	9,620
12		17	(a)	Portsmouth	L 0-2		15,199
13		24	(h)	Wolves	W 4-0	Gill, Binks 2, Mee	10,724
14		31	(a)	South Shields	W 4-3	Fishwick 2, Binks, Gill	10,178
15	Nov	7	(h)	Preston NE	W 3-1	Fishwick 2, Meredith	10,207
16		14	(a)	Stoke C	W 3-1	Meredith, Fishwick, Mee	8,548
17		21	(a)	Oldham A	L 2-3	Gill, Fishwick	12,058
18		28	(a)	Stockport C	L 3-4	Fishwick, Gill, Williams	4,500
19	Dec	5	(h)	Fulham	W 2-0	Meredith, Binks	6,786
20		12	(a)	Wolves	D 0-0		12,692
21		19	(h)	Sheffield W	W 1-0	Binks	8,931
22		25	(h)	Chelsea	D 0-0		13,690
23		26	(a)	Chelsea	W 3-2	Thorpe (pen), Meredith, Fishwick	29,139
24	Jan	2	(a)	Southampton	D 2-2	Downes 2	8,637
25		16	(h)	Nottingham F	W 3-0	Thorpe (pen), Fishwick 2	6,686
26		23	(a)	Derby C	L 2-5	Downes 2	14,694
27		30	(h)	Bradford C	W 3-0	Fishwick 2, Williams	8,061
28	Feb	6	(a)	Port Vale	L 0-5		9,207
29		13	(h)	Barnsley	W 4-0	Williams 3, Fishwick	8,620
30		25	(a)	Swansea T	L 1-6	Williams	16,998
31		27	(h)	Portsmouth	D 2-2	Fishwick, Downes	6,754
32	Mar	8	(a)	Clapton O	D 2-2	Crook, Watson	4,500
33		13	(h)	South Shields	W 1-0	Meredith	7,640
34		20	(a)	Preston NE	L 4-6	Crawford (og), Williams 2, Butler	20,000
35		27	(h)	Stoke C	D 0-0		7,756
36	Apr	2	(h)	Hull C	D 2-2	Thorpe (pen), Fishwick	13,676
37		3	(h)	Oldham A	W 2-1	Fishwick, Butler	14,636
38		5	(a)	Hull C	W 2-1	Wellock, Fishwick	7,365
39		10	(h)	Stockport C	W 4-1	Wellock, Fishwick 2, Meredith	7,610
40		17	(a)	Fulham	D 1-1	Butler	14,682
41		24	(h)	Swansea T	D 0-0		9,994
42	May	1	(a)	Sheffield W	L 0-2		20,575

FINAL LEAGUE POSITION: 6th in Division Two — Appearances

Goals

FA Cup

3	Jan	9	(h)	Swansea T	L 0-2		13,520

Appearances

Goals

Crompton	Leaver	Jones	Mercer	Curran	Benton	Meredith	Watson	Bedford	Williams	Mee	Jennings	Wright	Hamilton	Thorpe	Butler	Downes	Streets	Tremelling	Binks	Fishwick	Gill	Bradshaw	Best	Martin	Crook	Wood	Wellock	Tilbrook	Warren	Neal	
1	2	3	4	5	6	7	8	9	10	11																					1
	2	3		5	6		8	9	10	11	1	4	7																		2
	2	3		5	6	7	8	9	10	11	1	4																			3
	2	3		5	6	7	8	9	10	11	1	4																			4
1		3		5	6	7	8	9	10	11		4		2																	5
1	5	3			6	7	8		9			4		2	10	11															6
1		3		5	6	7	4	8	9	11				2	10																7
1		3		5	6	7	4	9	10	11				2			8														8
1	9	3		5	6	7	4			11				2			8	10													9
1		3		5	6		4			11		6		2	10		7		9												10
1		3		5	6	7	4			11				2	10		8		9												11
1		3		5	6	7	4			11				2	10		8		9												12
1		3		5	6	7	4			11				2					9	8	10										13
1		3		5	6	7	4			11				2					9	8	10										14
1		3		5	6	7	4			11				2					9	8	10										15
1		3		5	6	7	4			11				2					9	8	10										16
1		3		5	6	7	4			11				2					9	8	10										17
1				5	6	7	4		11					2					9	8	10	3									18
1				5	6	7	4			11				2					9	8	10	3									19
1		3		5	6	7	4			11				2					9	8	10										20
1	2			5	6	7	4		10	11				3					9		8										21
1	2			5	6	7	4							3		11			9	8	10										22
1	2			5	6	7	4							3		11			9	8	10										23
1	2			5	6	7	4							3		11			9	8	10										24
				5	6	7	4		10		1			2		11			9	8		3									25
				5	6	7	4		10					2		11				9	8	3	1								26
				5	6	7	4		10					2		11				9	8	3	1								27
					6	7	4		10					2		11				9	8	3	1	5							28
1					6	7	4		10					2		11		9	5	8		3									29
1					6	7	4		10					2		11		9	5	8		3									30
1					6	7	4		10					2		11			5	8		3			9						31
1					6	7	4		10							11			5	8		3			9	2					32
1					6	7	4					2			10	11			5	8					9		3				33
1					6	7	4		9			2			10	11			5								3	8			34
1					6	7	4		9			3		2	10	11			5	8											35
1					6	7	4					3		2	10	11			5	8					9						36
1						7	4							2	10	11			5	8		3					9		6		37
1						7	4					2			10	11			5	8		3					9		6		38
1						7	4					2			10	11			5	8		3					9		6		39
1					6	7	4					2			10	11			5	8		3					9				40
1					6	7	4					2			10	11			5	8		3					9				41
1					6		4					2			10	11			5	8		3					9			7	42
35	10	18	1	27	39	39	42	7	20	19	4	15	1	30	15	22	5	3	30	28	15	16	3	1	4	1	8	1	3	1	
	1				1	8	2	6	10	2		1		3	4	5			6	19	4				1		2				

1 own-goal

Crompton	Leaver	Jones	Mercer	Curran	Benton	Meredith	Watson	Bedford	Williams	Mee	Jennings	Wright	Hamilton	Thorpe	Butler	Downes	Streets	Tremelling	Binks	Fishwick	Gill	Bradshaw	Best	Martin	Crook	Wood	Wellock	Tilbrook	Warren	Neal	
1	2			5	6	7	4		8					3		11			9		10										3
1	1			1	1	1	1		1					1		1			1		1										

1926-27

Manager: Major Frank Buckley

1	Aug	28	(a)	Nottingham F	L 0-2		11,542
2		30	(h)	Reading	W 3-1	Downes, Wellock 2	12,958
3	Sep	4	(h)	Barnsley	W 6-1	Fishwick 3, Thorpe (pen), Ayres, Wellock	12,673
4		8	(a)	Reading	W 1-0	Wellock	16,005
5		11	(a)	Manchester C	L 1-2	Fishwick	34,885
6		18	(h)	Darlington	D 1-1	Fishwick	13,545
7		20	(a)	Swansea T	L 0-2		14,264
8		25	(a)	Portsmouth	L 0-5		14,429
9	Oct	2	(h)	Oldham A	W 2-0	Browell 2	14,599
10		9	(a)	Fulham	L 0-1		16,237
11		16	(h)	Wolves	L 2-3	Wellock, Fishwick	9,486
12		23	(a)	Hull C	L 0-3		11,363
13		30	(h)	Preston NE	L 2-3	Browell, Ayres	16,542
14	Nov	6	(a)	Chelsea	D 1-1	Binks	25,366
15		13	(h)	Bradford C	W 3-0	Curran, Crook (pen), Tremelling	5,498
16		20	(a)	Southampton	L 3-5	Tremelling 2, Crook (pen)	8,721
17		27	(h)	Port Vale	D 2-2	Tremelling, Crook	7,656
18	Dec	4	(a)	Middlesbrough	D 4-4	Downes 2, Fishwick, Tremelling	19,456
19		11	(h)	Clapton O	W 6-0	Fishwick, Tremelling 3, Crook, Downes	7,551
20		18	(a)	Notts C	W 3-2	Crook, Meredith, Tremelling	8,108
21		25	(a)	Grimsby T	L 1-2	Thorpe	15,492
22		27	(h)	Grimsby T	W 6-2	Crook 3, Tremelling 2, Downes	13,980
23	Jan	1	(h)	Swansea T	W 3-1	Tremelling, Fishwick, Browell	13,754
24		15	(h)	Nottingham F	D 2-2	Tremelling 2	7,536
25		22	(a)	Barnsley	L 1-6	Fishwick	7,533
26		29	(h)	Manchester C	L 2-4	Kelly, Fishwick	9,223
27	Feb	5	(a)	Darlington	W 3-1	Neal, Tremelling, Meredith	8,695
28		12	(h)	Portsmouth	W 2-0	Fishwick, Tremelling	8,465
29		19	(a)	Oldham A	W 3-1	Tremelling 2, Fishwick	14,446
30		26	(h)	Fulham	D 0-0		7,958
31	Mar	12	(h)	Hull C	W 4-0	Browell, Binks 2, Neal	9,195
32		19	(a)	Preston NE	L 1-4	Browell	24,089
33		21	(a)	Wolves	L 1-4	Browell	6,698
34		26	(h)	Chelsea	W 3-1	Neal, Tremelling 2	8,251
35	Apr	2	(a)	Bradford C	L 1-4	Tremelling	9,840
36		9	(h)	Southampton	W 3-2	Browell, Tremelling, Meredith	7,825
37		15	(h)	South Shields	W 6-1	Tremelling 2, Meredith 2, Browell, Downes	15,450
38		16	(a)	Port Vale	W 4-2	Tremelling 3, Meredith	10,749
39		18	(a)	South Shields	D 2-2	Tremelling, Browell	5,282
40		23	(h)	Middlesbrough	D 2-2	Tremelling, Browell	12,657
41		30	(a)	Clapton O	L 0-1		16,025
42	May	7	(h)	Notts C	W 5-0	Browell 3, Ayres, Tremelling	5,651

FINAL LEAGUE POSITION: 9th in Division Two

Appearances
Goals

FA Cup

3	Jan	8	(h)	Bolton W	L 1-3	Tremelling	16,297

Appearances
Goals

Crompton	Thorpe	Bradshaw	Watson	Binks	Benton	Meredith	Fishwick	Wellock	Ayres	Downes	Butler	Browell	Barnett	Tremelling	Neal	Wright	Crook	Best	Curran	Warren	Martin	Tilford	Kelly	Hargreaves	
1	2	3	4	5	6	7	8	9	10	11															1
1	2	3	4	5	6	7	8	9	10	11															2
1	2	3	4	5	6	7	8	9	10	11															3
1	2	3	4	5	6	7	8	9		11	10														4
1	2	3	4	5	6	7	8	9	10	11															5
1	2	3	4	5	6	7	8	9		11		10													6
1	2	3	4	5	6	7	8	9		11		10													7
1		3	4	5	6	7	8			11		10	2	9											8
1		3	4	5	6	7	8	9		11		10	2												9
1		3	4	5	6	7	8	9				10	2		11										10
1		3	4	5	6	7	8	9				10	2		11										11
1	2	3		5		7			8			9	6		11	4	10								12
	2	3	4	5		7	8	6	9	11		10						1							13
	2	3		9	6	7			8			10			11			1	4	5					14
	2	3	8	5	6	7								9	11		10	1	4						15
	2	3	6	5		7						8		9	11		10	1	4						16
	2	3	4			7	8							9	11		10	1	6		5				17
	2		4	5		7	8		6	11				9			10	1				3			18
	2		4	5	6	7	8			11				9			10	1				3			19
	2		4	5	6	7	8			11				9			10	1				3			20
	2		4	5	6	7	8			11				9			10	1				3			21
	2		4	5		7			6	11		8		9			10	1				3			22
	2		4	5		7	8		6	11		10		9				1				3			23
1	2				4	7	8		6	11				9			10				5	3			24
1	2		4			7	8		6	11				9			10				5	3			25
1	2	3	4	5	6	7	8			11					10								9		26
	2		4		6	7	8		5	11				9	10			1				3			27
	2		4		6	7	8		5	11				9			10	1				3			28
	2		4		6	7	8		5	11				9			10	1				3			29
	2		4		6	7	8		5	11				9			10	1				3			30
	2		4	9	6	7			5	11		8			10			1				3			31
	2		4	9	6	7			5	11		8					10	1				3			32
	2		4		6	7			5	11		8	3	9			10	1							33
	2		4		6	7			5			8		9	11		10	1				3			34
	2		4		6	7			5			8		9	11		10	1				3			35
	2		4		6	7			5			8		9	11		10	1				3			36
	2		4		6	7			5	11		8		9			10	1				3			37
	2				6	7						8	4	9	11		10	1				3		5	38
	2		4		6	7						8	3	9	11		10	1						5	39
1	2		4		6	7						8		9	11		10					3		5	40
1	2		4		6	7			5	11		10		9			8					3			41
1	2		4		6	7			5			8	3	9	11		10								42
18	38	18	38	25	34	42	25	11	25	28	1	24	9	26	17	1	25	24	4	1	3	21	1	3	
	2			3		6	13	5	3	6		14		30	3		8		1				1		

Crompton	Thorpe	Bradshaw	Watson	Binks	Benton	Meredith	Fishwick	Wellock	Ayres	Downes	Butler	Browell	Barnett	Tremelling	Neal	Wright	Crook	Best	Curran	Warren	Martin	Tilford	Kelly	Hargreaves	
	2		4	5		7			6	11		10		9			8	1				3			3
	1		1	1		1			1	1		1		1			1	1				1			
														1											

1927-28

Manager: Sydney Beaumont

No	Month	Day	Venue	Opponent	Result	Scorers	Attendance
1	Aug	27	(h)	Swansea T	D 2-2	Tremelling, Downes	15,771
2		29	(h)	Oldham A	L 1-2	Adlam (og)	16,690
3	Sep	3	(a)	Chelsea	L 0-3		36,529
4		5	(a)	Oldham A	L 0-6		14,542
5		10	(h)	Clapton O	L 0-1		12,337
6		17	(a)	West Brom A	L 3-6	Tufnell 2, Williams	19,605
7		24	(h)	Bristol C	W 6-2	Browell 3, Watson, Tufnell, Williams	12,509
8	Oct	1	(a)	Stoke C	L 0-2		9,293
9		8	(h)	Southampton	W 1-0	Williams	11,875
10		15	(a)	Notts C	L 1-3	Hampson	11,885
11		22	(h)	Manchester C	D 2-2	Hampson 2	17,013
12		29	(a)	Hull C	D 2-2	Neal, Hampson	9,067
13	Nov	5	(h)	Preston NE	W 4-1	Benton 2 (2 pens), Meredith, Tufnell	10,789
14		12	(a)	Nottingham F	L 1-4	Hampson	8,602
15		19	(h)	Leeds U	L 0-2		9,008
16		26	(a)	Wolves	W 4-2	Hampson 3, Downes	13,200
17	Dec	3	(h)	Port Vale	L 1-6	Hampson	7,662
18		10	(a)	South Shields	D 2-2	Downes, Hampson	5,130
19		17	(h)	Barnsley	L 1-3	Hampson	7,629
20		24	(a)	Fulham	D 2-2	Hampson, Neal	10,853
21		26	(h)	Reading	W 3-1	Fishwick 3	13,233
22		27	(a)	Reading	L 0-1		11,841
23		31	(a)	Swansea T	L 0-1		9,185
24	Jan	2	(h)	Grimsby T	L 4-5	Crook 2 (1 pen), Hampson, Ayres	10,347
25		7	(h)	Chelsea	L 2-4	Browell, Tremelling	8,704
26		21	(a)	Clapton O	W 5-2	Neal 2, Browell, Hampson 2	11,401
27		28	(h)	West Brom A	W 4-3	Hampson 2, Benton (pen), McIntyre	8,102
28	Feb	4	(a)	Bristol C	D 2-2	McIntyre, Browell	11,395
29		11	(h)	Stoke C	W 3-1	Meredith, Hampson, Browell	8,744
30		18	(a)	Southampton	L 0-2		12,229
31		25	(h)	Notts C	D 3-3	Fishwick, Neal, Meredith	9,423
32	Mar	3	(a)	Manchester C	L 1-4	Hampson	40,906
33		10	(h)	Hull C	W 2-1	Oxberry, Downes	9,988
34		17	(a)	Preston NE	L 1-2	Benton (pen)	22,341
35		24	(h)	Nottingham F	W 5-3	Hampson 4, Ramsay	8,977
36		31	(a)	Leeds U	L 0-4		19,630
37	Apr	6	(a)	Grimsby T	D 3-3	Tremelling, Hampson 2	15,097
38		7	(h)	Wolves	W 3-0	Neal, Browell, Oxberry	18,030
39		14	(a)	Port Vale	L 0-3		5,321
40		21	(h)	South Shields	W 4-1	Browell, Hampson 2, Tremelling	8,539
41		28	(a)	Barnsley	L 1-2	Hampson	4,949
42	May	5	(h)	Fulham	W 4-0	Hampson 3, Oxberry	14,466

FINAL LEAGUE POSITION: 19th in Division Two

Appearances
Goals

FA Cup

Round	Month	Day	Venue	Opponent	Result	Scorers	Attendance
3	Jan	14	(h)	Oldham A	L 1-4	Neal	10,349

Appearances
Goals

Crompton	Thorpe	Tilford	Watson	Ayres	Benton	Meredith	Browell	Tremelling	Crook	Downes	Malpas	Hobbs	Grimwood	Cowan	Williams	Tufnell	Hampson	Barnett	Neal	Wright	Grant	Brookes	Fishwick	Hughes	McIntyre	Purdy	Oxberry	Ramsay	
1	2	3	4	5	6	7	8	9	10	11																			1
1	2	3	4	5	6	7	8	9	10	11																			2
1	2	3	4	5	6	7	8	9	10	11																			3
1	2	3	4		6	7	8	9	10	11	5																		4
	2	3	4		6	7	8		10	11		1	5	9															5
	2	3	4		6	7	8			11		1	5		9	10													6
	2	3	4		6	7	8			11		1	5		9	10													7
	2	3	4		6	7	8			11		1	5		9	10													8
	2	3	4		6	7	8			11		1	5		9	10													9
	2	3	4		6	7				11		1	5		9	10	8												10
	2	3	4		6	7	8			11		1				10	9	5											11
	5	3	4		6	7	8					1				10	9	2	11										12
	5	3	4		6	7	8					1				10	9	2	11										13
	5	3	4		6	7	8					1				10	9	2	11										14
	5	3	4		6	7		9				1				10	9	2	11										15
	5	3	8		6	7	10			11		1				4	9			2									16
	5	3	8		6	7	10			11		1				4	9			2									17
	2	3	4				8			11		1				6	9		7		5	10							18
	2	3	4		8	7				11		1				6	9				5	10							19
	2				4	7						1				6	9	3	11		5	10	8						20
	2				4	7						1	5			6	9		11	3		10	8						21
			4			7						1	5			6	9	3	11	2		10	8						22
	2		4		6	7						1	5				9		11	3		10	8						23
	2			6	4	7			10			1					9		11	3	5		8	4					24
					4	7	10	8				1					9	3	11	2	5			4					25
					4	7	8	6				1					9	3	11	2	5				10				26
					4	7	8	6				1					9	3	11	2	5				10				27
						7	8	6				1					9	3	11	2	5				10				28
						7	8	6									9	3	11	2	5				10	1			29
					4	7	8	6								4	9	3	11	2	5				10	1			30
			4			7	8	6										3	11	2	5		9		10	1			31
					6	7		6									9	3	11	2	5					1	8	10	32
	2		4	5		7		6		11							9	3								1	8	10	33
	2		4	5		7				11							8	3								1	9	10	34
1	2		4	5		7		6		11							9	3									8	10	35
1	2		4	5		7		6		11							9	3									8	10	36
	2	3	4					6	7								9		11		5					1	8	10	37
1	2		4				10	6	7								9	3	11		5						8		38
1	2		4				10	6	7								9	3	11		5						8		39
	2		4				10	6	7								9	3	11		5					1	8		40
	2		4				10	6	7								9	3	11		5					1	8		41
	2		4				10	6	7								9	3	11		5					1	8		42
8	33	20	32	8	28	35	28	22	12	19	1	24	9	1	5	18	32	24	24	14	18	6	6	2	6	10	11	6	
			1	1	4	3	9	4	2	4					3	4	31		6				4		2		3	1	

1 own-goal

Crompton	Thorpe	Tilford	Watson	Ayres	Benton	Meredith	Browell	Tremelling	Crook	Downes	Malpas	Hobbs	Grimwood	Cowan	Williams	Tufnell	Hampson	Barnett	Neal	Wright	Grant	Brookes	Fishwick	Hughes	McIntyre	Purdy	Oxberry	Ramsay	
1					4	7	8	10								6	9	3	11	2	5								3
1					1	1	1	1								1	1	1	1	1	1								
																			1										

1928-29

Manager: Harry Evans (Honorary title)

1	Aug	25	(a)	Preston NE	L 1-3	Hampson	23,225
2		27	(a)	Swansea T	D 5-5	Hampson 2, Browell, Brookes 2	12,152
3	Sep	1	(h)	Chelsea	L 0-1		17,653
4		3	(h)	Swansea T	D 2-2	Hampson 2	12,899
5		8	(a)	Barnsley	L 1-3	Browell	7,312
6		15	(h)	Bristol C	W 2-1	Watson 2	14,135
7		22	(a)	Nottingham F	L 0-2		12,615
8		29	(h)	West Brom A	L 0-2		16,415
9	Oct	6	(a)	Clapton O	W 4-2	Hampson, Crook, Martin 2	12,222
10		13	(h)	Stoke C	W 2-0	Hampson, Watson	17,942
11		20	(a)	Middlesbrough	L 1-4	Hampson	15,727
12		27	(h)	Oldham A	W 4-0	Oxberry 2, Benton, Hampson	10,524
13	Nov	3	(a)	Southampton	L 2-8	Ramsay, Hampson	15,146
14		10	(h)	Reading	W 7-0	Hampson 5, Oxberry 2	6,638
15		17	(a)	Notts C	L 1-3	Wilson	13,987
16		24	(h)	Millwall	W 3-0	Hampson 2, Benton (pen)	6,829
17	Dec	1	(a)	Port Vale	L 0-1		8,244
18		8	(h)	Hull C	W 2-1	Oxberry, Benton (pen)	9,033
19		15	(a)	Tottenham H	W 2-1	Oxberry, Tremelling	15,729
20		22	(h)	Wolves	W 3-0	Hampson, Tremelling 2	7,262
21		25	(a)	Grimsby T	W 4-1	Hampson 3, Downes	15,437
22		26	(h)	Grimsby T	D 1-1	Hampson	15,337
23		29	(h)	Preston NE	W 3-2	Tremelling, Neal, Hampson	16,339
24	Jan	5	(a)	Chelsea	W 3-2	Neal, Tremelling, Hampson	20,069
25		19	(h)	Barnsley	L 0-1		8,937
26		26	(a)	Bristol C	L 2-3	Hampson 2	13,748
27	Feb	2	(h)	Nottingham F	D 2-2	Benton (pen), Hampson	6,997
28		9	(a)	West Brom A	D 2-2	Benton, Taylor	10,625
29		16	(h)	Clapton O	L 0-1		6,236
30		23	(a)	Stoke C	D 1-1	Hampson	12,538
31	Mar	2	(h)	Middlesbrough	W 3-0	Neal, Downes, Browell	10,440
32		9	(a)	Oldham A	L 2-4	Hampson, Neal	23,824
33		16	(h)	Southampton	W 3-0	Upton 2, Hampson	9,279
34		23	(a)	Reading	L 1-4	Upton	7,517
35		29	(h)	Bradford	W 3-0	Upton, Hampson 2	17,977
36		30	(h)	Notts C	W 3-2	Hampson, Brookes, Bisby (og)	16,049
37	Apr	1	(a)	Bradford	L 2-5	Hampson 2	14,125
38		6	(a)	Millwall	L 1-2	Browell	16,933
39		13	(h)	Port Vale	W 4-0	Hampson, Downes, Upton, Benton (pen)	8,696
40		20	(a)	Hull C	W 3-1	Brookes, Benton, Hampson	4,945
41		27	(h)	Tottenham H	D 2-2	Hampson, Upton	8,744
42	May	4	(a)	Wolves	W 5-1	Hampson 2 (1 pen), Upton, Downes, Neal	7,936

FINAL LEAGUE POSITION: 8th in Division Two

Appearances
Goals

FA Cup

3	Jan	12	(a)	Plymouth A	L 0-3		30,300

Appearances
Goals

Mercer	Wilson	Barnett	Watson	Grant	Tremelling	Ritchie	Oxberry	Hampson	Ramsay	Crook	Tilford	Benton	Browell	Brookes	Downes	Purdy	Hamilton	Tufnell	Robinson	Martin	Neal	Gibson	Taylor	Upton	Swift	
1	2	3	4	5	6	7	8	9	10	11																1
1	2		4	5		7		9			3	6	8	10	11											2
1	2		4	5		7		9			3	6	8	10	11											3
1	2		4	5		7		9			3	6	8	10	11											4
	2		4	5		7		9	10		3	6	8		11	1										5
1			4	5		11	9		10	7	3	6	8				2									6
1			4	5		11	8	9		7	3	6					2	10								7
1			4	5		7	8	9			3	6		10	11		2									8
1			4				8	9		7	3	6					2		5	10	11					9
1			4				8	9		7	3	6					2		5	10	11					10
1			4				8	9		7	3	6					2		5	10	11					11
1			4				8	9		7	3	6					2		5	10	11					12
1			4	5			10	9	8	7	3	6					2				11					13
1	5		4	6		7	8	9									3	10			11	2				14
1	5		4		10	7	8	9				6					3				11	2				15
1	5	3	4		10		8	9				6			7						11	2				16
1	5	3	4		10		8	9				6			7						11	2				17
	5	3	4		10		8	9				6			11	1					7	2				18
	5	3	4		10		8	9				6			11	1					7	2				19
	5	3	4		10		8	9				6			11	1					7	2				20
	5	3	4		10		8	9				6			11	1					7	2				21
		3	4		10		8	9				6			11	1			5		7	2				22
	5	3	4		10			9				6	8		11	1					7	2				23
	5	3	4		10		8	9				6			11	1					7	2				24
	5	3	4		10		8	9				6			11	1					7	2				25
	5	3	4	2				9				6		10	11	1					7		8			26
	5		4	2				9				6		10	11	1	3				7		8			27
	5		4	2				9		7		6		10		1	3				11		8			28
	5		4	2				9	5	7		6		10		1	3				11		8			29
			4	2			8	9	5			6		10	11	1	3				7					30
			4	2			8	9	5			6	10		11	1	3				7					31
			4	2			8	9	5			6	10		11	1	3				7					32
			4	2				9	5			6	10		11	1	3				7			8		33
			4	2				9	5			6	10		11	1	3				7			8		34
			4	2				9	5			6	10		11	1	3				7			8		35
			4	2		7		9	5				8	10	11	1	3									36
			4	2		7		9	5			6	10	6	11	1	3							8		37
			4	2				9	5			6	10		11		3				7			8	1	38
1		3	4	2				9	5			6		10	11						7			8		39
1			4	2				9	5			6		10	11		3				7			8		40
1			4	2				9	5			6		10	11		3				7			8		41
			4	2			10	9	5			6			11		3				7			8	1	42
19	20	13	42	27	12	12	24	41	17	10	12	39	14	14	30	21	25	2	5	4	32	12	4	9	2	
	1		3		5		6	40	1	1		7	4	4	4					2	5		1	7		

1 own-goal

Mercer	Wilson	Barnett	Watson	Grant	Tremelling	Ritchie	Oxberry	Hampson	Ramsay	Crook	Tilford	Benton	Browell	Brookes	Downes	Purdy	Hamilton	Tufnell	Robinson	Martin	Neal	Gibson	Taylor	Upton	Swift	
	5	3	4		10		8	9				6			11	1					7	2				3
	1	1	1		1		1	1				1			1	1					1	1				

1929-30

Manager: Harry Evans (Honorary title)

1	Aug	31	(h)	Millwall	W 4-3	Downes, Neal, Hampson, Ritchie	15,760
2	Sep	2	(h)	Bury	W 2-1	Hampson, Downes	16,918
3		7	(a)	Southampton	L 2-4	Hampson 2	10,113
4		9	(h)	Nottingham F	W 5-1	Upton 2, Downes, Hampson 2	14,182
5		14	(h)	Tottenham H	W 3-2	Hampson 2, Upton	14,913
6		21	(a)	West Brom A	L 1-5	Hampson	17,168
7		28	(h)	Bradford	W 1-0	Downes	18,870
8	Oct	5	(a)	Barnsley	W 4-2	Hampson 3, Lauderdale	8,353
9		12	(h)	Cardiff C	W 3-0	Tremelling, Hampson, Quinn	15,900
10		19	(a)	Preston NE	W 6-4	Lauderdale, Hampson 3, Downes 2	21,185
11		26	(h)	Bristol C	W 7-1	Downes 3, Hampson 2, Lauderdale, Upton	11,192
12	Nov	2	(a)	Notts C	W 2-0	Lauderdale, Hampson	13,282
13		9	(h)	Reading	W 4-2	Hampson 2, Upton, Quinn	10,757
14		16	(a)	Charlton A	W 4-1	Hall, Hampson, Upton 2	4,493
15		23	(h)	Hull C	L 1-2	Hampson	10,364
16		30	(a)	Stoke C	W 1-0	Hampson	11,546
17	Dec	7	(h)	Wolves	W 3-2	Neal, Hampson, Upton	9,608
18		14	(a)	Bradford C	D 1-1	Downes	21,644
19		21	(h)	Swansea T	W 3-0	Hampson 2, Downes	10,139
20		25	(h)	Chelsea	D 1-1	Ritchie	14,882
21		26	(a)	Chelsea	L 0-4		53,819
22		28	(a)	Millwall	L 1-3	Upton	21,745
23	Jan	1	(a)	Bury	W 1-0	Ritchie	17,963
24		4	(h)	Southampton	W 5-1	Hampson 3, Tremelling, Ritchie	12,574
25		18	(a)	Tottenham H	L 1-6	Quinn	24,946
26	Feb	1	(a)	Bradford	L 0-5		17,970
27		8	(h)	Barnsley	W 2-1	Downes, Hampson	11,785
28		15	(a)	Cardiff C	L 2-4	Watson, Broadhurst	12,730
29		22	(h)	Preston NE	W 5-1	Ritchie, Broadhurst, Upton 2, Hampson	15,347
30	Mar	1	(a)	Bristol C	W 1-0	Broadhurst	11,925
31		5	(h)	West Brom A	W 1-0	Hampson	10,225
32		8	(h)	Notts C	L 1-2	Broadhurst (pen)	13,733
33		15	(a)	Reading	D 1-1	Hampson	12,741
34		22	(h)	Charlton A	W 6-0	Hampson 4, Rattray, Upton	12,614
35		29	(a)	Hull C	W 3-0	Hampson 2, Broadhurst	10,113
36	Apr	5	(h)	Stoke C	L 0-2		13,679
37		12	(a)	Wolves	W 2-1	Hampson, Tremelling	13,444
38		18	(h)	Oldham A	W 3-0	Oxberry, Hampson, Downes	24,144
39		19	(h)	Bradford C	W 3-0	Hampson 2, Oxberry	18,163
40		21	(a)	Oldham A	W 2-1	Hampson, Oxberry	45,304
41		26	(a)	Swansea T	L 0-3		16,433
42	May	3	(a)	Nottingham F	D 0-0		6,044

FINAL LEAGUE POSITION: 1st in Division Two

Appearances
Goals

FA Cup

3	Jan	11	(h)	Stockport C	W 2-1	Browell 2	14,000
4		25	(a)	Hull C	L 1-3	Hampson	23,000

Appearances
Goals

Swift	Grant	Hamilton	Watson	Ramsay	Benton	Neal	Ritchie	Hampson	Oxberry	Downes	Wolfe	Upton	Tremelling	Quinn	Lauderdale	Tufnell	Hall	Jennings	Wilson	Brookes	Smalley	Pearson	Broadhurst	Browell	Gibson	Rattray	
1	2	3	4	5	6	7	8	9	10	11																	1
	2	3	4	5	6	7	8	9	10	11	1																2
	2	3	4	5	6	7	8	9		11	1	10															3
	2		4	3	6	7	8	9		11	1	10	5														4
	2		4	3	6		8	9		11	1	10	5	7													5
	2		4	3	6		8	9		11	1	10	5	7													6
	2		4	3	6			9		11	1	8	5	7	10												7
	2		4	3	6			9		11	1	8	5	7	10												8
	2		4	3	6			9		11	1	8	5	7	10												9
	2		4	3				9		11	1	8	5	7	10	6											10
	2		4	3				9		11	1	8	5	7	10	6											11
	2		4	3				9			1	8	5	7	10	6	11										12
	2		4	3				9			1	8	5	7	10	6	11										13
	2		4					9			1	8	5	7	10	6	11	3									14
	2		4	3				9			1	8	5	7	10	6	11										15
	2		4	3				9		11	1	8	5		10	6	7										16
	2		4	3		7		9		11	1	8	5		10	6											17
	2		4	3				9		11	1	8	5		10	6	7										18
	2		4	3				9		11	1	8	5		10	6	7										19
	2		4	3			10	9		11	1	8	5			6	7										20
	2		4	3			7	9	8	11	1		6		10				5								21
	2		4	3				9		11	1	8	5	7						6	10						22
	2		4	3			10	9		11	1		5	7		6					8						23
	2		4	3			10	9		11	1		5	7		6					8						24
	2		4	3			10	9		11	1		5	7		6					8						25
	2		4	3			7	9		11	1	8	5		10	6											26
	2			5			10	9		11			6	7		4		3				1	8				27
	2		7	5				9		11	1		6			4		3					8	10			28
	2		4	3			7	8		11		10	5			6						1	9				29
	2		4	3			7	9		11		10	5			6						1	8				30
			4	3			7	9		11		10	5			6						1	8		2		31
			4	3			7		9	11		10	5			6						1	8		2		32
	2			3				9		11		10	5			6			4			1	8			7	33
	2			3				9		11		10	5			6			4			1	8			7	34
	2			3				9		11		10	5			6			4			1	8			7	35
	2			3				9		11		10	5			6			4			1	8			7	36
	2		4	3				9	10	11			5						6			1	8			7	37
	2		4	3				9	10	11			5						6			1	8			7	38
	2		3					9	10	11		8	5			6			4			1				7	39
	2		3			11		9	10				5			6			4			1	8			7	40
	2		3					9	10	11			5			6			4			1	8			7	41
	2		3			7		9	10	11						6			4	5		1	8				42
1	40	3	37	37	9	7	17	41	10	37	26	29	38	16	15	29	8	3	11	2	4	15	15	1	2	9	
			1			2	5	45	3	13		12	3	3	4		1						5			1	

Swift	Grant	Hamilton	Watson	Ramsay	Benton	Neal	Ritchie	Hampson	Oxberry	Downes	Wolfe	Upton	Tremelling	Quinn	Lauderdale	Tufnell	Hall	Jennings	Wilson	Brookes	Smalley	Pearson	Broadhurst	Browell	Gibson	Rattray	
	2		4	3			10	9		11	1		5	7		6								8			3
	2		4				11	9			1	8	5	7		6		3						10			4
	2		2	1			2	2		1	2	1	2	2		2		1						2			
								1																2			

1930-31

Manager: Harry Evans (Honorary title)

1	Aug	30	(h)	Arsenal	L 1-4	Hampson	28,723
2	Sep	3	(a)	Manchester C	W 4-2	Carr, Hampson 2, Neal	34,908
3		6	(a)	Blackburn R	L 0-5		25,388
4		10	(h)	Portsmouth	D 2-2	Hall 2	20,611
5		13	(h)	Middlesbrough	W 3-2	Hampson 2, Quinn	20,050
6		17	(a)	Portsmouth	L 3-4	Hampson 2, Quinn	11,838
7		20	(h)	Leeds U	L 3-7	Upton, Benton, Hampson	25,743
8		27	(a)	Sunderland	W 4-2	Hampson 2, Quinn, Upton	20,087
9	Oct	4	(h)	Leicester C	W 5-4	Hampson 3, Oxberry, Upton	24,105
10		11	(a)	Birmingham	D 1-1	Hampson	23,453
11		18	(a)	Bolton W	L 0-1		26,651
12		25	(h)	Liverpool	L 1-3	Benton	14,998
13	Nov	1	(a)	Chelsea	L 0-3		32,775
14		8	(h)	Newcastle U	D 0-0		14,516
15		15	(a)	Manchester U	D 0-0		14,765
16		22	(h)	Aston Villa	D 2-2	Hutchison, Tremelling	12,054
17		29	(a)	Sheffield W	L 1-7	Broadhurst	17,393
18	Dec	6	(h)	West Ham U	L 1-3	Hutchison	12,115
19		13	(a)	Huddersfield T	L 1-10	Upton	11,932
20		20	(h)	Grimsby T	W 3-1	Hampson 2, Oxberry	11,427
21		25	(h)	Sheffield U	W 2-1	McMahon, Upton	18,575
22		26	(a)	Sheffield U	L 1-5	Oxberry	20,963
23		27	(a)	Arsenal	L 1-7	Carr	35,113
24	Jan	3	(h)	Blackburn R	D 1-1	Hampson	16,294
25		17	(a)	Middlesbrough	L 1-5	Hampson	16,060
26		28	(a)	Leeds U	D 2-2	Hampson 2	7,750
27		31	(h)	Sunderland	W 3-1	Lauderdale 2, Hampson	7,310
28	Feb	7	(a)	Leicester C	L 0-6		14,581
29		18	(h)	Birmingham	L 0-1		10,136
30		21	(h)	Bolton W	D 3-3	Oxberry, McLelland, Hampson	16,695
31		28	(a)	Liverpool	L 2-5	Oxberry, Hampson	13,732
32	Mar	7	(h)	Chelsea	W 2-1	Hampson (pen), McLelland	12,271
33		14	(a)	Newcastle U	W 2-0	Hampson, Rattray	13,303
34		21	(h)	Manchester U	W 5-1	Hampson 3 (1 pen), McLelland 2	13,612
35		28	(a)	Aston Villa	L 1-4	Longden	27,245
36	Apr	3	(h)	Derby C	W 1-0	Longden	22,993
37		4	(h)	Sheffield W	L 0-4		23,391
38		6	(a)	Derby C	L 2-3	Hampson 2	12,149
39		11	(a)	West Ham U	L 2-3	Oxberry, Hampson	15,514
40		18	(h)	Huddersfield T	D 1-1	Smalley	15,111
41		25	(a)	Grimsby T	L 2-6	Longden, Hampson	8,042
42	May	2	(h)	Manchester C	D 2-2	Oxberry, Watson	18,688

FINAL LEAGUE POSITION: 20th in Division One — Appearances / Goals

FA Cup

3	Jan	10	(a)	Hull C	W 2-1	Hampson, Upton	20,000
4		24	(a)	Southport	L 1-2	Downes	10,500

Appearances

Goals

Pearson	Grant	Watson	McMahon	Tremelling	Tufnell	Neal	Carr	Hampson	Oxberry	Downes	Ramsay	Benton	Quinn	Upton	Hall	Brookes	Shankley	Hutchison	Broadhurst	Rattray	O'Donnell J	Ritchie	Cardwell	Wilson	Wolfe	Lauderdale	Longden	McLelland	Smalley	
1	2	3	4	5	6	7	8	9	10	11																				1
1	2	3	4	5	6	7	8	9	10	11																				2
1	2	3	4	5	6	7	8	9	10	11																				3
1	2		4	5			10	9			3	6	7	8	11															4
1	2		4	5			10	9			3	6	7	8	11															5
1	2		4	5			10	9			3	6	7	8	11															6
1	2		4	5			10	9			3	6	7	8	11															7
1	2	4	5					9	10		3	6	7	8	11															8
1	2	4	5	6				9	10		3		7	8	11															9
1	2	4	5					9	10		3	6	7	8	11															10
1	2	4	5					9	10	11	3	6	7	8																11
1	2	4	5					9		11	3	6	7	8		10														12
1	2	4	5					9	10		3	6		8			7	11												13
1	2	4	5				8	9	10		3	6					7	11												14
1	2	4	5					9	10		3	6		8			7	11												15
1	2	4	6	5			8		10		3						7	11	9											16
1	2	4	6	5			10	9			3						7	11	8											17
1	2	4	6	5			10	8			3							11	9	7										18
1	2	4	5					9	10	11	3	6		8						7										19
1	2	4	5					9	10	11		6		8						7	3									20
1	2	4	5					9	10	11		6		8						7	3									21
1	2	4	5					9	10	11		6		8						7	3									22
1	2	4	5				10	9		11						6				7	3	8								23
1	2	4	5				10	9		11						6				7	3	8								24
1	2				6		10	9		11				8						7	3		4	5						25
	2	4	5					9	8	11		6								7	3				1	10				26
	2	4	5					9	8	11		6								7	3				1	10				27
1	2	4						9		11	5	6								7	3					10	8			28
1	2	4						9	8	11	6									7	3					10	5			29
1	2	4						9	8		6				11					7	3						5	10		30
1	2	4			6			9	8		5				11					7	3							10		31
1	2	4			6			9	8		5				11					7	3							10		32
1	2	4			6			9			5				11					7	3						8	10		33
1	2	4			6			9			5				11					7	3						8	10		34
1	2	4			6			9			5				11					7	3						8	10		35
1	2	4			6			9			5				11					7	3						8	10		36
1	2	4			6			9			5		7		11						3						8	10		37
1	2	4				11		9			5		7								3						8	10	6	38
1	2	4			6			9	8		5		7								3							10	11	39
1	2	4			6			9			5		7								3						8	10	11	40
1	2	4			6			9			5		7								3						8	10	11	41
1	2	4			6			9	8				7								3						5	10	11	42
40	42	37	26	11	15	4	14	41	23	16	30	18	15	16	15	3	5	6	3	19	23	2	1	1	2	4	12	13	5	
		1	1	1		1	2	32	7			2	3	5	2			2	1	1						2	3	4	1	

Pearson	Grant	Watson	McMahon	Tremelling	Tufnell	Neal	Carr	Hampson	Oxberry	Downes	Ramsay	Benton	Quinn	Upton	Hall	Brookes	Shankley	Hutchison	Broadhurst	Rattray	O'Donnell J	Ritchie	Cardwell	Wilson	Wolfe	Lauderdale	Longden	McLelland	Smalley	
1	2				6			9		11				8						7	3		4	5		10				3
1	2		5					9		11		6		8						7	3		4			10				4
2	2		1		1			2		2		1		2						2	2		2	1		2				
								1		1				1																

1931-32

Manager: Harry Evans (Honorary title)

1	Aug	29	(h)	Derby C	W 2-1	Hampson, Wilkinson	22,970
2		31	(h)	Sheffield U	W 2-0	Hampson, McLelland	19,052
3	Sep	5	(a)	West Brom A	L 0-4		19,320
4		9	(h)	Blackburn R	W 2-1	Wilkinson, Hampson	23,444
5		12	(h)	Birmingham	D 1-1	Wilkinson	19,063
6		19	(a)	Sunderland	L 0-4		14,901
7		21	(a)	Blackburn R	L 1-5	Oxberry	15,149
8		26	(h)	Manchester C	D 2-2	Hampson 2	25,031
9	Oct	3	(a)	Everton	L 2-3	McLelland 2	31,651
10		10	(h)	Arsenal	L 1-5	McLelland	29,576
11		17	(h)	Middlesbrough	L 1-2	Rattray	17,481
12		24	(a)	Liverpool	L 2-3	Hampson 2	20,742
13		31	(h)	Leicester C	L 2-3	Hampson 2	9,542
14	Nov	7	(a)	Aston Villa	L 1-5	Longden	40,448
15		14	(h)	Sheffield W	L 1-2	Douglas	12,160
16		21	(a)	West Ham U	D 1-1	Douglas	14,800
17		28	(h)	Grimsby T	W 4-3	Harrison, Hampson, Wilkinson, Longden	12,700
18	Dec	5	(a)	Bolton W	W 2-1	Hampson 2	14,294
19		12	(h)	Newcastle U	W 3-1	Hampson 2, Longden	13,410
20		19	(a)	Huddersfield T	L 0-5		11,072
21		25	(h)	Chelsea	L 2-4	Douglas 2	20,378
22		26	(a)	Chelsea	L 1-4	Hampson	38,569
23	Jan	2	(a)	Derby C	L 0-5		8,533
24		16	(h)	West Brom A	L 1-2	Douglas	12,269
25		30	(h)	Sunderland	W 3-2	Wilkinson, Douglas, Opp own-goal	14,547
26	Feb	3	(a)	Birmingham	L 0-3		5,829
27		6	(a)	Manchester C	L 1-7	Everest	24,739
28		13	(h)	Everton	W 2-0	Hampson 2	16,346
29		20	(a)	Arsenal	L 0-2		39,045
30		27	(a)	Middlesbrough	W 3-0	Douglas, A.Watson 2	11,371
31	Mar	5	(h)	Liverpool	D 2-2	Hampson, P.Watson	14,562
32		12	(a)	Leicester C	D 2-2	A.Watson 2 (1 pen)	14,558
33		19	(h)	Aston Villa	L 1-3	A.Watson (pen)	15,585
34		25	(h)	Portsmouth	D 1-1	Hampson	23,272
35		26	(a)	Sheffield W	L 0-3		13,101
36		28	(a)	Portsmouth	D 2-2	Hampson, Wilkinson	17,805
37	Apr	2	(h)	West Ham U	W 7-2	Douglas 2, A.Watson 2, Wilkinson 2, Hampson	13,092
38		9	(a)	Grimsby T	D 0-0		8,651
39		16	(h)	Bolton W	L 0-3		16,890
40		27	(a)	Newcastle U	D 2-2	Hampson 2	31,348
41		30	(h)	Huddersfield T	W 2-0	Longden, McLelland	15,675
42	May	7	(a)	Sheffield U	W 3-1	Douglas, McLelland, Wilkinson	12,388

FINAL LEAGUE POSITION: 20th in Division One

Appearances
Goals

FA Cup

3	Jan	9	(h)	Newcastle U	D 1-1	Hampson	14,000
R		13	(a)	Newcastle U	L 0-1		46,104

Appearances
Goals

Maggs	Grant	O'Donnell J	Watson A	Longden	Tufnell	Wilkinson	Upton	Hampson	McLelland	Lax	Quinn	Morfitt	Reece	Oxberry	Smalley	Rattray	Ramsay	Douglas	Wilson	Harrison	Brookes	McDonough	Everest	Watson P	No.
1	2	3	4	5	6	7	8	9	10	11															1
1	2	3	4	5	6		8	9	10	11	7														2
1	2	3	4	5	6	7	8	9	10	11															3
1	2	3	4	5	6	7	8	9	10	11															4
1	2	3	4	5	6	7		9	10	11		8													5
1	2	3	4	5	6	7	8	9	10	11															6
1	2		4	5	6			9	8	11	7		3	10											7
1	2	3	4	5			8	9		11	7			10	6										8
1	2	3	4	5	6	7	8	9	10	11															9
1	2	3	4	5			8	9	10	11					6	7									10
1	2	3	4	5			8	9	10	11					6	7									11
1	2	3	4	8				9	10		11				6	7	5								12
1	2	3	4	8				9	10		11				6	7	5								13
1	2			5			4	9			11			8	6	7	3	10							14
1	2			8	6	7		9							4		3	10	5	11					15
1	2	3		8	6	7		9							4			10	5	11					16
1	2	3		8	6	7		9							4			10	5	11					17
1	2			8	6	7	4	9									3	10	5	11					18
1	2			8	6	7	4	9									3	10	5	11					19
1	2			8	6	7	4	9									3	10	5	11					20
1	2		4	8		7		9									3	10	5	11	6				21
1	2			4	6	7		9						10			3	8	5	11					22
1	2	3		4	6	7		9						10				8	5	11					23
1	2	3		4	6	7		8		11								9	5	10					24
	2	3		4	6	7		8		11								9	5	10		1			25
	2	3		4	6	7		8										10	5	11		1	9		26
	2	3	4	5	6	7		8										10		11		1	9		27
	2	3	8	4		7		9									6	10		11		1		4	28
	2	3	8	4		7		9									6	10		11		1		5	29
	2	3	8	4		7		9		11							6	10				1		5	30
	2	3	8	4		7		9									6	10		11		1		5	31
	2	3	8	4		7		9		11							6	10				1		5	32
	2	3	8	4	6	7		9		11				10								1		5	33
	2	3	8	4	6	7		9	10	11												1		5	34
	2		8	4	6	7	10	9		11									5			1		3	35
	2		8	4		7	10	9		11							6		5			1		3	36
	2	3	8	4		7		9		11								10	5			1		6	37
	2	3	8	4		7		9		11								10	5			1		6	38
	2	3	8	4		7		9		11								10	5			1		6	39
	2	3	8	4		7		9		11								10	5			1		6	40
	2	3		4	6	7		9	8						11			10				1		5	41
	2	3		4	6	7		9	8						11			10				1		5	42
24	42	32	28	42	25	34	15	42	15	23	6	1	1	6	11	5	15	25	18	16	1	18	2	15	
			7	4		9		23	6					1		1		10		1			1	1	

1 own-goal

Maggs	Grant	O'Donnell J	Watson A	Longden	Tufnell	Wilkinson	Upton	Hampson	McLelland	Lax	Quinn	Morfitt	Reece	Oxberry	Smalley	Rattray	Ramsay	Douglas	Wilson	Harrison	Brookes	McDonough	Everest	Watson P	Round
1	2	3	8	4	6	7		9										10	5	11					3
1	2	3	8	4	6	7		9										10	5	11					R
2	2	2	2	2	2	2		2										2	2	2					
								1																	

1932-33

Manager: Harry Evans (Honorary title)

1	Aug	27	(a)	Sheffield W	L 1-4	Wilkinson	15,152
2		29	(h)	Leeds U	W 2-1	Hampson, McLelland (pen)	20,313
3	Sep	3	(h)	West Brom A	L 2-4	Hampson, McLelland	20,646
4		5	(a)	Leeds U	L 1-3	Hampson	9,171
5		10	(a)	Birmingham	L 1-2	McLelland (pen)	16,048
6		17	(h)	Sunderland	W 3-1	McLelland 2, Douglas	18,234
7		24	(a)	Manchester C	L 1-5	McLelland	25,175
8	Oct	1	(h)	Arsenal	L 1-2	McLelland (pen)	30,218
9		8	(a)	Everton	L 0-2		18,359
10		15	(h)	Leicester C	W 2-1	Hampson, Crawford	16,898
11		22	(a)	Portsmouth	L 1-2	Wilkinson	14,422
12		29	(h)	Chelsea	W 4-0	Hampson 3, Wilkinson	7,311
13	Nov	5	(a)	Aston Villa	L 2-6	Hampson, McLelland	29,371
14		12	(h)	Middlesbrough	W 3-1	Hampson 2, McLelland	12,104
15		19	(a)	Bolton W	L 0-1		14,468
16		26	(h)	Liverpool	W 4-1	Butterworth 2, Hampson 2	12,162
17	Dec	3	(a)	Huddersfield T	W 1-0	Butterworth	8,623
18		10	(h)	Sheffield U	L 0-3		12,909
19		17	(a)	Wolves	W 3-2	Hampson 2, Wilkinson	21,377
20		24	(h)	Newcastle U	L 0-4		14,053
21		26	(a)	Derby C	D 1-1	Wilkinson	21,862
22		27	(h)	Derby C	W 4-1	McLelland, Hampson, Douglas, Smailes	19,017
23		31	(h)	Sheffield W	L 3-4	Hampson 2, Wilkinson	13,689
24	Jan	2	(a)	Blackburn R	L 5-6	McLelland 2, Wilkinson, Douglas, Smailes	22,471
25		7	(a)	West Brom A	L 1-2	McLelland	17,280
26		21	(h)	Birmingham	L 0-1		10,352
27	Feb	1	(a)	Sunderland	D 1-1	McLelland	19,873
28		4	(h)	Manchester C	W 1-0	Hampson	13,399
29		11	(a)	Arsenal	D 1-1	McLelland	35,180
30		22	(h)	Everton	W 2-1	A.Watson, Cook (og)	12,050
31	Mar	4	(h)	Portsmouth	L 0-2		12,623
32		11	(a)	Chelsea	L 0-1		31,222
33		18	(h)	Aston Villa	W 6-2	P.Watson 3, Smailes 2, Crawford	15,729
34		28	(a)	Middlesbrough	L 0-2		10,724
35		30	(a)	Leicester C	L 0-3		7,904
36	Apr	1	(h)	Bolton W	L 1-3	Crawford	15,849
37		8	(a)	Liverpool	L 3-4	P.Watson 2, Crawford	16,384
38		14	(h)	Blackburn R	W 3-0	Smailes, P.Watson 2	26,365
39		15	(h)	Huddersfield T	D 1-1	Douglas	22,867
40		22	(a)	Sheffield U	L 0-1		8,945
41		29	(h)	Wolves	D 2-2	Upton, Douglas	16,007
42	May	6	(a)	Newcastle U	W 2-1	Upton, Reid	11,443

FINAL LEAGUE POSITION: 22nd in Division One

Appearances
Goals

FA Cup

3	Jan	14	(h)	Port Vale	W 2-1	McLelland (pen), Hampson	15,800
4		28	(h)	Huddersfield T	W 2-0	McLelland, Douglas	16,187
5	Feb	18	(a)	Sunderland	L 0-1		46,900

Appearances
Goals

McDonough	Grant	Everest	Longden	Watson P	Smalley	Wilkinson	McLelland	Hampson	Douglas	Bridge	Smith	Tufnell	Upton	Wassell	Reece	Watson A	Crawford	Butterworth	Lax	Rattray	Smailes	Reid	Roxburgh	Cardwell	
1	2	3	4	5	6	7	8	9	10	11															1
1	2	3	4	5	6	7	8	9	10	11															2
1	2	3	4	5		7	8	9	10	11	6														3
1	2	3	4	5		7	8	9		11		6	10												4
1			6	5		7	8	9		11			10	2	3	4									5
1			4	5		7	8	9	10	11				2	3		6								6
1			4	5		7	8	9	10	11				2	3		6								7
1		3		5		7	10	9						2		4	6	8	11						8
1		3		5		7	10	9						2		4	6	8	11						9
1		3		5	11	7	10	9						2		4	6	8							10
1		3		5	11	7	10	9						2		4	6	8							11
1		3		5	11	7	10	9						2		4		8		6					12
1		3		5		7	8	9	10					2		4	6			11					13
1		3		5		7	8	9	10					2		4	6			11					14
1		3		5		7	8	9	10					2		4	6			11					15
1		3		5		7		9	10					2		4	6	8		11					16
1		3		5			8	9	10					2		4	6	7		11					17
1		3		5			8	9	10					2		4	6	7		11					18
1		3		5		7	10	9						2		4	6	8			11				19
1		3		5		7	10	9						2		4	6	8			11				20
1	4	3		5		7	8	9	10					2			6				11				21
1		3		5		7	8	9	10					2		4	6				11				22
1		3		5		7	8	9	10					2		4	6				11				23
1		3		5		7	8	9	10					2		4	6				11				24
1		3		5		7	8	9	10					2		4	6				11				25
1		3		5		7	8	9	10					2		4	6				11				26
1	2	3		5		7	9		10							4	6	8			11				27
1	2	3		5		7		9	10							4	6	8			11				28
1	2	3		5			8	9	10							4	6				11	7			29
1	2	3		5			8	9	10							4	6				11	7			30
1	2	3		5				9	10							4	6	8			11	7			31
1	2	3		5			8	9	10							4	6				11	7			32
	2	3		9			8		10							4	6				11	7	1	5	33
	2	3		9			8		10							4	6				11	7	1	5	34
1	2	3		5			9	8	10							4	6				11	7			35
1	2	3		5			9	8	10							4	6				11	7			36
1	2	4		9			8		10					3		5					11	7		6	37
1	2			9			8		10					3		4	6				11	7		5	38
1	2			9			8		10					3		4	6				11	7		5	39
1		3		9			8	7	10					2		4	6				11			5	40
1		3		5			9		10				8	2		4	6				11	7			41
1		3		5				9	10				8	2		4	6				11	7			42
40	18	37	7	42	5	26	38	35	33	7	1	1	4	28	3	35	35	13	2	7	24	13	2	6	
				7		7	15	18	5				2			1	4	3			5	1			

1 own-goal

McDonough	Grant	Everest	Longden	Watson P	Smalley	Wilkinson	McLelland	Hampson	Douglas	Bridge	Smith	Tufnell	Upton	Wassell	Reece	Watson A	Crawford	Butterworth	Lax	Rattray	Smailes	Reid	Roxburgh	Cardwell	
1		3		5		7	8	9	10					2		4	6				11				3
1		3		5		7	8	9	10					2		4	6				11				4
1	2	3		5			8	9	10							4	6				11	7			5
3	1	3		3		2	3	3	3					2		3	3				3	1			
							2	1	1																

1933-34

Manager: Alex 'Sandy' McFarlane

No	Month	Day	Venue	Opponents	Result	Scorers	Attendance
1	Aug	26	(h)	Preston NE	L 1-2	Hampson	28,771
2		28	(a)	Fulham	L 0-1		14,948
3	Sep	2	(a)	Bradford C	L 0-1		13,199
4		4	(h)	Fulham	W 4-3	Butterworth 2, Hampson, T.Jones	20,791
5		9	(h)	Port Vale	W 1-0	Crawford	16,988
6		16	(a)	Notts C	D 1-1	Hampson	18,957
7		23	(h)	Swansea T	W 2-1	Smailes, Hampson	18,366
8		30	(a)	Millwall	D 0-0		18,243
9	Oct	7	(h)	Lincoln C	W 2-0	Hampson 2	18,599
10		14	(a)	Bury	W 5-2	Hampson 3, Thomson, Bussey	10,497
11		21	(h)	Oldham A	D 0-0		21,233
12		28	(a)	Burnley	L 2-3	Hampson, Dougall	18,150
13	Nov	4	(h)	Brentford	W 3-1	Smailes 2, Bussey	14,229
14		11	(a)	Bolton W	W 2-1	Smailes, Bussey	19,947
15		18	(h)	Manchester U	W 3-1	T.Jones, Hampson, Smailes	14,384
16		25	(a)	Plymouth A	W 3-0	Rattray 2, Hampson	21,533
17	Dec	2	(h)	West Ham U	D 1-1	Hampson	13,822
18		9	(a)	Nottingham F	D 0-0		10,282
19		16	(h)	Grimsby T	L 3-4	Rattray 2, Bussey	15,332
20		23	(a)	Bradford	W 2-1	T.Jones 2	10,465
21		25	(h)	Hull C	D 0-0		24,631
22		26	(a)	Hull C	L 0-3		15,002
23		30	(a)	Preston NE	L 0-3		23,361
24	Jan	6	(h)	Bradford C	W 3-2	Rattray, Smailes, Doherty	13,070
25		20	(a)	Port Vale	L 0-1		14,216
26	Feb	3	(a)	Swansea T	D 2-2	Bussey, Smailes	8,574
27		7	(h)	Notts C	W 2-1	Bussey, T.Jones	10,188
28		10	(h)	Millwall	D 2-2	Smailes, S.Jones	13,149
29		17	(a)	Lincoln C	D 2-2	Smailes, T.Jones	5,968
30		24	(h)	Bury	W 2-0	Bussey 2	14,811
31	Mar	3	(a)	Oldham A	L 0-2		9,393
32		10	(h)	Burnley	D 1-1	Brallisford	13,278
33		17	(a)	Brentford	L 0-1		16,461
34		24	(h)	Bolton W	D 1-1	Hall	17,464
35		30	(h)	Southampton	W 4-2	Hall, T.Jones, Smailes, Doherty	20,966
36		31	(a)	Manchester U	L 0-2		20,038
37	Apr	2	(a)	Southampton	L 2-3	Hall 2	10,221
38		7	(h)	Plymouth A	D 1-1	Hall	13,994
39		14	(a)	West Ham U	W 2-1	Doherty 2	14,170
40		21	(h)	Nottingham F	L 2-3	Rattray, P.Watson	10,396
41		28	(a)	Grimsby T	L 0-7		7,090
42	May	5	(h)	Bradford	D 1-1	Brallisford	8,252

FINAL LEAGUE POSITION: 11th in Division Two

Appearances
Goals

FA Cup

Round	Month	Day	Venue	Opponents	Result	Scorers	Attendance
3	Jan	13	(a)	Cheltenham T	W 3-1	Bussey, P.Watson, Doherty	12,000
4		27	(a)	Stoke C	L 0-3		24,000

Appearances
Goals

McDonough	Wassell	Everest	Watson A	Watson P	Crawford	Thomson	Robinson	Hampson	Douglas	Smailes	Shipman	Grant	Upton	Butterworth	Jones T	Varty	Rattray	Dougall	Bussey	Jones S	Doherty	Cardwell	Roxburgh	Wallace	Witham	Armes	Brallisford	Hall	Finan	
1	2	3	4	5	6	7	8	9	10	11																				1
1	2			5	6	7		9	10	11	3	4	8																	2
1	2			5	6	7	10	9		11	3	4		8																3
1	2			5	6	7		9		11	3	4		10	8															4
1	2		4	5	6	7		9			3			8	10	11														5
1	2		4	5	6			9		11	3			8	10		7													6
1	2			5	6	7		9		11	3			8	10			4												7
1	2			5	6	7		9		11	3			10				4	8											8
1	2			5	6	7		9		11	3			10				4	8											9
1	2			5	6	7		9		11	3				10			4	8											10
1	2			5		7		9		11	3				10			4	8	6										11
1	2			5		7		9		11	3				10			4	8	6										12
1	2			5	6	7		9		11	3				10			4	8											13
1	2			5	6	7		9		11	3				10			4	8											14
1	2			5	6			9		11	3				10		7	4	8											15
1	2			5	6			9		11	3				10		7	4	8											16
1	2			5				9		11	3				10		7	4	8	6										17
1	2			5	6			9		11	3				10		7	4	8											18
1	2			5	6			9		11	3				10		7	4	8											19
1	2			5				9		11	3				8		7	4		6	10									20
1	2			5				9		11	3				8		7	4		6	10									21
1	2			9	6					11	3			7	10			4	8			5								22
1	2			5				9		11	3				10		7	4	8	6										23
1	2	3		5						11					10		7	4	8	6	9									24
	2	3		5		7									10	11		4	8	6	9		1							25
	2			5		7				11	3				8			4	9	6	10		1							26
	2			5		7				11	3				8			4	9	6	10		1							27
	2			5		7				11	3			8				4	9	6	10		1							28
	2			5		7				11					8			4	9	6	10			1	3					29
	2			5						11					8			4	9	6	10			1	3	7				30
	2			5						11					8			4	9	6	10			1	3	7				31
	2			5		7				11					10			4	8	6				1	3		9			32
	3			5		7				11					10			4	8	6				1	2		9			33
	2			5		7				11					8			4		6	10			1	3			9		34
	2			5		7				11					8			4		6	10			1	3			9		35
	2			5		7				11					8			4		6	10			1	3			9		36
	2			5	6					11		4							8		10			1	3	7		9		37
	2			5	6			9		11		4			8						10			1	3			7		38
	2			5						11					8		7	4		6	10			1	3			9		39
	2			5						11					8		7	4		6	10			1	3			9		40
	2			5						11								4		6	10		1		3	7			8	41
				5	6	7				11	3							4			10			1	2		9		8	42
24	41	3	3	42	20	24	2	23	2	40	26	5	1	9	33	2	12	34	25	22	19	1	5	13	14	4	3	8	2	
				1	1	1		13		10				2	7		6	1	8	1	4						2	5		

McDonough	Wassell	Everest	Watson A	Watson P	Crawford	Thomson	Robinson	Hampson	Douglas	Smailes	Shipman	Grant	Upton	Butterworth	Jones T	Varty	Rattray	Dougall	Bussey	Jones S	Doherty	Cardwell	Roxburgh	Wallace	Witham	Armes	Brallisford	Hall	Finan	
1	2	3		5						11					10		7	4	8	6	9									3
	2	3		5		7				11					10			4	8	6	9		1							4
1	2	2		2		1				2					2		1	2	2	2	2		1							
				1															1		1									

1934-35

Manager: Alex 'Sandy' MacFarlane

1	Aug	25	(a)	Bury	W 5-1	Hampson 3, Finan, Smailes	13,006
2		27	(h)	Newcastle U	W 4-1	Thomas, Hampson 2, Smailes	25,303
3	Sep	1	(h)	Hull C	W 2-1	Hampson 2	18,447
4		8	(a)	Nottingham F	D 0-0		17,179
5		12	(a)	Newcastle U	L 1-4	Thomas	23,404
6		15	(h)	Brentford	D 2-2	Hampson, Dougall	24,223
7		22	(a)	Fulham	L 1-4	Hampson	26,656
8		29	(h)	Bradford	W 1-0	Oram	15,354
9	Oct	6	(a)	Plymouth A	W 2-1	Doherty, Oram	8,286
10		13	(h)	Norwich C	W 2-1	Hall, Watmough	15,889
11		20	(h)	Burnley	W 1-0	Oram	22,096
12		27	(a)	Swansea T	L 1-2	T.Jones	5,689
13	Nov	3	(h)	Manchester U	L 1-2	Hampson	15,663
14		10	(a)	Port Vale	D 2-2	Brallisford, Finan	11,428
15		17	(h)	Barnsley	W 3-0	Brallisford 2, Watmough	11,428
16		24	(a)	Sheffield U	D 1-1	Doherty	13,856
17	Dec	1	(h)	Bradford C	W 2-1	T.Jones, Watmough	9,576
18		8	(a)	Notts C	L 2-3	Hall, Watmough	10,067
19		15	(h)	Southampton	W 4-1	Smailes, S.Jones, Doherty 2	10,016
20		22	(a)	Bolton W	L 2-4	Hall, P.Watson (pen)	22,255
21		25	(h)	Oldham A	W 4-0	Smailes 2, T.Jones, Hall	18,427
22		26	(a)	Oldham A	W 3-2	Smailes, Doherty, Watmough	14,075
23		29	(h)	Bury	D 1-1	P.Watson (pen)	12,624
24	Jan	5	(a)	Hull C	D 2-2	Brallisford 2	10,670
25		19	(h)	Nottingham F	W 1-0	Doherty (pen)	11,819
26		26	(a)	Brentford	L 1-2	Doherty	13,087
27	Feb	2	(h)	Fulham	D 1-1	Doherty	11,032
28		9	(a)	Bradford	D 0-0		9,019
29		16	(h)	Plymouth A	W 4-1	Hampson 3, Doherty	7,484
30		23	(a)	Norwich C	D 1-1	Watmough	11,290
31	Mar	5	(a)	Burnley	W 2-1	Hampson, Smailes	8,992
32		9	(h)	Swansea T	W 2-1	Hampson, Finan	10,979
33		16	(a)	Manchester U	L 2-3	Doherty 2	25,704
34		23	(h)	Port Vale	W 3-1	Hampson, Watmough, Smailes	7,268
35		30	(a)	Barnsley	D 2-2	Watmough, Smailes	11,639
36	Apr	6	(h)	Sheffield U	W 1-0	Smailes	11,509
37		13	(a)	Bradford C	W 2-0	Doherty (pen), T.Jones	8,456
38		19	(h)	West Ham U	W 3-2	Hampson 2, T.Jones	29,626
39		20	(h)	Notts C	W 3-1	Hampson, Doherty (pen), Finan	15,434
40		22	(a)	West Ham U	L 1-2	Hampson	35,161
41		27	(a)	Southampton	L 0-2		6,758
42	May	4	(h)	Bolton W	D 1-1	Watmough	25,550

FINAL LEAGUE POSITION: 4th in Division Two

Appearances
Goals

FA Cup

3	Jan	12	(a)	Leicester C	L 1-2	Hall	18,000

Appearances
Goals

Wallace J	Wassell G	Witham R	Dougall R	Watson P	Jones S	Thomas R	Finan B	Hampson J	Jones T	Smailes J	Grant W	Brallisford A	Doherty P	Oram D	Watmough R	Shipman T	Cardwell L	Hall A	
1	2	3	4	5	6	7	8	9	10	11									1
1	2	3	4	5	6	7	8	9	10	11									2
1	2	3	4	5	6	7	8	9	10	11									3
1	2		4	5	6	7	8	9	10	11	3								4
1	2		4	5	6	7	8	9	10	11	3								5
1	2		4	5	6		8	9		11	3	7	10						6
1	2		4	5	6		8	9			3	7	10	11					7
1	2		4	5	6	7	8	9			3		10	11					8
1	2	3	4	5	6		8	9	10				7	11					9
1		3	4	5	6				10		2		8	11	7			9	10
1		3	4	5	6				10			9	8	11	7	2			11
1	2	3	4	5	6			9	10				8	11	7				12
1	2	3	4	5	6			9	10				8	11	7				13
1		3	4	2	6		8		10			9	11		7		5		14
1		3	4	2	6		8		10			9	11		7		5		15
1		3	4	2	6		8		10			9	11		7		5		16
1		3	4	2	6		8		10			9	11		7		5		17
1		3	4	2	6		8		10				11		7		5	9	18
1		2	4	3	6		8			11			10		7		5	9	19
1		3	4	2	6				8	11			10		7		5	9	20
1		3		2	6				8	11	4		10		7		5	9	21
1		3		2	6				8	11	4		10		7		5	9	22
1		3		2	6				8	11	4		10		7		5	9	23
1	2	3			6		8			11	4	9	10		7		5		24
1	2	3			6				8	11	4	9	10		7		5		25
1	2	3	4	9			10		8		5		11		7		6		26
1	2	3		9	6				8	11	4		10		7		5		27
1	2	3			6		10	9	8	11	4				7		5		28
1	2	3			6			9	8	11	4		10		7		5		29
1	2	3			6				8	11	4		10		7		5	9	30
1	2	3			6			9	8	11	4		10		7		5		31
1	2	3			6		8	9		11	4		10		7		5		32
1	2	3			6			9	8	11	4		10		7		5		33
1		3		2	6			9	8	11	4		10		7		5		34
1		3		2	6			9	8	11	4		10		7		5		35
1		3		2	6			9	8	11	4		10		7		5		36
1		3		2	6			9	8	11	4		10		7		5		37
1		3		2	6			9	8	11	4		10		7		5		38
1		3		2	6		8	9		11	4	7	10				5		39
1		3		2	6			9	8	11	4		10		7		5		40
1		3		2	6		10	9	8		4		11		7		5		41
1		3		2	6		10	9	8	11	4				7		5		42
42	21	37	21	34	41	6	22	25	35	28	28	10	35	7	32	1	29	8	
			1	2	1	2	4	20	5	10		5	13	3	9			4	

Wallace J	Wassell G	Witham R	Dougall R	Watson P	Jones S	Thomas R	Finan B	Hampson J	Jones T	Smailes J	Grant W	Brallisford A	Doherty P	Oram D	Watmough R	Shipman T	Cardwell L	Hall A	
1	2	3			6				8	11	4		10		7		5	9	3
1	1	1			1				1	1	1		1		1		1	1	
																		1	

1935-36

Manager: Joe Smith

1	Aug	31	(h)	Doncaster R	W 5-2	Oram, Finan 2, T.Jones, Doherty	20,649
2	Sep	4	(h)	Norwich C	W 2-1	Finan, Oram	19,259
3		7	(a)	Bury	D 1-1	Oram	12,276
4		11	(a)	Norwich C	W 1-0	Finan	22,337
5		14	(h)	West Ham U	W 4-1	Finan 2, Oram, Parr	22,082
6		16	(h)	Nottingham F	L 1-4	Doherty (pen)	13,738
7		21	(a)	Swansea T	L 0-1		13,276
8		28	(h)	Leicester C	L 3-5	Middleton 2, Watmough	24,409
9	Oct	3	(a)	Nottingham F	D 2-2	Doherty, T.Jones	8,325
10		5	(a)	Bradford	L 2-3	Oram, Watmough	11,410
11		12	(h)	Sheffield U	W 3-0	Watmough 2, Finan	19,684
12		19	(a)	Charlton A	D 1-1	Hampson	23,171
13		26	(h)	Hull C	W 4-1	T.Jones 2, Finan, Doherty	10,624
14	Nov	2	(a)	Barnsley	W 2-1	Oram, Watmough	9,075
15		9	(h)	Plymouth A	W 3-1	Finan 2, Doherty	12,415
16		16	(a)	Bradford C	L 1-2	Finan	13,231
17		23	(h)	Fulham	D 1-1	Doherty	12,353
18		30	(a)	Tottenham H	L 1-3	Finan	35,031
19	Dec	7	(h)	Manchester U	W 4-1	Doherty 2, T.Jones, Finan	13,218
20		14	(a)	Port Vale	D 2-2	Watmough 2	7,106
21		25	(a)	Burnley	L 2-3	Hampson, T.Jones	19,376
22		26	(h)	Burnley	W 2-0	Hampson, Doherty (pen)	15,579
23		28	(a)	Doncaster R	W 3-0	Finan 2, Watmough	12,373
24	Jan	4	(h)	Bury	L 2-3	Finan, T.Jones	11,758
25		18	(a)	West Ham U	L 1-2	Finan	19,362
26		29	(h)	Swansea T	D 1-1	Finan	7,862
27	Feb	1	(a)	Leicester C	L 1-4	T.Jones	18,095
28		8	(h)	Bradford	W 4-2	Finan 2, Doherty 2	9,936
29		20	(a)	Sheffield U	L 0-1		16,291
30		22	(h)	Charlton A	W 6-2	Finan 3, Hampson, Chandler, Brallisford	10,956
31		29	(a)	Manchester U	L 2-3	Finan 2	18,423
32	Mar	7	(h)	Bradford C	D 3-3	Finan, Cardwell, S.Jones	6,918
33		14	(a)	Plymouth A	L 2-3	Cardwell, Finan	13,761
34		21	(h)	Barnsley	W 3-0	Hampson, Cardwell, Opp own-goal	10,123
35		28	(a)	Fulham	L 2-4	Finan 2	18,250
36	Apr	4	(h)	Tottenham H	L 2-4	Finan, Opp own-goal	11,044
37		10	(h)	Southampton	W 2-1	Hampson, Finan	18,447
38		11	(a)	Hull C	W 3-0	T.Jones, Middleton, Cardwell (pen)	4,309
39		13	(a)	Southampton	L 0-1		11,911
40		18	(h)	Port Vale	W 3-1	T.Jones, S.Jones, Chandler	9,326
41		22	(h)	Newcastle U	W 6-0	Cardwell (pen), Finan 3, T.Jones 2	7,935
42		28	(a)	Newcastle U	L 0-1		7,765

FINAL LEAGUE POSITION: 10th in Division Two

Appearances
Goals

FA Cup

3	Jan	11	(h)	Margate	W 3-1	Finan, Watmough 2	13,800
4		25	(a)	Fulham	L 2-5	Finan, T.Jones	25,000

Appearances
Goals

Match	Wallace	Watson P	Witham	Dougall	Cardwell	Jones S	Watmough	Jones T	Finan	Doherty	Oram	Parr	Middleton	McIntosh	Butler	Shipman	Watson A	Hampson	Chandler	Bokas	Roxburgh	Wassell	Brallisford
1	1	2	3	4	5	6	7	8	9	10	11												
2	1	2	3	4	5	6			9	10	11	7	8										
3	1	2	3	4	5	6		8	9	10	11	7											
4	1	2	3	4	5	6		8	9	10	11	7											
5	1	2	3	4	5	6		8	9	10	11	7											
6	1	2	3	4	5	6		8	9	10	11	7											
7	1	2	3	4	5	6			9	10		7	8	11									
8	1	2	3	4	5	6	7		9	10			8	11									
9	1	2	3		5	6	7	8	9	10	11				4								
10	1	2			5	6	7	8	9	10	11					3	4						
11	1	2	3		5	6	7	8	9	10	11						4						
12	1	2	3		5	6	7	8	10		11						4	9					
13	1	2	3		5	6	7	8	9	10	11						4						
14	1	2	3		5	6	7	8	9	10	11						4						
15	1	2	3		5	6	7	8	9	10	11						4						
16	1	2	3		5	6	7	8	9	10	11						4						
17	1	2	3		5	6	7	8	9	10							4		11				
18	1	2	3		5	6	7	8	9	10							4		11				
19	1	2	3		5	6	7	10	9	11							4	8					
20	1	2	3		5	6	7	10	9	11							4	8					
21	1	2	3		5	6	7	10	9	11							4	8					
22	1	2	3		5		7	8		10	11						4	9		6			
23	1	2	3		5		7	8	9	10	11						4			6			
24	1	2	3		5	6	7	8	9	10	11									4			
25	1	2	3		5	6	7	8	9	10	11									4			
26			3		5	6	7	8	9	10					2				11	4	1		
27			3		5	6	7	10	9	11					2		4	8		4	1		
28					5	6	7		9	10	11					3	4	8			1	2	
29	1				5	6	7		9	10						3	4	8	11			2	
30	1				5	6			9	10						3	4	8	11			2	7
31	1			4	5	6		10	9							3		8	11			2	7
32	1			4	5	6		10	9							3		8	11			2	7
33	1			4	5	6		10	9							3		8	11			2	7
34	1	2	3	4	5	6		10	9					7				8	11				
35	1	2	3	4	5	6		10	9					7				8	11				
36	1		3		5	6		10	9				7				4	8	11			2	
37		5	3	2	4			10	9			7					6	8	11		1		
38		5	3	2	4			10	9				7				6	8	11		1		
39		5	3	2	4			10	9				7				6	8	11		1		
40		2	3	4	5	6		10	9			7						8	11		1		
41		2	3	4	5	6		10	9		11	7						8			1		
42	1	2	3	4	5	6		10	9		11	7						8					
	34	33	35	19	42	37	23	36	41	29	21	10	6	4	3	7	22	21	15	6	8	7	4
					5	2	8	12	34	11	6	1	3					6	2				1

2 own-goals

Round	Wallace	Watson P	Witham	Dougall	Cardwell	Jones S	Watmough	Jones T	Finan	Doherty	Oram	Parr	Middleton	McIntosh	Butler	Shipman	Watson A	Hampson	Chandler	Bokas	Roxburgh	Wassell	Brallisford
3	1	2	3		5	6	7	8	9	10	11									4			
4	1	2	3		5	6	7	8	9	10	11									4			
	2	2	2		2	2	2	2	2	2	2									2			
							2	1	2														

1936-37

Manager: Joe Smith

1	Aug	29	(a)	Leicester C	W 2-1	Finan 2	14,417
2		31	(h)	Tottenham H	D 0-0		23,875
3	Sep	5	(h)	West Ham U	W 1-0	Finan	20,671
4		12	(a)	Norwich C	W 2-1	Farrow, Cook	22,631
5		14	(h)	Bury	L 1-2	Hampson	17,933
6		19	(h)	Newcastle U	W 3-0	Hampson 2, Finan	26,962
7		21	(a)	Tottenham H	W 2-1	Watmough, Hampson	16,308
8		26	(a)	Bradford	L 1-2	Finan	11,256
9	Oct	3	(h)	Barnsley	D 1-1	Finan	22,839
10		10	(a)	Sheffield U	D 2-2	Finan, Watmough	22,399
11		17	(h)	Burnley	W 2-0	Finan, Watmough	22,529
12		24	(a)	Southampton	L 2-5	Hampson 2	16,779
13		31	(h)	Swansea T	W 3-2	Watmough 2, Hampson	12,719
14	Nov	7	(a)	Bradford C	W 4-1	T.Jones, Watmough, Finan 2	12,036
15		14	(h)	Aston Villa	L 2-3	Hampson, Finan	15,694
16		21	(a)	Chesterfield	W 4-0	Hampson, Finan 2, Farrow	15,116
17		28	(h)	Nottingham F	W 7-1	Finan 2, T.Jones 4, Watmough	12,294
18	Dec	5	(a)	Plymouth A	W 3-1	Hill, Watmough 2	24,737
19		12	(h)	Coventry C	W 3-0	T.Jones, Hill, Astley (og)	12,271
20		19	(a)	Doncaster R	W 4-0	Hill, T.Jones, Finan 2	13,435
21		25	(a)	Fulham	W 3-0	Finan, Hampson, T.Jones	22,855
22		26	(h)	Leicester C	W 6-2	Finan 2, Hill, Farrow (pen), Watmough, T.Jones	30,759
23		28	(h)	Fulham	W 3-1	T.Jones, Hampson, Hill	13,186
24	Jan	1	(a)	Bury	W 3-2	Hill, Finan, Hampson	34,386
25		2	(a)	West Ham U	L 0-3		26,229
26		9	(h)	Norwich C	L 0-2		12,999
27		23	(a)	Newcastle U	W 2-1	Hill 2	34,122
28		30	(h)	Bradford	W 6-0	Danskin (og), Finan, T.Jones 2, Hampson 2	8,923
29	Feb	6	(a)	Barnsley	L 1-2	Finan	14,013
30		13	(h)	Sheffield U	W 1-0	Finan	14,321
31		24	(a)	Burnley	L 0-3		9,051
32		27	(h)	Southampton	W 2-0	Finan, Watmough	11,058
33	Mar	6	(a)	Swansea T	D 1-1	Munro	13,686
34		13	(h)	Bradford C	W 4-2	Hampson, Farrow (pen), Finan, Watmough	12,857
35		20	(a)	Aston Villa	L 0-4		54,860
36		26	(h)	Blackburn R	W 2-0	Finan, Hampson	29,059
37		27	(h)	Chesterfield	L 0-1		21,668
38		29	(a)	Blackburn R	L 0-2		26,977
39	Apr	3	(a)	Nottingham F	D 1-1	Watmough	18,674
40		10	(h)	Plymouth A	D 1-1	Farrow	17,385
41		17	(a)	Coventry C	W 2-1	Munro, Finan	16,719
42		24	(h)	Doncaster R	D 1-1	Bowl	16,333

FINAL LEAGUE POSITION: 2nd in Division Two

Appearances
Goals

FA Cup

3	Jan	16	(a)	Luton T	D 3-3	Finan, Middleton, Watmough	13,000
R		20	(h)	Luton T	L 1-2	Finan	16,700

Appearances
Goals

Wallace	Blair	Witham	Hill	Cardwell	Jones S	Watmough	Hampson	Finan	Jones T	Cook	Butler	Parr	Farrow	Shipman	Bowl	Roxburgh	Hall	Munro	Lyon	Middleton	
1	2	3	4	5	6	7	8	9	10	11											1
1	2	3	4	5	6		8	9	10	11	7										2
1	2	3	4	5	6		8	9		11		7	10								3
1	2	3	4	5	6		8	9		11		7	10								4
1	2	3	4	5	6		8	9		11		7	10								5
1	2	3	4	5	6		8	9		11		7	10								6
1	2	3	4	5	6	7	8	9		11			10								7
1	2	3	4	5	6	7	8	9		11			10								8
1	2	3	4	5	6	7	8	9	10	11											9
1	2	3	4	5	6	7	8	9	10	11											10
1	2	3	4	5	6	7	8	9	10	11											11
1	2	3	4	5	6	7	8	9	10	11											12
1	2	3	4	5	6	7	8	9	10	11											13
1	2		4	5	6	7	8	9	10	11				3							14
1	2		4	5	6	7	8	9	10	11				3							15
1	2	3	11	5	6	7	8	9	10				4								16
1	2	3	11	5	6	7	8	9	10				4								17
1	2	3	11	5	6	7	8		10				4		9						18
	2	3	11	5	6	7	8	9	10				4			1					19
	2	3	11	5	6	7	8	9	10				4			1					20
	2	3	11	5		7	8	9	10				4			1	6				21
	2	3	11	5		7	8	9	10				4			1	6				22
	2	3	11	5			8	9	10	7			4			1	6				23
	2	3	11	5	6		8	9	10	7			4			1					24
	2	3	11	5	6		8	9	10	7			4			1					25
	2	3	11	5			8	9	10	7			4			1	6				26
1	2	3	11	5		7	8	9	10				4				6				27
1	2	3	11	5		7	8	9	10				4				6				28
1	2	3	11	5		7	8	9	10				4				6				29
1	2	3	11	5	6	7	8	9	10				4								30
1	2	3	11	5	6	7	8	9	10				4								31
1	2	3	11	5	6	7	8	9	10				4								32
1	2	3	11	5	6	7	8	9					4					10			33
1	2	3	11	5	6	7	8	9					4					10			34
1	2	3	11	5	6	7	8	9					4					10			35
1	2	3	11	5	6	7	8	9					4					10			36
1	2	3	11	5	6	7	8	9					4					10			37
1	2	3	11	5			8	9					4				6	7	10		38
1	2	3	11	5	6	7	8	9					4						10		39
1	2	3	11	5	6	7	8	9					4						10		40
1	2	3	11	5	6		8	9					4					7	10		41
1	2	3	11	5	6	7	8	9					4		10						42
34	42	40	42	42	34	31	42	41	26	19	1	4	33	2	2	8	8	7	4		
			8			13	16	28	12	1			5		1			2			

2 own-goals

Wallace	Blair	Witham	Hill	Cardwell	Jones S	Watmough	Hampson	Finan	Jones T	Cook	Butler	Parr	Farrow	Shipman	Bowl	Roxburgh	Hall	Munro	Lyon	Middleton	
1	2	3	11	5		7		9	10				4				6			8	3
1	2	3	11	5		7		9	10				4				6			8	R
2	2	2	2	2		2		2	2				2				2			2	
						1		2												1	

1937-38

Manager: Joe Smith

1	Aug	28	(a)	Huddersfield T	L 1-3	Hampson	17,768
2		30	(h)	Bolton W	D 2-2	Farrow, Finan	24,939
3	Sep	4	(h)	Everton	W 1-0	Finan	27,423
4		6	(a)	Bolton W	L 0-3		23,606
5		11	(a)	Wolves	L 0-1		30,820
6		16	(a)	Brentford	W 4-2	J.A.Blair 2, Munro, Cardwell	14,816
7		18	(h)	Leicester C	L 2-4	Hampson, J.A.Blair	31,443
8		20	(h)	Brentford	D 1-1	Opp own-goal	20,732
9		25	(a)	Sunderland	L 1-2	Hastings (og)	31,356
10	Oct	2	(h)	Derby C	D 1-1	Hall	29,662
11		9	(a)	Manchester C	L 1-2	Watmough	38,846
12		16	(h)	Chelsea	L 0-2		23,974
13		23	(a)	Portsmouth	W 2-1	J.A.Blair, Watmough	11,976
14		30	(h)	Stoke C	L 0-1		15,119
15	Nov	6	(a)	Leeds U	D 1-1	Hampson	18,438
16		13	(h)	Birmingham	L 0-3		13,975
17		20	(a)	Preston NE	L 0-2		30,815
18		27	(h)	Liverpool	L 0-1		14,617
19	Dec	4	(a)	Middlesbrough	D 2-2	Buchan 2	17,970
20		11	(h)	Grimsby T	D 2-2	Finan, Hampson	12,880
21		18	(a)	West Brom A	W 2-1	O'Donnell, Buchan	18,129
22		25	(h)	Arsenal	W 2-1	Farrow (pen), Buchan	23,229
23		27	(a)	Arsenal	L 1-2	Finan	54,163
24	Jan	1	(h)	Huddersfield T	W 4-0	Munro, O'Donnell 2, Farrow	22,362
25		15	(a)	Everton	L 1-3	Buchan	22,219
26		26	(h)	Wolves	L 0-2		13,216
27		29	(a)	Leicester C	W 1-0	Finan	13,873
28	Feb	5	(h)	Sunderland	D 0-0		16,682
29		12	(a)	Derby C	L 1-3	T.Jones	12,646
30		19	(h)	Manchester C	W 2-1	Munro, O'Donnell	19,764
31		26	(a)	Chelsea	W 3-1	Munro, Finan, O'Donnell	27,301
32	Mar	5	(h)	Portsmouth	W 2-0	Buchan, O'Donnell	19,407
33		12	(a)	Stoke C	W 3-1	Finan, Farrow, Buchan	24,961
34		19	(h)	Leeds U	W 5-2	Holley (og), Finan 2, Farrow, O'Donnell	18,029
35		26	(a)	Birmingham	D 1-1	T.Jones	19,902
36	Apr	2	(h)	Preston NE	W 1-0	O'Donnell	26,112
37		9	(a)	Liverpool	L 2-4	Finan, Buchan	31,475
38		15	(h)	Charlton A	W 1-0	Buchan	29,961
39		16	(h)	Middlesbrough	W 4-2	Buchan, O'Donnell, Finan 2	29,822
40		18	(a)	Charlton A	L 1-4	Buchan	25,602
41		23	(a)	Grimsby T	L 0-1		10,042
42		30	(h)	West Brom A	W 3-1	Buchan, O'Donnell, Johnston	13,506

FINAL LEAGUE POSITION: 12th in Division One

Appearances
Goals

FA Cup

3	Jan	8	(a)	Birmingham	W 1-0	T.Jones	40,000
4		22	(a)	Aston Villa	L 0-4		69,633

Appearances
Goals

Wallace	Blair D	Witham	Farrow	Cardwell	Jones S	Munro	Hampson	Finan	Jones T	McIntosh	Lyon	Hill	Blair JA	Watson	Hall	Watmough	Butcher	Butler	Johnston	Buchan	Murray	Roxburgh	Hayward	O'Donnell	Sibley	
1	2	3	4	5	6	7	8	9	10	11																1
1	2	3	4	5	6	7	8	9			10	11														2
1	2	3	4	5	6	7	8	9				11	10													3
1	2	3	4		6	7	8	9				11	10	5												4
1	2	3	8	5	6	11		9					10		4	7										5
1	2			5	6	11	8	9					10		4	7	3									6
1	2			5	6	11	8	9					10		4	7	3									7
1	2	3		5	6	11	8				9		10		4	7										8
1	2	3		5	6	11	8	9					10		4	7										9
1	2	3		5	6	11	8	9					10		4	7										10
1	2	3		5	6	11	8	9					10		4	7										11
1	2	3		5	6	11	8		10						4	7		9								12
1	2	3			6	11	8	9					10	5	4	7										13
1	2	3			6	11	8	9					10	5	4	7										14
1	2	3			6	11	8		10				9	5	4	7										15
1	2	3			6	11	8		10				9	5	4	7										16
1	2	3	4		5	11		10								7			6	8	9					17
	2	3	4			11		9	10							7			6	8		1	5			18
	2	3	4			7	10	11											6	8		1	5	9		19
	2	3				7	10	11							4				6	8		1	5	9		20
	2	3	4			7		11					10						6	8		1	5	9		21
	2	3	4			7	9	11					10						6	8		1	5			22
	2	3	4		6	7		11	10											8	9	1	5			23
	2	3	4		6	7		11	10											8		1	5	9		24
	2		4			7		11					10				3		6	8		1	5	9		25
	2	3	4		6	7		11	10									9		8		1	5			26
	2		4			7		9	10				11						6	8		1	5		3	27
	2		4		6	7		9	10				11							8		1	5		3	28
	2		4		6	7		9	10				11				5			8		1			3	29
	2		4			7			10				11						6	8		1	5	9	3	30
	2		4			7		11	10										6	8		1	5	9	3	31
	2		4		6	7		11	10											8		1	5	9	3	32
	2		4			7		11	10										6	8		1	5	9	3	33
	2		4			7		11	10										6	8		1	5	9	3	34
	2		4			7		11	10										6	8		1	5	9	3	35
	2		4			7		11	10										6	8		1	5	9	3	36
			4			7		9	10				11					2	6	8		1	5		3	37
	2		4			7		11	10										6	8		1	5	9	3	38
	2		4			7		11	10										6	8		1	5	9	3	39
	2		4			7		11	10										6	8		1	5	9	3	40
	2		4			7		11	10										6	8		1	5	9	3	41
	2		4		6	7		10											11	8		1	5	9	3	42
17	41	23	30	11	24	42	18	37	23	1	2	3	21	5	13	14	4	3	20	26	2	25	24	17	16	
			5	1		4	4	12	2				4		1	2			1	12				10		

3 own-goals

Wallace	Blair D	Witham	Farrow	Cardwell	Jones S	Munro	Hampson	Finan	Jones T	McIntosh	Lyon	Hill	Blair JA	Watson	Hall	Watmough	Butcher	Butler	Johnston	Buchan	Murray	Roxburgh	Hayward	O'Donnell	Sibley	
	2	3	4			7	9	11	10										6	8		1	5			3
	2	3	4			7		11			9		10						6	8		1	5			4
	2	2	2			2	1	2	1		1		1						2	2		2	2			
									1																	

1938-39

Manager: Joe Smith

1	Aug	27	(h)	Everton	L 0-2		29,647
2		31	(a)	Portsmouth	L 0-1		24,998
3	Sep	3	(a)	Wolves	D 1-1	F.O'Donnell	24,795
4		10	(h)	Aston Villa	L 2-4	Buchan 2	29,128
5		17	(a)	Sunderland	W 2-1	Buchan, Farrow (pen)	26,295
6		19	(h)	Brentford	W 4-1	F.O'Donnell, Munro, Buchan 2	21,970
7		24	(h)	Grimsby T	W 3-1	Buchan, Munro, F.O'Donnell	27,349
8		31	(a)	Derby C	L 1-2	Dawson	21,584
9	Oct	8	(h)	Chelsea	W 5-1	F.O'Donnell 3, Buchan 2	24,878
10		15	(a)	Manchester U	D 0-0		39,723
11		22	(h)	Stoke C	D 1-1	Munro	23,501
12		29	(a)	Preston NE	D 1-1	F.O'Donnell	29,443
13	Nov	5	(h)	Charlton A	D 0-0		16,135
14		12	(a)	Bolton W	W 1-0	Finan	35,782
15		19	(h)	Leeds U	L 1-2	Finan	16,612
16		26	(a)	Liverpool	L 0-1		26,752
17	Dec	3	(h)	Leicester C	D 1-1	Jones	14,255
18		10	(a)	Middlesbrough	L 2-9	Eastham, Munro	17,166
19		17	(h)	Birmingham	W 2-1	Finan, Buchan	11,855
20		24	(a)	Everton	L 0-4		24,040
21		26	(h)	Huddersfield T	D 1-1	Eastham	18,955
22		27	(a)	Huddersfield T	L 0-3		27,113
23		31	(h)	Wolves	W 1-0	Finan	16,134
24	Jan	14	(a)	Aston Villa	L 1-3	Lewis	34,190
25		25	(h)	Sunderland	D 1-1	Munro	13,237
26		28	(a)	Grimsby T	L 0-2		12,126
27	Feb	4	(h)	Derby C	D 2-2	Jones, Lewis	15,929
28		18	(h)	Manchester U	L 3-5	Astley 2, Buchan	15,253
29		25	(a)	Stoke C	D 1-1	Astley	22,886
30	Mar	8	(h)	Preston NE	W 2-1	Astley, Lewis	10,680
31		11	(a)	Charlton A	L 1-3	Dodds	16,668
32		15	(a)	Chelsea	D 1-1	Dodds	12,971
33		18	(h)	Bolton W	D 0-0		18,896
34		25	(a)	Leeds U	L 0-1		21,818
35	Apr	1	(h)	Liverpool	D 1-1	Astley	17,137
36		7	(h)	Arsenal	W 1-0	Finan	31,497
37		8	(a)	Leicester C	W 4-3	Dodds 2, Sharman (og), Eastham	14,679
38		10	(a)	Arsenal	L 1-2	H.O'Donnell	30,760
39		15	(h)	Middlesbrough	W 4-0	Dodds 4	13,733
40		22	(a)	Birmingham	L 1-2	Dodds	21,812
41		29	(a)	Brentford	D 1-1	Opp own-goal	12,761
42	May	6	(h)	Portsmouth	W 2-1	Dodds, Astley	15,947

FINAL LEAGUE POSITION: 15th in Division One

Appearances
Goals

FA Cup

3	Jan	7	(h)	Sheffield U	L 1-2	Lewis	15,000

Appearances
Goals

Roxburgh	Blair D	Sibley	Farrow	Hayward	Johnston	Munro	Buchan	O'Donnell F	Finan	Dawson	Blair JA	Wallace	Parr WW	Hall	Mauchline	Eastham	Ashworth	Jones	Lewis	Butler	Forster	McLaren	Astley	Burke	Dodds	O'Donnell H	Park	
1	2	3	4	5	6	7	8	9	10	11																		1
1	2	3	4	5	6	7	8	9	10	11																		2
1	2	3	4	5	6	7	8	9	10	11																		3
1	2	3	4	5	6	7	8	9		11	10																	4
	2	3	4	5	6	7	8	10	9	11		1																5
	2	3	4	5	6	7	8	10	9	11		1																6
	2	3	4	5	6	7	8	10	9	11		1																7
	2	3	4	5	6	7	8	10	9	11		1																8
	2	3	4	5	6	7	8	10	9	11		1																9
	2	3	4	5	6	7	8	10	9	11		1																10
	2	3	4	5	6	7	8	10	9	11		1																11
	2	3	4	5		8	10	9		11		1	7	6														12
	2	3	4	5	6	7	8	10	9			1			11													13
	2	3	4	5	6	7	8		9			1			11	10												14
	2	3	4	5	6	7			9		10	1			11	8												15
	2	3	4	5	6	7			9			1			11	8	10											16
	2	3	4	5	11	7	8		9			1				10		6										17
	2	3	4	5		7	8		9		11	1				10		6										18
	2	3	4	5	6	7	8		9			1				10			11									19
	2	3	4	5	6	7	8		9			1				10			11									20
	2		4	5	6	7	8					1				10	9		11	3								21
	2			5			8					1		4		10	9	6	11	3	7							22
	2		4	5	6	7	8		11			1				10			9	3								23
	2		4	5		7	8					1				10		6	9	3		11						24
	2			5	6	7	8		11			1		4		10				3			9					25
	2			5		7						1		4		10	9	6	11	3			8					26
	2		4	5		7	8					1				10		6	11	3			9					27
	2		4	5		7	8					1				10		6	11				9	3				28
1		2	4	5	6	7					10					8			11	3			9					29
		2	4	5	6	7	8					1				10			11	3			9					30
		2	4	5	6	7	8					1				10			11	3					9			31
	2	3	4	5	6		8					1									7	11	10		9			32
	2	3	4	5	6	7	8					1											10		9	11		33
	2		4	5	6	7	8					1								3			10		9	11		34
1	2		4	5	6	7										10				3			8		9	11		35
1	2		4	5	6				7							10				3			8		9	11		36
1	2		4	5	6				7							10				3			8		9	11		37
1		2		5	6		10		7					4						3			8		9	11		38
	2		4	5	6		10		7			1											8		9	11	3	39
	2	3	4	5	6		10		7			1											8		9	11		40
	2	3	4		6				7			1				10							8		9	11	5	41
	2	3	4	5	6		10		7			1											8		9	11		42
9	38	29	38	41	35	32	34	13	27	12	4	33	1	5	4	22	4	7	12	15	2	2	17	1	12	10	2	
			1			5	10	7	5	1						3		2	3				6		10	1		

2 own-goals

Roxburgh	Blair D	Sibley	Farrow	Hayward	Johnston	Munro	Buchan	O'Donnell F	Finan	Dawson	Blair JA	Wallace	Parr WW	Hall	Mauchline	Eastham	Ashworth	Jones	Lewis	Butler	Forster	McLaren	Astley	Burke	Dodds	O'Donnell H	Park	
	2		4	5	6	7	8		11			1				10			9	3								3
	1		1	1	1	1	1		1			1				1			1	1								
																			1									

1939-40

Manager: Joe Smith

1	Aug	26	(a)	Huddersfield T	W 1-0	Finan	15,558
2		28	(h)	Brentford	W 2-1	Finan, Dodds	21,633
3	Sep	2	(h)	Wolves	W 2-1	Dodds 2	17,366

FINAL LEAGUE POSITION: 1st in Division One when Football League abandoned upon outbreak of war

North-West Regional League

1	Oct	21	(a)	Blackburn R	D 1-1	Astley	4,000
2		28	(h)	Bury	W 1-0	Astley	4,500
3	Nov	11	(h)	Barrow	W 5-4	Dodds 3, Ashworth, Eastham	6,000
4		18	(a)	Southport	W 3-0	Hayward 2, Dodds	3,000
5		25	(a)	Accrington S	D 3-3	Dodds 2, Farrow	1,500
6	Dec	2	(a)	Bolton W	L 1-3	Lewis	2,777
7		9	(h)	Preston NE	W 3-0	Dodds (pen), Farrow, Astley	11,000
8		23	(a)	Burnley	D 1-1	Dodds	2,668
9	Jan	6	(h)	Carlisle U	D 2-2	Eastham, Ashworth	5,000
10	Feb	10	(h)	Blackburn R	W 3-2	Ainsley 2, Lewis	4,800
11		24	(a)	Bury	W 2-1	Dodds 2	3,000
12	Mar	9	(a)	Barrow	W 4-1	Opp own-goal, Munro 2, Ainsley	3,202
13		16	(h)	Southport	W 3-1	Finan, Eastham, Ainsley	5,000
14		23	(h)	Accrington S	W 8-1	Dodds 3, Buchan 4, Farrow	7,000
15		30	(h)	Bolton W	W 3-1	F.O'Donnell 2, Dodds	6,000
16	Apr	6	(a)	Preston NE	D 1-1	Dodds	4,000
17		13	(h)	Burnley	W 5-0	Dodds 2, Eastham 2, Ashworth	5,000
18		24	(h)	Rochdale	W 7-2	Dodds 3, Finan 2, Blair, Hayward	
19	May	13	(h)	Oldham A	W 11-2	Dodds 7, Astley 3, Finan	3,500
20		28	(a)	Rochdale	D 3-3	Finan, Dodds, Munro	
21	Jun	1	(a)	Carlisle U	L 1-3	Finan	
22		7	(a)	Oldham A	L 2-4	Dodds 2	1,835

FINAL LEAGUE POSITION: 3rd in North-West Regional League

League War Cup

1	Apr	20	(h)	Southport	W 4-0	Dodds 3, Astley	6,388
		27	(a)	Southport	W 5-2	Jones 2, Dodds, Eastham, Astley	2,300
2	May	4	(a)	Burnley	W 2-1	Dodds, Finan	7,857
		11	(h)	Burnley	W 3-1	Dodds 2, Munro	7,631
3		18	(a)	Barnsley	W 1-0	Dodds	10,796
QF		25	(h)	Newcastle U	L 0-2		7,800

1	2	3	4	5	6	7	8	9	10	11	
Wallace	Sibley	Butler	Farrow	Hayward	Johnston	Finan	Astley	Dodds	Buchan	O'Donnell	1
..	..	..	..	..	..	..	..	..	..	..	2
..	..	..	..	..	..	..	..	..	..	..	3

Roxburgh	Sibley	S.Jones	Farrow	Hayward	Johnston	Finan	Astley	Dodds	Eastham	Munro	1
..	..	..	..	..	..	..	..	..	..	..	2
..	..	..	..	..	..	..	Eastham	..	Ashworth	..	3
..	..	..	..	..	..	..	..	..	D.Blair	..	4
..	..	..	..	..	..	..	Astley	..	..	..	5
..	..	..	..	..	..	Munro	Eastham	Ashworth	..	Lewis	6
..	..	..	..	..	..	Finan	Astley	Dodds	Buchan	Munro	7
..	..	..	..	..	..	..	Eastham	..	D.Blair	..	8
..	..	..	..	..	..	..	..	Ashworth	Munro	Lewis	9
..	..	..	..	..	..	Astley	Ainsley	..	..	..	10
..	..	..	..	..	..	Finan	..	Dodds	Eastham	Munro	11
..	..	..	..	..	..	..	..	Astley	..	..	12
..	..	..	..	..	..	..	..	Dodds	..	..	13
..	..	..	..	..	..	..	..	..	Buchan	..	14
..	..	..	..	..	..	..	Eastham	..	F.O'Donnell	H.O'Donnell	15
..	..	..	..	..	..	..	Astley	..	Eastham	Munro	16
..	..	..	..	..	Ainsley	..	Eastham	..	Ashworth	..	17
..	..	..	..	..	D.Blair	..	..	..	D.Blair	..	18
..	..	..	..	..	Johnston	..	Astley	..	Eastham	..	19
..	..	..	..	Suart	Ainsley	..	Buchan	..	..	..	20
..	..	..	..	Cradwell	D.Blair	..	Ainsley	..	..	..	21
..	..	..	..	..	..	..	..	..	..	..	22

Roxburgh	Sibley	S.Jones	Farrow	Hayward	D.Blair	Finan	Astley	Dodds	Eastham	Munro	1
..	..	..	..	..	Johnston	..	..	..	..	..	
..	..	..	..	..	..	..	..	..	..	..	2
..	..	..	..	..	..	..	..	..	..	..	
..	..	..	..	..	..	..	..	..	..	..	3
..	..	..	..	..	..	..	..	..	Buchan	..	QF

Football League Division One
Appearances: Astley 3, Buchan 3, Butler 3, Dodds 3, Farrow 3, Finan 3, Hayward 3, Johnston 3, O'Donnell 3, Sibley 3, Wallace 3.
Goalscorers: Dodds 3, Finan 2

North-West Regional League
Appearances: Roxburgh 22, Sibley 22, S.Jones 22, Farrow 22, Hayward 19, Suart 1, Cardwell 2, Johnston 17, Ainsley 9, Blair 8, Finan 20, Munro 21, Astley 8, Eastham 18, Buchan 3, Dodds 18, Ashworth 5, F.O'Donnell 1, H.O'Donnell 1, Lewis 3.
Goalscorers: Dodds 30, Astley 6, Finan 6, Eastham 5, Ainsley 4, Buchan 4, Ashworth 3, Farrow 3, Hayward 3, Lewis 2, Munro 3, F.O'Donnell 2, Blair 1, Opponents' own-goal 1.

League War-Cup
Appearances: Astley 6, Dodds 6, Farrow 6, Finan 6, Hayward 6, Jones 6, Munro 6, Roxburgh 6, Sibley 6, Eastham 5, Johnston 5, Blair 1, Buchan 1, .
Goalscorers: Dodds 8, Astley 2, Eastham 1, Finan 1, Jones 1, Munro 1.

1940-41

Manager: Joe Smith

1	Jan	4	(h)	Bury	W 3-2	Buchan 2, Dodds	6,000
2		11	(a)	Bury	W 2-1	Buchan, O'Donnell	3,960
3		18	(a)	Manchester C	W 4-2	Buchan, Dodds, Johnson, Burbanks	1,000
4		25	(h)	Manchester C	W 2-1	Dodds 2	12,000
5	Feb	1	(a)	Stockport C	W 2-1	Dodds, Deverall	
6		8	(h)	Stockport C	W 9-2	Dodds 8, Deverall	
7	Mar	1	(h)	Chester	W 5-2	Dodds 2, Boulton 2, Deverall	5,000
8		8	(a)	Chester	L 3-4	Dodds, Burbanks, Buchan	2,000
9		15	(h)	Liverpool	W 6-4	Russell, Burbanks, Buchan, Dodds 3	7,000
10		22	(a)	Liverpool	W 6-2	C.Jones 3, Burbanks 2, Dodds	3,000
11		29	(h)	Manchester U	W 2-0	Dodds 2	4,000
12	Apr	5	(a)	Manchester U	W 3-2	Trigg, Johnston, Burbanks	2,000
13		12	(h)	Liverpool	D 0-0		4,000
14		14	(a)	Everton	D 2-2	Trigg 2	
15		19	(h)	Oldham A	W 6-2	Trigg 3, Buchan, C.Jones 2	4,000
16		26	(a)	Manchester C	L 0-2		4,000
17	May	3	(h)	Manchester C	D 1-1	C.Jones	6,000
18		10	(a)	Burnley	L 0-1		7,000
19		17	(a)	Preston NE	L 0-2		4,000
20		24	(h)	Burnley	W 3-0	C.Jones, Pope (pen), Murphy	2,000
21		31	(h)	Chester	W 4-2	Dodds 3, C.Jones	4,000
22	Jun	2	(h)	Preston NE	W 4-2	Dodds, Murphy, Stevenson, C.Jones	9,800

FINAL LEAGUE POSITION: 6th in North-Regional League

League War-Cup

1	Feb	15	(h)	Manchester C	L 1-4	Dodds	15,000
		22	(a)	Manchester C	W 1-0	Dodds	8,967

Matches number 1-4 & 18 also counted towards the Lancashire Cup. Matches 5 & 6 were Lancashire Cup only.

1	2	3	4	5	6	7	8	9	10	11	
Strong	Pope	S.Jones	Russell	Whittaker	Johnston	Finan	Ainsley	Dodds	Buchan	Burbanks	1
..	..	..	..	..	..	Burbanks	Buchan	..	Deverall	O'Donnell	2
..	..	..	Lowe	..	..	Johnson	..	..	..	Burbanks	3
..	..	..	Russell	..	..	..	..	..	..	..	4
..	..	..	..	..	..	..	..	..	..	..	5
..	..	..	..	..	..	..	..	..	..	..	6
..	Hughes	..	Pugh	..	..	P.Jones	..	..	Boulton	Deverall	7
..	Pope	..	Russell	..	..	..	..	..	..	Burbanks	8
..	Hughes	..	..	..	Pugh	Johnson	..	..	McFadyen	..	9
..	..	..	..	..	..	..	..	..	C.Jones	..	10
..	..	..	..	..	Johnston	..	..	..	McFadyen	..	11
..	Trigg	Hughes	..	Lowe	..	..	..	Trigg	..	..	12
..	Pope	S.Jones	..	Whittaker	..	..	..	C.Jones	Deverall	..	13
..	..	Hughes	..	..	..	..	..	Trigg	..	..	14
..	..	..	..	..	..	..	..	..	C.Jones	..	15
..	Hughes	S.Jones	..	..	..	..	..	..	..	..	16
..	Pope	Hughes	..	..	..	..	Boulton	..	..	..	17
..	..	..	..	..	..	..	Buchan	..	..	..	18
..	..	S.Jones	..	..	Powell	Fidden	Ottewell	..	Johnston	..	19
..	..	..	..	..	..	Johnson	Murphy	C.Jones	..	..	20
..	..	..	..	..	Johnston	Lowe	Buchan	Dodds	C.Jones	..	21
..	..	..	..	..	..	..	Murphy	..	Stevenson	C.Jones	22

Strong	Pope	S.Jones	Russell	Whittaker	Johnston	Johnson	Buchan	Dodds	Deverall	Burbanks	1
..	..	..	..	..	..	C.Jones	..	..	Boulton	..	

North Regional League
Appearances: Strong 22, Whittaker 21, Burbanks 20, Johnston 20, Russell 20, Buchan 18, S.Jones 17, Johnson 15, Pope 15, Dodds 13, Hughes 11, C.Jones 9, Deverall 8, Trigg 8, Lowe 4, Boulton 3, McFadyen 3, Pugh 3, P.Jones 2, Murphy 2, Powell 2, Ainsley 1, Fidden 1, Finan 1, O'Donnell 1, Ottewell 1, Stevenson 1.
Goalscorers: Dodds 26, C.Jones 9, Buchan 7, Burbanks 6, Trigg 6, Deverall 3, Boulton 2, Murphy 2, Johnson 1, Johnston 1, O'Donnell 1, Pope 1, Russell 1, Stevenson 1.

League War Cup
Appearances: Buchan 2, Burbanks 2, Dodds 2, Johnston 2, S.Jones 2, Pope 2, Russell 2, Strong 2, Whittaker 2, Boulton 1, Deverall 1, Johnson 1, C.Jones 1.
Goalscorers: Dodds 2.

1941-42

Manager: Joe Smith

1	Aug	30	(a)	Preston NE	L 1-3	Dodds	12,000
2	Sep	6	(h)	Preston NE	W 2-0	Dodds, Burbank	20,000
3		13	(h)	Southport	W 10-1	Dodds 3, Farrow, C.Jones 2, Whittaker 2, Opp own-goals 2	7,000
4		20	(a)	Southport	W 5-1	Dodds 2, Matthews, Dix, C.Jones	3,000
5		27	(a)	Bury	W 5-0	Johnston, Dodds, Dix 2, C.Jones	4,137
6	Oct	4	(h)	Bury	W 4-2	Pope, C.Jones, Dodds, Burbanks	6,000
7		11	(a)	Bolton W	W 6-2	Buchan 2, Dodds 3, Finan	5,203
8		18	(h)	Bolton W	W 2-1	Dix, Johnston	3,000
9		25	(a)	Blackburn R	L 1-2	Dodds	7,000
10	Nov	1	(h)	Blackburn R	W 4-1	Dodds 3, C.Jones	6,000
11		8	(h)	Halifax T	W 9-1	C.Jones 2, Dodds 4, Dix 2, Farrow	4,000
12		15	(a)	Halifax T	W 2-1	Dodds 2	10,000
13		22	(h)	Oldham A	W 5-1	Finan, Burbanks, C.Jones 3	6,000
14		29	(a)	Oldham A	W 3-0	Dodds 2, Dix	6,805
15	Dec	6	(a)	Burnley	D 2-2	Dodds 2	2,873
16		13	(h)	Burnley	W 9-0	Dix 2, Finan 3, C.Jones 3, Burbanks	4,000
17		20	(a)	Rochdale	W 5-0	Dodds 2, Burbanks 2, Opp own-goal	1,000
18		25	(h)	Rochdale	L 0-1		10,000

FINAL LEAGUE POSITION: 1st in Northern Section — First Competition

Northern Section — Second Competition

19	Dec	27	(h)	Stockport C	W 5-2	Dodds 2, C.Jones 2, Dix	6,000
20	Jan	3	(a)	Stockport C	L 1-2	Dix	2,000
21		10	(h)	Wolves	W 6-1	Matthews, Mortensen, Dodds 2, Dix, Burbanks	6,026
22		17	(a)	Wolves	L 0-1		4,972
23		24	(a)	Huddersfield T	D 3-3	C.Jones, Burbanks, Mortensen	4,375
24		31	(h)	Huddersfield T	W 4-2	Mortensen, Dodds 2, Dix	6,000
25	Feb	7	(h)	Liverpool	W 6-2	Dix 2, Dodds 3, C.Jones	10,000
26		14	(a)	Liverpool	W 3-1	C.Jones, Dix, Dodds	14,295
27		21	(a)	Tranmere R	D 2-2	Dodds, Cuthbertson	2,000
28		28	(h)	Tranmere R	W 15-3	Dodds 7, C.Jones 3, Dix 4, Burbanks	3,000
29	Mar	7	(h)	Burnley	W 13-0	Dodds 5, Mortensen 4, C.Jones 2, Burbanks 2	4,000
30		14	(a)	Everton	D 2-2	Dodds, Dix	12,000
31		21	(a)	Burnley	W 6-0	C.Jones, Dodds 2, Dix 3	5,091
32		28	(h)	Stoke C	W 4-0	Dodds 3, O'Donnell	4,000
33	Apr	11	(h)	Bolton W	W 7-1	Dix 3, Dodds 3, O'Donnell	4,000
34		18	(a)	Bolton W	L 1-2	Dix	3,760
35		25	(a)	Rochdale	L 0-2		3,000
36	May	2	(h)	Rochdale	W 5-1	Farrow 2, Lewis, Finan, Mortensen	4,000
37		9	(a)	Oldham A	W 8-2	C.Jones 5, Mortensen 2, Farrow (pen)	1,850
38		16	(h)	Oldham A	D 2-2	Dix, C.Jones	4,000
39		25	(h)	Liverpool	W 8-2	Finan 2, Mortensen 2, Dix 2, McEwan 2	4,000
40		30	(h)	Blackburn R	W 7-1	Dodds 5, Dix, Mortensen	10,000

FINAL LEAGUE POSITION: 2nd in Northern Section — Second Competition

1. Matches 19 to 28 in the Football League War Cup Qualifying section.
2. Blackpool drawn away to Manchester City on 6 April in Football League War Cup first round proper, but could not fulfill fixture due to travelling ban.
3. Matches 34-36 in Lancashire Cup.
4. Match 40 Lancashire Cup Final, Blackpool given bye in semi-final by Everton.

1	2	3	4	5	6	7	8	9	10	11	
Roxburgh	Pope	S.Jones	Powell	Whittaker	Johnston	Matthews	Dix	Dodds	Stevenson	Burbanks	1
..	..	..	Farrow	..	..	..	..	..	..	..	2
..	..	..	..	..	..	..	Buchan	..	C.Jones	..	3
..	..	..	..	..	..	..	Dix	..	..	..	4
..	..	..	Powell	Suart	..	..	..	..	..	..	5
..	..	..	Farrow	..	..	Finan	..	..	..	..	6
..	..	..	..	..	..	..	..	..	Buchan	..	7
..	..	..	..	..	..	..	..	C.Jones	..	O'Donnell	8
..	..	..	..	..	..	..	..	Dodds	..	Burbanks	9
..	..	..	..	..	..	Matthews	..	..	C.Jones	..	10
..	..	..	..	..	..	..	..	..	..	..	11
Strong	..	..	..	..	..	..	..	..	..	..	12
Savage	..	..	..	..	..	Dix	Mortensen	C.Jones	Finan	..	13
..	..	..	..	..	..	Matthews	Dix	Dodds	C.Jones	..	14
..	..	..	Powell	..	Barker	..	Finan	..	..	..	15
..	..	..	..	..	..	..	Dix	Finan	..	..	16
..	..	..	..	..	..	..	..	Dodds	..	..	17
..	..	..	..	..	Johnston	..	..	..	..	..	18

Savage	Pope	S.Jones	Powell	Suart	Johnston	Matthews	Dix	Dodds	C.Jones	Burbanks	19
..	..	..	..	..	..	..	..	..	..	..	20
..	Barker	Ancell	Farrow	..	..	..	Mortensen	..	Dix	..	21
..	Pope	S.Jones	Barker	Farrow	..	Finan	Dix	..	C.Jones	..	22
..	..	..	Farrow	Whittaker	..	Matthews	Mortensen	..	..	..	23
..	..	..	..	..	..	..	..	..	Dix	..	24
..	..	Barker	..	..	..	..	Dix	..	C.Jones	..	25
Roxburgh	..	..	..	Suart	..	..	..	..	..	..	26
..	..	S.Jones	Whittaker	..	Powell	McEwan	Cuthbertson	..	Mortensen	..	27
..	..	Barker	Farrow	..	Johnston	Matthews	Dix	..	C.Jones	..	28
..	..	..	Whittaker	..	..	..	Mortensen	..	..	..	29
Savage	..	..	Powell	Whittaker	..	..	Dix	..	..	..	30
Roxburgh	..	..	Farrow	..	..	..	..	..	..	O'Donnell	31
..	..	Williams	Powell	..	..	..	Mortensen	..	Finan	..	32
Savage	..	S.Jones	Farrow	Hayward	..	..	Dix	..	C.Jones	..	33
..	..	..	Powell	..	..	C.Jones	Farrow	Finan	Dix	..	34
..	..	..	Farrow	..	..	Matthews	Dix	Dodds	Finan	..	35
Roxburgh	..	Barker	..	..	..	Finan	Mortensen	C.Jones	O'Donnell	Lewis	36
..	..	..	..	..	..	..	..	..	Dix	..	37
..	..	..	..	..	..	..	..	..	..	..	38
..	..	..	..	Dykes	..	Matthews	..	Finan	..	McEwan	39
..	..	..	..	..	..	..	..	Dodds	..	Burbanks	40

Northern Section – First Competition

Appearances: S.Jones 18, Pope 18, Burbanks 17, Dix 16, Dodds 15, Johnston 15, C.Jones 14, Suart 14, Matthews 13, Farrow 12, Roxburgh 11, Finan 7, Powell 6, Savage 6, Buchan 4, Whittaker 4, Barker 3, Stevenson 2, Mortensen 1, O'Donnell 1, Strong 1.

Goalscorers: Dodds 28, C.Jones 14, Dix 9, Burbanks 6, Finan 5, Buchan 2, Farrow 2, Johnston 2, Whittaker 2, Matthews 1, Pope 1, Opponents' own-goals 3.

Northern Section – Second Competition

Appearances: Johnston 21, Pope 21, Dix 17, Dodds 17, Farrow 16, Matthews 16, C.Jones 15, Barker 13, Burbanks 13, Mortensen 11, Roxburgh 11, Savage 11, S.Jones 9, Finan 8, Whittaker 8, Suart 7, Hayward 6, O'Donnell 6, Powell 6, Lewis 3, Dykes 2, McEwan 2, Ancell 1, Cuthbertson 1, Williams 1.

Goalscorers: Dodds 37, Dix 23, C.Jones 17, Mortensen 13, Burbanks 5, Farrow 3, Finan 3, McEwan 2, O'Donnell 2, Cuthbertson 1, Lewis 1, Matthews 1.

1942-43

Manager: Joe Smith

1	Aug	29	(a)	Manchester C	W 3-1	S.Matthews, Mortensen, Dix	6,000
2	Sep	5	(h)	Manchester C	W 5-2	Dodds 3, Dix, Mortensen	5,000
3		12	(h)	Bury	W 9-1	O'Donnell 2, Finan 2, Dodds 4, Burbanks	
4		19	(a)	Bury	W 11-1	Dix 5, Dodds 4, Finan 2	4,500
5		26	(a)	Stockport C	W 6-0	Finan, Farrow, Burbanks, Johnston, Dix, Withington	3,000
6	Oct	3	(h)	Stockport C	W 6-2	Dodds 3, Finan 2, Johnston	7,000
7		10	(h)	Bolton W	W 2-0	Burbanks, Finan	4,000
8		17	(a)	Bolton W	W 2-0	Dodds 2	4,982
9		24	(a)	Rochdale	W 4-3	Dodds, Burbanks 2, Finan	1,500
10		31	(h)	Rochdale	W 5-0	Finan 2, Dodds, Dix 2	6,000
11	Nov	7	(h)	Southport	W 6-2	Dix 3, Dodds, Burbanks, Farrow	10,000
12		14	(a)	Southport	L 2-3	Dodds, Burbanks	6,000
13		21	(a)	Burnley	D 4-4	Finan 3, Burbanks	5,054
14		28	(h)	Burnley	W 5-1	Dodds 3, Farrow 2	5,000
15	Dec	5	(h)	Oldham A	W 8-3	Mortensen 2, Johnston 3, Burbanks, Colquhoun, Finan	3,500
16		12	(a)	Oldham A	W 4-1	Buchan 2, Burbanks, Finan	5,000
17		19	(a)	Blackburn R	W 4-2	Dodds 4	3,000
18		25	(h)	Blackburn R	W 7-2	Dodds 2, Finan 2, Dix 2, Shields	4,000

FINAL LEAGUE POSITION: 1st in Northern Section — First Competition

Northern Section — Second Competition

19	Dec	26	(h)	Southport	D 1-1	Finan	15,000
20	Jan	2	(a)	Southport	W 3-2	Farrow, Finan 2	4,000
21		9	(h)	Manchester U	D 1-1	Finan	5,000
22		16	(a)	Manchester U	L 3-5	Dix, Dodds 2	17,381
23		23	(a)	Blackburn R	D 3-3	Dodds 2, Dix	6,724
24		30	(h)	Blackburn R	W 4-2	Dodds 2, Dix 2	5,000
25	Feb	6	(h)	Oldham A	W 4-0	Burbanks, Dix 2, Dodds	6,000
26		13	(a)	Oldham A	D 1-1	Dix (pen)	4,304
27		20	(a)	Bolton W	D 1-1	S.Matthews	9,000
28		27	(h)	Bolton W	W 5-0	Dodds 2, C.Jones 2, Dix (pen)	5,000
29	Mar	6	(h)	Everton	W 4-1	Dodds 2, Dix (pen), Gardner	15,173
30		13	(a)	Everton	L 3-4	Dodds 2, Burbanks	35,000
31		20	(a)	Liverpool	L 1-3	Dix (pen)	40,000
32		27	(h)	Liverpool	W 5-0	Dodds 2, Finan 2, Dix (pen)	25,000
33	Apr	3	(h)	Manchester C	W 3-1	Dix 2, Opp own-goal	25,000
34		10	(a)	Manchester C	D 1-1	Dodds	53,205
35		17	(h)	Aston Villa	W 3-1	Farrow, Finan, Dix	28,000
36		24	(a)	Aston Villa	L 1-2	Gardner	50,000
37	May	1	(h)	Sheffield W	D 2-2	Finan, Burbanks	28,000
38		8	(a)	Sheffield W	W 2-1	Dodds, Gardner	47,657
39		15	(n)	Arsenal	W 4-2	Dix, Burbanks, Dodds, Finan	55,195

FINAL LEAGUE POSITION: 13th in Northern Section — Second Competition

1. Matches 19 to 26 were Football League War Cup qualifying competition.
2. Matches 27 to 38 were Football League War Cup knock-out competition from first round to final.
3. Match 37 was Challenge Cup Final played at Stamford Bridge, London.

1	2	3	4	5	6	7	8	9	10	11	
Roxburgh	Pope	Williams	Farrow	S.Jones	Hayward	Matthews	Mortensen	Withington	Dix	Burbanks	1
..	..	..	..	Hayward	Johnston	..	..	Dodds	..	..	2
..	..	..	Powell	..	..	..	O'Donnell	..	Finan	..	3
..	..	..	Farrow	..	..	..	Dix	..	..	..	4
..	..	..	..	..	..	Withington	O'Donnell	Finan	Dix	..	5
..	..	..	..	..	..	Matthews	Dix	Dodds	Finan	O'Donnell	6
..	..	..	..	..	..	McEwan	..	Finan	O'Donnell	Burbanks	7
..	..	..	..	..	..	Matthews	..	Dodds	Finan	..	8
..	..	..	..	..	..	C.Jones	..	..	..	..	9
..	..	..	..	..	..	Matthews	..	..	..	..	10
..	..	..	..	..	..	..	..	..	..	..	11
..	Horton	..	..	..	..	..	..	..	..	..	12
..	Pope	..	..	..	Powell	Shields	..	Finan	Johnston	..	13
..	Barker	..	Powell	..	Johnston	Matthews	Farrow	Dodds	Finan	..	14
..	..	Shaw	..	..	..	Colquhoun	Mortensen	Finan	Dix	..	15
..	Williams	..	Barker	..	Powell	..	Buchan	..	McEwan	..	16
..	Pope	Williams	Shaw	Farrow	Hayward	Matthews	Dix	Dodds	Finan	..	17
..	..	..	Farrow	S.Jones	Powell	..	..	..	..	Shields	18

1	2	3	4	5	6	7	8	9	10	11	
Roxburgh	Pope	Williams	Farrow	S.Jones	Powell	R.Matthews	Dix	Dodds	Finan	Shields	19
..	..	..	..	..	..	Finan	..	..	Burbanks	..	20
..	..	..	..	..	..	..	..	..	..	..	21
Savage	..	..	..	Hayward	Johnston	..	Shields	..	Dix	Burbanks	22
Roxburgh	..	..	..	..	..	S.Matthews	Dix	..	Finan	..	23
..	Barker	..	..	..	..	..	Finan	..	Dix	..	24
..	..	..	Powell	..	..	..	Dix	..	Finan	..	25
..	..	S.Jones	..	..	..	..	..	..	..	..	26
..	Pope	..	..	..	..	..	Buchan	..	..	..	27
..	..	..	Farrow	..	..	Finan	Dix	..	C.Jones	..	28
Savage	..	..	..	Atkinson	..	Gardner	..	..	Finan	..	29
Roxburgh	..	..	..	..	..	S.Matthews	..	..	C.Jones	..	30
..	Powell	Williams	..	..	..	Gardner	..	..	Finan	..	31
..	Pope	S.Jones	..	Hayward	..	S.Matthews	..	..	..	..	32
..	..	..	..	..	..	..	..	..	..	..	33
Savage	..	..	..	Johnston	Powell	..	..	..	..	..	34
..	..	..	..	Atkinson	..	Gardner	..	Finan	Johnston	..	35
..	..	..	..	Hayward	Johnston	..	..	Dodds	Finan	..	36
..	..	..	..	Johnston	Powell	S.Matthews	..	..	..	..	37
..	..	Hubbick	..	Hayward	Johnston	Gardner	..	..	..	..	38
..	..	..	..	..	..	S.Matthews	..	..	..	..	39

Northern Section – First Competition
Appearances: Roxburgh 18, Hayward 17, Williams 17, Burbanks 16, Finan 16, Dix 15, Farrow 15, Johnston 14, Pope 14, Dodds 12, Matthews 12, Powell 6, O'Donnell 4, Barker 3, Mortensen 3, Shaw 3, Colquhoun 2, S.Jones 2, McEwan 2, Shields 2, Withington 2, Buchan 1, Horton 1, C.Jones 1.
Goalscorers: Dodds 29, Finan 18, Dix 15, Burbanks 10, Johnston 5, Farrow 4, Mortenson 4, Buchan 2, O'Donnell 2, Colquhoun 1, Matthews 1, Shields 1, Withington 1.

Northern Section – Second Competition
Appearances: Burbanks 20, Dix 20, Dodds 20, Finan 20, Farrow 18, Johnston 18, Pope 17, S.Jones 14, Roxburgh 13, Hayward 12, S.Matthews 11, Powell 10, Savage 8, Williams 8, Gardner 5, Atkinson 4, Shields 4, Barker 3, Hubbick 2, C.Jones 2, Buchan 1, R.Matthews 1.
Goalscorers: Dodds 18, Dix 15, Finan 9, Burbanks 4, Gardner 3, Farrow 2, C.Jones 2, S.Matthews 1, Opponents' own-goal 1.

1943-44

Manager: Joe Smith

No.	Month	Day	Venue	Opponent	Result	Score	Scorers	Attendance
1	Aug	28	(h)	Rochdale	W	6-1	Finan 2, Beattie 2, McEwan, Farrow	5,000
2	Sep	4	(a)	Rochdale	W	6-2	Beattie 3, Farrow 2 (1 pen), McEwan	3,500
3		11	(h)	Manchester C	W	6-2	F.O'Donnell 2, Finan 2, McEwan 2	10,000
4		18	(a)	Manchester C	W	2-1	Hayward, Mortensen	17,500
5		25	(h)	Stockport C	W	3-2	Dix 2, Beattie	5,000
6	Oct	2	(a)	Stockport C	D	0-0		7,000
7		9	(a)	Bury	L	0-1		6,428
8		16	(h)	Bury	W	3-1	Beattie 3	6,000
9		23	(a)	Bolton W	W	2-1	H.O'Donnell, Dix	10,243
10		30	(h)	Bolton W	L	1-2	Dix	7,000
11	Nov	6	(a)	Blackburn R	D	1-1	Dodds	9,250
12		13	(h)	Blackburn R	W	8-0	Mortensen 4, Farrow 2 (1 pen), Dix, Dodds	8,000
13		20	(h)	Burnley	W	3-0	Dix 2, H.O'Donnell	10,000
14		27	(a)	Burnley	W	5-3	Mortensen 2, Dodds, Johnston, Matthews	8,744
15	Dec	4	(a)	Oldham A	D	1-1	Mortensen	7,927
16		11	(h)	Oldham A	W	3-1	Dodds 2, Mortensen	12,291
17		18	(a)	Southport	D	1-1	Mortensen	4,000
18		25	(h)	Southport	W	5-0	Dodds 3 (1 pen), Mortensen 2	25,000
FINAL LEAGUE POSITION: 1st in Northern Section — First Competition								

Northern Section — Second Competition

No.	Month	Day	Venue	Opponent	Result	Score	Scorers	Attendance
19	Dec	26	(h)	Blackburn R	D	2-2	Dix, Dodds	19,500
20	Jan	1	(a)	Blackburn R	L	1-3	Bradley	10,000
21		8	(a)	Southport	W	4-2	H.O'Donnell, Dodds, Mortensen, Dix	5,000
22		15	(h)	Southport	W	2-1	Dix (pen), Dodds	10,000
23		22	(a)	Bolton W	W	6-0	Finan 2, Dodds, Dix, H.O'Donnell, Kirkham	8,000
24		29	(h)	Bolton W	W	2-0	Dodds, Mortensen	10,254
25	Feb	5	(a)	Burnley	L	1-2	Finan	10,282
26		12	(h)	Burnley	L	1-3	H.O'Donnell	8,000
27		19	(h)	Rochdale	W	2-0	Dix, H.O'Donnell	8,000
28		26	(a)	Rochdale	W	2-0	Pearson, Dodds	10,000
29	Mar	4	(h)	Everton	W	7-1	Dix 3, Mortensen 2, Dodds 2	25,000
30		11	(a)	Everton	W	3-1	Dix, Mortensen 2	28,013
31		18	(h)	Rochdale	W	8-0	Mortensen 3, Dix 3, Dodds 2	25,000
32		25	(a)	Rochdale	L	1-2	H.O'Donnell	8,706
33	Apr	1	(h)	Bradford	D	2-2	Dodds 2	17,000
34		8	(a)	Bradford	W	2-1	Finan, Stephen (og)	32,810
35		15	(h)	Manchester C	D	1-1	Dodds	24,800
36		22	(a)	Manchester C	W	2-1	Finan, Tapping	55,000
37		29	(h)	Aston Villa	W	2-1	Dodds 2	26,800
38	May	6	(a)	Aston Villa	L	2-4	Dix, Pearson	54,824
FINAL LEAGUE POSITION: 7th in Northern Section — Second Competition								

1. Matches 19 to 28 were in Football League War Cup Qualifying Competition.
2. Matches 29 to 38 were in Football League War Cup Knock-out Competition from first round to final.

1	2	3	4	5	6	7	8	9	10	11	
Savage	Pope	Kinsell	Farrow	Powell	Johnston	Matthews	McEwan	Finan	Beattie	Burbanks	1
..	..	..	..	..	..	..	..	..	..	..	2
..	..	..	..	..	..	Johnson	..	F.O'Donnell	Finan	..	3
..	..	..	..	Hayward	..	Matthews	Dix	Finan	Mortensen	..	4
..	..	..	..	..	..	Johnson	..	..	Beattie	..	5
John	..	..	Butler	..	Cutting	..	..	..	..	..	6
Savage	..	Williams	Farrow	..	Johnston	Matthews	Johnson	McGahey	..	..	7
..	..	Kinsell	..	..	..	Johnson	Dix	Finan	..	..	8
..	..	..	..	..	..	Matthews	..	F.O'Donnell	..	H.O'Donnell	9
..	..	Williams	..	..	..	..	..	Mortensen	..	Burbanks	10
..	..	Kinsell	..	Suart	..	Finan	..	Dodds	..	H.O'Donnell	11
..	..	..	..	Hayward	..	Matthews	..	..	Mortensen	..	12
..	..	..	Powell	S.Jones	..	..	..	..	..	..	13
..	..	..	..	Hayward	..	..	Mortensen	..	Finan	..	14
..	..	..	..	..	..	..	..	..	..	..	15
..	..	S.Jones	..	..	..	..	Dix	..	Mortensen	..	16
..	..	..	Farrow	..	..	..	..	..	..	..	17
..	..	Kinsell	..	..	..	..	..	..	..	..	18

Savage	Pope	Kinsell	Farrow	Hayward	Johnston	Matthews	Dix	Dodds	Mortensen	H.O'Donnell	19
..	..	Sibley	Maxwell	Bradshaw	..	Whittingham	Williams	Finan	Bradley	..	20
..	..	Kinsell	Johnston	Hayward	S.Jones	Finan	Dix	Dodds	Mortensen	..	21
..	..	..	Tapping	S.Jones	Johnston	..	..	..	..	..	22
..	..	..	..	..	..	..	..	..	Kirkham	..	23
Roxburgh	..	..	Farrow	..	..	..	..	..	Mortensen	..	24
Savage	..	..	Tapping	..	..	Matthews	Kirkham	..	Finan	..	25
John	Garrett	Sibley	Gibbons	Davies	Majdesley	Finan	Dix	..	Watkin	..	26
Savage	Pope	Kinsell	Davies	Hayward	Johnston	Majdesley	..	Mortensen	Finan	..	27
..	..	..	..	S.Jones	..	Matthews	..	Dodds	..	Pearson	28
..	..	..	..	..	..	..	..	..	Mortensen	..	29
..	..	..	Tapping	Hayward	..	Finan	..	..	..	..	30
..	..	..	Davies	S.Jones	..	Matthews	..	..	..	..	31
..	..	..	Johnston	Hayward	S.Jones	..	..	..	..	H.O'Donnell	32
..	..	..	Davies	S.Jones	Johnston	Tapping	..	..	Finan	Pearson	33
..	..	..	Farrow	Hayward	S.Jones	Matthews	..	..	..	..	34
..	..	..	S.Jones	..	Johnston	..	..	..	..	..	35
..	..	..	..	..	..	Tapping	..	Finan	Mortensen	..	36
..	..	..	Johnston	..	S.Jones	Matthews	..	Dodds	Finan	..	37
..	..	..	..	..	..	..	..	..	..	..	38

Northern Section – First Competition
Appearances: Pope 18, Johnston 17, Savage 17, Kinsell 14, Farrow 13, Hayward 13, Matthews 13, Dix 12, Finan 10, Beattie 9, Burbanks 9, Mortensen 9, H.O'Donnell 9, Dodds 8, Powell 7, Johnson 5, S.Jones 3, McEwan 3, F.O'Donnell 2, Williams 2, Butler 1, Cutting 1, John 1, McGahey 1, Suart 1.
Goalscorers: Mortensen 12, Beattie 9, Dodds 8, Dix 7, Farrow 5, Finan 4, McEwan 4, F.O'Donnell 2, H.O'Donnell 2, Hayward 1, Johnston 1, Matthews 1.

Northern Section – Second Competition
Appearances: Pope 19, Dix 18, Johnston 18, Kinsell 18, Savage 18, Dodds 17, Finan 16, S.Jones 15, Hayward 10, Matthews 10, Mortensen 10, H.O'Donnell 10, Pearson 10, Davies 6, Tapping 6, Farrow 3, Kirkham 2, Majdesley 2, Sibley 2, Bradley 1, Bradshaw 1, Garrett 1, Gibbons 1, John 1, Maxwell 1, Roxburgh 1, Watkin 1, Whittingham 1, Williams 1.
Goalscorers: Dodds 15, Dix 13, Mortensen 9, H.O'Donnell 5, Finan 5, Pearson 2, Bradley 1, Kirkham 1, Tapping 1, Opponents' own-goal 1.

1944-45

Manager: Joe Smith

No.	Month	Day	Venue	Opponents	Result	Score	Scorers	Attendance
1	Aug	26	(a)	Rochdale	W	7-3	Finan 2, Farrow, Mortensen 3, Theurer	7,500
2	Sep	2	(h)	Rochdale	W	3-0	Eakin, Finan, F.O'Donnell	3,000
3		9	(h)	Bolton W	L	1-2	Pearson	8,000
4		16	(a)	Bolton W	L	0-1		10,148
5		23	(a)	Accrington S	W	4-3	Finan, Mortensen 3	5,500
6		30	(h)	Accrington S	W	6-0	F.O'Donnell 3, Finan 2, Pearson	8,000
7	Oct	7	(h)	Preston NE	D	1-1	Matthews	14,000
8		14	(a)	Preston NE	L	0-1		10,000
9		21	(a)	Southport	W	5-4	Pearson, Matthews, Finan, Farrow 2	5,000
10		28	(h)	Southport	W	10-2	Dodds 2, Mortensen 4, F.O'Donnell 2, Dix, Matthews	12,000
11	Nov	4	(h)	Oldham A	L	1-3	Larner	6,000
12		11	(a)	Oldham A	W	3-2	Porter (og), Farrow, Finan	7,135
13		18	(a)	Halifax T	L	3-4	Farrow, Paterson, Tweedy	7,000
14		25	(h)	Halifax T	W	4-2	Laing, Walsh 2, Tweedy	6,000
15	Dec	2	(h)	Burnley	L	0-2		5,000
16		9	(a)	Burnley	L	1-5	Tapping	6,335
17		16	(h)	Blackburn R	W	2-1	Davies, Tweedy	3,000
18		23	(a)	Blackburn R	D	2-2	Laing, F.O'Donnell	10,000

FINAL LEAGUE POSITION: 20th in Northern Section — First Competition

Northern Section — Second Competition

No.	Month	Day	Venue	Opponents	Result	Score	Scorers	Attendance
19	Dec	25	(a)	Preston NE	W	3-1	Bradford (og), Johnson, F.O'Donnell	9,000
20		26	(a)	Manchester C	D	1-1	F.O'Donnell	13,600
21		30	(h)	Preston NE	D	1-1	Laing	10,000
22	Jan	6	(a)	Burnley	L	0-2		9,643
23		13	(h)	Burnley	W	4-0	Mortensen, Dodds, Johnson, Fenton	12,000
24		20	(a)	Blackburn R	L	4-7	Jones, Walsh 3	800
25		27	(h)	Blackburn R	W	3-1	Johnson, Jones (pen), Fenton	6,000
26	Feb	3	(h)	Accrington S	L	0-3		8,000
27		10	(a)	Accrington S	L	2-4	Laing, Fenton	6,091
28		17	(a)	Rochdale	W	6-3	Finan 2, Fenton 3, Laing	5,000
29		24	(h)	Rochdale	W	4-0	Eastham 2, Farrow, Laing	6,000
30	Mar	3	(a)	Accrington S	L	1-4	Laing	5,500
31		10	(h)	Accrington S	L	1-2	Finan	8,000
32		17	(h)	Barnsley	L	0-2		8,000
33		24	(h)	Wrexham	W	2-0	Dodds, Worrall	12,000
34		31	(a)	Wrexham	D	2-2	Farrow, Worrall	17,081
35	Apr	2	(h)	Manchester U	W	4-1	Fenton 3, H.O'Donnell	14,000
36		7	(h)	Bolton W	L	1-4	Farrow (pen)	18,000
37		14	(a)	Bolton W	W	2-1	Worrall 2	13,613
38		21	(a)	Manchester C	W	1-0	Worrall	9,500
39		28	(h)	Manchester C	W	4-0	Mortensen 3, Farrow	5,000
40	May	5	(a)	Preston NE	W	8-1	Farrow 4, H.O'Donnell 3, Slater	3,000
41		12	(a)	Preston NE	W	4-0	Todd 2, Laing 2	3,000
42		19	(a)	Liverpool	L	0-2		16,807

FINAL LEAGUE POSITION: 16th in Northern Section — Second Competition

1. Matches 19 to 28 in Football League War Cup qualifying competition.
2. Matches 32 to 36 in Football League War Cup Knock-out Competition.
3. There were also six Lancashire Cup games played between dates 25 December 1944 to 5 May 1945. Unfortunately there are insufficient records on these games to include as statistics.

1	2	3	4	5	6	7	8	9	10	11	
Savage	Pope	S.Jones	Farrow	Davies	Paterson	Matthews	Mortensen	Finan	Theurer	F.O'Donnell	1
..	..	..	..	..	..	Cross	Eakin	..	Pearson	..	2
..	..	Rogerson	..	..	Edward	..	Bradley	..	..	..	3
..	..	S.Jones	..	Suart	Davies	Johnson	Tapping	..	F.O'Donnell	Pearson	4
..	..	Rogerson	..	..	S.Jones	Finan	Mortensen	F.O'Donnell	Bradley	..	5
..	..	Sibley	..	S.Jones	Paterson	Johnson	Finan	..	Larner	..	6
..	..	S.Jones	..	Suart	Davies	Matthews	H.O'Donnell	Finan	Mortensen	..	7
..	..	Franklin	..	..	..	Johnson	..	Tapping	Finan	..	8
..	..	..	..	Davies	Paterson	Matthews	Dix	Finan	Slater	..	9
Thorpe	..	S.Jones	..	..	..	..	..	Dodds	Mortensen	F.O'Donnell	10
..	..	Sibley	..	..	Tapping	Mortensen	Tweedy	Finan	Larner	..	11
..	..	S.Jones	..	..	Paterson	Johnson	Tapping	..	F.O'Donnell	Kirby	12
..	..	..	..	..	..	..	Tweedy	Tapping	Finan	F.O'Donnell	13
..	..	..	Walsh	..	..	Tweedy	Falla	Laing	F.O'Donnell	Kirby	14
..	Garrett	Kirby	Tapping	S.Jones	..	Matthews	Walsh	Revell	Larner	Killgallon	15
..	Davies	..	..	..	..	Johnson	Laing	..	Tweedy	F.O'Donnell	16
..	Franklin	..	..	Davies	..	..	Tweedy	..	Eastham	..	17
Roxburgh	Pope	..	..	..	..	..	Laing	F.O'Donnell	..	H.O'Donnell	18

1	2	3	4	5	6	7	8	9	10	11	
Roxburgh	Pope	Kirby	Tapping	Davies	Paterson	Johnson	Laing	F.O'Donnell	Eastham	H.O'Donnell	19
..	..	..	..	..	..	..	..	..	..	..	20
..	..	Sibley	..	..	Manley	..	..	..	..	..	21
Thorpe	..	S.Jones	..	..	..	..	..	Tweedy	..	..	22
..	..	Kirby	Paterson	..	S.Jones	..	Mortensen	Dodds	Fenton	..	23
Roxburgh	..	..	..	..	..	..	Laing	Walsh	..	..	24
Thorpe	..	..	..	..	..	..	..	Fenton	Eastham	..	25
..	..	..	..	..	Johnston	..	..	Walsh	..	..	26
..	..	..	Farrow	S.Jones	Laing	Eastham	Fenton	Finan	Mortensen	..	27
..	..	..	..	Davies	Paterson	..	..	..	Laing	Oakes	28
..	..	Galley	..	S.Jones	..	..	..	..	..	Kirby	29
..	..	..	..	..	..	..	..	..	..	..	30
..	..	..	..	..	..	..	..	..	..	..	31
Roxburgh	Sibley	Franklin	Paterson	Davies	S.Jones	Cross	Eastham	Dodds	Thomas	H.O'Donnell	32
..	..	Suart	Farrow	..	Paterson	Worrall	Forster	..	Tapping	..	33
..	..	Franklin	S.Jones	Farrow	Davies	..	Mortensen	Fenton	Bailey	..	34
..	..	..	..	..	..	..	..	..	..	..	35
..	..	Crook	Farrow	Davies	Paterson	..	Fenton	Dodds	Mortensen	..	36
..	..	..	..	..	..	..	Mortensen	Fenton	Bailey	..	37
..	Miller	Sibley	..	..	Todd	..	Tapping	Slater	..	..	38
..	..	..	..	..	..	..	Mortensen	..	Paterson	..	39
..	..	..	..	..	..	..	..	..	..	..	40
..	..	..	..	..	..	..	..	..	Laing	..	41
..	..	..	..	..	..	..	..	..	Paterson	..	42

Northern Section – First Competition
Appearances: Davies 15, Pope 15, F.O'Donnell 14, Farrow 13, Finan 12, S.Jones 12, Paterson 12, Savage 9, Tapping 9, Johnson 8, Pearson 8, Thorpe 8, Kirby 6, Matthews 5, Mortensen 5, Tweedy 5, Suart 4, Franklin 3, Laing 3, Larner 3, H.O'Donnell 3, Revell 3, Bradley 2, Cross 2, Dix 2, Eastham 2, Rogerson 2, Sibley 2, Walsh 2, Dodds 1, Eakin 1, Edward 1, Falla 1, Garrett 1, Killgallon 1, Roxburgh 1, Slater 1, Theurer 1.
Goalscorers: Mortensen 10, Finan 8, F.O'Donnell 7, Farrow 5, Matthews 3, Pearson 3, Tweedy 3, Dodds 2, Laing 2, Walsh 2, Davies 1, Dix 1, Eakin 1, Larner 1, Paterson 1, Tapping 1, Theurer 1, Opponents' own-goal 1.

Northern Section – First Competition
Appearances: Davies 20, H.O'Donnell 20, Paterson 17, Farrow 15, Roxburgh 15, Laing 13, Pope 13, Eastham 12, Fenton 12, Sibley 12, S.Jones 11, Kirby 11, Mortensen 10, Worrall 10, Thorpe 9, Johnson 8, Tapping 6, Finan 5, Miller 5, Slater 5, Todd 5, Bailey 4, Dodds 4, Franklin 3, Galley 3, F.O'Donnell 3, Crook 2, Manley 2, Walsh 2, Cross 1, Forster 1, Johnston 1, Oakes 1, Suart 1, Thomas 1, Tweedy 1.
Goalscorers: Fenton 9, Farrow 8, Laing 7, Worrall 5, H.O'Donnell 4, Mortensen 4, Johnson 3, Walsh 3, Finan 3, F.O'Donnell 2, Dodds 2, Jones 2, Eastham 2, Todd 2, Slater 1, Opponents' own-goal 1.

1945-46

Manager: Joe Smith

1	Aug	25	(a)	Bury	W 4-1	Mortensen 4	12,00
2		27	(h)	Preston NE	W 6-3	Fenton 2, H.O'Donnell 2, Mortensen, Buchan	15,78
3	Sep	1	(h)	Bury	W 3-1	Fenton 3	13,49
4		3	(a)	Preston NE	L 0-5		18,00
5		8	(h)	Blackburn R	W 5-2	Mortensen 2, Farrow 2, Fenton	16,17
6		12	(h)	Bolton W	D 1-1	Eastham	15,20
7		15	(a)	Blackburn R	D 1-1	Taylor (og)	6,95
8		22	(a)	Bradford	L 0-3		15,89
9		29	(h)	Bradford	L 0-1		15,59
10	Oct	6	(h)	Manchester C	W 5-4	Dodds 4, Fenton	14,22
11		13	(a)	Manchester C	W 4-1	Fenton 2, Dodds, Farrow	32,83
12		20	(a)	Newcastle U	D 2-2	Farrow, Mortensen	35,29
13		27	(h)	Newcastle U	D 1-1	H.O'Donnell	14,91
14	Nov	3	(h)	Sheffield W	W 5-1	Tapping, Mortensen 3, H.O'Donnell	14,08
15		10	(a)	Sheffield W	L 2-3	Withington, Mortensen	25,61
16		17	(a)	Huddersfield T	W 4-2	Dodds, Mortensen 2, H.O'Donnell	16,37
17		24	(h)	Huddersfield T	W 1-0	Dodds	14,45
18	Dec	1	(h)	Chesterfield	L 0-1		15,14
19		8	(a)	Chesterfield	W 3-0	Mortensen 2, Whittaker (og)	17,95
20		15	(a)	Barnsley	D 1-1	Blair	22,68
21		22	(h)	Barnsley	D 1-1	Farrow (pen)	10,24
22		25	(h)	Everton	W 5-2	H.O'Donnell 2, Blair 2, Mortensen	20,77
23		26	(a)	Everton	L 1-7	H.O'Donnell	53,98
24		29	(a)	Bolton W	D 1-1	Dodds	31,42
25	Jan	12	(a)	Leeds U	W 2-1	H.O'Donnell, Buchan	14,37
26		19	(h)	Leeds U	W 4-2	Mortensen 3, Blair	8,73
27	Feb	2	(a)	Manchester U	L 2-4	Mortensen 2	18,03
28		16	(h)	Sunderland	W 4-0	Mortensen, Farrow, Dodds 2	12,88
29		23	(h)	Sheffield U	L 1-2	Dodds	16,85
30	Mar	2	(a)	Sheffield U	L 2-4	Dodds 2	38,74
31		9	(a)	Middlesbrough	L 2-4	H.O'Donnell, Dodds	23,00
32		13	(a)	Sunderland	L 1-3	Finan	6,00
33		16	(h)	Middlesbrough	W 3-1	Blair 2, H.O'Donnell	10,00
34		23	(a)	Stoke C	L 3-6	Mortensen 2, Blair	18,00
35		27	(h)	Manchester U	L 1-5	Mortensen	10,00
36		30	(h)	Stoke C	W 3-2	Mortensen, H.O'Donnell, Dodds	15,00
37	Apr	6	(a)	Grimsby T	L 2-4	Mortensen 2	12,00
38		13	(h)	Grimsby T	W 5-3	Mortensen 3, Blair 2	10,00
39		19	(a)	Burnley	D 1-1	Mortensen	18,10
40		20	(h)	Liverpool	D 1-1	Buchan (pen)	7,00
41		22	(a)	Burnley	W 2-1	Mortensen, H.O'Donnell	14,00
42		27	(a)	Liverpool	L 0-4		20,00

FINAL LEAGUE POSITION: 9th in Football League (North)

FA Cup

3	Jan	5	(a)	Wrexham	W 4-1	Buchan, Mortensen, Blair, Dodds	14,10
		9	(h)	Wrexham	W 4-1	Dodds 3, H.O'Donnell	11,20
4		26	(h)	Middlesbrough	W 3-2	Mortensen 2, Dodds	17,16
		30	(a)	Middlesbrough	L 2-3*	H.O'Donnell, Mortensen	46,56
R	Feb	4	(n†)	Middlesbrough	L 0-1		30,00

*After two periods of extra-time. †Played at Elland Road, Leeds — after extra-time.

1	2	3	4	5	6	7	8	9	10	11	
Roxburgh	Sibley	Lewis	Farrow	S.Jones	Paterson	Matthews	Buchan	Mortensen	Eastham	H.O'Donnell	1
Wallace	Butler	..	..	Suart	..	Hobson	..	..	Fenton	..	2
Roxburgh	Suart	..	..	S.Jones	..	..	Eastham	Fenton	F.O'Donnell	..	3
..	Sibley	..	..	Suart	..	Matthews	..	F.O'Donnell	Fenton	..	4
..	Butler	..	Todd	..	Farrow	..	Mortensen	Fenton	Eastham	..	5
Wallace	Sibley	..	Farrow	..	Paterson	Hobson	Buchan	..	..	..	6
..	Butler	..	..	..	..	..	..	..	Cowell	..	7
Thorpe	..	..	..	..	Todd	Matthews	Withington	Mortensen	Larner	..	8
..	..	..	..	S.Jones	Paterson	Withington	Mortensen	Dodds	Fenton	..	9
..	Suart	..	Tapping	..	..	..	Laing	..	..	..	10
..	..	..	Farrow	..	Tapping	Fenton	Mortensen	Laing	Dodds	..	11
Roxburgh	..	..	..	..	..	Withington	..	Dodds	McLaren	..	12
..	..	..	..	..	..	Munro	Withington	Mortensen	Blair	..	13
..	Butler	..	..	..	..	Withington	Mortensen	Dodds	..	..	14
..	..	..	..	Suart	S.Jones	..	..	Tapping	..	..	15
..	..	..	..	..	Tapping	..	..	Dodds	..	..	16
..	..	..	..	..	..	Munro	..	..	..	..	17
..	..	..	Tapping	..	S.Jones	..	..	..	..	..	18
..	..	..	Todd	..	Kelly	Hobson	..	..	..	..	19
..	..	..	..	..	..	..	..	..	..	..	20
..	..	..	Farrow	..	Todd	..	..	McLaren	..	..	21
..	Sibley	..	..	S.Jones	Kelly	Buchan	..	Dodds	..	..	22
..	..	..	Tapping	..	..	..	..	..	..	..	23
..	Franklin	..	Sibley	..	Todd	Withington	..	..	..	..	24
..	Burke	..	Farrow	..	..	Hobson	Buchan	Astley	..	..	25
Wallace	..	..	..	Harper	..	..	Mortensen	Dodds	..	..	26
..	..	..	Tapping	Franklin	..	..	Munro	Mortensen	Eastham	Withington	27
Roxburgh	..	..	Farrow	Suart	..	Eastham	Mortensen	Dodds	Blair	H.O'Donnell	28
..	..	..	..	..	Kelly	Buchan	..	..	..	..	29
..	Lewis	Burke	..	..	..	Hobson	..	..	Eastham	..	30
..	Kennedy	Lewis	..	..	..	Finan	Buchan	..	Blair	..	31
Hesford	Burke	..	..	..	..	..	..	..	..	..	32
Thorpe	..	..	..	..	..	Hobson	..	..	..	..	33
Roxburgh	..	..	Kelly	..	Johnston	Matthews	Eastham	Mortensen	..	..	34
..	..	..	Farrow	Hayward	..	Hobson	Buchan	Dodds	Mortensen	..	35
Thorpe	..	..	Kelly	Suart	..	..	Mortensen	..	Buchan	..	36
..	Butler	..	Farrow	..	..	Buchan	..	Blair	Hobson	..	37
..	Suart	..	Kelly	S.Jones	..	Munro	Buchan	Dodds	Mortensen	Blair	38
..	..	..	..	..	..	..	..	Mortensen	Blair	H.O'Donnell	39
..	..	..	..	..	..	..	..	..	..	..	40
..	..	..	..	..	..	Hobson	..	..	..	..	41
..	..	Kennedy	..	..	..	..	..	..	..	..	42

Wallace	Burke	Lewis	Farrow	Suart	Todd	Buchan	Mortensen	Dodds	Blair	H.O'Donnell	3
..	..	..	..	S.Jones	..	..	..	..	..	..	
..	..	..	..	Suart	..	..	..	..	..	..	4
..	..	..	..	..	..	..	..	..	..	..	
..	..	..	..	..	Kelly	..	..	..	..	..	R

Football League (North)
Appearances: Lewis 41, H.O'Donnell 40, Mortensen 33, Suart 32, Farrow 28, Blair 26, Roxburgh 24, Dodds 23, S.Jones 19, Buchan 18, Hobson 17, Kelly 16, Butler 14, Thorpe 12, Burke 11, Tapping 11, Todd 10, Withington 10, Eastham 9, Fenton 9, Johnston 9, Paterson 8, Munro 7, Sibley 6, Matthews 5, Wallace 5, Finan 2, Franklin 2, Kennedy 2, Laing 2, McLaren 2, F.O'Donnell 2, Astley 1, Cowell 1, Harper 1, Hayward 1, Hesford 1, Larner 1.
Goalscorers: Mortensen 34, Dodds 15, H.O'Donnell 13, Blair 9, Fenton 9, Farrow 6, Buchan 3, Eastham 1, Finan 1, Tapping 1, Withington 1, Opponents' own-goals 2.

FA Cup
Appearances: Blair 5, Buchan 5, Burke 5, Dodds 5, Farrow 5, Lewis 5, Mortensen 5, H.O'Donnell 5, Wallace 5, Suart 4, Todd 4, S.Jones 1, Kelly 1.
Goalscorers: Dodds 5, Mortensen 4, H.O'Donnell 2, Blair 1, Buchan 1.

1946-47

Manager: Joe Smith

1	Aug	31	(a)	Huddersfield T	W 3-1	Mortensen, Blair, Munro	14,378
2	Sep	2	(h)	Brentford	W 4-2	Mortensen, W.Buchan 2, McIntosh	24,236
3		7	(h)	Wolves	W 2-0	Eastham, Mortensen	27,623
4		11	(a)	Portsmouth	W 1-0	Eastham	27,504
5		14	(a)	Sunderland	L 2-3	Eastham 2	40,653
6		18	(a)	Brentford	L 1-2	Mortensen	25,621
7		21	(h)	Aston Villa	W 1-0	Mortensen	27,452
8		23	(h)	Portsmouth	W 4-3	W.Buchan 3 (1 pen), Blair	18,517
9		28	(a)	Derby C	W 2-1	Mortensen, McIntosh	25,138
10	Oct	5	(h)	Arsenal	W 2-1	Mortensen, Dick	24,426
11		12	(a)	Preston NE	L 0-2		34,488
12		19	(h)	Manchester U	W 3-1	Farrow, Mortensen, Dick	26,307
13		26	(a)	Bolton W	D 1-1	McIntosh	35,896
14	Nov	2	(h)	Chelsea	W 1-0	Blair	23,365
15		9	(a)	Sheffield U	L 2-4	Mortensen (pen), Eastham	31,637
16		16	(h)	Grimsby T	L 2-3	McIntosh, Mortensen	17,511
17		23	(a)	Leeds U	L 2-4	H.O'Donnell, Mortensen	25,829
18		30	(h)	Liverpool	W 3-2	McIntosh, Blair, Mortensen	23,565
19	Dec	7	(a)	Stoke C	L 1-4	Dick	28,624
20		14	(h)	Middlesbrough	L 0-5		14,571
21		21	(a)	Charlton A	W 1-0	W.Buchan (pen)	13,417
22		25	(a)	Blackburn R	D 1-1	Mortensen	27,013
23		26	(h)	Blackburn R	W 1-0	Mortensen	25,576
24		28	(h)	Huddersfield T	W 2-1	Dick, W.Buchan (pen)	24,558
25	Jan	4	(a)	Wolves	L 1-3	Mortensen	49,482
26		18	(h)	Sunderland	L 0-5		20,049
27		25	(a)	Aston Villa	D 1-1	Mortensen	32,541
28	Feb	1	(h)	Derby C	W 2-1	Munro, Dick	16,042
29		8	(a)	Arsenal	D 1-1	Mortensen	31,111
30		15	(h)	Preston NE	W 4-0	Dick 2, Mortensen 2	28,907
31		22	(a)	Manchester U	L 0-3		30,823
32	Mar	1	(h)	Bolton W	L 0-1		20,356
33		8	(a)	Chelsea	W 4-1	Dick 2, W.Buchan, Mortensen	30,365
34		15	(h)	Sheffield U	W 4-2	Mortensen, Munro, Dick 2	17,307
35		22	(a)	Grimsby T	W 3-2	Mortensen 2, McKnight	13,452
36		29	(h)	Leeds U	W 3-0	Mortensen 2, McKnight	14,501
37	Apr	4	(a)	Everton	D 1-1	Jones (og)	63,617
38		5	(a)	Liverpool	W 3-2	Mortensen 2, W.Buchan	47,320
39		7	(h)	Everton	L 0-3		23,699
40		12	(h)	Stoke C	L 0-2		17,260
41		19	(a)	Middlesbrough	W 2-1	Eastham, Mortensen	28,849
42		28	(h)	Charlton A	D 0-0		16,771

FINAL LEAGUE POSITION: 5th in Division One

Appearances
Goals

FA Cup

3	Jan	11	(a)	Sheffield W	L 1-4	Mortensen	37,000

Appearances
Goals

Wallace	Sibley	Lewis	Buchan T	Suart	Johnston	Munro	Buchan W	Mortensen	Blair J	McIntosh	Eastham	Crossland	Kelly	Kennedy	Dick	Farrow	O'Donnell	Hayward	Shimwell	Nelson	McKnight	
1	2	3	4	5	6	7	8	9	10	11												1
1	2	3	4	5	6		8	9	10	11	7											2
1	2	3	4	5	6		8	9	10	11	7											3
1	2	3	4	5	6		8	9	10	11	7											4
1	2	3	4	5	6		8	9	10	11	7											5
1	2	3	4		6		8	9	10	11	7	5										6
1	2	3			6		8	9	10	11	7	5	4									7
1	2				6		8	9	10	11	7	5	4	3								8
1	2				6		8	9	10	11	7	5	4	3								9
1	2	3		5	6			9	10	11	7		4		8							10
1	2	3		5	6			9	10	11	7		4		8							11
1	2	3		5	6	7		9		11	10				8	4						12
1	2	3		5	6	7		9	10	11					8	4						13
1	2	3		5	6	7		9	10	11					8	4						14
1	2	3	4	5	6			9	10	11	7				8							15
1	2	3	4	5		7		9		11	10		6		8							16
1	2	3		5	6		7	8		9	10					4	11					17
1	2				6	7		9	10	11				3	8	4		5				18
1	2				6	7		9	10	11				3	8	4		5				19
1	2				6	7			10	11	8			3	9	4		5				20
1	2	3			6	7	10	9		11					8	4		5				21
1		3		5	6	7	10	9		11					8	4			2			22
1		3		5	6	7	10	9		11					8	4			2			23
1		3		5	6		10	9		11					8	4			2	7		24
1		3		5	6		10	9		11					8	4			2	7		25
1		3	4	5	6			8	10	11									2	7	8	26
1		3			6			9	11		10				8	4		5	2	7		27
1		3			6	7		9	11		10				8	4		5	2			28
1		3			6			9	11		10				8	4		5	2	7		29
1		3			6	8		9	11						10	4		5	2	7		30
1		3			6	8		9	11						10	4		5	2	7		31
1		3			6	8		9	11						10	4		5	2	7		32
1		3			6	7	8	9			10				11	4		5	2			33
1		3			6	7	8	9			10				11	4		5	2			34
1	3	3			6		10	9							11	4		5	2	7	8	35
1	3				6	7	10	9							11	4		5	2		8	36
1	3				6	7	10	9							11	4		5	2		8	37
1	3				6	7	10	9							11	4		5	2		8	38
1	3				6	7	10	9							11	4		5	2		8	39
1		6		3		7	8		10						11	4		5	2		9	40
1				3	6	7		9		11	10				8	4		5	2			41
1				3	6	7		9		11	10				8	4		5	2			42
42	26	31	9	21	40	24	23	40	25	28	22	4	6	5	31	28	1	20	21	9	7	
						3	9	28	4	5	6				11	1	1				2	

1 own-goal

Wallace	Sibley	Lewis	Buchan T	Suart	Johnston	Munro	Buchan W	Mortensen	Blair J	McIntosh	Eastham	Crossland	Kelly	Kennedy	Dick	Farrow	O'Donnell	Hayward	Shimwell	Nelson	McKnight	
1	3			5	6	7	10	9		11					8	4			2			3
1	1			1	1	1	1	1		1					1	1			1			
								1														

1947-48

Manager: Joe Smith

1	Aug	23	(h)	Chelsea	W 3-0	Mortensen 2, Opp own-goal	27,389
2		25	(a)	Huddersfield T	L 0-2		32,099
3		30	(a)	Everton	W 2-1	Mortensen, McKnight	59,665
4	Sep	1	(h)	Huddersfield T	W 4-0	McCormack 2, Mortensen, Farrow (pen)	29,555
5		6	(h)	Wolves	D 2-2	Buchan 2	31,663
6		8	(h)	Blackburn R	W 1-0	Matthews	28,137
7		13	(a)	Aston Villa	W 1-0	McKnight	56,004
8		15	(a)	Blackburn R	D 1-1	McCormack	27,790
9		20	(h)	Sunderland	L 0-1		25,343
10		27	(a)	Grimsby T	W 1-0	Mortensen	25,576
11	Oct	4	(h)	Manchester C	D 1-1	Mortensen	30,930
12		11	(a)	Burnley	L 0-1		52,869
13		18	(h)	Portsmouth	W 1-0	Johnston	17,719
14		25	(a)	Bolton W	L 0-1		45,037
15	Nov	1	(h)	Liverpool	W 2-0	McIntosh 2	23,999
16		8	(a)	Arsenal	L 1-2	McIntosh	67,057
17		15	(h)	Sheffield U	W 2-1	Mortensen, Farrow	19,794
18		22	(a)	Middlesbrough	L 0-4		38,936
19		29	(h)	Charlton A	W 3-1	Buchan 2 (1 pen), Mortensen	18,954
20	Dec	6	(a)	Manchester U	D 1-1	Mortensen	64,852
21		13	(h)	Preston NE	L 0-1		29,587
22		20	(a)	Chelsea	D 2-2	Farrow (pen), Mortensen	48,421
23		25	(h)	Stoke C	L 1-2	Mortensen	27,047
24		27	(a)	Stoke C	D 1-1	McIntosh	47,725
25	Jan	3	(h)	Everton	W 5-0	Dick 2, Mortensen 2, McIntosh	21,685
26		17	(a)	Wolves	D 1-1	Shorthouse (og)	46,383
27		31	(h)	Aston Villa	W 1-0	McIntosh	22,203
28	Feb	14	(h)	Grimsby T	W 3-1	McIntosh 2, Mortensen	21,612
29		21	(a)	Manchester C	L 0-1		31,445
30	Mar	6	(a)	Portsmouth	D 1-1	Mortensen	37,067
31		20	(a)	Liverpool	L 0-2		48,725
32		26	(h)	Derby C	D 2-2	Mortensen 2	30,445
33		27	(h)	Arsenal	W 3-0	Mortensen 2, McCall	32,678
34		29	(a)	Derby C	L 0-1		34,896
35	Apr	3	(a)	Sheffield U	L 1-2	Rickett	48,150
36		5	(h)	Bolton W	D 1-1	Mortensen	25,050
37		7	(h)	Burnley	L 0-1		16,732
38		10	(h)	Middlesbrough	W 1-0	McKnight	16,330
39		12	(a)	Sunderland	L 0-1		61,084
40		17	(a)	Charlton A	L 0-2		49,312
41		28	(h)	Manchester U	W 1-0	Mortensen	32,236
42	May	1	(a)	Preston NE	W 7-0	McIntosh 5, Munro, Rickett	26,610
							Appearances
							Goals

FINAL LEAGUE POSITION: 9th in Division One

FA Cup

3	Jan	10	(h)	Leeds U	W 4-0	Dick, McIntosh 2, Mortensen	23,000
4		24	(h)	Chester	W 4-0	Shimwell, Mortensen 2, Johnston	26,419
5	Feb	7	(h)	Colchester U	W 5-0	Munro, McIntosh 2, Mortensen 2	26,000
6		28	(a)	Fulham	W 2-0	Mortensen, McIntosh	32,000
SF	Mar	13	(n*)	Tottenham H	W 3-1†	Mortensen 3	67,500
F	Apr	24	(n‡)	Manchester U	L 2-4	Shimwell (pen), Mortensen	99,000
							Appearances
							Goals

*Played at Villa Park, Birmingham. †After extra-time. ‡Final played at Wembley Stadium.

Wallace	Shimwell	Suart	Farrow	Hayward	Johnston	Matthews	Munro	Mortensen	Dick	McIntosh	Kelly	Buchan	McCormack	Lewis	McKnight	McCall	Nelson	Robinson	Rickett	Garrett	Hobson	Crosland	Kennedy	
1	2	3	4	5	6	7	8	9	10	11														1
1	2	3	4	5		7	8	9	10	11	6													2
1	2	3	4	5		7		9			6	8	11		10									3
1	2	3	4	5	6	7		9		10		8	11											4
1	2	3	4	5	6	7		9		10		8	11											5
1	2	3	4	5	6	7		9		10		8	11											6
1	2	3	4	5	6	7		9				8	11		10									7
1	2	3		5	6	7						8	11	4	9	10								8
1	2	3		5	6					7		8	11	4	9	10								9
1	2	3		5	6	7	8	9					11	4		10								10
1	2	3		5	6	7	8	9					11	4		10								11
1	2	3	4	5	6	7	8	9	10	11														12
1	2	3	4	5	6		8	9	10				11				7							13
1	2	3	4	5	6	7		8		10		9	11											14
1	2	3		5	6	7	11	8		9				4		10								15
1	2	3		5	6	7	11	8		9				4		10								16
1	2	3	4	5	6	7	11	8		9						10								17
1	2	3	4	5	6	7	11	8		9						10								18
1	2	3		5	6	7		9		11	4	10			8									19
1	2	3		5	6	7		9		11	4	10			8									20
1	2	3		5	6	7		9		11	4	10			8									21
1	2	3	4	5	6	7	11	8		9						10								22
1	2	3	4	5	6	7	11	8		9						10								23
1	2	3	4	5	6	7	11	8		9						10								24
1	2	3	4	5		7	11	8	10	9	6													25
	2	3		5	4	7	11	8	10	9	6							1						26
	2	3		5	4	7	11	8	10	9	6							1						27
	2	3		5	4	7		8	10	9	6							1	11					28
	2	3		5	4		7	8	10	9	6		11					1						29
	2	3		5	4	7		8	10	9	6							1	11					30
	2	3		5	4	7		8	10	9	6							1	11					31
	2	3		5	4	7		8	10	9	6							1	11					32
	2	3		5	4	7	8	9			6					10		1	11					33
	2			5	4		8		9		6					10		1	11	3	7			34
		3		5	4	7		8		9	6					10		1	11	2				35
		3		5	4	7		8		9	6					10		1	11	2				36
		3					7		10	9	6	4			8			1	11	2		5		37
		3		5			7		10	9	6	4			8			1	11	2				38
	2	3		5	4	7	8	9			6					10		1	11					39
				5	4	7		8	10	9	6							1	11			2	3	40
	2			5	4	7		8		9	6					10		1	11			3		41
	2			5			8			9	6	4				10		1	11		7	3		42
25	37	38	16	41	36	35	23	36	16	33	23	14	12	6	9	18	1	17	14	5	2	4	1	
			3		1	1	1	21	2	13		4	3		3	1			2					

2 own-goals

Wallace	Shimwell	Suart	Farrow	Hayward	Johnston	Matthews	Munro	Mortensen	Dick	McIntosh	Kelly	Buchan	McCormack	Lewis	McKnight	McCall	Nelson	Robinson	Rickett	Garrett	Hobson	Crosland	Kennedy	
	2	3		5	4	7	11	8	10	9	6							1						3
	2	3		5	4	7	11	8	10	9	6							1						4
	2	3		5	4	7		8	10	9	6							1	11					5
	2	3		5	4	7	11	8	10	9	6							1						6
	2	3		5	4	7	11	8	10	9	6							1						SF
	2			5	4	7	8	9	10		6							1	11			3		F
	6	5		6	6	6	5	6	6	5	6							6	2			1		
	2				1		1	10	1	5														

1948-49

Manager: Joe Smith

1	Aug	21	(a)	Sheffield U	L 2-3	Munro, McCall	45,943
2		23	(h)	Manchester U	L 0-3		31,996
3		28	(h)	Aston Villa	W 1-0	Mortensen	29,815
4	Sep	1	(a)	Manchester U	W 4-3	Rickett, W.McIntosh 2, Kelly	54,046
5		4	(a)	Sunderland	D 2-2	W.McIntosh 2	48,750
6		6	(h)	Derby C	D 1-1	McCall	30,656
7		11	(h)	Wolves	L 1-3	Matthews	31,329
8		14	(a)	Derby C	L 1-3	W.McIntosh	32,082
9		18	(a)	Bolton W	D 2-2	Mortensen 2 (1 pen)	46,779
10		25	(h)	Liverpool	W 1-0	McCall	28,870
11	Oct	2	(a)	Preston NE	W 3-1	Mortensen 2, Matthews	38,280
12		9	(h)	Everton	W 3-0	Wardle (pen), W.McIntosh, Rickett	22,070
13		16	(a)	Chelsea	D 3-3	Mortensen, McCall 2	77,696
14		23	(h)	Birmingham C	W 1-0	Rickett	25,126
15		30	(a)	Middlesbrough	L 0-1		44,780
16	Nov	6	(h)	Newcastle U	L 1-3	Mortensen (pen)	30,676
17		13	(a)	Portsmouth	D 1-1	Mortensen (pen)	44,869
18		20	(h)	Manchester C	D 1-1	W.McIntosh	22,412
19		27	(a)	Charlton A	D 0-0		45,727
20	Dec	4	(h)	Stoke C	W 2-1	McCall 2	22,984
21		11	(a)	Burnley	L 0-2		37,969
22		18	(h)	Sheffield U	L 0-3		17,086
23		25	(h)	Huddersfield T	D 0-0		29,244
24		26	(a)	Huddersfield T	L 0-1		41,232
25	Jan	1	(a)	Aston Villa	W 5-2	Munro, Mortensen, Kelly, Rickett, Matthews	48,392
26		15	(h)	Sunderland	D 3-3	Mortensen 2, McCall	18,917
27		22	(a)	Wolves	L 1-2	Shimwell	54,088
28	Feb	12	(h)	Bolton W	W 1-0	J.McIntosh	23,210
29		19	(a)	Liverpool	D 1-1	J.McIntosh	52,294
30		26	(h)	Preston NE	D 2-2	J.McIntosh 2	27,487
31	Mar	5	(a)	Everton	L 0-5		75,548
32		12	(h)	Chelsea	W 2-1	Mortensen 2	20,292
33		19	(a)	Manchester C	D 1-1	Mortensen	38,973
34		26	(h)	Charlton A	L 0-1		18,065
35	Apr	2	(a)	Newcastle U	L 1-3	Fenton	62,672
36		9	(h)	Portsmouth	W 1-0	Adams	18,723
37		15	(h)	Arsenal	D 1-1	Mortensen	28,818
38		16	(a)	Birmingham C	D 1-1	Mortensen	34,726
39		18	(a)	Arsenal	L 0-2		45,047
40		23	(h)	Middlesbrough	D 1-1	Mortensen	23,128
41		30	(a)	Stoke C	L 2-3	McCall, Shimwell (pen)	18,640
42	May	7	(h)	Burnley	D 1-1	Mortensen	21,626

FINAL LEAGUE POSITION: 16th in Division One

Appearances
Goals

FA Cup

3	Jan	8	(a)	Barnsley	W 1-0	Mortensen	31,700
4		29	(a)	Stoke C	D 1-1	Mortensen	47,000
R	Feb	4	(h)	Stoke C	L 0-1		29,100

Appearances
Goals

Robinson	Shimwell	Suart	Johnston	Hayward	Kelly	Matthews	McCall	Mortensen	Munro	Rickett	Wardle	McIntosh W	Wright	Fenton	Farm	Adams	Davidson	Garrett	McIntosh J	McKnight	Kennedy	Hobson	
1	2	3	4	5	6	7	8	9	10	11													1
1	2	3	4	5	6	7	10	9	8	11													2
1	2	3	4	5	6	7	10	9	8		11												3
1	2	3	4	5	6		10	8		7	11	9											4
1	2	3	4	5	6		10	8		7	11	9											5
1		3		5	6		10	8		7	11	9	2	4									6
1		2		5	6	7	10	8			11	9	3	4									7
1		2		5	6	7	10	8			11	9	3	4									8
	2	3	4	5	6	7	10	8			11	9			1								9
	2	3		5	6		10			8	11	9		4	1	7							10
	2		4	5	6	7	10	8		9	11		3		1								11
	2		4	5	6		10		8	7	11	9	3		1								12
	2		4	5	6	7	10	8		9	11		3		1								13
	2	3	4	5	6		10		7	9	11				1		8						14
	2	3	4	5	6	7	10	8		9	11				1								15
	2	3	4	5	6	7	10	8		9	11				1								16
	2	3	4	5	6	7	10	8		9	11				1								17
	2	3	4	5	6	7		10		8	11	9			1								18
	2	3	4	5		7	10	8			11	9		6	1								19
	2	3	4	5		7	10	8			11	9		6	1								20
	2	3	4	5	6	7	10			8	11	9		.	1								21
	2	3	4	5		7	10			8	11	9		6	1								22
	2	3	4	5	6	7	10		8	11		9			1								23
	2	3	4	5	6	7	10		8	11					1			9					24
	2	3	4	5	6	7		8	10	11					1			9					25
	2	3	4	5	6	7	10	8		11					1				9				26
	2	3	4	5	6	7	10	8		11					1				9				27
	2	3	4	5	6	7		8			11				1				9	10			28
	2	3	4	5	6	7		8			11				1				9	10			29
		3	4	5	6	7		8			11				1				9	10	2		30
	2	3	4	5	6		8	9			11				1					10		7	31
	2	3	4	5	6		8	9							1	11	10					7	32
	2	3	4	5	6		8	9							1	11	10					7	33
	2	3	4	5	6			8							1	11	10		9			7	34
		3		5	6	7	9	8						4	1	11	10	2					35
	2	3		5	6		8				11			4	1	7	10		9				36
	2	3	4	5	6			8			11				1	7	10		9				37
	2	3	4	5	6			8			11				1	7	10		9				38
	2	3	4	5	6		11	8						10	1			9	7				39
	2	3	4	5	6		11	8							1	7	10		9				40
	2	3	4	5	6	7	11	8							1		10		9				41
	2	3	4	5			11	8		7				6	1		10		9				42
8	37	39	36	42	38	26	34	34	8	22	27	14	6	11	34	9	11	4	13	4	1	4	
	2				2	3	9	18	2	4	1	7		1		1			4				

Robinson	Shimwell	Suart	Johnston	Hayward	Kelly	Matthews	McCall	Mortensen	Munro	Rickett	Wardle	McIntosh W	Wright	Fenton	Farm	Adams	Davidson	Garrett	McIntosh J	McKnight	Kennedy	Hobson	
	2	3	4	5	6	7		8	10	11					1			9					3
	2	3	4	5	6	7	10	8		11					1				9				4
	2	3	4	5	6	7	10	8		11					1				9				R
	3	3	3	3	3	3	2	3	1	3					3			1	2				
								2															

1949-50

Manager: Joe Smith

1	Aug	20	(h)	Huddersfield T	W 4-1	McIntosh, Shimwell (pen), Rickett, McCall	29,712
2		22	(h)	Middlesbrough	D 1-1	McCall	28,243
3		27	(a)	Portsmouth	W 3-2	McIntosh, Mortensen 2	46,927
4		31	(a)	Middlesbrough	L 0-2		47,870
5	Sep	3	(h)	Wolves	L 1-2	Mortensen	31,854
6		5	(h)	Newcastle U	D 0-0		27,182
7		10	(a)	Aston Villa	D 0-0		60,337
8		17	(h)	Charlton A	W 2-0	Shimwell (pen), Mortensen	31,707
9		24	(a)	Manchester C	W 3-0	Mortensen, Johnston, McIntosh	57,931
10	Oct	1	(h)	Fulham	D 0-0		33,340
11		8	(a)	Sunderland	D 1-1	Mortensen	64,889
12		15	(h)	Liverpool	D 0-0		33,675
13		22	(a)	Arsenal	L 0-1		66,391
14		29	(h)	Bolton W	W 2-0	Mortensen 2	23,233
15	Nov	5	(a)	Birmingham C	W 2-0	Mortensen 2	34,045
16		12	(h)	Derby C	W 1-0	Mortensen	17,257
17		26	(h)	Manchester U	D 3-3	Shimwell (pen), McIntosh, Johnston	27,742
18	Dec	3	(a)	Chelsea	D 1-1	McCall	47,636
19		10	(h)	Stoke C	W 4-2	Slater 2, McIntosh, Franklin (og)	18,430
20		17	(a)	Huddersfield T	W 1-0	Mortensen	28,107
21		24	(h)	Portsmouth	W 2-1	McCall 2	25,953
22		26	(a)	Burnley	D 0-0		49,815
23		27	(h)	Burnley	W 2-0	Mortensen, McIntosh	31,074
24		31	(a)	Wolves	L 0-3		51,400
25	Jan	14	(h)	Aston Villa	W 1-0	Mortensen	23,743
26		21	(a)	Charlton A	W 2-1	Mortensen, McIntosh	44,701
27	Feb	4	(h)	Manchester C	D 0-0		23,780
28		18	(a)	Fulham	L 0-1		32,131
29		25	(h)	Sunderland	L 0-1		21,317
30	Mar	8	(a)	Liverpool	W 1-0	Mudie	33,464
31		11	(h)	West Brom A	W 3-0	Mortensen 2, Slater	23,104
32		18	(a)	Manchester U	W 2-1	Mortensen 2 (1 pen)	55,517
33		25	(h)	Birmingham C	D 1-1	Mortensen	20,733
34	Apr	1	(a)	Derby C	D 0-0		28,862
35		7	(a)	Everton	L 0-3		71,008
36		8	(h)	Arsenal	W 2-1	Mortensen 2	32,022
37		10	(h)	Everton	L 0-1		22,942
38		15	(a)	Bolton W	D 0-0		25,800
39		22	(h)	Chelsea	D 0-0		26,006
40		26	(a)	West Brom A	L 0-1		23,671
41		29	(a)	Stoke C	D 1-1	McKnight	17,444
42	May	6	(a)	Newcastle U	L 0-3		35,274

FINAL LEAGUE POSITION: 7th in Division One

Appearances
Goals

FA Cup

3	Jan	7	(h)	Southend U	W 4-0	Slater 3 (1 pen), Mortensen	24,532
4		28	(h)	Doncaster R	W 2-1	McIntosh, McKnight	31,362
5	Feb	11	(a)	Wolves	D 0-0		53,597
R		14	(h)	Wolves	W 1-0	Mortensen	29,050
6	Mar	4	(a)	Liverpool	L 1-2	Mortensen (pen)	48,000

Appearances
Goals

Farm	Shimwell	Suart	Johnston	Hayward	Kelly	Matthews	Mortensen	McIntosh	McCall	Rickett	Garrett	Wright	Lewis	Crosland	Slater	Wardle	Davidson	McKnight	Hobson	Kennedy	Adams	Mudie	Perry	Falconer	
1	2	3	4	5	6	7	8	9	10	11															1
1	2	3	4	5	6	7	8	9	10	11															2
1		3	4	5	6	7	8	9	10	11	2														3
1		2	4	5	6	7	8	9	10	11		3													4
1		2	4	5	6	7	8	9	10	11			3												5
1			4	5	6	7	8	9	10	11			3	2											6
1			4	5	6	7	8	9	10				3	2	11										7
1	2		4	5	6	7	8	9	10				3			11									8
1	2		4	5	6	7	8	9	10				3			11									9
1	2		4	5	6	7	8	9	10		3					11									10
1	2		4	5	6	7	8	9	10		3					11									11
1	2		4	5	6	7		9	8	11	3						10								12
1	2		4	5	6	7	8	9	10	11	3														13
1	2		4	5	6	7	9		10		3					11		8							14
1	2		4	5	6	7	9		8		3				10	11									15
1	2		4	5	6	7	9		8		3				10	11									16
1	2		4	5	6	7		9	8		3					11	10								17
1	2		4	5	6	7	9		8		3					11	10								18
1	2		4	5	6	7		9	8		3				10	11									19
1	2		4	5	6	7	9	10	8		3					11									20
1	2		4	5	6	7	9	10	8		3					11									21
1	2		4	5	6	7	9	10	8		3					11									22
1	2		4	5	6	7	9	10	8		3					11									23
1	2		4	5	6	7	9	10	8		3					11									24
1	2		4	5	6	7	9		8						10					3	11				25
1	2		4	5	6	7	9	10	8		3										11				26
1	2		4		6	7	9		8		3			5			10				11				27
1	2		4	5	6		9	10			3					11		8	7						28
1			4		6		9	10			3			5				8	7	2	11				29
1	2		4		6		8	10				3		5		11			7			9			30
1	2		4		6		8	11				3		5	10				7			9			31
1	2		5		6		8					3			10			4	7			9	11		32
1	2		4		6		8	10				3		5					7			9	11		33
1	2		4		6		8					3		5	10				7			9	11		34
1	2		4		6		8	10				3		5					7			9	11		35
1			4		6		9		10		2	3		5		11							7	8	36
1			4		6		9		10		2	3		5		11							7	8	37
1			4		6			9			2	3		5	10	11							7	8	38
1	2		4		6	7	9	10				3		5									11	8	39
1	2		4			7	9		8			3		6			10	5					11		40
1	2				6	7	8					3		5		11		4				9	10		41
1					6	7	8		10		2	3		5				4				9	11		42
42	32	5	40	27	41	31	38	29	31	8	24	14	5	16	9	21	5	7	8	2	4	8	11	4	
	3		2				22	7	5	1					3			1				1			

1 own-goal

Farm	Shimwell	Suart	Johnston	Hayward	Kelly	Matthews	Mortensen	McIntosh	McCall	Rickett	Garrett	Wright	Lewis	Crosland	Slater	Wardle	Davidson	McKnight	Hobson	Kennedy	Adams	Mudie	Perry	Falconer	
1			4	5	6	7	9	8			3				10					2	11				3
1	2			5	6	7	9	8			3				10	11		4							4
1	2		4	5	6	7	9	10				3				11		8							5
1	2		4	5	6		9	10				3				11		8	7						R
1			4		6		9	10				3		5				8	7	2	11				6
5	3		4	4	5	3	5	5			2	3		1	2	3		4	2	2	2				
							3	1							3			1							

1950-51

Manager: Joe Smith

1	Aug	19	(a)	Tottenham H	W 4-1	Johnston 2, Mortensen, Kelly	64,978
2		21	(h)	Burnley	L 1-2	Slater	33,161
3		26	(h)	Charlton A	D 0-0		25,484
4		29	(a)	Burnley	D 0-0		38,688
5	Sep	2	(a)	Manchester U	L 0-1		55,090
6		4	(h)	Fulham	W 4-0	Mudie, McKnight 3	28,051
7		9	(h)	Wolves	D 1-1	Johnston	32,204
8		13	(a)	Fulham	D 2-2	Slater, Perry	39,761
9		16	(a)	Sunderland	W 2-0	Mudie, Watson (og)	56,204
10		23	(h)	Aston Villa	D 1-1	Mortensen	33,298
11		30	(a)	Derby C	L 1-4	Mortensen	32,471
12	Oct	7	(h)	Chelsea	W 3-2	Slater 2, Mortensen	29,240
13		14	(a)	Portsmouth	L 0-2		47,829
14		21	(h)	West Brom A	W 2-1	Mudie 2	30,536
15		28	(a)	Newcastle U	L 2-4	Mortensen, Harvey (og)	61,008
16	Nov	4	(h)	Everton	W 4-0	Mudie 2, Mortensen, Perry	20,902
17		11	(a)	Stoke C	L 0-1		39,894
18		18	(h)	Huddersfield T	W 3-1	Withers 3	19,724
19		25	(a)	Middlesbrough	L 3-4	Mudie 2, Mortensen	40,487
20	Dec	2	(h)	Sheffield W	W 3-2	Mortensen, Johnston, Withers	19,732
21		9	(a)	Arsenal	D 4-4	Withers, Mortensen 2, Barnes (og)	54,445
22		16	(h)	Tottenham H	L 0-1		22,203
23		23	(a)	Charlton A	W 3-2	Mortensen, Mudie 2	27,220
24		25	(h)	Liverpool	W 3-0	Mortensen 2, Mudie	31,867
25		26	(a)	Liverpool	L 0-1		54,121
26		30	(h)	Manchester U	D 1-1	Perry	22,864
27	Jan	13	(a)	Wolves	D 1-1	Mortensen	49,028
28		20	(h)	Sunderland	D 2-2	Perry, Stephenson	22,797
29	Feb	3	(a)	Aston Villa	W 3-0	Mudie, Mortensen, Johnston	55,093
30		17	(h)	Derby C	W 3-1	Mortensen 2, Johnston	21,002
31		28	(a)	Chelsea	W 2-0	Mortensen, Mudie	36,074
32	Mar	4	(h)	Portsmouth	W 3-0	Brown 2 (1 pen), Mortensen	23,521
33		17	(h)	Newcastle U	D 2-2	Mortensen, Mudie	24,825
34		23	(h)	Bolton W	W 2-0	Mortensen, Johnston	33,627
35		24	(a)	Everton	W 2-0	Mortensen 2	61,387
36		26	(a)	Bolton W	W 2-1	Mortensen 2	42,265
37		31	(h)	Stoke C	W 3-0	Mortensen 2, Brown	23,106
38	Apr	4	(a)	West Brom A	W 3-1	Mudie 2, Mortensen	39,459
39		7	(a)	Huddersfield T	L 1-2	Mortensen	52,479
40		14	(h)	Middlesbrough	W 2-1	Mudie, McIntosh	16,300
41		21	(a)	Sheffield W	L 1-3	Mortensen	53,420
42	May	2	(h)	Arsenal	L 0-1		23,044

FINAL LEAGUE POSITION: 3rd in Division One — Appearances / Goals

FA Cup

3	Jan	6	(a)	Charlton A	D 2-2	Perry, Mortensen	37,000
R		10	(h)	Charlton A	W 3-0	Mortensen 2, Mudie	28,000
4		27	(h)	Stockport C	W 2-1	Mortensen, Mudie	31,190
5	Feb	10	(h)	Mansfield T	W 2-0	Mudie, Brown	33,016
6		24	(h)	Fulham	W 1-0	Brown (pen)	33,000
SF	Mar	11	(n*)	Birmingham C	D 0-0		73,000
R		15	(n†)	Birmingham C	W 2-1	Mortensen, Perry	70,114
F	Apr	28	(n‡)	Newcastle U	L 0-2		100,000

*Played at Maine Road, Manchester. †Played at Goodison Park, Liverpool. ‡Played at Wembley Stadium. — Appearances / Goals

Farm	Shimwell	Wright	Johnston	Hayward	Kelly	Matthews	McCall	Mortensen	Slater	Wardle	Mudie	McIntosh	McKnight	Garrett	Hobson	Perry	Withers	Brown	Crosland	Fenton	Ainscough	Stephenson	Adams	
1	2	3	4	5	6	7	8	9	10	11														1
1	2	3	4	5	6	7	8	9	10	11														2
1	2	3	4	5	6	7	8	9	10	11														3
1	2	3	4	5	6	7		9	10	11	8													4
1	2	3	4	5	6	7			10	11	8	9												5
1	2	3	4	5	6	7			10	11	8		9											6
1	2	3	4	5	6	7		9	10	11	8													7
1	2	3	4	5	6	7		9	10		8					11								8
1		3	4	5	6	7		9	10	11	8			2										9
1	2	3	4	5	6	7		9	10		8					11								10
1	2		4	5	6	7		9	10		8			3		11								11
1	2		4	5	6			9	10		8			3	7	11								12
1	2		4	5	6	7		9	10		8			3		11								13
1	2		4	5	6	7			10		8	9		3		11								14
1	2		4	5	6	7		9	10		8			3		11								15
1	2		4	5	6	7		9	10		8			3		11								16
1	2		4	5	6	7			10		8	9		3		11								17
1	2		4	5	6	7		9			8			3		11	10							18
1	2		4	5	6	7		9			8			3		11	10							19
1	2		4	5	6	7		9			8			3		11	10							20
1	2		4	5	6	7		9			8			3		11	10							21
1	2		4	5	6	7		9			8			3		11	10							22
1	2	3	4	5	6	7		9			8					11		10						23
1	2	3	4	5	6	7		9			8					11		10						24
1	2		4		6						8	9		3	7	11		10	5					25
1	2				6	7		9			8			3		11		10	5	4				26
1	2		4		6	7		9			8			3		11		10			5			27
1	2		4		6	7		9			8			3		11			5			10		28
1	2		4	5	6	7		9			8					11		10	3					29
1	2		4	5	6	7		9			8			3		11		10						30
1	2		4	5		7		9			8			3		11		10		6				31
1	2			5		7		9			8	4		3		11		10		6				32
1	2		4	5				9		11	8			3	7			10		6				33
1	2		4	5		7		9		11	8			3				10		6				34
1	2		4	5		7		9		11	8			3				10		6				35
1	2		4	5	6	7		9		11	8			3				10						36
1	2		4	5	6	7		9			8			3		11		10						37
1	2		4	5	6	7		9			8			3		11		10						38
1	2		4		6	7		9			8			3		11		10			5			39
1	2			5	6						8	9	4	3		11	10						7	40
1	2			5	6	7		9			8		4	3		11	10							41
1	2		4	5	6	7		9	10		8			3		11								42
42	41	12	38	37	37	38	3	36	18	12	39	6	3	30	3	30	7	16	4	6	2	1	1	
			7		1			30	4		17	1	3			4	5	3				1		

3 own-goals

Farm	Shimwell	Wright	Johnston	Hayward	Kelly	Matthews	McCall	Mortensen	Slater	Wardle	Mudie	McIntosh	McKnight	Garrett	Hobson	Perry	Withers	Brown	Crosland	Fenton	Ainscough	Stephenson	Adams	
1	2		4		6	7		9			8			3		11		10	5					3
1	2		4		6	7		9			8			3		11		10	5					R
1	2		4		6	7		9			8			3		11		10	5					4
1	2		4	5	6	7		9			8			3		11		10						5
1	2		4	5		7		9			8			3		11		10		6				6
1	2		4	5	6	7		9			8			3		11		10						SF
1	2		4	5	6	7		9			8			3		11		10						R
1	2		4	5	6	7		9	10		8			3		11								F
8	8		8	5	7	8		8	1		8			8		8		7	3	1				
								5			3					2		2						

1951-52

Manager: Joe Smith

1	Aug	18	(h)	Chelsea	L 1-2	Mortensen	31,172
2		22	(a)	Portsmouth	W 3-1	Perry, Yeull (og), Mortensen	41,825
3		25	(a)	Huddersfield T	W 3-1	Mudie, McEvoy (og), Brown	33,584
4		27	(h)	Portsmouth	D 0-0		30,628
5	Sep	1	(h)	Wolves	W 3-2	Mortensen 2, Mudie	32,074
6		5	(a)	Preston NE	L 1-3	Mortensen	40,809
7		8	(a)	Sunderland	W 3-1	Mortensen, Matthews, Withers	55,163
8		10	(h)	Preston NE	L 0-3		36,120
9		15	(h)	Aston Villa	L 0-3		31,783
10		22	(a)	Derby C	D 1-1	Slater	26,655
11		29	(h)	Manchester C	D 2-2	Mortensen, Slater	33,858
12	Oct	6	(a)	Burnley	L 0-2		34,855
13		13	(h)	Charlton A	L 1-2	Mortensen	35,724
14		20	(a)	Fulham	W 2-1	Mortensen 2	43,509
15		27	(h)	Middlesbrough	D 2-2	Mortensen, Brown	23,195
16	Nov	3	(a)	West Brom A	D 1-1	Brown	43,045
17		10	(h)	Newcastle U	W 6-3	Perry, Mortensen 2, Taylor, Robinson, Brown	28,611
18		17	(a)	Bolton W	L 0-1		38,990
19		24	(h)	Stoke C	W 4-2	Brown 2, Robinson, Hobson	18,536
20	Dec	1	(a)	Manchester U	L 1-3	Perry	35,977
21		8	(h)	Tottenham H	W 1-0	Taylor	14,821
22		15	(a)	Chelsea	L 1-2	W.Wright	38,912
23		22	(h)	Huddersfield T	W 3-1	Mortensen 2, Brown	14,923
24		25	(a)	Liverpool	D 1-1	Mortensen	41,198
25		26	(h)	Liverpool	W 2-0	Mortensen 2	27,414
26		29	(a)	Wolves	L 0-3		32,496
27	Jan	5	(h)	Sunderland	W 3-0	Perry, Mortensen 2	22,252
28		19	(a)	Aston Villa	L 0-4		33,613
29		26	(h)	Derby C	W 2-1	Taylor 2	18,337
30	Feb	9	(a)	Manchester C	D 0-0		47,528
31		16	(h)	Burnley	W 1-0	Mortensen	26,079
32	Mar	1	(a)	Charlton A	L 0-2		42,572
33		8	(h)	Fulham	W 4-2	Taylor, Mortensen 3	18,600
34		15	(a)	Middlesbrough	L 0-1		35,094
35		22	(h)	West Brom A	W 2-0	Mortensen, Millard (og)	20,128
36	Apr	5	(h)	Bolton W	W 1-0	Mortensen	17,374
37		7	(a)	Newcastle U	W 3-1	Brown 3	47,316
38		11	(h)	Arsenal	D 0-0		32,186
39		12	(a)	Stoke C	W 3-2	Brown 3	24,895
40		14	(a)	Arsenal	L 1-4	Brown (pen)	48,445
41		19	(h)	Manchester U	D 2-2	Mudie 2	29,118
42		26	(a)	Tottenham H	L 0-2		45,991

FINAL LEAGUE POSITION: 9th in Division One

Appearances
Goals

FA Cup

3	Jan	12	(a)	West Ham U	L 1-2	Johnston	38,600

Appearances
Goals

Farm	Shimwell	Garrett	Johnston	Hayward	Kelly	Matthews	Mudie	Mortensen	Brown	Perry	Hobson	Wright J	Withers	Fenton	McIntosh	Slater	Stephenson	Taylor	Robinson	Wright W	Crosland	
1	2	3	4	5	6	7	8	9	10	11												1
1	2	3	4	5	6	7	8	9	10	11												2
1	2	3	4	5	6		8	9	10	11	7											3
1		2	4	5	6	7	8	9	10	11		3										4
1		2	4	5	6	7	8	9	10	11		3										5
1		2	4	5	6	7		9	10	11		3	8									6
1	2			5	6	7		8		11		3	10	4	9							7
1	2			5	6	7		8		11		3	10	4	9							8
1	2			5	6	7		9		11		3		4		8	10					9
1	2			5	6	7	8	9		11		3		4		10						10
1	2			5	6	7	8	9		11		3		4		10						11
1		2	4	5	6	7		9	10	11		3				8						12
1		2		5	6	7		9	10	11		3		4				8				13
1	2	3		5	6	7		9	10	11				4				8				14
1	2	3		5	6	7		9	10	11				4				8				15
1	2	3		5		7		9	10	11				4				8	6			16
1	2	3		5		7		9	10	11				4				8	6			17
1	2	3		5		7		9	10	11				4				8	6			18
1	2	3	4	5				9	10	11	7							8	6			19
1	2	3	4	5					10	11	7			6		9		8				20
1	2	3	4	5					10	11	7			6				8		9		21
1	2	3	4	5					10	11	7							8	6	9		22
1	2	3	4	5				9	10	11	7							8	6			23
1	2	3	4	5				9	10	11	7							8	6			24
1	2	3	4	5	6			9	10	11	7							8				25
1	2	3	4	5	6			9	10	11	7							8				26
1	2	3	4	5				9	10	11	7							8	6			27
1	2	3	4	5	6			9	10	11	7							8				28
1	2	3	4	5	6			9	10	11	7							8				29
1	2	3	4	5	6			9	10	11	7							8				30
1	2	3	4	5	6	7		9	10	11								8				31
1	2	3	4	5	6	7		9	10	11								8				32
1	2	3	4	5	6			9	8	11								10		7		33
1	2	3	4	5	6			9	8	11	7							10				34
1	2	3	4	5	6			9	8	11	7							10				35
1	2		4	5	6			9	8		7	3	11					10				36
1		2	4	5	6			9	8		7	3						10	11			37
1		2	4	5	6			9	10		7	3						8	11			38
1		2	4		6				10		7	3					9	8		11	5	39
1		2	4		6				10		7	3					9	8		11	5	40
1	2	3	4	5	6		9		10		7		11					8				41
1	2	3	4	5	6		9		10		7		11					8				42
42	33	36	31	40	32	19	9	35	37	35	22	15	6	13	2	5	3	30	10	5	2	
						1	4	26	14	4	1		1			2		5	2	1		

3 own-goals

Farm	Shimwell	Garrett	Johnston	Hayward	Kelly	Matthews	Mudie	Mortensen	Brown	Perry	Hobson	Wright J	Withers	Fenton	McIntosh	Slater	Stephenson	Taylor	Robinson	Wright W	Crosland	
1	2	3	4	5		7		9	10	11								8	6			3
1	1	1	1	1		1		1	1	1								1	1			
			1																			

1952-53

Manager: Joe Smith

1	Aug	23	(a)	Portsmouth	W 2-0	Brown, Mortensen	43,478
2		25	(h)	Preston NE	D 1-1	Mortensen	36,159
3		30	(h)	Bolton W	W 3-0	Barrass (og), Matthews, Taylor	31,317
4	Sep	6	(a)	Aston Villa	W 5-1	Brown 3, Taylor, Mortensen	52,688
5		10	(a)	Chelsea	L 0-4		47,632
6		13	(h)	Sunderland	W 2-0	Mortensen, Perry	35,350
7		15	(h)	Chelsea	W 3-1	Mortensen, Perry, Matthews	28,892
8		20	(a)	Wolves	W 5-2	Mortensen, Matthews, Perry, Taylor, Brown	48,598
9		27	(h)	Charlton A	W 8-4	Hammond (og), Brown 3, Mortensen, Garrett, Matthews, Taylor	33,498
10	Oct	4	(a)	Arsenal	L 1-3	Taylor	66,642
11		11	(h)	Burnley	W 4-2	Mortensen, Perry 2, Brown (pen)	35,671
12		18	(a)	Tottenham H	L 0-4		53,928
13		25	(h)	Sheffield W	L 0-1		28,162
14	Nov	1	(a)	Cardiff C	D 2-2	Hobson, Taylor	43,662
15		8	(h)	Newcastle U	L 0-2		33,712
16		15	(a)	West Brom A	W 1-0	Mortensen	33,712
17		22	(h)	Middlesbrough	D 1-1	Brown	19,934
18		29	(a)	Liverpool	D 2-2	Taylor, Perry	32,336
19	Dec	6	(h)	Manchester C	W 4-1	Mortensen, Taylor, Brown 2	19,496
20		13	(a)	Stoke C	L 0-4		19,118
21		20	(h)	Portsmouth	W 3-2	Taylor, Fenton, Perry	13,562
22		25	(h)	Manchester U	D 0-0		27,778
23		27	(a)	Manchester U	L 1-2	Mortensen	49,934
24	Jan	1	(a)	Preston NE	L 2-4	Hobson, Perry	30,696
25		3	(a)	Bolton W	L 0-4		36,572
26		17	(h)	Aston Villa	D 1-1	Mudie	21,258
27		24	(a)	Sunderland	D 1-1	Hepton	53,653
28	Feb	7	(h)	Wolves	W 2-0	Brown 2	21,702
29		21	(h)	Arsenal	W 3-2	Mudie 2, Brown	30,034
30		23	(a)	Charlton A	L 0-2		15,913
31	Mar	3	(a)	Burnley	W 1-0	Perry	20,874
32		8	(h)	Tottenham H	W 2-0	Mudie, Perry	26,796
33		15	(a)	Sheffield W	L 0-2		59,794
34		25	(h)	Cardiff C	L 0-1		15,227
35		28	(a)	Newcastle U	W 1-0	Taylor	41,205
36	Apr	3	(h)	Derby C	W 2-1	Mortensen, Taylor	27,382
37		4	(h)	West Brom A	W 2-0	Mortensen 2	30,592
38		6	(a)	Derby C	D 1-1	Mortensen	24,795
39		11	(a)	Middlesbrough	L 1-5	Durie	38,847
40		15	(h)	Stoke C	D 1-1	Perry	13,284
41		18	(h)	Liverpool	W 3-1	Perry, Garrett, Mudie	20,073
42		25	(a)	Manchester C	L 0-5		35,507

FINAL LEAGUE POSITION: 7th in Division One

Appearances
Goals

FA Cup

3	Jan	10	(a)	Sheffield W	W 2-1	Matthews, Taylor	60,199
4		31	(h)	Huddersfield T	W 1-0	Garrett	29,239
5	Feb	14	(h)	Southampton	D 1-1	Perry	27,543
R		18	(a)	Southampton	W 2-1	Horton (og), Brown	30,000
6		28	(a)	Arsenal	W 2-1	Taylor, Brown	68,000
SF	Mar	21	(n*)	Tottenham H	W 2-1	Perry, Mudie	68,221
F	May	2	(n†)	Bolton W	W 4-3	Mortensen 3, Perry	100,000

*Played at Villa Park, Birmingham. †Played at Wembley Stadium.

Appearances
Goals

Farm	Shimwell	Garrett	Johnston	Crosland	Kelly	Matthews	Taylor	Mortensen	Brown	Perry	Robinson	Mudie	Frith	Sharratt	Fenton	Hobson	Ainscough	Wright W	McKnight	Durie	Hepton	Hall	
1	2	3	4	5	6	7	8	9	10	11													1
1		2	4	5	6	7	8	9	10	11	3												2
1		2	4	5	6	7	8	9	10	11			3										3
1	2	3	4	5	6	7	8	9	10	11													4
1	2	3	4	5	6	7	8	9	10	11													5
1	2	3	4	5	6	7	8	9	10	11													6
1	2	3	4	5	6	7		9	10	11		8											7
1	2	3	4	5	6	7	8	9	10	11													8
1	2	3	4	5	6	7	8	9	10	11													9
1	2		4	5	6	7	8	9	10	11			3										10
1	2		4	5	6	7	8	9	10	11			3										11
	2		4	5	6	7	8	9		11		10	3	1									12
1	2	3	4	5			8	9	10	11					6	7							13
1	2	3	4	5			8	9	10	11					6	7							14
1	2	3	4		6		8	9	10	11						7	5						15
1	2	3	5		6		8	9	10	11					4	7	5						16
1	2	3	5		6		8	9	10	11					4	7							17
1	2	3	5		6		8	9	10	11					4	7							18
1	2	3	5		6		8	9	10	11					4	7							19
1	2	3	5		6		8	9	10	11					4	7							20
1	2	3	4	5			8	9	10	11					6	7							21
1	2	3	4	5			8	9	10	11					6			7					22
1	2	3	4	5			8	9	10	11					6			7					23
1	2	3	4	5	6		8	9	10	11						7							24
1	2	3	4	5	6		8	9	10	11						7							25
1	2	3	5			7	10		9	11		8			6				4				26
1	2	3	5			7	10		9	11		8			6						4		27
1	2	3	4	5		7	10		9	11		8			6								28
1		3	4	5	6	7	8		10	11		9	2										29
1		3	4	5	6	7	8		10	11		9	2										30
1	2	3	4	5	6	7	8			11		9								10			31
1	2	3	4	5	6	7	8			11		9								10			32
1		3			6		8	10		11		9	2		4	7	5						33
1	2	3	5		6	7	8	9							4			11		10			34
1	2	3	5		6		8	9				10			4	7				11			35
1	2	3	5		6	7	8	9				10			4			11					36
1	2	3	5		6	7	8	9				10			4			11					37
1	2	3	5		6			9				8			4	7		11		10			38
1	2	3	5		6	7	8	9				10			4					11			39
		3	5		6		8	9		11		10	2		4	7						1	40
	2	3	5		6	7	8	9		11		10			4							1	41
1		3	5	6				9		11		10	2		4	7				8			42
39	35	39	41	25	33	24	39	35	29	36	1	18	9	1	23	16	3	6	1	7	1	2	
		2				4	11	15	15	12		5			1	2				1	1		

2 own-goals

Farm	Shimwell	Garrett	Johnston	Crosland	Kelly	Matthews	Taylor	Mortensen	Brown	Perry	Robinson	Mudie	Frith	Sharratt	Fenton	Hobson	Ainscough	Wright W	McKnight	Durie	Hepton	Hall	
1	2	3	5			7	10		9	11		8			6				4				3
1	2	3	4	5		7	10		9	11		8			6								4
1	2	3	4	5		7	10		9	11		8			6								5
1	2	3	4	5		7	10		9	11		8			6								R
1	2	3	5		6	7	8		10	11		9			4								6
1	2	3	5		6	7	8	10		11		9			4								SF
1	2	3	5			7	8	9		11	6	10			4								F
7	7	7	7	3	2	7	7	2	5	7	1	7			7				1				
		1				1	2	3	2	3		1											

1 own-goal

1953-54

Manager: Joe Smith

1	Aug	20	(h)	Chelsea	W 2-1	Mortensen 2	28,440
2		23	(a)	Burnley	L 1-2	Mortensen	41,574
3		27	(a)	Sheffield U	W 4-3	Mortensen 3, Mudie	35,171
4		29	(h)	Burnley	W 2-0	Mortensen 2	18,113
5	Sep	5	(h)	Huddersfield T	W 3-1	Mortensen, Mudie, Fenton	34,507
6		7	(h)	Portsmouth	D 1-1	Mudie	30,914
7		12	(a)	Aston Villa	L 1-2	Mortensen	37,284
8		16	(a)	Portsmouth	D 4-4	Mudie 2, Mortensen, Perry	28,703
9		19	(h)	Wolves	D 0-0		35,074
10		26	(a)	Sunderland	L 2-3	Perry, Mudie	60,998
11	Oct	3	(h)	Manchester C	W 2-0	Mudie 2	35,666
12		10	(a)	Charlton A	L 2-4	Mortensen, Fenton (pen)	56,664
13		17	(h)	Sheffield W	L 1-2	Mortensen	35,910
14		24	(a)	Middlesbrough	W 1-0	Taylor	39,416
15		31	(h)	West Brom A	W 4-1	Mortensen, Taylor 2, Perry	27,106
16	Nov	7	(a)	Preston NE	W 3-2	Fenton (pen), Brown, Mortensen	31,886
17		14	(h)	Tottenham H	W 1-0	Taylor	19,667
18		21	(a)	Manchester U	L 1-4	Perry	29,464
19		28	(h)	Bolton W	D 0-0		29,464
20	Dec	5	(a)	Liverpool	L 2-5	Taylor 2	47,320
21		12	(h)	Newcastle U	L 1-3	Perry	19,896
22		19	(a)	Chelsea	L 1-5	Mudie	34,865
23		26	(h)	Arsenal	D 2-2	Brown 2	29,347
24		28	(a)	Arsenal	D 1-1	Perry	63,661
25	Jan	1	(a)	Newcastle U	L 1-2	Brown	44,343
26		2	(h)	Sheffield U	D 2-2	Taylor 2	20,470
27		16	(a)	Huddersfield T	D 0-0		25,733
28		23	(h)	Aston Villa	W 3-2	Stephenson, Perry 2	16,629
29	Feb	6	(a)	Wolves	L 1-4	Stephenson	27,795
30		13	(h)	Sunderland	W 3-0	Perry, Brown 2	23,058
31		24	(a)	Manchester C	W 4-1	Matthews 2, Brown, Perry	22,515
32		27	(h)	Charlton A	W 3-1	Stephenson 2, Taylor	21,619
33	Mar	6	(a)	Sheffield W	W 2-1	Mudie, Brown	41,619
34		13	(h)	Middlesbrough	D 0-0		20,334
35		20	(a)	West Brom A	L 1-2	Mudie	53,019
36		31	(h)	Preston NE	W 4-2	Taylor 2, Durie, Mortensen	16,674
37	Apr	4	(a)	Tottenham H	D 2-2	Perry, Mortensen	43,870
38		11	(h)	Manchester U	W 2-0	Mortensen, Perry	25,996
39		17	(h)	Cardiff C	W 4-1	Brown, Mortensen, Taylor, Perry	26,194
40		18	(a)	Bolton W	L 2-3	Brown, Perry	40,291
41		20	(a)	Cardiff C	W 1-0	Perry	44,508
42		25	(h)	Liverpool	W 3-0	Mortensen 2, Brown	18,651

FINAL LEAGUE POSITION: 6th in Division One

Appearances
Goals

FA Cup

3	Jan	9	(h)	Luton T	D 1-1	Mortensen	25,242
R		13	(a)	Luton T	D 0-0*		20,000
2R		18	(n†)	Luton T	D 1-1*	Johnston	33,000
3R		25	(n‡)	Luton T	W 2-0	Perry, Stephenson	39,000
4		30	(a)	West Ham U	D 1-1	Brown	37,000
R	Feb	3	(h)	West Ham U	W 3-1	Perry 2, Brown	27,120
5		20	(a)	Port Vale	L 0-2		40,500

*After extra-time. †Played at Villa Park, Birmingham. ‡Played at the Molineux Grounds, Wolverhampton.

Appearances
Goals

Farm	Shimwell	Garrett	Fenton	Johnston	Kelly	Matthews	Taylor	Mortensen	Mudie	Perry	Durie	Hobson	Wylie	Wright	Crosland	Brown	Robinson	McKnight	Harris	Frith	Stephenson	Gratrix	Ainscough	
1	2	3	4	5	6	7	8	9	10	11														1
1	2	3	4	5	6	7	8	9	10	11														2
1	2	3	4	5	6	7	8	9	10	11														3
1	2	3	4	5	6	7	8	9	10	11														4
1	2	3	4	5	6	7		9	8	11	10													5
1	2	3	4	5	6	7	8	9	10	11														6
1	2	3	4	5	6		8	9	10	11		7												7
1	2	3	4	5	6		8	9	10	11		7												8
1	2	3	4	5	6	7	8	9	10	11														9
1	2	3	4	5	6	7	8	9	10	11														10
	2	3	4	5	6	7	8	9	10	11			1											11
1	2		4		6	7	8	9	10	11				3	5									12
1	2	3	4	5	6	7	8	9		11						10								13
1	2	3	4	5		7	8	9		11						10	6							14
1	2	3	4	5		7	8	9		11						10	6							15
1	2		4	5	6	7	8	9		11				3		10								16
1	2	3	4	5	6	7	8	9		11						10								17
1	2	3	4	5	6	7	8	9		11						10								18
1	2	3	4	5		7	8	9		11						10	6							19
1	2	3	4	5		7	8	9		11						10	6							20
1	2	3	4	5			8	9	10	11		7				6								21
		3	4				8	9	10	11		7	1	3	5	6								22
	2	4		4	6	7		9	8	11			1		5	10								23
	2	4		4	6	7		9	8	11			1		5	10								24
	2	4		4	6			9	8	11		7	1		5	10								25
	2	4		4	6	7	8	9		11			1		5	10								26
1	2	4			6		8		9	11					5	10		4	7					27
1	2	4			6		8		10	11					5				7	4	9			28
1	2		4	6					8	11					5	10			7	3	9			29
1	2		4	5	6		8		7	11						10				3	9			30
1	2		4	5	6	7	8			11						10				3	9			31
1	2		4	5	6	7	8			11						10				3	9			32
1	2		4	5	6	7			8	11						10				3	9			33
1			4	5	6	7	8			11						10				3	9	2		34
1			4	5	6	7	8		9	11						10				3		2		35
			4	5	6	7	8	9		11	10		1	3								2		36
			4	5	6	7	8	9		11	10		1	3								2		37
1			4	5	6	7	8	9		11				3		10						2		38
1			4	5	6	7	8	9		11				3		10						2		39
1			4	5	6	7	8	9		11				3		10						2		40
1		3	4		6				8	11						10			7		9	2	5	41
1		3	4	5	6	7	8	9		11						10						2		42
34	32	28	36	37	35	32	35	32	24	42	3	5	8	8	9	27	4	1	4	8	8	9	1	
			3			2	12	21	11	15	1					11					4			

Farm	Shimwell	Garrett	Fenton	Johnston	Kelly	Matthews	Taylor	Mortensen	Mudie	Perry	Durie	Hobson	Wylie	Wright	Crosland	Brown	Robinson	McKnight	Harris	Frith	Stephenson	Gratrix	Ainscough	
1	2	3	4	5	6	7	8	9		11						10								3
1	2	3	4	5	6	7	8	9		11						10								R
1	2	3		4	6	7	8		9	11					5	10								2R
1	2		4			7	8			11					5	10	6			3	9			3R
1	2		4	5	6	7	8			11						10				3	9			4
1	2		4	5	6	7	8			11						10				3	9			R
1	2		4	5	6	7	8			11						10				3	9			5
7	7	3	6	6	6	7	7	2	1	7					2	7	1			4	4			
				1				1		3						2					1			

1954-55

Manager: Joe Smith

1	Aug	21	(a)	Huddersfield T	W 3-1	Mortensen, Perry, Taylor	35,793
2		23	(h)	Bolton W	L 2-3	Fenton, Taylor	33,915
3		28	(h)	Manchester U	L 2-4	Mortensen, Fenton	31,855
4	Sep	1	(a)	Bolton W	L 0-3		47,013
5		4	(a)	Wolves	L 0-1		50,203
6		11	(h)	Aston Villa	L 0-1		31,417
7		16	(a)	Charlton A	D 3-3	Mudie, Durie, Mortensen	16,354
8		18	(a)	Sunderland	L 0-2		51,556
9		20	(h)	Charlton A	D 1-1	Perry	20,164
10		25	(h)	Tottenham H	W 5-1	Brown 2, Fenton (pen), Stephenson, Perry	34,626
11	Oct	2	(a)	Sheffield W	L 1-2	Stephenson	31,415
12		9	(h)	Preston NE	L 1-2	Brown	36,264
13		16	(a)	Sheffield U	L 1-2	Stephenson	26,007
14		23	(h)	Chelsea	W 1-0	Fenton (pen)	19,694
15		30	(a)	Leicester C	D 2-2	Mortensen 2	40,655
16	Nov	6	(h)	Newcastle U	W 2-0	Paterson (og), Perry	20,701
17		13	(a)	Everton	W 1-0	Mudie	57,137
18		20	(h)	Manchester C	L 1-3	Mudie	21,734
19		27	(a)	Cardiff C	W 2-1	McKenna, Taylor	19,823
20	Dec	4	(h)	Arsenal	D 2-2	Taylor, Stephenson	16,348
21		11	(a)	West Brom A	W 1-0	Stephenson	33,614
22		18	(h)	Huddersfield T	D 1-1	Taylor	17,579
23		25	(h)	Portsmouth	D 2-2	Mudie 2	25,004
24		27	(a)	Portsmouth	L 0-3		43,896
25	Jan	1	(a)	Manchester U	L 1-4	Perry	54,774
26		15	(h)	Wolves	L 0-2		14,704
27		22	(a)	Aston Villa	L 1-3	Brown	30,161
28	Feb	5	(h)	Sunderland	D 0-0		21,899
29		12	(a)	Tottenham H	L 2-3	Hepton, Wright	47,386
30		19	(h)	Sheffield W	W 2-1	Fenton (pen), Hepton	18,959
31		26	(a)	Preston NE	L 1-3	J.Kelly	30,853
32	Mar	5	(h)	West Brom A	W 3-1	Fenton (pen), Matthews, Brown	20,430
33		12	(a)	Chelsea	D 0-0		55,227
34		19	(h)	Leicester C	W 2-0	Mudie 2	24,185
35	Apr	2	(h)	Everton	W 4-0	Taylor, Mortensen, Perry, McKenna	19,269
36		8	(a)	Burnley	W 1-0	Mortensen	35,212
37		9	(a)	Arsenal	L 0-3		59,381
38		11	(h)	Burnley	W 1-0	Mortensen	32,881
39		16	(h)	Cardiff C	D 0-0		21,832
40		23	(a)	Manchester C	W 6-1	Perry 3, Mortensen 2, Brown	44,839
41		25	(a)	Newcastle U	D 1-1	Mortensen	41,380
42		30	(h)	Sheffield U	L 1-2	Perry	19,681

FINAL LEAGUE POSITION: 19th in Division One

Appearances
Goals

FA Cup

3	Jan	8	(h)	York C	L 0-2		26,030

Appearances
Goals

Farm	Shimwell	Garrett	Fenton	Johnston	Kelly H	Matthews	Taylor	Mortensen	Brown	Perry	Withers	Gratrix	Stephenson	Mudie	Robinson	McKenna	Durie	Frith	Armfield	Kelly J	Smith	Hepton	Wylie	Wright	Harris	
1	2	3	4	5	6	7	8	9	10	11																1
1	2	3	4	5	6	7	8	9	10	11																2
1	2	3	4	5	6	7	8	9	10		11															3
1	2	3	4	5	6	7	8	9	10		11															4
1		3	4	5	6	7	8			11		2	9	10												5
1		3	4	5	6	7	8	9		11		2		10												6
1		3	4	5			8	9				2		10	6	7	11									7
1		3	4	5			8	9				2		10	6	7	11									8
1		3	4	5		7	8	9		11		2		10	6											9
1		3	4	5		7	8		10	11		2	9		6											10
1		3	4	5			8		10	11		2	9		6	7										11
1		3	4	5		7	8	9	10			2			6		11									12
1		3	4	5	6	7	8		10			2	9			11										13
1	2	3	4	5	6	7	8	9	10	11																14
1	2	3	4	5	6	7	8	9		11				10												15
1	2	3	4	5	6	7		9		11			10	8												16
1	2	3	4	5	6	7	8	9						10		11										17
1	2	3	4	5	6	7	8	9		11				10												18
1	3		4	5	6		8	9		11		2		10		7										19
1		3	4	5	6	7	8	9				2	11	10												20
1		3	4	5	6	7	8	9				2	11	10												21
1			4	5	6	7	8	9				2	11	10				3								22
1			4	5	6	7	8			11		2	9	10				3								23
1				5	6		8			11		3	9	10		7			2	4						24
1			4	5	6	7	8	9		11		3		10					2							25
1		3	4	5	6	7						2	10			11				8	9					26
1		3	4	5	6	7			10	11		2								8		9				27
1		3	4	5	6	7			10	11		2								8		9				28
		3	4	5	6	7			10			2								8		9	1	11		29
		3	4	5	6	7			10			2								8		9	1	11		30
		3	4	5	6	7			10			2								8		9	1	11		31
1		3	4	5	6	7			9	11		2		10						8						32
1		3	4	5	6	7	8		9	11		2		10												33
1		3	4	5	6	7	8	9		11		2		10												34
1		3	4	5	6		8	9		11		2		10		7										35
1		3	4	5	6		8	9		11		2		10		7										36
1		3	4	5	6		8	9		11		2		10		7										37
1		3	4	5		7	8	9				2		10						6					11	38
1		3	4	5	6	7	8	9		11		2		10												39
1		3	4	5	6	7	8	9	10	11		2														40
1		3	4	5	6		8	9	10	11		2				7										41
1	3	5	4		6	7	8	9	10	11		2														42
39	11	37	41	41	35	33	34	28	19	27	2	33	11	24	6	12	3	2	2	9	1	5	3	3	1	
			6			1	6	11	6	10			5	7		2	1			1		2		1		

1 own-goal

Farm	Shimwell	Garrett	Fenton	Johnston	Kelly H	Matthews	Taylor	Mortensen	Brown	Perry	Withers	Gratrix	Stephenson	Mudie	Robinson	McKenna	Durie	Frith	Armfield	Kelly J	Smith	Hepton	Wylie	Wright	Harris	
1		3		5	6	7	10	9		11		2		8						4						3
1		1		1	1	1	1	1		1		1		1						1						

1955-56

Manager: Joe Smith

1	Aug	20	(h)	Arsenal	W 3-1	Taylor, Perry, Mortensen	30,928
2		22	(a)	Burnley	W 2-0	Perry 2	35,226
3		27	(a)	Portsmouth	D 3-3	Perry 3	37,072
4		29	(h)	Burnley	D 1-1	Taylor	25,774
5	Sep	3	(h)	Sunderland	W 7-3	Perry 3, Mudie 2, Mortensen 2	34,546
6		5	(h)	Chelsea	W 2-1	Fenton (pen), Mortensen	30,563
7		10	(a)	Aston Villa	D 1-1	Perry	52,000
8		17	(h)	Wolves	W 2-1	Mortensen, Matthews	38,098
9		24	(a)	Manchester C	L 0-2		63,925
10	Oct	1	(h)	Cardiff C	W 2-1	Fenton (pen), Perry	33,451
11		8	(a)	Luton T	L 1-3	Mudie	24,473
12		15	(h)	Charlton A	W 5-0	Durie 2, Mudie 3	34,247
13		22	(a)	Sheffield U	L 1-2	Mudie	23,753
14		29	(h)	Preston NE	L 2-6	Fenton (pen), Farm	25,692
15	Nov	5	(a)	Newcastle U	W 2-1	Brown, Mudie	54,692
16		12	(h)	Birmingham C	W 2-0	Taylor, Mudie	21,967
17		19	(a)	West Brom A	W 2-1	Brown, Taylor	37,910
18		26	(h)	Manchester U	D 0-0		26,240
19	Dec	3	(a)	Tottenham H	D 1-1	Mudie	51,162
20		10	(h)	Everton	W 4-0	Mudie 3, Perry	16,796
21		17	(a)	Arsenal	L 1-4	Evans (og)	45,086
22		25	(h)	Portsmouth	L 2-3	Perry, Fenton	24,182
23		26	(h)	Huddersfield T	W 4-2	Perry, Brown, Mudie, Lythgoe	27,628
24		27	(a)	Huddersfield T	L 1-3	Mudie	41,626
25		31	(a)	Sunderland	D 0-0		41,626
26	Jan	14	(h)	Aston Villa	W 6-0	Mudie 2, Matthews, Brown 2 (2 pens), Perry	15,844
27		21	(a)	Wolves	W 3-2	Mudie, Brown (pen), Taylor	46,322
28	Feb	4	(h)	Manchester C	L 0-1		17,012
29		11	(a)	Cardiff C	L 0-1		36,000
30		18	(h)	Luton T	W 3-2	Durie 2, Perry	18,562
31		25	(a)	Charlton A	W 2-1	Taylor 2 (1 pen)	30,234
32	Mar	3	(h)	West Brom A	W 5-1	Matthews, J.Kelly, Durie, Mudie 2	19,768
33		10	(a)	Preston NE	D 3-3	Durie 2, Perry	38,058
34		17	(h)	Newcastle U	W 5-1	Taylor, Mudie 2, Perry, Durie	23,740
35		24	(a)	Birmingham C	W 2-1	Durie, Perry	47,933
36		30	(h)	Bolton W	D 0-0		34,764
37		31	(h)	Sheffield U	D 1-1	Durie	27,272
38	Apr	2	(a)	Bolton W	W 3-1	Durie 2, Perry	35,471
39		7	(a)	Manchester U	L 1-2	Durie	62,277
40		14	(h)	Tottenham H	L 0-2		19,257
41		21	(a)	Everton	L 0-1		57,823
42		28	(a)	Chelsea	L 1-2	Durie	35,247

FINAL LEAGUE POSITION: 2nd in Division One

Appearances
Goals

FA Cup

3	Jan	11	(a)	Manchester C *	L 1-2	Perry	42,517

*After a game abandoned after 50 minutes because of fog.

Appearances
Goals

Farm	Shimwell	Garrett	Fenton	Gratrix	Kelly H	Matthews	Taylor	Mortensen	Mudie	Perry	Wright	McKenna	Armfield	Durie	Brown	Kelly J	Lythgoe	Frith	Fawcett	Snowdon	Harris	
1	2	3	4	5	6	7	8	9	10	11												1
1	2		4	5	6	7	8	9	10	11	3											2
1	2		4	5	6	7	8	9	10	11	3											3
1	2		4	5	6		8	9	10	11	3	7										4
1	2		4	5	6	7	8	9	10	11	3											5
1	2		4	5	6	7	8	9	10	11	3											6
1	2		4	5	6	7	8	9	10	11	3											7
1	2		4	5	6	7	8	9	10	11	3											8
1			4	5	6	7	8	9	10	11	3		2									9
1			4	5	6		8	9	10	11	3	7	2									10
1			4	5	6		8	9	10	11	3	7	2									11
1			4	5	6	7	8		9	11	3		2	10								12
1			4	5	6		8		9	11	3	7	2	10								13
1			4	5	6	7	8		9	11	3		2	10								14
1			4	5	6	7	8		9	11	3		2		10							15
1			4	5	6	7	8		9	11	3		2		10							16
1			4	5	6	7	8		9	11	3		2		10							17
1			4	5	6	7	8		9	11	3		2		10							18
1			4	5	6	7	8		9	11	3		2		10							19
1			4	5	6	7	8		9	11	3		2		10							20
1			4	5	6	7	8		9	11	3		2		10							21
1			4	5	6	7	8		9	11	3		2		10							22
1			4	5	6	7			9	11	3		2		10		8					23
1		3		5	6	7			9	11			2		10	4	8					24
1		3	4	5	6				9	11		7	2		10		8					25
1		3		5	6	7	8		9	11			2		10	4						26
1				5	6	7	8		9	11	3		2		10	4						27
1				5	6	7	8		9	11	3		2		10	4						28
1				5	6	7			9	10	3				8	4		2	11			29
1				5	6	7			9	11	3		2	10	8	4						30
1				5	6	7	8		9	11	3		2	10		4						31
1				5	6	7	8		9	11	3		2	10		4						32
1				5	6	7	8		9	11	3		2	10		4						33
1				5	6	7	8		9	11	3		2	10		4						34
1				5	6	7	8		9	11	3			10		4		2				35
1				5	6	7	8		9	11	3		2		10	4						36
1				5	6	7	8		9	11	3		2	10		4						37
1			6	5		7	8		9	11	3		2	10		4						38
1				5	6	7	8		9	11	3		2	10		4						39
1				5	6	7	8		9		3		2	10	11	4						40
1					6	7	8		9	11	3		2	10		4				5		41
1					6		8		9	11	3		2	10		4				5	7	42
42	8	4	25	40	41	36	37	11	42	41	38	5	32	15	18	18	3	2	1	2	1	
1			4			3	8	5	22	20				14	6	1	1					

1 own-goal

Farm	Shimwell	Garrett	Fenton	Gratrix	Kelly H	Matthews	Taylor	Mortensen	Mudie	Perry	Wright	McKenna	Armfield	Durie	Brown	Kelly J	Lythgoe	Frith	Fawcett	Snowdon	Harris	
1		3	4	5	6	7	8		9	11			2	10								3
1		1	1	1	1	1	1		1	1			1	1								
										1												

1956-57

Manager: Joe Smith

1	Aug	18	(a)	Bolton W	L 1-4	Durie	33,310
2		22	(a)	Everton	W 3-2	Durie 3	55,442
3		25	(h)	Wolves	W 3-2	Durie, Mudie 2	28,482
4		27	(h)	Everton	W 5-2	Mudie 2, Brown, Matthews, J.Kelly	14,709
5	Sep	1	(a)	Aston Villa	L 2-3	Mudie, Brown	46,000
6		3	(h)	Tottenham H	W 4-1	Brown 2, Durie, Matthews	28,460
7		8	(h)	Luton T	W 4-0	Mudie, Brown, Durie, Wright	32,112
8		15	(a)	Sunderland	L 2-5	Mudie 2	45,914
9		22	(h)	Charlton A	W 3-2	Mudie 2, J.Kelly	34,199
10		29	(a)	Manchester C	W 3-0	Mudie, Fenton, Taylor	39,358
11	Oct	6	(a)	Burnley	D 2-2	Booth, Mudie	27,678
12		13	(h)	Preston NE	W 4-0	Fenton, Dunn (og), Mudie 2	36,006
13		20	(a)	Sheffield W	W 2-1	Brown, Perry	46,395
14		27	(h)	Manchester U	D 2-2	Durie, Mudie	32,632
15	Nov	3	(a)	Birmingham C	D 2-2	Taylor, Mudie	35,597
16		10	(h)	West Brom A	L 0-1		18,839
17		17	(a)	Portsmouth	D 0-0		26,466
18		24	(h)	Newcastle U	L 2-3	Mudie, Durie	18,258
19	Dec	1	(a)	Chelsea	D 2-2	Brown, Mudie	45,327
20		8	(h)	Cardiff C	W 3-1	Brown 2, Durie	16,623
21		15	(h)	Bolton W	W 4-2	Durie, Mudie, Fenton (pen), Brown	17,556
22		22	(a)	Wolves	L 1-4	Brown	21,302
23		25	(h)	Leeds U	D 1-1	Brown	20,517
24		26	(a)	Leeds U	L 0-5		22,689
25		29	(h)	Aston Villa	D 0-0		16,777
26	Jan	12	(a)	Luton T	W 2-0	Mudie, Durie	16,564
27		19	(h)	Sunderland	L 1-2	Mudie	18,702
28	Feb	2	(a)	Charlton A	W 4-0	Ufton (og), Mudie 2, Brown	31,746
29		9	(h)	Manchester C	W 4-1	Perry 2, Harris, Mudie	21,101
30		23	(a)	Manchester U	W 2-0	Perry, Durie	42,602
31	Mar	2	(h)	Sheffield W	W 3-1	Perry, Mudie, Durie	18,444
32		9	(a)	Cardiff C	W 4-3	Durie 4	16,000
33		16	(h)	Birmingham C	W 3-1	Perry, Taylor, Mudie	17,610
34		30	(h)	Portsmouth	W 5-0	Mudie 2, Durie, Harris, Dickinson (og)	14,972
35	Apr	3	(a)	West Brom A	W 3-1	Smith 3	6,397
36		6	(a)	Newcastle U	L 1-2	Smith	31,810
37		13	(h)	Chelsea	W 1-0	Mudie	17,176
38		19	(a)	Arsenal	D 1-1	Perry	50,270
39		20	(a)	Preston NE	D 0-0		35,887
40		22	(h)	Arsenal	L 2-4	Mudie, Durie	24,118
41		27	(a)	Tottenham H	L 1-2	Mudie	49,878
42	May	1	(h)	Burnley	W 1-0	Mudie	13,919
	FINAL LEAGUE POSITION: 4th in Division One						Appearances
							Goals

FA Cup

3	Jan	5	(a)	Bolton W	W 3-2	Mudie 2, Durie	42,515
4		26	(h)	Fulham	W 6-2	Mudie 4, Lampe (og), Durie	26,248
5	Feb	16	(h)	West Brom A	D 0-0		32,707
R		20	(a)	West Brom A	L 1-2	Perry	48,054
							Appearances
							Goals

Farm	Armfield	Garrett	Kelly J	Gratrix	Kelly H	Matthews	Taylor	Mudie	Durie	Perry	Starkey	Wright	Brown	Barnes	Fenton	Booth	Harris	Frith	McKenna	Shimwell	Smith	Snowdon	Peterson	
1	2	3	4	5	6	7	8	9	10	11														1
1	2	3	4	5	6	7	8	9	10	11														2
1	2	3	4	5	6	7	8	9	10		11													3
1	2		4	5	6	7		9	10			3	8	11										4
1	2		4	5	6	7		9	10	11		3	8											5
1	2		4	5	6	7		9	10	11		3	8											6
1	2		4	5	6	7		9	10	11		3	8											7
1	2		4	5	6	7		9	10	11		3	8											8
1	2		4	5	6	7		9	10	11		3	8											9
1	2		4	5		7	8	9	10	11		3			6									10
1	2		4	5			8	9	10	11		3			6	7								11
1	2		4	5		7	8	9	10	11		3			6									12
1	2		4	5		7	8		10	11		3	9		6									13
1	2		4	5		7	8	9	10	11		3			6									14
1	2		4	5			8	9	10	11		3			6		7							15
1	2		4	5		7	8	9	10	11		3			6									16
1	2		4	5			8	9	10	11		3			6		7							17
1	2		4	5			8	9	10	11		3			6		7							18
1	2		4	5		7	8	9		11			10		6			3						19
1	2		4	5		7	8	9	11				10		6			3						20
1	2		4	5			8	9	11				10		6			3	7					21
1	2		4	5			8	9		11			10		6			3	7					22
1	2		4	5			8	9		11			10		6			3	7					23
1	2		4	5				9	10	11			8		6			3	7					24
1	2	3	4	5				9	10	11			8		6				7					25
1	2	3	4	5				9	8	11			10		6				7					26
1	2		4	5		7		9	8	11			10		6					3				27
1	2	3	4	5		7	8	9		11			10		6									28
1	2	3	4	5			8	9	10	11					6		7							29
1	2	3	4	5		7	8	9	10	11					6									30
1	2	3	4	5		7	8	9	10	11					6									31
1	2	3	4	5		7	8	9	10	11					6									32
1	2	3	4	5		7	8	9	10	11					6									33
1	2	3	4	5			8	9	10	11					6		7							34
1	2	3	7	5	6		8		10					11	4						9			35
1	2	3		5	6		8		10	11					4				7		9			36
1	2	3		5	6	7		9	10	11												4	8	37
1	2	3	4	5	6	7	8	9		11													10	38
1		3	4	5	6		8	9	10	11								2	7					39
1		3	4	5	6		8	9	10	11								2					7	40
1			4	2	6		8	9	10	11								3				5	7	41
1				2	6		8	9	10	11		3									4	5	7	42
42	38	18	39	42	17	24	31	39	37	37	1	16	17	2	27	1	5	9	8	1	3	3	5	
			2			2	3	32	20	7		1	13		3	1	2				4			

3 own-goals

Farm	Armfield	Garrett	Kelly J	Gratrix	Kelly H	Matthews	Taylor	Mudie	Durie	Perry	Starkey	Wright	Brown	Barnes	Fenton	Booth	Harris	Frith	McKenna	Shimwell	Smith	Snowdon	Peterson	
1	2	3	4	5		7		9	8	11			10		6									3
1	2		4	5		7	8	9	10	11					6			3						4
1	2	3	4	5		7	8	9	10	11					6									5
1	2	3	4	5		7	8	9	10	11					6									R
4	4	3	4	4		4	3	4	4	4			1		4			1						
								6	2	1														

1 own-goal

1957-58

Manager: Joe Smith

1	Aug	24	(h)	Leeds U	W 3-0	Durie, Perry, Taylor	26,700
2		26	(h)	Luton T	L 1-2	Perry	21,099
3		31	(a)	Bolton W	L 0-3		28,584
4	Sep	4	(a)	Luton T	L 0-2		19,511
5		7	(h)	Arsenal	W 1-0	Taylor	31,486
6		9	(h)	Manchester U	L 1-4	Mudie	34,181
7		14	(a)	Wolves	L 1-3	Perry	38,496
8		18	(a)	Manchester U	W 2-1	Mudie 2	40,763
9		21	(h)	Aston Villa	D 1-1	Taylor	31,079
10	Oct	5	(h)	Sunderland	W 7-0	Durie 2, Charnley 2, Taylor 2, Perry	33,172
11		12	(a)	Sheffield W	W 3-0	Mudie, Peterson, Durie	30,332
12		19	(h)	Manchester C	L 2-5	Mudie 2	28,322
13		26	(a)	Nottingham F	W 2-1	Perry, Durie	41,736
14	Nov	2	(h)	Chelsea	W 2-1	Durie, Peterson	17,817
15		9	(a)	Newcastle U	W 2-1	Mudie 2	36,410
16		16	(h)	Burnley	L 2-4	Mudie, H.Kelly (pen)	21,641
17		20	(a)	Everton	D 0-0		47,665
18		23	(a)	Birmingham C	D 0-0		32,168
19		30	(h)	Portsmouth	W 2-1	Mudie, Harris	14,722
20	Dec	7	(a)	West Brom A	D 1-1	Durie	27,900
21		14	(h)	Tottenham H	L 0-2		14,938
22		21	(a)	Leeds U	L 1-2	Taylor	32,500
23		25	(h)	Leicester C	W 5-1	Mudie, Perry 2, Peterson 2	16,696
24		26	(a)	Leicester C	L 1-2	Durie	33,052
25		28	(h)	Bolton W	L 2-3	Mudie, Harris	19,858
26	Jan	11	(a)	Arsenal	W 3-2	Charnley 2, Douglas (og)	38,667
27		18	(h)	Wolves	W 3-2	Taylor, Durie, Perry	17,953
28	Feb	1	(a)	Aston Villa	D 1-1	Taylor	45,000
29		15	(a)	Sunderland	W 4-1	Durie 2, Perry, Mudie	28,127
30		22	(h)	Sheffield W	D 2-2	H.Kelly (pen), Charnley	13,771
31	Mar	1	(a)	Manchester C	L 3-4	Perry 2, Durie	30,621
32		8	(h)	Nottingham F	W 3-0	Perry 2, Durie	16,492
33		15	(a)	Chelsea	W 4-1	Mudie 2, Charnley, Perry	49,471
34		22	(h)	Birmingham C	W 4-2	Mudie, Charnley, Perry 2	11,549
35		29	(a)	Burnley	L 1-2	Perry	20,771
36	Apr	4	(h)	Preston NE	L 1-2	Mudie	29,029
37		5	(h)	Newcastle U	W 3-2	H.Kelly (pen), Charnley, Mudie	18,719
38		7	(a)	Preston NE	L 1-2	Charnley	32,626
39		12	(a)	Portsmouth	W 2-1	Perry, Durie	25,391
40		19	(h)	West Brom A	W 2-0	Charnley 2	17,327
41		23	(h)	Everton	L 0-1		12,981
42		26	(a)	Tottenham H	L 1-2	Charnley	37,632

FINAL LEAGUE POSITION: 7th in Division One

Appearances
Goals

FA Cup

3	Jan	5	(a)	West Ham U	L 1-5	H.Kelly (pen)	34,000

Appearances
Goals

Farm	Armfield	Wright	Kelly J	Gratrix	Fenton	Matthews	Taylor	Mudie	Durie	Perry	Smith	Kelly H	Charnley	Peterson	Garrett	Harris	Gregson	Martin	Snowdon	Hauser	
1	2	3	4	5	6	7	8	9	10	11											1
1	2	3	4	5	6	7	8	9	10	11											2
1	2	3	4	5	6	7	8		10	11	9										3
1	2	3	8	5	4	7				11		6	9	10							4
1	2		4	5	6	7	8	9		11				10	3						5
1	2		4	5	6	7	8	9		11				10	3						6
1	2		4	5	6	7		8		11			9	10	3						7
1		3	4	5			8	9		11		6		10	2	7					8
1		3	4	5		7	8	9		11		6		10	2						9
1	2		4	5		7	8		10	11		6	9		3						10
1	2		4	5		7	8	9	10			6		11	3						11
1	2		4	5		7	8	9	10	11		6			3						12
1	2		4	5		7	8	9	10	11		6			3						13
1	2		4	5		7		9	10	11		6		8	3						14
1	2	3	4	5		7		9	10	11		6		8							15
1	2		4	5		7		9	10	11		6		8	3						16
1	2	3	4	5		7		9	10	11		6		8							17
1	2	3	4	5		7		9	10	11		6		8							18
1	2	3	4	5				9	10	11		6		8		7					19
1	2	3	4	5				9	10	11		6		8		7					20
1	2	3	4	5		7		9	10	11		6		8							21
1	2	3	4	5		7	8	9	10	11		6									22
1	2	3		5	4	7	8	9		11		6		10							23
1	2	3		5	4	7	8	9		11		6		10							24
1	2	3		5	4			9	10	11		6		8		7					25
1		3	4	5		7		8	11			6	9	10	2						26
1		3	4	5		7	8		10	11		6	9		2						27
1		3	4	5		7	8		10	11		6	9		2						28
1		3	4	5		7		8	10	11		6	9		2						29
1		3	4	5		7		8	10	11		6	9		2						30
1		3	4	5		7		8	10	11		6	9		2						31
1	2	3	4	5		7		8	10	11		6	9								32
1		3	4	5		7		8	10	11		6	9		2						33
1		3	4	5				8	10	11		6	9	7	2						34
1		3	4	5				8	10	11		6	9	7	2						35
1	2	3	4	5				8	10	11		6	9				7				36
1	2	3	4	5				8	10	11		6	9				7				37
1	2	3	4	5				8	10	11		6	9				7				38
1		3	4	5				8	10	11		6	9	7	2						39
1		3	4	5		7			10	11		6	9	8	2						40
1			4	5					10	11		6	9	7				3	5	8	41
1			4	5				10		11		6	9	7	2			3		8	42
42	27	31	39	42	10	30	16	35	33	40	1	36	20	25	23	4	3	2	1	2	
							8	18	14	18		3	12	4		2					

1 own-goal

Farm	Armfield	Wright	Kelly J	Gratrix	Fenton	Matthews	Taylor	Mudie	Durie	Perry	Smith	Kelly H	Charnley	Peterson	Garrett	Harris	Gregson	Martin	Snowdon	Hauser	
1	2	3	4	5		7			10	11		6	9	8							3
1	1	1	1	1		1			1	1		1	1	1							
												1									

1958-59

Manager: Ron Suart

1	Aug	23	(a)	Tottenham H	W 3-2	Charnley 2, Mudie	57,043
2		25	(h)	Newcastle U	W 3-0	Gregson, Charnley, Durie	25,231
3		30	(h)	Manchester U	W 2-1	Perry, H.Kelly (pen)	36,719
4	Sep	3	(a)	Newcastle U	L 0-1		45,000
5		6	(a)	Wolves	L 0-2		46,219
6		8	(h)	Blackburn R	D 1-1	Mudie	31,752
7		13	(h)	Portsmouth	D 1-1	H.Kelly (pen)	26,035
8		15	(a)	Blackburn R	D 0-0		30,947
9		20	(a)	Aston Villa	D 1-1	Charnley	27,000
10		27	(h)	West Ham U	W 2-0	Snowdon, Mudie	32,626
11	Oct	4	(a)	Nottingham F	L 0-2		31,784
12		11	(h)	Burnley	D 1-1	Mudie	31,744
13		18	(a)	Bolton W	L 0-4		37,045
14		25	(h)	Everton	D 1-1	Perry	19,426
15	Nov	1	(a)	Leicester C	W 3-0	Durie, J.Kelly, Garrett	31,642
16		8	(h)	West Brom A	D 1-1	Mudie	18,666
17		15	(a)	Leeds U	D 1-1	Mudie	29,252
18		22	(h)	Manchester C	D 0-0		19,200
19		29	(a)	Arsenal	W 4-1	Charnley 2, Mudie, Durie	54,792
20	Dec	6	(h)	Luton T	W 3-0	Charnley, Mudie, Perry	14,140
21		13	(a)	Birmingham C	L 2-4	Charnley, Mudie	16,747
22		20	(h)	Tottenham H	D 0-0		12,939
23		25	(h)	Preston NE	W 4-2	Perry 3, J.Kelly	24,411
24		26	(a)	Preston NE	W 3-0	Charnley 2, J.Kelly	36,450
25	Jan	3	(a)	Manchester U	L 1-3	Fenton (pen)	61,720
26		31	(a)	Portsmouth	W 2-1	Charnley, Perry	23,556
27	Feb	7	(h)	Aston Villa	W 2-1	Durie, Charnley	13,704
28		16	(a)	West Ham U	L 0-1		28,332
29		21	(h)	Nottingham F	W 1-0	Durie	13,228
30	Mar	7	(h)	Bolton W	W 4-0	Charnley 2, Durie, Mudie	21,072
31		14	(a)	Everton	L 1-3	Charnley	34,562
32		17	(a)	Burnley	L 1-3	Peterson	15,887
33		21	(h)	Leicester C	W 2-1	Perry 2	11,479
34		27	(h)	Chelsea	W 5-0	Perry 2, Mudie 2, Charnley	19,887
35		28	(a)	West Brom A	L 1-3	Mudie	30,100
36		30	(a)	Chelsea	L 1-3	Durie	40,534
37	Apr	4	(h)	Leeds U	W 3-0	Charnley 3	14,089
38		11	(a)	Manchester C	W 2-0	Durie, Perry	28,118
39		13	(h)	Wolves	L 0-1		22,328
40		18	(h)	Arsenal	L 1-2	Mudie	17,118
41		20	(h)	Birmingham C	W 2-0	Charnley, Durie	12,260
42		28	(a)	Luton T	D 1-1	Fenton	17,720

FINAL LEAGUE POSITION: 8th in Division One

Appearances
Goals

FA Cup

3	Jan	10	(a)	Southampton	W 2-1	Charnley 2	29,265
4		24	(a)	Bristol C	D 1-1	Charnley	42,594
R		28	(h)	Bristol C	W 1-0	Durie	25,933
5	Feb	14	(h)	West Brom A	W 3-1	Charnley 2, Durie	30,415
6		28	(h)	Luton T	D 1-1	Charnley	30,634
R	Mar	4	(a)	Luton T	L 0-1		30,069

Appearances
Goals

Farm	Garrett	Wright	Kelly J	Gratrix	Kelly H	Matthews	Mudie	Charnley	Durie	Perry	Gregson	Armstrong	Snowdon	Barnes	Armfield	Hauser	Starkey	Fenton	Martin	Peterson	Fawcett	
1	2	3	4	5	6	7	8	9	10	11												1
1	2	3	4	5	6		8	9	10	11	7											2
1	2	3	4	5	6	7	8	9	10	11												3
1	2	3	4	5	6		8	10				7	9	11								4
1	2	3	4	5	6		8	10		11			9	7								5
1	2	3	4	5	6	7	8	9	10	11												6
1	2	3	4	5	6	7	8	9	10	11												7
1	3		4	5	6		8	9	10	11				7	2							8
1	3		4	5	6	7	8	9	10	11					2							9
1	3		4	5	6	7	8		10	11			9		2							10
1	3		4	5	6		8		10	11			9	7	2							11
1	3		4	5	6	7	8		10	11			9		2							12
1	3		4	5	6		8		11	7			9		2		10					13
1	3		4	5	6	7	8		10	11			9		2							14
1	3		8	5	6	7	9		10	11					2	4						15
1		3	8	5	6	7	9		10	11					2	4						16
1		3	4	5	6	7	8	9	10	11					2							17
1		3	4	5	6	7	8	9	10	11					2							18
1		3	4	5	6	7	8	9	10	11					2							19
1		3	4	5	6		8	9	10	11				7	2							20
1		3	4	5	6		8	9	10	11				7	2							21
1		3	4	5	6	7	8	9	10	11					2							22
1		3	10	5	6	7	8	9		11					2	4						23
1		3	8	5			7	9	10	11					2	4		6				24
1		3		5		7	8	9	10	11					2	4		6				25
1	3		8		6		7	9	10	11			5		2	4						26
1	3			5	6	7	8	9	10	11					2	4						27
1	3		8	5	6		7	9	10	11					2	4						28
1	3		8	5	6			9	10	11					2	4				7		29
1			10	5	6	7	8	9	11						2	4			3			30
1	3		10	5	6		8	9	11						2	4				7		31
1	3				6		8	9	10				5	11		4			2	7		32
1	3			5	6		8	9	10	11						4			2	7		33
1	3			5	6	7	8	9		11					2	4				10		34
1	3			5	6		8	9	10	11					2	4				7		35
1	3			5	6		8	9	10	11					2	4				7		36
1			6	2			8	9	10	11			5			4			3	7		37
1	3			5	6		8	9	10	11					2	4				7		38
1	3			5	6		8	9	10	11					2	4				7		39
1			6	5			8	9	10	11					2	4			3	7		40
1			6	5			8	9	10	11					2	4			3	7		41
1	3			5				9	10	11					2	4		6		8	7	42
42	28	17	32	40	36	19	40	35	38	38	1	1	10	7	32	22	1	3	6	13	1	
	1		3		2		14	20	9	12	1		1					2		1		

Farm	Garrett	Wright	Kelly J	Gratrix	Kelly H	Matthews	Mudie	Charnley	Durie	Perry	Gregson	Armstrong	Snowdon	Barnes	Armfield	Hauser	
1		3		5	6	7	8	9	10	11					2	4	3
1		3		5	6	7	8	9	10	11					2	4	4
1		3		5	6	7	8	9	10	11					2	4	R
1		3		5	6	7	8	9	10	11					2	4	5
1		3		5	6	7	8	9	10	11					2	4	6
1		3	10	5	6	7	8	9	11						2	4	R
6		6	1	6	6	6	6	6	6	5					6	6	
								6	2								

1959-60

Manager: Ron Suart

1	Aug	22	(h)	Bolton W	W 3-2	Charnley 2, Mudie	29,216
2		26	(a)	Luton T	W 1-0	Charnley	19,095
3		29	(a)	Fulham	L 0-1		42,611
4		31	(h)	Luton T	D 0-0		22,008
5	Sep	5	(h)	Nottingham F	L 0-1		25,987
6		9	(a)	Leicester C	D 1-1	Mudie	28,089
7		12	(a)	Sheffield W	L 0-5		29,328
8		14	(h)	Leicester C	D 3-3	J.Kelly, Mudie, Armfield	20,494
9		19	(h)	Wolves	W 3-1	Mudie 3	35,303
10		26	(a)	Arsenal	L 1-2	Mudie	47,473
11	Oct	3	(h)	Manchester C	L 1-3	Durie	33,226
12		10	(a)	Burnley	W 4-1	Kaye, Durie 3	26,620
13		17	(h)	Leeds U	D 3-3	Kaye, Durie, Peterson	22,301
14		24	(a)	West Ham U	L 0-1		32,455
15		31	(h)	Preston NE	L 0-2		27,796
16	Nov	7	(a)	West Brom A	L 1-2	Mudie	30,700
17		14	(h)	Newcastle U	W 2-0	Charnley, Kaye	15,667
18		21	(a)	Birmingham C	L 1-2	Charnley	24,783
19		28	(h)	Tottenham H	D 2-2	Charnley, Durie	17,085
20	Dec	5	(a)	Manchester U	L 1-3	Kaye	45,558
21		12	(h)	Chelsea	W 3-1	Durie, Charnley, Martin	12,410
22		19	(a)	Bolton W	W 3-0	Perry 2, Peterson	17,308
23		25	(a)	Blackburn R	L 0-1		27,600
24		26	(h)	Blackburn R	W 1-0	Charnley	30,071
25	Jan	2	(h)	Fulham	W 3-1	Perry, Kaye, Durie	17,046
26		16	(a)	Nottingham F	D 0-0		20,722
27		23	(h)	Sheffield W	L 0-2		16,343
28	Feb	6	(a)	Wolves	D 1-1	Charnley	36,347
29		13	(h)	Arsenal	W 2-1	Mudie, Perry	14,868
30		27	(h)	Manchester U	L 0-6		23,966
31	Mar	5	(a)	Leeds U	W 4-2	Durie, Charnley 3	23,127
32		9	(a)	Manchester C	W 3-2	Kaye, Charnley 2	19,653
33		12	(h)	West Ham U	W 3-2	Perry 2, Charnley	14,515
34		19	(a)	Chelsea	W 3-2	Charnley, Perry 2	40,262
35		26	(h)	West Ham A	W 2-0	Durie, Kaye	16,190
36	Apr	2	(a)	Newcastle U	D 1-1	Kaye (pen)	31,182
37		9	(h)	Birmingham C	L 0-1		13,595
38		15	(a)	Everton	L 0-4		65,719
39		16	(a)	Preston NE	L 1-4	Charnley	26,126
40		18	(h)	Everton	D 0-0		25,697
41		23	(h)	Burnley	D 1-1	Charnley	23,733
42		30	(a)	Tottenham H	L 1-4	Perry	49,823

FINAL LEAGUE POSITION: 11th in Division One

Appearances
Goals

FA Cup

3	Jan	9	(h)	Mansfield T	W 3-0	Durie 3	18,812
4		30	(a)	Blackburn R	D 1-1	Kaye	51,223
R	Feb	3	(h)	Blackburn R	L 0-3		31,975

Appearances
Goals

Farm	Armfield	Martin	Kelly J	Gratrix	Kelly H	Kaye	Mudie	Charnley	Peterson	Perry	Hauser	Durie	Garrett	Snowdon	Hill	Matthews	Waiters	Crawford	Fawcett	Green	Burrows	Smethurst	
1	2	3	4	5	6	7	8	9	10	11													1
1	2	3	4	5	6	7	8	9	10	11													2
1	2	3	4	5	6	7	8	9	10	11													3
1	2	3	4	5		7	8	9		11	6	10											4
1	2		4	5		7	8	9		11	6	10	3										5
1	2		4		6	7	8	9		11		10	3	5									6
1	2		4		6	7	8	9		11		10	3	5									7
1	2		4	5	6	7	9		8	11		10	3										8
1	2	3	4	5	6	7	9		8	11		10											9
1	2	3	4	5	6	7	9		8	11		10											10
1	2	3	4	5	6		9		8	11		10			7								11
1	2	3	4	5	6	11	9		8			10			7								12
1	2	3	4	5	6	11	9		8			10			7								13
1	2	3	4	5	6	11	9		8			10			7								14
1	2	3		5	6	11	9		8		4	10				7							15
1	2	3		5	6	11	8	9			4	10				7							16
1	2	3	6	5		10	8	9		11	4					7							17
1	2	3	6	5		10	8	9		11	4					7							18
1	2	3	6	5		7		9	8	11	4	10											19
1	2	3	6	5		7		9	8	11	4	10											20
1	2	3	6	5		7		9	8	11	4	10											21
1	2	3	6	5		7		9	8	11	4	10											22
1	2	3	6	5		7	10	9	8	11	4												23
	2	3	6	5		7		9	8	11	4	10					1						24
	2	3	6	5		7		9	8	11	4	10					1						25
1	2	3	6	5		7	8	9		11	4	10											26
1	2	3	6	5		7	8	9		11	4	10											27
	2	3		5	6		8	9			4					7	1	10	11				28
	2	3		5	6		8	9		11	4					7	1	10					29
	2	3		5	6		8	9		11	4					7	1	10					30
	2	3	4	5		8		9		11		6				7	1			10			31
	2	3	4	5		8		9		11		6				7	1			10			32
	2	3	4	5		8		9		11		6				7	1			10			33
	2	3	4	5		8		9		11		6				7	1			10			34
	2	3	4	5		8	10	9		11		6				7	1						35
	2	3	4	5		7	8	9		11		6					1			10			36
		3	4	5		8	10	9		11		6				7	1				2		37
	2	3	4	5	6	8		9		11						7	1			10			38
	2	3	4	5			8	9				6			7		1		11			10	39
	2	3	4	5		11	8	9				6			7		1			10			40
	2	3	4	5		8	10	9		11		6			7		1						41
	2	3	4	5		8	10	9		11		6				7	1						42
25	41	38	37	40	18	37	31	34	18	34	18	32	4	2	7	15	17	3	2	7	1	1	
	1	1	1			8	9	18	2	9		10											

Farm	Armfield	Martin	Kelly J	Gratrix	Kelly H	Kaye	Mudie	Charnley	Peterson	Perry	Hauser	Durie	
1	2	3	6	5		7		9	8	11	4	10	3
1	2	3		5	6	7	8	9		11	4	10	4
1	2	3		5	6	7	8	9		11	4	10	R
3	3	3	1	3	2	3	2	3	1	3	3	3	
						1						3	

1960-61

Manager: Ron Suart

No	Month	Date	Venue	Opponent	Result	Scorers	Attendance
1	Aug	20	(a)	Leicester C	D 1-1	Charnley	27,062
2		22	(h)	Tottenham H	L 1-3	Mudie	27,656
3		27	(h)	Aston Villa	W 5-3	Charnley 2, Kaye, Mudie, Durie	16,821
4		31	(a)	Tottenham H	L 1-3	Lea	46,684
5	Sep	3	(a)	Wolves	L 0-1		34,036
6		5	(h)	Everton	L 1-4	Charnley	24,945
7		10	(h)	Bolton W	L 0-1		17,166
8		14	(a)	Everton	L 0-1		46,923
9		17	(a)	West Ham U	D 3-3	Charnley 2, Mudie	23,521
10		24	(h)	Chelsea	L 1-4	Charnley	26,546
11	Oct	1	(a)	Preston NE	L 0-1		17,445
12		8	(h)	Fulham	L 2-5	Charnley 2	20,623
13		15	(a)	Sheffield W	L 0-4		31,424
14		22	(h)	Nottingham F	W 4-0	Charnley 2, Durie, Opp own-goal	15,733
15		29	(a)	Burnley	W 2-1	Durie, Perry	28,889
16	Nov	5	(h)	Cardiff C	W 6-1	Charnley 3, Perry, Durie, Parry	13,457
17		12	(a)	Newcastle U	L 3-4	Charnley, Parry, Durie	26,657
18		19	(h)	Arsenal	D 1-1	Charnley	15,417
19	Dec	3	(h)	Birmingham C	L 1-2	Charnley	11,720
20		10	(a)	West Brom A	L 1-3	Charnley	14,300
21		17	(h)	Leicester C	W 5-1	Charnley 2, Mudie, J.Kelly, Perry	8,752
22		24	(h)	Blackburn R	W 2-0	Perry, Charnley (pen)	19,379
23		27	(a)	Blackburn R	L 0-2		18,200
24		31	(a)	Aston Villa	D 2-2	Parry 2	30,000
25	Jan	21	(a)	Bolton W	L 1-3	Charnley (pen)	15,909
26	Feb	4	(h)	West Ham U	W 3-0	Crawford, Parry, Charnley	9,947
27		11	(a)	Chelsea	D 2-2	Crawford, Parry	21,993
28		18	(h)	Preston NE	L 0-1		20,541
29		25	(a)	Fulham	L 3-4	Charnley, Hauser 2	19,342
30	Mar	4	(h)	Wolves	W 5-2	Perry 2, Parry, Durie, Charnley	15,312
31		11	(a)	Nottingham F	D 0-0		29,646
32		15	(h)	Sheffield W	L 0-1		17,738
33		21	(h)	Burnley	D 0-0		19,391
34		24	(a)	Cardiff C	W 2-0	Charnley, Horne	20,000
35		31	(h)	Manchester U	W 2-0	Peterson, Opp own-goal	30,885
36	Apr	1	(h)	West Brom A	L 0-1		20,809
37		3	(a)	Manchester U	L 0-2		39,169
38		8	(a)	Arsenal	L 0-1		36,301
39		15	(h)	Newcastle U	W 2-1	Parry, Charnley	19,381
40		19	(a)	Manchester C	D 1-1	Crawford	28,269
41		22	(a)	Birmingham C	W 2-0	Peterson, Crawford	17,834
42		29	(h)	Manchester C	D 3-3	Hauser 2, Opp own-goal	20,838

FINAL LEAGUE POSITION: 20th in Division One

Appearances
Goals

FA Cup

Round	Month	Date	Venue	Opponent	Result	Scorers	Attendance
3	Jan	7	(a)	Scunthorpe U	L 2-6	Mudie, Charnley	19,303

Appearances
Goals

League Cup

Round	Month	Date	Venue	Opponent	Result	Scorers	Attendance
2	Sep	28	(a)	Leeds U	D 0-0		13,064
R	Oct	5	(h)	Leeds U	L 1-3*	Durie	9,614

*After extra-time

Appearances
Goals

Waiters	Armfield	Martin	Kelly J	Gratrix	Durie	Matthews	Lea	Charnley	Kaye	Campbell	Mudie	Hill	Salt	Crawford	James	Garrett	Hauser	Green	Parry	Perry	West	Chi Doy	Peterson	Horne	Singleton	
1	2	3	4	5	6	7	8	9	10	11																1
1	2	3	4	5	6	7		9	10	11	8															2
1	2	3	4	5	6	7	8	9	11		10															3
1	2	3	4	5	6		8	9	11		10	7														4
1	2	3	4	5	6		8	9	11		10	7														5
1	2	3	4	5	6	7	8	9		11	10															6
1	2	3	4	5	10		8	9	11			7	6													7
1	2	3	4	5				9	7	11	8		6	10												8
1	2	3	4	5		7		9	8	11	10		6													9
1	2	3	4	5	11	7		9	8		10		6													10
1	2	3	4		10		8		7	11	9		6		5											11
1		3	6		10			9		11		7			5	2	4	8								12
1	2		4	5	11	7		9	8		10		6			3										13
1	2		4	5	8	7		9					6			3			10	11						14
1	2		4	5	8	7		9					6			3			10	11						15
1	2		4	5	8	7		9					6			3			10	11						16
1	2		4	5	8	7		9		11			6			3			10							17
1	2		4	5	8	7		9					6			3			10	11						18
1	2		4	5	8	7		9					6			3			10	11						19
1	2		4		8	7		9					6		5	3			10	11						20
1	2		4	5		7		9			8		6			3			10	11						21
1	2		4	5		7		9			8		6			3			10	11						22
1	2		4	5		7		9			8		6			3			10	11						23
1	2		4	5	11	7		9			8		6			3			10							24
	2		4	5	6			9			8	7				3			10		1	11				25
	2		8	5	6			9		7				10		3	4		11		1					26
	2			5	6			9		7				10		3	4		11		1		8			27
	2			5	6			9		7				10		3	4		11		1		8			28
	2			5	6	7		9								3	4		10	11	1		8			29
	2			5	6	7		9								3	4		10	11	1		8			30
	2			5	6	7		9								3	4		10	11	1		8			31
	2			5	6	7		9								3	4		10		1		8	11		32
	2			5	6	7		9								3	4		10		1		8	11		33
	2			5	6			9				7				3	4		10		1		8	11		34
	2	3		5				9				7	6				4		10		1		8	11		35
	2	3		5	6			9				7					4		10		1		8	11		36
	2			5	6			9				7				3	4		10	11	1		8			37
	2	3		5	6	7		9									4		10		1		8	11		38
		3		5	6	7		9						8		2	4		10		1		11			39
	2			5	6	7		9						8		3	4		10		1		11			40
	2	3		5	6	7		9						8			4		10		1		11			41
	2	3		5	6			9				7		8			4		10		1		11			42
24	40	18	26	39	36	27	7	41	11	11	15	10	18	8	3	26	18	1	29	13	18	1	16	6		
			1		6		1	27	1		4			4			4		8	6			2	1		
																										3 own-goals
	2		4	5		7		9			8		6			3			10	11	1					3
	1		1	1		1		1			1		1			1			1	1	1					
								1			1															
1	2	3	4		10		8		7	11	9		6		5											2
1		3	4	9	10					11		7	6		5								8		2	R
2	1	2	2	1	2		1		1	2	1	1	2		2								1		1	
					1																					

1961-62

Manager: Ron Suart

1	Aug	19	(h)	Tottenham H	L 1-2	Charnley	29,023
2		21	(h)	Blackburn R	W 2-1	Charnley (pen), Peterson	21,680
3		26	(a)	Cardiff C	L 2-3	Horne, Charnley	22,700
4		28	(a)	Blackburn R	D 1-1	Horne	22,400
5	Sep	2	(h)	Manchester U	L 2-3	Charnley 2 (1 pen)	28,156
6		4	(h)	West Ham U	W 2-0	Horne, Hill	19,838
7		9	(a)	Wolves	D 2-2	Charnley 2 (1 pen)	22,669
8		16	(h)	Nottingham F	L 1-3	Charnley	23,737
9		18	(a)	West Ham U	D 2-2	Hauser, Parry	25,528
10		23	(a)	Aston Villa	L 0-5		31,700
11		30	(h)	Chelsea	W 4-0	Charnley 3, Peterson	24,191
12	Oct	7	(a)	Arsenal	L 0-3		41,166
13		14	(h)	Bolton W	W 2-1	Horne, Peterson	22,062
14		21	(a)	Leicester C	W 2-0	Charnley 2 (1 pen)	17,424
15		28	(h)	Ipswich T	D 1-1	Parry	19,773
16	Nov	4	(a)	Birmingham C	D 1-1	Charnley	19,007
17		11	(h)	Everton	D 1-1	Durie	23,026
18		18	(a)	Fulham	W 1-0	Parry	18,592
19		25	(h)	Sheffield W	L 1-3	Chi Doy	16,569
20	Dec	2	(a)	Manchester C	W 4-2	Charnley 2, Horne, Peterson	15,971
21		9	(h)	West Brom A	D 2-2	Crawford, Peterson	13,076
22		16	(a)	Tottenham H	L 2-5	Charnley, Opp own-goal	42,734
23		23	(h)	Cardiff C	W 3-0	Parry 2, Charnley	13,961
24		26	(a)	Sheffield U	L 1-2	Peterson	22,757
25	Jan	13	(a)	Manchester U	W 1-0	Hauser	27,082
26		20	(h)	Wolves	W 7-2	Charnley 4, Hauser, Perry, Crawford	12,852
27	Feb	3	(a)	Nottingham F	W 4-3	Charnley, Parry 2, Perry	17,828
28		10	(h)	Aston Villa	L 1-2	Parry	13,039
29		16	(a)	Chelsea	L 0-1		24,276
30		24	(h)	Arsenal	L 0-1		13,728
31	Mar	3	(a)	Bolton W	D 0-0		14,831
32		10	(h)	Leicester C	W 2-1	Charnley, Hauser	10,952
33		17	(a)	Ipswich T	D 1-1	Charnley	22,521
34		24	(h)	Birmingham C	W 1-0	Hauser	11,854
35		30	(a)	Everton	D 2-2	Peterson, Charnley	38,302
36	Apr	3	(h)	Sheffield U	L 2-4	Parry, Hauser	11,199
37		7	(h)	Fulham	W 2-1	Charnley, Parry	10,641
38		14	(a)	Sheffield W	L 2-3	Green, Parry	18,090
39		20	(a)	Burnley	L 0-2		34,132
40		21	(h)	Manchester C	W 3-1	Charnley, Green, Parry	19,954
41		23	(h)	Burnley	D 1-1	Charnley	31,660
42		28	(a)	West Brom A	L 1-7	Charnley	17,462

FINAL LEAGUE POSITION: 13th in Division One

Appearances
Goals

FA Cup

3	Jan	6	(h)	West Brom A	D 0-0		19,250
R		10	(a)	West Brom A	L 1-2	Hauser	27,061

Appearances
Goals

League Cup

1	Sep	13	(h)	Port Vale	W 2-1	Charnley, Parry	10,494
2	Oct	4	(a)	Leyton O	D 1-1	Oates	9,910
R		30	(h)	Leyton O	W 5-1	Parry 2, Charnley 3	6,098
3	Nov	5	(a)	Workington	W 1-0	Green	10,035
4	Feb	6	(h)	Sheffield U	D 0-0		11,127
R	Mar	27	(a)	Sheffield U	W 2-0	Parry, Charnley	12,895
SF	Apr	11	(a)	Norwich C	L 1-4	Peterson	19,231
		16	(h)	Norwich C	W 2-0	Horne, Charnley	9,124

Appearances
Goals

Match	West	Armfield	Martin	Hauser	Gratrix	Durie	Horne	Peterson	Charnley	Parry	Perry	Hill	Green	Oates	Crawford	Matthews	Waiters	Thompson	Chi Doy	Cranston	Harvey	Halsall	James	Napier
1	1	2	3	4	5	6	7	8	9	10	11													
2	1	2	3	4	5	6	11	8	9	10		7												
3	1	2	3	4	5	6	11	8	9	10		7												
4	1	2	3	4	5	6	11	7	9	10			8											
5	1	2	3	4	5	6	11	7	9	10			8											
6	1	2	3	4	5	6	11	8	9	10		7												
7	1	2	3	4	5	6	11	8	9	10		7												
8	1	2	3	4	5	6		7	9	10			8	11										
9	1	2	3	4	5	6			9	10	11	7			8									
10	1	2	3	4	5	6			9	10	11	7			8									
11	1	2	3	4	5	6		8	9	10				11		7								
12	1	2	3	4	5	6		8	9	10				11		7								
13			3		5	6	11	8	9	10		7			4		1	2						
14			3		5	6	11	8	9	10		7			4		1	2						
15		2	3		5	6	11	8	9	10		7			4		1							
16			3		5	6	11	8	9	10		7			4		1	2						
17		9	3		5	6	11	8		10		7			4		1	2						
18		2	3		5	6	11		9	10		7	8		4		1							
19		2	3		5	6	11		9	10		7			4		1		8					
20		2	3		5	6	11	8	9	10		7			4		1							
21		2	3		5	6	11	8	9	10		7			4		1							
22		2	3		5	6	11	8	9	10		7			4		1							
23		2	3		5	6	11	8	9	10		7			4		1							
24		2	3		5	6	11	8	9	10		7			4		1							
25		2	3	8	5	6			9	10	11	7			4		1							
26		2	3	8	5				9	10	11	7			4		1			6				
27		2	3	8	5	6			9	10	11	7			4		1							
28		2	3	8	5	6			9	10	11	7			4		1							
29		2		8	5	6			9	10	11	7			4		1	3						
30		2	3		5	10		8	9		11	7			4		1			6				
31		2	3	8	5	6			9	10	11	7			4		1							
32		2	3	8	5	6	11		9	10		7			4		1							
33		2	3	8	5	6	11		9	10		7			4						1			
34		2	3	8	5	6	11		9	10		7			4						1			
35		2	3	8	5	6		10	9	11		7			4						1			
36			3	8	5	6		10	9	11		7			4			2			1			
37		2	3		5	6	11	8	9	10		7			4						1			
38			3		5	6	11		9	10		7	8		4						1		5	
39		2	3		5		11		9	10		7	8		4					6	1			
40		2	3		5	6	11		9	10		7	8		4							1		
41		2	3		5	6			9	10		7	8	11	4							1		
42		2	3		5	6	11		9	10		7	8		4						1			
	12	37	41	23	42	40	27	24	41	41	10	36	9	4	32	2	20	6	1	3	8	2	1	
				6		1	5	7	30	12	2	1	2		2				1					

1 own-goal

Round	West	Armfield	Martin	Hauser	Gratrix	Durie	Horne	Peterson	Charnley	Parry	Perry	Hill	Green	Oates	Crawford	Matthews	Waiters	Thompson	Chi Doy	Cranston	Harvey	Halsall	James	Napier
3		2	3		5	6	11	8	9	10		7			4		1							
R		2	3	8	5	6			9	10	11	7			4		1							
		2	2	1	2	2	1	1	2	2	1	2			2		2							
				1																				

Round	West	Armfield	Martin	Hauser	Gratrix	Durie	Horne	Peterson	Charnley	Parry	Perry	Hill	Green	Oates	Crawford	Matthews	Waiters	Thompson	Chi Doy	Cranston	Harvey	Halsall	James	Napier
1	1	2	3	4	5	6		7	9	10	11				8									
2	1	2	3	4	5	6	7	8	9	10				11										
R			3		5	6	11	8	9	10		7			4		1	2						
3		2	3		5	6	11			10		7	8		4		1							9
4		2	3	8	5	6			9	10	11	7			4		1							
R		2	3	8	5	6	11		9	10		7			4						1			
SF			3		5	6	11	8	9	10		7			4			2			1			
		2	3		5	6	11		9	10		7	8		4						1			
	2	6	8	4	8	8	6	4	7	8	2	6	2	1	7		3	2			3			1
							1	1	6	4			1	1										

1962-63

Manager: Ron Suart

No	Month	Day	Venue	Opponents	Result	Score	Scorers	Attendance
1	Aug	18	(a)	Liverpool	W	2-1	Charnley, Horne	51,207
2		20	(h)	Ipswich T	W	1-0	Horne	23,305
3		25	(h)	Wolves	L	0-2		23,823
4		28	(a)	Ipswich T	L	2-5	Durie, Charnley (pen)	21,079
5	Sep	1	(a)	Aston Villa	D	1-1	Horne	35,006
6		3	(h)	Nottingham F	W	2-1	Horne, Green	19,737
7		8	(h)	Tottenham H	L	1-2	Charnley	31,773
8		11	(a)	Nottingham F	L	0-2		19,032
9		14	(a)	West Ham U	D	2-2	McPhee 2	24,745
10		22	(h)	Manchester C	D	2-2	Charnley 2 (1 pen)	29,461
11		29	(a)	Burnley	L	0-2		28,345
12	Oct	6	(h)	Manchester U	D	2-2	McPhee, Charnley	33,242
13		13	(a)	Leyton O	W	2-0	Parry 2	17,156
14		20	(h)	Fulham	D	0-0		17,115
15		27	(a)	Sheffield W	D	0-0		20,227
16	Nov	3	(h)	West Brom A	L	0-2		12,528
17		10	(a)	Everton	L	0-5		39,317
18		17	(h)	Bolton W	W	3-1	Durie, Charnley, Quinn	12,272
19		24	(a)	Leicester C	D	0-0		21,832
20	Dec	1	(h)	Birmingham C	D	1-1	Durie	12,955
21		8	(a)	Arsenal	L	0-2		23,767
22		15	(h)	Liverpool	L	1-2	Quinn	16,271
23	Jan	19	(a)	Tottenham H	L	0-2		25,710
24	Feb	23	(a)	Manchester U	D	1-1	Charnley (pen)	43,121
25	Mar	2	(h)	Leyton O	W	3-2	Quinn (pen), McPhee, Opp own-goal	11,732
26		9	(a)	Fulham	L	0-2		8,954
27		16	(h)	Sheffield W	L	2-3	Charnley 2	10,141
28		20	(h)	Burnley	D	0-0		16,445
29		23	(a)	West Brom A	W	2-1	McPhee, Parry	14,829
30		25	(a)	Blackburn R	D	3-3	Parry, Crawford, Charnley	9,900
31		29	(h)	Aston Villa	W	4-0	Charnley 3, Parry	10,690
32	Apr	6	(a)	Bolton W	L	0-3		14,486
33		8	(h)	Leicester C	D	1-1	Charnley (pen)	16,765
34		13	(h)	Everton	L	1-2	Quinn	27,842
35		15	(h)	Sheffield U	W	3-1	Charnley, Quinn 2	16,746
36		16	(a)	Sheffield U	D	0-0		21,637
37		20	(a)	Birmingham C	W	6-3	Crawford, Durie, Charnley 3, Opp own-goal	15,396
38		23	(h)	Blackburn R	W	4-1	Charnley, McPhee, Quinn 2	16,446
39		27	(h)	Arsenal	W	3-2	Charnley 2, Lea	13,864
40	May	4	(a)	Manchester C	W	3-0	Crawford 2, Lea	19,062
41		9	(a)	Wolves	L	0-2		14,889
42		13	(h)	West Ham U	D	0-0		12,434
FINAL LEAGUE POSITION: 13th in Division One								Appearances
								Goals

FA Cup

Round	Month	Day	Venue	Opponents	Result	Score	Scorers	Attendance
3	Mar	4	(a)	Norwich C	D	1-1	McPhee	26,002
R		6	(h)	Norwich C	L	1-3	Quinn	15,559
								Appearances
								Goals

League Cup

Round	Month	Day	Venue	Opponents	Result	Score	Scorers	Attendance
2	Sep	24	(a)	Manchester C	D	0-0		12,064
R	Oct	8	(h)	Manchester C	D	3-3	Horne, Watt, Parry	10,508
2R		15	(a)	Manchester C	L	2-4	McPhee 2	12,237
								Appearances
								Goals

Waiters	Armfield	Martin	Crawford	Gratrix	Durie	Ball	Green	Charnley	Parry	Horne	James	Hill	McPhee	Watt	Thompson	Oates	Cranston	Lea	Quinn	Napier	Turner	Prentis	
1	2	3	4	5	6	7	8	9	10	11													1
1	2	3	4	5	6	7	8	9	10	11													2
1	2	3	4	5	6	7	8	9	10	11													3
1	2	3	4		6	7	8	9	10	11	5												4
1	2	3	4		6		8	9		11	5	7	10										5
1	2	3	4		6		8	9		11	5	7	10										6
1	2	3	4		6		8	9		11	5	7	10										7
1	2	3	4		6	7	8	9		11	5		10										8
1	2	3	4		6		8	9		11	5		10	7									9
1	2	3	4		6		8	9		11	5	7	10										10
1	2	3	4	5	6			9	10	11		7	8										11
1	2	3	4	5	6			9	10	11			8	7									12
1	2	3	4	5	6			9	10	11			8	7									13
1		3	4	5	6			9	10	11			8	7	2								14
1	2	3	4	5	6			9	10			7	8			11							15
1	2	3	4	5				9	10	11			8	7			6						16
1	2	3	4	5	10		8	9	11								6	7					17
1	2	3	4	5	10			9	11				6					7	8				18
1	2	3	4	5	10			9	11				6					7	8				19
1	2	3	4	5	10			9		11			6					7	8				20
1	2	3	4	5	10			9	11			7	6						8				21
1	2	3	10	5	6			9	11			7	4						8				22
1	2	3		5	6			10		11		7	4						8	9			23
1	2	3	4	5	6				11				10					7	8	9			24
1	2	3		5	6		10	9	11				4					7	8				25
1	2	3	10	5	6			9	11				4					7	8				26
1	2	3	10	5	6			9	11				4					7	8				27
1	2	3	10	5	6			9	11				4					7	8				28
1	2	3	10	5	6			9	11				4					7	8				29
1	2	3	10	5	6			9	11				4					7	8				30
1	2	3	10	5	6			9	11				4					7	8				31
1		3	10	5	6			9	11				4		2			7	8				32
1	2	3	10	5	6			9	11				4					7	8				33
1	2	3	10	5	6			9	11				4					7	8				34
1	2	3	10	5	6			9	11				4					7	8				35
1	2	3	10	5	6			9	11				4					7	8				36
1	2	3	10	5	6			9	11				4					7	8				37
1	2	3	10	5	6			9	11				4					7	8				38
1	2	3	10	5	6			9	11				4					7	8				39
1	2	3	10	5	6			9	11				4					7	8				40
1		3	10	5				9	11				4		2		6	7	8				41
42	39	42	40	35	40	5	12	41	34	17	7	9	37	5	3	1	3	23	25	2			42
			4		4		1	22	5	4			6					2	8				

2 own-goals

Waiters	Armfield	Martin	Crawford	Gratrix	Durie	Ball	Green	Charnley	Parry	Horne	James	Hill	McPhee	Watt	Thompson	Oates	Cranston	Lea	Quinn	Napier	Turner	Prentis	
1	2	3	4	5	6			9	11				10					7	8				3
1	2	3		5	6			9	11				10					7	8		4		R
2	2	2	1	2	2			2	2				2					2	2		1		
													1						1				

Waiters	Armfield	Martin	Crawford	Gratrix	Durie	Ball	Green	Charnley	Parry	Horne	James	Hill	McPhee	Watt	Thompson	Oates	Cranston	Lea	Quinn	Napier	Turner	Prentis	
1	2	3	4	5	6			9		11		7	10					8					2
1	2	3	4	5	6			9	10	11			8	7									R
1		3	4	5	6			9	10	11			8	7								2	2R
3	2	3	3	3	3			3	2	3		1	3	2				1				1	
									1	1			2	1									

1963-64

Manager: Ron Suart

1	Aug	24	(h)	Sheffield U	D 2-2	Quinn, Parry	18,037
2		26	(a)	West Ham U	L 1-3	Charnley	25,533
3		31	(a)	Liverpool	W 2-1	McPhee, Charnley	45,767
4	Sep	2	(h)	West Ham U	L 0-1		18,407
5		7	(h)	Aston Villa	L 0-4		16,885
6		11	(a)	Manchester U	L 0-3		47,363
7		14	(a)	Tottenham H	L 1-6	Charnley	38,138
8		16	(h)	Manchester U	W 1-0	Charnley	29,806
9		21	(h)	Wolves	L 1-2	Ball	25,231
10		28	(a)	Stoke C	W 2-1	Ball, Durie	27,377
11		30	(h)	Fulham	W 1-0	Oates	13,757
12	Oct	5	(h)	Nottingham F	W 1-0	Durie	22,397
13		12	(a)	Burnley	L 0-1		20,025
14		19	(h)	Ipswich T	D 2-2	Parry, Charnley	14,666
15		26	(a)	Bolton W	D 1-1	Charnley	14,359
16	Nov	2	(h)	Everton	D 1-1	Charnley	24,834
17		9	(a)	Birmingham C	L 2-3	Crawford, Ball	17,536
18		16	(h)	West Brom A	W 1-0	Oates	11,047
19		23	(a)	Arsenal	L 3-5	McPhee, Ball, Charnley	33,871
20		30	(h)	Leicester C	D 3-3	Ball, Charnley 2	10,534
21	Dec	7	(a)	Sheffield W	L 0-1		20,156
22		14	(a)	Sheffield U	L 0-1		13,868
23		21	(h)	Liverpool	L 0-1		13,254
24		26	(h)	Chelsea	L 1-5	Durie	17,563
25		28	(a)	Chelsea	L 0-1		34,380
26	Jan	11	(a)	Aston Villa	L 1-3	Ball	14,191
27		18	(h)	Tottenham H	L 0-2		13,955
28	Feb	1	(a)	Wolves	D 1-1	Horne	16,345
29		8	(h)	Stoke C	W 1-0	Oates	14,452
30		15	(a)	Nottingham F	W 1-0	Oates	17,008
31		22	(h)	Burnley	D 1-1	Green	12,938
32		29	(a)	Fulham	D 1-1	Oates	12,199
33	Mar	7	(h)	Bolton W	W 2-0	McPhee, Ball	12,242
34		13	(a)	West Brom A	L 1-2	Green	22,459
35		20	(h)	Birmingham C	W 3-0	McPhee, Oates 2	10,203
36		27	(a)	Blackburn R	W 2-1	Horne 2	23,039
37		28	(a)	Everton	L 1-3	Horne	49,504
38		30	(h)	Blackburn R	W 3-2	Ball 2, Rowe	20,165
39	Apr	4	(h)	Arsenal	L 0-1		14,067
40		11	(a)	Leicester C	W 3-2	Ball 2, Oates	15,189
41		18	(h)	Sheffield W	D 2-2	McPhee, Horne	12,908
42		25	(a)	Ipswich T	L 3-4	Ball 2, Lea	11,187
FINAL LEAGUE POSITION: 18th in Division One							Appearances
							Goals

FA Cup

3	Jan	4	(a)	West Brom A	D 2-2	Charnley, Opp own-goal	22,459
R		8	(h)	West Brom A	L 0-1		21,241
							Appearances
							Goals

League Cup

2	Sep	25	(h)	Charlton A	W 7-1	Charnley 4, Durie, Oates, Ball	6,771
3	Oct	30	(a)	Norwich C	L 0-1		15,326
							Appearances
							Goals

	Waiters	Armfield	Martin	McPhee	Gratrix	Cranston	Lea	Quinn	Charnley	Crawford	Parry	Horne	Durie	Green	Harvey	Hill	Ball	Oates	Cooper	Thompson	Fisher	James	Turner	Rowe
1	1	2	3	4	5	6	7	8	9	10	11													
2	1	2	3	4	5	6	7	8	9		10	11												
3	1	2	3	4	5		7	8	9		10	11	6											
4	1	2	3	4	5		7	8	9		10	11	6											
5	1	2	3	4	5		7	8	9		10	11	6											
6	1	2	3	10	5		7	8	9		11		6	4										
7		2	3	10	5			8	9		11		6	4	1	7								
8		2	3		5	6		10	9	4		7			1		8	11						
9		2	3		5	6		10	9	4		7			1		8	11						
10	1	2	3		5	6	7		9	4			10				8	11						
11	1	2	3		5	6	7		9	4			10				8	11						
12	1	2	3		5	6	7			4			10				8	11	9					
13	1		3		5	6	7		9	4			10				8	11		2				
14	1	2	3		5	6	7		9	4	11		10				8							
15	1	2	3		5	6			9	4	11					7	8				10			
16	1	2	3	10		6	7		9	4	11						8					5		
17	1	2	3	10		6	7		9	4							8	11				5		
18	1	2		10		6			9					4		7	8	11		3		5		
19	1			10	2	6			9		11			4		7	8			3		5		
20	1	2	3	10		6	7		9		11			4			8					5		
21	1	2	3	10		6	7		9		11			4			8					5		
22	1	2	3			6			9		10			4			7	11				5	8	
23	1		3			6			9	4	10					7	8	11		2		5		
24	1		3			6				8	10		9	4		7		11		2		5		
25	1		3	4	5	6			9		10	11	8			7				2				
26	1	2	3	4	5	6			9		10	11				7	8							
27	1	2	3	4	5	6			9		10	11				7	8							
28	1	2	3		5		7		9			11		6			8	10						6
29	1	2	3	4	5		7		9			11		6			8	10						
30	1	2	3	4	5		7					11		6			8	10	9					
31	1	2	3	4	5		7					11		6			8	10	9					
32	1	2	3	8	5		7					11		6				10	9					4
33	1	2	3	9	5		7					11		6			8	10						4
34	1	2	3	9	5		7					11		6			8	10						4
35	1	2	3	9	5		7					11		6			8	10						4
36	1	2	3	9	5		7					11		6			8	10						4
37	1	2	3	8	5		7		9		10	11		6										4
38	1		3	9	5		7					11		6			8	10		2				4
39	1	2	3	9	5		7			4		11		6			8	10						
40	1		3	9	5		7					11		6			8	10		2				4
41	1	2	3	9	5		7					11		6			8	10						4
42	1	2	3	9	5		7					11		6			8	10						4
	39	35	40	30	34	22	30	9	28	14	20	24	12	23	3	9	31	25	4	8	1	9	1	11
				5			1	1	10	1	2	5	3	2			13	8						1

	Waiters	Armfield	Martin	McPhee	Gratrix	Cranston	Lea	Quinn	Charnley	Crawford	Parry	Horne	Durie	Green	Harvey	Hill	Ball	Oates	Cooper	Thompson	Fisher	James	Turner	Rowe
3	1	2	3	4	5	6			9		10	11				7	8							
R	1	2	3	4	5	6			9		10	11				7	8							
	2	2	2	2	2	2			2		2	2				2	2							
									1															

1 own-goal

	Waiters	Armfield	Martin	McPhee	Gratrix	Cranston	Lea	Quinn	Charnley	Crawford	Parry	Horne	Durie	Green	Harvey	Hill	Ball	Oates	Cooper	Thompson	Fisher	James	Turner	Rowe
2		2	3		5	6	7		9	4			10		1		8	11						
3	1	2	3			6			9	4	11		10	8		7						5		
	1	2	2		1	2	1		2	2	1		2	1	1	1	1	1				1		
									4				1				1	1						

1964-65

Manager: Ron Suart

1	Aug	22	(a)	Burnley	D 2-2	Oates 2	15,773
2		24	(h)	Blackburn R	W 4-2	Charnley, Lea, Rowe, Opp own-goal	22,381
3		29	(h)	Sheffield W	W 1-0	Ball	18,461
4	Sep	2	(a)	Blackburn R	L 1-4	Charnley	20,315
5		5	(a)	Liverpool	D 2-2	Charnley 2	45,646
6		7	(h)	Leeds U	W 4-0	Oates, Charnley 2, Ball	26,310
7		12	(h)	Aston Villa	W 3-1	Oates, Charnley, Ball	22,795
8		16	(a)	Leeds U	L 0-3		35,973
9		19	(a)	Wolves	W 2-1	Charnley, Oates	22,260
10		26	(h)	Sunderland	W 3-1	Lea, Ball (pen), Oates	31,291
11		28	(h)	Tottenham H	D 1-1	Oates	26,436
12	Oct	5	(a)	Leicester C	L 2-3	Oates, Charnley	18,727
13		10	(a)	Sheffield U	W 3-1	Horne, Ball, Charnley	20,839
14		17	(h)	Everton	D 1-1	Charnley	31,855
15		24	(a)	Birmingham C	L 0-3		15,800
16		31	(h)	West Ham U	L 1-2	Green	14,383
17	Nov	7	(a)	West Brom A	W 3-1	Rowe, Ball 2	17,500
18		14	(h)	Manchester U	L 1-2	Oates	31,129
19		21	(a)	Fulham	D 3-3	Ball 3	16,587
20		28	(h)	Nottingham F	L 0-2		14,047
21	Dec	5	(a)	Stoke C	L 2-4	Rowe, Oates	17,360
22		12	(h)	Burnley	L 2-4	Oates 2	11,000
23		19	(a)	Sheffield W	L 1-4	McPhee	16,172
24		26	(a)	Chelsea	L 0-2		30,581
25	Jan	2	(h)	Liverpool	L 2-3	Charnley 2	21,363
26		16	(a)	Aston Villa	L 2-3	Green, Charnley	17,403
27		23	(h)	Wolves	D 1-1	Horne	11,992
28	Feb	6	(a)	Sunderland	L 0-2		36,759
29		13	(h)	Leicester C	D 1-1	Charnley	10,367
30		20	(h)	Sheffield U	D 2-2	Charnley, Moir	10,160
31		27	(a)	Everton	D 0-0		35,267
32	Mar	6	(h)	Birmingham C	W 3-1	Armfield, Rowe, Moir	11,464
33		13	(a)	Tottenham H	L 1-4	Moir	26,295
34		20	(h)	West Brom A	W 3-0	Robson, Waddell 2	11,168
35		22	(a)	Manchester U	L 0-2		42,318
36	Apr	3	(h)	Fulham	W 3-0	Waddell, Armfield, Robson	11,972
37		10	(a)	Nottingham F	L 0-2		16,595
38		16	(h)	Arsenal	D 1-1	Ball (pen)	18,620
39		17	(h)	Stoke C	D 1-1	Charnley	18,263
40		19	(a)	Arsenal	L 1-3	Charnley	17,063
41		23	(a)	West Ham U	L 1-2	Moir	22,702
42		26	(h)	Chelsea	W 3-2	Charnley 3	16,008

FINAL LEAGUE POSITION: 17th in Division One

Appearances
Goals

FA Cup

3	Jan	11	(a)	Stoke C	L 1-4	Ball	38,651

Appearances
Goals

League Cup

2	Sep	23	(h)	Newcastle U	W 3-0	Ball (pen), Horne (pen), Lea	13,670
3	Oct	26	(a)	Sunderland	L 1-4	Charnley	20,540

Appearances
Goals

Waiters	Armfield	Thompson	Rowe	Gratrix	Green	Lea	Ball	Charnley	Oates	Horne	Prentis	Turner	James	Cranston	Parry	Fisher	McPhee	Crawford	Loyden	Moir	Robson	Waddell	
1	2	3	4	5	6	7	8	9	10	11													1
1	2	3	4	5	6	7	8	9	10	11													2
1		3	4	5	6	7	8	9	10	11	2												3
1	2	3		5	6	7	8	9	10	11		4											4
1	2	3			6	7	8	9	10				5	4	11								5
1	2	3			6	7	8	9	10				5	4	11								6
1	2	3			6	7	8	9	10				5	4	11								7
1	2	3			6	7	8	9	10				5	4	11								8
1	2	3	4		6	7	8	9	10	11			5										9
1	2	3	4		6	7	8	9	10	11			5										10
1	2	3	4		6	7	8	9	10	11			5										11
1	2	3	4		6	7	8	9	10	11			5										12
1	2	3	4		6	7	8	9	10	11			5										13
1	2	3	4		6	7	8	9	10	11			5										14
1	2	3			6	7	8	9	10	11			5	4									15
1	2	3	4		6		8	9	7	11			5			10							16
1	2	3	4		6		8	9	10	11			5				7						17
1	2	3	5		6	7	8	9	10	11							4						18
1	2	3	5		6	7	8	9	10	11							4						19
1	2	3	5		6	7	8	9	10	11							4						20
1	2	3	4		6	7	8	9	11				5				10						21
1	2	3	4		6	7	8	9	11				5				10						22
1		3			6	7	8	5	10	11			2				9	4					23
1	2	3	4		6	7		9	10	11			5				8						24
1	2	3	4		6			8	10	11			5				7		9				25
1	2	3			6	7	8	9		11			5			10	4						26
1	2	3			6	7	8	9		11			5			10	4						27
1	2	3			6	7	8	9	10	11			5				4						28
1	2	3			6	7	8	10					5				4		9	11			29
1	2	3	10		6		8	9		11			5				4			7			30
1	2	3	10		6		8	9		11			5				4			7			31
1	2	3	10		6		8	9		11			5				4			7			32
1	2	3			6		8	9		11			5				4			7	10		33
1	2	3			6		8		11				5				4			7	10	9	34
1	2	3			6		8		11				5				4			7	10	9	35
1	2	3			6		8		11				5				4			7	10	9	36
1	2	3			6			8	11				5				4			7	10	9	37
1	2	3			6		8			11			5				4			7	10	9	38
1	2		3		6	7	8	9					5				4			11	10		39
1	2	3			6	7	8	9					5				4			11	10		40
1	2		3		6	7	8	9					5				4			11	10		41
1	2	3			6	10	8	9		11			5				4			7			42
42	40	40	23	4	42	30	39	38	30	28	1	1	35	5	4	3	26	1	2	14	9	5	
	2		4		2	2	11	21	12	2							1			4	2	3	

1 own-goal

Waiters	Armfield	Thompson	Rowe	Gratrix	Green	Lea	Ball	Charnley	Oates	Horne	Prentis	Turner	James	Cranston	Parry	Fisher	McPhee	
1	2	3	4		6	7	10	8		11			5				9	3
1	1	1	1		1	1	1	1		1			1				1	
							1											

Waiters	Armfield	Thompson	Rowe	Gratrix	Green	Lea	Ball	Charnley	Oates	Horne	Prentis	Turner	James	Cranston	Parry	Fisher	
1	2	3	4		6	7	8	9		11			5			10	2
1		3			6	7	8	9		11	2		5	4		10	3
2	1	2	1		2	2	2	2		2	1		2	1		2	
						1	1	1		1							

1965-66

Manager: Ron Suart

1	Aug	21	(h)	Fulham	D 2-2	Charnley, Green	15,280
2		24	(a)	Burnley	L 1-3	Charnley	15,509
3		27	(a)	Tottenham H	L 0-4		36,118
4		30	(h)	Burnley	L 1-3	Robson	17,723
5	Sep	4	(h)	Liverpool	L 2-3	Charnley, Robson	25,616
6		6	(h)	Leicester C	W 4-0	Robson, Moir, Ball, Armfield	15,640
7		11	(a)	Aston Villa	L 0-3		21,615
8		14	(a)	Leicester C	W 3-0	Ball, Charnley, Robson	24,153
9		18	(h)	Sunderland	L 1-2	Green	28,277
10		25	(a)	West Ham U	D 1-1	Charnley	20,740
11	Oct	9	(a)	Chelsea	W 1-0	Charnley	28,022
12		16	(h)	Arsenal	W 5-3	Charnley 3 (1 pen), Ball (pen), Thompson	19,533
13		23	(a)	Everton	D 0-0		33,766
14		30	(h)	Manchester U	L 1-2	Ball	24,703
15	Nov	6	(a)	Newcastle U	L 0-2		33,853
16		13	(h)	West Brom A	D 1-1	Robson	12,642
17		20	(a)	Nottingham F	L 1-2	Ball	19,549
18		27	(h)	Sheffield W	W 2-1	Lea, Robson	9,807
19	Dec	4	(a)	Northampton T	L 1-2	Ball (pen)	14,404
20		11	(h)	Stoke C	D 1-1	Ball (pen)	11,837
21		25	(h)	Blackburn R	W 4-2	Turner, Waddell, Charnley, Ball	20,851
22	Jan	1	(h)	Chelsea	L 1-2	Ball	14,065
23		8	(a)	Stoke C	L 1-4	Ball (pen)	20,276
24		15	(h)	Everton	W 2-0	Charnley, Opp own-goal	14,588
25		29	(a)	Fulham	D 0-0		12,093
26	Feb	5	(h)	Tottenham H	D 0-0		13,103
27		19	(a)	Liverpool	L 1-4	James	45,047
28		26	(h)	Aston Villa	L 0-1		11,075
29	Mar	5	(a)	Arsenal	D 0-0		21,881
30		12	(a)	Sunderland	L 1-2	Oates	26,246
31		19	(h)	West Ham U	W 2-1	Charnley, Ball	10,559
32		26	(a)	Leeds U	W 2-1	Lea 2	30,727
33		28	(h)	Leeds U	W 1-0	Ball	19,017
34	Apr	4	(a)	Sheffield W	L 0-3		20,945
35		8	(h)	Sheffield U	W 2-1	Ball 2 (1 pen)	17,483
36		9	(a)	West Brom A	L 1-2	Charnley	15,000
37		11	(a)	Sheffield U	W 1-0	Ball	15,196
38		16	(h)	Nottingham F	L 0-3		10,354
39		20	(h)	Newcastle U	D 1-1	Charnley	12,446
40		27	(a)	Manchester U	L 1-2	Robson	26,953
41		30	(h)	Northampton T	W 3-0	Lea, Moir, Ball (pen)	15,295
42	May	2	(a)	Blackburn R	W 3-1	Charnley 2, Moir	7,487
	FINAL LEAGUE POSITION: 13th in Division One						Appearances
							Goals

FA Cup

3	Jan	22	(h)	Manchester C	D 1-1	James	23,937
R		24	(a)	Manchester C	L 1-3	Charnley	52,661
							Appearances
							Sub Appearances
							Goals

League Cup

2	Sep	22	(h)	Gillingham	W 5-2	Charnley 2, Lea, Ball, (pen), Horne	6,717
3	Oct	13	(h)	Darlington	L 1-2	Green	8,204
							Appearances
							Goals

Waiters	Armfield	Thompson	McPhee	James	Rowe	Moir	Ball	Charnley	Green	Lea	Oates	Craven	Fisher	Robson	Horne	Turner	Prentis	Waddell	Taylor	Brown	Hughes	Conway	
1	2	3	4	5	6	7	8	9	10	11													1
1	2	3	4	5	6	7	8	9	10	11													2
1	2		4	5			8	9	10	11	7	3	6										3
1	2		4	5		7	8	9	6	11		3		10									4
1	2				5	7	8	9	6			3	4	10	11								5
1	2		6		5	7	8	9				3	4	10	11								6
1	2		6		5	7	8	9				3	4	10	11								7
1	2		12		5	7	8	9	6			3*	4	10	11								8
1	2		12		5*	7	8	9	6			3	4	10	11								9
1		2		5		7	8	9	6	10		3	4		11								10
1	2		7	5			8	9	6	10*	12	3	4		11								11
1	2	3		5		7	8	9	6		11			10		4							12
1	2	3		5		7	8	9	6		11			10		4							13
1*		3	12	5		7	8	9	6		11			10		4	2						14
1	2	3	4	5		7	8	9	6					10	11								15
1	2	3	4	5		7	8	9	6	11				10									16
1		3	4	5		7	8	9	6	11				10			2						17
1		3	4	5			8	9	6	7				10	11		2						18
1	2	3	4	5		7	8	9	6					10	11								19
1	2	3	4	5		7	8	9	6		11							10					20
1		3		5		7	8	9	6		11					4	2	10					21
1	2	3		5		7	8	9	6		11*				12	4		10					22
1	2	3		5		7	8	9	6				12	10	11	4*							23
1	2	3		5			8	9	6	7			4		11			10					24
	2	3		5	6	7	8	9		11	10		4						1				25
	2	3		5	6		8	9		7	10		4		11				1				26
1	2	3		5	4		8	9	6	7	10				11								27
1	2	3		5	4	11	8*		6	7			10			12		9					28
1	2	3	7	5	4		8	10			11		6	12				9*					29
1	2	3	7	5	6		8	9	10		11		4										30
1		3	12	5			8	9	6*	7	11		4				2	10					31
1	2	3	6	5			8	9		7	11		4					10					32
1	2	3	6	5			8	9		7	11		4					10					33
1	2	3	6	5			8	9		7	11		4					10					34
1	2	3	6	5			8	9		7	11		4	10									35
1	2	3	6	5			8	9		7	11		4	10									36
1	2	3	6	5		10	8	9		7	11		4										37
1	2	3	6	5			8	9		7	11		4	10									38
1	2	3	6	5			8	9		11			4					10		7			39
1	2	3	6	5			8	9		7			4	12	11*			10					40
1	2	3	6	5		7	8	9		11			4					10					41
1		2	6	5		11		9		8			4					10		7	2		42
40	35	34	26	37	13	25	41	41	26	26	20	9	26	18	15	6	5	14	2	2	1		
			4								1		1	2	1	1							
	1	1		1		3	16	16	2	4	1			7		1		1					

1 own-goal

Waiters	Armfield	Thompson	McPhee	James	Rowe	Moir	Ball	Charnley	Green	Lea	Oates	Craven	Fisher	Robson	Horne	Turner	Prentis	Waddell	Taylor	Brown	Hughes	Conway	
1	2	3		5			8	9	6	7			4		11			10					3
1	2	3	10	5			8	9	6	7			4		11								R
2	2	2	1	2			2	2	2	2			2		2			1					
				1				1															

Waiters	Armfield	Thompson	McPhee	James	Rowe	Moir	Ball	Charnley	Green	Lea	Oates	Craven	Fisher	Robson	Horne	Turner	Prentis	Waddell	Taylor	Brown	Hughes	Conway	
1	2					7	8	9	6	10		3			11	4						5	2
1	2		7	5			8	9	6	10		3	4		11								3
2	2		1	1		1	2	2	2	2		2	1		2	1						1	
							1	2	1	1					1								

1966-67

Manager: Ron Suart/Stan Mortensen

1	Aug	20	(a)	Sheffield W	L 0-3		21,008
2		22	(h)	Leicester C	D 1-1	Charnley	17,031
3		27	(h)	Southampton	L 2-3	Lea, Charnley	15,258
4		31	(a)	Leicester C	L 0-3		22,005
5	Sep	3	(a)	Sunderland	L 0-4		24,941
6		5	(h)	Liverpool	L 1-2	Waddell	24,377
7		10	(h)	Aston Villa	L 0-2		15,238
8		17	(a)	Arsenal	D 1-1	Skirton	28,928
9		24	(h)	Manchester C	L 0-1		25,761
10	Oct	1	(a)	Burnley	L 0-1		16,645
11		8	(a)	Manchester U	L 1-2	Charnley	33,555
12		15	(a)	Tottenham H	W 3-1	Charnley 2, Skirton	36,459
13		22	(h)	Newcastle U	W 6-0	Moir 2, Skirton 2, Charnley, Robson	21,202
14		29	(a)	Nottingham F	L 0-2		22,083
15	Nov	5	(h)	Tottenham H	D 2-2	Lea, Moir	16,524
16		12	(a)	Sheffield U	D 1-1	Moir	16,224
17		19	(h)	Stoke C	L 0-1		16,172
18		26	(a)	Everton	W 1-0	Skirton	38,127
19	Dec	3	(h)	Fulham	L 0-1		13,518
20		10	(a)	Leeds U	D 1-1	Skirton	28,466
21		17	(h)	Sheffield W	D 1-1	Robson	10,862
22		26	(h)	West Ham U	L 1-4	Charnley (pen)	26,901
23		27	(a)	West Ham U	L 0-4		29,360
24		31	(a)	Southampton	W 5-1	Fisher, Charnley 3, Suddick	21,336
25	Jan	7	(h)	Sunderland	D 1-1	Suddick	14,669
26		14	(a)	Aston Villa	L 2-3	Suddick 2	16,889
27		21	(h)	Arsenal	L 0-3		12,028
28	Feb	4	(a)	Manchester C	L 0-1		27,840
29		11	(h)	Burnley	L 0-2		16,681
30		25	(a)	Manchester U	L 0-4		47,155
31	Mar	4	(h)	Nottingham F	D 1-1	Skirton	14,003
32		18	(a)	Newcastle U	L 1-2	Moir	30,550
33		24	(a)	Chelsea	W 2-0	Charnley, Skirton (pen)	37,852
34		25	(h)	Leeds U	L 0-2		22,548
35		27	(h)	Chelsea	L 0-2		16,186
36	Apr	1	(a)	West Brom A	L 1-3	Lea	18,304
37		8	(h)	Sheffield U	L 0-1		6,619
38		15	(a)	Stoke C	L 0-2		12,259
39		22	(h)	Everton	L 0-1		13,823
40		29	(a)	Fulham	D 2-2	Oates, Charnley	14,867
41	May	6	(h)	West Brom A	L 1-3	Charnley	9,986
42		13	(a)	Liverpool	W 3-1	Charnley, Oates, Robson	28,773

FINAL LEAGUE POSITION: 22nd in Division One

Appearances
Sub Appearances
Goals

FA Cup

3	Jan	28	(a)	Birmingham C	L 1-2	Charnley	27,603

Appearances
Sub Appearances
Goals

League Cup

2	Sep	14	(h)	Manchester U	W 5-1	Charnley 3 (1 pen), Lea, Waddell	15,570
3	Oct	5	(h)	Chelsea	D 1-1	Robson	13,520
R		17	(a)	Chelsea	W 3-1	Skirton 2, Moir	20,240
4		26	(h)	Fulham	W 4-2	Charnley 2, Moir, Robson	15,349
5	Dec	7	(h)	West Ham U	L 1-3	Charnley	15,831

Appearances
Sub Appearances
Goals

Waiters	Armfield	Thompson	Fisher	James	Green J	Lea	Turner	Charnley	Waddell	Moir	Rowe	Hughes	Brown	Robson	Taylor	Craven	McPhee	Skirton	Oates	Suddick	Ingram	Thomas	Green A	
1	2	3	4	5	6	7	8	9	10	11														1
1	2	3	4	5	10	7		9	8	11	6													2
1	2	3	4	5	10*	7		9	8	11	6	12												3
1	2	3	4	5		11		9	8		6	10	7											4
1		3	4	5		11		9	8		6	3	7	10										5
	2	3		5		11	10	9	8	7	4	6			1									6
	2	3	4	5		11		9	8	7		6			1		10							7
1		2	12	5	6	11		9	8			4				3		7*	10					8
1		2		5	6	11		9	8			4	7			3			10					9
1		2	8	5	6	11		9		10		3	7				4							10
1		2	4	5*		11		9		10		3	7	8		12	6							11
1	6	2	4			11		9		10		3		8			5	7						12
1		2	4			11		9		10	6	3		8			5	7						13
1		2	4			11		9		10	6	3		8			5	7						14
1	6	2	4	12		11*		9		10		3		8			5	7						15
1	4	2		5		11		9		10		3		8			6	7						16
1	4	2	10	5		7		9				3		8			6		11					17
1	2		4	5		11		9		10		3		8			6	7						18
1	2		4	5		11		9		10		3		8			6	7						19
1	2		4	5		11		9		10		3		8			6	7						20
1	2		4	5		11		9		10		3		8			6	7						21
1	2*		12	5	6			9		11		3		8			4	7		10				22
1		2	4			11		9				3		8			6	7		10				23
1		2	4	5	10	7		9				3		8			6			11				24
1		2		5	10	7		9			4	3		8			6			11				25
1	2	3		5	10	7		9				6		8			4			11				26
1	2	3	4	5		7		9		10				8			6			11				27
1		2		5				9			4	3	7*	8		6	12		11	10				28
1		2	4*	5		11		9		8		3		12		6		7		10				29
1	4	2		5				9				3		10		6		7	11	8				30
1	2	3		5*	4			9		8				12		6		7	11	10				31
1	2	3			4			9		8				5		6		7	11	10				32
1	2	3				8		9			5			4		6		7	11	10				33
1	2	3				8		9			5			4		6		7	11	10				34
1	2	3								8	5			4		6		7	11	10	9			35
1	2	3				8		9			5			4		6		7	11	10				36
		2		5		8								4		3	6	7	10	11	9	1		37
	2			5		8		10						4	1	3	6	7		11	9			38
	2	3		5	8	7		9						4			6		11	10		1		39
	2	3		5	10	8		9						4			6	7	11			1		40
	2	3		5	6	8		9									4	7	11			1	10	41
	2	3		5		8		9						4			6	7	11	10		1		42
34	29	36	21	33	15	36	2	40	9	22	13	26	6	30	3	13	25	25	16	19	3	5	1	
			2	1								1		2		1	1							
			1			3		14	1	5				3				8	2	4				

Waiters	Armfield	Thompson	Fisher	James	Green J	Lea	Turner	Charnley	Waddell	Moir	Rowe	Hughes	Brown	Robson	Taylor	Craven	McPhee	Skirton	Oates	Suddick	Ingram	Thomas	Green A	
1		2	4	5	10	7		9				3		8			6			11				3
1		1	1	1	1	1		1				1		1			1			1				
								1																

Waiters	Armfield	Thompson	Fisher	James	Green J	Lea	Turner	Charnley	Waddell	Moir	Rowe	Hughes	Brown	Robson	Taylor	Craven	McPhee	Skirton	Oates	Suddick	Ingram	Thomas	Green A	
1	2*	3	12	5	6	11		9	8			4	7						10					2
1		2	4	5		11		9		10		3	7	8			6							3
1		2	4			11	6*	9		10		3	12	8			5	7						R
1		2	4			11		9		10	6	3		8			5	7						4
1	2		4	5		11		9		10		3		8			6	7						5
5	2	4	4	3	1	5	1	5	1	4	1	5	2	4			4	3	1					
			1										1											
						1		6	1	2				2				2						

1967-68

Manager: Stan Mortensen

No	Month	Day	Venue	Opponent	Result	Scorers	Attendance
1	Aug	19	(a)	Preston NE	W 2-0	Ingram, Charnley (pen)	21,499
2		21	(h)	Ipswich T	D 0-0		19,634
3		26	(h)	Millwall	l 1-4	Charnley	14,886
4		29	(a)	Ipswich T	D 1-1	Ingram	18,286
5	Sep	2	(a)	Hull C	W 1-0	Skirton	16,558
6		4	(h)	Huddersfield T	W 2-0	Ingram, Opp own-goal	17,674
7		9	(h)	Middlesbrough	W 3-0	Ingram, Skirton (pen), Oates	24,346
8		16	(a)	Bristol C	W 4-2	Ingram 2, Skirton 2	13,193
9		23	(h)	Birmingham C	W 1-0	Ingram	25,572
10		30	(a)	Bolton W	W 2-1	Oates, Green	16,452
11	Oct	7	(a)	Rotherham U	W 2-1	Ingram 2	6,725
12		14	(h)	Crystal P	W 2-0	Charnley, Armfield	20,905
13		21	(a)	Aston Villa	L 2-3	Ingram, Suddick	21,620
14		24	(a)	Millwall	D 1-1	Ingram	17,189
15		28	(h)	Queen's Park R	L 0-1		21,635
16	Nov	11	(h)	Cardiff C	W 3-1	Ingram, Robson, Skirton	11,324
17		18	(a)	Charlton A	W 2-0	Ingram, Robson	12,690
18		25	(h)	Norwich C	L 0-2		12,554
19	Dec	2	(a)	Portsmourth	L 1-3	Skirton	35,038
20		9	(h)	Derby C	D 1-1	McPhee	11,113
21		16	(h)	Preston NE	W 4-1	Milne, Craven 2, Green	16,291
22		26	(h)	Carlisle U	D 1-1	Suddick	20,732
23		30	(a)	Carlisle U	W 3-1	Oates, Skirton, Ingram	12,679
24	Jan	6	(h)	Hull C	W 3-1	Ingram 2, Green	13,227
25		13	(a)	Middlesbrough	D 0-0		19,748
26		20	(h)	Bristol C	D 1-1	Skirton (pen)	13,032
27	Feb	3	(a)	Birmingham C	W 2-1	Skirton 2	28,008
28		10	(h)	Bolton W	D 1-1	Suddick	19,183
29		24	(h)	Rotherham U	D 1-1	James	13,689
30	Mar	2	(a)	Crystal P	L 1-3	Skirton	11,860
31		9	(a)	Plymouth A	D 2-2	Ingram, James	8,688
32		16	(h)	Aston Villa	W 1-0	Milne	14,361
33		23	(a)	Queen's Park R	L 0-2		18,498
34		30	(h)	Plymouth A	W 2-0	White, Brown	14,586
35	Apr	3	(a)	Blackburn R	L 1-2	Skirton	13,655
36		6	(a)	Cardiff C	W 3-1	Skirton, Suddick 2	14,439
37		13	(h)	Charlton A	W 2-0	Skirton 2	17,095
38		15	(h)	Blackburn R	W 2-1	Suddick, Opp own-goal	21,865
39		20	(a)	Norwich C	W 2-1	Rowe, Suddick	16,501
40		27	(h)	Portsmouth	W 2-0	White 2	17,042
41	May	4	(a)	Derby C	W 3-1	White, Skirton, Suddick	20,635
42		11	(a)	Huddersfield T	W 3-1	Suddick, Skirton, Opp own-goal	11,603

FINAL LEAGUE POSITION: 3rd in Division Two

Appearances
Sub Appearanc
Goals

FA Cup

Rd	Month	Day	Venue	Opponent	Result	Scorers	Attendance
3	Jan	27	(h)	Chesterfield	W 2-1	Green, Opp own-goal	21,457
4	Feb	17	(a)	Sheffield U	L 1-2	Skirton	25,517

Appearances
Sub Appearanc
Goals

League Cup

Rd	Month	Day	Venue	Opponent	Result	Scorers	Attendance
2	Sep	12	(a)	Newport C	W 1-0	Milne	12,000
3	Oct	11	(a)	Manchester C	D 1-1	Craven	27,633
R		18	(h)	Manchester C	L 0-2		23,405

Appearances
Sub Appearanc
Goals

	Thomas	Armfield	Thompson	Milne	James	McPhee	Green	Rowe	Charnley	Ingram	Lea	Craven	Suddick	Skirton	Taylor	Mowbray	Oates	Alcock	Brown	Robson	White	Marsden	Dean	Hutchison
1	1	2	3	4	5	6	7*	8	9	10	11	12												
2	1	2	3	4	5	6		8	9	10	11		7											
3	1	2	3	4	5	6	8		9	10	11			7										
4		2	12	4	5	6	10			9*		8		7	1	3	11							
5		2		4	5	6	10			9		8		7	1	3	11							
6		2		4		6	10*			9	12	8		7	1	3	11	5						
7		2		4	5	6	10			9		8		7	1	3	11							
8		2		4	5	6	10			9		8		7	1	3	11							
9		2		4	5	6	10			9		8		7	1	3	11							
10		2		4	5	6	10			9		8		7	1	3	11							
11		2		4	5	6	10			9*		8		7	1	3	11		12					
12		2		4	5	6	10		9			8		7	1	3	11							
13		2		4	5	6	11			9		8	10	7	1	3								
14		2		4	5	6	10			9		8	11	7	1	3								
15		2		4	5	6	10			9	12	8	11	7	1	3*								
16		2		4	5	6	10			9	11	3		7	1					8				
17		2		4	5	6	10			9	11	3		7	1					8				
18		2		4		6	10			9	11	3		7	1			5		8				
19		2		4	5	6	10*	12		9		8		7	1	3	11							
20		2		4	5	6				9		8	12	7*	1	3	11		10					
21		2		4	5	6	7			9		8	11		1	3	10							
22		2		4	5*	6	7			9		8	11	12	1	3	10							
23		2	3	4		6	8	5		9			11	7	1		10							
24		2	3	4		6	8	5		9			11	7	1		10							
25		2*	3	4		6	8	5		9		12	11	7	1		10							
26		2	3	4		6	8	5		9		12	11	7*	1		10							
27		2	3	4		6	8	5		9			11	7	1		10							
28			3	4		6	8	5		9		2	11	7	1		10							
29		2	3		5	6	8	10*		9		4	11	7	1								12	
30		2	3	4	5	6	7					8		11	1		10					9		
31		2	3	4	5*	6	7			9		8		11	1		10	12						
32		2		4		6	7			12		8		11	1	3	10*	5			9			
33		2		4		6	7			10		8		11*	1	3	12	5			9			
34		2		8	5	6						4	10		1	3			7		9			11
35		2		8	5	6						4	10	7	1	3					9			11
36		2			5	6	8	4					10	7	1	3					9			11
37		2			5	6	8	4					10	7	1	3					9			11
38		2			5	6	8	4					10	7	1	3					9			11
39		2			5	6	8	4					10	7	1	3					9			11
40		2			5	6	8	4*				12	10	7	1	3					9			11
41		2			5	6	8					4	10	7	1	3					9			11
42		2			5	6	8					4	10	7	1	3					9			11
	3	41	12	34	32	42	38	14	4	30	6	29	22	37	39	27	22	4	2	3	11	1		9
			1					1		1	2	4	1	1			1	1	1				1	
		1		2	2	1	3	1	3	17		2	9	17			3		1	2	4			

3 own-goals

	Thomas	Armfield	Thompson	Milne	James	McPhee	Green	Rowe	Charnley	Ingram	Lea	Craven	Suddick	Skirton	Taylor	Mowbray	Oates
3		2*	3	4		6	8	5		9		12	11	7	1		10
4		2	3	4	5	6	8	10				9	11	7	1		
		2	2	2	1	2	2	2		1		1	2	2	2		1
												1					
							1							1			

1 own-goal

	Thomas	Armfield	Thompson	Milne	James	McPhee	Green	Rowe	Charnley	Ingram	Lea	Craven	Suddick	Skirton	Taylor	Mowbray	Oates	Alcock	Brown
2		2		4	5	6	10			9	7	8			1	3	11		
3		2		4	5	6	10		9			8		7	1	3	11		
R			2	4	5	6	10		9			8		7	1	3	11*		12
		2	1	3	3	3	3		2	1	1	3		2	3	3	3		
																			1
				1								1							

1968-69

Manager: Stan Mortensen

1	Aug	10	(h)	Hull C	W 2-0	White 2	16,755
2		17	(a)	Derby C	D 1-1	Green	24,760
3		21	(a)	Oxford U	D 0-0		14,120
4		24	(h)	Bristol C	D 2-2	Milne, Green	15,767
5		28	(a)	Blackburn R	D 1-1	White	21,062
6		31	(a)	Aston Villa	W 1-0	Brown	18,919
7	Sep	7	(h)	Bolton W	W 1-0	Suddick	22,668
8		14	(a)	Millwall	W 2-1	Suddick, White	13,198
9		16	(h)	Preston NE	D 1-1	James	27,975
10		21	(h)	Fulham	D 2-2	Brown, Hutchison	15,765
11		28	(a)	Sheffield U	L 1-2	Green	15,997
12	Oct	5	(a)	Huddersfield T	L 1-2	Suddick	13,023
13		7	(h)	Blackburn R	L 0-1		21,154
14		12	(h)	Portsmouth	D 1-1	White	16,407
15		19	(a)	Carlisle U	L 0-1		10,519
16		26	(h)	Crystal P	W 3-0	Suddick, McPhee, James	15,224
17	Nov	2	(a)	Charlton A	D 0-0		14,906
18		9	(h)	Cardiff C	L 1-2	Hutchison	12,085
19		16	(a)	Birmingham C	L 0-1		22,206
20		23	(h)	Bury	W 6-0	Rowe 3, Brown, Suddick 2	10,499
21		30	(a)	Norwich C	W 1-0	Rowe	15,128
22	Dec	7	(h)	Middlesbrough	D 1-1	James	13,356
23		14	(a)	Portsmouth	L 0-1		16,961
24		21	(h)	Carlisle U	W 1-0	Rowe	11,619
25		28	(h)	Huddersfield T	D 0-0		20,319
26	Jan	11	(h)	Charlton A	L 2-3	Brown, Milne (pen)	11,475
27		25	(a)	Crystal P	W 2-1	Craven, Johnston (pen)	17,003
28	Feb	1	(h)	Birmingham C	W 2-1	Brown, Suddick	11,294
29		12	(a)	Cardiff C	L 0-1		24,229
30		22	(a)	Middlesbrough	L 1-2	Craven	18,672
31	Mar	1	(a)	Hull C	D 2-2	Alcock, Craven	10,896
32		8	(h)	Derby C	L 2-3	Brown, Craven	18,853
33		15	(a)	Bristol C	D 1-1	Suddick	16,079
34		19	(h)	Norwich C	W 2-1	Green, Brown	9,536
35		22	(h)	Aston Villa	D 1-1	James	12,148
36		26	(a)	Bury	L 0-2		6,675
37		29	(a)	Bolton W	W 4-1	Suddick 2, Brown (pen), Rowe	9,029
38	Apr	5	(h)	Sheffield U	D 1-1	Suddick	13,857
39		7	(h)	Oxford U	W 1-0	Suddick	11,155
40		8	(a)	Preston NE	L 0-1		17,233
41		12	(a)	Fulham	D 0-0		7,154
42		19	(h)	Millwall	W 1-0	Green	9,524

FINAL LEAGUE POSITION: 8th in Division Two

Appearances
Sub Appearance
Goals

FA Cup

3	Jan	4	(a)	Coventry C	L 1-3	Brown	28,357

Appearances
Sub Appearance
Goals

League Cup

2	Sep	4	(a)	Wrexham	D 1-1	White	15,102
R		9	(h)	Wrexham	W 3-0	Hutchison, Suddick, Craven	17,063
3		25	(h)	Manchester C	W 1-0	White	23,795
4	Oct	16	(h)	Wolves	W 2-1	Suddick, Marsden	16,466
5		29	(a)	Arsenal	L 1-5	Green	32,321

Appearances
Sub Appearanc
Goals

Taylor	Armfield	Mowbray	Milne	James	McPhee	Skirton	Green	White	Suddick	Hutchison	Rowe	Oates	Brown	Craven	Alcock	Thompson	Marsden	Johnston	Bentley	Thomas	Fisher	
1	2	3	4	5	6	7	8	9	10	11												1
1	2	3	4	5	6	7	8	9	10	11												2
1	2	3	4	5	6	7	8	9	10	11												3
1	2	3	4	5	6	7	8	9	10	11												4
1	2	3	4*	5	6	7	8	9	10	11				12								5
1	2	3		5	6			9	10	11		7	8	4								6
1	2*	3	4	5	6		8	9	10	11		12	7									7
1		3		5	6	11	8	9	10	7	4			2								8
1		3		5	6	7	8	9	10	11	4			2								9
1		3	4	5	6		8	9	10	11			7	2								10
1			4	5	6	7	8	9	10	11				2		3						11
1	2		8	5	6	9	7		10	11				4*		3	12					12
1			4	5	6	7	8		10	11			12		2	3	9*					13
1	2		4*	5	6	7	8	9	10	11	12					3						14
1	2		7*	5	6		8		10	11	4		12			3	9					15
1	2			9	6		8		10	11	4		7		5	3						16
1	2			5	6	7	8		9	11	4*		10	12		3						17
1	2			5	6	7	8	9		11	4		10			3						18
1	2		4	5	6	7	8	9	10	11						3						19
1	2			5	6		8		10	11	9		7	4		3						20
1	2			5	6		8		10	11	9		7	4		3						21
1	2		12	5	6		8		10	11*	9		7	4		3						22
1		2	10	5	6		8		11		9		7	4		3		5				23
1	2		12	5	6		8	10*	11		9		7	4		3						24
1	2			5	6		8	10	11		9		7	4		3						25
1	2		8	9	6				10	11			7	4		5			3			26
1	2			5	6		8		10	11	9*			4	12			7	3			27
1	2			5			8		9	11			7	4	6			10	3			28
1	2			5			8		9	11			7	4	6			10	3			29
1	2			5	11		8		9				7	4	6			10	3			30
1	2			5			8		9	11			7	4	6			10	3			31
1	2			5	12		8		9	11			7	4	6			10*	3			32
1	2		10	5	6		8	9	11				7	4					3			33
1	2		10	5	6		8	9	11				7	4					3			34
		2	10*	5	6		8	9	11		12		7	4					3	1		35
				5	6		8	9	10	11			7	4					3	1	2	36
	2			5	6		8		11		9		7	10	4				3	1		37
	2			5	6		8		11		9		7		4			10	3	1		38
1	2			5	6		10	9	11	7			8		4				3			39
1	2			5	6		10	9	11	7			8		4				3			40
1	2			5	6		10		11	7	8				4		9		3			41
1	2*		12	5	6		8		11		9		7	10	4				3			42
38	34	12	18	42	38	14	40	22	41	32	17	1	27	25	13	16	3	8	17	4	1	
			3		1						2	1	2	2	1		1					
			2	4	1		5	5	12	2	6		8	4	1			1				

Taylor	Armfield	Mowbray	Milne	James	McPhee	Skirton	Green	White	Suddick	Hutchison	Rowe	Oates	Brown	Craven	Alcock	Thompson	Marsden	Johnston	Bentley	Thomas	Fisher	
	2		12	5	6		8	10*	11		9		7	4		3				1		3
	1			1	1		1	1	1		1		1	1		1				1		
			1																			
													1									

Taylor	Armfield	Mowbray	Milne	James	McPhee	Skirton	Green	White	Suddick	Hutchison	Rowe	Oates	Brown	Craven	Alcock	Thompson	Marsden	Johnston	Bentley	Thomas	Fisher	
1	2	3		5	6			9	10	11		7	8	4								2
1		3		5	6	7	8		10	11	4			2				9				R
1	2	3*	12	5	6	7	8	9	10	11				4								3
1	2			5	6	7	8		10	11	4						3	9				4
1	2			9	6		8		10	11	4		7			5	3					5
5	4	3		5	5	3	4	2	5	5	3	1	2	3		1	2	2				
			1																			
							1	2	2	1				1				1				

1969-70

Manager: Les Shannon

1	Aug	9	(h)	Portsmouth	W 2-1	Burns, Craven	15,844
2		16	(a)	Norwich C	L 1-3	Pickering	17,149
3		18	(h)	Blackburn R	D 0-0		21,038
4		23	(h)	Birmingham C	W 2-0	Brown (pen), Opp own-goal	17,495
5		26	(a)	Queen's Park R	L 1-6	Pickering (pen)	19,227
6		29	(a)	Hull C	L 0-1		9,701
7	Sep	6	(h)	Swindon T	W 3-2	Brown, Craven, Suddick	17,201
8		13	(a)	Huddersfield T	L 0-2		10,575
9		15	(h)	Preston NE	D 0-0		19,741
10		20	(h)	Watford	L 0-3		14,859
11		27	(a)	Middlesbrough	W 2-0	Burns, Suddick	20,268
12	Oct	4	(h)	Cardiff C	W 3-2	Suddick, Pickering, Craven	18,115
13		6	(h)	Norwich C	D 0-0		12,485
14		11	(a)	Millwall	W 3-1	Pickering, James, Suddick	11,516
15		18	(a)	Sheffield U	W 3-2	Burns, Pickering 2	15,876
16		25	(h)	Bolton W	D 1-1	Craven	17,179
17	Nov	1	(a)	Charlton A	W 2-0	McPhee, Craven	13,610
18		8	(h)	Leicester C	D 1-1	Brown	13,074
19		12	(a)	Blackburn R	L 1-2	Suddick	17,393
20		15	(a)	Aston Villa	D 0-0		24,942
21		22	(h)	Oxford U	W 1-0	Johnston	10,968
22		29	(a)	Bristol C	L 1-2	Hutchison	14,818
23	Dec	6	(h)	Carlisle U	D 1-1	Armfield	9,766
24		13	(h)	Huddersfield T	W 2-0	Suddick, Craven	12,587
25		26	(a)	Birmingham C	W 3-2	Hutchison, James, Suddick	29,548
26	Jan	10	(a)	Watford	W 1-0	Pickering	12,052
27		17	(h)	Middlesbrough	D 1-1	Burns	15,154
28		31	(a)	Cardiff C	D 2-2	Burns, Suddick	24,717
29	Feb	7	(h)	Millwall	D 1-1	Pickering (pen)	10,297
30		14	(a)	Portsmouth	W 3-2	Pickering, Craven, Suddick	13,949
31		21	(a)	Bolton W	W 2-0	Craven, Pickering	14,131
32		28	(h)	Charlton A	W 2-0	Pickering 2	13,083
33	Mar	14	(h)	Bristol C	W 1-0	Bentley	13,657
34		18	(h)	Hull C	L 0-1		15,724
35		21	(a)	Carlisle U	W 2-1	Suddick, Murray	8,212
36		28	(h)	Aston Villa	W 2-1	Pickering 2 (1 pen)	17,352
37		30	(h)	Sheffield U	W 1-0	Craven	24,432
38		31	(a)	Leicester C	D 0-0		32,784
39	Apr	4	(h)	Queen's Park R	D 1-1	Craven	19,516
40		7	(a)	Swindon T	D 1-1	Burns	28,520
41		13	(a)	Preston NE	W 3-0	Pickering 3	34,000
42		18	(a)	Oxford U	L 0-2		9,190

FINAL LEAGUE POSITION: 2nd in Division Two

Appearances
Sub Appearances
Goals

FA Cup

3	Jan	3	(a)	Arsenal	D 1-1	Hutchison	32,210
R		15	(h)	Arsenal	W 3-2	Suddick, Pickering, Burns	24,801
4		24	(h)	Mansfield T	L 0-2		23,715

Appearances
Sub Appearances
Goals

League Cup

2	Sep	3	(h)	Gillingham	W 3-1	Suddick, Rowe, Bentley	10,797
3		24	(a)	Crystal P	D 2-2	Suddick, James	17,990
R	Oct	1	(h)	Crystal P	L 0-1		13,973

Appearances
Sub Appearances
Goals

Thomson	Armfield	Bentley	Alcock	James	Craven	Burns	Milne	Pickering	Suddick	Hutchison	Brown	McPhee	Hughes	Wann	Rowe	Hatton	White	Mowbray	Johnston	Taylor	Thomas	Murray	
1	2	3	4	5	6	7	8	9	10	11													1
1	2	3	4	5	6	7	8	9	10	11													2
1	2	3	4	5	6	7		9	10	11	8												3
1	2	3	4	5	6	7		9	10	11	8												4
1	2	3	5		4	7*	12	9	10	11	8	6											5
1	2	3	5		12		4		10	11	7*	6	8		9								6
1	2	3	5		9		4		10	11	7				8	6							7
1	2	3		5	9		4		10	11	7				8	6							8
1	2	3		5	9		4		10	11	7			12	8*	6							9
1	2	3	4	5	8				10	11	7			12		6	9*						10
1	2			5	4	7		9	10	11		12				6		3	8*				11
	2			5	4	7	8	9	10	11*		12				6		3		1			12
	2			5	9	11	8*		10			4	7			6		3		1	12		13
	2			5	8	7		9	10	11		4				6		3		1			14
1	2	12		5	8	7		9	10	11*		4				6		3					15
1	2			5	8	7*		9	10	11		4	12			6		3					16
1	2			5	8			9	10	11	7	4				6		3					17
1	2			5	8			9	10	11	7	4				6		3					18
1	2			5	8			9	10	11	7	4				6		3					19
1	2	12		5	8	7*		9	10	11		4				6		3					20
1	2			5	8			9	10	11		4				6		3	7				21
1	2	12		5				9	10	11	7*	4			8	6		3					22
1	2	12		5		8		9	10	11	7*	4				6		3					23
1		3		5	8	7		9	10	11		4				6		2					24
1		3		5	8	7		9	10	11		4				6		2					25
1	2	12		5	8	7*		9	10	11		4				6		3					26
1	2	8		5	8	7			10	11*		4			12	6		3					27
1	2	3		5	9	7		9	10	11		4*				6		12					28
1	2	3		5	8	7*		9	10	11	12	4				6							29
1	2	4		5	8	7		9	10*	11		12				6		3					30
1	2	4		5	8	7		9	10	11		12				6*		3					31
1	2	4		5	8	7		9	10	11						6		3					32
1	2	4		5	8	7*		9	10	11	12					6		3					33
1	2	4	5		8*			9	10	11	12					6		3				7	34
1	2	4		5	8	12		9	10	11*						6		3				7	35
1	2	4		5	8	12		9	10	11						6		3				7*	36
1	2	3		5	8	7		9	10	11		4				6							37
1	2	3		5	8			9	10	11		4				6						7	38
1	2	3		5	8			9	10	11		4				6						7	39
1	2	3		5	8*	7		9	10	11		4				6		12					40
1	2	3		5	8	7		9	10	11		4				6							41
1	2	3		5	8	7*		9	10	11		4				6						12	42
39	40	28	9	38	39	27	8	35	42	41	13	25	2		5	36	1	24	2	3		5	
		5			1	2	1				3	4	1	2	1			2			1	1	
	1	1		2	10	6		17	10	2	3	1							1			1	

1 own-goal

Thomson	Armfield	Bentley	Alcock	James	Craven	Burns	Milne	Pickering	Suddick	Hutchison	Brown	McPhee	Hughes	Wann	Rowe	Hatton	White	Mowbray	Johnston	Taylor	Thomas	Murray	
1	2	6		5	8	7		9	10	11		4						3					3
1	2	12		5	8	7		9	10	11		4*				6		3					R
1	2	3		5	8	7		9	10*	11		4				6		12					4
3	3	2		3	3	3		3	3	3		3				2		2					
		1																1					
						1		1	1	1													

Thomson	Armfield	Bentley	Alcock	James	Craven	Burns	Milne	Pickering	Suddick	Hutchison	Brown	McPhee	Hughes	Wann	Rowe	Hatton	White	Mowbray	Johnston	Taylor	Thomas	Murray	
1		3	5		2		4		10	11	7	6	9		8								2
1	2	3	5		4	7		9	10	11		6							8				3
1	2			5	4	7	12	9	10	11		6						3	8*				R
3	2	2	2	1	3	2	1	2	3	3	1	3	1		1			1	2				
							1																
		1		1					2						1								

1970-71

Manager: Les Shannon/Bob Stokoe

1	Aug	15	(a)	Huddersfield T	L 0-3		22,787
2		17	(h)	Liverpool	D 0-0		23,818
3		22	(h)	West Brom A	W 3-1	Pickering 2, Brown	22,162
4		26	(a)	Manchester C	L 0-2		37,197
5		29	(a)	Newcastle U	W 2-1	Craven 2	33,270
6	Sep	2	(a)	Crystal P	L 0-1		26,296
7		5	(h)	Southampton	L 0-3		18,035
8		12	(a)	Tottenham H	L 0-3		19,894
9		19	(h)	Everton	L 0-2		30,705
10		26	(a)	Manchester U	D 1-1	Burns	46,647
11	Oct	3	(h)	Stoke C	D 1-1	Burns	25,324
12		10	(a)	Nottingham F	L 1-3	Burns	16,615
13		17	(h)	Huddersfield T	D 2-2	Green, Burns	21,006
14		24	(h)	Chelsea	L 3-4	Pickering 2, Suddick	24,940
15		31	(a)	West Ham U	L 1-2	Green	26,239
16	Nov	7	(h)	Arsenal	L 0-1		17,115
17		14	(a)	Leeds U	L 1-3	Craven	32,921
18		21	(a)	Derby C	L 0-2		28,237
19		28	(h)	Ipswich T	L 0-2		13,048
20	Dec	5	(a)	Wolves	L 0-1		22,623
21		12	(h)	Coventry C	W 1-0	Craven	11,381
22		19	(a)	West Brom A	D 1-1	James	17,862
23		26	(h)	Burnley	D 1-1	Burns	28,371
24	Jan	9	(a)	Liverpool	D 2-2	Burns, Pickering	42,939
25		16	(h)	Manchester C	D 3-3	Craven, Pickering 2	29,356
26		30	(a)	Ipswich T	L 1-2	Burns	17,509
27	Feb	6	(h)	Wolves	L 0-2		19,054
28		13	(a)	Coventry C	L 0-2		18,633
29		20	(h)	Derby C	L 0-1		17,892
30		27	(h)	West Ham U	D 1-1	Kemp	15,689
31	Mar	6	(a)	Chelsea	L 0-2		26,530
32		13	(h)	Leeds U	D 1-1	Craven	27,401
33		20	(a)	Arsenal	L 0-1		37,372
34		27	(a)	Southampton	D 1-1	Burns	17,833
35	Apr	3	(h)	Newcastle U	L 0-1		14,637
36		10	(a)	Burnley	L 0-1		14,495
37		12	(h)	Tottenham H	D 0-0		16,541
38		13	(a)	Stoke C	D 1-1	Hutchison	13,916
39		17	(h)	Nottingham F	L 2-3	McGrotty, Craven	10,028
40		24	(a)	Everton	D 0-0		26,286
41		26	(h)	Crystal P	W 3-1	Craven, Burns 2	8,905
42	May	1	(h)	Manchester U	D 1-1	Green	29,857

FINAL LEAGUE POSITION: 22nd in Division One

Appearances
Sub Appearances
Goals

FA Cup

3	Jan	2	(h)	West Ham U	W 4-0	Green 2, Craven, Mowbray	21,814
4		23	(a)	Hull C	L 0-2		34,752

Appearances
Sub Appearances
Goals

League Cup

2	Sep	9	(h)	Newport C	W 4-1	Suddick, Bentley, Coleman, Rowe	9,878
3	Oct	7	(h)	Bristol C	L 0-1		10,877

Appearances
Sub Appearances
Goals

Thomson	Armfield	Bentley	Craven	James	Hatton	Murray	Brown	Pickering	Suddick	Hutchison	Mowbray	Hughes	Nicholson	Rowe	Johnston	Coleman	Alcock	McNicholas	Burns	Green	Blacklaw	Wann	Kemp	Taylor	Ramsbottom	Suddaby	McGrotty	Burridge	
1	2	3	4	5	6	7*	8	9	10	11	12																		1
1	2	4	8	5	6		7	9	10	11	3																		2
1	2	4	8	5	6		7	9	10	11	3																		3
1	2	4	8	5	6		7*	9	10	11	3	12																	4
1	2	4	8	5	6				10	11	3	7*		9	12														5
1	2	4	8	5	6				10	7	3			9		11													6
1	2	4	8		6			9	10	7	3*	12				11	5												7
1	2	4	3		6			9	10*	11				8		7	5	12											8
1	2	4	3		6					11		9		8		10*	5		7	12									9
1	2*	10	9	5	4				12	11	3						6		7	8									10
1	2	10	9	5	4				8	11	3						6		7										11
1		10	9	5	4	12				8	3		2			11*	6		7										12
		10		5	4			9		11	3		2				6		7	8	1								13
1	2	6	12	5	4			9*	10	11	3								7	8									14
1	2	6		5	4*				10	11	3	9							7	8		12							15
1	2	10	4	5					7	11	3						6		9	8									16
1	2	3	9	5						11					4		6		7	8		10							17
1	2	3	9	5				7		11					4		6		12	8		10*							18
1	2	3	9	5		12				11					8*	10	6			7			4						19
	2	3	9		6				12	11*						10	5		7	8			4	1					20
	2		9		6		12			11	3					10*	5		7	8			4	1					21
		3	9	12	6					11	2					10*	5		7	8			4	1					22
		3	9		6					11	2					10	5		7	8			4	1					23
	2		9	5	6			12		11*	3					10			7	8			4	1					24
	2		8	5	6*			9	12		3					10			11	7			4	1					25
1	2		8	5	6			9			3					10			11	7			4						26
1	2	12	8	5	6			9			3					10			11*	7			4						27
1		3	9	5	6			10*			2					11			12	7			8			4			28
	2	3*	10	5	6			9		11					12					7			8		1	4			29
	2		9	5	6				12	11						10			7*	8			4		1	3			30
	2		9	5	6					11	8				12	10*			7				4		1	3			31
		3	9	5					10	11	2								7			8	4		1	6			32
			9	5	6				10	11							2		7	8			4		1	3			33
			9	5	3				10	11	4						2		7	8					1	6			34
		3	9	5	2				10	11	4								7	8					1	6			35
		3	9	5	2					11					4				7*	8		10			1	6	12		36
		3	9	5	2					11			12		4					8		10*	7	1		6			37
		3	9	5						11			4	8	10		2		12				7*	1		6			38
		3	9	5	2					11					4				12	8		10		1		6*	7		39
		3	9	5	2					11			12		4		6			8		10					7*	1	40
		3	9	5	2					11			12		4		6		7	8		10*						1	41
	2	12	9	5	3					11					4*		6		7	8		10						1	42
21	27	32	39	35	36	1	4	14	16	38	25	3	3	5	10	17	21		26	28	1	9	17	9	8	12	2	3	
		2	1	1		2	1	1	4		1	2	3		3			1	4	1		1					1		
			8	1			1	7	1	1									10	3			1				1		

Thomson	Armfield	Bentley	Craven	James	Hatton	Murray	Brown	Pickering	Suddick	Hutchison	Mowbray	Hughes	Nicholson	Rowe	Johnston	Coleman	Alcock	McNicholas	Burns	Green	Blacklaw	Wann	Kemp	Taylor	Ramsbottom	Suddaby	McGrotty	Burridge	
	2		9	5	6					11	3					10			7	8			4	1					3
	2		8	5	6*			9	12		3					11				7			4	1		10			4
	2		2	2	2			1		1	2					2			1	2			2	2		1			
									1																				
			1								1									2									

Thomson	Armfield	Bentley	Craven	James	Hatton	Murray	Brown	Pickering	Suddick	Hutchison	Mowbray	Hughes	Nicholson	Rowe	Johnston	Coleman	Alcock	McNicholas	Burns	Green	Blacklaw	Wann	Kemp	Taylor	Ramsbottom	Suddaby	McGrotty	Burridge	
1		4	3	5	6*			9	10	11			2	8		7		12											2
1	2		9*	5	4				8	10	3		12			11	6		7										3
2	1	1	2	2	2			1	2	2	1		1	1		2	1		1										
													1					1											
		1							1					1		1													

1971-72

Manager: Bob Stokoe

1	Aug	14	(h)	Swindon T	W 4-1	James 2, Ainscow, Green	13,004
2		16	(h)	Cardiff C	W 3-0	Green, James 2	19,253
3		21	(a)	Millwall	L 0-1		12,053
4		28	(h)	Sheffield W	W 1-0	Hatton	16,557
5	Sep	1	(a)	Portsmouth	W 3-1	Burns, James 2	16,058
6		4	(a)	Hull C	L 0-1		18,288
7		11	(h)	Norwich C	L 1-2	Hatton	15,960
8		18	(a)	Watford	L 0-1		10,575
9		25	(h)	Birmingham C	D 1-1	Suddick	22,610
10		28	(a)	Bristol C	L 0-4		20,352
11	Oct	2	(a)	Middlesbrough	L 0-1		18,671
12		9	(h)	Orient	W 4-1	Burns 2, Suddaby, Ainscow	14,657
13		16	(a)	Swindon T	L 0-1		10,346
14		23	(h)	Queen's Park R	D 1-1	Lennard	16,417
15		30	(a)	Fulham	L 1-2	Lennard	11,020
16	Nov	6	(h)	Carlisle U	W 2-0	James, Suddick (pen)	12,769
17		13	(a)	Sunderland	D 0-0		17,240
18		20	(h)	Luton T	L 0-1		8,432
19		27	(a)	Oxford U	L 1-3	Suddick (pen)	7,894
20	Dec	4	(h)	Preston NE	D 1-1	Dyson	18,912
21		11	(a)	Charlton A	W 3-2	Lennard, Dyson, Burns	9,598
22		18	(h)	Hull C	D 1-1	Burns	9,349
23		27	(a)	Burnley	L 1-2	Lennard	21,977
24	Jan	1	(h)	Watford	W 5-0	Lennard, Suddaby, Burns 3	10,745
25		8	(a)	Sheffield W	W 2-1	Burns, Hatton	17,113
26		22	(h)	Bristol C	W 1-0	Suddick	9,923
27		29	(a)	Cardiff C	W 4-3	Burns, Suddick (pen), Dyson 2	11,719
28	Feb	12	(a)	Queen's Park R	W 1-0	Dyson	13,690
29		19	(h)	Fulham	W 2-1	Suddick, Lennard	11,480
30		26	(a)	Carlisle U	L 0-2		9,985
31	Mar	4	(h)	Sunderland	D 1-1	Suddick	10,989
32		11	(a)	Orient	W 1-0	Burns	11,582
33		18	(h)	Millwall	D 0-0		12,916
34		25	(a)	Norwich C	L 1-5	Burns	23,605
35	Apr	1	(h)	Burnley	W 4-2	Suddick, Dyson 3	15,931
36		3	(h)	Middlesbrough	W 3-1	Burns, Bentley, Dyson	13,726
37		4	(a)	Birmingham C	L 1-2	Dyson	45,181
38		8	(a)	Luton T	W 4-1	Dyson, Simpkin, Burns, Opp own-goal	7,270
39		15	(h)	Oxford U	W 2-0	Burns, Suddick	10,131
40		22	(a)	Preston NE	W 4-1	Suddick (pen), Burns, Ainscow, Dyson	19,819
41		24	(h)	Portsmouth	L 1-2	Hutchison	10,507
42		29	(h)	Charlton A	W 5-0	Burns, James, Hutchison, Hatton, Opp own-goal	8,884

FINAL LEAGUE POSITION: 6th in Division Two

Appearances
Sub Appearances
Goals

FA Cup

3	Jan	15	(h)	Chelsea	L 0-1		22,135

Appearances
Sub Appearances
Goals

League Cup

2	Sep	8	(a)	Bournemouth	W 2-0	Hutchison, Burns	15,649
3	Oct	5	(h)	Colchester U	W 4-0	Suddick, Green, Burns 2	11,042
4		26	(h)	Aston Villa	W 4-1	Suddick, Green, James, Hutchison	20,193
5	Nov	17	(a)	Tottenham H	L 0-2		30,099

Appearances
Sub Appearances
Goals

Burridge	Hatton	Bentley	Booth	Alcock	Suddaby	Ainscow	Green	James	Suddick	Burns	Hardcastle	Johnston	Craven	Hutchison	Wann	Ramsbottom	Fuschillo	Harrison	Lennard	Kemp	Simpkin	Dyson	Mann	Wood	Match
1	2	3	4	5	6	7	8	9	10	11															1
1	2	3	4	5	6	7	8	9	10	11															2
1	2	3	4	5	6	7*	8	9	10	11		12													3
1	2	3	4	5	6	7*	8	9	10	11			12												4
1	2	3	4	5	6		8	9	10	7				11											5
1	2	3	4	5	6		8	9	10	7*			12	11											6
	2	3	4	5	6		8	9	10	7*				11	12	1									7
	2	3	4*	5	6		8	9	10	7				11	12	1									8
	2	3*	4	5	6	12	8	9	10	7				11		1									9
	2		4	5	6	7	8	9	10						11	1	3								10
1	2		4*	5	6	12	8	9	10	7					11			3							11
1	2			5	4	7	8	9	10	11								3	6						12
1	2			5	4		8	9	7*	11				12				3	10		6				13
1	2			5	4		8	9*	7	11				12				3	10		6				14
1	2			5	4			9	10	12				7				3*	11		6	8			15
1	2			5	4			3	8	11*				7					10	12	6	9			16
1	2		10*	5	4					11				7	12					8	6	9	3		17
1	2			5	4				8	11				7					10*	12	6	9	3		18
1	2			5	4			12	8	11									10*	7	6	9	3		19
1	2			5	4			6	8	7	3			11					10			9			20
1	3			5*	4			6	8	7	2			11					10		12	9			21
1	2				4	12		5	8	7				11			3*		10		6	9			22
1	2				4	12		5	8	7	3			11					10		6*	9			23
1	2				4	12		5	8	7	3*			11					10		6	9			24
1	2	3			4			5	8	7				11					10		6	9			25
1	2*	3			4	12		5	8	7				11					10		6	9			26
1		3		2	4	12		5	8*	7				11					10		6	9			27
1	2	3			4			5	8	7				11					10		6	9			28
1		3			4			5	8	7	2			11					10		6	9			29
1	2	3			4			5	8	7		12		11*					10		6	9			30
1	2	3			4			5	8	7	12			11					10		6	9*			31
1	2				4			5	8	11	3			7					10		6	9			32
1	2				4			5	8	11	3			7				12	10*		6	9			33
1	2			12	4			5	8	11	10			7				3*			6	9			34
1	2				4			5	8	11	3	12		7					10*		6	9			35
1	2	10			4	12		5	8	11	3			7							6*	9			36
1	2	3			4	10		5	8	7				11							6	9			37
1	2	3			4			5	8	11	10			7							6	9			38
	2	3			4			5	8	11	10			7							6	9		1	39
	4	3			5	12			8	11	2			7					10*		6	9		1	40
	2	3			4	12		5	8	11	10			7							6*	9		1	41
	2	3		4		10		5	8	11	6			7								9		1	42
34	40	23	12	23	41	8	14	38	41	40	15			32	2	4	2	6	23	2	27	28	3	4	
				1		10		1		1	1	3	2	2	3			1		2	1				
	4	1			2	3	2	8	10	17				2					6		1	12			

2 own-goals

Burridge	Hatton	Bentley	Booth	Alcock	Suddaby	Ainscow	Green	James	Suddick	Burns	Hardcastle	Johnston	Craven	Hutchison	Wann	Ramsbottom	Fuschillo	Harrison	Lennard	Kemp	Simpkin	Dyson	Mann	Wood	Round
1	2	3			4	12		5	8	7				11					10		6*	9			3
1	1	1			1			1	1	1				1					1		1	1			
						1																			

Burridge	Hatton	Bentley	Booth	Alcock	Suddaby	Ainscow	Green	James	Suddick	Burns	Hardcastle	Johnston	Craven	Hutchison	Wann	Ramsbottom	Fuschillo	Harrison	Lennard	Kemp	Simpkin	Dyson	Mann	Wood	Round
	2	3	4	5	6		8	9	10	7				11		1									2
1	2		4	5	6	7	8	9	10	11								3							3
1	2			5	4		8	9	10	11				7				3			6				4
1	2		10	5	4			9*		11				7	12					8	6		3		5
3	4	1	3	4	4	1	3	4	3	4				3		1		2		1	2		1		
															1										
							2	1	2	3				2											

1972-73

Manager: Bob Stokoe

1	Aug	12	(a)	Huddersfield T	L 0-1		12,840
2		19	(h)	Brighton & HA	W 6-2	Hutchison 2, Burns, Lennard, Bentley, Dyson	10,894
3		26	(a)	Cardiff C	W 2-1	Dyson, Lennard	12,401
4		28	(h)	Sunderland	D 0-0		14,797
5	Sep	2	(h)	Millwall	W 2-1	Burns, Dyson	9,494
6		9	(a)	Swindon T	D 0-0		10,069
7		16	(h)	Orient	D 1-1	Burns	10,471
8		23	(a)	Burnley	L 3-4	Suddick 2, Ainscow	14,591
9		26	(a)	Carlisle U	W 3-2	Ainscow, Suddick, Barton	10,969
10		30	(h)	Middlesbrough	L 0-1		14,714
11	Oct	7	(a)	Luton T	D 2-2	Hutchison, Ainscow	12,073
12		14	(h)	Oxford U	W 2-1	Ainscow, Burns	11,589
13		17	(h)	Aston Villa	D 1-1	Rafferty	15,043
14		21	(a)	Fulham	L 0-2		8,644
15		28	(h)	Queen's Park R	W 2-0	Rafferty, Suddick	14,160
16	Nov	4	(h)	Carlisle U	D 0-0		9,564
17		11	(a)	Aston Villa	D 0-0		31,651
18		18	(h)	Bristol C	W 3-0	Alcock, Dyson, Suddick	8,341
19		25	(a)	Hull C	W 2-1	Ainscow, Rafferty	8,988
20	Dec	2	(h)	Portsmouth	W 3-1	Dyson, Ainscow, Suddick	8,409
21		9	(a)	Preston NE	W 3-0	Ainscow 3	15,822
22		16	(h)	Sheffield W	L 1-2	Hatton	10,270
23		23	(a)	Nottingham F	L 0-4		10,078
24		26	(h)	Burnley	L 1-2	Rafferty	25,277
25		30	(a)	Brighton & HA	W 2-1	Ainscow, Alcock	18,001
26	Jan	20	(a)	Millwall	D 1-1	Suddick	8,700
27		27	(h)	Swindon T	W 2-0	Suddick (pen), Rafferty	8,277
28	Feb	2	(a)	Middlesbrough	L 0-2		10,464
29		10	(a)	Orient	L 0-2		4,923
30		17	(h)	Huddersfield T	D 1-1	Rafferty	8,593
31		28	(a)	Sheffield W	L 0-2		13,930
32	Mar	3	(h)	Luton T	D 1-1	Suddick	6,947
33		7	(h)	Cardiff C	W 1-0	Rafferty	5,303
34		10	(a)	Oxford U	W 1-0	Dyson	7,911
35		17	(h)	Fulham	W 2-0	Alcock, Dyson	8,019
36		24	(a)	Queen's Park R	L 0-4		15,714
37		31	(h)	Hull C	W 4-3	James, Dyson, Burns, Suddick	5,645
38	Apr	7	(a)	Portsmouth	L 0-1		6,768
39		14	(h)	Preston NE	W 2-0	Rafferty, Burns	12,195
40		21	(a)	Bristol C	L 0-3		11,537
41		23	(h)	Nottingham F	W 2-0	Dyson, Lennard	8,322
42		28	(a)	Sunderland	L 0-1		26,921

FINAL LEAGUE POSITION: 7th in Division Two

Appearances
Sub Appearances
Goals

FA Cup

3	Jan	13	(a)	Bradford C	L 1-2	Suddick (pen)	14,205

Appearances
Sub Appearances
Goals

League Cup

2	Sep	6	(a)	Bournemouth	D 0-0		10,577
R		11	(h)	Bournemouth	D 1-1*	Suddick	8,685
2R		18	(n†)	Bournemouth	W 2-1*	Hatton, Barton	2,337
3	Oct	4	(a)	Newcastle U	W 3-0	Parker, Barton, Suddick (pen)	19,810
4		31	(h)	Birmingham C	W 2-0	Burns 2	13,332
5	Nov	21	(a)	Wolves	D 1-1	Dyson	17,312
R		28	(h)	Wolves	L 0-1		19,812

*After extra-time. †Played at Villa Park, Birmingham.

Appearances
Sub Appearances
Goals

Burridge	Hardcastle	Bentley	James	Suddaby	Barton	Hutchison	Suddick	Dyson	Lennard	Burns	Ainscow	Wood	Hatton	Simpkin	Alcock	Fuschillo	Parker	Rafferty	McGrotty	Tully	O'Neil	
1	2	3*	4	5	6	7	8	9	10	11	12											1
		3	4	5	6	7	8	9	10*	11	12	1	2									2
		3	4	5	6	7	8	9	10		11*	1	2	12								3
	12	3	4	5	6	7	8	9	10	11		1	2*									4
	2	3	4*	5	6	7	8	9	10	11		1			12							5
	2	3		5	6		8	9	7	11		1			4	6						6
	2*	3		5	6	7	8		10	11	9	1			4		12					7
1		3	9	5	6	7	8		10	11*	12		2		4							8
1		3	4	5	10	7	8		6	11	9		2									9
1		3	4		10	7	8	9*	6		11		2		5	12						10
1		3	4	5	6	7*	8			11	10		2			12	9					11
1		3	4	5	6		8		10	11	7		2					9				12
1	12	3	4	5	6		8		10*	11	7		2					9				13
1		3	4	5	6		8	9		11	7		2			12	10*					14
1	12	3	4	5	6		8	10		7*	11		2					9				15
1	7	3		5	6*		8	10			11		2	12	4			9				16
1		3		5			8	10	6	7	11		2		4			9				17
1		3		5			8	10	6	7	11		2		4			9				18
1	12	3	6*	5			8		10	7	11		2		4			9				19
1	10	3	12	5			8	10*		7	11		2		4			9				20
1	6	3		5			8		10	7	11		2		4			9				21
1	6*	3	12	5			8		10	7	11		2		4			9				22
1		3	12	5			8	10	6*	7	11		2		4			9				23
1	3			5			8	10		7	11		2		4			9		6		24
1	3			5	10		8			7	11		2		4			9		6		25
1	2	3	5				8			7	11			10	4			9			6	26
1	2	3	4				8			7	11			6	5			9			10	27
1	2	3	4				8			7	11			6	5			9			10	28
	2	3	4	5			8			7	11	1		6*				9	12		10	29
		3	4	5	2		8			7	10	1						9		11	6	30
		3	11	6			10	12		7	8	1	2		12			9*			4	31
		3	5	6			8*			7	11	1	2		4			9		12	10	32
		3	5	6			8	10		7	11	1	2		4			9				33
		3	5	6			8	10		7	11	1	2		4			9				34
		3	5	6			8	10		7	11	1	2		4			9				35
		3	5	6			8	10		7	11	1	2		4			9				36
		3	5	6			8	10		7	11	1	2		4			9				37
		3	5	6			8	10	12	7*	11	1	2		4			9				38
		3	5	6			8	10		7	11	1	2		4			9				39
		3	5	6			8	10	12	7	11*	1	2		4			9				40
		3	5	6			8	10	12	7		1	2		4			9*		11		41
	12	3	5	6*			8	10	9	7		1	2		4					11		42
22	14	40	31	38	18	10	42	25	19	39	34	20	33	4	28	1	2	29		5	7	
	5		3					1	3		3			2	2	3	1		1	1		
		1	1		1	3	10	9	3	6	10		1		3			8				

Burridge	Hardcastle	Bentley	James	Suddaby	Barton	Hutchison	Suddick	Dyson	Lennard	Burns	Ainscow	Wood	Hatton	Simpkin	Alcock	Fuschillo	Parker	Rafferty	McGrotty	Tully	O'Neil	
1		3	5	4		11	8	9	10	7	12		2	6*								3
1		1	1	1		1	1	1	1	1			1	1								
											1											
							1															

Burridge	Hardcastle	Bentley	James	Suddaby	Barton	Hutchison	Suddick	Dyson	Lennard	Burns	Ainscow	Wood	Hatton	Simpkin	Alcock	Fuschillo	Parker	Rafferty	McGrotty	Tully	O'Neil	
	2	3		5	10	7	8	9	6	11		1			4							2
	2	3		5	6	7	8	9*	12	11	10	1			4							R
1		3		5	6	7	8*		10		11		2		4	12	9					2R
1		3	4	5	6	7	8			11	10		2				9					3
1	10	3	4	5	6		8	9		11*	7		2		12							4
1	12	3	6	5			8	9*	10	7	11		2		4							5
1	12	3	6	5			8	9	10*	7	11		2		4							R
5	3	7	4	7	5	4	7	5	4	6	6	2	5		5		2					
	2								1						1	1						
					2		2	1		2			1				1					

1973-74

Manager: Harry Potts

No	Month	Day	Venue	Opponents	Result	Scorers	Attendance
1	Aug	25	(h)	West Brom A	L 2-3	Alcock, Suddaby	14,236
2	Sep	1	(a)	Sheffield W	D 0-0		15,834
3		8	(h)	Millwall	W 1-0	Burns	9,442
4		12	(a)	Fulham	D 0-0		9,301
5		15	(a)	Orient	L 2-3	Davies, Burns	7,352
6		17	(h)	Crystal P	W 1-0	Rafferty	9,323
7		22	(h)	Middlesbrough	D 0-0		14,784
8		29	(a)	Luton T	L 0-3		10,365
9	Oct	2	(a)	Crystal P	W 2-1	James, Burns	18,080
10		6	(h)	Notts C	L 0-1		11,072
11		13	(a)	Cardiff C	L 0-1		7,693
12		20	(h)	Nottingham F	D 2-2	James, Davies	8,107
13		22	(h)	Fulham	W 2-0	Alcock 2	5,526
14		27	(a)	Bristol C	W 1-0	Dyson	13,896
15	Nov	3	(h)	Portsmouth	W 5-0	Suddick, Walsh, Burns 2, Alcock	6,535
16		10	(a)	Preston NE	W 3-1	Alcock 2, Walsh	21,580
17		17	(h)	Swindon T	W 2-0	Alcock, Bentley	7,404
18		24	(a)	Hull C	L 0-1		9,004
19	Dec	1	(h)	Sunderland	L 0-2		11,000
20		8	(a)	Carlisle U	W 3-2	Bentley, Suddick, Alcock	6,641
21		15	(a)	Oxford U	D 2-2	Alcock, Hatton	5,001
22		22	(h)	Luton T	W 3-0	Burns 3	7,796
23		26	(a)	Bolton W	D 1-1	Opp own-goal	18,150
24		29	(a)	Millwall	D 2-2	Burns, Dyson	8,848
25	Jan	1	(h)	Sheffield W	D 0-0		11,362
26		12	(h)	Orient	D 1-1	Burns	8,760
27		19	(a)	West Brom A	D 1-1	Ainscow	17,727
28	Feb	2	(h)	Oxford U	W 2-0	Burns, Suddick	5,508
29		9	(a)	Middlesbrough	D 0-0		21,913
30		16	(h)	Cardiff C	W 2-1	Ainscow 2	7,410
31		23	(a)	Notts C	W 3-0	Dyson 2, Burns	11,092
32	Mar	2	(h)	Bolton W	L 0-2		18,575
33		16	(a)	Nottingham F	L 0-2		15,724
34		19	(h)	Bristol C	D 2-2	James, Davies	7,710
35		23	(h)	Preston NE	W 3-0	Alcock, Walsh, Suddick (pen)	13,243
36		30	(a)	Portsmouth	D 0-0		9,693
37	Apr	6	(h)	Hull C	L 1-2	Burns	8,159
38		13	(a)	Swindon T	L 0-1		4,655
39		15	(a)	Aston Villa	W 1-0	Dyson	18,351
40		16	(h)	Aston Villa	W 2-1	Suddick, Dyson	10,787
41		20	(h)	Carlisle U	W 4-0	Dyson, Alcock 2, Suddick (pen)	15,777
42		27	(a)	Sunderland	L 1-2	Burns	22,331

FINAL LEAGUE POSITION: 5th in Division Two

Appearances
Sub Appearar
Goals

FA Cup

Rd	Month	Day	Venue	Opponents	Result	Scorers	Attendance
3	Jan	5	(a)	Southampton	L 1-2	Dyson	16,212

Appearances
Sub Appeara
Goals

League Cup

Rd	Month	Day	Venue	Opponents	Result	Scorers	Attendance
2	Oct	9	(h)	Birmingham C	D 1-1	Burns	7,943
R		16	(a)	Birmingham C	L 2-4	Burns 2	16,880

Appearances
Sub Appeara
Goals

Wood	Hatton	Bentley	Alcock	James	Suddaby	Burns	Suddick	Davies	McEwan	Tully	Rafferty	Fuschillo	Walsh	Hardcastle	Curtis	Dyson	Burridge	Hart	Harrison	Ainscow	Evanson	
1	2	3	4	5	6	7	8	9	10	11*	12											1
1	2	3	4	5	6	7	8	9	10	11												2
1	2	3	4	5	6	7	8	9		11		10										3
1	2	3	4	5	6	7		9		11		10	8									4
1		3	4	5	6	7		9		11		10	8*	12	2							5
1	2	3	4	5	6	11		9			8		7		10							6
1	2	3	4	5	6	7	8	9			10		11									7
1	2	3	4	5	6	7	8	9			10		11*		12							8
1	3		4	5	6	7	8	9			10*	11			12	12						9
1	2	3	4	5	6	7	8	9			10	11										10
1	2	3	4	5	6	7	8	9	11							10						11
1		3	4	5	6	7	8	9	11*		10				2	12						12
		3	4	5	6	7	8	9					11		2		1	10				13
	10	3	4	5	6	7	8						11		2	9	1					14
	3	10	4	5	6	7	8						11		2	9	1					15
	3	10	4	5	6	7	8						11		2	9	1					16
		10	4	5	6	7	8						11		2	9	1		3			17
	3	10	4	5	6	7	8						11		2	9	1					18
	3	10	4	5	6	7	8						11		2	9	1					19
	3	10	4	5	6	7	8						11		2	9	1					20
	3	10	4	5	6	7	8						11*		2	9	1		12			21
	3	10	4	5	6	7	8						12		2	9	1			11*		22
	3	10	4	5	6	7	8								2	9	1			11		23
	3	10	4	5	6	7	8								2	9	1			11		24
	3*	10	4	5	6	7	8						12		2	9	1			11		25
		10	4	5	6	7	8						12		2	9	1		3	11*		26
		10	4	5	6	7	8								2	9	1		3	11		27
		10	4	5	6	7	8								2	9	1		3	11		28
		10	4	5	6	7	8								2	9	1		3	11		29
		10	4	5		7	8								2	9	1	6	3	11		30
		3	4	5		7	8								2	9	1	6		11	10	31
		3	4	5	6	7	8								2	9	1			11	10	32
	12	3	4	5	6	7	8								2	9*	1			11	10	33
	2	3	4	5	6	7	8	9					12				1			11	10*	34
	2		4	5	6	7	8	9					11				1		3		10	35
	2		4	5	6	7	8	9									1		3	11	10	36
	2		4	5	6	7	8	9					12				1		3	11*	10	37
	2	4		5	6	7	8						10			9	1		3*	11	12	38
	2	10	4	5	6	7	8									9	1		3	11		39
	2	10	4	5	6	7	8									9	1		3	11*	12	40
	2	11	4	5	6	7	8									9	1		3	12	10*	41
	2	11	4	5	6	7	8									9	1		3		10	42
12	30	38	41	42	40	42	39	17	4	5	6	5	16		25	26	30	3	14	18	9	
	1										1		5	1	1	2			1	1	2	
	1	2	12	3	1	14	6	3			1		3			7				3		

1 own-goal

Wood	Hatton	Bentley	Alcock	James	Suddaby	Burns	Suddick	Davies	McEwan	Tully	Rafferty	Fuschillo	Walsh	Hardcastle	Curtis	Dyson	Burridge	Hart	Harrison	Ainscow	Evanson	
		10	4	5	6	7	8								2	9	1		3	11		3
		1	1	1	1	1	1								1	1	1		1	1		
																1						

Wood	Hatton	Bentley	Alcock	James	Suddaby	Burns	Suddick	Davies	McEwan	Tully	Rafferty	Fuschillo	Walsh	Hardcastle	Curtis	Dyson	Burridge	Hart	Harrison	Ainscow	Evanson	
1	2	3	4	5	6	7	8	9	11							10						2
1	2	3	4	5	6	7	8	9	11	10												R
2	2	2	2	2	2	2	2	2	2	1						1						
						3																

1974-75

Manager: Harry Potts

1	Aug	17	(a)	Norwich C	L 1-2	Bentley	18,551
2		20	(h)	Orient	D 0-0		9,314
3		24	(h)	Bolton W	W 2-1	Dyson, Ainscow	15,513
4		27	(a)	Orient	D 0-0		7,314
5		31	(a)	Southampton	D 1-1	Walsh	14,694
6	Sep	7	(h)	Millwall	W 1-0	Walsh	5,579
7		14	(a)	Oldham A	L 0-1		11,926
8		21	(h)	York C	D 1-1	Walsh	7,927
9		24	(h)	Cardiff C	W 4-0	Parker, Hart, Davies, Opp own-goal	5,597
10		28	(a)	Bristol R	W 3-1	Hart, Walsh (pen), Parker	10,968
11	Oct	5	(h)	Hull C	L 1-2	Hart	8,406
12		12	(a)	Aston Villa	L 0-1		25,763
13		19	(h)	Manchester U	L 0-3		22,211
14		22	(a)	Bolton W	D 0-0		12,574
15		26	(a)	Portsmouth	D 0-0		10,143
16	Nov	2	(h)	Sheffield W	W 3-1	Tong 2, Ainscow	6,243
17		9	(a)	Sunderland	L 0-1		24,939
18		16	(h)	Oxford U	D 0-0		5,342
19		23	(a)	Bristol C	W 1-0	Hatton (pen)	11,584
20		30	(a)	Fulham	L 0-1		6,416
21	Dec	7	(h)	Notts C	W 3-1	Ainscow, Walsh, Dyson	4,922
22		14	(h)	Norwich C	W 2-1	Hart, Walsh	6,683
23		21	(a)	Nottingham F	D 0-0		8,480
24		26	(h)	Oldham A	W 1-0	Walsh	12,491
25		28	(a)	West Brom A	L 0-2		14,924
26	Jan	11	(a)	Notts C	D 0-0		10,601
27		18	(h)	Fulham	W 1-0	Alcock	6,710
28	Feb	1	(h)	Sunderland	W 3-2	Alcock, Davies, Walsh	16,151
29		8	(a)	Sheffield W	D 0-0		14,342
30		15	(h)	Bristol C	W 2-0	Ainscow, Bentley	8,687
31		22	(a)	Oxford U	D 0-0		7,476
32	Mar	1	(h)	Southampton	W 3-0	Walsh 2, Alcock	8,831
33		8	(a)	Cardiff C	D 1-1	Bentley	8,134
34		15	(h)	Bristol R	D 0-0		8,019
35		22	(a)	Millwall	D 0-0		7,506
36		29	(h)	Nottingham F	D 0-0		11,640
37		31	(h)	West Brom A	W 2-0	Alcock, Opp own-goal	11,611
38	Apr	1	(a)	York C	D 0-0		8,234
39		5	(h)	Portsmouth	D 2-2	Walsh 2 (1 pen)	6,543
40		12	(a)	Hull C	L 0-1		6,027
41		19	(h)	Aston Villa	L 0-3		20,762
42		26	(a)	Manchester U	L 0-4		58,769

FINAL LEAGUE POSITION: 7th in Division Two

Appearances
Sub Appearances
Goals

FA Cup

3	Jan	4	(a)	Plymouth A	L 0-2		23,143

Appearances
Sub Appearances
Goals

League Cup

2	Sep	11	(a)	Chester C	L 1-3	Walsh	5,854

Appearances
Sub Appearances
Goals

Burridge	Hatton	Bentley	Alcock	James	Suddaby	Tong	Suddick	Dyson	Evanson	Walsh	Curtis	Moore	Parker	Harrison	Evans	Hart	Ainscow	Davies	Wood	McEwan	Ronson	
1	2	3	4	5	6	7*	8	9	10	11	12											1
1		3	4	5	6		8	9			12	7	10*	11	12							2
1	2*	10		5	6		8	9			12	7		3		4	11					3
1	7	3		5	6			9	8		2			11		4	10					4
1	7	3		5	6			9*	8	12	2			11		4	10					5
1	5	3			6		7		8	9	2			11		4	10					6
1	5	3		2	6		7		8	9	12		10*	11		4						7
1	2	3		5	6	8			10*	7	12			11		4		9				8
1	2	3		5*	6	8					10	7	12	11		4		9				9
	2	3*			6	8				7	5	10	12	11		4		9	1			10
	2	3			6	8			10*	7	5		12	11		4		9	1			11
	2	3		4	6	8			10	7*	5			11			9	12	1			12
	4*	10		5	6	12			11	7	2			3			8	9	1			13
1	4	10			6	9			11	7	2			3		5	8					14
1	4	10			6	9			11	7	2			3		5	8					15
1	2	10			6	7			11	9	4			3		5	8					16
1	2	10			6	7*			11	9	4			3	12	5	8					17
1	2	10			6				11	9	4		12	3	7*	5	8					18
1	2	10			6				11		4		9	3	7	5	8					19
1	2	10			6				11	12	4		9*	3	7	5	8					20
1	4	3	6			7		10	11	9	2					5	8					21
1	4	3	6			7		10*	11	9	2					5	8	12				22
1	4	3	6			7		10	11	9	2					5	8					23
1	4	3	6			7		10	11	9	2					5	8					24
1	4	3	6			7*		10	11	9		2				5	8			12		25
1	3		6	4		7			11*	10	2	12				5	8	9				26
1	4		6	3		7			11	9	2					5	8	10				27
1	3	10	6						11	9	2			5		4	7	8				28
1	3	10	6			12			11	9	2*			5		4	7	8				29
1	6	10	5						11	7	2			3		4	8	9				30
1	6	10	5			9			11	7	2			3		4	8					31
1	6	10	5			11				7	2			3		4	8	9				32
1	6	10	5						11	7	2			3		4	8	9				33
1	6	10	5			12			11	7	2			3		4	8*	9				34
1	4	10	5			8			11	7	2		9	3		6						35
1	6	10	5						11	7	2			3		4		9			8	36
1	6	10	5			8			11	7	2			3		4		9				37
1	4	10*	5		12				11	7	2		8	3		6		9				38
1	6		8		5				10	7	2			3		4	11	9				39
1	6		5*			8			11	7	2	12	9	3		4	10					40
1	6*				5	8			11	9	2		12	3		4	10				7	41
1	2		3		5	8			11	7	12		9*	3	6		10					42
38	41	36	23	12	23	24	5	10	37	35	36	5	8	34	4	37	31	17	4		2	
					1	3				2	5	2	5		2			2		1		
	1	3	4			2		2		12			2			4	4	2				

2 own-goals

Burridge	Hatton	Bentley	Alcock	James	Suddaby	Tong	Suddick	Dyson	Evanson	Walsh	Curtis	Moore	Parker	Harrison	Evans	Hart	Ainscow	Davies	Wood	McEwan	Ronson	
1	4	3	6			12			11	9	2	7*				5	8	10				3
1	1	1	1						1	1	1	1				1	1	1				
						1																

Burridge	Hatton	Bentley	Alcock	James	Suddaby	Tong	Suddick	Dyson	Evanson	Walsh	Curtis	Moore	Parker	Harrison	Evans	Hart	Ainscow	Davies	Wood	McEwan	Ronson	
1		3	5	7	6	12			8	9	2			11		4	10*					2
1		1	1	1	1				1	1	1			1		1	1					
						1																
									1													

1975-76

Manager: Harry Potts

No	Month	Day	Venue	Opponent	Result	Score	Scorers	Attendance
1	Aug	16	(a)	Fulham	D	0-0		8,863
2		19	(a)	Hull C	L	0-1		5,304
3		23	(h)	Orient	W	1-0	Tong	6,626
4		30	(a)	Sunderland	L	0-2		23,576
5	Sep	6	(h)	Oldham A	D	1-1	Walsh	8,862
6		13	(a)	Charlton A	D	1-1	Walsh	9,190
7		20	(h)	Southampton	W	4-3	Walsh 3 (1 pen), Moore	9,564
8		24	(a)	Blackburn R	W	2-0	Walsh, Moore	11,048
9		27	(a)	Bristol C	L	0-2		10,240
10	Oct	4	(h)	Luton T	W	3-2	Suddaby 2, Walsh	7,854
11		11	(h)	Portsmouth	D	0-0		8,351
12		18	(a)	Chelsea	L	0-2		16,924
13		25	(h)	Bristol R	L	1-4	Suddick	9,019
14	Nov	1	(a)	Bolton W	L	0-1		17,274
15		4	(h)	Nottingham F	D	1-1	Ainscow	5,851
16		8	(h)	West Brom A	L	0-1		8,271
17		15	(a)	Oxford U	W	3-1	Walsh, Suddaby, Ainscow	4,316
18		22	(h)	Chelsea	L	0-2		8,595
19		29	(h)	Notts C	W	1-0	Walsh	6,103
20	Dec	6	(a)	Plymouth A	W	2-1	Walsh 2	12,422
21		12	(a)	Orient	W	1-0	Tong	4,337
22		20	(h)	Fulham	D	1-1	Weston	6,379
23		26	(a)	Carlisle U	L	0-1		11,532
24		27	(h)	York C	D	0-0		7,939
25	Jan	10	(h)	Charlton A	W	2-1	Walsh 2 (1 pen)	5,748
26		17	(a)	Oldham A	L	0-1		11,734
27		31	(h)	Hull C	D	2-2	Alcock, Ronson	4,966
28	Feb	7	(a)	Nottingham F	L	0-3		8,582
29		21	(h)	Oxford U	W	2-0	Walsh, Smith	4,423
30		24	(h)	Blackburn R	D	1-1	Hart	8,772
31		28	(a)	Bristol R	D	1-1	Smith	6,686
32	Mar	6	(h)	Bolton W	D	1-1	Smith	18,548
33		13	(a)	Portsmouth	L	0-2		8,394
34		20	(a)	Notts C	W	2-1	Smith 2	10,427
35		27	(h)	Plymouth A	D	0-0		5,497
36		31	(a)	West Brom A	D	0-0		20,729
37	Apr	3	(h)	Bristol C	W	2-1	Moore, Walsh	8,273
38		10	(a)	Southampton	L	1-3	Suddaby	21,758
39		17	(h)	Carlisle U	W	2-1	Walsh, Hart	8,382
40		19	(a)	York C	D	1-1	Ronson	3,800
41		20	(h)	Sunderland	W	1-0	Walsh	16,768
42		24	(a)	Luton T	L	0-3		8,757

FINAL LEAGUE POSITION: 10th in Division Two

Appearances
Sub Appearances
Goals

FA Cup

Rd	Month	Day	Venue	Opponent	Result	Score	Scorers	Attendance
3	Jan	3	(h)	Burnley	W	1-0	Bentley	20,573
4		24	(a)	Southampton	L	1-3	Alcock	21,553

Appearances
Sub Appearances
Goals

League Cup

Rd	Month	Day	Venue	Opponent	Result	Score	Scorers	Attendance
2	Sep	10	(a)	Peterborough U	L	0-2		6,987

Appearances
Sub Appearances
Goals

Burridge	Curtis	Harrison	Suddaby	Tong	Alcock	Walsh	Suddick	Ronson	Moore	Ainscow	McEwan	Hart	Bentley	Dyson	Hatton	Betts	Wood	Evanson	Weston	Smith	
1	2	3	4	5	6	7	8	9	10	11											1
1	2	3	5	6	4	7	8			11		9	10								2
1	2	3	5	6	4	7	8			11		9	10								3
1	2	3	5	10*	4	7	8		12	11		9	6								4
1	2	3	5	10*	4	7	8	12		11			6	9							5
1	2		5	10		12	8		7	11		4	6	9*	3						6
1	2		5			9	8	7	11	10		4	3		6						7
	2		5			9	8	7	11	10		4	3		6		1				8
	2		5			9	8	7	11	10		4	3		6		1				9
	2	11	5			9	8	7		10		4	3		6		1				10
	2	12	5	7*		9	8		11	10		4	3		6		1				11
	2	3		5		7	8		10	9		4	11		6		1				12
	2	3	5		12	9	8			10		4	11		6		1	7*			13
	2	3	5			9	8		7	10		4	11		6		1				14
	2	3	5			9	7	10	11	8		4			6		1				15
		3	5		2	9	7	10	11	8		6			4		1				16
		3	5	2		9	7	10*	11	8		6			4	12	1				17
		3	5	11	12	9	8	7*	6	10		4			2		1				18
		3*	5	7	6	9	8			11		4			2	10	1		12		19
			5	7	6	9				11*		4	3		2	10	1	12	8		20
			5	7	6	9					4		3		2	11	1	8	10		21
				7	6	9				8*	4	5	3		2	12	1	11	10		22
		12	5	7	6	9						4	3		2	11	1	8	10*		23
		3	5	7*	6	9		8			12	4	10		2		1	11			24
		8	5		6	9			12		4	7	3		2		1	11	10		25
		8			6	9			2	5*	4	7	3			12	1	11	10		26
		3			6	9		12	8		4	5	2				1	7*	11	10	27
		3	11		6	9		7	8		4	5	2				1			10	28
		3	5			9		7	11	8		4	6		2		1			10	29
		3	5			9		7	11	8		4	6		2		1			10	30
		3	5			9				8	7	4	6		2		1		11	10	31
		3	5			9				8	7	4	6		2		1		11	10	32
		3	5		6	9				11	4		3		2		1	12	10*	7	33
		3	5		6	9				10	4		11		2		1	7		8	34
		3	5		6	9	8			10	4		11		2		1	7			35
			5		6	9	8	11	10		4		3		2		1	7			36
			5		6	9	8		11	10	4		3		2		1	7			37
			5		6	9	8		11	10	4		3		2		1	7			38
		3	5			9	8			7	4	6	10		2		1	11			39
		6	5			9	8	11		10		4	3		2		1	7			40
		3	5			9	8	4		7		6	10		2		1	11			41
		6	5			9	8	11		10	12	4	3		2		1	7*			42
7	15	30	38	16	22	41	27	17	20	35	15	33	36	2	34	4	35	17	10	8	
		2			2	1		2	1		2					3		2	1		
			4	2	1	17	1	2	3	2		2							1	5	

Burridge	Curtis	Harrison	Suddaby	Tong	Alcock	Walsh	Suddick	Ronson	Moore	Ainscow	McEwan	Hart	Bentley	Dyson	Hatton	Betts	Wood	Evanson	Weston	Smith	
		8	5		6*	9			12		4	7	3		2		1	11	10		3
		3			6	9			8		4	5	10		2		1	7	11		4
		2	1		2	2			1		2	2	2		2		2	2	2		
									1												
					1								1								

Burridge	Curtis	Harrison	Suddaby	Tong	Alcock	Walsh	Suddick	Ronson	Moore	Ainscow	McEwan	Hart	Bentley	Dyson	Hatton	Betts	Wood	Evanson	Weston	Smith	
1	2	3*	5	12		7	8	10		11			6	9	4						2
1	1	1	1			1	1	1		1			1	1	1						
				1																	

1976-77

Manager: Allan Brown

1	Aug	21	(a)	Bristol R	W 4-1	Hatton 2, Suddick, Opp own-goal	5,845
2		24	(h)	Oldham A	L 0-2		12,974
3		28	(h)	Orient	W 3-0	Hart, Walsh 2 (1 pen)	7,928
4	Sep	4	(a)	Blackburn R	W 1-0	Walsh (pen)	10,173
5		11	(h)	Millwall	W 4-2	Ronson, Walsh 2, Suddick	8,881
6		18	(a)	Notts C	L 0-2		9,598
7		25	(h)	Chelsea	L 0-1		19,041
8	Oct	2	(a)	Bolton W	W 3-0	Hatton, Walsh 2 (1 pen)	18,680
9		9	(h)	Plymouth A	L 0-2		12,647
10		12	(a)	Carlisle U	D 1-1	Bentley	8,427
11		16	(h)	Nottingham F	W 1-0	Walsh	17,089
12		23	(a)	Cardiff C	D 2-2	Hatton, Spence	12,178
13		30	(h)	Wolves	D 2-2	Spence, Hart	21,005
14	Nov	6	(a)	Hull C	D 2-2	Walsh, Hatton	9,541
15		13	(h)	Sheffield U	W 1-0	Walsh	13,506
16		20	(a)	Charlton A	W 2-1	Hart, Walsh	12,045
17		27	(h)	Fulham	W 3-2	Hart, Hatton, Walsh	16,779
18	Dec	4	(a)	Luton T	D 0-0		9,163
19		18	(a)	Southampton	D 3-3	Bentley, Walsh 2	14,918
20		27	(h)	Carlisle U	D 0-0		17,075
21		28	(a)	Burnley	D 0-0		19,640
22	Jan	1	(h)	Hull C	D 0-0		12,503
23		15	(a)	Oldham A	L 0-1		12,411
24		22	(h)	Bristol R	W 4-0	Walsh (pen), Hart, Ainscow, Bentley	9,288
25	Feb	12	(h)	Blackburn R	D 1-1	Ainscow	14,922
26		14	(h)	Hereford U	W 2-1	Walsh 2	8,535
27		19	(a)	Millwall	D 1-1	Walsh	10,561
28		26	(h)	Notts C	D 1-1	Walsh	10,275
29	Mar	1	(a)	Wolves	L 1-2	Hatton	23,879
30		5	(a)	Chelsea	D 2-2	Ronson, Spence	27,412
31		12	(h)	Bolton W	W 1-0	Ronson	23,659
32		19	(a)	Plymouth A	L 0-2		8,893
33		26	(a)	Nottingham F	L 0-3		16,658
34	Apr	2	(h)	Cardiff C	W 1-0	Hart	7,351
35		9	(h)	Burnley	D 1-1	Walsh	14,526
36		12	(a)	Sheffield U	W 5-1	Walsh 3, Hatton, Ronson	18,357
37		16	(h)	Charlton A	D 2-2	Walsh 2 (1 pen)	8,686
38		23	(a)	Fulham	D 0-0		10,956
39		30	(h)	Luton T	W 1-0	Hatton	9,277
40	May	7	(a)	Hereford U	D 1-1	Finnigan	5,312
41		10	(a)	Orient	W 1-0	Walsh	4,730
42		14	(h)	Southampton	W 1-0	Hatton	10,768

FINAL LEAGUE POSITION: 5th in Division Two

Appearances
Sub Appearan
Goals

FA Cup

3	Jan	8	(h)	Derby C	D 0-0		19,442
R		19	(a)	Derby C	L 2-3	Walsh, Spence	21,433

Appearances
Sub Appearan
Goals

League Cup

2	Aug	31	(h)	Birmingham C	W 2-1	Ronson, Hatton	12,203
3	Sep	21	(h)	Arsenal	D 1-1	Walsh	18,983
R		28	(a)	Arsenal	D 0-0		27,195
2R	Oct	5	(a)	Arsenal	L 0-2		26,791

Appearances
Sub Appearar
Goals

Wood	Curtis	Bentley	Hart	Suddaby	Tong	Ronson	Suddick	Ainscow	Hatton	Harrison	Moore	Walsh	Gardner	Farley	Hockaday	Spence	Weston	McEwan	Summerbee	Finnigan	Milligan	Wilson	
1	2	3	4	5	6	7	8	9	10	11													1
1	2	3	5	6	4	7*	8	11	10		12	9											2
1	2	3	5	6	4	7	8		10		11	9											3
1	2	3	5	6	4	7	8		10		11	9											4
1	2	3	5	6	4	7	8		10		11	9											5
1	2	3	5	6	4	7	8		10		11*	9			12								6
1		3	5	6		4	8		10	12	11*	9	2		7								7
1		11	5	6		4	8	7	10*	3		9	2		12								8
1		3	5	6		4	8	7	10			9	2	11									9
1		11	5	6		4	8	7	10	3		9	2										10
1		11	5	6		4		7	10	3		9	2			8							11
1		11	5	6		4		7	10	3		9	2			8							12
1		11	5	6		4	7		10	3		9	2			8							13
1		11	5	6		4			10	3		9	2			8	7						14
1		11	5	6		4			10	3	12	9	2			8	7*						15
1		11	5	6		4			10	3		9	2			8	7						16
1		11	5	6		4			10	3		9	2			8	7						17
1		11	5	6		4			10	3		9	2			8	7						18
1	2	11*	5	6		4			10	3		9				8	7	12					19
1	2	11	5	6		4			10	3		9				8	7						20
1	2	11	5	6		4			10	3		9				8	7						21
1	2	11	5	6	10	4				3		9				8			7				22
1	2	11	5	6	12	4*		7	10	3		9				8							23
1	2	11	5	6		4		7	10	3		9				8							24
1	2	11	5	6		4		7	10	3		9				8							25
1	2	11	5	6		4		7	10*	3	8	9				12							26
1	2	11	5	6		4		7	10	3	8	9											27
1	2	11	5	6		4		7	10	3	8*	9				12							28
1	2	11	5	6		4		7	10	3		9				8							29
1	2	11	5	6		4		7	10	3		9				8							30
1	2	11	5	6		4		7	10	3		9				8							31
1		11	5	6					10	3		9	2			8	7	12	4*				32
1	2	11*	5	6	12	4		7	10	3		9				8							33
1			5	6	11*	4			10	3		9	2		7			12	8				34
1		11	8	6		4				3		9	2		7*	12		5		10			35
1		11	5	6		4			10	3		9	2			7		8					36
1		11	5	6		4			10	3		9	2			7*		8		12			37
1		11	5	6		4			10	3		9	2			7		8					38
1		11	5	6		4			10	3		9	2			7*		8		12			39
1		11	5	6	12	4			10	3*		9	2					8		7			40
1			5	6	11	4						9	2					8		7	3	10	41
1			5	6	11	4			10			9	2					8		7	3		42
42	20	39	42	42	10	41	11	17	39	33	8	41	22	1	3	24	9	8	3	4	2	1	
					3					1	2				2	3		3		2			
		3	6			4	2	2	10			26				3				1			

1 own-goal

Wood	Curtis	Bentley	Hart	Suddaby	Tong	Ronson	Suddick	Ainscow	Hatton	Harrison	Moore	Walsh	Gardner	Farley	Hockaday	Spence	Weston	McEwan	Summerbee	Finnigan	Milligan	Wilson	
1	2	11	5	6		4		7	10	3		9				8							3
1	2	11	5	6		4		7	10	3		9				8							R
2	2	2	2	2		2		2	2	2		2				2							
												1				1							

Wood	Curtis	Bentley	Hart	Suddaby	Tong	Ronson	Suddick	Ainscow	Hatton	Harrison	Moore	Walsh	Gardner	Farley	Hockaday	Spence	Weston	McEwan	Summerbee	Finnigan	Milligan	Wilson	
1	2	3	5	6	4	7	8		10		11	9											2
1		3	5	6		4	8		10		11	9	2		7								3
1		3	5	6		4	8		10	12		9	2		7		11*						R
1		11	5	6		4	12	7	10	3		9	2									8*	2R
4	1	4	4	4	1	4	3	1	4	1	2	4	3		2		1					1	
							1			1													
						1			1			1											

1977-78

Manager: Allan Brown

No	Month	Day	Venue	Opponents	Result	Scorers	Attendance
1	Aug	20	(h)	Oldham A	D 1-1	Suddaby	11,021
2		23	(a)	Orient	W 4-1	Finnigan, Hatton 3	5,328
3		27	(a)	Charlton A	L 1-3	Walsh	6,449
4	Sep	3	(h)	Bristol R	W 3-1	Walsh 2, Hatton	8,219
5		10	(a)	Blackburn R	W 2-1	Walsh, Chandler	8,211
6		17	(h)	Tottenham H	L 0-2		17,077
7		24	(a)	Notts C	D 1-1	Finnigan	7,200
8	Oct	1	(h)	Cardiff C	W 3-0	Hatton 3	8,704
9		4	(h)	Crystal P	W 3-1	Hart, Hatton 2	9,369
10		8	(a)	Fulham	D 1-1	Ronson	9,190
11		15	(a)	Hull C	L 0-2		6,800
12		22	(h)	Luton T	W 2-1	Ronson, Ainscow	12,167
13		29	(a)	Burnley	W 1-0	Ainscow	11,225
14	Nov	5	(h)	Sheffield U	D 1-1	Hatton	10,625
15		12	(a)	Southampton	L 0-2		18,356
16		19	(h)	Millwall	D 2-2	Hatton, Hart	7,224
17		26	(a)	Stoke C	W 2-1	Walsh 2	15,132
18	Dec	3	(h)	Brighton & HA	L 0-1		9,704
19		10	(a)	Mansfield T	W 3-1	Hatton, Ainscow, Walsh	6,975
20		17	(h)	Southampton	L 0-1		8,640
21		26	(a)	Sunderland	L 1-2	Hatton	30,628
22		27	(h)	Bolton W	L 0-2		25,789
23		31	(h)	Orient	D 0-0		6,911
24	Jan	2	(a)	Oldham A	L 1-2	Walsh	15,308
25		14	(h)	Charlton A	W 5-1	Hatton 3, Hart, Walsh	6,206
26		21	(a)	Bristol R	L 0-2		7,304
27	Feb	4	(h)	Blackburn R	W 5-2	Hatton 4, Waldron	12,416
28		11	(a)	Tottenham H	D 2-2	Ronson, Walsh	28,707
29		25	(a)	Cardiff C	L 1-2	Tong	7,322
30	Mar	7	(h)	Notts C	D 2-2	Walsh (pen), Groves	6,783
31		11	(h)	Hull C	W 3-0	Tong, Chandler, Ainscow	6,220
32		18	(a)	Luton T	L 0-4		6,041
33		25	(a)	Bolton W	L 1-2	Walsh (pen)	20,506
34		27	(h)	Sunderland	D 1-1	Tong	9,872
35		28	(h)	Burnley	D 1-1	Walsh	13,393
36	Apr	1	(a)	Sheffield U	D 0-0		12,804
37		8	(h)	Stoke C	D 1-1	Wilson	12,201
38		15	(a)	Millwall	L 0-2		5,553
39		18	(h)	Fulham	L 1-2	Walsh (pen)	4,695
40		22	(h)	Mansfield T	L 1-2	Hatton	5,376
41		25	(a)	Crystal P	D 2-2	McEwan, Opp own-goal	11,115
42		29	(a)	Brighton & HA	L 1-2	Hatton	33,431

FINAL LEAGUE POSITION: 20th in Division Two

Appearances
Sub Appearan
Goals

FA Cup

Round	Month	Day	Venue	Opponents	Result	Scorers	Attendance
3	Jan	7	(a)	West Brom A	L 1-4	Hatton	21,306

Appearances
Sub Appearar
Goals

League Cup

Round	Month	Day	Venue	Opponents	Result	Scorers	Attendance
2	Aug	30	(h)	Sheffield W	D 2-2	Walsh (pen), Hatton	10,101
R	Sep	5	(a)	Sheffield W	L 1-3	Hart	13,260

Appearances
Sub Appearai
Goals

Hesford	Gardner	Harrison	Hart	McEwan	Suddaby	Ainscow	Tong	Walsh	Hatton	Finnigan	Sinclair	Ronson	Milligan	Chandler	Ward	Weston	Groves	Waldron	Wilson	Thompson	Hockaday	
1	2	3	4	5	6	7	8	9	10	11*	12											1
1	2	3	4	5	6		8	9	10	11		7										2
1	2	3	4	6	5		8	9	10	11		7										3
1	2	3	5	7	6		8	9	10	11		4										4
	2	3		5	6	7		9	10	11		4		8								5
	2	3	5	12	6	7*		9	10	11		4		8	1							6
	2*	3	4	5	6	7		9	10	11		12			1	8						7
		3	4	5	6	7		9	10	11			2		1	8						8
		3	4	5	6	8		9	10			7	2		1	11						9
		3	4	5	6	8		9	10			7	2		1	11						10
		3	4	5	6	8		9	10			7	2		1	11						11
	2		4	5	6	8		9	10	12		7	3*		1	11						12
	2	3	4	5	6	8		9	10			7			1	11						13
	2	3	4	5	6	8		9	10			7			1	11						14
	2	3	4	5	6	8		9	10	12		7			1	11*						15
	2	3	4	5	6	8		9	10	11		7*			1	12						16
	2	3	4	5	6	8		9	10						1	7	11					17
	2	3	4	5	6	8		9	10			12			1	7*	11					18
		3	5	2	6	7	8	9	10			4			1		11					19
		3	5	2	6	7	8	9	10			4*			1		11	12				20
			5	2	6	7	8	9	10						1	3	11	4				21
	2	3	5		6	7		9	10						1	8	11	4*	12			22
	2	3	5	4	6	8		9	10			7			1		11					23
	2		4	5	6	8		9	10			7	3		1		11					24
		3	4	5	6	8		9	10			7			1			11		2		25
		3	4	5	6	8		9	10			7			1	12		11*		2		26
	2	3	4	5				9	10			7		8	1			11		6		27
	2		4	5		10		9				7		8	1	3		11		6		28
			4	5			6	9			12	7	3		1		11	10	8	2*		29
				5	6		7	9				4	3	8	1		11	10	2			30
	2			5	6*	10	7	9				4	3	8	1			11	12			31
	2			5	6	10	7*	9				4	3	8	1			11	12			32
1	2			5	6	10	12	9				4		8				11	7*	3		33
1	2			5	6	10	7		9			4		8			12	11*		3		34
1	2			5	6	8	7	9	10			4	3					11				35
1	2				6	8	4	9*	10				3	7			12	11	5			36
1	2			5	6	8	4		10				3	7*			12	11	9			37
1	2				6	8*	4		10				3	7			9	11	5	12		38
1	2			5	6		12	9	10			8		7*		3		11		4		39
1	2			5	6	11*	7	9	10			8	3				12			4		40
1	2			5	6	11	7	9	10			8				3				4		41
1	2			5	6	11	7	9	10			8				3				4		42
14	31	23	28	38	39	35	19	39	36	9		32	15	13	28	17	11	17	6	11		
				1			2			1	2	2				2	4	1	3	1		
			3	1	1	4	3	14	22	2		3		2			1	1	1			

1 own-goal

Hesford	Gardner	Harrison	Hart	McEwan	Suddaby	Ainscow	Tong	Walsh	Hatton	Finnigan	Sinclair	Ronson	Milligan	Chandler	Ward	Weston	Groves	Waldron	Wilson	Thompson	Hockaday	
	2		4	5	6	8		9	10			7	3	12	1		11*					3
	1		1	1	1	1		1	1			1	1		1		1					
														1								
									1													

Hesford	Gardner	Harrison	Hart	McEwan	Suddaby	Ainscow	Tong	Walsh	Hatton	Finnigan	Sinclair	Ronson	Milligan	Chandler	Ward	Weston	Groves	Waldron	Wilson	Thompson	Hockaday	
1	2	3	5		6		8	9*	10	11	12	4									7	2
1	2	3	5*	7	6		8	9	10	11		4	12									R
2	2	2	2	1	2		2	2	2	2		2									1	
											1		1									
			1					1	1													

1978-79

Manager: Bob Stokoe

1	Aug	19	(h)	Oxford U	W 1-0	Davidson	6,215
2		22	(a)	Watford	L 1-5	Wilson	11,812
3		26	(a)	Rotherham U	L 1-2	Davidson	4,572
4	Sep	2	(h)	Carlisle U	W 3-1	Spence 3	7,789
5		9	(a)	Shrewsbury T	L 0-2		4,179
6		12	(h)	Chesterfield	D 0-0		6,244
7		16	(h)	Walsall	W 2-1	Spence, McEwan (pen)	8,153
8		23	(a)	Swindon T	W 1-0	Sermanni	6,607
9		26	(h)	Gillingham	W 2-0	Wagstaffe, Davidson	5,772
10		30	(a)	Colchester U	L 1-3	Hockaday	3,007
11	Oct	7	(h)	Lincoln C	W 2-0	Spence, Chandler	7,080
12		14	(a)	Southend U	L 0-4		6,374
13		18	(a)	Exeter C	L 0-3		3,993
14		21	(h)	Mansfield T	W 2-0	Chandler, Weston	6,663
15		28	(a)	Plymouth A	D 0-0		8,886
16	Nov	4	(h)	Sheffield W	L 0-1		9,403
17		11	(a)	Carlisle U	D 1-1	Chandler	6,505
18		18	(h)	Rotherham U	L 1-2	Suddaby	6,085
19	Dec	9	(h)	Peterborough U	D 0-0		4,280
20		23	(h)	Chester C	W 3-0	Spence 2, Kellow	4,106
21		26	(a)	Tranmere R	W 2-0	Ronson, Thompson	3,481
22		30	(a)	Swansea C	L 0-1		12,549
23	Feb	3	(a)	Gillingham	L 0-2		6,146
24		6	(a)	Walsall	L 1-2	Kellow	3,711
25		10	(h)	Colchester U	W 2-1	Spence 2	3,446
26		20	(h)	Hull C	W 3-1	Kellow, Weston, Spence	3,636
27		24	(h)	Southend U	L 1-2	Spence	4,566
28	Mar	3	(a)	Mansfield T	D 1-1	Spence	4,829
29		6	(a)	Bury	W 3-1	Spence 2, Jones	4,575
30		10	(h)	Plymouth A	D 0-0		4,879
31		14	(a)	Chesterfield	W 3-1	Ronson 2, Kellow	4,638
32		20	(h)	Shrewsbury T	W 5-0	McEwan 2 (1 pen), Kellow 2, Suddaby	5,330
33		24	(h)	Watford	D 1-1	McEwan	9,253
34		28	(a)	Oxford U	L 0-1		2,924
35		31	(a)	Brentford	L 2-3	Weston 2	6,360
36	Apr	7	(h)	Bury	L 1-2	Kellow	5,451
37		13	(a)	Chester C	L 2-4	Thompson, Jones	4,439
38		14	(h)	Tranmere R	W 2-0	Spence, Jones	4,798
39		16	(a)	Hull C	D 0-0		6,000
40		21	(h)	Swansea C	L 1-3	Kellow	5,977
41		24	(h)	Exeter C	D 1-1	Kellow	3,136
42		28	(a)	Peterborough U	W 2-1	Kellow 2	4,004
43	May	5	(h)	Brentford	L 0-1		3,464
44		7	(a)	Lincoln C	W 2-1	Hockaday 2	1,949
45		15	(h)	Swindon T	W 5-2	Chandler, Malone, McEwan (pen), Hockaday, Spence	4,191
46		17	(a)	Sheffield W	L 0-2		7,310

FINAL LEAGUE POSITION: 12th in Division Three

Appearances
Sub Appearances
Goals

FA Cup

1	Nov	25	(h)	Lincoln C	W 2-1	McEwan (pen), Chandler	4,375
2	Dec	16	(a)	Bury	L 1-3	Kellow	6,519

Appearances
Sub Appearances
Goals

League Cup

1	Aug	12	(a)	Carlisle U	D 2-2	McEwan 2 (1 pen)	5,100
		16	(h)	Carlisle U	W 2-1	Davidson, Opp own-goal	6,617
2		30	(h)	Ipswich T	W 2-0	Davidson 2	10,029
3	Oct	4	(h)	Manchester C	D 1-1	Spence	18,868
R		10	(a)	Manchester C	L 0-3		26,213

Appearances
Sub Appearances
Goals

Ward	Gardner	Thompson	Wilson	Suddaby	McEwan	Spence	Tong	Holden	Davidson	Wagstaffe	Hockaday	Waldron	Chandler	Pashley	Ronson	Hesford	Sermanni	Bissell	Weston	Hall	Malone	Milligan	May	Kellow	Jones	Kerr	Dowes	
1	2	3	4	5	6	7*	8	9	10	11	12																	1
1	2	3	4	5	6	9	8		10			7*	12															2
1	2	4	8	5	6	9		12	10	11	7*			3														3
1	2	4		5	6	9			10		7		11	3	8													4
1	2	4		5	6	9		7	10	11*			12	3	8													5
1	2	4		5	6	9			10	11	7*		12	3	8													6
1	2	4		5	6	9			10	11	7		12	3	8*													7
	2	4		5	6	9*			10	11	12		7	3		1	8											8
	2	4		5	6	9			10	11*	12		7	3	8	1												9
	2	4		5	6	9					11		7	3	8	1	12	10*										10
	2	4		5	6	9			10	12	7		11	3	8*	1												11
	2	4		5	6	9			10		11*		7	3	8	1			12									12
1	2	4	12	5	6	9			10	11*				3	8				7									13
1	2	4	10*	5	6	9				11			12	3	8				7									14
1	2	4		5	6	9*				11			7	3	8		12		10									15
1	2*	4		5	6	9				11			7	3	8		12		10									16
1		4		5	6	9				11			7	3	8				10		2							17
1				8	6	9					12	10	7	3					11		2		4*	8				18
	2	4			6				12				7	3		1	8		10*		12			9	11			19
		4		5	6	9			10	12				3	8	1					2			7	11*			20
		4		5	6	9			10	11				3	8	1					2			7				21
		4		5	6	9			10	11*				3	8	1					2			7	12			22
		4	9	5	6				10	11*				3	8	1			12		2				7			23
		4*		5	6				10					3	8	1	12		11		2			7	9			24
			4	5	6	9			10	115				3	8	1					2			7	12			25
				5	6	9			10				11	3		1	8		4		2			7*	12			26
		12		5	6	9			10				11	3		1	8		4		2			7*				27
		4		5	6	9			10			8*	12	3		1			11		2				7			28
		4		5	6	9			10					3	8	1			11		2				7			29
		4		5	6	9			10					3		1			11		2				7	8		30
		4		5	6	9								3	10	1			11		2			7		8		31
				5	6	9						4		3	10	1			11		2			7		8		32
				5	6	9						4		3	10	1			11		2			7		8		33
		4		5	6	9			12					3	10*	1			11		2			7		8		34
			4*	5	6	9								3	10	1			11		2			7	12	8		35
			12	5	6	9							10	3		1			11	4	2			8		7*		36
		4		5	6	9					7		10	3*		1			11		2			8	12			37
	3	4		5	6	9					7					1			11		2			8	10			38
		4			6	9										1	7		11		2	3	5	8			10	39
		4			6	9									10	1	7*		11		2	3	5	8	12			40
	3	4		5	6	9									10	1			11		2			8	7			41
	3	4		5	6	9					12				10	1			11		2			8	7*			42
	3	4		5	6	9					7				10	1			11*		2			8	12			43
		4		5	6	9					7		3		10	1			11		2*			8	12			44
	12	4		5*	6	9					7		3		10	1			11		2			8				45
	2	4	12		6						7		11		10	1			3*		2		5	8	9			46
13	22	38	7	42	46	42	2	2	23	16	13	5	18	35	32	33	6	1	29	1	29	2	4	25	11	7	1	
	1	1	3					1	2	2	5		6				4		2		1				7			
		2	1	2	5	16			3	1	4		4		3		1		4		1			11	3			

Ward	Gardner	Thompson	Wilson	Suddaby	McEwan	Spence	Tong	Holden	Davidson	Wagstaffe	Hockaday	Waldron	Chandler	Pashley	Ronson	Hesford	Sermanni	Bissell	Weston	Hall	Malone	Milligan	May	Kellow	Jones	Kerr	Dowes	
	4			5	6	9				11*	12		7	3		1	8		10		2							1
	2	8		5	6	9			12					3	11*	1					4			10	7			2
	2	1		2	2	2				1			1	2	1	2	1		1		2			1	1			
									1		1																	
					1								1											1				

Ward	Gardner	Thompson	Wilson	Suddaby	McEwan	Spence	Tong	Holden	Davidson	Wagstaffe	Hockaday	Waldron	Chandler	Pashley	Ronson	Hesford	Sermanni	Bissell	Weston	Hall	Malone	Milligan	May	Kellow	Jones	Kerr	Dowes	
1	2		6	5	4	9*	8	12	10	11	7											3						1
1	2		4	5	6	7	8	9*	10	11	12											3						
1	2	4		5	6	9			10		7		11	3	8													2
	2	4		5	6	9*			10	12	11		7	3	8	1												3
	2	4		5	6	9			10		11		7	3	8	1												R
3	5	3	2	5	5	5	2	1	5	2	4		3	3	3	2						2						
								1		1	1																	
					2	1			3																			

1 own-goal

1979-80

Manager: Stan Ternent/Alan Ball

1	Aug	18	(h)	Gillingham	W 2-1	Pashley, McEwan	5,253
2		21	(a)	Bury	L 0-3		4,028
3		25	(a)	Grimsby T	L 3-4	B.Smith, Kellow, Wilson	7,306
4	Sep	1	(h)	Wimbledon	W 3-0	Wilson, Kerr, Weston	4,556
5		7	(a)	Southend U	W 2-1	Wilson, Kellow	5,600
6		15	(h)	Rotherham U	W 3-2	Wilson, Kellow, McEwan	7,807
7		18	(a)	Sheffield U	L 1-3	Kellow	15,198
8		22	(h)	Blackburn R	W 2-1	McEwan 2 (1 pen)	10,193
9		29	(a)	Plymouth A	D 2-2	Kellow, Jones	5,693
10	Oct	3	(h)	Sheffield U	L 2-3	Doyle, McEwan	10,392
11		6	(a)	Exeter C	L 0-1		3,769
12		10	(h)	Bury	L 1-2	Kerr	5,955
13		13	(h)	Brentford	W 5-4	Pashley, McEwan, Kellow 2, Spence	5,386
14		19	(a)	Colchester U	L 1-3	Weston	4,383
15		23	(a)	Chesterfield	D 0-0		4,967
16		27	(h)	Swindon T	L 0-1		5,741
17	Nov	3	(a)	Gillingham	D 1-1	McEwan (pen)	6,518
18		7	(h)	Chesterfield	D 2-2	Doyle, McEwan	3,484
19		10	(h)	Sheffield W	D 1-1	Bowey	8,355
20		17	(a)	Millwall	L 0-2		5,979
21	Dec	1	(a)	Mansfield T	D 1-1	Hockaday	4,324
22		8	(h)	Reading	W 5-2	Kellow 2, Harrison 2, Spence	3,834
23		21	(a)	Barnsley	L 1-2	Kellow	8,567
24		26	(h)	Hull C	D 2-2	Weston, Kellow	4,535
25		29	(a)	Chester C	L 0-1		4,212
26	Jan	5	(h)	Oxford U	L 1-2	McEwan (pen)	4,003
27		12	(a)	Wimbledon	W 2-1	Jones, Morris	2,688
28		18	(h)	Southend U	W 1-0	Noble	4,286
29		26	(h)	Grimsby T	L 0-3		4,932
30	Feb	9	(a)	Blackburn R	L 0-2		14,446
31		16	(h)	Plymouth A	L 1-3	Fletcher	3,302
32		23	(a)	Brentford	L 1-2	Pashley	6,400
33		29	(h)	Colchester U	W 1-0	Kellow	5,594
34	Mar	8	(a)	Swindon T	L 1-2	Morris	9,517
35		15	(h)	Exeter C	W 1-0	Fletcher	4,155
36		18	(a)	Carlisle U	L 0-2		3,793
37		22	(a)	Sheffield W	L 1-4	Fletcher	19,552
38		29	(h)	Millwall	D 2-2	Noble, Fletcher	4,357
39	Apr	4	(h)	Barnsley	D 1-1	Morris	10,049
40		5	(a)	Hull C	L 1-3	McEwan (pen)	5,428
41		7	(h)	Carlisle U	W 2-1	Bamber, McEwan	6,054
42		12	(a)	Oxford U	W 2-0	Fletcher, Harrison	3,582
43		19	(h)	Mansfield T	D 1-1	Fletcher	5,677
44		26	(a)	Reading	W 1-0	McEwan (pen)	5,865
45	May	3	(h)	Chester C	D 0-0		5,928
46		6	(a)	Rotherham U	W 2-0	Morris, Fletcher	4,497

FINAL LEAGUE POSITION: 18th in Division Three

Appearances
Sub Appearances
Goals

FA Cup

1	Nov	24	(h)	Wigan A	D 1-1	McEwan	11,277
R		28	(a)	Wigan A	L 0-2		14,589

Appearances
Sub Appearances
Goals

League Cup

1	Aug	11	(h)	Rochdale	D 1-1	McEwan	5,842
		14	(a)	Rochdale	W 1-0	Spence	3,910
2		29	(a)	Peterborough U	D 0-0		4,326
	Sep	5	(h)	Peterborough U	L 0-1		5,254

Appearances
Sub Appearances
Goals

McAlister	Thompson	Pashley	Doyle	Suddaby	McEwan	Kerr	Kellow	Spence	Smith B	Weston	Wilson	Malone	Gardner	Jones	Hockaday	Hesford	Ashurst	Harrison	Bowey	Bamber	Noble	Morris	Fletcher	MacDougall	Drummy	Brockbank	Seward	Smith P	Chandler	
1	2	3	4	5	6	7	8	9*	10	11	12																			1
1	2	3	4	5	6	7	8	9	10	11																				2
1	2	3	4	5	6	7	8	9*	10	11	12																			3
1	2	3	4	5	6	7	8		10	11	9																			4
1		3	4	5	6		8		10	11	9	7	2																	5
1		3	4	5	6		8		11	10	9	7	2																	6
1		3	4	5	6		8		11	10	9	7	2																	7
1		3	4	5	6	12	8		10	11	9*	7	2																	8
1		3	4	5	6	12	8		10	11*		7	2	9																9
1	5	3	4		6		8		10	11*	9	7	2		12															10
1	7	3	4*	5	6	12	8		10		9		2		11															11
1	6	3		5		4	8	9	10	11*	12	7	2																	12
1	7	3		5	6	4	8*	9	10	12		11	2																	13
1	7	3*		5	6	4		9	10	12		11	2	8																14
	7			5	6	4		9	10	3		11	2	8		1														15
	7		4	5	6		8	9	10	3		11	2			1														16
		3	4		6	7	8	9	10	11		2				1	5													17
		3	4		6	7	8	9	10	11		25		12		1	5													18
	6	3	8		4		10	9		11			2			1	5		7											19
	6	3	8		4		10	9		11	12		2			1	5		7*											20
		3	8		4		10	9		11		5*	2		7	1		6		12										21
		3	8		4		10	9		11			2		7	1	5	6												22
1	12	3	8		4		10	9*		11			2		7		5	6												23
1	12	3	8		4		10	9*		11			2		7		5	6												24
	6	3	8		4		10			11*			2		12	1	5	7		9										25
	6	3	8		4		10						2			1	5	11		9		7								26
	6	3	8				10					4	2	9		1	5	11				7								27
	6	3	8				10						2	9		1	5	11			4	7								28
	6	3	8				10*			12		5	2	9		1		11			4	7								29
	6	3	8				10		12			5	2	9*		1		11			4	7								30
		3	6				8*			11		5	2			1		10			4	7	9			12				31
	5	3	6				8			11		2	12			1		10		9*	4	7								32
	5	3	6		12		8						2			1	4	10			11	7	9*							33
	5*	3	6		12		8						2			1	4	10			11	7	9							34
		3	6		5	12							2			1	4	11				7	8	9*	10					35
		3	6		5								2			1	4	11				7	9	8	11					36
		3	5		6	8							2			1	4					7	9		10			11		37
		3			6								2			1	5	11			4	7	9	8	10					38
		3	10		6					11			2			1	5				4*	7	9	8	12					39
		3	10		6					11			2			1	5		4			7	9	8						40
		3*	4		5					10			2			1	6	11		8		7	9				12			41
		3	12		6					10			2			1	5	11		8*	4	7	9							42
		3	12		5					10			2			1	6	11		8*	4	7	9							43
		3			5					10			2			1	6	11			4	7	9	8						44
		3			5					10			2			1	6	11			4	7	9	8						45
		3			5					10			2			1	6	11			4	7	9	8						46
16	22	44	36	15	37	11	32	16	18	32	7	19	39	7	5	30	25	23	3	6	14	21	15	8	4			1		
	2		2		2	4			1	3	4		1	1	2					1					1	1	1			
		3	2		12	2	12	2	1	3	4			2	1			3	1	1	2	4	7							

McAlister	Thompson	Pashley	Doyle	Suddaby	McEwan	Kerr	Kellow	Spence	Smith B	Weston	Wilson	Malone	Gardner	Jones	Hockaday	Hesford	Ashurst	Harrison	Bowey	Bamber	Noble	Morris	Fletcher	MacDougall	Drummy	Brockbank	Seward	Smith P	Chandler	
	6	3	8		4		10	9*		11	12		2		7	1	5													1
		3	8		4		10	9		11*			2		7	1	5	6		12										R
	1	2	2		2		2	2		2			2		2	2	2	1												
											1									1										
					1																									

McAlister	Thompson	Pashley	Doyle	Suddaby	McEwan	Kerr	Kellow	Spence	Smith B	Weston	Wilson	Malone	Gardner	Jones	Hockaday	Hesford	Ashurst	Harrison	Bowey	Bamber	Noble	Morris	Fletcher	MacDougall	Drummy	Brockbank	Seward	Smith P	Chandler	
1	2	3	4	5	6	7	8	9		10					11*														12	1
1	2	3	4	5	6	7	8	9		10	11																			
1	2	3	8	5	4	7	9		10	11		6																		2
1	2	3	4	5	6	7	8		11	10	9*	12																		
4	4	4	4	4	4	4	4	2	2	4	2	1			1															
												1																	1	
					1			1																						

1980-81

Manager: Alan Ball/Allan Brown

No	Month	Day	Venue	Opponent	Result	Scorers	Attendance
1	Aug	16	(a)	Swindon T	W 2-1	Hockaday, Fletcher	7,108
2		20	(h)	Rotherham U	D 0-0		10,427
3		23	(a)	Huddersfield T	D 1-1	Morris	9,490
4		30	(h)	Portsmouth	L 0-2		8,352
5	Sep	5	(a)	Fulham	W 2-1	Sbragia, Morris	4,940
6		13	(h)	Hull C	D 2-2	Morris, Harrison	6,138
7		16	(a)	Sheffield U	L 2-4	Hockaday, Gardner	13,331
8		20	(h)	Brentford	L 0-3		6,738
9		27	(a)	Walsall	D 2-2	Morris 2	4,227
10	Oct	1	(h)	Sheffield U	W 2-1	Thompson 2	8,995
11		4	(h)	Gillingham	W 4-0	Morris 2, Hockaday, Thompson	6,588
12		7	(a)	Millwall	D 0-0		3,363
13		11	(a)	Plymouth A	W 2-0	Morris 2	10,698
14		18	(h)	Colchester U	D 1-1	Williams	6,997
15		22	(h)	Chesterfield	L 0-3		8,062
16		25	(a)	Charlton A	L 1-2	Morgan	6,838
17		28	(a)	Carlisle U	L 0-2		3,588
18	Nov	1	(h)	Newport C	L 2-4	McEwan (pen), Ashurst	4,556
19		8	(a)	Oxford U	W 2-0	Ball 2 (1 pen)	3,038
20		11	(a)	Rotherham U	L 0-4		6,367
21		15	(h)	Swindon T	D 1-1	Entwistle	3,758
22		29	(a)	Reading	L 0-3		3,968
23	Dec	6	(h)	Exeter C	D 0-0		3,597
24		20	(a)	Barnsley	L 0-2		10,862
25		26	(h)	Chester C	L 2-3	Morgan, Bamber	4,878
26		27	(a)	Burnley	L 1-4	Bamber	10,667
27	Jan	10	(a)	Colchester U	L 2-3	Morris, Ball	2,378
28		17	(h)	Reading	D 0-0		3,273
29		24	(a)	Portsmouth	D 3-3	Morris, Thompson, Hockaday	13,265
30		31	(h)	Huddersfield T	L 1-2	Ball (pen)	9,431
31	Feb	7	(a)	Hull C	L 1-2	Ball	5,315
32		14	(h)	Fulham	L 0-2		3,792
33		21	(h)	Walsall	W 1-0	Ashurst	3,894
34		28	(a)	Brentford	L 0-2		5,850
35	Mar	4	(h)	Millwall	D 0-0		5,534
36		7	(a)	Gillingham	L 1-3	Ashurst	3,424
37		14	(h)	Plymouth A	W 1-0	Morris	3,933
38		21	(a)	Chesterfield	L 2-3	Thompson, Noble	5,959
39		25	(h)	Charlton A	L 0-2		4,230
40		28	(h)	Carlisle U	L 0-1		4,531
41	Apr	4	(a)	Newport C	L 1-3	Williams	4,514
42		12	(h)	Oxford U	D 1-1	Bamber	3,188
43		17	(a)	Chester C	L 1-2	Entwistle	2,804
44		18	(h)	Burnley	D 0-0		7,198
45		25	(h)	Barnsley	W 1-0	Entwistle	7,648
46	May	2	(a)	Exeter C	D 0-0		3,864

FINAL LEAGUE POSITION: 23rd in Division Three

Appearances
Sub Appearanc
Goals

FA Cup

No	Month	Day	Venue	Opponent	Result	Scorers	Attendance
1	Nov	22	(h)	Fleetwood T	W 4-0	Entwistle, Morris, Hockaday 2	10,897
2	Dec	13	(a)	Doncaster R	L 1-2	Williams	6,398

Appearances
Sub Appearan
Goals

League Cup

No	Month	Day	Venue	Opponent	Result	Scorers	Attendance
1	Aug	9	(a)	Walsall	W 3-2	McEwan 2 (1 pen), Morris	5,496
		13	(h)	Walsall	W 3-1	Morris, Fletcher, Ashurst	9,781
2		26	(a)	Everton	L 0-3		20,156
	Sep	3	(h)	Everton	D 2-2	McEwan (pen), Morris	10,579

Appearances
Sub Appearar
Goals

Hesford	Gardner	Williams	Doyle	McEwan	Ashurst	Morris	Hockaday	Fletcher	Ball	Harrison	Noble	Brockbank	Greenall	MacDougall	Welsh	Sbragia	Deary	Pashley	Bamber	Simmonite	Morgan	Thompson	Rush	Entwistle	Conn	
1	2	3	4	5	6	7	8	9	10	11																1
1	2	3	4	5	6	7	8		10*	11	9	12														2
1	2	3	4	5		7	8	9*		11	10		6	12												3
1	2	3	4	5		7	8	9*			10		6	12	11											4
1	2	3	4	5		7	8			11				9		6	10									5
1	2	3	4	5		7	8			11				9		6	10									6
1	2	3	4	5		7	8		10					9*		6		11	12							7
1		3	4	5			8		10	7						6		11	9	2						8
1		3		5		10	8	9*	4							6	11			2	7	12				9
1		3		5		10	8		4							6	11			2	7	9				10
1		3		5		10	8		4							6	11			2	7	9				11
1		3		5		10	8		4							6	11			2	7	9				12
1		3		6	9	10	8		4							5	11			2	7					13
1		3		6	9	10	8		4							5*	11			2	7	12				14
1		3		6	5	10	8		4								11			2	7	9				15
		3		6	4	9	10		8				5				11*			2	7	12	1			16
		3		8	5	10	9		4				6							2	7	11	1			17
		11		6	5	10	9		4			3	12						8	2*	7		1			18
1		3	9		2	10	8		4				6			5		11			7					19
1		3	9		2	10	11*		7	12			5			4		6						8		20
1		3	8	5	2	10			4				6					11			7			9		21
1		3		6	2	10	8		4				5					11			7			9		22
1		3		6	2	10	8		4	7								11				5		9		23
1		3		6	2	10			4			12						11	8		7*	5		9		24
1	2	3		6		10			4									11	8		7	5		9		25
1	2	3		6		10			4									11	8		7	5		9		26
1	2				5	10	8		4	9*		12				6		3		11	7					27
1	2				6	10	8		4	9						5		3		11	7					28
1	2				6	10	8		4	9								3		11*	7	5		12		29
					6	10	8		4	9								3	12	2*	7	5	1	11		30
1	2						12		4	9		11				6		3	8		7	5		10		31
1					6	10	11		4	9								3		2	7	5		8		32
1	12				6	10	11		4	9								3		2*	7	5		8		33
1	2				6	10	8		4	9		11						3			7*	5		12		34
1	2			7	6	10	11			9		8*				4		3				5		12		35
1		3		7	6	10	11*			9	4	8				5		2						12		36
1	2			4	5	10					11					6		3	12		7	9*			8	37
1	2	12		4	5	10				8	11					6		3				9		7*		38
1	2	11		4	5	10	12			7	8					6*		3				9				39
1				6	2	10	8			9	4					12		3			7	5			11*	40
1		8		6	2	10	7			9	4							3	11			5				41
1	2			6		10	12			9	4		5					3	11		7				8*	42
1	2			6		10				8	4					5		3	11		7			9		43
1	2	4		6		10	12			8						5*		3	11		7			9		44
1	2			6		10				8	4		5					3	11		7			9		45
1	2			6		10				8	4		5					3	11	7				9		46
42	23	30	11	36	28	44	33	4	30	26	13	5	11	3	1	22	10	30	12	18	30	21	4	16	3	
	1	1					3			1		3	1	2		1			3			3		4		
	1	2		1	3	12	4	1	5	1	1					1			3		2	5		3		

Hesford	Gardner	Williams	Doyle	McEwan	Ashurst	Morris	Hockaday	Fletcher	Ball	Harrison	Noble	Brockbank	Greenall	MacDougall	Welsh	Sbragia	Deary	Pashley	Bamber	Simmonite	Morgan	Thompson	Rush	Entwistle	Conn	
1		3	8	6	2	10	12		4				5					11*			7			9		1
1		3		6	2	10	8		4	7								11				5		9		2
2		2	1	2	2	2	1		2	1			1					2			1	1		2		
							1																			
		1				1	2																	1		

Hesford	Gardner	Williams	Doyle	McEwan	Ashurst	Morris	Hockaday	Fletcher	Ball	Harrison	Noble	Brockbank	Greenall	MacDougall	Welsh	Sbragia	Deary	Pashley	Bamber	Simmonite	Morgan	Thompson	Rush	Entwistle	Conn	
1	3		4	6	2	7	8		10					9	11			5								1
1	2	3	4*	5	6	7	8	9	10	11					12											
1	2	3	4	5		7	8	9		11	10		6													2
1	2	3	4	5		7	8		10	11				9		6										
4	4	3	4	4	2	4	4	2	3	3	1		1	2	1	1		1								
															1											
				3	1	3		1																		

1981-82

Manager: Allan Brown

1	Aug	29	(h)	Stockport C	W 2-0	Blair, Morris	4,556
2	Sep	5	(a)	Scunthorpe U	D 1-1	Noble	2,200
3		12	(h)	Crewe A	W 5-0	Bamber, Goddard 2, Morris, Hockaday	4,506
4		19	(a)	Darlington	D 2-2	Bamber, Morris	2,085
5		22	(a)	Rochdale	D 0-0		2,763
6		26	(h)	Hull C	W 3-1	Bamber 2, Morris	4,838
7		30	(h)	Halifax T	W 7-1	Bamber 3, Hockaday, Simmonite, Noble, Harrison	5,084
8	Oct	3	(a)	Mansfield T	D 2-2	Hockaday, McEwan (pen)	3,466
9		10	(h)	Torquay U	W 2-1	Noble, Morris	6,716
10		13	(a)	Northampton T	W 1-0	Morris	2,376
11		17	(a)	Aldershot	L 2-3	Pashley, Bamber	2,000
12		20	(a)	York C	W 4-0	Hockaday, Morris, Blair, Noble	2,657
13		31	(a)	Sheffield U	L 1-3	McEwan	15,566
14	Nov	4	(h)	Bury	D 1-1	Blair	7,805
15		7	(a)	Peterborough U	L 1-3	McEwan (pen)	5,442
16		11	(h)	Port Vale	L 2-3	Noble, Morris	4,785
17		14	(h)	Bournemouth	L 0-3		4,665
18	Dec	4	(a)	Colchester U	L 1-2	Bamber	3,875
19	Jan	9	(h)	Scunthorpe U	W 2-0	Morris 2	4,136
20		13	(h)	Tranmere R	L 1-2	Bamber	3,329
21		30	(h)	Darlington	W 1-0	Entwistle	3,336
22	Feb	1	(a)	Stockport C	W 3-2	Entwistle, Bamber, Hockaday	3,008
23		5	(a)	Crewe A	D 1-1	Opp own-goal	2,513
24		10	(h)	Rochdale	D 1-1	Entwistle	3,294
25		13	(h)	Mansfield T	L 2-3	McEwan (pen), Hockaday	3,017
26		17	(h)	Northampton T	W 1-0	Noble	2,231
27		20	(a)	Halifax T	D 0-0		2,245
28		27	(a)	Torquay U	D 1-1	Harrison	2,177
29	Mar	3	(h)	Bradford C	W 1-0	Stewart	4,009
30		6	(h)	Aldershot	L 0-2		2,655
31		10	(h)	York C	W 3-1	Brockbank, McEwan (pen), Bamber	2,164
32		13	(a)	Port Vale	L 0-2		3,439
33		20	(h)	Sheffield U	L 0-1		7,542
34		27	(h)	Peterborough U	D 2-2	Bamber 2	2,855
35		30	(a)	Wigan A	L 1-2	Morgan (pen)	7,329
36	Apr	3	(a)	Bournemouth	L 0-1		5,146
37		9	(h)	Wigan A	L 1-2	Hockaday	9,439
38		10	(a)	Tranmere R	L 1-3	Morgan	1,828
39		17	(h)	Colchester U	D 0-0		2,298
40		21	(a)	Hereford U	L 1-2	Opp own-goal	2,617
41		24	(a)	Bradford C	L 0-1		4,898
42		28	(a)	Hartlepool U	D 2-2	Noble, Bamber	1,387
43	May	1	(h)	Hereford U	W 1-0	Noble	1,881
44		4	(a)	Hull C	L 0-1		3,206
45		8	(h)	Hartlepool U	D 2-2	Stewart 2	1,824
46		11	(a)	Bury	W 1-0	Noble	2,041

FINAL LEAGUE POSITION: 12th in Division Four

Appearances
Sub Appearances
Goals

FA Cup

1	Nov	21	(a*)	Horden CW	W 1-0	Harrison	4,465
2	Jan	2	(a)	Kettering T	W 3-0	Harrison, Wann, Morris	4,439
3		5	(a)	Barnsley	W 2-0	Bamber, Morris	13,429
4		23	(h)	Queen's Park R	D 0-0		10,227
R		26	(a)	Queen's Park R	L 1-5	Entwistle	11,712

*Played at the Victoria Ground, Hartlepool.

Appearances
Sub Appearances
Goals

League Cup

1	Sep	2	(a)	Bradford C	L 1-3	Bamber	3,374
		16	(h)	Bradford C	D 0-0		5,722

Appearances
Sub Appearances
Goals

Hesford	Simmonite	Pashley	Blair	Greenall	McEwan	Morris	Noble	Bamber	Hockaday	Harrison	Morgan	Wann	Hart	Pollard	Goddard	Entwistle	Sbragia	Gardner	Rush	Fletcher	Deary	McEvoy	Stewart	Brockbank	Butler	Bardsley		
1	2	3	4	5	6	7	8	9	10*	11	12																	1
1	2	3		5		7	8	9	10*	11		4	6	12														2
1	2	3	4	5		7	8*	9	12	11			6		10													3
1	2	3	4		6	7	8*	9	12	11			5		10													4
1	2	3	4	5		7	8	9		11			6		10													5
1	2	3	4		6	7	8*	9	12	11			5		10													6
1	2	3	4*		6	7	8	9	10	11		12	5															7
1	2	3	4		6	7	8		10*	11		12	5			9												8
1	2	3	4		6	7	8	9	10	11			5															9
1	2	3	4		6	7	8	9	10	11							5											10
1		3	4		6	7	8	9	10	11		12	5					2*										11
1		3	4		6	7	8	9	10*	11		12	5					2										12
		3	4		6	7	8		10	11		12	5			9*		2	1									13
		3	4		6	7	8		10	11*			5			9		2	1	12								14
		3	4*		6	7	8	9	10			11	5				12	2	1									15
	2	3	4		6	7	8	9	10*			11	5						1		12							16
	2	3	4			7	8	9		11*			5				6		1		12	10						17
1	2	3	4			7	8	9	10	11		6	5															18
1	2	3	4		6*	7	8	9	10	11		5									12							19
1	2	3	4			7	8	9	10	11		5*	12								6							20
1		3	4	5		7	8	9	10			6				11					2							21
1		3	4	5		7	8	9	10	12		6				11*					2							22
1		3	4	5	12		8	9	10*	11		6				7					2							23
1		3	4	5			8	9*		11	7	6				10					2		12					24
1		3	4		5		8	9	12	11*	7	6				10					2							25
1		10	4		6		8		9			5				11		2			7			3				26
1		10	4		6		8		9			5*				11		2			7		12	3				27
1		10	4	12	6		8		9	5								2			7		11*	3				28
1		7	4		6		8	9	10	5								2					11	3				29
		7	4		6		8	9	10	5								2	1		12		11*	3				30
1		10			6		8	9	4	5	7							2					11	3				31
1		10			6		8	9	7	5						12		2			4		11*	3				32
1	2	10			6		8	9	7	5*		12				11					4			3				33
1	2	11			6			9	10		7		5								4		8	3				34
1	2	10	6					9	11	12	7		5								4	8*		3				35
1	2	11*	6				4	9	10	12	7		5									8		3				36
1	2	11					6	9	10	12	7		5								4	8*		3				37
1	2	11		12			6*	9	10	8	7		5								4			3				38
1	2	11		5			6			8	7										4	10	9	3				39
1	2	11		5			6	9	8	4*	7										12		10	3				40
1	2	11	8*	5			6	9	10				7								4		12	3				41
	2	11	12	5			10	9	8		7*		6						1		4			3				42
1	2	11	4	5			10	9	7				6								8			3				43
1	2	11*	4	5			10	9	7				6								8		12	3				44
1	2	3	4*	5			10	9	7	11			6								8		12					45
1	2	11	4	5			7														8	10	9		3	6		46
39	29	46	36	16	24	22	44	38	37	29	11	13	26		4	11	2	12	7		22	6	9	19	1	1		
			1	2	1				4	4		6	1	1		1	1			1	5		5					
	1	1	3		5	10	9	15	7	2	2				2	3							3	1				

2 own-goals

Hesford	Simmonite	Pashley	Blair	Greenall	McEwan	Morris	Noble	Bamber	Hockaday	Harrison	Morgan	Wann	Hart	Pollard	Goddard	Entwistle	Sbragia	Gardner	Rush	Fletcher	Deary	McEvoy	Stewart	Brockbank	Butler	Bardsley		
1	2	3	4		6	7	8	9	10	11			5															1
1	2	3	4		6	7	8	9	10	11		5																2
1	2	3	4		6	7	8	9	10	11		5																3
1	2*	3	4		6	7	8	9	10	11		5									12							4
1		3	4			7	8	9	10	11*		5	6			12					2							R
5	4	5	5		4	5	5	5	5	5		4	2								1							
																1					1							
						2		1		2		1				1												

Hesford	Simmonite	Pashley	Blair	Greenall	McEwan	Morris	Noble	Bamber	Hockaday	Harrison	Morgan	Wann	Hart	Pollard	Goddard	Entwistle	Sbragia	Gardner	Rush	Fletcher	Deary	McEvoy	Stewart	Brockbank	Butler	Bardsley	
1	2	3	4*	5	6	7		9	10	11		8	12														1
1	2	3	4		6	7	8	9	10	11			5														
2	2	2	2	1	2	2	1	2	2	2		1	1														
													1														
								1																			

1982-83

Manager: Sam Ellis

1	Aug	28	(a)	Mansfield T	L 1-2	Hockaday	2,627
2	Sep	4	(h)	Swindon T	W 2-1	Pashley (pen), Bamber	3,593
3		7	(h)	Bury	D 1-1	Bamber	4,292
4		11	(a)	Bristol C	D 0-0		4,681
5		18	(h)	Wimbledon	D 1-1	Hockaday	3,929
6		25	(a)	Colchester U	L 1-4	Pashley (pen)	2,918
7		29	(a)	Chester C	W 2-1	Bamber, Deary	2,256
8	Oct	2	(h)	Darlington	W 2-0	Hockaday, Bamber	4,059
9		9	(h)	Halifax T	D 0-0		4,150
10		16	(a)	Rochdale	L 1-3	Bamber	2,001
11		19	(h)	York C	D 1-1	Deary	2,765
12		23	(h)	Hereford U	W 5-1	Downes (pen), Stewart 2, Bamber 2	3,405
13		30	(a)	Port Vale	L 0-1		5,449
14	Nov	2	(h)	Torquay U	W 1-0	Bamber	2,734
15		6	(h)	Crewe A	W 2-0	Mayo, Bamber	3,443
16		13	(a)	Northampton T	L 1-2	Hockaday	1,893
17		27	(a)	Aldershot	L 1-2	Downes (pen)	2,003
18	Dec	4	(h)	Hull C	D 1-1	Pashley	3,395
19		18	(h)	Scunthorpe U	W 3-1	Hockaday, Downes (pen), Bamber	2,860
20		27	(a)	Stockport C	L 0-3		3,673
21		28	(h)	Tranmere R	L 0-2		3,563
22	Jan	1	(a)	Hartlepool U	L 1-2	Jeffrey	1,569
23		3	(h)	Peterborough U	L 0-3		2,383
24		15	(h)	Mansfield T	W 2-1	I.Richardson, Opp own-goal	2,217
25		22	(a)	Bury	L 1-4	I.Richardson	3,263
26		29	(h)	Chester C	D 1-1	Stewart	2,054
27	Feb	5	(h)	Colchester U	L 1-2	Hetzke	1,747
28		15	(a)	York C	L 0-2		2,937
29		18	(a)	Halifax T	L 0-2		2,366
30		26	(h)	Rochdale	W 1-0	McNiven	2,373
31	Mar	2	(a)	Torquay U	W 3-1	Hockaday, Noble, Deary	1,802
32		5	(a)	Hereford U	D 0-0		1,755
33		12	(h)	Port Vale	W 2-0	Noble, Hetzke	4,519
34		19	(a)	Crewe A	L 1-3	Stewart	2,538
35		26	(h)	Northampton T	D 0-0		2,054
36	Apr	1	(h)	Stockport C	D 0-0		3,126
37		2	(a)	Tranmere R	D 1-1	Pritchett	1,831
38		9	(a)	Hull C	L 1-3	Deary	8,555
39		12	(a)	Darlington	W 1-0	Stewart	1,333
40		16	(h)	Bristol C	L 1-4	McNiven	2,209
41		19	(a)	Swindon T	D 3-3	McNiven, Hockaday, Deary	2,408
42		23	(a)	Scunthorpe U	L 3-4	McNiven 2, Greenall	2,791
43		30	(h)	Aldershot	W 4-1	Hockaday, Deary, Stewart, Opp own-goal	1,994
44	May	4	(a)	Peterborough U	L 1-3	Stewart	1,636
45		7	(a)	Wimbledon	L 0-5		2,717
46		14	(a)	Hartlepool U	L 1-2	Serella	2,184

FINAL LEAGUE POSITION: 21st in Division Four

Appearances
Sub Appearances
Goals

FA Cup

1	Nov	20	(h)	Horwich RMI	W 3-0	Pashley, Bamber, Deary (pen)	5,280
2	Dec	11	(a)	Preston NE	L 1-2	Brockbank	14,148

Appearances
Sub Appearances
Goals

League Cup

1	Sep	1	(a)	Chester C	W 2-1	Bamber, Serella	2,557
1		14	(h)	Chester C	W 5-1	Serella, Hetzke, Deary, Stewart, Pashley (pen)	3,429
2	Oct	5	(a)	Northampton T	D 1-1	Bamber	2,490
2		26	(h)	Northampton T	W 2-1	Downes (pen), Bamber	3,249
3	Nov	9	(a)	Luton T	L 2-4	Bamber, Pashley	6,409

Appearances
Sub Appearances
Goals

Hesford	Simmonite	Brockbank	Deary	Hetzke	Greenall	Noble	Hockaday	Bamber	Pashley	Downes	Stewart	Serella	Butler J	Hart	Jeffrey	Mayo	Bardsley	Pritchett	Scott	Richardson I	Richardson P	McNiven	Bramhall	
1	2	3	4	5	6	7*	8	9	10	11	12													1
1	2	3	4	5		7*	8	9	10	11	12	6												2
1	2	3	4	5			8	9	10	11	7	6												3
1	2	3	4	5		7	8		10		9	6	11											4
1	2	3	4	5		7	11	9	10		8	6												5
1	2	3	4	5		7	11	9	10		8	6												6
1	2		4	5			7	9	10	11	8	6		3										7
1	2			5			7	9	10	11	8	6		3	4									8
1	2		5		6	12	7	9	10	11	8*			3	4									9
1	2		10		5		7	9	3	11		6	12		4	8*								10
1	2		4	5			7	9	10	11	8	6		3										11
1	2		4	5			7	9	10	11	8	6		3										12
1	2		4	5			7	9	10	11		6		3		8								13
1	2		4	5			7	9	10	11		6		3		8								14
1	2		4	5			7	9	10	11	12	6*		3		8								15
1	2		4	5			7	9	10	11	12	6		3		8*								16
1			4	5			7	9	10	11		6			8		2	3						17
1			4*	5		12	7	9	10	11		6			8		2	3						18
1		3	4	5		12	7*	9	10	11		6			8		2							19
		3	4	5		12		9	10	11*		6			8		2		1	7				20
			4	5				9	10		11	6			8		2	3	1	7				21
1			4	5			7	9	10		11	6			8		2	3		12				22
1			4	5			7	9	10	11	7	6			8		2	3						23
1			4	5			7		10	11	9	6					2	3		8	7			24
1			4	5			7		2	11	9	6						3		8	10			25
1			4	5	12		7		10	11*	9	6					2	3			8			26
1			4*	5	6	12	7		10	11	9						2	3			8			27
1			4	5	6	9	7		11		10				8		2	3						28
1			4	5	6	10*	7		11		9	12			8		2	3						29
1			4	5	6	10	7		11		9						2	3				8		30
1			4	5	6	10	7		11		9						2	3				8		31
1			4	5	6	10	7*		11		9				12		2	3				8		32
1			4	5	6	10	7		11		9				12		2	3*				8		33
1			4	5	6	10	7		11	3	9						2					8		34
1			4	5	6	10	7		11		9		3				2					8		35
1			4	5	6	10	7		11		9						2	3				8		36
1			4	5	6*	10	7		11	9							2	3				8	12	37
1			4		6	10	7		5	11	9						2	3				8		38
1			4	5	6	10	7		11		9						2	3				8		39
1			4	5	6	10*	7	12	11		9						2	3				8		40
1			4	5	6		7	10	11		9						2	3				8		41
1			4	5	6	10	7		11		9						2	3				8		42
1			4	5	6	10	7		11		9						2	3				8		43
1			4	5	6		7		11	12	9		10*				2	3				8		44
1			4		6			7*	11	10	9	5					2	3				8	12	45
1			4	7	6	10		11*	2		9	5						3				8	12	46
44	16	8	45	42	23	21	40	25	46	23	34	26	3	9	12	5	28	26	2	4	4	17		
					1	5		1		1	4	1	1		2					1			3	
			6	2	1	2	8	10	3	3	7	1			1	1		1		2		5		

2 own-goals

Hesford	Simmonite	Brockbank	Deary	Hetzke	Greenall	Noble	Hockaday	Bamber	Pashley	Downes	Stewart	Serella	Butler J	Hart	Jeffrey	Mayo	Bardsley	
1			4	5		8	7	9	10	11*		6		3	12		2	1
1		12		5		4	7*	9	10	11		6	3		8		2	2
2			1	2		2	2	2	2	2		2	1	1	1		2	
		1													1			
		1	1					1	1									

Hesford	Simmonite	Brockbank	Deary	Hetzke	Greenall	Noble	Hockaday	Bamber	Pashley	Downes	Stewart	Serella	Butler J	Hart	Jeffrey	
1		3	4	5		7	8	9	10	11		6	2			1
1	2	3	4	5		7	8	9	10			6	11			
1	2	3			5		7	9	10	11	8			6	4	2
1	2		4	5			7	9	10	11	8	6		3		
1	2		4	5			7	9	10	11	8	6		3		3
5	4	3	4	4	1	2	5	5	5	4	3	4	2	3	1	
			1	1				4	2	1	1	2				

1983-84

Manager: Sam Ellis

1	Aug	27	(h)	Reading	W 1-0	Mercer	3,429
2	Sep	3	(a)	Colchester U	L 1-2	Serella	2,169
3		6	(a)	Bury	D 0-0		2,953
4		10	(h)	Northampton T	L 2-3	McNiven, Serella	3,216
5		17	(a)	Swindon T	D 0-0		2,867
6		24	(h)	Crewe A	W 3-0	Deary (pen), Greenall, Windridge	4,198
7		27	(h)	Mansfield T	W 2-0	Hetzke, Mercer	3,467
8	Oct	1	(a)	York C	L 0-4		4,058
9		8	(h)	Rochdale	L 0-2		3,126
10		18	(a)	Wrexham	W 1-0	Deary (pen)	2,005
11		22	(h)	Chesterfield	W 1-0	McNiven	4,206
12		29	(a)	Stockport C	W 2-1	Mercer, McNiven	2,602
13	Nov	1	(h)	Bristol C	W 1-0	Windridge	4,344
14		5	(h)	Darlington	W 3-1	Greenall, Hetzke, Mercer	3,843
15		9	(a)	Chester C	W 2-0	Stewart, Mercer	2,286
16		12	(a)	Doncaster R	L 1-2	Greenall	4,604
17		26	(a)	Hereford U	W 2-1	Windridge, Mercer	2,801
18	Dec	3	(h)	Peterborough U	L 1-2	Deary	4,439
19		17	(h)	Torquay U	W 1-0	Hetzke (pen)	3,955
20		26	(a)	Tranmere R	L 2-3	Mercer, Windridge	3,492
21		27	(h)	Hartlepool U	W 1-0	Hetzke (pen)	4,562
22		31	(a)	Halifax T	L 0-1		1,958
23	Jan	2	(h)	Aldershot	W 5-0	McNiven, Hetzke (pen), Windridge, Britton 2	3,193
24		14	(a)	Reading	L 0-2		4,923
25		21	(h)	Swindon T	D 1-1	Stewart	3,474
26	Feb	4	(h)	York C	W 3-0	Mercer, Britton, Moore	6,010
27		11	(a)	Crewe A	L 1-2	Stewart	4,042
28		14	(a)	Bristol C	D 1-1	Hetzke	7,413
29		25	(a)	Chesterfield	D 1-1	Windridge	3,281
30	Mar	3	(h)	Wrexham	W 4-0	Opp own-goal, Britton 2, Walsh	3,798
31		10	(h)	Doncaster R	W 3-1	Mercer, Stewart 2	6,062
32		17	(a)	Rochdale	L 0-1		3,115
33		20	(a)	Northampton T	W 5-1	Walker 3, Greenall, Stewart	1,318
34		24	(h)	Chester C	D 3-3	Stewart 3	4,746
35		31	(a)	Mansfield T	D 1-1	Hetzke (pen)	2,007
36	Apr	7	(h)	Bury	D 1-1	Stewart	4,513
37		10	(h)	Stockport C	D 1-1	Stonehouse	3,971
38		14	(a)	Peterborough U	L 0-4		2,921
39		20	(a)	Hartlepool U	W 1-0	Stonehouse	1,817
40		21	(h)	Tranmere R	L 0-1		4,055
41		28	(h)	Hereford U	W 3-1	Deary 3	2,413
42	May	1	(h)	Colchester U	W 3-2	McNiven, Stonehouse 2	3,131
43		5	(a)	Aldershot	L 2-3	McNiven, Britton	2,936
44		7	(h)	Halifax T	W 4-0	Britton 3, Stonehouse	2,324
45		12	(a)	Torquay U	L 0-1		1,592
46		18	(a)	Darlington	L 0-2		1,177

FINAL LEAGUE POSITION: 6th in Division Four

Appearances
Sub Appearances
Goals

FA Cup

1	Nov	19	(a)	Gainsborough T	W 2-0	Mercer, McNiven	2,557
2	Dec	10	(a)	Bangor C	D 1-1	Mercer	3,785
R		13	(h)	Bangor C	W 2-1	Deary, Stewart	5,013
3	Jan	7	(h)	Manchester C	W 2-1	McNiven, Opp own-goal	15,377
4		28	(a)	Oxford U	L 1-2	Mercer	10,759

Appearances
Sub Appearances
Goals

League Cup

1	Aug	30	(h)	Walsall	W 2-1	Bardsley, McNiven	3,353
	Sep	13	(a)	Walsall	L 1-3	Stewart	2,879

Appearances
Sub Appearances
Goals

O'Rourke	Bardsley	Pritchett	Rodaway	Hetzke	Greenall	Windridge	Mercer	Stewart	Ferns	McNiven	Deary	Serella	Steele	Dyer	Downes	Siddall	Britton	Pierce	Moore	Walsh	Stonehouse	Walker	Brand	Davies	
1	2	3	4	5	6	7	8	9	10	11															1
1	2	3	4	5		7	8	12	10	11*	9	6													2
1	2	3	4	5		7	8	9	10		11	6													3
1	2	3	4	5		7*	8	12	10	11	9	6													4
1	2	3	4	5	6	7	8	9	10		11														5
1	2	3	4	5	6	7	8	9*	10	12	11														6
	2	3	4	5	6	7*	8	12	10	9	11		1												7
	2	3	4	5	6	7		8	10	9	11		1												8
	2	3	4	5	6	7	8	9	10				1	11											9
	2		4	5	6	7	8	9	3	11	10					1									10
	2		4	5	6	7	8	9	3	11	10					1									11
	2		4	5	6	7	8	9	3	11	10					1									12
	2		4	5	6	7	8	9	3	11	10					1									13
	2		4	5	6	7	8*	9	3	11	10			12		1									14
	2		4	5	6	7	8	9	3	11	10					1									15
	2		4*	5	6	7	8	9	3	11	10					1	12								16
			4	5	6	7	8		3	11	10	2					9	1							17
			4	5	6	7	8	12	3*	11	10	2					9	1							18
			4	5	6		8	9	3	11	10*			12			7	1	2						19
		10*	4	5	6	12	8	9	3	11							7	1	2						20
			4	5	6	10	8	9	3*	11				12			7	1	2						21
			4	5	6	10	8	9	3	11*				12			7	1	2						22
			4	5	6	10	8	9	3	11							7	1	2						23
				5	6	10	8	9	3	11				4			7	1	2						24
				5	6		8	9		11		3		4	10		7	1	2						25
			4	5	6	10	8	9*		11	12						7	1	2	3					26
			4	5		10	8	9	3	11							7	1	2	6					27
			4	5		10	8	9	3	11*				12			7	1	2	6					28
			4	5	6	11	8	9	10*		12						7	1	2	3					29
			4	5	6	11	8	9*		12	10						7	1	2	3					30
				5	6	11	8	9	10		4						7	1	2	3					31
				5	6	11	8*	9	10	12	4						7	1	2	3					32
			4	5	6			9		11	10						7	1	2	3		8			33
			4	5	6			9		12	10						7*	1	2	3	11	8			34
			4	5	6	12		9			10						7	1	2	3	11	8*			35
			4	5	6	7		9	12	8	10							1	2	3*	11				36
			4	8	5	10*		9	3								7	1	2	6	11	12			37
			4	10	5			9	3								7	1	2	6	11	8			38
			4	10	6			9	3								7	1	2	5	11	8			39
			4	10	6			9	3		12						7*	1	2	5	11	8			40
			4					9	3		8	6		10			7	1	2	5	11				41
			4	5				9	3	10	8						7	1	2	6	11				42
		12	4	5	6	9				10		3*					7	1	2		11	8			43
			4	5	6			9									7		2	3	11	10	1	8	44
			4	5	6			9	10		12						7*		2	3	11		1	8	45
				5	6			9	10		4						7		2	3	11		1	8	46
6	16	10	41	45	39	32	31	40	37	28	27	8	3	4	1	7	29	27	28	20	13	8	3	3	
		1				2		4	1	4	4			5			1					1			
				7	4	6	9	10		6	6	2					9		1	1	5	3			

1 own-goal

O'Rourke	Bardsley	Pritchett	Rodaway	Hetzke	Greenall	Windridge	Mercer	Stewart	Ferns	McNiven	Deary	Serella	Steele	Dyer	Downes	Siddall	Britton	Pierce	Moore	Walsh	Stonehouse	Walker	Brand	Davies	
			4	5	6	7*	8		3	11	10			12	2		9	1							1
		3	4	5	6		8	9		11	10	2					7	1							2
			4	5	6		8	9	3	11	10	2					7	1							R
			4	5	6	10	8	9	3	11							7	1	2						3
				5	6	10*	8	9		11	12	3		4			7	1	2						4
		1	4	5	5	3	5	4	3	5	3	3		1	1		5	5	2						
											1			1											
							3	1		2	1														

1 own-goal

O'Rourke	Bardsley	Pritchett	Rodaway	Hetzke	Greenall	Windridge	Mercer	Stewart	Ferns	McNiven	Deary	Serella	Steele	Dyer	Downes	Siddall	Britton	Pierce	Moore	Walsh	Stonehouse	Walker	Brand	Davies	
1	2	3	4	5	6	7*	8		10	11	9			12											1
1	2	3	4	5		7*	8	9	10	12	11	6													
2	2	2	2	2	1	2	2	1	2	1	2	1													
										1				1											
	1							1		1															

1984-85

Manager: Sam Ellis

1	Aug	28	(a)	Halifax T	W 2-0	Stonehouse 2 (1 pen)	1,870
2	Sep	1	(h)	Exeter C	W 3-0	Deary 2 (1 pen), Dyer	3,663
3		8	(a)	Colchester U	D 1-1	Deary (pen)	1,772
4		15	(h)	Darlington	D 0-0		4,722
5		18	(h)	Port Vale	D 1-1	Deary	4,902
6		22	(a)	Chesterfield	L 1-2	Dyer	3,947
7		29	(h)	Chester C	W 3-1	Hetzke, Windridge, Dyer	4,566
8	Oct	2	(a)	Swindon T	L 1-4	Dyer	2,501
9		6	(h)	Aldershot	W 1-0	Stonehouse (pen)	3,824
10		13	(a)	Scunthorpe U	D 1-1	Stonehouse	2,366
11		20	(h)	Bury	D 0-0		5,100
12		23	(a)	Tranmere R	L 0-3		2,084
13		27	(h)	Northampton T	W 2-1	Britton, Stonehouse (pen)	3,577
14	Nov	3	(a)	Southend U	W 4-1	Dyer, Greenall 2, Windridge	1,904
15		7	(a)	Peterborough U	L 0-2		4,296
16		10	(h)	Stockport C	W 4-1	Stonehouse 2 (1 pen), Windridge 2	3,428
17		24	(a)	Hereford U	L 1-2	Stonehouse	3,588
18	Dec	1	(h)	Mansfield T	W 1-0	Stonehouse	2,796
19		7	(a)	Stockport C	W 3-1	Dyer, Britton, Malley (og)	2,428
20		15	(a)	Torquay U	W 2-0	Hetzke 2	1,252
21		22	(a)	Wrexham	W 2-1	Britton, Dyer	2,109
22		26	(h)	Rochdale	W 3-0	Stewart 2, Windridge	5,641
23		29	(h)	Hartlepool U	W 2-1	Walsh, Stewart	4,778
24	Jan	1	(a)	Crewe A	W 2-0	Stewart, Davis (og)	4,008
25		5	(h)	Halifax T	D 1-1	Stonehouse	5,184
26	Feb	2	(a)	Chester C	D 0-0		3,307
27		19	(h)	Swindon T	W 1-0	Stewart	3,382
28		23	(h)	Southend U	W 1-0	Britton	4,272
29	Mar	2	(a)	Northampton T	W 1-0	Stewart	1,860
30		5	(h)	Tranmere R	L 1-2	Teasdale	4,885
31		9	(a)	Bury	L 0-1		7,978
32		16	(h)	Scunthorpe U	W 1-0	Deary (pen)	3,937
33		23	(a)	Aldershot	L 0-1		2,260
34		26	(h)	Colchester U	D 1-1	Deary	4,057
35		30	(h)	Peterborough U	W 4-2	Deary 2 (1 pen), Conroy, O'Keefe	3,809
36	Apr	2	(h)	Chesterfield	W 1-0	O'Keefe	7,144
37		6	(a)	Rochdale	D 1-1	Windridge	3,555
38		9	(h)	Crewe A	W 6-1	Cegielski, Windridge 2, Deary 2, Hetzke	6,653
39		17	(a)	Exeter C	D 1-1	Stonehouse	1,847
40		20	(h)	Hereford U	W 2-0	Deary (pen), Britton	5,585
41		22	(a)	Port Vale	D 1-1	Hetzke	3,725
42		27	(a)	Mansfield T	D 1-1	Greenall	3,030
43	May	1	(a)	Darlington	W 4-0	Conroy, O'Keefe, Stewart, Deary	7,021
44		4	(h)	Torquay U	D 3-3	O'Keefe 2, Deary (pen)	7,855
45		6	(a)	Hartlepool U	W 2-0	O'Keefe, Dyer	2,196
46		11	(h)	Wrexham	D 0-0		6,093

FINAL LEAGUE POSITION: 2nd in Division Four

Appearances
Sub Appearances
Goals

FA Cup

1	Nov	17	(h)	Altrincham	L 0-1		4,486

Appearances
Sub Appearances
Goals

League Cup

1	Aug	28	(h)	Chester C	W 1-0	Deary	3,318
	Sep	5	(a)	Chester C	W 3-0	Dyer, Deary (pen), Stewart	3,001
2		25	(a)	Manchester C	L 2-4	Windridge, Greenall	13,344
	Oct	9	(h)	Manchester C	L 1-3	Britton	10,960

Appearances
Sub Appearances
Goals

O'Rourke	Moore	Ferns	Conroy	Hetzke	Greenall	Britton	Stonehouse	Stewart	Deary	Dyer	Davies	Walsh	Windridge	Murphy	Bailey	Donovan	Teasdale	Price	Crainie	Cegielski	O'Keefe	
1	2	3	4	5	6	7	8	9	10	11												1
1	2		4	5	6	7		9	10	11	8	3										2
1	2		4	5	6	7		9	10	11	8	3										3
1	2	12	4	5	6	7		9*	10	11	8	3										4
1	2		4	5	6	7			10	11	8	3	9*	12								5
1	2		4	5*	6	7		9	10	11	8	3	12									6
1	2		4	5	6	7		9	10*	11	12	3	8									7
1	2	10	4*	5	6	7				11	9	3	8	12								8
1	2		4	5	6	7	10			11	9	3	8									9
1	2		4	5	6	7	10			11*	9	3	8	12								10
1	2		4	5	6	7	10				9		8		3	11						11
1	2		4	5	6	7	10				12	9*	8		3	11						12
1	2		4	5	6	7	10*			11	9		8	12	3							13
1	2		4	5	6	7	10			11	9	3	8*	12								14
1	2		4	5	6	7	10			11		3	8	9								15
1	2		4	5	6	7	10			11	9	3	8									16
1	2		4	5	6	7	10	9		11		3	8									17
1	2		4	5	6	7	10	9		11		3	8									18
1	2		4	5	6	7	10	9		11		3	8									19
1	2*		4	5	6	7	10	9	12	11		3	8									20
1	2		4	5	6	7	10	9		11		3	8									21
1	2	5	4		6	7*	10	9	12	11		3	8									22
1	2	5	4		6	7	10	9	12	11		3	8*									23
1	2		4	5	6	7	10*	9	12	11		3	8									24
1	2	12	4	5	6	7	10	9	8*	11		3										25
1	2	12			6	7	10	9	4	11		3	8									26
1	2	3			6	7	10	9	4	11*		5	8				12					27
1	2	5*			6	7	10	9	4	11		3	8				12					28
1	2		4		6	7		9	5	11		3	8				10					29
1	2		8		6	7	10	9	4	11*		5	3				12					30
1	2		8		6	7	10*	9	4	11		5	3				12					31
1	2		8		6	7		9	4	11*		5		12				3	10			32
1	2		8		6	7		9	4	11*		5		12				3	10			33
1	2		8		6	7		9	4			5	11					3	10			34
1	2		8		6	7		9	4				12					3	11*	5	10	35
1	2		8		6	7		9*	4			5	12					3	11		10	36
1	2		8		6	7	12		4	11*		5	9					3			10	37
1	2		8	5		7			4				9				12	3	11	6	10*	38
1	2		4	5		7	11				8*		9				12	3		6	10	39
1	2		8	5	6	7	11		4			3	9								10	40
1	2		8	5	6	7	11*		4				9					3		12	10	41
1	2		8	5	6	7		9	4	12		3*	11								10	42
1	2		8	5	6	7		9	4				11					3			10	43
1	2*		8	5	6	7		9	4	12			11					3			10	44
1					6	7		9	4	11	8		2					3		5	10	45
1					6	7		9	4	11	8		2					3		5	10	46
46	44	6	41	30	44	46	26	31	28	34	15	35	36	1	3	2	1	13	6	5	12	
		2					1		3	2	2		3	7			6			1		
			2	5	3	5	11	7	13	8		1	8				1			1	6	

2 own-goals

O'Rourke	Moore	Ferns	Conroy	Hetzke	Greenall	Britton	Stonehouse	Stewart	Deary	Dyer	Davies	Walsh	Windridge	Murphy	Bailey	Donovan	Teasdale	Price	Crainie	Cegielski	O'Keefe	
1	2		4	5	6	7	10		11		9*	3	8	12								1
1	1		1	1	1	1	1		1		1	1	1									
														1								

O'Rourke	Moore	Ferns	Conroy	Hetzke	Greenall	Britton	Stonehouse	Stewart	Deary	Dyer	Davies	Walsh	Windridge	Murphy	Bailey	Donovan	Teasdale	Price	Crainie	Cegielski	O'Keefe	
1	2	3	4	5	6	7		9	10	11	8											1
1	2		4	5	6	7		9	10	11	8	3										
1	2		4	5	6	7	12	9	10	11*		3	8									2
1	2	12	4	5	6	7	10			11	9*	3	8									
4	4	1	4	4	4	4	1	3	3	4	3	3	2									
		1					1															
					1	1		1	2	1			1									

1985-86

Manager: Sam Ellis

1	Aug	17	(a)	Reading	L 0-1		3,190
2		24	(h)	Notts C	L 1-3	O'Keefe	4,011
3		26	(a)	Darlington	L 1-2	O'Keefe	3,548
4		31	(h)	Swansea C	W 2-0	Deary (pen), Dyer	3,085
5	Sep	7	(a)	Derby C	W 2-1	O'Keefe 2 (1 pen)	10,102
6		14	(h)	York C	L 0-2		4,053
7		17	(a)	Bournemouth	W 4-1	Dyer 2, O'Keefe, Nightingale (og)	3,039
8		21	(h)	Cardiff C	W 3-0	Davies, O'Keefe, Deary	3,783
9		28	(a)	Bristol C	L 1-2	O'Keefe	6,570
10	Oct	1	(h)	Doncaster R	W 4-0	Dyer, O'Keefe 3 (1 pen)	4,121
11		5	(h)	Gillingham	D 2-2	Deary, O'Keefe (pen)	4,571
12		12	(a)	Wigan A	D 1-1	O'Keefe	5,993
13		19	(h)	Bury	W 5-0	O'Keefe 2 (1 pen), Davies, Deary, Hetzke	5,496
14		22	(a)	Chesterfield	W 2-1	Windridge, Davies	3,720
15		26	(h)	Brentford	W 4-0	Hetzke, Stewart 2, Windridge	5,448
16	Nov	2	(a)	Lincoln C	W 3-0	Hetzke, Stonehouse, Deary	2,373
17		5	(a)	Wolves	L 1-2	Dyer	3,690
18		9	(h)	Bristol R	W 4-2	Hetzke, Dyer 2, Windridge	4,707
19		23	(a)	Walsall	D 1-1	Greenall	5,161
20		30	(h)	Plymouth A	D 1-1	Stonehouse (pen)	6,184
21	Dec	14	(a)	Newport C	D 1-1	Stewart	1,991
22		22	(a)	Notts C	W 2-1	Stonehouse, Dyer	5,926
23		26	(h)	Bolton W	D 1-1	Stewart	9,473
24		28	(h)	Darlington	D 0-0		5,595
25	Jan	1	(a)	Rotherham U	L 1-4	Walsh	4,200
26		11	(a)	Swansea C	L 0-2		5,705
27		18	(h)	Reading	D 0-0		5,295
28	Feb	1	(h)	Derby C	L 0-1		6,732
29		4	(h)	Chesterfield	L 0-1		2,998
30		22	(a)	Cardiff C	L 0-1		2,430
31		25	(h)	Lincoln C	W 2-0	Deary, Hodson (og)	1,995
32	Mar	1	(h)	Bristol C	W 2-1	Butler, Deary (pen)	3,366
33		4	(a)	Doncaster R	D 0-0		2,316
34		8	(a)	Gillingham	D 2-2	O'Keefe (pen), Oakes (og)	4,537
35		15	(h)	Wigan A	L 1-2	O'Keefe (pen)	6,218
36		22	(a)	Brentford	D 1-1	Britton	3,528
37		29	(h)	Rotherham U	W 2-1	Thomson, Davies	4,007
38		31	(a)	Bolton W	W 3-1	Thomson, Stewart, O'Keefe	7,878
39	Apr	5	(h)	Wolves	L 0-1		4,563
40		12	(a)	Bristol R	L 0-1		3,472
41		19	(h)	Walsall	W 2-1	Stewart (pen), Hawker (og)	2,964
42		22	(a)	Bury	L 1-4	Stewart (pen)	2,738
43		26	(a)	Plymouth A	L 1-3	Stewart	14,978
44		29	(h)	Bournemouth	W 2-0	Law, Davies	2,259
45	May	3	(h)	Newport C	D 0-0		3,407
46		6	(a)	York C	L 0-3		3,370

FINAL LEAGUE POSITION: 12th in Division Three

Appearances
Sub Appearances
Goals

FA Cup

1	Nov	16	(a)	Lincoln C	W 1-0	West (og)	2,596
2	Dec	7	(h)	Altrincham	L 1-2	Stewart	5,037

Appearances
Sub Appearances
Goals

League Cup

1	Aug	20	(a)	Preston NE	L 1-2	Davies	4,704
	Sep	3	(h)	Preston NE	L 1-3	Greenall	5,043

Appearances
Sub Appearances
Goals

O'Rourke	Moore	Walsh	Deary	Hetzke	Greenall	Britton	O'Keefe	Stewart	Windridge	Dyer	Butler	Conroy	Matthews	Davies	Law	Stonehouse	Thomson	Sendall	Ronson	Morgan	
1	2	3	4	5	6	7	8	9	10	11											1
1	2	3	4	5*	6	7	10	9	12	11		8									2
1	2	3*	8		6	7	10			9	11	4	5	12							3
1	2		8		6	7	10	9		11	3	4			5						4
1	2		8		6		10	9		11	3	4		7	5						5
1	2	3	8		6		10	9		11		4		7	5						6
1	2	3	8		6		10	9		11		4		7	5						7
1	2	3	8		6		10	9		11		4		7	5						8
1	2	3*	8		6		10	9		11		4		7	5	12					9
1	2		8	3	6		10*	9		11		4		7	5		12				10
1	2		8	5	6		10	9		11		4		7	3						11
1	2		8	5	6		10	9		11		4		7	3						12
1	2		8	5	6		10	9		11		4*		7	3	12					13
1	2		8	5	6		10*	9	12	11				7	3	4					14
1	2		8	5	6	12		9	10	11				7*	3	4					15
1	2		8	5	6	12		9	10	11				7*	3	4					16
1	2			5	6	8		9	10	11				7	3	4					17
1	2			5	6	8		9	10	11				7	3	4					18
1	2			5	6	8		9	10	11				7	3	4					19
1	2			5	6	8		9	10	11				7	3	4					20
1	2	3	4	5	6	7		9	10	11						8					21
1		3	4	5	6	7		9*	8	11	2					10		12			22
1		3	8	5	6	7*		9	10	11	2				12	4					23
1		3	8	5	6			9*	10	11	2			7	12	4					24
1		3	8	5	6				10	11	2			7	9	4					25
1	2		8	5	6				9	11	10			7	3	4					26
1	2			5	6	7		9	10*	11				12	3	4			8		27
1	2		4	5	6	7*		9		11				8	3		12		10		28
1	2		4	5	6	12		9		11				8*	3		7		10		29
1	2		4	5	6	7		9		11		8*		12	3		10				30
1	2		8			10		9		11	3	4		7	5		6				31
1	2	3	8		6	7	12	9		11	10	4			5						32
1	2	3	8		6		12	9		11	10	4		7*	5						33
1	2	5	8		6		12	9		11	3	4		7*			10				34
1	2	5	8		6	12	10	9		11	3	4*					7				35
1	2	3*			6	8	10	9		11		4		12	5		7				36
1	2		8		6	7	10			11	3	4*		12	5		9				37
1	2*		4		6	7	10	9		11	12			3	5		8				38
1	2	6	4			7	10	9		11*	3			12	5		8				39
1	2	6	4			7		9			3*			10	5		8	12		11	40
1	2	3	8		6	7		9				4			5		10*	12		11	41
1	2	3	4		6	7*		9				8			5		10	12		11	42
1	2	3	8		6			9				4		7	5		10	11			43
1	2	3	4		6	12		9				8		7	5		10*	11			44
1	2*	3	8		6	10		9				4		7	5			11		12	45
1	2	3	8		6*	10		9			4			7	5			11		12	46
46	42	25	40	23	43	25	19	42	14	39	17	25	1	30	37	14	14	4	3	3	
						5	3		2		1			6	2	2	2	4		2	
		1	7	4	1	1	17	8	3	8	1			5	1	3	2				

4 own-goals

O'Rourke	Moore	Walsh	Deary	Hetzke	Greenall	Britton	O'Keefe	Stewart	Windridge	Dyer	Butler	Conroy	Matthews	Davies	Law	Stonehouse	Thomson	Sendall	Ronson	Morgan	
1	2			5	6	8		9	10	11				7	3	4					1
1	2	3	8	5	6			9	10	11				7		4					2
2	2	1	1	2	2	1		2	2	2				2	1	2					
								1													

1 own-goal

O'Rourke	Moore	Walsh	Deary	Hetzke	Greenall	Britton	O'Keefe	Stewart	Windridge	Dyer	Butler	Conroy	Matthews	Davies	Law	Stonehouse	Thomson	Sendall	Ronson	Morgan	
1	2	3	4		6	7	10		5	11		8		9							1
1	2		8		6	7*	10	9		11	3	4	5			12					
2	2	1	2		2	2	2	1	1	2	1	2	1	1							
																1					
					1									1							

1986-87

Manager: Sam Ellis

No	Month	Day	Venue	Opponent	Result	Scorers	Attendance
1	Aug	23	(h)	Chesterfield	D 0-0		4,032
2		30	(a)	Fulham	W 1-0	Stewart	3,903
3	Sep	6	(h)	Carlisle U	L 1-2	Thomson	4,188
4		14	(a)	Doncaster R	D 2-2	Stewart 2 (1 pen)	3,338
5		16	(a)	Swindon T	W 6-2	Taylor 2, Dyer 2, Mayes, Stewart	6,662
6		20	(h)	Wigan A	W 5-1	Mayes 3, Taylor, Butler	4,905
7		27	(a)	Bristol R	D 2-2	Mayes, Methven	3,417
8		30	(h)	Port Vale	W 2-0	Methven 2	4,585
9	Oct	4	(h)	Walsall	D 1-1	Dyer	5,554
10		11	(a)	Middlesbrough	W 3-1	Taylor 2, Stewart	11,470
11		18	(h)	Notts C	W 3-1	Mayes, Taylor, Stewart	5,325
12		21	(a)	Bolton W	L 0-1		6,534
13	Nov	1	(h)	Bristol C	W 1-0	Butler	4,370
14		4	(a)	Gillingham	L 1-2	Walsh	5,951
15		8	(h)	Rotherham U	W 1-0	Methven	3,578
16		22	(a)	Brentford	D 1-1	Taylor	4,471
17		29	(h)	Newport C	D 1-1	Deary	3,281
18	Dec	6	(a)	Mansfield T	D 1-1	Stewart	2,931
19		13	(h)	Bury	D 1-1	Walsh	3,412
20		26	(h)	York C	W 2-1	Stewart 2 (1 pen)	4,515
21		27	(a)	Chester C	W 4-1	Davies, Butler, Deary, Taylor	4,002
22	Jan	3	(h)	Brentford	W 2-0	Taylor, Stewart (pen)	4,384
23		24	(a)	Carlisle U	L 1-3	Davies	3,048
24	Feb	3	(a)	Bournemouth	D 1-1	Stewart	6,242
25		7	(h)	Swindon T	D 1-1	Stewart (pen)	4,839
26		13	(a)	Wigan A	L 1-4	Madden	6,857
27		17	(a)	Chesterfield	D 1-1	Stewart	2,468
28		21	(h)	Bristol R	W 6-1	Taylor 2, Davies, Madden, Stewart 2 (1 pen)	3,434
29		28	(a)	Port Vale	W 6-1	Stewart 3 (1 pen), Davies, McGinley, Madden	3,765
30	Mar	3	(a)	Bristol C	L 1-3	Stewart	10,769
31		7	(h)	Mansfield T	L 1-2	Stewart (pen)	3,032
32		10	(a)	Darlington	D 1-1	Windridge	1,600
33		14	(a)	Notts C	L 2-3	Thomson, Stewart (pen)	5,920
34		17	(h)	Bolton W	D 1-1	Taylor	4,717
35		21	(h)	Middlesbrough	L 0-1		7,132
36		28	(a)	Walsall	L 1-2	Madden	5,061
37	Apr	4	(a)	Rotherham U	L 0-1		2,653
38		7	(h)	Fulham	W 1-0	Thomson	1,902
39		11	(h)	Gillingham	L 0-1		2,558
40		18	(h)	Darlington	W 2-1	Thomson, Davies	2,612
41		20	(a)	York C	D 1-1	Taylor	2,694
42		25	(h)	Bournemouth	L 1-3	Methven	2,866
43		28	(h)	Doncaster R	D 1-1	Davies	1,638
44	May	2	(a)	Newport C	D 1-1	Taylor	1,247
45		4	(h)	Chester C	W 1-0	Deary	2,069
46		9	(a)	Bury	L 1-4	Madden	2,198

FINAL LEAGUE POSITION: 9th in Division Three

Appearances
Sub Appearances
Goals

FA Cup

Round	Month	Day	Venue	Opponent	Result	Scorers	Attendance
1	Nov	15	(a)	Middlesbrough	L 0-3		11,205

Appearances
Sub Appearances
Goals

League Cup

Round	Month	Day	Venue	Opponent	Result	Scorers	Attendance
1	Aug	26	(h)	Preston NE	D 0-0		3,929
	Sep	2	(a)	Preston NE	L 1-2	Deary	5,914

Appearances
Sub Appearances
Goals

Siddall	Matthews	Walsh	Law	Methven	Greenall	Deary	Thomson	Stewart	O'Keefe E	Dyer	Davies	Sendall	Butler	Taylor	Mayes	Moore	McAteer	McGinley	Priest	Powell	O'Keefe V	Windridge	Bradshaw	Morgan	Jones	Madden	
1	2	3	4	5	6	7	8	9	10	11																	1
1		3	4	5	6	7	8	9		11	2	10*	12														2
1		3	4	5	6	7	8	9	10*	11	2		12														3
1	2*	3	4	5		7	8	9		11	6	12		10													4
1		3	4	5		6	8*	9		10	2		12	11	7												5
1		3	4	5		6		9		10	2		8	11*	7	12											6
1		3	4	5		6		9		10	2		8	11	7												7
1		3	4	5		6	8	9		10	2		12	11*	7												8
1		3	4	5		6	8	9		10	2*		12	11	7												9
1		3	4	5		6	8	9		10			2	11	7												10
1		3	4	5		6	8	9		10			2*	11	7			12									11
1	12	3	4	5		6	8			10	2	9*		11	7												12
1		3	4	5		6	8*	9		10	2		12	11	7												13
1	7*	3	4	5		6		9		10	2		8	11	12												14
1		3	4	5		6	10	9			2		8	11	7												15
1		3		5		6		9		10	2		8	11	7*	4		12									16
1		3	4	5		6		9		10	2		8	11	7*			12									17
1		3	4	5		6	7	9		10	2		8	11													18
1		3	4	5			8	9		10	7		2	11					6								19
			4*	5		6	8	9		10	7		2	11			3	12		1							20
	4			5		6	8*	9		10	7		2	11			3	12			1						21
1	4			5		6	8	9		10	7		2	11			3										22
1	6*	3		8		4	7	9		10	8		2				11					12					23
1		3	4	5		6	8	9		10	7		2	11													24
1		3	4	5		6	8	9		10	7*		2	11			12										25
1		3	4	5		6	8*	9			7		2	11				12								10	26
1	2		4	5		6	8	9			7			11			3									10	27
1	2		4*	5		6		9			7		10	11			3	12								8	28
1	2		4	5		6		9			7		8*	11			3	12								10	29
1	2		4	5		6	8	9			7			11			3									10	30
1	2		4	5		6	8*	9			7		11				3	12								10	31
1	2	4		5		6		9			7		10				3					11				8	32
1		4		5		6	8	9			7			2			3					11				10	33
1		4		5		6	9				7			11			3	2*				8		12		10	34
1	2			5		6	9				7		8	11			3					12		4*		10	35
1	6			5			9				7		2	11								10		3	4	8	36
1	6			5		7	9*						2	11			3	10						12	4	8	37
1		6		5		8	9				7		2	11			3							12	4	10*	38
1		6*		5		7	9				8		2	11			3					12		10	4		39
		6		5		7	9				8		2*	11			3			1		12		10	4		40
	2	6		5		7	9*				8			11			3			1		12			4	10	41
	2	6		5		7					8			9			3			1				11	4	10	42
	4	6		5		8					7		3	9						1		2*	12	11		10	43
	2	6		5		7	9				8		3	11						1			12		4*	10	44
	4	6*		5		8	9				7		3	11						1			2	12		10	45
	2			5		8	9				7		3	11						1		12	4	6*		10	46
37	21	34	27	46	3	44	36	32	2	24	42	2	22	40	12	1	19	2	1	8	1	5	2	7	8	19	
	1											1	6		1	1	1	9				5	3	4			
		2		5		3	4	21		3	6		3	14	6			1				1				5	

Siddall	Matthews	Walsh	Law	Methven	Greenall	Deary	Thomson	Stewart	O'Keefe E	Dyer	Davies	Sendall	Butler	Taylor	Mayes	Moore	McAteer	McGinley	Priest	Powell	O'Keefe V	Windridge	Bradshaw	Morgan	Jones	Madden	
1		3*	4	5		6	8	9			2		10†	11	7	12		14									1
1		1	1	1		1	1	1			1		1	1	1												
																1		1									

Siddall	Matthews	Walsh	Law	Methven	Greenall	Deary	Thomson	Stewart	O'Keefe E	Dyer	Davies	Sendall	Butler	Taylor	Mayes	Moore	McAteer	McGinley	Priest	Powell	O'Keefe V	Windridge	Bradshaw	Morgan	Jones	Madden	
1	2*	3	4	5	6	7	8	9		11	12	10															1
1		5	4		6	7	8	9		11	2	10*	3	12													
2	1	2	2	1	2	2	2	2		2	1	2	1														
											1			1													
						1																					

1987-88

Manager: Sam Ellis

No	Month	Day	Venue	Opponents	Result	Scorers	Attendance
1	Aug	15	(a)	Gillingham	D 0-0		4,430
2		22	(h)	Walsall	L 1-2	Cunningham	4,614
3		29	(a)	Bury	L 1-3	Walwyn	3,053
4		31	(h)	Bristol R	W 2-1	Cunningham 2 (1 pen)	3,319
5	Sep	5	(a)	Brighton & HA	W 3-1	Cunningham 2, Taylor	7,166
6		12	(h)	Chester C	L 0-1		4,035
7		15	(a)	Doncaster R	L 1-2	Cunningham	1,558
8		19	(a)	Brentford	L 1-2	Walwyn	3,886
9		26	(h)	Preston NE	W 3-0	Walwyn 2, Madden (pen)	8,406
10		29	(a)	York C	W 3-1	Cunningham, Morgan, Madden	2,559
11	Oct	3	(h)	Fulham	W 2-1	Madden 2 (1 pen)	4,973
12		17	(h)	Sunderland	L 0-2		8,476
13		20	(a)	Grimsby T	D 1-1	Taylor	2,260
14		24	(h)	Wigan A	D 0-0		4,821
15		31	(a)	Mansfield T	D 0-0		3,321
16	Nov	3	(h)	Bristol C	W 4-2	Morgan, Taylor, Madden 2 (1 pen)	3,140
17		7	(h)	Rotherham U	W 3-0	Deary, Taylor, Madden	3,447
18		22	(a)	Port Vale	D 0-0		3,594
19		28	(h)	Northampton T	W 3-1	Cunningham, Walwyn, Morgan	3,593
20	Dec	12	(a)	Chesterfield	D 1-1	Taylor	2,279
21		19	(h)	Southend U	D 1-1	Walwyn	3,277
22		26	(a)	Preston NE	L 1-2	Madden	11,155
23		28	(h)	Notts C	D 1-1	Coughlin	4,627
24	Jan	1	(h)	Bury	W 5-1	Butler, Cunningham, Morgan, Madden, Deary	4,240
25		2	(a)	Chester C	D 1-1	Madden	3,093
26		16	(h)	Brentford	L 0-1		3,911
27	Feb	6	(h)	Brighton & HA	L 1-3	Lester	4,081
28		13	(a)	Notts C	W 3-2	Morgan, Taylor 2	5,794
29		20	(h)	Gillingham	D 3-3	Coughlin, Taylor, Walwyn	3,045
30		23	(a)	Walsall	L 2-3	Taylor 2 (1 pen)	4,252
31		27	(a)	Fulham	L 1-3	Walwyn	4,072
32	Mar	1	(h)	York C	W 2-1	Taylor, Methven	2,249
33		5	(a)	Sunderland	D 2-2	Taylor, Walwyn	15,513
34		12	(h)	Aldershot	W 3-2	Taylor, Walwyn, Cunningham	2,661
35		19	(h)	Mansfield T	W 2-0	Taylor 2 (1 pen)	2,847
36		25	(a)	Wigan A	D 0-0		4,505
37		29	(a)	Aldershot	D 0-0		2,091
38	Apr	2	(a)	Rotherham U	W 1-0	Deary	3,001
39		4	(h)	Port Vale	L 1-2	Taylor	5,516
40		9	(a)	Bristol C	L 1-2	Taylor	6,460
41		15	(h)	Doncaster R	W 4-2	Madden, Taylor 2, Walwyn	2,291
42		23	(h)	Grimsby T	W 3-0	Walwyn, Taylor 2	2,558
43		27	(a)	Bristol R	L 0-2		3,546
44		30	(a)	Northampton T	D 3-3	Walwyn, Methven, Morgan	5,730
45	May	2	(h)	Chesterfield	W 1-0	Walwyn	2,950
46		7	(a)	Southend U	L 0-4		5,541

FINAL LEAGUE POSITION: 10th in Division Three

Appearances
Sub Appearances
Goals

FA Cup

Round	Month	Day	Venue	Opponents	Result	Scorers	Attendance
1	Nov	14	(a)	Bishop Auckland	W 4-1	Deary, Madden, Taylor 2	2,462
2	Dec	6	(a)	Northwich V	W 2-0	Madden, Walwyn	2,528
3	Jan	9	(a)	Scunthorpe U	D 0-0		6,217
R		12	(h)	Scunthorpe U	W 1-0	Madden	6,227
4		30	(h)	Manchester C	D 1-1	Sendall	10,835
R	Feb	3	(a)	Manchester C	L 1-2	Deary	26,503

Appearances
Sub Appearances
Goals

League Cup

Round	Month	Day	Venue	Opponents	Result	Scorers	Attendance
1	Aug	18	(h)	Chester C	W 2-0	Cunningham, Methven	3,114
		26	(a)	Chester C	L 0-1		2,147
2	Sep	23	(h)	Newcastle U	W 1-0	Cunningham	7,691
	Oct	7	(a)	Newcastle U	L 1-4	Morgan	20,805

Appearances
Sub Appearances
Goals

Siddall	Davies	Morgan	Matthews	Methven	Jones	Cunningham	Madden	Walwyn	Deary	Taylor	Butler	Bradshaw	Walsh	Rooney	Lancashire	McAteer	Hutchison	Coughlin	Lester	Shaw	Muggleton	Powell	Wright	Sendall	
1	2	3	4	5	6	7	8	9	10	11															1
1	2	3	4	5	6*	7	8	9	10	11†	12		14												2
1	2	3	4	5	14		8*	9	10	11†	7		6	12											3
1	2	3	4	5		7		9	10	11	8		6												4
1	2	3	4	5		7	8	9	10	11			6												5
1	2*	3	4	5	14	7	8	9	10	11	12†		6												6
1		3	4	5		7	8	9	10	11*		2	6			12									7
1	2	3	4	5*	10	7	8	9		11			6			12									8
1		3	4	12	10	7	8†	9		11			6*		14	12	2								9
1	2	3	4	12	10*	7†	8			11			6		14	12	9								10
1	2	3	4	5		7	8	12		11			6			10	9*								11
1	2	3	4	5			8	9	7	11			6			10*	12								12
1	2*	3	4	5		7		9	8	11			6			10†	12								13
1		3	4	5		7		9	8†	11	12		6		2*	10	14								14
1		3		5	6	7	2	9	8	11		4				10									15
1	2*	3		5		7	8	9	6	11		4			12	10									16
1	2	3		5			8	9	6	11	12	4			7*	10									17
1	2	3		5	14	6	8*	9	7	11†	12	4				10									18
1		3		5†	12	8	2	9	7	11		4	6*		14	10									19
1	2	3		5		8		9		11		4	6			10		7							20
1	2*	3		5	6	7	14	9		11	12	4†				10		8							21
1		3		5	6	7	2	9*		11	12	4				10		8							22
1		3		5	6	7	9		12	11	2	4*				10		8							23
1	12	3		5	6	7†	9		14	11	2					10		8	4*						24
1	12	3		5	6	7	9†		14	11	2*					10		8	4						25
1	2	3		5	6	7	9		10						12	11		8	4*						26
1	2*	3†			6	9	14		10	11	12		5					8	4	7					27
	2	3		12	5*	9	14		10	11			6					8	4†	7	1				28
	2*	3		5†	12		10	9		11			6			14		8	4	7	1				29
1	2	3			5	10	14	9†		11	12		6					8	4	7*					30
1	2	3			5	10	12	9	7	11			6					8	4*						31
1	2	3		5		10		9	7	11	4*		6					8		12					32
1	2	3		5		10		9	7	11	4*		6					8		12					33
1	2	3	6	5	8	10		9	4	11									7						34
1	2	3	6	5	8*	10		9	4	11				12					7						35
1	2	3	6	5	8	10		9	4	11								7							36
1	2	3	4	5	8			9	10	11	6							7							37
1	2	3	4	5	6			9	10	11*	7†		12	14				8							38
1	2	3	6	5	8*	10		9	7	11			12					4							39
1		3*	2	5		10		9	7	11†		12	6	8				4							40
	2	3	8	5		10	6	9	7*	11		12							4			1			41
	2	3	8	5		10	6*	9	7	11				12				4				1			42
	2	3	8	5		10	6*	9	7			11	12					4				1			43
	2†	3	8	12		10	14	9	7			6*	5	11				4				1			44
	2	3	8	12		10		9	7			6†	5*	11				4				1	14		45
	2	3	8			10		9	7			6	5	11				4				1			46
38	36	46	27	37	22	40	25	38	34	41	9	14	25	4	2	16	3	24	11	4	2	6			
	2			5	5		8	1	3		9	2	4	4	5	5	3			2			1		
		6		2		10	11	14	3	21	1							2	1						

Siddall	Davies	Morgan	Matthews	Methven	Jones	Cunningham	Madden	Walwyn	Deary	Taylor	Butler	Bradshaw	Walsh	Rooney	Lancashire	McAteer	Hutchison	Coughlin	Lester	Shaw	Muggleton	Powell	Wright	Sendall	
1	2	3		5	6		8*	9	7	11	14	4		12		10†									1
1	2*	3			5		8	9	7	11	12	4	6			10									2
1	2	3			6	7	9		10	11			5					8	4						3
1	2	3		12	6	7	9		10				5			11*		8	4						R
1	2	3			6			9	10	11			5	7*				8	4					12	4
1	2	3			6		12	9	10	11	7		5					8	4*						R
6	6	6		1	6	2	4	4	6	5	1	2	5	1		3		4	4						
				1			1				2			1										1	
							3	1	2	2														1	

Siddall	Davies	Morgan	Matthews	Methven	Jones	Cunningham	Madden	Walwyn	Deary	Taylor	Butler	Bradshaw	Walsh	Rooney	Lancashire	McAteer	Hutchison	Coughlin	Lester	Shaw	Muggleton	Powell	Wright	Sendall	
1	2	3	4	5	6	7	8	9	10	11*	12														1
1	2	3	4	5			8	9	10	11	7		6												
1	2*	3	4		10	7	8	9		11			6		12	5									2
1	2	3	4*	5		7	8	9		11			6			10	12								
4	4	4	4	3	2	3	4	4	2	4	1		3			2									
											1				1		1								
		1		1		2																			

1988-89

Manager: Sam Ellis

1	Aug	27	(a)	Chester C	D 1-1	Cunningham	3,496
2	Sep	3	(h)	Notts C	L 0-1		4,669
3		10	(a)	Preston NE	L 0-1		8,779
4		17	(h)	Mansfield T	D 1-1	Garner	4,021
5		20	(h)	Bristol C	D 2-2	Davies, Taylor	3,413
6		24	(a)	Chesterfield	W 2-0	Garner, Taylor	2,128
7		30	(a)	Wigan A	L 1-2	Taylor	4,141
8	Oct	4	(h)	Northampton T	W 3-1	Cunningham, Thompson, Deary	3,034
9		8	(a)	Bolton W	D 2-2	Cunningham, Morgan	7,106
10		15	(h)	Sheffield U	L 1-2	Coughlin (pen)	8,471
11		22	(h)	Port Vale	W 3-2	Cunningham, Madden, Coughlin (pen)	7,045
12		25	(a)	Wolves	L 1-2	Morgan	12,104
13		29	(h)	Cardiff C	W 1-0	Garner	3,849
14	Nov	5	(a)	Fulham	D 1-1	Garner	4,760
15		8	(a)	Gillingham	L 0-1		3,541
16		12	(h)	Aldershot	W 4-0	Garner 2, Coughlin (pen), Deary	2,690
17		26	(h)	Swansea C	D 0-0		3,443
18	Dec	3	(a)	Huddersfield T	D 1-1	Cunningham	5,738
19		17	(h)	Bristol R	D 1-1	Garner	3,240
20		26	(a)	Brentford	L 0-1		6,021
21		30	(a)	Reading	L 1-2	Cunningham	5,554
22	Jan	2	(h)	Bury	D 2-2	Cunningham, Coughlin (pen)	4,199
23		14	(a)	Notts C	D 1-1	Morgan	4,748
24		21	(h)	Preston NE	W 1-0	Thompson	8,951
25		28	(a)	Mansfield T	W 1-0	Madden	2,738
26	Feb	4	(h)	Wigan A	W 2-0	Deary 2	4,221
27		11	(a)	Northampton T	L 2-4	Thompson 2	3,033
28		18	(h)	Bolton W	W 2-0	Cunningham, Thompson	5,552
29		25	(a)	Sheffield U	L 1-4	Garner	11,317
30		28	(h)	Wolves	L 0-2		6,482
31	Mar	4	(a)	Port Vale	L 0-1		6,306
32		11	(h)	Fulham	L 0-1		3,014
33		18	(h)	Chester C	D 1-1	Deary	2,795
34		25	(a)	Bury	D 0-0		3,717
35		27	(h)	Brentford	L 0-3		3,053
36	Apr	1	(a)	Bristol R	L 0-1		5,355
37		4	(a)	Southend U	L 1-2	Methven	2,795
38		8	(h)	Reading	L 2-4	Garner, Davies	2,792
39		15	(a)	Bristol C	W 2-1	Walwyn 2	5,096
40		22	(h)	Chesterfield	L 1-2	Garner	3,321
41		29	(a)	Aldershot	L 0-1		1,763
42	May	1	(h)	Gillingham	W 4-1	Walwyn, Matthews, O'Shea (og), Garner	2,152
43		6	(h)	Huddersfield T	W 2-1	Thompson, Madden	4,070
44		9	(h)	Southend U	W 3-2	Thompson 2, Madden	3,999
45		13	(a)	Swansea C	W 2-1	Coughlin, Davies (og)	3,494
46		16	(a)	Cardiff C	D 0-0		3,426

FINAL LEAGUE POSITION: 19th in Division Three

Appearances
Sub Appearances
Goals

FA Cup

1	Nov	19	(h)	Scunthorpe U	W 2-1	Cunningham, Garner	3,974
2	Dec	10	(h)	Bury	W 3-0	Cunningham, Garner, Deary	5,324
3	Jan	7	(h)	Bournemouth	L 0-1		5,317

Appearances
Sub Appearances
Goals

League Cup

1	Aug	30	(a)	Carlisle U	D 1-1	Deary	2,336
	Sep	6	(h)	Carlisle U	W 3-0	Garner 2, Taylor	2,955
2		27	(h)	Sheffield W	W 2-0	Coughlin, Cunningham	5,492
	Oct	12	(a)	Sheffield W	L 1-3*	Morgan	12,237
3	Nov	1	(a)	Tranmere R	L 0-1		9,454

*After extra-time, Blackpool won on away-goals rule.

Appearances
Sub Appearances
Goals

Siddall	Gore	Burgess	Deary	Methven	Elliott	Davies	Cunningham	Garner	Coughlin	Wright	Walwyn	Thompson	Morgan	Taylor	Walsh	Matthews	Madden	Kelly	O'Keefe	Rooney	
1	2	3	4	5	6	7	8	9*	10	11	12										1
1	2*	3	4	5	6	7	8	9†	10		14	12	11								2
1		2	4	5*	6	7	8	9	10			12	3	11							3
1		2	4	5	6	7	8	9	10*		14	12	3†	11							4
1		2	4	5	6	7	8	9†	10*		14	12	3	11							5
1		2	4	5	6	7	8	9	10		14	12	3*	11†							6
1		2	4	5	6		8	9	10		7*		3	11		12					7
1		2	4	5	6*		8	9	10	11†		12	3			7	14				8
	6	2	4	5			8	9	10			11*	3			7	12	1			9
	6	2	4	5			8	9	10		7	11*	3				12	1			10
	14	2	4	5†	6		8	9	10			11	3			7*	12	1			11
	11	2	4	12	6		8	9	10†			14	3			7*	5	1			12
	7	2	4	5	6		8	9	10		12		3				11*	1			13
1	7	2	4	5	6		8	9	10			11	3								14
1	7	2	4	5	6		8	9	10		12	11*	3†	14							15
1		2	4	5*	6	7	8	9	10	14	12		3	11†							16
1		2	4*	5	6		8	9	10				3	11†	7	14	12				17
1		2	4	5	6		8	9	10			14	3	11†	7*		12				18
1		2	4	5	6	12	8	9	10			11	3*				7				19
1		2	4	5	6	7	8	9	10		14		3*		12		11†				20
1		2		5	6	7	8	9	10	11*	12		3		4						21
1		2	14	5	6	7	8	9	10	11*	12		3		4†						22
1	4	2		5	6	7	8	9	10		11		3								23
1	4	2	10	5*	6	7	8	9			12†	14	3				11				24
1	4	2	5		6	7	8	9				10	3				11				25
1	4	2	5		6	7*	8	9	12			10	3				11				26
1	4†	2	7	5			8	9	6		12	10	3		14		11*				27
	4†	2	7	5		14	8	9	6		12	10	3				11*		1		28
		2	7	5†	6	14	8	9	4		11	10*	3		12				1		29
		2	7	5*	6	11	8	9	4		12	10	3						1		30
		2	7	5	6	11	8	9	4		12	10	3						1		31
		2	7	5	6	11		9	4	12	8	10*	3						1		32
		2	7	5	6	11		9	4		8	10	3						1		33
1	7	2	4	5	6	11*		9	10			12	3				8				34
1	8*	2	7	5	6	11			4			10	3			12	9				35
1	7*	2		5	6	12		9	4	11		10	3				8				36
1		2	4	5	6	7		9		11		10	3*				8			12	37
1		2	10	5	6	7		9	4	11		12	3*				8				38
1	10	2	6	5	4	7		9	8		12					3*	11				39
1	11	2			6	7		9	10	3	8	5*	12				4				40
1		2		5	6	7		9	10	11†	8*	4	3			14	12				41
1		2		5	6			9	10	11	8	4	3			7					42
1	12	2	14	5	6*				10†	11	8	4	3			7	9				43
1		2		5	6	12			10	11	8	4	3			7*	9				44
1		2		5					10	11	8	4	3		6	7	9				45
1		2			6			12	10	11	8*	4	3		5	7	9				46
35	19	46	35	41	41	25	31	41	42	14	13	25	43	8	6	10	20	5	6		
	2		2	1		5		1	1	2	17	11	1	1	4	4	7			1	
			5	1		2	8	11	5		3	8	3	3		1	4				

2 own-goals

Siddall	Gore	Burgess	Deary	Methven	Elliott	Davies	Cunningham	Garner	Coughlin	Wright	Walwyn	Thompson	Morgan	Taylor	Walsh	Matthews	Madden	Kelly	O'Keefe	Rooney	
1		2	4	5	6	7	8	9	10				3	11							1
1		2	4	5	6		8	9	10*			11	3		12		7				2
1		2	4	5	6	7	8	9	10		12		3							11*	3
3		3	3	3	3	2	3	3	3			1	3	1			1			1	
											1				1						
			1				2	2													

Siddall	Gore	Burgess	Deary	Methven	Elliott	Davies	Cunningham	Garner	Coughlin	Wright	Walwyn	Thompson	Morgan	Taylor	Walsh	Matthews	Madden	Kelly	O'Keefe	Rooney	
1	2	3	4	5	6	7	8	9	10	11*		12									1
1		2	4†	5	6	7	8	9	10*			12	3	11			14				
1		2	4	5	6	7*	8	9	10		12		3	11							2
1	12	2	4	5			8	9	10		11†		3		6*	7	14				
1	7	2	4*	5	6		8	9	10		11	12	3								3
5	2	5	5	5	4	3	5	5	5	1	2		4	2	1	1					
	1										1	3					2				
			1				1	2	1				1	1							

1989-90

Manager: Jimmy Mullen

1	Aug	19	(h)	Wigan A	D 0-0		4,561
2		26	(a)	Notts C	W 1-0	Burgess	4,852
3	Sep	2	(h)	Shrewsbury T	L 0-1		4,109
4		9	(a)	Bristol C	L 0-2		7,172
5		16	(h)	Crewe A	L 1-3	Briggs	4,722
6		23	(a)	Mansfield T	W 3-0	Gabbiadini 2, Diamond	2,629
7		26	(a)	Preston NE	L 1-2	Madden	8,920
8		30	(h)	Birmingham C	W 3-2	Overson (og), Garner (pen), Gabbiadini	5,737
9	Oct	6	(h)	Reading	D 0-0		3,321
10		14	(a)	Leyton O	L 0-2		4,126
11		17	(a)	Northampton T	L 2-4	Briggs, Garner (pen)	3,098
12		21	(h)	Cardiff C	W 1-0	Owen	3,502
13		28	(a)	Rotherham U	D 1-1	Garner	5,570
14		31	(h)	Bury	L 0-1		4,184
15	Nov	4	(a)	Bristol R	D 1-1	Madden	5,520
16		11	(h)	Brentford	W 4-0	Madden 2 (1 pen), Eyres, Morgan	2,512
17		25	(h)	Tranmere R	L 0-3		4,106
18	Dec	2	(a)	Swansea C	D 0-0		4,020
19		16	(h)	Fulham	L 0-1		2,548
20		26	(a)	Bolton W	L 0-2		9,944
21		30	(a)	Chester C	L 0-2		2,405
22	Jan	1	(h)	Huddersfield T	D 2-2	Methven, Garner (pen)	5,097
23		13	(h)	Notts C	D 0-0		3,146
24		20	(a)	Wigan A	D 1-1	Garner	3,179
25	Feb	3	(h)	Mansfield T	W 3-1	Owen, Garner (pen), Richards	4,402
26		10	(a)	Crewe A	L 0-2		3,978
27		13	(a)	Shrewsbury T	D 1-1	Eyres	2,300
28		23	(a)	Tranmere R	L 2-4	Garner (pen), Eyres	7,873
29	Mar	3	(h)	Walsall	W 4-3	Bradshaw, Eyres, Methven, Groves	3,174
30		6	(a)	Birmingham C	L 1-3	Richards	6,738
31		10	(h)	Preston NE	D 2-2	Brook, Garner (pen)	8,108
32		13	(h)	Bristol C	L 1-3	Brook	3,227
33		17	(a)	Reading	D 1-1	Owen	3,752
34		20	(h)	Leyton O	W 1-0	Richards	2,746
35		24	(h)	Northampton T	W 1-0	Eyres	3,290
36		27	(a)	Walsall	D 1-1	Richards	3,134
37		31	(a)	Cardiff C	D 2-2	Eyres, Brook	2,850
38	Apr	7	(h)	Rotherham U	L 1-2	Brook	3,508
39		10	(a)	Bury	L 0-2		3,131
40		14	(a)	Huddersfield T	D 2-2	Coughlin, Gouck	4,845
41		16	(h)	Bolton W	W 2-1	Brook, Eyres	5,438
42		21	(a)	Fulham	D 0-0		3,816
43		24	(h)	Chester C	L 1-3	Methven	3,724
44		28	(a)	Brentford	L 0-5		4,784
45		30	(h)	Swansea C	D 2-2	Owen, Brook	1,842
46	May	5	(h)	Bristol R	L 0-3		6,776

FINAL LEAGUE POSITION: 23rd in Division Three

Appearances
Sub Appearar
Goals

FA Cup

1	Nov	18	(h)	Bolton W	W 2-1	Eyres, Garner	7,309
2	Dec	9	(h)	Chester C	W 3-0	Brook, Burgess, Owen	4,099
3	Jan	6	(h)	Burnley	W 1-0	Methven	8,091
4		27	(h)	Torquay U	W 1-0	Owen	6,781
5	Feb	18	(h)	Queen's Park R	D 2-2	Groves, Eyres	9,641
R		21	(a)	Queen's Park R	D 0-0*		15,323
2R		26	(a)	Queen's Park R	L 0-3		12,775

*After extra-time

Appearances
Sub Appeara
Goals

League Cup

1	Aug	22	(h)	Burnley	D 2-2	Briggs, Garner	4,540
		29	(a)	Burnley	W 1-0	Bradshaw	6,083
2	Sep	19	(a)	Barnsley	D 1-1	Gabbiadini	7,515
	Oct	3	(h)	Barnsley	D 1-1*	Briggs	5,259
3	Oct	25	(a)	Exeter C	L 0-3		6,508

*After extra-time, Blackpool won 5-4 on penalties.

Appearances
Sub Appeara
Goals

McIlhargey	Burgess	Morgan	Gore	Briggs	Matthews	Bradshaw	Sinclair	Garner	Coughlin	Wright	Madden	Methven	Owen	Eyres	Thompson	Elliott	Diamond	Gabbiadini	Bartram	Davies	Brook	Hawkins	Wood	Jones	Groves	Gouck	Richards	Gayle	
1	2	3	4	5	6	7*	8	9†	10	11	12	14																	1
1	2	3	4	5		6		9*	10	11	8	7	12																2
1	2	3	4†	5	14	11		10*	8	7	9	6			12														3
1	2	3	4	5	10	11*		9		7		6			8	12													4
1	2	3	4	5	14			10		12			7	11*		6†	8	9											5
1	2	3	4	11				10				5	7			6	8	9											6
1	2*	3	4	11		6†		10	14	12	8	5	7					9											7
1	2	3	4	11				10	8			5	7			6		9											8
1	2	3	4	11				10	8	12		5	7			6*		9											9
1	2	3	4	11	6*		12	10	8			5	7	9															10
1	2	3	4*	11			9	10	8	6		5	7	12															11
1	2	3		6			9*	10	8	12		5	7	11	4														12
	2			11				10	4	3	8	5	7			6			1			9							13
	2			11				10	4	3	8	5	7*	12		6			1			9							14
	2	3		11			12	10	4		8	5	7			6			1			9*							15
	2	3		11				10†			8	5	7*	9		6			1	12		14							16
1		3	2		7†			10	4*		8	5	12	11		6				14	9								17
	7	3	2					10	4		8	5	9	11		6			1										18
	2	3*	7					10	4			5	9	11		6			1	12	8								19
	2*		7					10	4	3	14	5	9†	11		6			1	12	8								20
		12	7		14			10	4	3		5		11		6			1	2†	9	8*							21
		3	7					10	4	2		5	9	11		6			1		8								22
1		3	7					10	4	2		5	9*	11		6					8	12							23
1		3	7	11		8		10	4*	2		5	9†			6	14			12									24
1		3	7			14		10†	4	2		5	9*	12		6									8		11		25
1		3	7			14		10	4†	2		5		11*		6				12					8		9		26
1		3	7			9		10	4	2		5		12		6*									8		11		27
1		3	7			6†		10	4	2		5	14	12							9				8*		11		28
1		3†	7			6		10	4*	2		5		9						14	12				8		11		29
1		3	7			6†		10		2		5		9						14	8*	12			4		11		30
1		3*	7			12		10		2		5		9						6	8				4		11		31
		3	7					10		2*		5		9		6				12	8		1		4		11		32
			2			3		10	7†			5	12	9*		6					8		1		4	14	11		33
						3		10	7			5		9		6				2	8		1		4		11		34
						3		10				5		9		6				7	8		1	2	4		11		35
						3		10				5		9		6				7	8		1	2	4		11		36
						3		10				5	12	9*		6				7	8		1	2	4		11		37
		12	6			3	14	10	11*			5		9						7	8†		1	2	4				38
		3	6					10	11			5		9						7	8		1	2	4				39
		3	6					10	7*			5		9							8		1	2	12	4	11		40
		3	6					10	7			5		9						2	8		1		4	12	11*		41
		3	6		2			10	11			5		9						7	8		1			4			42
		3	6		14			10	7†			5	12	9						2	8		1			4	11*		43
		3			6		12	10	11			5	7	9						2	8*		1			4			44
		3			6	11†	7	10*				5	12	9						2	14		1		8	4			45
		3			6	14	7	12				8	11†	9						2	8		1		10*	4			46
22	19	36	34	17	8	17	5	45	33	20	9	44	21	30	2	25	2	5	9	14	23	4	15	6	18	6	16		
		2			4	4	4	1	1	4	2	1	7	5	1	1	1			9	2	3			1	2			
	1	1		2		1		8	1		4	3	4	7			1	3			6				1	1	4		

1 own-goal

McIlhargey	Burgess	Morgan	Gore	Briggs	Matthews	Bradshaw	Sinclair	Garner	Coughlin	Wright	Madden	Methven	Owen	Eyres	Thompson	Elliott	Diamond	Gabbiadini	Bartram	Davies	Brook	Hawkins	Wood	Jones	Groves	Gouck	Richards	Gayle	
1		3			7*			10	4		8	5		11		6				12	9					2			1
1	2	3						10	4			5	9	11		6*				12	8					7			2
1		3						10	4	2		5	9	11		6					8					7			3
1		3				12		10	4*	2		5	9†	11		6				14					8	7			4
1		3				6		10	4	2		5	12	11							9*				8	7			5
1		3*				6		10		2		5	4†	11			14			12	9				8	7			R
1		3†				6		10	4*	2		5	14	11						12	9				8	7			2R
7	1	7			1	3		7	6	5	1	7	4	7		4					6				4	7			
						1							2				1			5									
	1							1				1	2	2							1				1				

McIlhargey	Burgess	Morgan	Gore	Briggs	Matthews	Bradshaw	Sinclair	Garner	Coughlin	Wright	Madden	Methven	Owen	Eyres	Thompson	Elliott	Diamond	Gabbiadini	Bartram	Davies	Brook	Hawkins	Wood	Jones	Groves	Gouck	Richards	Gayle	
1	2	3	4	5				9	10	11	8	7		6*	12														1
1	2	3	4	5		11		10	8	7	9	6																	
1	2	3*	4	11				10		12	14	5	7			6	8†	9											2
1	2*	3	4†	11				10	8	12		5	7	14		6		9											
	2	3		11				10	8	6	12	5	7		4*							9						1	3
4	5	5	4	5		1		5	4	3	2	5	3	1	1	2	1	2				1						1	
										2	2			1	1														
				2		1		1										1											

1990-91

Manager: Graham Carr/Billy Ayre

No	Month	Date	Venue	Opponents	Result	Scorers	Att
1	Aug	25	(a)	Scunthorpe U	L 0-2		3,024
2	Sep	1	(h)	Rochdale	D 0-0		3,357
3		8	(a)	Northampton T	L 0-1		4,300
4		15	(h)	Wrexham	W 4-1	Stant, Eyres, Phillips (og), Rodwell	3,497
5		18	(h)	Burnley	L 1-2	Stant	4,737
6		22	(a)	Chesterfield	D 2-2	Groves, Garner (pen)	3,549
7		29	(h)	Hartlepool U	W 2-0	Eyres, Groves	3,181
8	Oct	3	(a)	Scarborough	W 1-0	Groves	1,713
9		6	(a)	Torquay U	L 1-2	Stant	2,884
10		13	(h)	Darlington	L 1-2	Garner	4,092
11		20	(h)	Gillingham	W 2-0	Stant, Eyres	3,041
12		22	(a)	Stockport C	D 0-0		4,337
13		27	(a)	Halifax T	L 3-5	Rodwell 2, Stant	1,945
14	Nov	3	(h)	Walsall	L 1-2	Groves	3,233
15		10	(h)	Aldershot	W 4-2	Sinclair, Taylor, Garner (pen), Lancaster	2,065
16		24	(a)	Doncaster R	L 0-1		2,113
17	Dec	1	(a)	Hereford U	D 1-1	Bamber	2,588
18		15	(h)	Maidstone U	D 2-2	Garner, Bamber	2,341
19		23	(a)	Carlisle U	L 0-1		5,195
20		26	(h)	Peterborough U	D 1-1	Garner	3,658
21		29	(h)	Lincoln C	W 5-0	Groves 2 (1 pen), Bamber 2, Eyres	2,519
22	Jan	1	(a)	York C	W 1-0	Horner	3,115
23		12	(a)	Rochdale	L 1-2	Bamber	2,621
24		19	(h)	Scunthorpe U	W 3-1	Bamber 2, Garner	2,494
25		26	(a)	Wrexham	W 1-0	Garner (pen)	2,393
26	Feb	5	(h)	Chesterfield	W 3-0	Bamber, Horner, Garner	2,357
27		16	(h)	Doncaster R	W 2-0	Taylor, Horner	3,533
28		23	(a)	Aldershot	W 4-1	Bamber 2, Garner 2	2,164
29	Mar	2	(h)	Hereford U	W 3-0	Bamber 2, Richards	3,636
30		9	(a)	Maidstone U	D 1-1	Richards	2,253
31		12	(h)	Scarborough	W 3-1	Richards, Taylor, Bamber	3,798
32		16	(a)	Hartlepool U	W 2-1	Horner, Rodwell	2,840
33		19	(a)	Darlington	D 1-1	Willis (og)	4,108
34		23	(h)	Torquay U	W 1-0	Bamber	4,778
35		30	(a)	Peterborough U	L 0-2		7,721
36	Apr	2	(h)	Carlisle U	W 6-0	Bamber 2, Horner, Groves (pen), Rodwell, Richards	5,368
37		6	(a)	Lincoln C	W 1-0	Bamber	4,003
38		13	(h)	York C	W 1-0	Groves	5,086
39		17	(h)	Cardiff C	W 3-0	Groves, Horner, Rodwell	4,813
40		20	(a)	Gillingham	D 2-2	Davies, Horner	3,028
41		23	(a)	Burnley	L 0-2		18,398
42		27	(h)	Stockport C	W 3-2	Eyres, Garner 2	8,590
43		30	(h)	Halifax T	W 2-0	Rodwell, Groves	5,883
44	May	2	(a)	Cardiff C	D 1-1	Garner (pen)	1,793
45		7	(h)	Northampton T	W 2-1	Eyres, Groves	7,298
46		11	(a)	Walsall	L 0-2		8,051

FINAL LEAGUE POSITION: 5th in Division Four

Appearances
Sub Appeara
Goals

Play-offs

Rd	Month	Date	Venue	Opponents	Result	Scorers	Att
SF	May	19	(a)	Scunthorpe U	D 1-1	Rodwell	6,536
		22	(h)	Scunthorpe U	W 2-1	Eyres 2	7,596
F		31	(n†)	Torquay U	D 2-2‡	Groves, Curran (og)	21,615

†Played at Wembley Stadium. ‡After extra-time, Torquay won 5-4 on penalties.

Appearances
Sub Appeara
Goals

FA Cup

Rd	Month	Date	Venue	Opponents	Result	Scorers	Att
1	Nov	17	(h)	Grimsby T	W 2-0	Groves, Garner	4,175
2	Dec	10	(a)	Huddersfield T	W 2-0	Groves, Jackson (og)	6,329
3	Jan	5	(h)	Tottenham H	L 0-1		9,563

Appearances
Sub Appeara
Goals

League Cup

Rd	Month	Date	Venue	Opponents	Result	Scorers	Att
1	Aug	28	(a)	Darlington	D 0-0		2,254
	Sep	4	(h)	Darlington	D 1-1*	Brook	1,696

*After extra-time, Darlington won on away-goals rule.

Appearances
Sub Appeara
Goals

McIlhargey	Gore	Bradshaw	Groves	Briggs	Wright M	Sinclair	Brook	Lancaster	Garner	Eyres	Taylor	Rodwell	Wright A	Stant	Davies	Hedworth	Horner	Gouck	Smalley	Owen	Barber	Bamber	Richards	
1	2	3†	4	5	6	7	8*	9	10	11	12	14												1
1	2		4	5	6	7	8	9*	10	11	12		3											2
1	2		4	5*	6	7		9	10	11†		14	3	8	12									3
1	6		4			12		9†	10	11		7	3	8*	14	2	12							4
1	6		4			12		9	10	11		7	3	8†	12	2*	14							5
1	6		4			8			10	11		7	3	9	2		5							6
1	6		4			8			10	11		7*	3	9	12	2	5							7
1	6		4			8			10	11		7	3	9		2	5							8
1			4			8			10*	11		7	3	9	12	2	5		6					9
1			4	5		14	8†		10	11		7	3	9	12	2			6*					10
1			4	5		8			10	11		7	3	9		2			6					11
1			4	5		8			10	11		7	3	9		2			6					12
1	12		4			8			10	11		7	3	9	14	2*	5		6†					13
1			4			12		8*	10	11	14	7	3	9†	2		5		6					14
1	6		4			9		8	10		11*	7	3		2		5			12				15
1	6		4	5		9*			10	11	12	7	3			2	8							16
	6		4	5		9			10			7	3			2	8				1	11		17
1	6		4	5		9			10			7	3		2		8*					11	12	18
	6		4	5		9			10	11*		7	3		2		8				1		12	19
1	6		4	5		9			10*	14		7†	3		2		8					11	12	20
1	6		4	5		9				11		7	3		2		8					10		21
1	6		4	5		9	12			11*		7	3		2		8					10		22
1	6		4*	5		12			10	11		7	3		2		8					9		23
1	6		4						10		11	7	3		2	5	8					9		24
1	6		4						10		11	7	3		2	5	8					9		25
1	6		4			14			10	12	11*	7†	3		2	5	8					9		26
1	6		4			12			10		11	7*	3		2	5	8					9		27
1	6		4						10		11	7	3		2	5	8					9*	12	28
1	6		4						10*		11	7	3		2	5	8					9	12	29
1	6		4	5						14	11	7†	3			2	8*	12				9	10	30
1	6		4	5							11	7	3		8	2						9	10	31
1	6		4	5						12	11*	7	3		2		8	14				9	10†	32
1	6		4	5							11	7	3		2		8					9	10	33
1	6		4	5						12	11†	7*	3		2		8	14				9	10	34
1	6		4	5						12	11*	7	3		2		8†	14				9	10	35
1	6		4							11	14	7	3		2	5*	8	12†				9	10	36
1	6		4	5		2				11		7	3				8					9	10	37
1	6		4	5					12	11		7	3		2		8					9	10*	38
1	6		4	5					12	11		7	3		2		8					9*	10	39
1	6		4	5		12			10*	11		7	3		2		8						9	40
1	6		4	5		12		14	10	11		7*	3		2		8						9†	41
1	6		4	5		12			10	11		7	3		2		8						9*	42
1	6		4	5					10	11		7	3		2		8					9*	12	43
1	6		4	5		12			10	11		7	3		2		8						9*	44
1	6		4	5					10	11		7	3		2		8						9	45
1	6		4	5†		12			10	11	14	7	3		2		8						9*	46
44	40	1	46	30	3	19	3	7	34	30	13	43	45	12	30	20	37		6		2	23	16	
	1					12	1	1	2	6	6	2			7		2	5		1			6	
			11			1		1	13	6	3	7		5	1		7					17	4	

2 own-goals

McIlhargey	Gore	Bradshaw	Groves	Briggs	Wright M	Sinclair	Brook	Lancaster	Garner	Eyres	Taylor	Rodwell	Wright A	Stant	Davies	Hedworth	Horner	Gouck	Smalley	Owen	Barber	Bamber	Richards	
1	6		4	5					10	11	9	7	3		2		8							SF
1	6		4	5*		12			10	11	9	7	3		2		8							
1	6		4			12			10	11	8	7	3		2*		5					9		F
3	3		3	2					3	3	3	3	3		3		3					1		
						2																		
			1							2		1												

1 own-goal

McIlhargey	Gore	Bradshaw	Groves	Briggs	Wright M	Sinclair	Brook	Lancaster	Garner	Eyres	Taylor	Rodwell	Wright A	Stant	Davies	Hedworth	Horner	Gouck	Smalley	Owen	Barber	Bamber	Richards	
1	6		4	5*		9			10			7	3		12	2	8						11	1
1	6		4	5		12			10	11*		7	3			2	8						9	2
1	6		4	5		9			10			7	3			2	8					11		3
3	3		3	3		2			3	1		3	3			3	3					1	2	
						1									1									
			2						1															

1 own-goal

McIlhargey	Gore	Bradshaw	Groves	Briggs	Wright M	Sinclair	Brook	Lancaster	Garner	Eyres	Taylor	Rodwell	Wright A	Stant	Davies	Hedworth	Horner	Gouck	Smalley	Owen	Barber	Bamber	Richards	
1	6	3	4	5		7	8	9*	10	11			2										12	1
1	6	3†	4	5		7	8	9*	10	11	12	14	2											
2	2	2	2	2		2	2	2	2	2			2											
											1	1											1	
							1																	

1991-92

Manager: Billy Ayre

1	Aug	17	(h)	Walsall	W 3-0	Horner, Eyres, Garner	4,141
2		24	(a)	Carlisle U	W 2-1	Rodwell, Bamber	4,369
3		31	(h)	Scunthorpe U	W 2-1	Groves, Opp own-goal	3,273
4	Sep	3	(a)	York C	L 0-1		2,686
5		7	(a)	Mansfield T	D 1-1	Bamber	2,629
6		14	(h)	Cardiff C	D 1-1	Horner	3,931
7		17	(h)	Gillingham	W 2-0	Bamber 2	3,035
8		20	(a)	Doncaster R	W 2-0	Bamber, Taylor	2,428
9		28	(h)	Rotherham U	W 3-0	Groves, Rodwell, Eyres	5,356
10	Oct	5	(a)	Northampton T	D 1-1	Sinclair	3,355
11		13	(h)	Lincoln C	W 3-0	Groves (pen), Horner, Bamber	5,086
12		19	(a)	Barnet	L 0-3		5,085
13	Nov	2	(h)	Scarborough	D 1-1	Groves	3,057
14		5	(a)	Aldershot	W 5-2	Rodwell 3 (1 pen), Groves, Bamber	1,685
15		9	(a)	Chesterfield	D 1-1	Taylor	4,917
16		19	(h)	Wrexham	W 4-0	Sinclair 2, Bamber 2	2,842
17		23	(h)	Crewe A	L 0-2		4,534
18		30	(h)	Halifax T	W 3-0	Bamber 2, Groves	3,118
19	Dec	14	(a)	Rochdale	L 2-4	Rodwell, Bamber	2,892
20		21	(h)	Carlisle U	W 1-0	Bamber	3,440
21		26	(a)	Walsall	L 2-4	Bamber, Eyres	4,675
22		28	(a)	Scunthorpe U	L 1-2	Groves	4,271
23	Jan	1	(h)	York C	W 3-1	Gouck, Bamber, Eyres	3,534
24		4	(a)	Maidstone U	D 0-0		1,774
25		11	(h)	Burnley	W 5-2	Rodwell 2, Kerr, Bamber, Garner	8,007
26		18	(a)	Hereford U	W 2-1	Bamber 2	3,008
27	Feb	8	(a)	Wrexham	D 1-1	Garner (pen)	4,053
28		12	(a)	Halifax T	W 2-1	Rodwell, Bamber	2,158
29		15	(h)	Rochdale	W 3-0	Groves, Gouck, Eyres	4,632
30		18	(h)	Barnet	W 4-2	Groves, Rodwell, Bamber, Eyres	5,149
31		22	(a)	Burnley	D 1-1	Bamber	18,215
32		29	(h)	Maidstone U	D 1-1	Garner	4,136
33	Mar	3	(h)	Hereford U	W 2-0	Groves, Bamber	3,560
34		10	(h)	Aldershot	W 1-0	Eyres	3,728
35		14	(a)	Scarborough	W 2-1	Bamber, Eyres	1,965
36		21	(h)	Chesterfield	W 3-1	Rodwell, Davies, Bamber	4,447
37		28	(a)	Crewe A	L 0-1		4,913
38		31	(a)	Cardiff C	D 1-1	Bamber	8,430
39	Apr	4	(h)	Mansfield T	W 2-1	Bamber 2	6,055
40		11	(a)	Gillingham	L 2-3	Horner, Eyres	3,684
41		14	(h)	Doncaster R	W 1-0	Eyres (pen)	4,353
42		20	(a)	Rotherham U	L 0-2		8,992
43		25	(h)	Northampton T	W 1-0	Bamber	5,915
44	May	2	(a)	Lincoln C	L 0-2		7,884

FINAL LEAGUE POSITION: 4th in Division Four

Appearances
Sub Appearar
Goals

Play-offs

SF	May	10	(a)	Barnet	L 0-1		5,629
		13	(h)	Barnet	W 2-0	Groves, Garner (pen)	7,588
F		23	(n*)	Scunthorpe U	D 1-1†	Bamber	22,741

*Played at Wembley Stadium. †After extra-time, Blackpool won 4-3 on pens

Appearances
Sub Appeara
Goals

FA Cup

1	Nov	16	(h)	Grimsby T	W 2-1	Groves, Bamber	4,074
2	Dec	7	(h)	Hull C	L 0-1		4,554

Appearances
Sub Appeara
Goals

League Cup

1	Aug	20	(a)	Mansfield T	W 3-0	Bamber 2, Opp own-goal	2,124
		27	(h)	Mansfield T	W 4-2	Bamber 3, Groves	2,155
2	Sep	24	(h)	Barnsley	W 1-0	Bamber	4,123
	Oct	8	(a)	Barnsley	L 0-2*		6,315

*After extra-time

Appearances
Sub Appeara
Goals

McIlhargey	Davies	Wright	Groves	Stoneman	Gore	Rodwell	Horner	Bamber	Garner	Eyres	Richards	Gouck	Hedworth	Sinclair	Taylor	Briggs	Brook	Burgess	Murray	Mitchell	Bonner	Howard	Kerr	Kearton	Leitch	Cook	Murphy	
1	2†	3	4	5	6	7	8*	9	10	11	12	14																1
1	2	3	4	5	6	7		9	10	11		8	14															2
1	2	3	4		6	7	5	9	10	11	12	8*																3
1	2	3	4	5†	6	7	8	9	10*	11	12	14																4
1	2	3	4		6	7	8	9	10	11			5															5
1	2	3	4		6	7	8	9	10†	11			5	14														6
1	2	3	4		6	7	8	9†	12	11				14	10*	5												7
1	2	3*	4		6	7	8	9	12	11				10		5												8
1	2	3	4		6	7	8	9		11				10		5												9
1	2	3	4		6	7	8	9		11				10		5												10
1	2	3	4		6	7	8	9		11				10		5												11
1	2*	3	4	12	6	7	8	9		11				10†	14	5												12
1			4		6	7	8	9		11				14		5	10†	2	3*	12								13
1			4	3	6	7	8*	9		11				10†		5		2			12	14						14
1			4	3	6	7		9		11				10	14	5†		2			8							15
1	12		4	3	6	7	8†	9		11				10	14	5		2*										16
1	12		4	3	6*	7	8†	9		11				10	14	5		2										17
1	2		4	3		7		9	12	11			6	10*	14	5					8†							18
1	2*		4	3	6	7		9	11			8†	5	10	14						12							19
1			4	3	6	7		9		11		8		10		5		2										20
1			4	3	6	7		9	12	11		8*		10†	14	5		2										21
1			4	3	6	7		9	5	11		8			10			2										22
1			4	3	6	7		9	10	11		8						2	3									23
1			4	3	6	7		9	10	11		8						2					5					24
			4	3	6	7		9	10	11		8						2					5	1				25
	2		4		6	7		9	10	11		8				5							3	1				26
	2*		4		6	7		9	10	11		8		12		5							3	1				27
	2		4		6	7		9	10	11		8				5							3	1				28
	2		4		6	7*	14	9	10	11		8†		12		5							3	1				29
	2		4		6	7		9	10	11		8				5							3	1				30
	2		4		6	7*		9	10	11		8		12		5							3	1				31
	2		4		6		14	9	10	11		8†		7*		5							3	1	12			32
	2		4		6		8	9†	10*	11		14		12		5							3	1	7			33
	2†		4		6	7	8	9		11		14		12		5							3	1	10*			34
	2		4		6	7	8	9	10*	11				12		5							3	1				35
	2		4		6	7	8	9	10	11				12		5†							3	1	14*			36
			4		6	7	8	9	10	11		5						2						1		3		37
			4		6	7*	8	9	10	11		5		12				2						1		3		38
	2		4		6	7*	8	9	10	11		5												1	12	3		39
1	2*		4	14	6	7	8	9	10	11		5†													12	3		40
1			4	5	6	7	8	9	10*	11				12				2								3		41
1			4		6	7†	8	9	10	11		14		12		5		2								3*		42
1	12		4	5	6	7†	8	9		11				10*				2							14	3		43
1			4	5	6	7	8	9		11				10				2								3		44
29	27	12	44	18	43	42	27	44	27	43		20	4	16	2	26	1	17	2		2		13	15	2	8		
	3			2			2		4		3	5		13	7					1	2	1			5			
	1		10			11	4	28	4	10		2		3	2								1					

1 own-goal

McIlhargey	Davies	Wright	Groves	Stoneman	Gore	Rodwell	Horner	Bamber	Garner	Eyres	Richards	Gouck	Hedworth	Sinclair	Taylor	Briggs	Brook	Burgess	Murray	Mitchell	Bonner	Howard	Kerr	Kearton	Leitch	Cook	Murphy	
1	7*		4		6	14	8	9		11		5†		10				2	12							3		SF
1	5		4		6	7	8	9	10	11								2								3		
1	5*		4		6	7	8†	9	10	11				14				2								3	12	F
3	3		3		3	2	3	3	2	3		1		1				3								3		
						1								1					1								1	
			1					1	1																			

McIlhargey	Davies	Wright	Groves	Stoneman	Gore	Rodwell	Horner	Bamber	Garner	Eyres	Richards	Gouck	Hedworth	Sinclair	Taylor	Briggs	Brook	Burgess	Murray	Mitchell	Bonner	Howard	Kerr	Kearton	Leitch	Cook	Murphy	
1			4	3	6	7	8	9		11				10		5		2										1
1	2*		4	3		7		9	12				6	10*	11						8	14					5	2
2	1		2	2	1	2	1	2		1			1	2	1	1		1			1	1					1	
									1																			
			1					1																				

McIlhargey	Davies	Wright	Groves	Stoneman	Gore	Rodwell	Horner	Bamber	Garner	Eyres	Richards	Gouck	Hedworth	Sinclair	Taylor	Briggs	Brook	Burgess	Murray	Mitchell	Bonner	Howard	Kerr	Kearton	Leitch	Cook	Murphy	
1	2	3	4	5	6	7		9	10	11		8																
1	2	3	4*	5	6	7		9	10	11	12	8																1
1	2*	3	4		6	7	8	9	12	11				10		5												
1	2	3	4	12	6	7*	8	9		11				10		5												2
4	4	4	4	2	4	4	2	4	2	4		2		2		2												
				1					1		1																	
			1					6																				

1 own-goal

Blackpool Against Other Clubs

(League Matches Up To 1991-92 Season)

	P	W	D	L	F	A
AFC Bournemouth	6	2	1	3	8	9
Aldershot	14	6	2	6	30	18
Arsenal	72	13	21	38	84	142
Aston Villa	62	20	16	26	90	109
Barnet	2	1	0	1	4	5
Barnsley	64	20	16	28	89	99
Birmingham City	72	31	15	26	110	111
Blackburn Rovers	42	20	11	11	68	59
Bolton Wanderers	82	27	22	33	98	116
Bradford	26	9	6	11	39	44
Bradford City	32	17	3	12	52	38
Brentford	26	8	5	13	42	43
Brighton & HA	6	3	0	3	13	10
Bristol City	62	23	14	25	78	88
Bristol Rovers	18	7	5	6	32	25
Burnley	92	26	26	40	101	134
Burton U/Swifts	20	9	8	3	31	19
Burton Wanderers	2	1	0	1	6	3
Bury	50	16	13	21	76	74
Cardiff City	46	25	11	10	86	48
Carlisle United	28	13	6	9	40	29
Charlton Athletic	46	24	10	12	95	58
Chelsea	76	28	14	34	108	130
Chester City	20	6	7	7	28	26
Chesterfield	42	13	16	13	48	47
Colchester United	14	3	4	7	17	25
Coventry City	16	11	1	4	29	13
Crewe Alexandra	12	5	1	6	22	14
Crystal Palace	18	10	2	6	30	20
Darlington	18	8	6	4	26	16
Darwen	6	5	0	1	14	5
Derby County	54	18	15	21	76	87
Doncaster Rovers	22	12	5	5	45	22
Everton	46	15	11	20	55	66
Exeter City	8	2	4	2	6	6
Fulham	90	35	28	27	122	106
Gainsborough Trin	30	9	9	12	38	42
Gillingham	18	6	6	6	30	24
Glossop	32	13	10	9	47	46
Grimsby Town	56	19	15	22	94	100
Halifax Town	12	6	3	3	24	11
Hartlepool United	10	6	2	2	16	10
Hereford United	14	9	3	2	25	11
Huddersfield Town	56	22	15	19	82	89
Hull City	78	23	24	31	103	108
Ipswich Town	10	1	5	4	16	18
Leeds United	58	19	14	25	78	93
Leicester City	84	36	18	30	141	138
Leyton Orient	58	24	16	18	82	56
Lincoln City	44	28	8	8	84	33
Liverpool	40	13	9	18	62	72

	P	W	D	L	F	A
Loughborough T	6	5	0	1	16	7
Luton Town	26	11	5	10	38	37
Maidstone United	4	0	4	0	4	4
Manchester City	56	16	17	23	94	109
Manchester United	80	20	16	44	92	145
Mansfield Town	24	10	10	4	36	23
Middlesbrough	52	15	14	23	73	93
Millwall	28	9	13	6	36	34
Nelson	2	1	1	0	4	3
New Brighton	4	0	1	3	2	8
Newcastle United	48	21	7	20	89	76
Northampton Town	20	11	3	6	35	25
Norwich City	16	8	2	6	19	23
Nottingham Forest	66	22	17	27	83	97
Notts County	42	16	11	15	63	60
Oldham Athletic	32	11	5	16	43	51
Oxford United	20	11	5	4	24	13
Peterborough U	12	2	3	7	12	25
Plymouth Argyle	22	9	8	5	33	25
Portsmouth	60	24	21	15	96	82
Port Vale	52	22	9	21	80	87
Preston NE	70	25	11	34	123	118
Queen's Park R	8	2	2	4	6	15
Reading	20	8	5	7	31	25
Rochdale	12	3	4	5	13	14
Rotherham United	26	14	3	9	37	28
Scarborough	4	3	1	0	7	3
Scunthorpe United	10	5	2	3	17	13
Sheffield United	52	18	11	23	77	86
Sheffield Wed	58	17	11	30	68	110
Shrewsbury Town	4	1	1	2	6	4
South Shields	18	9	3	6	39	27
Southampton	36	15	5	16	68	69
Southend United	10	5	1	4	14	17
Stockport County	50	21	14	15	70	57
Stoke City	50	17	16	17	69	74
Sunderland	54	16	17	21	81	8[illegible]
Swansea City	26	7	10	9	35	42
Swindon Town	22	10	7	5	37	25
Torquay United	10	6	2	2	15	9
Tottenham Hotspur	50	11	13	26	64	103
Tranmere Rovers	12	2	1	9	12	24
Walsall	24	8	5	11	34	48
Watford	6	2	1	3	8	10
West Brom Albion	72	28	12	32	103	125
West Ham United	40	14	10	16	61	59
Wigan Athletic	12	2	5	5	14	15
Wimbledon	4	2	1	1	6	[illegible]
Wolves	90	32	16	42	135	14[illegible]
Wrexham	8	6	2	0	17	[illegible]
York City	20	9	6	5	26	2[illegible]

Blackpool in 1905-06. Back row (left to right): Threlfall, Gow, Parkinson, Hull, Johnson, Scott, Rothwell (trainer). Front: Duckworth, Birkett, Hancock, Connor, Bate. Inset left: C.Ramsden (chairman). Right: T.Barcroft (secretary).

Blackpool in 1937-8. Back row (left to right): Farrell, Hayward, Cardwell, Wallace, Roxburgh, Witham, S.Jones, Lyon. Middle: Butcher, Johnston, Hall, Joe Smith (manager), D.Blair, T.W.Jones, Munro. Front: Finan, Buchan, J.Blair, O'Donnell.

Blackpool in Other Competitions

FA Charity Shield

1953
Oct 12 v Arsenal (h) 1-3
Mortensen
Farm; Shimwell, Garrett, Fenton, Johnston, Kelly, Matthews, Taylor, Mortensen, Mudie, Perry.
Att: 39,853

Anglo-Italian Cup

1970-71
May 26 v Verona (h) 3-3
Burns, Suddick, Nicholson
Burridge; Nicholson, Hatton, McGrotty(Johnston), James(Alcock), Suddaby, Burns, Green, Craven, Suddick, Hutchison.
Att: 9,917
May 29 v AS Roma (h) 1-3
Burns
Burridge; Johnston, Hatton, McGrotty, Alcock, Suddaby, Burns, Suddick, Craven, Wann, Hutchison.
Att: 11,000
Jun 1 v Verona (a) 4-1
Alcock, Suddaby, Wann, Hutchison
Burridge; Bentley, Hatton, Ainscow(Wann), Alcock, Suddaby, Burns, Green, Craven, Suddick, Hutchison.
Att: 10,000
Jun 4 v AS Roma (h) 2-1
Bentley, Hutchison
Burridge; Bentley, Hatton, Ainscow, Alcock, Suddaby, Burns, Green, Craven, Suddick, Hutchison.
Att: 12,000
Final
Jun 12 v Bologna (a) 2-1 aet
Craven, Burns
Burridge; Bentley, Hatton, Ainscow(Wann), Alcock, Suddaby, Burns, Green, Craven(Johnston), Suddick, Hutchison.
Att: 40,000

1971-72
Jun 1 v Sampdoria (a) 4-1
Hill 2, Dyson, James
Burridge; Hatton, Bentley, Suddaby, James, Hardcastle, Hutchison, Suddick, Dyson, Hill (Ainscow), Burns.
Att: 15,000
Jun 4 v Lanerossi Vicenza (a) 2-0
Burns, Suddick
Burridge; Hatton, Bentley, Suddaby, James, Alcock, Hutchison, Suddick, Dyson, Hill(Ainscow), Banks.
Att: 5,000
Jun 7 v Sampdoria (h) 2-0
Burns, Hill
Burridge; Hatton, Bentley, Suddaby, James, Ainscow, Hutchison, Suddick, Dyson, Hill, Burns.
Att: 12,588
Jun 10 v Lanerossi Vicenza (h) 10-0
Burns 4, Hill 2, Ainscow, Suddick, James, Opp own-goal
Burridge; Alcock, Bentley(Harrison), Suddaby, James, Ainscow, Hutchison, Suddick, Dyson, Hill, Burns.
Att: 10,761
Final
Jun 24 v AS Roma (a) 1-3
Alcock
Burridge; Hatton, Bentley, Suddaby, James, Ainscow, Hutchison, Suddick, Dyson, Hill(Alcock), Burns.
Att: 75,000

1972-73
Feb 25 v Torino (a) 1-0
Burns
Wood; O'Neil, Bentley, Hatton, Suddaby, Alcock, Burns, Ainscow, Rafferty, Lennard(Dyson), Tully.
Att: 4,881
Mar 21 v Como (h) 3-0
Ainscow 2, Dyson
Wood; Hatton, Bentley, Alcock, James, Suddaby, Burns, Suddick, Rafferty, Dyson, Ainscow. Subs: Burridge, Simpkin, McGrotty.
Att: 6,717
Apr 4 v Bologna (a) 1-0
Rafferty
Wood; Hatton, Bentley, Alcock, James, Suddaby, Burns, Suddick, Rafferty, Dyson, Ainscow. Subs: Burridge, Hardcastle, Simpkin, Barton.
Att: 5,049
May 2 v AS Roma (h) 2-1
James, Suddick
Wood; Hatton, Bentley, Alcock, James, Simpkin, Burns, Suddick, Dyson, Ainscow(Parker), Lennard. Subs: Burridge, Fuschillo, Curtis, Tully.
Att: 6,823

Watney Cup

1972-73
Round 1
Jul 29 v Peterborough United (a) 0-0
Burridge(Wood); Hatton, Bentley, James, Suddaby, Lennard, Hutchison(Ainscow), Suddick, Dyson, Barton, Burns.
Blackpool lost 7-6 on penalties

Texaco Cup

1974-75

Aug 3 v Manchester City (h) 1-1
Dyson
Burridge; Hatton, Bentley, James, Suddaby, Evanson, Walsh, Suddick, Dyson, Tong, Ainscow. Subs: Wood, Curtis.
Att: 12,342

Aug 6 v Oldham Athletic (h) 1-2
Dyson
Burridge; Hatton, Bentley, Alcock, Hart, Suddaby, Tong, Suddick, Dyson, Evanson, Walsh. Subs: Wood, Harrison.
Att: 9,359

Aug 10 v Sheffield United (a) 2-1
Suddick, Dyson
Burridge; Hatton, Bentley, Alcock, James, Suddaby, Tong, Suddick, Dyson, Evanson, Walsh. Subs: Wood, Curtis.
Att: 8,945

Anglo-Scottish Cup

1975-76

Aug 2 v Manchester City (h) 1-0
Hart
Burridge; Hatton, Bentley, Hart, Alcock, Suddaby, Ainscow, Suddick, Dyson, Evanson, Walsh. Subs: Wood, Harrison.
Att: 11,038

Aug 6 v Sheffield United (h) 1-1
Walsh (pen)
Burridge; Hatton, Bentley, Hart, Alcock, Suddaby, Walsh, Suddick, Dyson, Evanson, Ainscow. Sub: Wood, Harrison.
Att: 7,518

Aug 9 v Blackburn Rovers (a) 2-3
Suddick, Tong
Burridge; Hatton, Bentley, Hart, Alcock, Tong, Walsh, Suddick, Ronson, Evanson(Harrison), Ainscow. Sub: Wood.
Att: 9,774

1976-77

Aug 7 v Bolton Wanderers (a) 0-0
Wood; Curtis, Bentley, Hart, Suddaby, Suddick, Tong, Ainscow, Moore, Walsh(Harrison), Hatton. Sub: King.
Att: 9,402

Aug 9 v Blackburn Rovers (a) 0-1
Wood; Curtis, Bentley, Tong, Suddaby, Hart, Hockaday(Moore), Suddick, Ainscow, Hatton, Harrison. Sub: King.
Att: 6,608

Aug 11 v Burnley (h) 2-1
Hatton, Suddick
Wood; Curtis, Bentley, Tong(Hockaday), Suddaby, Hart, Ronson, Suddick, Ainscow, Hatton, Harrison. Sub: King.
Att: 9,386

1977-78

Aug 6 v Blackburn Rovers (a) 1-3
Walsh
Wood; Gardner, Harrison, Ronson, McEwan, Suddaby, Hart, Tong, Walsh, Hatton, Finnigan. Subs: Hesford, Milligan.
Att: 5,074

Aug 9 v Burnley (a) 4-0
Walsh 3, Hatton
Wood; Gardner, Harrison, Ronson, McEwan, Suddaby, Hart, Tong, Walsh, Hatton, Finnigan. Subs: Hesford, Milligan.
Att: 5,497

Aug 13 v Bolton Wanderers (h) 0-1
Wood; Gardner, Harrison, Ronson, McEwan, Suddaby, Hart, Tong, Walsh, Hatton, Finnigan. Subs: Hesford, Milligan.
Att: 8,155

Mickey Walsh

1978-79
Aug 2 v Preston North End (a) 2-4
Davidson, Tong
Hesford; Gardner, Milligan, McEwan, Suddaby, Waldron, Chandler, Tong, Hockaday, Tynan, Davidson. Sub: Wilson.
Att: 9,952
Aug 5 v Blackburn Rovers (h) 0-1
Ward(Hesford); Gardner, Waldron, McEwan, Suddaby, Tong, Chandler, Hockaday, Holden(Spence), Tynan, Davidson.
Att: 6,554
Aug 8 v Burnley (a) 1-3
Holden
Hesford; Gardner, Fleming, Waldron, McEwan, Wilson, Hockaday, Tynan(Holden), Spence, Tong, Bowey.
Att: 4,750

1979-80
Aug 1 v Blackburn Rovers (h) 2-2
Spence, Opp own-goal
McAlister; Thompson, Weston, Doyle, Suddaby, McEwan, Hockaday, Kerr, Spence, Kellow, Smith. Subs: Hesford, Jones.
Att: 6,348
Aug 4 v Preston North End (a) 1-3
McEwan (pen)
McAlister; Thompson, Pashley, Doyle, Suddaby, McEwan, Kerr, Kellow, Jones, Weston, Hockaday. Subs: Hesford, Bowey.
Att: 8,159
Aug 7 v Burnley (h) 3-2
Kerr, Kellow, Opp own-goal
McAlister; Thompson, Pashley, Doyle, Suddaby, McEwan, Kerr, Kellow, Spence(Jones), Weston, Hockaday. Sub: Hesford.
Att: 5,003

1980-81
Jul 30 v Blackburn Rovers (h) 2-0
Bamber, McEwan
Hesford; Ashurst, Brockbank, Doyle, Sbragia, McEwan, Morris, Hockaday, Bamber, Ball, Welsh.
Att: 7,522
Aug 2 v Carlisle United (a) 2-1
Pashley, Fletcher
Hesford; Gardner, Pashley, Doyle, Sbragia, Ashurst, Morris, MacDougall, Fletcher, Ball, Noble.
Att: 2,814
Aug 5 v Preston North End (a) 1-0
Hockaday
Hesford; Ashurst, Brockbank, Doyle, Sbragia, McEwan, Morris, Hockaday, MacDougall, Ball, Welsh. Subs: Bamber, Deary.
Att: 7,181
Quarter-final (1st leg)
Sep 9 v Kilmarnock (h) 2-1
MacDougall, Harrison
Rush; Gardner, Williams, Doyle, McEwan, Sbragia, Morris, Hockaday(Collins), MacDougall, Deary (Seward), Harrison.
Att: 4,904
Quarter-final (2nd leg)
Oct 14 v Kilmarnock (a) 2-4
Thompson, Hendrick
Rush; Simmonite, Williams, Doyle, Ashurst, Sbragia (Bamber), Morris(Hendrick), McEwan, Thompson, Hockaday, Deary.
Att: 2,700

Football League Group Cup

1981-82
Aug 15 v Preston North End (a) 1-2
Morris
Hesford; Gardner(Simmonite), Pashley, Blair, Thompson, McEwan, Morgan, Bamber(Pollard), Entwistle, Morris, Harrison.
Att: 6,102
Aug 18 v Carlisle United (a) 0-1
Hesford; Simmonite, Pashley, Greenall, McEwan, Blair, Noble, Harrison, Entwistle, Morris, Bamber.
Att: 2,530
Aug 22 v Burnley (h) 0-0
Hesford; Simmonite, Pashley, Greenall, McEwan, Blair, Morgan, Pollard, Entwistle(Hockaday), Bamber, Harrison.
Att: 3,464

Lancashire Manx Cup

1982-83
Aug 14 v Blackburn Rovers (a) 2-2
Bamber 2
Hesford; Simmonite, Brockbank, Deary, Hetzke, Serella, Downes, Noble, Bamber, Stewart(Hockaday), Pashley.
Att: 2,559
Aug 17 v Preston North End (h) 2-1
Greenall, Deary
Hesford; Simmonite, Brockbank, Deary, Greenall, Serella, Downes, Noble, Bamber, Stewart(Hockaday), Pashley.
Att: 3,824
Aug 21 v Bolton Wanderers (h) 2-1
Hockaday, Noble
Hesford; Simmonite, Brockbank, Deary, Greenall, Serella, Noble, Hockaday, Bamber, Pashley, Downes.
Att: 2,661

1983-84
Aug 13 v Blackburn Rovers (a) 2-4
Hetzke, Stewart
Pierce; Bardsley, Pritchett, Deary, Hetzke, Westwell, Windridge, Ferns, Mercer, Stewart, McNiven.
Att: 1,780
Aug 16 v Preston North End (h) 2-3
Mercer, Hetzke
Pierce; Bardsley, Westwell, Deary, Hetzke, Serella, O'Donnell(Dyer), Mercer, Stewart(McNiven), Ferns, Windridge.
Att: 2,700
Aug 20 v Burnley (a) 0-0
Pierce; Bardsley, Pritchett, Deary, Hetzke, Greenall, Windridge, Mercer, Stewart(Dyer), Ferns, McNiven.
Att: 3,954

1984-85

Aug 11 v Burnley (a) 0-1
O'Rourke(Clarke); Moore, Walsh, Conroy, Hetzke, Greenall, Davies(Dyer), Stonehouse, Stewart, Britton, Ferns.
Att: 2,035

Aug 14 v Wigan Athletic (h) 0-0
O'Rourke; Moore, Walsh, Conroy(Davies), Hetzke, Greenall, Britton, Stonehouse, Stewart, Deary, Dyer.
Att: 1,633

Aug 18 v Rochdale (h) 1-0
Hetzke
O'Rourke; Turnbull, Ferns, Conroy, Hetzke(Walsh), Greenall, Britton, Stonehouse, Stewart, Deary (Davies), Dyer.
Att: 1,363

1985-86

Aug 3 v Preston North End (a) 2-1
O'Keefe 2
O'Rourke; Moore(Davies), Walsh, Conroy(Britton), Hetzke, Greenall, Stonehouse, O'Keefe, Stewart, Deary, Dyer.
Att: 3,281

Aug 7 v Blackburn Rovers (a) 0-6
O'Rourke; Matthews, Walsh, Britton, Hetzke(Scott), Greenall, Windridge, O'Keefe, Stewart(Davies), Stonehouse, Dyer.
Att: 1,628

Aug 10 v Wigan Athletic (h) 1-1
Stewart
Harrington; Matthews, Windridge, Deary, Walsh, Greenall, Britton, O'Keefe, Stewart, Stonehouse, Dyer.
Att: 1,683

1986-87

Aug 9 v Bury (a) 3-3
Deary, Sendall 2
O'Rourke; Davies, Walsh(Butler), Law, Methven, Greenall, Thomson, Deary, Stewart, O'Keefe(Sendall), Dyer. Subs: Siddall, Moore.
Att: 1,392

Aug 12 v Blackburn Rovers (h) 0-0
Siddall; Davies, Walsh, Law, Methven, Greenall, Thomson, Deary, Stewart, Sendall, Dyer. Subs: O'Rourke, Matthews, Taylor, Morgan, Butler.
Att: 2,138

Aug 16 v Rochdale (h) 0-0
O'Rourke; Matthews, Morgan(Butler), Law, Walsh, Methven, Davies, Thomson, Stewart, Deary, Dyer. Subs: Siddall, Moore, McGinley, Sendall.
Att: 1,175

1987-88

Aug 1 v Burnley (a) 2-0
Walwyn, Deary
Siddall; Davies, Morgan, Matthews, Methven, Walsh(Jones), Cunningham, Madden(Bradshaw), Walwyn, Deary, Taylor. Subs: Powell, Butler.
Att: 2,508

Aug 4 v Bolton Wanderers (h) 0-0
Siddall; Davies(Butler), Bradshaw, Matthews, Methven, Walsh, Cunningham, Madden, Walwyn, Deary, Taylor. Subs: Jones, Rooney, Powell, Morgan.
Att: 2,593

Aug 7 v Blackburn Rovers (a) 2-3
Madden, Opp own-goal
Siddall; Butler, Bradshaw, Matthews, Methven, Jones, Cunningham, Madden, Walwyn, Deary, Taylor (Maguire). Subs: Morgan, Rooney, Walsh, Lancashire.
Att: 2,527

1988-89

Aug 6 v Blackburn Rovers (h) 2-2
Cunningham, Methven
Siddall; Burgess, Morgan, Deary, Methven, Elliott, Davies, Madden, Cunningham, Coughlin, Taylor.
Att: 2,987

Aug 9 v Preston North End (h) 1-1
Taylor
Siddall; Burgess(Gore), Morgan, Deary, Methven, Elliott, Davies, Wright, Cunningham(Walwyn), Coughlin, Taylor.
Att: 3,335

Aug 13 v Burnley (h) 2-1
Deary (pen), Cunningham
Siddall; Burgess, Morgan(Gore), Deary, Methven, Elliott, Davies(Thompson), Wright, Cunningham, Coughlin, Taylor.
Att: 3,042

1989-90

Aug 5 v Rochdale (a) 0-0
McIlhargey; Burgess, Morgan, Gore, Briggs, Matthews, Thompson(Bradshaw), Madden, Sinclair, Coughlin, Wright.
Att: 1,083

Aug 8 v Preston North End (h) 2-0
Wright, Madden
McIlhargey; Burgess, Morgan, Gore, Briggs, Matthews, Thompson, Madden, Sinclair(Eyres), Coughlin(Bradshaw), Wright.
Att: 3,608

Aug 12 v Bury (a) 0-0
McIlhargey; Burgess, Morgan, Gore, Briggs, Matthews, Methven, Madden, Garner, Coughlin, Wright.
Att: 1,564

Final

Aug 15 v Blackburn Rovers (h) 0-1
McIlhargey; Burgess, Morgan, Gore, Briggs, Matthews, Methven, Madden(Bradshaw), Garner (Sinclair), Coughlin, Wright.
Att: 4,685

1990-91

Aug 11 v Burnley (a) 2-2
Garner, Lancaster
McIlhargey; Westwell, Bradshaw, Groves, Briggs, Gore, Sinclair(Rodwell), Brook, Taylor(Lancaster), Garner, Eyres.
Att: 3,060

Aug 14 v Bolton Wanderers (a) 0-2
McIlhargey; Davies, Bradshaw, Groves, Briggs, Gore, Rodwell(Sinclair), Brook, Lancaster(Taylor), Garner, Eyres.
Att: 1,588

Aug 18 v Wigan Athletic (a) 2-3
Sinclair 2
McIlhargey; Davies, Bradshaw, Groves, Briggs, Gore, Sinclair, Taylor(Rodwell), Lancaster, Garner, Eyres.
Att: 862

1991-92
Aug 3 v Wigan Athletic (a) 1-1
Bamber
McIlhargey; Davies, Wright, Groves, Briggs, Horner(Gore), Rodwell, Taylor(Lancaster), Bamber, Garner, Eyres.
Att: 1,245
Aug 7 v Bolton Wanderers (h) 1-2
Opp own-goal
McIlhargey(Gawthorpe); Davies, Wright, Groves, Briggs, Gore, Rodwell, Lancaster, Bamber, Garner, Roderick(Sinclair).
Att: 1,573
Aug 10 v Rochdale (a) 1-2
Gore
Baker; Davies, Wright, Groves, Briggs(Stoneman), Gore, Rodwell, Gouck, Bamber, Garner, Roderick (Richards).
Att: 950

Associate Members Cup

1983-84
Feb 22 v Chester City (a) 1-2 aet
Serella
Pierce; Butler, Walsh, Deary, Serella, Greenall, Dyer, Windridge, Bramhall(Davies), Ferns, Britton (McNiven).
Att: 1,046

1984-85
Jan 23 v Tranmere Rovers (h) 2-1
Deary, Teasdale
O'Rourke; Moore(Davies), Ferns, Deary, Hetzke, Walsh(Matthews), Britton, Teasdale, Stewart, Stonehouse, Dyer.
Att: 1,523
Jan 29 v Tranmere Rovers (a) 1-4
Britton
O'Rourke; Moore, Ferns, Deary, Walsh, Windridge, Britton(Davies), Teasdale, Stewart, Stonehouse, Dyer. Sub: Matthews.
Att: 1,170

Freight/Rover Trophy

1985-86
Jan 23 v Wrexham (h) 2-2
Davies, Thomson
O'Rourke; Moore, Price(Morgan), Conroy, Hetzke, Walsh, Sendall, Ronson(Davies), Stewart, Thomson, Dyer.
Att: 1,611

Feb 10 v Port Vale (a) 1-3
Thomson
O'Rourke; Moore, Law, Deary, Hetzke, Greenall, Davies, Ronson, Stewart, Thomson, Dyer. Subs: Stonehouse, Sendall.
Att: 1,569

1986-87
Dec 2 v Bolton Wanderers (a) 0-1
Siddall; Matthews, Walsh, Law, Methven, Deary, McGinley, Butler, Stewart, Dyer, Taylor. Subs: Morgan, Mayes.
Att: 3,395
Dec 9 v Burnley (h) 2-3
Dyer, Stewart
O'Rourke; Matthews, Walsh, Law(Mayes), Methven(Butler), Deary, Thomson, McGinley, Stewart, Dyer, Davies.
Att: 1,448

1987-88
Oct 28 v Chester City (a) 1-2
Madden
Siddall; Butler, Morgan, Matthews(Madden), Methven, Walsh(Bradshaw), Cunningham, Deary, Walwyn, McAteer, Taylor.
Att: 1,226
Nov 24 v Carlisle United (h) 0-1
Siddall; Davies, Morgan(Walsh), Bradshaw, Methven, Jones, Deary, Cunningham, Walwyn, Butler (Matthews), Taylor.
Att: 1,491

Sherpa Van Trophy

1988-89
Nov 22 v Wigan Athletic (a) 2-1
Cunningham, Morgan
Siddall; Burgess, Morgan, Deary, Methven, Elliott, Matthews(Gore), Cunningham, Garner, Coughlin, Taylor(Madden).
Att: 1,217
Dec 6 v Rochdale (h) 2-0
Madden 2
Siddall; Burgess, Wright, Deary, Methven, Elliott(Rooney), Gore(Garner), Cunningham, Madden, Coughlin, Thompson.
Att: 1,228
Jan 17 v Rotherham United (h) 4-3
Davies, Cunningham, Thompson, Madden
Siddall; Burgess, Morgan, Gore(Thompson), Methven, Walsh, Davies, Cunningham, Garner, Coughlin, Walwyn(Madden).
Att: 1,620
Feb 21 v Halifax Town (a) 2-0
Walwyn, Methven
O'Keefe; Burgess, Morgan, Coughlin(Davies), Methven, Elliott, Deary, Cunningham, Garner, Thompson, Walwyn. Sub: Gore.
Att: 3,289
Northern Semi-final
Mar 21 v Scarborough (h) 1-0 aet
Coughlin (pen)
Siddall; Burgess, Morgan, Coughlin, Methven, Elliott,

Deary, Walwyn(Gore), Garner, Thompson(Madden), Davies.
Att: 4,286
Northern Final (1st leg)
Apr 11 v Bolton Wanderers (a) 0-1
Siddall; Burgess, Morgan(Wright), Coughlin, Methven, Elliott, Davies, Madden, Garner, Deary, Gore. Sub: Thompson.
Att: 10,345
Northern Final (2nd leg)
Apr 18 v Bolton Wanderers (h) 1-1 aet (agg 1-2)
Garner (pen)
Siddall; Burgess, Wright(Thompson), Coughlin, Methven, Elliott, Davies, Walwyn, Garner, Deary, Gore(Madden).
Att: 9,027

Keith Walwyn

Leyland DAF Cup

1989-90
Nov 7 v Wrexham (a) 0-1
Bartram; Burgess, Morgan, Coughlin, Methven, Elliott, Owen, Madden, Hawkins(Eyres), Garner (Wright), Briggs.
Att: 1,092
Nov 28 v Bury (h) 4-0
Garner, Owen 2, Opp own-goal
McIlhargey; Gore, Morgan, Coughlin, Methven, Elliott, Davies, Madden, Owen, Garner, Eyres. Subs: Hawkins, Wright.
Att: 1,405
Jan 19 v Chester City (h) 0-1
Bartram; Wright, Morgan, Coughlin, Briggs, Elliott, Gore, Hawkins, Owen, Garner, Diamond(Bradshaw). Sub: Davies.
Att: 1,433

1990-91
Nov 27 v Tranmere Rovers (a) 0-4
McIlhargey; Hedworth(Taylor), Wright, Groves, Briggs, Gore, Rodwell, Horner, Sinclair(Lancaster), Garner, Eyres.
Att: 3,901
Dec 18 v Bolton Wanderers (h) 3-0
Groves, Sinclair, Horner
McIlhargey; Davies, Wright, Groves, Briggs, Gore, Rodwell, Horner, Sinclair, Garner, Bamber. Subs: Richards, Gouck.
Att: 2,579
Jan 22 v Halifax Town (a) 1-0
Taylor
McIlhargey; Davies, Wright, Groves, Hedworth, Gore, Rodwell, Horner, Bamber, Garner, Taylor. Subs: Eyres, Sinclair.
Att: 1,267
Jan 29 v Tranmere Rovers (a) 0-2
McIlhargey; Davies, Wright, Groves, Hedworth, Gore, Rodwell(Sinclair), Horner, Bamber, Garner, Taylor (Eyres).
Att: 4,129

Autoglass Trophy

1991-92
Oct 22 v Burnley (h) 1-3
Rodwell
McIlhargey; Davies(Brook), Wright, Groves, Briggs, Gore, Rodwell, Horner(Taylor), Bamber, Sinclair, Eyres.
Att: 2,805
Dec 17 v Doncaster Rovers (a) 2-2
Rodwell, Bamber
McIlhargey; Davies(Taylor), Stoneman, Groves, Hedworth, Gore, Rodwell, Gouck, Bamber, Sinclair, Garner(Bonner).
Att: 613
Jan 21 v Huddersfield Town (a) 1-1
Garner
McIlhargey, Davies, Kerr, Groves, Briggs, Gore, Rodwell, Gouck, Bamber, Garner, Eyres. Subs: Sinclair (2), Horner (8).
Att: 1,585
Blackpool lost 3-1 on penalties

Blackpool Internationals

Many players won additional caps with other clubs but the totals given here are solely for appearances made while Blackpool players. Before 1924 there was only one 'Ireland' team. In that year the Republic of Ireland began separate matches and that position is reflected here.

England

Armfield J.C. – 1958-59 v Brazil, Peru, Mexico, United States; 1959-60 v Yugoslavia, Spain, Hungary, Scotland; 1960-61 v Luxembourg, Portugal, Spain, Mexico, Italy, Austria, Wales, Northern Ireland, Scotland; 1961-62 v Austria, Sweden, Peru, Wales, Northern Ireland, Scotland, Luxembourg, Portugal, Hungary, Argentina, Bulgaria, Brazil; 1962-63 v France (twice), Brazil, East Germany, Sweden, Northern Ireland, Wales, Scotland; 1963-64 v Rest of World, Wales, Northern Ireland, Scotland; 1965-66 v Yugoslavia, Finland (43 app, 0 goals).
Ball A.J. – 1964-65 v Yugoslavia, West Germany, Sweden; 1965-66 v Scotland, Spain, France, Denmark, Uruguay, Argentina, Portugal, West Germany (twice), Poland (twice) (14 apps, 1 goal).
Bedford H. – 1922-23 v Sweden, 1924-25 v Northern Ireland (2 apps, 1 goal)
Charnley R.O. – 1962-63 v France (1 app, 0 goals).
Garrett T.H. – 1951-52 v Scotland, Italy; 1953-54 v Wales (3 apps, 0 goals).
Hampson J. – 1930-31 v Northern Ireland, Wales; 1932-33 v Austria (3 apps, 5 goals)

Jimmy Hampson scores for England against Austria at Stamford Bridge in December 1932.

Stan Matthews and Harry Johnston take to the field at Stamford Bridge for the 1950 FA Charity Shield match between the FA Canadian Touring Team and England's World Cup XI.

Johnston H. – 1946-47 v Scotland, Holland; 1950-51 v Scotland; 1952-53 v Argentina, Chile, Uruguay, United States; 1953-54 v Wales, Northern Ireland, Hungary (10 apps, 0 goals).
Matthews S. – 1946-47 v Switzerland, Portugal; 1947-48 v Scotland, Wales, Northern Ireland, Belgium, Italy; 1948-49 v Scotland, Wales, Northern Ireland, Denmark, Switzerland; 1949-50 v Spain; 1950-51 v Northern Ireland, Scotland; 1953-54 v

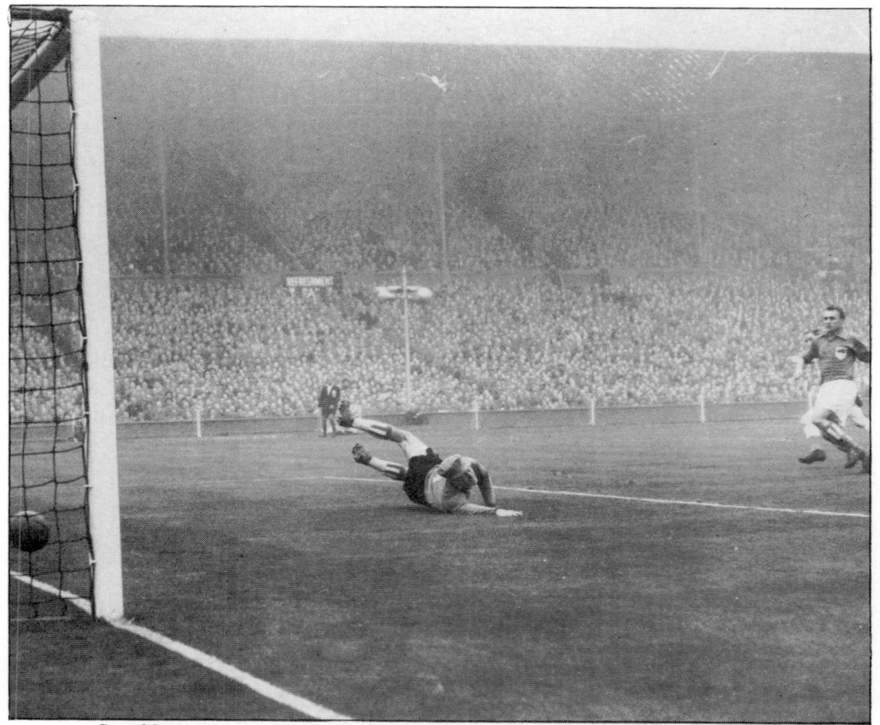

Stan Mortensen on target for England against the Rest of Europe at Wembley in 1953.

Northern Ireland, Rest of Europe, Hungary, Belgium, Uruguay; 1954-55 v Northern Ireland, Wales, Scotland, France, West Germany, Spain, Portugal; 1955-56 v Wales, Brazil; 1956-57 v Scotland, Wales, Northern Ireland, Yugoslavia, Denmark (twice), Republic of Ireland (36 apps, 3 goals).
Mortensen S.H. – 1946-47 v Portugal; 1947-48 v Wales, Scotland, Northern Ireland, Belgium, Sweden, Italy; 1948-49 v Scotland, Wales, Northern Ireland, Sweden, Norway; 1949-50 v Scotland, Wales, Northern Ireland, Italy, Portugal, Belgium, Chile, United States, Spain; 1950-51 v Scotland, Argentina; 1953-54 v Rest of Europe, Hungary (25 apps, 23 goals).
Perry W. – 1955-56 v Northern Ireland, Scotland, Spain (3 apps, 2 goals).
Shimwell E. – 1948-49 v Sweden (1 app, 0 goals).
Taylor E. – 1953-54 v Hungary (1 app, 0 goals).
Waiters A.K. – 1963-64 v Republic of Ireland, Brazil; 1964-65 v Wales, Belgium, Holland (5 app, 0 goals).

Scotland

Blair J.A. – 1946-47 v Wales (1 app, 0 goals).
Brown A.D. – 1951-52 v United States, Denmark, Sweden; 1952-53 v Wales; 1953-54 v Wales, England, Norway (twice), Finland, Austria, Uruguay (11 apps, 3 goals).

Blackpool's Jackie Mudie causes some problems at Wembley in April 1957. The England defenders are Ronnie Clayton, Alan Hodgkinson and Duncan Edwards.

Farm G.N. – 1952-53 v Wales, Northern Ireland, England, Sweden; 1953-54 v Northern Ireland, Wales, England; 1958-59 v West Germany, Holland, Portugal (10 app, 0 goals).
Green A. – 1970-71 v Belgium (sub), Portugal (sub), Northern Ireland, England; 1971-72 v Wales, England (sub) (6 apps, 0 goals).
Kelly H.T. – 1951-52 v United States (1 app, 0 goals).
Mudie J.K. – 1956-57 v Wales, Northern Ireland, England, Yugoslavia, Switzerland, Spain (twice), W.Germany; 1957-58 v Northern Ireland, England, Wales, Switzerland, Hungary, Poland, Yugoslavia, Paraguay, France (17 apps, 9 goals).
Munro A.D. – 1937-38 v Holland (1 app, 0 goals).
O'Donnell F. – 1936-37 v Holland (1 app, 0 goals).
Watson P.R. – 1933-34 v Austria (1 app, 0 goals).

Wales

Astley D.J. – 1938-39 v France (1 app, 1 goal).
Davies R.W. – 1973-74 v Poland (1 app, 0 goals).
Griffiths F.J. – 1899-1900 v England, Scotland (2 apps, 0 goals).
James E.G. – 1965-66 v Brazil (twice), Chile; 1966-67 v Northern Ireland; 1967-68 v Scotland; 1970-71 v Czechoslovakia, Scotland, England, Northern Ireland, (9 apps, 0 goals).

Northern Ireland

Butler M.P. – 1938-39 v Wales (1 app, 0 goals).
Doherty P.D. – 1934-35 v England, Wales; 1935-36 v England, Scotland (4 apps, 0 goals).
Jones S. – 1933-34 v Wales (1 app, 1 goal).
Spence D.W. – 1976-77 v Holland (sub), West Germany (sub), England (sub), Scotland (sub), Wales (sub), Iceland (sub); 1978-79 v Republic of Ireland, Denmark (sub), England (sub), Bulgaria (sub), England (sub), Scotland, Wales, Denmark; 1979-80 v Republic of Ireland (15 apps, 3 goals).

Republic of Ireland

Walsh M. – 1975-76 v Norway Poland; 1976-77 v France (sub), Poland (4 apps, 1 goal).

'B' Internationals

Name	Country	Year	Apps	Gls
Crosland J.R.	England	1950	2	0
Wright J.	England	1950	1	0
Kelly H.T.	Scotland	1952-53	2	0
Perry W.	England	1955-56	2	2
Gratrix R.	England	1956	1	0
Taylor E.	England	1956	1	0

Under-23 Internationals

Armfield J.C.	England	1956-59	9	0
West G.	England	1961	1	0
Hill S.T.	England	1961-62	4	1
Crawford J.R.B.	England	1962	1	0
James E.	Wales	1964-65	2	0
Ball A.J.	England	1964-65	8	2
Johnston J.	Northern Ireland	1969	1	0
Hughes J.I.	Wales	1970-73	2	0
Hutchison T.	Scotland	1971	1	0

Under-21 International

Hesford I.	England	1982-83	7	0

England Youth

West G.	1960-61	7	0
Willder F.	1962	4	0
Wojciechowicz S.	1970	3	0
Bardsley D.J.	1983	1	0
Greenall C.A.	1981	5	0
Hesford I.	1978	1	0
Stewart P.A.	1982-83	2	0
Wright A.	1990-92	8	0

Jimmy Armfield (left) won nine Under-23 caps as well as his many honours at full international level. Ian Hesford (right) was capped seven times for the Under-21s.

Blackpool's famous forward line of the 1950s. From left to right are Stan M

Taylor, Stan Mortensen, Allan Brown and Bill Perry taking a gentle training jog.

Blackpool Career Records

Player	Seasons played	League		FA Cup		FL Cup		Total	
		App	Gls	App	Gls	App	Gls	App	Gls
Adams R.	1948-49 to 1950-51	14	1	2	0	0	0	16	1
Ainscough J.	1950-51 to 1953-54	6	0	0	0	0	0	6	0
Ainscow A.	1971-72 to 1977-78	178/14	28	5/2	0	10	0	193/16	28
Alcock T.	1967-68 to 1975-76	184/6	21	4	1	15/1	0	203/7	22
Allen W.	1901-02	6	0	0	0	0	0	6	0
Anderson G.	1900-91 to 1903-04	78	29	0	0	0	0	78	29
Anderson T.	1903-04	2	0	0	0	0	0	2	0
Anderton W.	1901-02 to 1906-07	102	10	0	0	0	0	102	10
Appleton L.	1914-15 to 1919-20	33	3	0	0	0	0	33	3
Armes S.	1933-34	4	0	0	0	0	0	4	0
Armfield J.	1954-55 to 1970-71	569	6	33	0	25	0	627	6
Armstrong D.	1958-59	1	0	0	0	0	0	1	0
Ashurst J.	1979-80 to 1980-81	53	3	4	0	2	1	59	4
Ashworth J.F.	1938-39	4	0	0	0	0	0	4	0
Astley D.	1938-39 to 1939-40	20	6	0	0	0	0	20	6
Atherton W.	1898-99	13	0	0	0	0	0	13	0
Ayres G.	1926-27 to 1927-28	33	4	1	0	0	0	34	4
Baddeley A.	1908-09	32	3	2	0	0	0	34	3

Player	Seasons played	League		FA Cup		FL Cup		Total	
		App	Gls	App	Gls	App	Gls	App	Gls
Bailey I.	1984-85	3	0	0	0	0	0	3	0
Bainbridge J.	1910-11 to 1920-21	114	11	4	0	0	0	118	11
Baker L.H.	1919-29 to 1922-23	21	0	0	0	0	0	21	0
Ball A.	1962-63 to 1965-66 and 1980-81	146	45	7	1	8	3	161	40
Bamber D.	1979-80 to 1982-83 and 1990-91 to 1991-92	152/5	75	10/1	3	11	11	173/6	89
Banks J.	1897-98 to 1898-99	11	0	0	0	0	0	11	0
Barber F.	1990-91	2	0	0	0	0	0	2	0
Barcroft A.T.	1901-02	1	0	0	0	0	0	1	0
Bardsley D.	1981-82 to 1983-84	45	0	2	0	2	1	49	1
Barnes R.	1956-57 to 1958-59	9	0	0	0	0	0	9	0
Barnett L.H.	1926-27 to 1928-29	46	0	2	0	0	0	48	0
Barrass M.	1919-20 to 1924-25	168	53	12	1	0	0	180	54
Barton F.	1972-73	18	1	0	0	5	2	23	3
Bartram V.	1989-90	9	0	0	0	0	0	9	0
Bate T.	1905-06	24	1	1	0	0	0	25	1
Baverstock H.	1921-22 to 1922-23	18	0	0	0	0	0	18	0
Baxendale J.	1900-01	11	0	0	0	0	0	11	0
Beare H.	1920-21 to 1925-26	169	112	11	6	0	0	180	118
Bennett L.	1903-04 to 1905-06	42	13	0	0	0	0	42	13
Bentley W.	1968-69 to 1976-77	289/7	11	10/1	1	19	2	318/8	14
Benton W.	1920-21 to 1930-31	353	24	18	0	0	0	371	24

W.Benton

S.Binks

Player	Seasons played	League		FA Cup		FL Cup		Total	
		App	Gls	App	Gls	App	Gls	App	Gls
Berry E.	1919-20	5	1	0	0	0	0	5	1
Best G.A.	1925-26 to 1926-27	27	0	1	0	0	0	28	0
Betts H.	1975-76	4/3	0	0	0	0	0	4/3	0
Billington S.	1901-02	1	0	0	0	0	0	1	0
Binks S.	1925-26 to 1926-27	55	9	2	0	0	0	57	9
Birch W.	1907-08	13	0	0	0	0	0	13	0
Birchall J.	1900-01 to 1902-03	86	3	0	0	0	0	86	3
Birkett B.	1896-97 to 1906-07	215	44	4	0	0	0	219	44
Bisell S.	1978-79	1	0	0	0	0	0	1	0
Blacklaw A.	1970-71	1	0	0	0	0	0	1	0
Blair D.	1936-37 to 1938-39	121	0	5	0	0	0	126	0
Blair J.A.	1937-38 to 1946-47	50	8	1	0	0	0	51	8
Blair R.	1981-82	36/1	3	5	0	2	0	43/1	3
Bokas F.	1935-36	6	0	2	0	0	0	8	0
Bonner M.	1991-92	2/2	0	1	0	0	0	3/2	0
Booth D.	1971-72	12	0	0	0	3	0	15	0
Booth K.	1956-57	1	1	0	0	0	0	1	1
Booth R.	1912-13 to 1919-20	96	5	4	0	0	0	100	5
Boulton A.	1900-01 to 1901-02	56	1	0	0	0	0	56	1
Bowey K.	1979-80	3	1	0	0	0	0	3	1
Bowl H.T.	1936-37	2	1	0	0	0	0	2	1
Bowman T.	1896-97 to 1897-98	38	2	0	0	0	0	38	2
Bradshaw G.	1924-25 to 1926-27	43	0	0	0	0	0	43	0

Player	Seasons played	League		FA Cup		FL Cup		Total	
		App	Gls	App	Gls	App	Gls	App	Gls
Bradshaw M.	1986-87 to 1990-91	34/9	1	5/1	0	3	1	42/10	2
Bradshaw R.	1908-09 to 1911-12	29	0	4	0	0	0	33	0
Bradshaw T.D.	1896-97	17	5	0	0	0	0	17	5
Brallisford A.	1933-34 to 1935-346	17	8	0	0	0	0	17	8
Bramhall N.	1982-83	0/3	0	0	0	0	0	0/3	0
Brand D.	1983-84	3	0	0	0	0	0	3	0
Bridge A.	1932-33	7	0	0	0	0	0	7	0
Briggs E.	1989-90 to 1991-92	75	2	4	0	9	2	88	4
Brindley H.	1907-08	19	2	1	0	0	0	20	2
Britton I.	1983-84 to 1985-86	100/6	15	7	0	6	1	113/6	16
Broadhurst C.	1929-30 to 1930-31	18	6	0	0	0	0	18	6
Brockbank A.	1979-80 to 1982-83	32/4	1	0/1	1	3	0	35/5	2
Brook G.	1989-90 to 1991-92	27/3	6	6	1	2	1	35/3	8
Brookes S.	1927-28 to 1931-32	26	4	0	0	0	0	26	4
Brooks J.S.	1901-02	3	1	0	0	0	0	3	1
Brooks L.	1914-15	2	0	0	0	0	0	2	0
Browell T.	1926-27 to 1929-30	67	27	4	2	0	0	71	29
Brown A.	1905-06	3	0	0	0	0	0	3	0
Brown A.	1950-51 to 1956-57	163	68	22	6	0	0	185	74
Brown F.	1920-21 to 1922-23	10	0	3	0	0	0	13	0
Brown N.	1913-14	13	2	0	0	0	0	13	2
Brown R.	1965-66 to 1970-71	54/7	13	1	1	5/2	0	60/9	14
Buchan T.	1913-14	24	2	0	0	0	0	24	2

Player	Seasons played	League		FA Cup		FL Cup		Total	
		App	Gls	App	Gls	App	Gls	App	Gls
Buchan T.	1946-47	9	0	0	0	0	0	9	0
Buchan W.	1937-38 to 1947-48	100	35	4	0	0	0	104	35
Burder M.J.	1900-01 to 1901-02	35	0	0	0	0	0	35	0
Burgess D.	1988-89 to 1991-92	85	1	5	1	10	0	100	2
Burke P.	1913-14 to 1920-21	18	0	0	0	0	0	18	0
Burke R.	1938-39	1	0	0	0	0	0	1	0
Burns M.	1969-70 to 1973-74	174/7	53	7	1	15	8	196/7	62
Burridge J.	1970-71 to 1975-76	134	0	4	0	10	0	148	0
Burrows A.	1959-60	1	0	0	0	0	0	1	0
Burt J.	1909-10 to 1910-11	7	2	0	0	0	0	7	2
Bussey W.	1933-34	25	8	2	1	0	0	27	9
Butcher W.R.M.	1937-38	4	0	0	0	0	0	4	0
Butler B.	1985-86 to 1987-88	48/16	5	2/2	0	3/1	0	53/19	5
Butler H.	1923-24 to 1926-27	45	14	0	0	0	0	45	14
Butler J.	1981-82 to 1982-83	4/1	0	1	0	2	0	7/1	0
Butler M.	1935-36 to 1939-40	25	0	1	0	0	0	26	0
Butterworth A.	1932-33 to 1933-34	22	5	0	0	0	0	22	5
Cahill R.	1911-12	21	0	0	0	0	0	21	0
Campbell H.	1960-61	11	0	0	0	2	0	13	0
Cardwell G.	1897-98	6	0	0	0	0	0	6	0
Cardwell L.	1930-31 to 1937-38	132	6	11	0	0	0	143	6
Carr S.	1930-31	14	2	0	0	0	0	14	2
Carruthers S.L.	1923-24	2	0	0	0	0	0	2	0

Player	Seasons played	League App	League Gls	FA Cup App	FA Cup Gls	FL Cup App	FL Cup Gls	Total App	Total Gls
Carthell S.	1898-99	4	1	0	0	0	0	4	1
Carthy S.	1903-04	16	1	0	0	0	0	16	1
Cegielski C.	1984-85	5/1	1	0	0	0	0	5/1	1
Chadwick E.	1904-05	34	8	1	0	0	0	35	8
Chandler J.	1977-78 to 1979-80	31/6	6	1/1	1	3	0	35/7	7
Chandler W.	1935-36	15	2	0	0	0	0	15	2
Chapman R.	1912-13	2	0	0	0	0	0	2	0
Charles J.	1912-13 to 1923-24	228	30	13	3	0	0	241	33
Charlton T	1913-14	22	3	1	0	0	0	23	3
Charnley R.	1957-58 to 1967-68	363	193	21	10	23	19	407	222
Chi Doy C.	1960-61 to 1961-62	2	1	0	0	0	0	2	1
Clarke J.	1896-97	13	6	0	0	0	0	13	6
Clarke T.	1906-07 to 1911-12	141	0	6	1	0	0	147	1
Clarke W.	1911-12	6	1	4	0	0	0	10	1
Clarkin J.	1896-97 to 1897-98	54	11	0	0	0	0	54	11
Clennel S.	1910-11	32	18	1	1	0	0	33	19
Clough A.	1921-22	1	0	0	0	0	0	1	0
Coleman A.	1970-71	17	0	2	0	2	1	21	1
Collier J.	1906-07	2	0	0	0	0	0	2	0
Colville G.	1896-97	5	0	0	0	0	0	5	0
Conn D.	1980-81	3	0	0	0	0	0	3	0
Connor J.	1905-06 to 1914-15	282	13	17	0	0	0	299	13
Connor P.	1896-97	4	1	0	0	0	0	4	1

Player	Seasons played	League		FA Cup		FL Cup		Total	
		App	Gls	App	Gls	App	Gls	App	Gls
Conroy M.	1984-85 to 1985-86	66	2	1	0	6	0	73	2
Conway A.	1965-66	0	0	0	0	1	0	1	0
Cook L.	1904-05	7	0	1	0	0	0	8	0
Cook M.	1991-92	11	0	0	0	0	0	11	0
Cook W.	1936-37	19	1	0	0	0	0	19	1
Cookson W.S.	1902-03	33	8	0	0	0	0	33	8
Cooper J.E.	1963-64	4	0	0	0	0	0	4	0
Copestake L.	1905-06 to 1906-07	19	1	0	0	0	0	19	1
Coughlin R.	1987-88 to 1989-90	99/2	8	13	0	9	1	121/2	9
Cowan W.	1927-28	1	0	0	0	0	0	1	0
Cowie S.	1911-12	3	0	0	0	0	0	3	0
Cox J.	1897-98 and 1909-10 to 1911-12	85	18	1	0	0	0	86	18
Crainie R.	1984-85	6	0	0	0	0	0	6	0
Cranston W.	1961-62 to 1964-65	33	0	2	0	3	0	38	0
Craven J.	1965-66 to 1971-72	154/11	24	7/1	1	13	2	174/12	27
Crawford B.	1932-33 to 1933-34	55	5	3	0	0	0	58	5
Crawford B.	1959-60 to 1964-65	98	11	3	0	12	0	113	11
Crewdson R.	1904-05 to 1912-13	209	0	11	0	0	0	220	0
Crompton L.	1924-25 to 1927-28	87	0	9	0	0	0	96	0
Crook M.S.	1925-26 to 1928-29	51	12	1	0	0	0	52	12
Crosland J.	1946-47 to 1953-54	64	0	10	0	0	0	74	0
Crosswaithe H.	1906-07	1	0	0	0	0	0	1	0

Player	Seasons played	League		FA Cup		FL Cup		Total	
		App	Gls	App	Gls	App	Gls	App	Gls
Cunningham A.	1987-88 to 1988-89	71	18	5	2	8	3	84	23
Curran A.	1921-22 to 1926-27	98	3	11	0	0	0	109	3
Curtis J.	1973-74 to 1976-77	96/6	0	4	0	3	0	103/6	0
Dale G.	1909-10 to 1912-13	40	0	3	1	0	0	43	1
Darlington E.	1905-06	4	0	0	0	0	0	4	0
Davidson D.	1948-49 to 1949-50	16	0	0	0	0	0	16	0
Davidson V.	1978-79	23/2	3	0/1	0	5	3	28/3	6
Davies J.	1903-04	1	0	0	0	0	0	1	0
Davies M.	1983-84 to 1991-92	228/34	15	13/6	0	16/1	1	257/41	16
Davies S.	1912-13	3	0	0	0	0	0	3	0
Davies W.	1973-74 to 1974-75	34/2	5	1	0	2	0	37/2	5
Dawson E.	1938-39	12	1	0	0	0	0	12	1
Dawson H.	1908-09 to 1910-11	26	4	2	0	0	0	28	4
Dean B.	1967-68	0/1	0	0	0	0	0	0/1	0
Deary J.	1980-81 to 1988-89	285/17	43	17/2	5	20	5	322/19	53
Dewhurst W.A.	1898-99	2	0	0	0	0	0	2	0
Diamond A.	1989-90	2/1	1	0/1	0	1	0	3/2	1
Dick G.	1946-47 to 1947-48	47	13	7	1	0	0	54	14
Dickson J.	1898-99	1	0	0	0	0	0	1	0
Didymus E.	1909-10	3	0	0	0	0	0	3	0
Dodds E.	1938-39 to 1939-40	15	13	0	0	0	0	15	13
Doherty P.	1933-34 to 1935-36	83	28	5	1	0	0	88	29
Dollins J.	1911-12 to 1912-13	18	1	4	1	0	0	22	2

Player	Seasons played	League		FA Cup		FL Cup		Total	
		App	Gls	App	Gls	App	Gls	App	Gls
Donachie J.	1920-21	19	1	0	0	0	0	19	1
Donovan T.	1984-85	2	0	0	0	0	0	2	0
Donnelly S.	1896-97	14	5	0	0	0	0	14	5
Dorrington J.	1900-01 to 1904-05	78	0	0	0	0	0	78	0
Dougall R.	1933-34 to 1935-36	74	2	2	0	0	0	76	2
Douglas T.	1931-32 to 1933-34	60	15	5	1	0	0	65	16
Douglas W.	1896-97 to 1897-98	60	0	0	0	0	0	60	0
Dowes A.	1978-79	1	0	0	0	0	0	1	0
Downes P.	1925-26 to 1930-31	152	32	6	1	0	0	158	33
Downes R.	1982-83 to 1983-84	24/1	3	3	0	4	1	31/1	4
Downhall J.	1911-12	1	0	0	0	0	0	1	0
Doyle R.	1979-80 to 1980-81	47/2	2	3	0	8	0	58/2	2
Drain T.	1909-10	4	0	0	0	0	0	4	0
Drummy D.	1979-80	4/1	0	0	0	0	0	4/1	0
Duckworth T.C.	1902-03 to 1905-06	34	5	4	0	0	0	39	5
Dumper J.	1919-20	1	0	0	0	0	0	1	0
Dunkley A.	1906-07	15	3	1	0	0	0	16	3
Durie D.	1952-53 to 1963-64	296	84	19	7	15	2	330	93
Dyer A.	1983-84 to 1986-87	101/7	19	3/1	0	8/1	1	112/9	20
Dyke A.S.	1921-22	1	0	0	0	0	0	1	0
Dyson K.	1971-72 to 1975-76	91/3	30	3	1	7	1	101/3	32
Eastham G.	1938-39 to 1946-47	44	9	1	0	0	0	45	9
Edge T.	1922-23	5	0	0	0	0	0	5	0

Player	Seasons played	League App	League Gls	FA Cup App	FA Cup Gls	FL Cup App	FL Cup Gls	Total App	Total Gls
Elliott S.	1988-89 to 1989-90	66/1	0	7	0	6	0	79/1	0
Elmore G.	1909-10	34	6	0	0	0	0	34	6
Elston H.	1898-99	10	0	0	0	0	0	10	0
Entwistle W.	1980-81 to 1981-82	27/5	6	2/1	2	0	0	29/6	8
Evans A.	1909-10 to 1911-12	39	0	4	0	0	0	43	0
Evans A.	1974-75	4/2	0	0	0	0	0	4/2	0
Evans L.	1898-99 to 1902-03	56	6	0	0	0	0	56	6
Evanson J.	1973-74 to 1975-76	63/4	0	3	0	1	0	67/4	0
Everest J.	1931-32 to 1933-34	42	1	5	0	0	0	47	1
Exton E.	1898-99	1	0	0	0	0	0	1	0
Eyres D.	1989-90 to 1991-92	109/11	25	9	2	7/1	0	125/12	27
Fairhurst H.	1919-20 to 1920-21	47	0	3	0	0	0	50	0
Falconer G.	1949-50	4	0	0	0	0	0	4	0
Farley J.	1976-77	1	0	0	0	0	0	1	0
Farm G.	1948-49 to 1959-60	465	1	47	0	0	0	512	1
Farrow G.	1936-37 to 1947-48	148	15	6	0	0	0	154	15
Fawcett R.	1955-56 to 1959-60	4	0	0	0	0	0	4	0
Fenton E.	1948-49 to 1958-59	195	20	19	0	0	0	214	20
Ferns P.	1983-84 to 1984-85	43/3	0	3	0	3/1	0	49/4	0
Finan R.	1933-34 to 1939-40	173	85	7	4	0	0	180	89
Finnigan T.	1976-77 to 1977-78	13/3	3	0	0	2	0	15/3	3
Fisher H.	1963-64 to 1968-69	52/3	1	3	0	7/1	0	62/4	1
Fishwick A.	1925-26 to 1927-28	59	36	0	0	0	0	59	36

Player	Seasons played	League		FA Cup		FL Cup		Total	
		App	Gls	App	Gls	App	Gls	App	Gls
Fiske W.	1907-08 to 1913-14	217	0	7	0	0	0	224	0
Fletcher F.A.	1898-99	32	0	0	0	0	0	32	0
Fletcher P.	1979-80 to 1981-82	19/1	7	0	0	2	1	21/1	8
Forbes J.	1923-24	19	0	0	0	0	0	19	0
Ford J.	1921-22	1	0	0	0	0	0	1	0
Foster J.	1901-02	28	6	0	0	0	0	28	6
Francis E.	1905-06 to 1906-07	37	11	6	1	0	0	43	12
Frith D.	1952-53 to 1956-57	30	0	5	0	0	0	35	0
Fuschillo P.	1971-72 to 1973-74	8/3	0	0	0	0/1	0	8/4	0
Gabbiadini R.	1989-90	5	3	0	0	2	1	7	4
Gadsden E.	1923-24 to 1924-25	8	0	0	0	0	0	8	0
Gamble G.F.	1898-99	9	3	0	0	0	0	9	3
Gardner P.	1976-77 to 1981-82	149/3	1	5	0	14	0	168/3	1
Garner A.	1988-89 to 1991-92	152/8	37	13/1	4	14/1	3	179/10	44
Garrett T.	1947-48 to 1960-61	306	3	28	1	0	0	334	4
Gattins A.	1904-05	1	0	0	0	0	0	1	0
Gavin P.	1920-21 to 1921-22	48	0	4	0	0	0	52	0
Gayle M.	1989-90	0	0	0	0	1	0	1	0
Gibson W.	1928-29 to 1929-30	14	0	1	0	0	0	15	0
Gill J.	1925-26	15	4	1	0	0	0	16	4
Gillett N.	1896-97 and 1901-02	5	0	0	0	0	0	5	0
Gillow W.B.	1912-13 to 1913-14	25	2	2	0	0	0	27	2
Gladwin C.	1908-09 to 1912-13	89	0	6	0	0	0	95	0

Player	Seasons played	League		FA Cup		FL Cup		Total	
		App	Gls	App	Gls	App	Gls	App	Gls
Goddard P.	1981-82	4	2	0	0	0	0	4	2
Gore I.	1988-89 to 1991-92	142/3	0	4	0	12/1	0	158/4	0
Gosling G.	1898-99	1	0	0	0	0	0	1	0
Gouck A.	1989-90 to 1991-92	27/12	3	7	0	2	0	36/12	3
Goulding P.A.	1909-10 to 1910-11	15	0	1	0	0	0	16	0
Gow J.	1904-05 to 1907-08	61	4	6	0	0	0	67	4
Grant W.	1927-28 to 1934-35	220	0	8	0	0	0	228	0
Gratrix R.	1953-54 to 1964-65	400	0	23	0	13	0	436	0
Green A.	1966-67 to 1971-72	121/1	13	5	3	10	3	136/1	19
Green J.	1959-60 to 1966-67	135	9	4	0	8	2	147	11
Green R.	1913-14 to 1914-15	31	4	2	0	0	0	33	4
Greenall C.	1980-81 to 1986-87	179/4	9	9	0	12	2	200/4	11
Gregson C.W.S.	1914-15	3	0	0	0	0	0	3	0
Gregson J.	1957-58 to 1958-59	4	1	0	0	0	0	4	1
Grimwood J.	1927-28	9	0	0	0	0	0	9	0
Groves A.	1977-78	11/4	1	1	0	0	0	12/4	1
Groves P.	1989-90 to 1991-92	114/1	24	9	4	6	1	129/1	29
Grundy W.A.	1906-07 to 1908-09	63	26	2	1	0	0	65	27
Hacking J.	1921-22 to 1924-25	33	0	0	0	0	0	33	0
Hall A.	1933-34 to 1938-39	42	10	3	1	0	0	45	11
Hall J.	1978-79	1	0	0	0	0	0	1	0
Hall T.	1952-53	2	0	0	0	0	0	2	0
Hall W.	1929-30 to 1930-31	23	3	0	0	0	0	23	3

Player	Seasons played	League App	League Gls	FA Cup App	FA Cup Gls	FL Cup App	FL Cup Gls	Total App	Total Gls
Halsall L.	1897-98	5	1	0	0	0	0	5	1
Halsall S.	1961-62	2	0	0	0	0	0	2	0
Halstead F.D.	1920-21	1	0	0	0	0	0	1	0
Hamilton J.	1928-29 to 1929-30	28	0	0	0	0	0	28	0
Hamilton S.E.	1924-25 to 1925-26	2	0	0	0	0	0	2	0
Hampson J.	1927-28 to 1937-38	361	248	12	4	0	0	373	252
Hancock H.	1905-06	27	6	5	3	0	0	32	9
Hardcastle P.	1971-72 to 1973-74	29/6	0	0	0	3/2	0	32/8	0
Hardman P.H.	1900-01 to 1902-03	71	10	0	0	0	0	71	10
Hargreaves H.	1926-27	3	0	0	0	0	0	3	0
Harris S.	1953-54 to 1957-58	15	4	0	0	0	0	15	4
Harrison F.	1898-99	2	0	0	0	0	0	2	0
Harrison G.	1931-32	16	1	2	0	0	0	18	1
Harrison S.	1971-72 to 1977-78	140/6	2	5	0	8/1	2	153/7	4
Harrison W.	1898-99	1	0	0	0	0	0	1	0
Harrison W.	1979-80 to 1981-82	78/5	6	7	2	5	0	90/5	8
Hart N.	1981-82 to 1982-83	35/1	0	3	0	4/1	0	42/2	0
Hart P.	1973-74 to 1977-78	143	15	6	0	7	1	156	16
Harvey A.	1961-62 to 1963-64	11	0	0	0	4	0	15	0
Hateley A.	1898-99	4	1	0	0	0	0	4	1
Hatton D.	1969-70 to 1975-76	250/1	7	9	0	14	1	273/1	8
Hatton R.	1976-77 to 1977-78	75	32	3	1	6	2	84	35
Hawkins N.	1989-90	4/3	0	0	0	1	0	5/3	0

J.Heathcote

M.Holden

Player	Seasons played	League		FA Cup		FL Cup		Total	
		App	Gls	App	Gls	App	Gls	App	Gls
Hawser P.	1957-58 to 1961-62	83	10	10	1	4	0	97	11
Haywood E.	1937-38 to 1951-52	275	0	22	0	0	0	297	0
Heathcote J.	1919-20 to 1921-22	89	33	4	0	0	0	93	33
Hedworth C.	1990-91 to 1991-92	24	0	4	0	0	0	28	0
Hepton S.	1952-53 to 1954-55	6	3	0	0	0	0	6	3
Hesford I.	1977-78 to 1982-83	202	0	13	0	15	0	230	0
Heslop T.	1912-13	29	4	2	0	0	0	31	4
Hetzke S.	1982-83 to 1985-86	140	18	10	0	10	1	160	19
Heywood F.	1902-03 and 1904-05	34	4	0	0	0	0	34	4
Higginson W.	1901-02	3	0	0	0	0	0	3	0
Hill F.	1936-37 to 1937-38	45	8	2	0	0	0	47	8
Hill S.	1959-60 to 1963-64	71	1	4	0	9	0	84	1
Hird H.	1922-23	4	0	0	0	0	0	4	0
Hoade S.J.	1909-10 to 1910-11	25	3	3	0	0	0	28	3
Hobbs F.W.	1927-28	24	0	0	0	0	0	24	0
Hobson A.	1947-48 to 1953-54	60	3	2	0	0	0	62	3
Hockaday D.	1976-77 to 1982-83	131/16	24	10/2	2	19/1	0	160/19	26
Hodgson J.	1903-04	2	0	0	0	0	0	2	0
Hogg R.	1904-05	27	4	0	0	0	0	27	4
Holden M.	1978-79	2/1	0	0	0	1/1	0	3/2	0
Hollingworth J.	1905-06	10	0	1	0	0	0	11	0
Horne D.	1960-61 to 1965-66	117/1	17	6	0	13	4	136/1	21
Horner P.	1990-91 to 1991-92	70/4	11	4	0	2	0	76/4	11

Player	Seasons played	League App	League Gls	FA Cup App	FA Cup Gls	FL Cup App	FL Cup Gls	Total App	Total Gls
Howard A.	1991-92	0/1	0	0/1	0	0	0	0/2	0
Howard J.	1911-12	1	0	0	0	0	0	1	0
Howard S.	1919-20 to 1920-21	9	0	0	0	0	0	9	0
Howson E.W.	1898-99 to 1900-01	22	0	0	0	0	0	22	0
Hoyle T.	1898-99	21	1	0	0	0	0	21	1
Hughes D.	1903-04	1	0	0	0	0	0	1	0
Hughes E.	1965-66 to 1966-67	27/1	0	1	0	5	0	33/1	0
Hughes J.	1969-70 to 1970-71	5/3	0	0	0	1	0	6/3	0
Hughes R.A.	1927-28	2	0	0	0	0	0	2	0
Hull A.	1902-03 to 1905-06	116	0	6	0	0	0	122	0
Hunter T.	1919-30 to 1920-21	13	4	0	0	0	0	13	4
Hutchison A.	1930-31	6	2	0	0	0	0	6	2
Hutchison T.	1967-68 to 1972-73 and 1987-88	165/5	10	6	1	17/1	3	188/6	14
Ingram G.	1966-67 to 1967-68	33/1	17	1	0	1	0	35/1	17
Jacklin W.	1919-20	1	0	0	0	0	0	1	0
James E.G.	1960-61 to 1974-75	395/6	22	14	1	31	2	440/6	25
Jeffrey W.	1982-83	12/2	1	1/1	0	1	0	14/3	1
Jennings P.	1925-26 and 1929-30	7	0	0	0	0	0	7	0
Johnson S.	1905-06 to 1906-07	34	1	5	0	0	0	39	1
Johnston H.	1937-38 to 1954-55	398	11	40	3	0	0	438	14
Johnston J.	1968-69 to 1971-72	20/6	2	2	0	4	1	26/6	3
Jolly A.	1904-05	5	0	0	0	0	0	5	0

Player	Seasons played	League		FA Cup		FL Cup		Total	
		App	Gls	App	Gls	App	Gls	App	Gls
Jones G.	1978-79 to 1979-80	18/8	5	1	0	0	0	19/8	5
Jones H.	1922-23 to 1925-26	96	0	9	0	0	0	105	0
Jones J.	1898-99	3	0	0	0	0	0	3	0
Jones J.	1903-04 to 1905-06	19	0	0	0	0	0	19	0
Jones J.	1912-13 to 1919-20	113	0	3	0	0	0	116	0
Jones P.	1986-87 to 1987-88 and 1989-90	36/5	0	6	0	2	0	42/5	0
Jones S.	1933-34 to 1938-39	165	6	5	0	0	0	170	6
Jones T.	1933-34 to 1937-38	153	38	8	2	0	0	161	40
Kaye A.	1959-60 to 1960-61	48	9	3	1	1	0	52	10
Keach W.	1897-98	16	0	0	0	0	0	16	0
Kearns A.	1904-05	15	3	0	0	0	0	15	3
Kearton J.	1991-92	15	0	0	0	0	0	15	0
Keenan H.	1912-13 to 1922-23	101	3	8	0	0	0	109	3
Kellow A.	1978-79 to 1979-80	57	23	3	1	4	0	64	24
Kelly G.	1988-89	5	0	0	0	0	0	5	0
Kelly H.	1946-47 to 1959-60	428	8	40	1	0	0	468	9
Kelly J.	1954-55 to 1960-61	200	9	9	0	2	0	211	9
Kemp F.	1970-71 to 1971-72	19/2	1	2	0	1	0	22/2	1
Kennedy G.	1946-47 to 1949-50	9	0	2	0	0	0	11	0
Kent P.W.	1919-20	5	0	0	0	0	0	5	0
Kerr D.	1991-92	13	1	0	0	0	0	13	1
Kerr R.	1978-79 to 1979-80	18/4	2	0	0	4	0	22/4	2

Player	Seasons played	League App	League Gls	FA Cup App	FA Cup Gls	FL Cup App	FL Cup Gls	Total App	Total Gls
Kidd J.	1910-11 to 1914-15	61	0	7	0	0	0	68	0
Killean E.	1903-04	5	0	0	0	0	0	5	0
King H.	1907-08	10	1	0	0	0	0	10	1
Kirkham J.	1898-99	3	0	0	0	0	0	3	0
Lancashire G.	1987-88	2/5	0	0	0	0/1	0	2/6	0
Lancaster D.	1990-91	7/1	1	0	0	2	0	9/1	1
Lane J.	1913-14 to 1919-20	94	65	5	2	0	0	99	67
Latheron E.	1908-09	1	0	0	0	0	0	1	0
Lauderdale J.	1929-30 to 1930-31	19	6	2	0	0	0	21	6
Lavery J.	1906-07	16	0	0	0	0	0	16	0
Law N.	1985-86 to 1986-87	64/2	1	2	0	2	0	68/2	1
Lax W.	1931-32 to 1932-33	25	0	0	0	0	0	25	0
Lea L.	1960-61 to 1967-68	158/2	13	6	0	13	3	177/2	16
Leadbetter J.	1897-98 to 1900-01	65	10	0	0	0	0	65	10
Leaver J.	1920-21 to 1925-26	106	4	11	0	0	0	117	4
Leitch G.	1991-92	2/5	0	0	0	0	0	2/5	0
Lennard D.	1971-72 to 1972-73	42/3	9	2	0	4/1	0	48/4	9
Lester M.	1987-88	24	2	4	0	0	0	28	2
Lewis T.	1938-39	12	3	1	1	0	0	13	4
Lewis W.	1946-47 to 1949-50	42	0	0	0	0	0	42	0
Longden E.	1930-31 to 1932-33	61	7	2	0	0	0	63	7
Lovett W.	1920-21	2	0	0	0	0	0	2	0
Lowe W.	1904-05 to 1907-08	11	0	0	0	0	0	11	0

Player	Seasons played	League		FA Cup		FL Cup		Total	
		App	Gls	App	Gls	App	Gls	App	Gls
Lowson E.	1921-22 to 1922-23	5	0	0	0	0	0	5	0
Loyden E.	1964-65	2	0	0	0	0	0	2	0
Lyon H.	1908-09	8	2	1	0	0	0	9	2
Lyon T.K.	1936-37 to 1937-38	6	0	1	0	0	0	7	0
Lythgoe D.	1955-56	3	1	0	0	0	0	3	1
McAllister T.	1979-80	16	0	0	0	4	0	20	0
McAteer A.	1986-87 to 1987-88	35/6	0	3	0	2	0	40/6	0
McCall A.	1947-48 to 1950-51	86	15	2	0	0	0	88	15
McCulloch J.	1912-13	1	0	0	0	0	0	1	0
McDonough F.J.B.	1931-32 to 1933-34	82	0	4	0	0	0	86	0
Macdougall E.	1979-80 to 1980-81	11/2	0	0	0	2	0	13/2	0
McEvoy A.	1981-82	6	0	0	0	0	0	6	0
McEwan M.	1903-04 to 1904-05	44	1	1	0	0	0	45	1
McEwan S.	1973-74 to 1981-82	204/9	24	13	2	16	6	233/9	32
McEwan W.	1973-74 to 1974-75	4/1	0	0	0	2/1	0	6/2	0
McGinley P.	1986-87	2/9	1	1	0	0	0	3/9	1
McGinn A.	1919-20 to 1924-25	132	2	10	1	0	0	142	3
McGrotty W.	1970-71 to 1971-72	2/2	1	0	0	0	0	2/2	1
McHardie D.	1897-98	24	0	0	0	0	0	24	0
McIlhargey S.	1989-90 to 1991-92	101	0	12	0	10	0	123	0
McIntosh J.	1935-36 to 1937-38 and 1946-47 to 1948-49	79	22	8	5	0	0	87	27
McIntosh W.	1924-25	1	0	0	0	0	0	1	0

Player	Seasons played	League App	League Gls	FA Cup App	FA Cup Gls	FL Cup App	FL Cup Gls	Total App	Total Gls
McIntosh W.	1948-49 to 1951-52	51	15	5	1	0	0	56	16
McIntyre S.	1927-28	6	2	0	0	0	0	6	2
McIvenney J.	1922-23	16	4	1	0	0	0	17	4
McKenna J.	1954-55 to 1956-57	25	2	0	0	0	0	25	2
Mackenzie A.	1923-24	6	1	0	0	0	0	6	1
McKnight G.	1946-47 to 1953-54	32	9	5	1	0	0	37	10
McLaren M.	1938-39	2	0	0	0	0	0	2	0
McLelland J.	1930-31 to 1932-33	66	25	3	2	0	0	69	27
McNicholas J.	1970-71	0/1	0	0	0	0/1	0	0/2	0
McNiven D.	1982-83 to 1983-84	45/4	11	5	2	1/1	1	51/5	14
McPhee J.	1962-63 to 1969-70	249/10	15	13	1	19	2	281/10	18
Madden C.	1986-87 to 1989-90	73/17	24	6/1	3	6/4	0	85/22	27
Maggs P.	1931-32	24	0	2	0	0	0	26	0
Malone R.	1978-79 to 1979-80	48/1	1	2	0	1/1	0	51/2	1
Malpas A.	1927-28	1	0	0	0	0	0	1	0
Mann A.	1971-72	3	0	0	0	1	0	4	0
Marsden A.	1967-68 to 1968-69	4/1	0	0	0	2	0	6/1	0
Marsh C.	1919-20 to 1920-21	5	0	0	0	0	0	5	0
Martin A.	1922-23 to 1928-29	25	2	0	0	0	0	25	2
Martin B.	1957-58 to 1963-64	187	1	9	0	13	0	209	1
Martin J.	1896-97 to 1897-98	52	17	0	0	0	0	52	17
Matthews N.	1985-86 to 1989-90	67/9	1	1	0	7	0	75/9	1
Matthews S.	1947-48 to 1961-62	391	17	49	1	0	0	440	18

Player	Seasons played	League		FA Cup		FL Cup		Total	
		App	Gls	App	Gls	App	Gls	App	Gls
Mauchline R.	1938-39	4	0	0	0	0	0	4	0
May S.	1978-79	4	0	0	0	0	0	4	0
Mayes A.	1986-87	12/1	6	1	0	0	0	13/1	6
Mayo J.	1982-83	5	1	0	0	0	0	5	1
Mayor F.	1898-99	2	0	0	0	0	0	2	0
Mee G.W.	1920-21 to 1925-26	216	21	14	0	0	0	230	21
Mercer K.	1983-84	31	9	5	3	2	0	38	12
Mercer W.	1925-26 to 1928-29	20	0	0	0	0	0	20	0
Meredith J.	1923-24 to 1927-28	190	27	10	3	0	0	200	30
Metcalfe R.S.	1911-12	3	0	1	1	0	0	4	1
Methven C.	1986-87 to 1989-90	168/7	11	12/1	1	14	1	194/8	13
Middleton J.	1935-36 to 1936-37	10	3	2	1	0	0	12	4
Miller P.	1903-04	3	0	0	0	0	0	3	0
Miller P.E.	1908-09 to 1910-11	41	13	2	0	0	0	43	13
Miller W.	1910-11	6	0	0	0	0	0	6	0
Millership H.	1912-13 to 1914-15	30	0	0	0	0	0	30	0
Milligan L.	1976-77 to 1978-79	19	0	1	0	2/1	0	22/1	0
Milne G.	1967-68 to 1969-70	60/4	4	2/1	0	4/2	1	66/7	5
Milne W.	1911-12	21	6	2	1	0	0	23	7
Mingay H.	1919-20 to 1923-24	155	0	7	0	0	0	162	0
Mitchell F.J.	1914-15	5	0	0	0	0	0	5	0
Mitchell N.	1991-92	0/1	0	0	0	0	0	0/1	0
Mitchell T.	1911-12	3	0	0	0	0	0	3	0

Player	Seasons played	League		FA Cup		FL Cup		Total	
		App	Gls	App	Gls	App	Gls	App	Gls
Moir I.	1964-65 to 1966-67	61	12	0	0	5	2	66	14
Moore D.	1983-84 to 1986-87	115/1	1	6/1	0	6	0	127/2	1
Moore K.	1974-75 to 1976-77	33/5	3	2/1	0	2	0	37/6	3
Morfitt J.W.	1931-32	1	0	0	0	0	0	1	0
Morgan H.	1904-05	25	4	1	1	0	0	26	5
Morgan S.	1985-86 to 1989-90	135/9	10	16	0	13	2	164/9	12
Morgan W.	1980-81 to 1981-82	41	4	1	0	0	0	42	4
Morley F.	1909-10 to 1911-123	80	22	1	0	0	0	81	22
Morris C.	1979-80 to 1981-82	87	26	7	3	6	3	100	32
Morris J.J.	1906-07	17	4	0	0	0	0	17	4
Mortensen S.	1946-47 to 1955-56	325	197	29	25	0	0	354	222
Mount C.	1896-97	9	5	0	0	0	0	9	5
Mowbray H.	1967-68 to 1970-71	88/3	0	4/1	1	8	0	100/4	1
Mudie J.	1949-50 to 1960-61	324	144	31	11	1	0	356	155
Muggleton C.	1987-88	2	0	0	0	0	0	2	0
Munro A.	1936-37 to 1948-49	136	17	10	1	0	0	146	18
Murphy A.	1984-85	1/7	0	0/1	0	0	0	1/8	0
Murphy J.	1991-92	0/1	0	1	0	0	0	1/1	0
Murray J.	1969-70 to 1970-71	6/3	1	0	0	0	0	6/3	1
Murray M.	1991-92	2/1	0	0	0	0	0	2/1	0
Murray R.	1937-38	2	0	0	0	0	0	2	0
Musgrove C.	1905-06	4	0	0	0	0	0	4	0
Napier P.	1961-62 to 1962-63	2	0	0	0	1	0	3	0

Player	Seasons played	League		FA Cup		FL Cup		Total	
		App	Gls	App	Gls	App	Gls	App	Gls
Neal R.	1925-26 to 1930-31	85	17	2	1	0	0	87	18
Nelson S.	1946-47 to 1947-48	10	0	0	0	0	0	10	0
Nesbitt B.	1911-12	12	4	0	0	0	0	12	4
Nicholson P.	1970-71	3/3	0	0	0	1/1	0	4/4	0
Nightingale A.	1898-99	5	0	0	0	0	0	5	0
Noble P.	1979-80 to 1982-83	92/5	14	7	0	4	0	103/5	14
Norris R.	1896-97 to 1898-99	58	5	0	0	0	0	58	5
Oates G.	1961-62 to 1968-69	119/3	26	1	0	7	2	127/3	28
O'Doherty E.	1919-20 and 1922-23	2	0	0	0	0	0	2	0
O'Donnell F.	1937-38 to 1946-47	30	17	1	0	0	0	31	17
O'Donnell H.	1938-39 to 1946-47	14	2	1	0	0	0	15	2
O'Donnell J.	1930-31 to 1931-32	55	0	4	0	0	0	59	0
O'Keefe E.	1984-85 to 1986-87	33/3	23	0	0	2	0	35/3	23
O'Keefe V.	1986-87 to 1988-89	7	0	0	0	0	0	7	0
O'Neil T.P.	1972-73	7	0	0	0	0	0	7	0
Oram D.	1934-35 to 1935-36	28	9	2	0	0	0	30	9
O'Rourke W.	1983-84 to 1985-86	98	0	3	0	8	0	109	0
Owen A.	1911-12	2	0	1	0	0	0	3	0
Owen G.	1989-90 to 1990-91	21/8	4	4/2	2	3	0	28/10	6
Owers E.H.	1907-08	9	3	0	0	0	0	9	3
Oxberry J.	1927-28 to 1931-32	74	20	1	0	0	0	75	20
Pagnam F.	1912-13 to 1913-14	23	1	0	0	0	0	23	1
Park W.	1938-39	2	0	0	0	0	0	2	0

B.Nesbitt

F.O'Donnell

W.Rookes

Player	Seasons played	League		FA Cup		FL Cup		Total	
		App	Gls	App	Gls	App	Gls	App	Gls
Parker S.	1972-73 to 1974-75	10/6	2	0	0	2	1	12/6	3
Parkinson J.	1896-97 to 1908-09	365	52	10	1	0	0	375	53
Parkinson R.	1896-97	8	1	0	0	0	0	8	1
Parr H.	1896-97 to 1898-99	85	2	0	0	0	0	85	2
Parr W.W.	1935-36 to 1938-39	15	1	0	0	0	0	15	1
Parry R.	1960-61 to 1964-65	128	27	7	0	11	5	146	32
Pashley T.	1978-79 to 1982-83	201	7	13	1	15	2	229	10
Pearson A.	1906-07	4	0	0	0	0	0	4	0
Pearson H.	1929-30 to 1930-31	55	0	2	0	0	0	57	0
Pentland F.	1903-04	8	5	0	0	0	0	8	5
Perry W.	1949-50 to 1961-62	394	119	40	10	2	0	436	129
Peterson B.	1956-57 to 1961-62	101	16	3	0	5	1	109	17
Pickering F.	1969-70 to 1970-71	49/1	24	4	1	3	0	56/1	25
Pickford P.	1903-04	1	0	0	0	0	0	1	0
Pierce G.	1983-84	27	0	5	0	0	0	32	0
Pollard S.	1981-82	0/1	0	0	0	0	0	0/1	0
Popplewell S.	1920-21	1	0	0	0	0	0	1	0
Powell R.	1986-87 to 1987-88	14	0	0	0	0	0	14	0
Power J.	1921-22	18	6	1	0	0	0	19	6
Pratt T.	1904-05	8	2	0	0	0	0	8	2
Prentis J.	1962-63 to 1965-66	6	0	0	0	2	0	8	0
Price N.	1984-85	13	0	0	0	0	0	13	0
Priest P.	1986-87	1	0	0	0	0	0	1	0

Player	Seasons played	League		FA Cup		FL Cup		Total	
		App	Gls	App	Gls	App	Gls	App	Gls
Pritchett K.	1982-83 to 1983-84	36/1	1	1	0	2	0	39/1	1
Purdy A.	1927-28 to 1928-29	31	0	1	0	0	0	32	0
Quinn C.	1929-30 to 1931-32	37	6	2	0	0	0	39	6
Quinn P.	1910-11 to 1919-20	152	16	5	1	0	0	157	17
Quinn P.	1962-63 to 1963-64	34	9	2	1	0	0	36	10
Rafferty W.	1972-73 to 1973-74	35/1	9	0	0	0	0	35/1	9
Raisbeck L.	1905-06	15	0	0	0	0	0	15	0
Ramsay S.	1927-28 to 1931-32	105	2	2	0	0	0	107	2
Ramsbottom N.	1970-71 to 1971-72	12	0	0	0	1	0	13	0
Ratcliffe A.	1920-21	13	2	2	2	0	0	15	4
Rattray C.	1929-30 to 1933-34	52	9	3	0	0	0	55	9
Reece H.J.	1931-32 to 1932-33	4	0	0	0	0	0	4	0
Reeves G.	1912-13	4	0	0	0	0	0	4	0
Reid A.	1932-33	13	1	1	0	0	0	14	1
Reid G.H.	1920-21	3	2	0	0	0	0	3	2
Reid W.H.	1907-08 to 1908-09	32	3	1	0	0	0	33	3
Reilly J.	1904-05 to 1905-06	2	0	0	0	0	0	2	0
Richards C.	1989-90 to 1991-92	32/98	8	2	0	0/2	0	34/11	8
Richardson I.	1982-83	4/1	2	0	0	0	0	4/1	2
Richardson J.E.	1920-21 to 1921-22	32	0	3	0	0	0	35	0
Richardson P.	1982-83	4	0	0	0	0	0	4	0
Rickett W.	1947-48 to 1949-50	44	7	5	0	0	0	49	7
Rimmer H.	1906-07 to 1907-08	20	0	0	0	0	0	20	0

Player	Seasons played Seasons played	League App	League Gls	FA Cup App	FA Cup Gls	FL Cup App	FL Cup Gls	Total App	Total Gls
Ritchie A.	1928-29 to 1929-30	31	5	2	0	0	0	33	5
Robinson C.	1928-29	5	0	0	0	0	0	5	0
Robinson C.	1951-52 to 1954-55	21	2	3	0	0	0	24	2
Robinson J.	1947-48 to 1948-49	25	0	6	0	0	0	31	0
Robinson T.E.	1933-34	2	0	0	0	0	0	2	0
Robson J.	1964-65 to 1967-68	60/4	14	1	0	4	2	65/4	16
Robson W.	1913-14 to 1914-15	46	0	1	0	0	0	47	0
Rodaway W.	1983-84	41	0	4	0	2	0	47	0
Rodwell A.	1990-91 to 1991-92	90/3	19	5	0	4/1	0	99/4	19
Rookes J.	1903-04	23	5	0	0	0	0	23	5
Rookes W.	1913-14 to 1921-22	98	4	7	0	0	0	105	4
Rooney S.	1987-88 to 1988-89	4/5	0	2/1	0	0	0	6/6	0
Ronson W.	1974-75 to 1978-79 and 1985-86	127/4	12	4	0	10	1	141/4	13
Rose F.	1907-08	6	0	0	0	0	0	6	0
Rosebroom F.	1921-22 to 1922-23	20	2	0	0	0	0	20	2
Rowe G.	1963-64 to 1970-71	101/4	12	4	0	7	2	112/4	14
Roxburgh A.	1932-33 to 1938-39	57	0	3	0	0	0	60	0
Rush P.	1980-81 to 1981-82	11	0	0	0	0	0	11	0
Rushton F.	1913-14	1	0	0	0	0	0	1	0
Salt S.	1960-61	18	0	1	0	2	0	21	0
Sanderson C.	1905-06	2	1	0	0	0	0	2	1
Sbragia R.	1980-81 to 1981-82	24/2	1	0	0	1	0	25/2	1

Player	Seasons played	League		FA Cup		FL Cup		Total	
		App	Gls	App	Gls	App	Gls	App	Gls
Scarr J.G.	1896-97 to 1898-99	10	0	0	0	0	0	10	0
Scott J.	1898-99 to 1908-09	309	15	10	0	0	0	319	15
Scott L.	1982-83	2	0	0	0	0	0	2	0
Sendall R.	1985-86 to 1987-88	6/5	0	0/1	1	2	0	8/6	1
Serella D.	1982-83 to 1983-84	34/1	3	5	0	5	2	44/1	5
Sermani L.	1978-79	1	0	0	0	0	0	1	0
Seward P.	1979-80	0/1	0	0	0	0	0	0/1	0
Shankley J.	1930-31	5	0	0	0	0	0	5	0
Sharatt H.	1952-53	1	0	0	0	0	0	1	0
Sharp C.	1913-14	3	0	0	0	0	0	3	0
Shaw G.	1909-10 to 1910-11	6	0	0	0	0	0	6	0
Shaw G.	1987-88	4/2	0	0	0	0	0	4/2	0
Shimwell E.	1946-47 to 1956-57	288	5	36	2	0	0	324	7
Shipman T.	1933-34 to 1936-37	36	0	0	0	0	0	36	0
Sibbald J.	1914-15 to 1921-22	74	15	3	2	0	0	77	17
Sibley E.	1937-38 to 1946-47	74	0	1	0	0	0	75	0
Siddall B.	1983-84 and 1986-87 to 1988-89	117	0	10	0	11	0	138	0
Simmonite G.	1980-81 to 1982-83	63	1	4	0	6	0	73	1
Simpkin C.	1971-72 to 1972-73	31/3	1	2	0	2	0	35/3	1
Sinclair B.	1977-78	0/2	0	0	0	0/1	0	0/3	0
Sinclair T.	1989-90 to 1991-92	41/32	4	4/1	0	4	0	49/33	4
Singleton T.	1960-61	0	0	0	0	2	1	2	1

		League		FA Cup		FL Cup		Total	
Player	Seasons played	App	Gls	App	Gls	App	Gls	App	Gls
Skirton A.	1966-67 to 1968-69	76/1	25	2	1	8	2	86/1	28
Slater W.J.	1949-50 to 1951-52	32	9	3	3	0	0	35	12
Smailes J.	1932-33 to 1934-35	92	25	6	0	0	0	98	25
Smalley A.	1929-30 to 1932-33	25	1	0	0	0	0	25	1
Smalley P.	1990-91	6	0	0	0	0	0	6	0
Smethurst P.	1959-60	1	0	0	0	0	0	1	0
Smith B.	1979-80	18/1	1	0	0	2	0	20/1	1
Smith K.	1954-55 to 1957-58	4	4	0	0	0	0	4	4
Smith M.	1975-76	8	5	0	0	0	0	8	5
Smith P.	1979-80	1	0	0	0	0	0	1	0
Smith W.	1932-33	1	0	0	0	0	0	1	0
Snowdon B.	1955-56 to 1959-60	18	1	0	0	0	0	18	1
Speight T.	1900-01	5	0	0	0	0	0	5	0
Spence D.	1976-77 to 1979-80	82/3	21	6	1	7	2	95/3	24
Spencer J.	1911-12	1	0	0	0	0	0	1	0
Spencer S.	1903-04	1	1	0	0	0	0	1	1
Stant P.	1990-91	12	5	0	0	0	0	12	5
Starkey H.	1956-57 to 1958-59	2	0	0	0	0	0	2	0
Steele S.	1983-84	3	0	0	0	0	0	3	0
Stephenson C.	1908-09	1	0	0	0	0	0	1	0
Stephenson L.	1950-51 to 1954-55	23	10	4	1	0	0	27	11
Sterling R.L.	1908-09	1	0	0	0	0	0	1	0
Stewart P.	1981-82 to 1986-87	188/13	56	7	2	10	3	205/13	61

Player	Seasons played	League		FA Cup		FL Cup		Total	
		App	Gls	App	Gls	App	Gls	App	Gls
Stirzaker H.	1896-97 to 1902-03	154	13	0	0	0	0	154	13
Stonehouse K.	1983-84 to 1985-86	53/3	19	3	0	1/2	0	57/5	19
Stoneman P.	1991-92	18/2	0	2	0	2/1	0	22/3	0
Streets S.	1924-25 to 1925-26	14	2	4	2	0	0	18	4
Stroud W.	1921-22	2	0	0	0	0	0	2	0
Stuart A.	1896-97 to 1898-99	44	1	0	0	0	0	44	1
Suart R.	1946-47 to 1949-50	103	0	9	0	0	0	112	0
Suddaby P.	1970-71 to 1979-80	330/1	10	10	0	30	0	370/1	10
Suddick A.	1966-67 to 1976-77	305/5	65	10/1	2	26/1	9	34/7	76
Summerbee M.G.	1976-77	3	0	0	0	0	0	3	0
Swan A.	1906-07 to 1908-09	26	1	1	0	0	0	27	1
Swarbrick L.	1903-04	1	0	0	0	0	0	1	0
Swift F.	1928-39 to 1929-30	3	0	0	0	0	0	3	0
Taylor A.	1965-66 to 1970-71	94	0	4	0	8	0	106	0
Taylor E.	1951-52 to 1957-58	222	53	20	2	0	0	242	55
Taylor J.	1928-29	4	1	0	0	0	0	4	1
Taylor M.	1986-87 to 1991-92	107/14	43	8	2	6/2	1	121/16	46
Taylor T.	1900-01	4	0	0	0	0	0	4	0
Teasdale J.	1984-85	1/6	1	0	0	0	0	1/6	1
Thomas P.	1966-67 to 1969-70	12/1	0	1	0	0	0	13/1	0
Thomas R.	1934-35	6	2	0	0	0	0	6	2
Thompson C.	1988-89 to 1989-90	27/12	8	1	0	1/4	0	29/16	8
Thompson F.	1896-97	6	0	0	0	0	0	6	0

Player	Seasons played	League App	League Gls	FA Cup App	FA Cup Gls	FL Cup App	FL Cup Gls	Total App	Total Gls
Thompson F.	1914-15	3	0	0	0	0	0	3	0
Thompson H.	1977-78 to 1980-81	92/7	7	3	0	7	0	102/7	7
Thompson J.	1923-24	6	1	0	0	0	0	6	1
Thompson L.	1961-62 to 1968-69	155/1	2	7	0	11	0	173/1	2
Thomson C.	1985-86 to 1986-87	50/2	6	1	0	2	0	53/2	6
Thomson H.	1969-70 to 1970-71	60	0	3	0	5	0	68	0
Thomson R.	1933-34	24	1	1	0	0	0	25	1
Thorpe L.	1910-11 to 1913-14	92	1	6	0	0	0	98	1
Thorpe P.	1924-25 to 1927-28	113	5	2	0	0	0	115	5
Threlfall E.	1900-01 to 1910-11	320	10	11	2	0	0	331	12
Tilbrook C.	1925-26	1	0	0	0	0	0	1	0
Tilford A.	1926-27 to 1928-29	53	0	1	0	0	0	54	0
Tillotson S.	1907-08 to 1908-09	18	0	0	0	0	0	18	0
Tong D.	1974-75 to 1978-79	71/8	7	0/2	0	5/3	0	76/13	7
Tongue B.	1908-09	4	0	0	0	0	0	4	0
Topping R.	1905-06	3	0	0	0	0	0	3	0
Tremelling L.	1919-20	7	0	0	0	0	0	7	0
Tremelling W.	1924-25 to 1930-31	114	43	5	1	0	0	119	44
Tufnell S.	1927-28 to 1932-33	90	4	6	0	0	0	96	4
Tulloch B.	1914-15 to 1923-24	178	0	8	0	0	0	186	0
Tully K.	1972-73 to 1973-74	10/1	0	0	0	1	0	11/1	0
Turley H.	1913-14 to 1914-15	11	0	0	0	0	0	11	0
Turner P.	1962-63 to 1966-67	10/1	3	1	0	2	0	13/1	3

L.Thorpe

D.Wagstaff

Player	Seasons played	League		FA Cup		FL Cup		Total	
		App	Gls	App	Gls	App	Gls	App	Gls
Upton W.S.	1928-29 to 1933-34	74	25	4	1	0	0	78	26
Varty W.C.	1933-34	2	0	0	0	0	0	2	0
Waddell R.	1964-65 to 1966-67	28	5	1	0	1	1	30	6
Waddington J.	1904-05 and 1907-08	32	6	1	0	0	0	33	6
Wagstaffe D.	1978-79	16/2	1	1	0	2/1	0	19/2	1
Waiters A.	1959-60 to 1966-67	258	0	10	0	18	0	286	0
Wake B.	1906-07	3	0	0	0	0	0	3	0
Waldron A.	1977-78 to 1978-79	22/1	1	0	0	0	0	22/1	1
Walker C.	1983-84	8/1	3	0	0	0	0	8/1	3
Walker T.	1908-09	7	2	0	0	0	0	7	2
Wallace J.	1933-34 to 1947-48	243	0	7	0	0	0	250	0
Walters C.E.	1910-11	6	0	0	0	0	0	6	0
Walsh M.	1973-74 to 1977-78	172/8	72	6	1	8	3	186/8	76
Walsh M.	1983-84 to 1988-89	145/8	5	8/1	0	10	0	163/9	5
Walwyn K.	1987-88 to 1988-89	51/18	17	4/1	1	6/1	0	61/20	18
Wann D.	1969-70 to 1971-72	11/6	0	0	0	0/1	0	11/7	0
Wann D.	1981-82	13/6	0	4	1	1	0	18/6	1
Ward R.	1977-78 to 1978-79	41	0	1	0	3	0	45	0
Wardle W.	1948-49 to 1950-51	60	1	3	0	0	0	63	1
Warren H.	1924-25 to 1926-27	5	0	0	0	0	0	5	0
Wassell G.	1932-33 to 1935-36	97	0	5	0	0	0	102	0
Watkinson A.	1921-22 to 1922-23	10	1	0	0	0	0	10	1
Watmough R.	1934-35 to 1937-38	100	32	5	3	0	0	105	35

Player	Seasons played	League		FA Cup		FL Cup		Total	
		App	Gls	App	Gls	App	Gls	App	Gls
Watson A.	1922-23 to 1935-36	373	22	17	0	0	0	390	22
Watson P.	1931-32 to 1937-38	171	11	7	1	0	0	178	12
Watt J.	1962-63	5	0	0	0	2	1	7	1
Wellock M.	1923-24 to 1926-27	26	7	0	0	0	0	26	7
Welsh A.	1980-81	1	0	0	0	1/1	0	2/1	0
West G.	1960-61 to 1961-62	30	0	1	0	2	0	33	0
Weston J.	1975-76 to 1979-80	97/8	8	5	0	5	0	107/8	8
Weston W.	1907-08 to 1908-09	42	5	1	0	0	0	43	5
Whalley A.	1908-09	5	2	1	1	0	0	6	3
White H.	1922-23 to 1924-25	70	18	6	1	0	0	76	19
White T.	1967-68 to 1969-70	34	9	1	0	2	2	37	11
Whiteside F.	1908-09	6	0	0	0	0	0	6	0
Whittingham R.	1907-08 to 1908-09	53	28	0	0	0	0	53	28
Whittingham S.	1908-09 to 1909-10	48	0	3	0	0	0	51	0
Whittle W.	1903-04	4	0	0	0	0	0	4	0
Wilcox T.	1906-07	37	0	1	0	0	0	38	0
Wilkinson A.	1924-25	5	0	0	0	0	0	5	0
Wilkinson F.	1912-13	15	1	0	0	0	0	15	1
Wilkinson J.	1931-32 to 1932-33	60	16	4	0	0	0	64	16
Williams E.L.	1898-99	22	1	0	0	0	0	22	1
Williams G.	1980-81	30/1	2	2	1	3	0	35/1	3
Williams W.D.	1924-25 to 1927-28	26	13	1	0	0	0	27	13
Wilson B.	1976-77 to 1979-80	21/10	6	0	0	5/1	0	26/11	6

Player	Seasons played	League App	League Gls	FA Cup App	FA Cup Gls	FL Cup App	FL Cup Gls	Total App	Total Gls
Wilson F.	1897-98	23	1	0	0	0	0	23	1
Wilson G.	1911-12 to 1919-20	83	14	7	0	0	0	90	14
Wilson H.	1928-29 to 1931-32	50	1	4	0	0	0	54	1
Windridge D.	1983-84 to 1986-87	87/12	18	6	0	5	1	98/12	19
Winstanley G.	1896-97	2	0	0	0	0	0	2	0
Witham R.	1933-34 to 1937-38	149	0	7	0	0	0	156	0
Withers A.	1950-51 to 1954-55	15	6	0	0	0	0	15	6
Wolfe G.	1929-30 to 1930-31	28	0	2	0	0	0	30	0
Wolstenholme A.	1909-10 to 1911-12	76	14	5	1	0	0	81	15
Wolstenholme T.	1902-03 to 1904-05	91	0	1	0	0	0	92	0
Wood G.	1971-72 to 1976-77 and 1989-90	132	0	4	0	8	0	144	0
Wood J.W.	1922-23 to 1925-26	58	0	1	0	0	0	59	0
Wright A.	1987-88 to 1991-92	94/7	0	8	0	10/2	0	112/9	0
Wright J.	1948-49 to 1958-59	157	1	10	0	0	0	167	1
Wright J.W.	1902-03	7	0	0	0	0	0	7	0
Wright M.	1990-91	3	0	0	0	0	0	3	0
Wright R.	1925-26 to 1927-28	30	1	1	0	0	0	31	1
Wright W.	1951-52 to 1954-55	14	2	1	0	0	0	15	2
Wylie R.	1953-54 to 1954-55	11	0	0	0	0	0	11	0
Yarnall H.G.	1914-15	9	1	0	0	0	0	9	1

SUBSCRIBERS

Presentation Copies

1 Blackpool Football Club

2 The Football League • 3 The Football Association

4 Owen Oysten • 5 David Hatton

6 Geoff Warburton • 7 Roy Calley

8 J A Harris
9 Richard Hawkings
10 Richard Todd
11 Andrew Roberts
12 Brian Pendlebury
13 Christopher John Cooper
14 Paul Devonport
15 Mr Charles D Whittle
16 Bernard Anderson
17 Paul Lavery
18 John Terence Cooper
19 P Tweed
20 Garry Richardson
21 Anthony Carl Shaw
22 L G Kelshaw
23 Peter Lawrenson
24 Alan J Gibbons
25 C Hockridge
26 Michael Dixon
27 John D Woodman
28 Lawrence Wright
29 Trevor Paul Bamber
30 Mr John Curtis
31 Stephen Creer
32 J Bonnar and K Harvey
33 Malcolm Anderson
34 Barry Shaw
35 John Campbell
36 John O'Malley
37 Andrew Bennett
38 Phil Hatton
39 Harry Bradley
40 T W Lord
41 Darren Horn
42 Philip Robert Cardwell
43 Robert Cardwell
44 Mr Duncan Simpson
45 N A Lee
46 Mr Elgar Williams
47 Philip Greenwood
48 Martin M Lord
49 Robert Poole
50 Stephen Peter Harding
51 Peter Hogg
52 Michael Anthony Lee
53 Gareth Tucker
54 Tony Scarborough
55 Derek Booth
56 John P Ferguson
57 Roy Thomson
58 Peter Manock
59 Christopher R Blackburn
60 Peter Duerden
61 Don Wiseman
62 John Wiseman
63 Gary Wiseman
64 Richard James Plowman
65 David Flanagan
66 John Houghton
67 Skellington Family
68 J D Holden
69 Stuart John Edwards
70 David Thompson
71 Mr Neil Parkinson
72 Matthew Wright
73 Charles W Hill
74 G F Alderson
75 Tim Rutter
76 P J Heyworth
77 Peter Antony Blundell
78 Paul Darch
79 Roland Wyke
80 Stephen Wilson Mather
81 Andy Wadsworth
82 Rod Stother
83 David Gregory
84 Mark Potter
85 G S Holden
86 David Billington
87 Alan Edwards
88 A O Ward
89 Nigel F Marsden
90 J P Wright
91 John Keith Sutton
92 Paul Anthony Roger Page
93 Paul Mountford
94 Andrew Dyer
95 Ian C Wylde
96 J R Bateson
97 Geoffrey William Arthur Nixon
98 David J Turner
99 Thomas W Givanovich
100 Colin C Taylor
101 Barbara Leigh
102 Andrew Monkman
103 Kenneth Monkman
104 N J Fail
105 Christopher McCulloch
106 Vincent Howcroft
107 R E Gregson

108 Raymond Harrison
109 Steve Abernethy
110 Andrew Ross
111 Harold Moorby
112 Roy Corns
113 Rhodri Richard Davies
114 James Peter Lee
115 Leonard H W Hall
116 Mark C Wright
117 Stewart Chapman
118 Gareth Wynne Evans
119 Anthony Edge
120 John McCaskill
121 Peter Scott
122 Keith Woodcock
123 Bernard Joseph White
124 John Webster
125 Paul Knight
126 Andrew Knight
127 Kevin Bradshaw
128 Andrew Roberts
129 Stewart Edge
130 Bill Sandwell
131 Kieran Heaney
132 James Bryson
133 Joshua Bryson
134 Michael J Hargreaves
135 Graham J E Smith
136 Stewart Graham Swallow
137 Timothy C J Paisley
138 Tim Paisley
139 William Jackson
140 Mr Mark Strickland
141 Mr R Poole
142 Mr R Poole
143 Jennie Isabel Cookson
144 Mr Stephen Dickinson
145 John D Cross
146 Peter Mark Danson
147 David Whiteley
148 Allan H Sumner
149 Dave Tomlinson
150 Mr Donald O'Shea
151 Marco Vidoretti
152 Paul Wright
153 Joseph W Bootle
154 D W Standing
155 Stephen Moore
156 Malcolm Andrew
157 Barry M Sanderson
158 Michael Keith Booth
159 Harry Sumner
160 Geoff Taylor
161 Daniel Gordon Drew
162 F L Sharpe
163 Anthony M O'Brien
164 Mr D S Asquith
165 Stewart Coleman
166 Stephen Anthony Ormerod
167 Barry Hartley
168 Derek Brian Jones
169 Roy Walker
170 Pietro Simone
171 Tony Alman
172 Barrie John Keith Lamb
173 Steve Cobb
174 Barry Mauger
175 Malcolm Williams
176 Mick Bye
177 Robert Taylor
178 David Travis
179 R M P Duck
180 Mr Alan Morris
181 Chris Compton
182 John Macdonald
183 Kenneth Douglas Macdonald
184 Peter T Windle
185 Carl T Goode
186 Jonathan Westhead
187 Kevin Booker
188 Robert F Bolsom
189 Mr E A Alder
190 Mr Paul N Ogden
191 Peter G Johnson
192 Paul Hawkings
193 Andrew Miller
194 Stephen Paul Fletcher
195 Geoffrey Burrows
196 Keith Burrows
197 Mr Chris Simon Beveridge
198 Stephen A Smith
199 Ian Robinson
200 Mr Harold Stephen Bowden
201 Dr J P Bound
202 Mr J R Liggins
203 W Grundy
204 S J Hallt
205 Anthony Balaam
206 Barrie Balaam
207 Jonathan Leach
208 Alan Gordon Whalley
209 John Macdonald
210 Peter D Broome
211 Frank Kirby
212 Rodney Palmer
213 David Clifton
214 Michael R Eastwood
215 S Quarmby
216 James E Birch
217 Geoff Birch
218 Adam Robert Cooper
219 Chris Hull
220 'A Tangerine Stag'
221 Gordon Stewart
222 Nick Edwards
223 Kenneth B Gumley
224 Ian Costain
225 Mark Chandler
226 Robert Anthony Kavanagh
227 Steven Ferrier
228 Alan Keightley
229 Andrew Schofield
230 Robert Derrick Lawson
231 Mr Stephen R Ogden

232 Mr Rennie Parker
233 Mr Jonathan Parker
234 Stanley Winn
235 Les Hughes
236 Dr David W Cartmell
237 Neil W Tomlinson
238 Mark R Jones
239 John Stuart Smith
240 Keith Jenkinson
241 Patrick Jenkinson
242 Matthew Jenkinson
243 D A Haythornthwaite
244 D A Haythornthwaite
245 Bernard L Skinner
246 Anthony Woodgate
247 Michael Paul Thomason
248 Ronald Ashcroft
249 Mr Craig Kevin Benson
250 Kim Turner
251 Michael Hemingway
252 Stephen Yarwood
253 Brian Southern
254 Laurence Wilson
255 T Peter Fielding
256 Paul A Lupton
257 Derek Croft
258 David Mellows Facer
259 Lee David Carson
260 Malcolm Leaver
261 Bob Boardman
262 Ian G Vickers
263 Mark Dugdale
264 Michael Briggs
265 Paul A Hodgson
266 Andrew Giblin
267 P Cogle
268 Roy K Shoesmith
269 Mark Smith
270 Peter Bamford
271 Bruce Evans
272 David Keats
273 David R Earnshaw
274 Fred Lee
275 Sports Marketing
276 Gary Wynne
277 Anthony Jones
278 L Dixon
279 D T Bryant
280 Brian Spridgens
281 David Fisher
282 John Marriott
283 Phil Pearson
284 A Horner
285 Steven F Thomas
286 B H Standish
287 Geoffrey Hall
288 David Coulson
289 J S Pyke
290 Malc Hartley
291 Peter Pickup
292 S Simpson
293 John Allen
294 Phillip Hart
295 Raymond Shaw
296 A Sullivan
297 Roger Hudson
298 Alan Chapman
299 P J Cooke
300 Mr A J Davis (Jnr)
301 Mark Hillary
302 Keith Ruddick
303 John Schofield
304 Mr Ian Wilson
305 A R Milns
306 Andrew Pearson
307 Ian M Dacre
308 Harrison Fidler
309 Willy Østby
310 Bjørn Langerud
311 Philip H Whitehead
312 Derek Hyde
313 David Downs
314 Richard Wells
315 Mr Harry Kay
316 K P Wood
317 Donald Noble
318 John Ferreday
319 Paul Bannister
320 Ann Bone
321 Philip Defriez
322 Geoffrey Wright
323 Ian Willott
324 Terry Holt
325 Mr Peter Woodhead
326 Stephen Rydzkowski
327 Tony Armstrong
328 Duncan Watt
329 David Dickens
330 Phil Hollow
331 Colin Sillet
332 David J Godfrey
333 Michael Joyce
334 R S Shackleton
335 Ian Petrie
336 John Lathan
337 J Ringrose
338 Cleve Fortt
339 Peter Marsh
340 Stephen Todd
341 George David Petch
342 Barry Roy Green
343 Harold Löhr
344 Garnett Makinson
345 Derek Wheatcroft
346 Garth Dykes
347 J Kay
348 D C Lofthouse
349 J A Hartley
350 D Walker
351 Rick E Hoyle
352 Brian H Hobbs
353 Colin Jose
354 C J Morton
355 F Beale
356 T D Culshaw
357 Mr A G C Matthews
358 John Butlin
359 Mr Jack Moore
360 Mr Christopher Shaw

361 Mr Peter Elliott
362 Christer Svensson
363 Trond Isaksen
364 B R Butler
365 Dave Smith
366 M, B, & N Yelton
367 David Sullivan
368 Maurice Curtin
369 R A Sproule
370 Simon Jelf
371 Jonny Stokkeland
372 Dave Harrison
373 Riccardo Rossi
374 D Bidgood
375 J Gardiner
376 Mike Purkiss
377 John Clancy
378 John Gray
379 Moira & Frederick Furness
380 G W Burrans
381 Ian & Sue Carden
382 Alan G Bird
383 David Gregg
384 Errick Peterson
385 Michael McConkey
386 Ian Harraden
387 Julian M Holmes
388 David W Marsh
389 Christopher Bromiley
390 T Bryan Carney
391 R Peter Bailey
392 Stanley A Robinson
393 Phil Bradbury
394 Andrew Neale Eaton
395 Paul Jerome
396 Paul Vibert
397 Chris Hooker
398 Jeff Haigh
399 Ruth Worthington
400 Michael Worthington
401 J R Eastwood
402 Nick Wolstencroft
403 Paul Clarke
404 Paul Clarke
405 M R Pearce
406 Göran Schönhult
407 Keith Coburn
408 Angus W Rodger
409 Jordan Thomas
410 M Stapleton
411 John Downs
412 P T Davies
413 Brian Hall
414 George E Butterworth
415 Miss Ruth E Aspinall
416 W J Hope
417 Jim Walker
418 Nicholas Brown
419 John Quarnberg
420 Gilbert Monnereau
421 Stephen Hickson
422 S A Roberts
423 Gerald Hill
424 Mr B J Stewart
425 William Grier
426 Mike Young
427 Norman Green
428 Michael Andrew Shepherd
429 Mr John M South
430 Mr Stephen J South
431 Mr Craig R South
432 Martin Boak
433 Russell Boak
434 Stuart J Raistrick
435 Len Gibson
436 Barry Bradshaw
437 Kerry Rowe
438 Paul James Allen
439 Alan Hindley
440 A & J A Waterman
441 Dave Hillam
442 Mr Ken Nicholson
443 Darren Duckett
444 Phil Moore
445 Bernie & Adam Mearns
446 Steven Elsender
447 Mr Derek Ainsworth
448 Mr Kevin Ainsworth
449 Brian Tabner
450 Dave Green
451 R H Bubb
452 Peter Marks
453 Philip Brown
454 Richard Dougal
455 Jeremy Fawbert
456 J K Lane
457 Andrew M J Richardson
458 Andrew A Yule
459 Nicholas G Bithell
460 David W Bithell
461 Richard Stocken
462 Stephane Daugan
463 Mike Jackman
464 David J Simmons
465 J Musgrove
466 Duncan Pierce
467 Iain R M Love
468 A G Stevenson
469 John Evans
470 Ms Val Peeters
471 David Kirk
472 Rainer Jürgens
473 Charles B Ducker
474 Mike, Hilary, Edward & Warwick Brown
475 Gordon Small
476 Ian Griffiths
477 Gary Bragg
478 L A Zammit
479 Ormond Hesketh
480 W R Mitchell
481 Surapot Saengchote
482 John van den Elsen
483 Andrew Robert Yates
484 Geoffrey James Turner
485 Ian V Bentley
486 Tony Hodgson

487 Mr R Nesbitt
488 Mr D G Hargreaves
489 E N Hayton
490 Mervyn Powell
491 N P Shaw
492 C Minchin
493 W D Phillips
494 R A Kelly
495 D Lumb
496 H Thompson
497 R W Lane
498 D Lamming
499 P Baxter
500 S B Emms
501 R G Woolman
502 M Simons
503 A Bogaards
504 A Axelsson
505 E Kautonen
506 M Swart
507 G D Painter
508 I Green
509 Q C M Olsthoorn
510 A Young
511 C Cameron
512 A L Tweddell
513 G Juva
514 K M Torgrimsen
515 D Helliwell
516 A H Atkins
517 S Ramnefjell
518 A P J M Otten
519 Lars-Olof Wendler
520 I Stromberg
521 M Sirriani
522 A Johansson
523 S P Tomlin
524 S Laski
525 J A Retter
526 Niall Mac Sweeney
527 T Chorley
528 B Smith
529 William Reed
530 John Harrison
531 J Mulrennan
532 Haydock & Fletcher
533 Derry Good
534 John Osgerby
535 Bob Whiteside
536 Kenneth Harrison
537 Mark Ward
538 Chris Lowry
539 Steve Ward
540 J Buitenga
541 John & Neil Storey